PRAISE FOR

A People's History of the American Revolution

"Ray Raphael shows that, like the Civil Rights Movement, the American Revolution was the product of local people, not just Washington, Jefferson, and Franklin."

—James Loewen,
author of *Lies My Teacher Told Me*

"This is an exciting distillation of the discoveries of a generation of scholars about ordinary people in the American Revolution. . . . A very readable, thought-provoking book."

—Alfred Young,
author of *The Shoemaker and the Tea Party*

"Raphael succeeds admirably in bringing to life the excitement, upheaval, and complexity of plebian Americans' participation in the War of Independence. Drawing on a broad array of published eyewitness accounts and displaying a firm command of recent social-historical scholarship, he offers a reliable, extensively documented, and frequently riveting account of how various bodies of 'the people' tried to make the Revolution their own."   —*William and Mary Quarterly*

"The unique value of Raphael's work lies in its mining, from extant primary sources, of the extraordinary recollections of ordinary witnesses to history."   —*Booklist*

"Raphael . . . is relentlessly aggressive and unsentimental. He takes the traditional narrative of the American Revolution and shatters it into rough and contradictory but mesmerizing fragments. If a PBS documentary were ever made of Raphael's book, exploding cannons and heated arguments, rather than soothing fiddles, would have to provide the soundtrack. . . . The nervy energy of this *People's History* is an arresting antidote to the air of self-satisfied triumphalism that so many Americans casually assume each July Fourth."   —*Fresh Air* (NPR)

"Fascinating and scrupulously researched."   —*Seattle Times*

"He has fashioned a mosaic—history from the bottom up—with impressive skill."

—*London Times*

Allan Ridley

About the Author

RAY RAPHAEL is the author
of numerous books, including
*An Everyday History of Some-
where, The Men from the Boys:
Rites of Passage in Male America,*
and *Tree Talk: The People and
Politics of Timber.* He lives in
northern California.

A People's History of the American Revolution

ALSO BY RAY RAPHAEL

An Everyday History of Somewhere

Edges: Human Ecology of the Backcountry

Tree Talk: The People and Politics of Timber

Cash Crop: An American Dream?

The Teacher's Voice

The Men from the Boys: Rites of Passage in Male America

Little White Father: Redick McKee on the California Frontier

More Tree Talk: The People, Politics, and Economics of Timber

A People's History of the American Revolution

How Common People Shaped the Fight for Independence

RAY RAPHAEL

SERIES EDITOR

HOWARD ZINN

Perennial

An Imprint of HarperCollins*Publishers*

A hardcover edition of this book was published in 2001 by The New Press. It is here
reprinted by arrangement with The New Press.

A PEOPLE'S HISTORY OF THE AMERICAN REVOLUTION.
Copyright © 2002, 2001 by Ray Raphael.
All rights reserved. Printed in the United States of America. No part of this book may
be used or reproduced in any manner whatsoever without written permission except in
the case of brief quotations embodied in critical articles and reviews. For information
address The New Press,
450 West 41st Street, New York, NY 10036.

HarperCollins books may be purchased for educational, business, or sales promotional
use. For information please write: Special Markets Department,
HarperCollins Publishers Inc.,
10 East 53rd Street, New York, NY 10022.

First Perennial edition published 2002.

Library of Congress Cataloging-in-Publication Data
Raphael, Ray.
    A people's history of the American Revolution : how common people shaped the
fight for independence / Ray Raphael.—1st ed.
        p. cm.
    Originally published: New York : The New Press, 2001.
    Includes index.
    ISBN 0-06-000440-1
    1. United States—History—Revolution, 1775–1783. 2. United States—History—
Revolution, 1775–1783—Social aspects. 3. United States—History—Revolution,
1775–1783—Personal narratives. I. Title.

E208 .R25 2002
973.3—dc21
                                                                    2002016992

03   04   05   06   WB/RRD   10   9   8   7   6   5   4

For Marie

The research for *A People's History of the American Revolution* was made possible, in part, by a fellowship from the National Endowment for the Humanities.

CONTENTS

FOREWORD TO THE PERENNIAL EDITION

The libraries are bursting with books on the American Revolution, but not one like this. The publishers and the public never seem to tire of the same old story—the great battles, the military heroes, the wisdom of the Founding Fathers. Thomas Jefferson and John Adams, as I write this, are subjects of bestselling biographies. Multivolume sets of their papers, and those of the other leaders, are being published.

It is an approach to history which, in every society, serves the interests of the privileged and powerful, because, by ignoring ordinary people, it reinforces their feelings of powerlessness. We are not surprised when the narratives given to the public in totalitarian states deify the leaders and reduce the citizenry to ciphers. But we are startled when it is suggested to us that in liberal democratic states such as ours, boasting freedom of expression and a pluralism of ideas, there is a similar exaltation of leaders, with everyone else barely visible.

Surely, it is time to break with that habit in the interests of democracy. And Ray Raphael gives us a good start.

Howard Zinn

SERIES PREFACE

Turning history on its head opens up whole new worlds of possibility. Once, historians looked only at society's upper crust: the leaders and others who made the headlines and whose words and deeds survived as historical truth. In our lifetimes, this has begun to change. Shifting history's lens from the upper rungs to the lower, we are learning more than ever about the masses of people who did the work that made society tick.

Not surprisingly, as the lens shifts the basic narratives change as well. The history of men and women of all classes, colors, and cultures reveals an astonishing degree of struggle and independent political action. Everyday people played complicated historical roles, and they developed highly sophisticated and often very different political ideas from the people who ruled them. Sometimes their accomplishments left tangible traces; other times, the traces are invisible but no less real. They left their mark on our institutions, our folkways and language, on our political habits and vocabulary. We are only now beginning to excavate this multifaceted history.

The New Press People's History Series will roam far and wide through human history, revisiting old stories in new ways, and introducing altogether new accounts of the struggles of common people to make their own history. Taking the lives and viewpoints of common people as its point of departure, the series will reexamine subjects as different as the Renaissance, the Industrial Revolution, the Cold War, the settlement of the New World, World War II, and the American Civil War.

A people's history does more than add to the catalog of what we already know. These books will shake up readers' understanding of the past—just as common people throughout history have shaken up their always changeable worlds.

Howard Zinn
Boston, 2000

A People's History of the American Revolution

INTRODUCTION

Real people, not paper heroes, made and endured the American Revolution. Witness:

- In September of 1776, when the Reverend Ammi R. Robbins was making his rounds among patients of the Continental Army, he came upon "one very sick youth from Massachusetts" who asked the reverend to save him because he felt he was not fit to die. "Do, sir, pray for me," pleaded the youth, whose name and age were not reported. "Will you not send for my mother? If she were here to nurse me I could get well. O my mother, how I wish I could see her; she was opposed to my enlisting: I am now very sorry. Do let her know I am sorry!" Robbins did not send for the boy's mother; instead, he "endeavored to point him to the only source of peace, prayed and left him; he cannot live long."[1]

- In 1773, as white patriots complained they were being reduced to a state of slavery, four African Americans from Massachusetts petitioned a member of the assembly:

  Sir, The efforts made by the legislative of this province in their last sessions to free themselves from slavery, gave us, who are in that deplorable state, a high degree of satisfaction. We expect great things from men who have made such a noble stand against the designs of their *fellow*-men to enslave them.[2]

The slaves were only requesting one day a week to labor for themselves, but the assembly took no action.

• Lydia Mintern Post, a Long Island housewife with strong patriotic feelings, was forced to quarter some Hessian troops during the British occupation. When the Hessians received their monthly ration of rum, the hostess wrote, "we have trying and grievous scenes to go through; fighting, brawls, drumming and fifing, and dancing the night long; card and dice playing, and every abomination going on under our very roofs." Whether drunk or not, the soldiers would "take the fence rails to burn, so that the fields are left open, and the cattle stray away and are often lost; burn fires all night on the ground, and to replenish them, go into the woods and cut down all the young saplings, thereby destroying the growth of ages." What bothered Lydia the most, however, was that the Hessians made baskets for her daughters and taught German to her son. "The children are fond of them," she conceded. "I fear lest they should contract evil."[3]

• In June of 1776, fifteen-year-old Joseph Plumb Martin threatened to run off and board a privateer if his grandparents did not allow him to enlist in the army. Despite some "misgivings," he wanted someday to come "swaggering back" to tell tales of his "hair-breadth 'scapes." All his older friends were signing up, and Joseph did not wish to be left behind:

> I one evening went off with a full determination to enlist at all hazards. When I arrived at the place of rendezvous I found a number of young men of my acquaintance there. The old bantering began. "Come, if you will enlist, I will," says one. "You have long been talking about it," says another. "Come, now is the time." Thinks I to myself, I will not be laughed into it or out of it. I will act my own pleasure after all. But what did I come here for tonight? Why, to enlist. Then enlist I will. So seating myself at the table, enlisting orders were immediately presented to me. I took up the pen, loaded it with the fatal charge, made several mimic imitations of writing my

name, but took especial care not to touch the paper with the pen until an unlucky wight who was leaning over my shoulder gave my hand a stroke, which caused the pen to make a woeful scratch on the paper. "O, he has enlisted," said he. "He has made his mark; he is fast enough now." Well, thought I, I may as well go through with this business now as not. So I wrote my name fairly upon the indentures. And now I was a *soldier*, in name at least, if not in practice.[4]

- Dr. Abner Beebe of East Haddam, Connecticut, was known to speak "very freely" in favor of the Crown. Although he had committed no other crime,

  he was assaulted by a Mob, stripped naked, & hot Pitch was poured upon him, which blistered his Skin. He was then carried to a Hog Sty & rubbed over with Hogs Dung. They threw the Hog's Dung in his Face, & rammed some of it down his Throat; & in that condition exposed to a Company of Women. His House was attacked, his Windows broke, when one of his Children was sick, & a Child of his went in Distraction upon this Treatment. His Gristmill was broke, & Persons prevented from grinding at it, & from having any Connections with him.[5]

- Two months before the battles of Lexington and Concord, the British sent Colonel Leslie with 240 men to seize arms and ammunition which the rebels had stored in Salem. As the troops approached town, residents halted their progress by lifting the Northfield drawbridge. Several inhabitants climbed onto the raised leaf of the bridge and engaged in a shouting match with Colonel Leslie on the other side. William Gavett, an eyewitness, reported the incident:

  In the course of the debate between Colonel Leslie and the inhabitants, the colonel remarked that he was upon the King's Highway and would not be prevented passing over the bridge.
  Old Mr. James Barr, an Englishman and a man of much

nerve, then replied to him: "It is *not* the King's Highway; it is a road built by the owners of the lots on the other side, and no king, country or town has anything to do with it."[6]

Colonel Leslie was taken aback, but he pressed the issue; James Barr held firm, knowing he was in the right. In the end, Leslie promised to march only fifty rods "without troubling or disturbing anything" if the residents of Salem would lower the bridge. The bridge came down, Leslie kept his word, and the opening battle of the American Revolution was postponed. Old James Barr had taken on the British empire with a few simple words.

• Phebe Ward, of East Chester, New York, wrote a letter to her husband Edmund on June 6, 1783:

> Kind Husband
>   I am sorry to aquant you that our farme is sold. . . . thay said if I did not quitt posesion that thay had aright to take any thing on the farme or in the house to pay the Cost of a law sute and imprisen me I have sufered most Every thing but death it self in your long absens pray Grant me spedy Releaf or God only knows what will be com of me and my frendsles Children
>   thay say my posesion was nothing youre husband has firfeted his estate by Joining the British Enemy with a free and vollentary will and thereby was forfeted to the Stat and sold
>   All at present from your cind and Loveing Wife
>
>   phebe Ward
>
>   pray send me spedeay anser[7]

• In 1780 the British General Henry Clinton, not wanting to offend the civilian population, urged his subordinates: "For God's sake no irregularities." But animosities ran strong in South Carolina, and the soldiers couldn't resist; Major James Wemyss, for instance, burned fifty houses as he marched through the northeastern part of the state. In 1781 the American governor, John Rutledge, issued a proclamation against plundering, while General Nathanael Greene threatened to impose the death penalty on any of his soldiers who were caught marauding. But the American calls for restraint were likewise unheeded, and the state legislature, unable to provide support for the troops, soon gave legal sanction to acts of plunder. Each side took its turn running over the terrain, destroying or consuming everything in sight. After the fighting subsided, General William Moultrie reported the net effect: a countryside that had once been filled with

> live-stock and wild fowl of every kind, was now destitute of all. It had been so completely checquered by the different parties, that not one part of it had been left unexplored; consequently, not the vestiges of horses, cattle, hogs, or deer, &c. was to be found. The squirrels and birds of every kind were totally destroyed. . . . [N]o living creature was to be seen, except now and then a few camp scavengers, picking the bones of some unfortunate fellows, who had been shot or cut down, and left in the woods above ground.[8]

This was the Revolutionary War: soldiers who were not yet men; women who lost their homes; liberty achieved and liberty denied; a devastated landscape in the South, much like in the Civil War: the American Revolution was our first civil war, pitting neighbors against neighbors and splitting families apart. Much of the violence, unsanctioned by any formal military organization, took place in houses and barns and public streets; even in some of the major battles, British troops were conspicuously absent. After the royal army surrendered at Yorktown in 1781, fighting continued to rage across the South as warring factions refused to lay down their arms and settle up.

Once the war was over, most survivors did not wish to dwell on the myriad human tragedies which clouded the sense of victory. In the words of John Shy, "Much about the event called the Revolutionary War had been very painful and was unpleasant to remember; only the outcome was unqualifiedly pleasant; so memory, as ever, began to play tricks with the event."[9] Almost before the blood had cooled, surviving patriots turned the victims into heroes and created a whitewashed mythology eulogizing the so-called founding fathers. The majestic ideals of Thomas Jefferson, the persuasive words of Sam Adams and Tom Paine, the seasoned wisdom of Ben Franklin, the inspirational leadership of George Washington—great men with great ideas were the midwives to American liberty. The rebels had dumped tea, issued declarations, and killed a few redcoats who deserved their fates—but they had inflicted no mass carnage. Americans preferred to believe that their nation was conceived in an epiphany of republican glory.

The leaders of the new nation had a particular interest in selective memory as they utilized patriotic fervor to forge a viable union. According to historian Charles Royster,

> Charles Thomson, the longtime secretary of Congress, probably knew more about the administration and politics of the Revolutionary War than any other American, but he refused to publish a history of the Revolution: "I could not tell the truth without giving great offense. Let the world admire our patriots and heroes. Their supposed talents and virtues (where they were so) by commanding imitation will serve the cause of patriotism and our country." According to another version of his refusal, he concluded by saying, "I shall not undeceive future generations." Before he died, Thomson burned his papers.[10]

Americans of later generations have commandeered the Revolution. When workers tried to form a labor party in 1829, they pleaded: "Awake, then from your slumbers; and insult not the memories of the heroes of '76, by exhibiting to the world, that what they risked their lives, their fortunes, and their sacred honor to obtain, you do not think worth preserving."[11] When Philadelphia laborers went on strike in 1835 for the ten-hour day, they distributed a circular: "We claim BY THE BLOOD OF OUR FATHERS, shed on our battlefields in the war of the Revolution, the rights of American citizens."[12] In a very different cause, William L. Yancey of Alabama called for the white people of the South in 1860 to fight once again for their independence, "to produce spirit enough ... to call forth a Lexington, to fight a Bunker's hill."[13] After Lincoln was elected president that same year, confederates in South Carolina tried to form a group of "Minute Men" to go to Washington and prevent the inauguration.[14] A century later, right-wing anticommunists once again invoked memories of the Revolution as they organized their own groups of "Minutemen."

In the American mind, the *outcome* of the Revolution has always overshadowed the event itself. In 1958 Henry Steele Commager and Richard B. Morris concluded their monumental compilation of primary sources with telling remarks:

> The American Revolution was costly in lives and in property, and more costly in the terror and the fear and the violence that, as in all wars, fell so disproportionately on the innocent and the weak. Yet by comparison with other wars of comparable magnitude, before and since, the cost was not high. Notwithstanding the ruthlessness and even the ferocity with which it was waged, it did little lasting damage, and left few lasting scars. Population increased all through the war; the movement into the West was scarcely interrupted; and within a few years of peace, the new nation was bursting with prosperity and buoyant with hope. Independence stimulated both material and intellectual enterprise. ... Of few other wars can it be said that so much was gained at so little lasting cost, either in lives snuffed out, or in a heritage of hatred.[15]

In fact, a greater percentage of the American population perished in the Revolutionary War than in World War I, World War II, or the Vietnam War; only the Civil War was more deadly.

Even now, popular images of the Revolution continue to focus on its legacy rather than on the war itself. The past serves as a mirror to reflect present agendas: conservatives see the Revolution as a noble struggle against an intrusive government, a precedent (and implicitly a justification) for their own antigovernment leanings; liberals view the Revolution as a critical step towards political democracy and social equality; radicals tend to focus on the failure of the Revolution to achieve those same objectives, particularly with respect to women, African Americans, and Native Americans. Hardcore realists, meanwhile, treat our so-called war of independence as one more chapter in mankind's struggle for dominance and power, same as it ever was. For each and every political orientation, the American Revolution, always flexible, is there to offer support. Rhetoric and ideology were paramount in our nation's founding; they remain so today as we try to discover who we are by examining our roots.[16]

But what about the people themselves? Behind the myths, concealed by all the political agendas and self-serving talk, lie flesh-and-blood human beings, our real-life founding fathers—and founding mothers, too. Who were these people? That is what I wish to explore in this book.

That very term—"the people"—is suspect; more often than not, it serves as an invitation to yet more rhetoric. Then, as now, the people were many and varied:

- They were citizens-turned-soldiers, both men and boys, some who fought eagerly in the name of liberty, others who joined the army for lack of better alternatives.

- They were women—some widowed, some who cooked and washed for the troops, many who stayed at home to tend to business while the men went to war.

- They were African Americans who sought their freedom in any way they could—by writing petitions, serving in the army as substitutes for whites who had been drafted, or escaping to fight with the British—but who for the most part remained slaves at war's end, subjected to treatment at least as harsh as before.

- They were Native Americans—a few siding with the patriots, more siding with the British—who either joined or resisted alliances in search of their own sovereignty, much like the rebellious colonists.

- They were loyalists who endured a merciless persecution—citizens from all locations and classes, their loyalty based sometimes on a pure sense of allegiance, often on self-interest or prior antagonisms with the local patriot leadership.

- They were neutrals—Quakers and Moravians opposed to all wars, people from various walks of life who saw no particular advantage in joining either side, and countless, nameless individuals from that great mass of humanity which, throughout history, has tried to overlook public affairs in favor of private pursuits.

- They were city dwellers—bakers, cobblers, joiners, laborers, seamen—who took active roles in meetings and demonstrations and who filled the musters (either willingly or not) of local militias.

- They were farmers, mostly small, who left their animals and crops to fight in the militias for short periods of time, or who managed to stay at home, leaving the fighting to others.

- They were lawyers and merchants, local elites who tried to call the shots—some serving as political representatives or military officers, some profiteering from wartime shortages and inflation.

- They were slaveholding planters who held their world together with violence disguised as gentility, and who struggled—some consciously, others not—with the basic contradiction of waging a war in the name of freedom while denying freedom to others.

- They were victimizers and victims—men who started the war, other men who fought the war, men and women alike who died or suffered.

- They were true believers and nonbelievers—and many who had to compromise their patriotic ideals in the struggle for material survival as the war wreaked havoc on the domestic economy.

These and more were the faces of the American Revolution.
    In particular, I wish to explore what the Revolution meant for

the common people of the times, the men and women who did not enjoy the special privileges afforded by wealth, prestige, or political authority.[17] The surfeit of attention given to famous personalities has eclipsed the stories of lesser known folk and falsely skewed the telling of the Revolutionary War.

A simple shift of the lens—from George Washington to his slaves, to the soldiers he commanded, to the Indians he displaced—reveals incidents and events, facts and figures, portraits and personalities of great historical significance. It is time to replace, or at least supplement, the traditional picture of the Revolution with an elaborate mosaic of new scenes and different characters. This is beginning to happen. Historians today are breaking down the amorphous mass of "Revolutionary America" into more discrete groups as they try to understand how the idiosyncrasies of location, class, race, relationship, and gender colored the revolutionary experience. Farm wives and shoemakers and slaves and tenant farmers are finally being given their due.

When we look into forgotten corners, we find evidence that helps us deconstruct and reconstruct the American Revolution. There was more to it than Bunker Hill, George Washington crossing the Delaware, and Benedict Arnold's betrayal. Once we make the simple decision to include common people, we are forced to rewrite the story:

> Late in the summer of 1774, more than half a year before the "shot heard round the world," tens of thousands of plain farmers seized political authority from Crown-appointed officials in all of Massachusetts outside Boston. Hats in hand, judges and members of the governor's council resigned their posts; muskets in tow, the farmers took over. This was the true beginning of the American Revolution; the later battles at Lexington and Concord constituted a counterrevolution as the British tried to regain control of a countryside they had previously lost.
>
> Few of the patriots who cried so loudly about taxation without representation bore arms for more than brief periods of time. Buying their way out and hiring substitutes, those with property to protect left the fighting to poor men and boys with no farms or businesses of their own. Militiamen deserted by the droves; Continental soldiers mutinied for lack of food and pay.

While some women spun for the cause of liberty or gave up their tea, others devoted their lives to service in the Continental Army. Although most "camp followers," as they were called, joined the Revolution for lack of other alternatives, these poor women contributed more than their share as they starved and froze and fell ill along with the soldiers.

In Maryland, Delaware, New York, and the southern backcountry, many struggling farmers fought their own Revolution—against the patriot elite. It was a time to rise up and rebel, but not all the rebelling was directed against the British. Sometimes, when the rich called themselves patriots, the poor became loyalists in response.

Some 80,000 people—one in every thirty free Americans—belonged to pacifistic communities (Quakers, Shakers, Moravians, Mennonites, Amish, Dunkers, Schwenkfelders) which opposed the Revolutionary War on religious grounds.

The Revolution constituted the most sweeping and devastating Indian war in American history. All Native Americans east of the Mississippi were affected, and many lost their lands. The war accentuated divisions among and within the tribes as the majority sided with the Crown, the minority with the rebels. After the war, when American settlers no longer had to compete with the British, encroachment on native lands proceeded with unprecedented speed.

When tens of thousands of slaves sought their freedom by fleeing to the British, a great number perished from disease—the final death toll approximated that of revolutionary soldiers. In the North, some slaves gained their freedom by serving in the military for their masters; in the South, slaves fled to the woods and swamps to establish their own maroon communities. Freedom was the name of the game—and the stakes were much higher for African Americans than for patriots who complained they were "slaves" to Parliament.

These happenings, crucial to a comprehensive understanding of the Revolution, have been ignored in the mythic tale of our nation's founding. It is time to break from the mold. By uncovering the stories of farmers, artisans, and laborers, we discern how plain folk helped create a revolution strong enough to evict the British Empire from the thirteen colonies. And by digging deeper still, we learn how people with no political standing—women, Native Americans, African Americans—altered the shape of a war conceived by others.

RANK-AND-FILE REBELS

Street Action

In November of 1747 the people of Boston rose up with great anger. The problem started when some fifty British sailors, seeking a better life in the New World, deserted from HMS *Lark*. Commodore Charles Knowles responded by ordering a predawn sweep of the waterfront to find the deserters and, failing that, to impress other warm bodies into service on the *Lark*. Later that morning, according to an eyewitness, a "body of men arose I believe with no other motive than to rescue if possible the captivated . . . and to protest this form of like barberous abusage."

This was not the first time impressment gangs swept through the wharves and taverns of Boston, and every time they did, they met resistance. In 1741 a crowd beat up the sheriff and stoned a justice of the peace who supported impressment. In 1742 a crowd attacked the commanding officer of the *Astrea* and destroyed a barge belonging to the Royal Navy. In 1745 protestors beat up the commander of HMS *Shirley* and battered a deputy sheriff unconscious; later that year they rioted again when a press gang killed two seamen.

Already versed in the art of protesting, several thousand rioters against the Knowles impressment once again challenged authority. They placed a deputy sheriff in the stocks, seized officers of the *Lark* as hostages, broke the windows of the Council chamber, and confronted the royal governor with "very indecent, rude expressions." Governor Shirley, understandably frightened, abandoned his mansion and retreated to an island in the harbor.

On the mainland, the people reigned supreme. They literally shored the British Navy (or so they thought). Seizing a barge which they mistakenly thought belonged to the Crown, scores of burly laborers, brash apprentices, and hardened seamen "dragged it, with as much seeming ease through the streets as if it had been in the water," first to the governor's mansion and then to the Commons, where they set it ablaze.

Governor Shirley called out the militia, but only the officers showed up—the rest of the militiamen, it seems, were part of the crowd. Commodore Knowles then announced he would bombard Boston from his warships, but his threat was empty: the greatest damage would no doubt accrue to the property of the rich, not the rioters. The laboring classes of Boston remained firmly in control of their city for three days until Governor Shirley negotiated the release of most of the impressed seamen.[1]

Throughout the eighteenth century, common people who could not even vote engaged in collective public actions concerning issues that directly affected their lives. In the absence of a civil police force, people came together to enforce community norms. They tore down bawdy houses. They kept people with smallpox from entering their towns. Women demonstrated against unfaithful husbands.

Rioters acted in various relationships with the law. Sometimes they *became* the law, organized into the *posse comitatus*, the power of the county, which enjoyed the official sanction of the state. At other times they were only the "mob," short for *mobile vulgus*, the rootless lower class of English society. The rich and powerful often tried to discredit crowd action by calling attention to the lower-class status of rioters, but they could not always suppress the will of the people so forcefully expressed. Riots, with their direct objectives and moral urgency, effectively offset the arbitrary power or inattention of harsh rulers. Common people felt well within their rights to liberate impressed seamen or commandeer a few loaves of overpriced bread.[2]

Following in this tradition, American colonists took to the streets to demonstrate their opposition to the British taxation which followed the French and Indian War. On August 14, 1765, in response to the imposition of a stamp tax on all legal documents, a Boston crowd numbering in the thousands beheaded an effigy of Andrew Oliver, the Massachusetts stamp distributor. After witnessing the destruction of his personal property, Oliver announced he would resign. Heartened by such quick and clear results, crowds in other cities and towns followed suit. In Charleston, South Carolina, angry protestors hung an effigy of the stamp collector along with a figure of the devil. "Whoever shall dare attempt to pull down these effigies," they announced, "had better been born with a stone about his neck, and cast into the sea." That evening, two thousand people carted the effigies around town, burned them, staged a mock funeral, and mourned the loss of "American Liberty."[3] Similar demonstrations were held up and down the continent; in Connecticut, for example, crowds in New London, Norwich, Lebanon, Windham, West Haven, Fairfield, and Milford dramatized their discontent with the Stamp Act. By the end of 1765 the stamp distributors in all colonies except Georgia had resigned their posts.

Some of these Stamp Act rioters displayed feelings having little or nothing to do with the British Parliament. For many poor laborers and seamen, the riots afforded opportunities to demonstrate pent-up antagonisms toward rich merchants and officials who flaunted their wealth or abused their power. In Charleston, eighty sailors "armed with Cutlasses and Clubs" visited the home of Henry Laurens, a wealthy merchant, who claimed they "not only menaced very loudly but now & then handled me pretty uncouthly." In the words of historian Marcus Rediker, the sailors were "warm with drink and rage."[4] Rioters in Newport moved from the usual hanging of effigies to the destruction of homes. In New York, hit hard by the postwar depression in the shipbuilding trade, hundreds of unemployed mariners raised the stakes of the protests. On the night the Stamp Act was to take effect they rampaged the city, breaking

windows of British sympathizers and announcing to Governor Coldon that "you'll die a Martyr to your own Villainy . . . and that
every Man, that assists you, Shall be, surely, put to Death." After
hanging Coldon's effigy, the crowd carted it around in the governor's own prize chariot, which they later burned. The rioters focused upon images of wealth and pretention. Breaking into the
house of Major Thomas James, they chopped up furniture, threw
china to the ground, ripped open featherbeds, vandalized the garden.
In the end, they forced Colden to hand over all the stamps.[5]

In Boston laborers and seamen leveled their sights on prominent
royalists such as Thomas Hutchinson, the lieutenant governor and
chief justice of Massachusetts, who justified poverty because it produced "industry and frugality."[6] Twelve days after forcing Andrew
Oliver's resignation, the crowd attacked three luxurious mansions,
including Hutchinson's. Historian Gary Nash reconstructs that second wave of rioting in vivid detail:

> Catching the chief justice and his family at the dinner table,
> the crowd smashed in the doors with axes, sent the family
> packing, and then systematically reduced the furniture to splin-
> ters, stripped the walls bare, chopped through inner partitions
> until the house was a hollow shell, destroyed the formal gar-
> dens in the rear of the mansion, drank the wine cellar dry, stole
> £900 sterling in coin, and carried off every movable object of
> value except some of Hutchinson's books and papers, which
> were left to scatter in the wind.[7]

According to William Gordon, a contemporary of the rioters, "Gentlemen of the army, who have seen towns sacked by the enemy,
declare they never before saw an instance of such fury."[8]

Was Boston in the midst of class warfare? Not exactly, but the
poor had definitely been getting poorer as the rich got richer. Since
the late 1600s, the richest 5 percent of the population had increased
their share of the taxable assets from 30 percent to 49 percent, while
the wealth owned by the poorest half of the population had decreased from 9 percent to a mere 5 percent.[9] Throughout New
England, increasing numbers of people tried to scratch out a living

from depleted farmland, leading to a rise in the number of "strolling poor" who wandered the countryside in search of work. Each village in turn "warned out" these migrants to keep them from the local relief rolls; seaport towns also warned them out, but to little avail. Faced with no other opportunities, the poor congregated in the larger ports such as Boston, Newport, and New York where they could work odd jobs or ship out to sea.

The mob was thereby on the increase, getting angrier as well as larger. "From your Labour and Industry," wrote a radical from Boston, "arises all that can be called Riches, and by your Hands it must be defended: Gentry, Clergy, Lawyers, and military Officers, do all support their Grandeur by your Sweat, and at your Hazard." A New Yorker wrote:

> Some individuals . . . by the Smiles of Providence, or some other means, are enabled to roll in their four whell'd Carriages, and can support the expense of good Houses, rich Furniture, and Luxurious Living. But is it equitable that 99, rather 999, should suffer for the Extravagance or Grandeur of one? Especially when it is considered that Men frequently owe their Wealth to the impoverishment of their Neighbors? [10]

Not all Stamp Act protesters felt class antagonisms. Many merchants, lawyers, and other colonists of comfortable means objected only to the abuse of power by the British Parliament. These "Whigs," as they called themselves, talked about the rights of Englishmen, not violent social upheaval. (The "Whigs," who took their name from the liberal political party in Great Britain, labeled their opponents "Tories," after the conservative party that was pushing for stern measures in the colonies.) The issue, the Whigs believed, was simple and straightforward—no taxation without representation—and the wanton destruction of property only served to discredit their cause. Historians William Pencak and Pauline Maier have shown that the Sons of Liberty from Boston were at least as wealthy as Boston loyalists, while the Sons of Liberty from Newport, Charleston, and other areas came from the "respectable Populace" as well. [11]

These prosperous patriots had more of an interest in protecting property than destroying it. In New York, leading Whigs such as Robert Livingston and several ship captains tried to tame the throngs. In Newport, patriot leaders supposedly tried to quell the riots by offering money, clothes and "everything he would have" to John Webber, a young transient who appeared to have influence with the mob.[12] Whigs and lower-class rioters vied for control: Who would define the issues? Whose revolt was this, anyway?

In Boston, the leader of the Boston Stamp Act rioting was Ebenezer MacIntosh, a debt-ridden shoemaker from the South End whose father, one of the strolling poor, had been warned out of Boston when Ebenezer was in his teens. Appointed a fireman for Engine Company No. 9 in 1760, MacIntosh rose to prominence in the annual Pope's Day riots. Every year on November 5, to mark the anniversary of an aborted Catholic conspiracy to blow up Parliament in 1605, Boston's artisans and laborers staged dramatizations depicting the pope beside a giant effigy of the devil, suitably coated with tar and feathers. Early in the day, working-class youths solicited money for feasting and drinking from more prosperous inhabitants throughout Boston, who dared not refuse. As the day and the drinking progressed, competition between the North Enders and the South Enders turned violent, with paramilitary street gangs fighting for the honor of torching the stage sets in giant bonfires. On the surface, this fighting served no greater purpose—and yet, every November 5, lower-class Bostonians owned the town while genteel society huddled indoors.

Seventeen sixty-five was different. During the Stamp Act riots in August, North Enders and South Enders had worked side by side, destroying mansions in their wrath. Upper-class citizens nervously awaited the approach of November 1, the day the Stamp Act was supposed to take effect, with its close conjunction to November 5. What might happen if the mob ceased to expend its destructive energy upon itself? Boston's selectmen called out a military watch.

On November 5, 1765, Boston's working class marched en masse past the statehouse to display its power, with Ebenezer MacIntosh firmly in command.[13] Refraining from the usual street brawls, the combined North Enders and South Enders, two thousand strong, appeared as a formidable political force. While royal authority quivered, however, affluent Whigs relaxed: MacIntosh and other leaders had been bought. With the avowed intention of uniting the North and South Ends, the Whigs had provided a feast for the street leaders at a popular tavern, carefully dividing the guests into five different classes according to rank. For the Pope's Day parade they furnished pompous military regalia and bestowed official-sounding titles on key men. When MacIntosh marched at the head, he wore a blue and gold uniform, gilded armor, and a hat laced with gold. There were no riots on Pope's Day in 1765.

Although the Whigs prevailed in this instance, their relationship with street leaders remained ambivalent. On the one hand, they issued official disclaimers to the destruction of property, and they even went so far as to forbid "Negroes," supposedly more prone to destructive acts, from marching in the Pope's Day parade.[14] But they also needed to continue some sort of alliance with lower-class elements, and they did make it clear that British officials would receive no help whatsoever in identifying or punishing any of the August rioters. Street fighters needed this kind of protection; legally powerless and vulnerable, they could have suffered severely from sanctions for their actions. Prosperous leaders and lower-class activists each filled their roles, even if they evidenced different types of behavior and expressed different goals. They formed an alliance for their mutual benefit, although the alliance was not permanent, and it did not extend to personal loyalty: when Ebenezer MacIntosh was thrown into debtors' prison in 1770, not a single rich rebel offered to bail him out.[15] And when Whig leaders celebrated the anniversary of the Stamp Act protests in subsequent years, they did so with expensive feasts to which the actual rioters were not invited.[16]

Any effective challenge to British authority required a broad base of support, and class antagonisms helped motivate many who might not have responded to abstract legal issues. "Taxation without representation" was real for those who voted and paid taxes; for those who did neither, other symbols loomed larger. In Virginia the lower classes resented horse racing and gambling, customs of the plantation gentry. In New York theatrical productions were disrupted by "disorderly persons (in a Riotous Manner)."[17] A play in the Chapel Street theater, according to newspaper accounts, was "interrupted by the multitude who broke open the doors and entered with noise and tumult," shouting "Liberty, Liberty." Patrons were driven into the street, "their Caps, Hats, Wigs, Cardinals, and Cloaks . . . torn off (thro' Mistake) in the Hurray." The rioters "immediately demolished the House, and carried the pieces to the Common, where they consumed them in a Bonfire."[18] Why was the theater so hated? Theatergoers dressed in high fashion, arrived in carriages, and spent their money on frivolities. A New Yorker writing under the name of "Philander" complained that season tickets sold for as much as fifty pounds, while poor people starved. Another writer felt "it highly improper that such Entertainments should be exhibited at this time of public distress, when great Numbers of poor people can scarcely find means of subsistence."[19]

The boycott of tea, the most enduring component of American resistance, was imbued with class connotations. Historian Barbara Clark Smith describes the specific cultural milieu of teatime:

> Tea parties in genteel parlors required an elaborate material culture—some if not all of the following items: teapots and their rests, teacups and saucers, tea canisters, teakettles or urns, teaspoons and spoon dishes, sugar bowls, sugar tongs, cream jugs, slop bowls, strainers, tea trays, and tea tables—plus plates and utensils for any food consumed with the tea.[20]

Although some common folk might enjoy a sip now and again, the major consumers of tea participated in a ritual activity which was prohibitively expensive for the vast majority of colonists.[21]

Abstinence from tea came easily to commoners, but those with a tea-drinking habit had a more difficult time. At issue was not merely the ritual but the tea itself—strong tea, invigorating tea, heavily caffeinated tea. For that morning or late afternoon rush, affluent colonists turned to Bohea and brewed it dark. (Lighter teas such as Souchong and Hyson accounted for only about 10 percent of American imports.) Patriot leaders and newspaper editors, hoping to convince confirmed tea drinkers to change their habits, circulated wild rumors: tea was bad for your health, tea bred fleas, tea was packed tightly into chests by the stomping of barefoot Chinese.[22] They touted substitutes such as sassafras, sage, and "Labrador," widely hailed as superior to all imported varieties. But real tea drinkers knew the truth: none of the local imitations gave that buzz. Labrador, according to a convention of ladies from Worcester, Massachusetts, had a "debilitating" quality which led to social "frigidity."[23] The only viable substitute for tea was coffee, and it is no mere coincidence that between 1770 and the 1790s per capita coffee consumption in the United States increased more than sevenfold.[24] Although it too was imported, coffee did not carry the same social or political stigma as tea. Americans started brewing beans instead of leaves during the Revolution and never looked back.

The politics of tea contributed to a transformation of social relationships. When rumor spread that Isaac Jones of Weston, Massachusetts, had been selling tea at his tavern, thirty patriots disguised with war paint broke all his windows, smashed his bowls, mugs, and china, drank all his liquor, and then forced him to apologize for his crime.[25] The lower and middle classes confiscated tea whenever they could, intimidating and humiliating the offenders. Enforcement of the tea boycott turned class rank upside down: by insisting that those who could afford tea cease their indulgences, ordinary people exerted power over their "betters."

Tea helped unite opposition to British policy, for the resistance to the tax on tea dovetailed nicely with lower-class resentments. Tea was an easy target, a symbol both of Parliament's arrogance and a crumbling social hierarchy. By identifying the British and their loyalist allies as purveyors of a decadent European culture— tea drinking theatergoers who dressed in fancy clothes and enforced oppressive laws—Whig leaders and street fighters were able to unite around a common enemy. Some thought they were opposing taxation and protecting liberty and property; others (who paid no taxes and had little property to protect) flailed against symbols of wealth and the intrusive military presence which kept the rich in power. However they defined their issues, colonists of varying backgrounds joined in a crusade infused with a sense of righteousness.

At no time was this alliance of American interests more evident than during the Boston Tea Party. On November 28, 1773, the ship *Dartmouth* landed in Boston harbor filled with 114 chests of East India Company tea, subject to minimal import duties. If the tea were unloaded and sold, Parliament's ability to tax the colonists would be reaffirmed and the boycott of tea would be seriously undermined by cheap prices. Legally, however, the tea could not be returned to England. What was to be done? During the three weeks that followed thousands of citizens from Boston and nearby towns met repeatedly to discuss possible strategies, while some maintained a continuous watch over the *Dartmouth* and two other ships which joined it at Griffin's Wharf. The town meeting was extended to include "the whole body of the people"—women, apprentices, African Americans, and servants were allowed to participate. Thomas Hutchinson described one meeting as consisting "principally of the Lower ranks of the People & even Journeymen Tradesmen were brought in to increase the number & the Rabble were not excluded yet there were divers Gentlemen of Good Fortunes among them."[26]

On December 16, the day before customs officials were entitled to seize the cargo and land it themselves, an estimated 5,000 people traveled through a cold, steady rain to gather at the Old South Meeting House. (The entire population of Boston at the time was only about 16,000, children included.) The deadline for action had arrived. The meeting decided to send Francis Rotch, captain of the *Dartmouth*, to make one final appeal to the governor to allow his ship to return to England, its cargo intact. In Rotch's absence, and even as the speeches continued, informal preparations for a dramatic response were in the making. By the time Rotch returned at 5:45 P.M., Old South was lit only by candles. He announced that the governor had refused to bend. Sam Adams then rose to say that he saw nothing more that the people of Boston could do to save their country. Could this have been an earnest admission of defeat? Not likely. Indian war whoops, described by a Tory observer as "an hideous Yelling," came from outside, quickly answered by calls from the meeting house. Witnesses remember the various cries: "Boston harbor a tea-pot tonight!" "Hurrah for Griffin's Wharf!" "The Mohawks are come!"[27]

Who were those Mohawks? According to Joshua Wyeth, a journeyman blacksmith, "It was proposed that young men, not much known in town and not liable to be easily recognized should lead in the business . . . [M]ost of the persons selected for the occasion were apprentices and journeymen, as was the case with myself."[28] Unlike the mob of the Stamp Act riots, however, this was a contained and disciplined cadre. No extraneous looting or destruction of property was permitted. A padlock accidentally broken was supposedly replaced, while the few men who tried to grab some tea for themselves were severely reprimanded and ridiculed.

Indeed, Griffin's Wharf was strangely quiet that night; according to John Adams, "Boston was never more still and calm."[29] The rain had stopped, the moon was out. A large crowd gathered on shore, watching in silence as the chosen crews, numbering fewer than a hundred, chopped open 342 chests of tea and dumped them into the chilly water.[30] One witness claimed to hear the sounds of the hatchets from a considerable distance. By nine o'clock the mission had been accomplished and the crowd disbursed without any further disturbance. John Adams wrote in his diary: "This is the most magnificent Movement of all. There is a Dignity, a Majesty, a Sublimity in this last Effort of the Patriots that I greatly admire."[31] No small part of that "sublimity" was the manner in which rich rebels and rabble had joined in common cause. Some made speeches; others dumped tea; all were included in the process.

A Shoemaker's Tale

Peter Oliver, the Crown-appointed chief justice of Massachusetts, had a simple explanation for the tumultuous events in Boston during the 1760s and 1770s: James Otis, Jr., had vowed "that if his Father was not appointed a Justice of the superior Court, he would set the Province in a Flame." The riotous crowds, incapable of thinking or acting for themselves, were just following the commands of Otis and his friends:

They always had their Geniuses, who (by the *Mob Whistle*, as horrid as the *Iroquois Yell* . . .) could fabricate the Structure of

Rebellion from a single Straw. . . . As for the People in general, they were like the Mobility of all Countries, perfect Machines, wound up by any Hand who might first take the Winch.[32]

Anne Hulton, sister of the customs commissioner, also believed the rebellion was directed by "the Leader, who Governs absolutely, the Minds & the Passions of the people," although unlike Oliver, she did not state who that "Leader" happened to be.[33]

The notions of Oliver and Hulton seem patently absurd, but history texts for over two centuries have followed their lead every time they explain the actions of the Boston "mob" in terms of propagandists like Sam Adams. The theory of "diffusion"—ideas spreading from top down, from the few to the many—still informs much of our telling of history.

But that's not always the way history works. Except in totalitarian societies, people (even common people) tend to pursue, of their own volition, their personal interests and the interests of their communities. This was certainly true during the years leading up to the American Revolution. Witness the experiences of George Robert Twelves Hewes, a poor shoemaker who involved himself in the heart of the action.[34]

As a youth, Hewes said in his memoirs, he was "exposed of course to all the mischiefs to which children are liable in populous cities." At the age of six, while gathering wood chips at the waterfront, he jumped aboard some floating planks, fell in, and almost drowned. After nursing him back to health, his mother flogged him. A year later his father died, and young George was sent off to school. He ran away; the school mistress locked him in a dark closet; he dug his way out. Hewes recalled his education at the next school as "little more than a series of escapes" from being whipped. Unable to control her son, his mother Abigail sent him to live with an uncle in Wrentham, where George was made to endure the monotonous routine of farm life. Upon reaching the age of apprenticeship, he was placed under the care of a shoemaker named Downing who tried to keep him in line with a cowhide. Even so, Hewes recounted incidents of breaking curfew, fooling his master, and stealing food. Again George tried to escape, this time by joining the military during the French and Indian War. The recruiters, however, were under orders to "enlist no Roman-Catholic, nor any under five feet two inches high without their shoes." George, at five-one, was rejected. After heightening his heels and "stuffing his stocking with paper and rags," he tried again, but the examining officer was not so easily fooled. He went to the waterfront to enlist on a British ship of war, but his older brothers interfered and sent him back to his master.

In 1763, upon reaching the age of twenty-one, Hewes set up shop as an independent shoemaker. He was never very successful. In 1768 George married the daughter of a washerwoman. During his courtship, he went into debt in order to obtain "a sappled coat & breeches of fine cloth." Unable to pay off this liability, he landed in debtors prison two years later. "For want of Goods or Estate of the within named George Robt Twelve Hewes, I have taken his bodey & committed him to his majesty's gaol in Boston," wrote the constable. After getting out of jail, he and his family lived with relatives and as lodgers; in 1771, the only year for which the Boston records still survive, he was not taxed for any property.

George Robert Twelves Hewes, in short, was precisely the sort of person whom critics labeled as "rabble"—he was poor, he was saucy, and he was at home in the streets of Boston. His political education seems to have started in 1768 with the occupation of Boston by 4,000 British troops—approximately one for every four civilians. The soldiers' presence affected Hewes personally. They stopped him after curfew, letting him proceed only after he offered them a few swigs of rum. One cheated him out of a pair of shoes. He witnessed another robbing a woman "of her bonnet, cardinal muff and tippet." In addition to this petty harassment, the British troops, hoping to augment their meager wages, competed for work in their off-hours with laborers and lower-class craftsmen like himself.

The tension between soldiers and civilians reached a climax early in 1770. On February 23—a marketing day, and thereby a school holiday—a large crowd dominated by school boys and apprentices gathered near the shop of Theophilus Lilly, who had been dealing imported goods against the wishes of Boston's patriots. From inside the store, Ebenezer Richardson, a customs informer employed by the Crown, fired his gun toward the assembled throng and killed an eleven-year-old boy, Christopher Seider. A week later, only a block from Hewes' shop, a fight broke out between moonlighting soldiers and civilian workers. Two days after that, according to Hewes, a British sentry abused a barber's apprentice who was trying to collect a bill, inspiring a band of boys to harass the British troops under Captain Preston. "I was soon on the ground among them," Hewes claimed. The boys threw snowballs; the troops responded by charging their hecklers, swinging guns and clubs. Hewes himself received a blow on his shoulder. Despite repeated orders from Preston, the gathering, which had swollen to include men as well as boys, refused to disperse. According to Hewes, he and the others "were in the king's highway, and had as good a right to be there" as did the soldiers. Perhaps so, but the troops fired into the crowd nonetheless.

Of the five who were killed in the Boston Massacre, Hewes knew four: a ropewalk worker, a sailor, and two apprentices. He stood right next to James Caldwell, the sailor, catching him as he fell and helping to carry him quickly to a doctor. He then ran to tell Caldwell's captain. All that night, Hewes remained in the thick of the action. The next day he gave a deposition, summarized by historian Alfred Young:

> At 1:00 A.M., like many other enraged Bostonians, he went home to arm himself. On his way back to the Town House with a cane he had a defiant exchange with Sergeant Chambers of the 29th Regiment and eight or nine soldiers, "all with very large clubs or cutlasses." A soldier, Dobson, "ask'd him how he far'd; he told him very badly to see his townsmen shot in such a manner, and asked him if he did not think it was a dreadful thing." Dobson swore "it was a fine thing" and "you shall see more of it." Chambers "seized and forced" the cane from Hewes, "saying I had no right to carry it. I told him I had as good a right to carry a cane as they had to carry clubs." [35]

In the wake of the massacre, the Boston town meeting was extended to include the body of the people. Those too poor, like Hewes, or too young, like the apprentices, were implicitly acknowledged as actors in this dynamic public drama. Conservatives who objected to the participation of the lower classes were shouted down by men who argued "that if they had no Property they had Liberty, and their posterity might have property."[36] Hewes attended these meetings, marched in the funeral procession, gave a deposition, and watched the various murder trials which followed the killings. He had become, in the words of Young, "a citizen, a political man."[37]

The shoemaker's career as a street activist peaked during the Boston Tea Party. On a cold night in December of 1773, Hewes recalled years later, he had dressed as an Indian and covered his face and hands with coal dust.

I fell in with many who were dressed, equipped and painted as I was . . . When we arrived at the wharf, there were three of our number who assumed authority to direct our operations, to which we readily submitted. They divided us into three parties, for the purpose of boarding the three ships which contained tea at the same time. . . .

The commander of the division to which I belonged, as soon as we were on board the ship, appointed me boatswain, and ordered me to go to the captain and demand of him the keys to the hatches and a dozen candles. I made the demand accordingly, and the captain promptly replied, and delivered the articles; but requested me at the same time to do no damage to the ship or rigging. We then were ordered by our commander to open the hatches, and take out all the chests of tea and throw them overboard, and we immediately proceeded to execute his orders; first cutting and splitting the chests with our tomahawks, so as thoroughly to expose them to the effects of the water. In about three hours from the time we went on board, we had thus broken and thrown overboard every tea chest to be found in the ship; while those in the other ships were disposing of the tea in the same way, at the same time. We were surrounded by British armed ships, but no attempt was made to resist us. We then quietly retired to our several places of residence, without having any conversation with each other, or taking any measures to discover who were our associates. [38]

Why was a lowly shoemaker with neither military experience nor political connection chosen as a leader? George Hewes was well known on the Boston waterfront for his whistling talent, and a whistler could obviously out-perform a nonwhistler at conspiratorial tasks conducted in the dead of night. In the true spirit of the Revolution, George Robert Twelves Hewes was promoted to serve as a boatswain not because of his status but because of his ability: he could pucker and blow.

In January of 1774, George Hewes was the focal point of yet another political skirmish in the prelude to war. The occasion was a chance encounter with a well known Tory named John Malcolm, a customs informer who recently had been "genteely tarr'd and feather'd." According to the *Massachusetts Gazette*,

> Mr. George-Robert-Twelves Hewes was coming along Fore-Street, near Captain Ridgway's, and found the redoubted John Malcolm, standing over a small boy, who was pushing a little sled before him, cursing, damning, threatening and shaking a very large cane with a very heavy ferril on it over his head. . . . Mr. Hewes conceiving if he struck him with that weapon he must have killed him out-right, came up to him, and said to him, Mr. Malcolm I hope you are not going to strike this boy with that stick.
>
> Malcolm returned, you are an impertinent rascal, it is none of your business. Mr. Hewes then asked him, what had the child done to him. . . . Malcolm on that damned Mr. Hewes, called him a vagabond, and said he would let him know he should not speak to a gentleman in the street. Mr. Hewes returned to that, he was neither a rascal nor a vagabond, and though a poor man was in as good credit in town as he was. Malcolm called him a liar, and said he was not, nor ever would be. Mr. Hewes retorted, be that as it will, I never was tarred nor feathered any how. On this Malcolm struck him, and wounded him deeply in the forehead, so that Mr. Hewes for some time lost his senses. Capt. Godfrey, then present, interposed, and after some altercation, Malcolm went home.

That evening a crowd intervened on Hewes behalf, taking Malcolm from his house and dragging him on a sled through the streets "amidst the huzzas of thousands." Over the objections of some gentlemen, they had their way with their prisoner. The *Gazette* continued:

> [T]hey proceeded to elevate Mr. Malcolm from his sled into a cart, and stripping him to buff and breeches, gave him a modern jacket [tar and feathers] and hied him away to liberty-tree, where they proposed to him to renounce his present commission, and swear that he would never hold another inconsistent with the liberties of his country; but this he obstinately refusing, they then carted him to the gallows, passed a rope around his neck, and threw the other end over the beam as if they intended to hang him: But this manoeuvre he set at defiance. They then basted him for some time with a rope's end, and threatened to cut his ears off, and on this he complied, and they then brought him home.[39]

The class overtones of the argument between Hewes and Malcolm are clear: in revolutionary Boston a simple shoemaker no longer had to yield ground to his betters. In the Malcolm incident, as with the massacre and tea party, Hewes seized the moment, challenged authority, responded to injustice, and stood up for what he perceived as his rights or his interests. His behavior, which gentlemen might consider impudent, was defended by others of his own class, who acted collectively in the public arena.

George Hewes, an actual person within that anonymous "mob" so slandered by loyalist opponents, certainly knew his own mind. He did not need James Otis or Sam Adams to tell him what to do. Lower-class patriots such as Hewes, animated by their own concerns, became increasingly insolent and dangerous to the established order. Together with his cohorts, this Boston shoemaker engaged in purposive political activity with revolutionary consequences.[40]

While die-hard Tories like Peter Oliver and Anne Hulton continued to insist that most revolutionaries were mindless machines, other members of the privileged classes started to get the message. On the eve of the Revolution, Gouverneur Morris, while observing a crowd action in New York City, noted this with considerable trepidation:

These sheep, simple as they are, cannot be pulled as heretofore. In short, there is no ruling them; and now, to leave the metaphor, the heads of the mobility grow dangerous to the gentry; and how to keep them down is the question. . . . The mob begin to think and to reason. Poor reptiles: it is with them a vernal morning, they are struggling to cast off their winter's slough, they bask in the sunshine, and ere noon they will bite, depend on it. The gentry begin to fear this. . . . I see, and I see it with fear and trembling, that if the disputes with Great Britain continue, we shall be under the worst of all possible dominions; we shall be under the domination of a riotous mob.[41]

And for the elite who didn't get it on their own, the laboring classes made their message loud and clear. A Charleston minister who derided "*mechanics* and country *clowns*" was quickly dismissed by members of his congregation, who proudly boasted "that mechanics and country clowns (infamously so-called), are the real, and absolute masters of Kings, Lords, Commons and Priests."[42]

Country Rebellions

Prerevolutionary civil unrest was not limited to urban areas. From South Carolina to the Canadian border, a host of disturbances troubled the countryside. Each had its own set of causes, its own course of action, its own resolution, but all demonstrated the instability of an American society still in the making, and all used violent confrontation as a means of settling public disputes. Although British imperial policy did not figure prominently in most of these clashes, the repeated resistance to civil authority tilled the soil for the revolution which followed.

In 1764 an estimated 1,500 white settlers from western Pennsylvania marched toward Philadelphia demanding protection from Indians who were allegedly committing "horrid Ravages, cruel murders, and most shocking Barbarities." The "Paxton Boys," as they were called, were disappointed that no "Premium for Indian Scalps" had been offered by the Quaker-controlled government, and they expressed their disappointment by slaughtering a number of friendly Native Americans.[43]

In 1767 the settlers of the South Carolina backcountry also complained about the lack of governmental protection from an "infernal Gang of Villains"—white men this time—who looted and burned houses, stole stock, raped women, and generally "perpetrated such shocking Outrages thro'out the Back Settlements, as is past Description."[44] Lacking county sheriffs and courts to administer law and order, respectable citizens felt they had no choice but to regulate society on their own. For the following three years, the interior of South Carolina came under the control of vigilante "Regulators" who tracked down the bandits, captured and tried them, and administered punishment: flogging, forced labor, exile, and, in some cases, hanging.

In North Carolina another group of Regulators, claiming that corrupt local officials "continually Squez'd and oppressed poor . . . families" through taxation and extortion, declared they would curb "abuses of Power" by paying no more taxes until their grievances were addressed.[45] Gathering in large numbers they intimidated their enemies, disrupted the courts, and freed their leaders from jails. Although the Regulator movement in the North Carolina backcountry involved an overwhelming 80 percent of the white male residents, in 1771 the Regulators were defeated in a full-scale military confrontation with the colonial government that left more than 25 killed and 160 wounded.[46] Forced to disband, over 6,000 former Regulators repudiated their past misdeeds by signing oaths of allegiance to the Crown. In this trial run at Revolution—featuring an oppressive government accused by ordinary citizens of unfair taxation and abuses of power—the rebels lost.

In New York and New Jersey, rural unrest centered upon conflict between tenants or squatters on the one hand and large proprietors on the other. Numerous armed uprisings threatened social stability in various locations from the 1740s through the 1770s, with contested land claims generally at the heart of the conflict. When powerful New Jersey proprietors evicted small farmers from disputed land in 1746, the farmers, acting collectively, prevented anyone else from working the fields by ruining their crops and tearing down their fences. After some were jailed for their actions, others turned out in force "with clubbs, Axes and Crow barrs" to free them.[47]

These ordinary people, fighting for their land and their livelihood, voiced great anger. One promised that if the proprietor John Coxe jailed any more people, "they wod go . . . & pull Coxe's House down abot his Ears." Another said of Samuel Nevill, a county judge and assemblyman, "Damn him for a Son of a Bitch, I wish I cod see him, I'd be the death of him."[48] Even though the evictions were upheld by legal and martial force, simple farmers had challenged the established hierarchy in a manner reminiscent of the "Levellers" of the English countryside during the seventeenth century.

Isolated conflicts occurred on large manors in New York during the 1750s, but it was not until 1766 that land disputes culminated in a major rebellion. Spurred in part by the Stamp Act riots in New York City, tenants on some of the estates refused to pay their rent. In April an angry crowd from the Van Cortlandt Manor, complaining of rising rents, short leases, and frequent evictions, decided to march toward New York City to liberate prisoners and tell John Van Cortlandt they would "pull down his House in Town" if he did not give them "a grant forever of his Lands." Encouraged by tales of the city's mob, the insurgents "expected to be assisted by the poor people" when they arrived in Manhattan. But the poor people of New York, not directly concerned with the tenants' problems, offered no assistance and the marchers quickly retreated.[49]

In June the Livingston Manor erupted, along with portions of the Van Rensselaer holdings. A crowd of 200 "marched to murther the Lord of the Manor and level his house, unless he would sign leases for 'em agreeable to their form."[50] The rioters did not make good on their threat, but they did vent their anger on Robert Abraham Van Deusen, a tenant who occupied disputed land by favor of his landlord. When Van Deusen refused to give ground, "sixty or seventy" men "pulled him out by the Hair of his Head, beat his Son, turned out his Wife and Children, threw out his Goods and destroyed a part of them, tore off the Roof of his House and then went away."[51] When a sheriff with posse arrived on the scene a week later, the insurgents, well armed, were able to fight to a stalemate. Four died and many more were wounded in a conflict which seemed to be escalating daily.

The uprisings of 1766 challenged the ability of landed proprietors to maintain control of the countryside. According to one report, "Seventeen hundred of the Levellers with fire arms are collected at Poughkeepsie. All the jails broke open through all the countries."[52] These "Levellers," proud and boastful, no longer ceded to the authority of the landlords: Joseph Paine claimed that he had "Girdled, & cutt down several thousands" of trees on Livingston Manor and that "he would go & destroy the timber as he pleased & Robert Livingston kiss his a—s."[53] Most significantly, they understood the importance of collective action: they declared "that if any Tenants setld without the Rest they should be destroyed."[54] Local authorities, unable to quell the uprising, had to resort in the end to the assistance of British troops.

Again, the 1766 uprisings in New York foreshadowed the greater conflict that followed: angry farmers, apparently powerless, stood tall in the face of their rulers, who had to be bailed out by the British Army. The tenant rebellions of the middle colonies, along with the Regulator movements in the South, contributed indirectly to the coming Revolution by chipping away at the notion that a few men of prestige and privilege could exploit those beneath them with impunity. Rural unrest, as Edward Countryman observes, presented a more serious threat to the existing order than did the urban mob:

> Townsmen almost always went unarmed, except for stones and sticks. They acted and then dispersed. They organized quickly and posed no real challenge to institutions of power. Country people, however, were much more likely to be armed, if only because most farmers kept a gun or two for hunting. They were much more likely to attack the symbols of authority. They broke up courts; they kidnapped judges and sheriffs; they opened jails.[55]

Perhaps country rebels had more to gain, or at least more to lose: they fought for either their land, which was equivalent to their livelihood, or for their personal safety.

Street actions and rural uprisings did not follow an exact script, nor did they lead in a linear progression toward a break with England. Conflicts were many and varied, each shaped heavily by local circumstance: the riots against smallpox inoculations in Norfolk in 1768 and 1769 were directed at Tories, while inoculation protests in Marblehead in 1774 zeroed in on Whig proprietors of a smallpox hospital.[56] But at least in part, the medium was the message. Historian Paul Gilje, defining a "riot" as "any group of twelve or more people attempting to assert their will immediately through the use of force outside the normal bounds of law," has discovered evidence of 150 riots in the thirteen colonies from 1765 through 1769—and there were undoubtedly more he did not detect. During the early 1770s, according to Gilje, the rioting contined on a similar scale.[57] These prerevolutionary disturbances advanced a social climate conducive to violent confrontation. Tenants who wielded axes against their landlords or poor folk who tore apart theaters were not protesting against Parliament, but they were becoming accustomed to expressing rage, resisting authority, and taking public policy into their own hands. They questioned, they challenged, they refused to submit. Modern historians call it an end to deference; in the minds of the contemporary elite, it seemed like insolence. The hierarchical society which Euro-American colonists had brought with them from the Old World was beginning to crumble. Many common people on the eve of the Revolution would not accept conditions that were presented to them by those with more power, status, or money. They were primed to become rebels.

Frontier Swagger

Ethan Allen, a settler in the Green Mountain region of northeastern New York, was one of these upstarts not awed by his "superiors." Allen was found guilty of assault twice within a month. When hauled into court the second time, he exposed "his naked body and in a threatening manner with his fist lifted up repeated these malicious words three times: 'You lie you dog,' and also did with a loud voice say that he would spill the blood of any that opposed him."[58] Later, when the Governor of New York issued a proclamation not to his liking, Allen issued a proclamation of his own: the Governor could "stick it in his ars."[59] On another occasion, after burning down the house of one of his enemies, Allen offered some parting words: "Go your way now, and complain to that damned Scoundrel your Governor. God damn your Governor, Laws, King, Council, and Assembly."[60] This man, showing no deference whatsoever, embodied the spirit of arrogance which led first to local rebellion and finally to national revolution.

Why and how did a frontier ruffian like Ethan Allen rise to a position of power and influence? At the close of the French and Indian War, many land-hungry settlers purchased cheap claims in northern New England between the Connecticut River and Lake Champlain. The titles came cheaply primarily because they were fraudulent: although the Crown had given the region to New York, Governor Benning Wentworth of New Hampshire declared on his own authority that the area came under his jurisdiction. Breaking the land down into affordable units, Wentworth sold deeds to the sons of New England yeomen who hoped to start farms with little capital. Papers in hand, the Yankees set out in considerable numbers to inhabit the future state of Vermont.

But New York speculators also held title to those lands, and late in 1769 two Yorkers tried to evict settlers who possessed Wentworth grants. Sensing the dangerous precedent this might set, several owners of Wentworth papers decided to fight the evictions in court. They hired Ethan Allen, who had recently moved to the area, to find a lawyer and pursue the case, but the deck was stacked against the defendants: two of the presiding judges, the attorney general, and the plaintiff's lawyer all held New York deeds in the disputed area. The outcome was a foregone conclusion, but after the trial Allen spoke provocatively to the victorious attorney and the attorney general: "The gods of the hills are not the gods of the valley." When his opponents asked what he meant by this cryptic remark, he replied: "If you will accompany me to the hills of Bennington, the sense will be made clear." The New York attorneys chose to remain in Albany.[61]

Upon returning to Bennington, Allen met with other holders of Wentworth deeds in Stephen Fay's tavern, a two-and-a-half-story unpainted structure guarded by a large but shabby stuffed catamount, or mountain lion, perched on top of a twenty-foot pole. It was here at the Catamount tavern that Allen, his brothers, brothers-in-law, cousins, and other defenders of the New Hampshire deeds formed themselves into the Green Mountain Boys, an unauthorized militia with the single goal of intimidating anyone holding or enforcing New York titles. Over the next several years Ethan Allen and the Green Mountain Boys burned houses and haystacks, demolished fences, and threatened the personal safety of their opponents, taking special care to blacken their own faces with soot or dress as Indians to add that special touch of terror. "They assemble themselves together in the night time," wrote a scared New York official near Bennington, "and throw down all the Yorker fences, etc., and drive the Cattle into the fields and meadows and destroy both Grass and Corn, and do every mischief they can think of."[62] William Cockburn, a New York surveyor, wrote that he had to quit his job for fear of Allen, who was lurking "in the woods with another party blacked and dressed like Indians."[63] Ann Grant, another Yorker, complained that the region had become "a refuge for the vagabonds and banditti of the continent."[64]

According to biographer Michael Bellesiles, Allen carefully cultivated his image as a mad savage, turning his "frontier swagger into an art form."[65] Making ample use of political theater, he became master of the braggart's bluff; violence, he discovered, worked just as well if only implied. Once he seized two New York sheriffs, locking them in separate rooms. During the night he and his friends dangled life-size effigies outside each of their windows; in the morning each prisoner saw that the other had been hanged. He then arranged for them to "escape," one at a time. Each one, retreating quickly to the safety of Albany, spread tales of Allen's barbarity. The eventual discovery of the trick only added to Allen's unsavory reputation.[66]

Humiliation offered more possibilities for creative staging than crude physical abuse. Charles Jellison, another biographer, describes what happened to Dr. Samuel Adams of Arlington:

> Adams was set upon and taken by surprise by a small band of Green Mountain Boys, who carted him away to Stephen Fay's tavern. There in the long room, with Ethan presiding, his case

was heard by the Bennington Committee of Safety, which wasted little time in finding him guilty of being a public nuisance. His punishment, at Ethan's suggestion, was to be public humiliation. Tied securely to an armchair, the doctor was hoisted by ropes to the top of the tavern signpost. There, twenty feet off the ground and on eye-level with the Fay's stuffed catamount, he dangled in his armchair for two hours while the assembled inhabitants of Bennington looked on with wonder and amusement. At the end of his sentence the doctor, noticeably chastened, was lowered, warned to mend his ways, and dismissed by the committee. "This mild and exemplary disgrace," according to Ira [Allen], "had a salutary effect upon the Doctor, and many others." [67]

In trials such as this, the Green Mountain Boys did not argue the finer points of law. The rights of the accused were limited to an opportunity to apologize and repent. Hearings were conducted in taverns; juries adjourned to barns; prisoners were detained in outhouses. The trials were not about justice but politics: they mobilized support, they humiliated those who would not go along with the program, they intimidated the undecided with these blatant displays of power.

Although the Green Mountain Boys were certainly terrorists, their goal was not to kill or inflict pain but to convert. As they gained in strength, they actually minimized the likelihood of bloodshed, for nobody dared oppose them. Ironically, intimidation served to limit armed confrontation; the more violent the image, the less violent the reality. During the height of the controversy in the five years preceding the Revolutionary War, not a single person was killed in the disputed area on the west side of the Green Mountains. Once, when a pitched battle seemed imminent, Ethan Allen caused the enemy to flee simply by hurling invectives. [68]

The Green Mountain Boys drew obvious parallels between their own struggle with a tyrannical governor and the troubles which other New Englanders were having with a tyrannical king. In both cases, distant rulers tried to impose their wills on ordinary people; they taxed, they evicted, they deprived the people of what was rightfully theirs. The Green Mountain Boys fought only to secure their property, and thereby their liberty. Liberty and property—wasn't this the basis of discontent with England as well?

In April of 1775, when armed hostilities broke out between Massachusetts and England, the Green Mountain Boys controlled all of the west side of the mountains and were making inroads into the east side. But their victory was in no way assured. What if the British army came to the aid of New York, as it had during the 1766 uprisings in the Hudson Valley? Clearly, it was in the best interests of the Green Mountain Boys to remove the British army from New York and elsewhere—in other words, to join in the revolution which was evolving all around them. For both practical and ideological reasons, the Green Mountain Boys were happy to merge their own local cause with the greater struggle for power in North America. Of all the prerevolutionary land conflicts, only the battle over the Wentworth claims led seamlessly into the Revolution itself. The Green Mountain Boys, experienced freedom fighters by the time the war broke out, figured prominently in all the military campaigns of the Northeast. Their battlefield contributions have been heralded, but these flamboyant rebels also pioneered in the creative display of civil disorder which lay at the heart of the American Revolution.

Politics Out-of-Doors

People become radicalized by their own political actions, as the Green Mountain Boys so clearly demonstrated.[69] Particular acts of oppression can motivate them, pamphlets and propaganda might stir them, but it is the engagement in collective and purposive activity that turns ordinary people into revolutionaries.

American patriots from New Hampshire, Massachusetts, Rhode Island, Connecticut, New York, New Jersey, Pennsylvania, Delaware, Maryland, Virginia, North Carolina, South Carolina, and Georgia were willing to wage war in 1775 and declare their independence in 1776 because they had participated for the better part of a decade in what would appear as a simple and nonviolent political protest: an economic boycott of British imported goods. Although the riots also played a part, all the Stamp Act protests and tea parties and Regulator movements and land uprisings, even when considered together, involved only a modest fraction of the colonial populace. The nonimportation movement, by contrast, involved the majority of free Americans in one manner or another. On the most basic level, many citizens agreed to refrain from specified private behavior: the consumption of British imports. But private behavior, in this case, was imbued with a great deal of public meaning. By agreeing not to buy certain products, a man or a woman took a stance in support of a well-defined political program. A person did not have to cast a vote or tear down a mansion in order to make a statement. Even those who could never afford imported goods in the first place were able to participate by forcing others to comply.

Nonimportation started as a response to the Sugar Act of 1764 and the Stamp Act of 1765. By reducing their trade in luxury items, such as the gloves given out at funerals, and by forestalling on the payment of debts, merchants in Boston and other port towns hoped to place economic pressure on their British trading partners. The strategy was simple: create a constituency in England that would push for the repeal of colonial taxation. The effects of nonimportation would be felt throughout the British economy: facing decreased demand, glove makers and weavers in England would be forced to lay off workers, who would then riot. John Adams wrote: "I'de rather the Spittlefield weavers should pull down all the houses in old England, and knock the brains out of all the wicked men there, than this country should lose their liberty."[70]

The strategy worked. Unemployed workers in England started rioting. On January 17, 1766, a group of London merchants, claiming that the collapse of their colonial trade was leading them to "utter ruin," pleaded with Parliament to repeal the Stamp Act.[71] Merchants from other British towns presented similar petitions, and in March the Stamp Act was repealed.

When the Townshend Acts of 1767 placed new duties on glass, lead, paint, tea, and paper, Whig leaders again promoted nonimportation as an acceptable alternative to mob violence. The movement was initiated by merchants, but agreements soon circulated "among the people for general signing."[72] Artisans and laborers, hoping to spur the development of local manufacturing, enthusiastically embraced nonimportation. Patriots in Charleston followed Boston's example by holding meetings which were as "full . . . as possible" so that their resolutions would be seen as *"the Sense of the Whole Body."*[73]

As participation broadened, however, the nature of the movement changed. A 1768 agreement in Boston had requested only that the signers "give a constant preference" to merchants who refrained from importation; two years later, Bostonians voted to withhold "for ever hereafter . . . not only all commercial Dealings, but every Act and Office of Common Civility" to four men who refused to participate.[74] In Virginia, millers refused to grind the corn of an Anglican minister who had preached against "the danger and sin of rebellion," while doctors declined to treat his sick wife and children.[75] In Lancaster, Pennsylvania, advocates of nonimportation pledged "never [to] have any fellowship or correspondence" with importers or the consumers of imported goods and to "publish his or their names to the world . . . as a lasting monument to infamy."[76] In a society tightly bound within well-defined communities, social ostracism served as a potent weapon.

Large and vocal crowds which visited the homes of nonparticipants had "a more powerful Effect in reducing . . . such Culprits to Reason than the most convincing Arguments that could be used."[77] In July of 1769, the erection of a scaffold finally convinced Thomas Richardson, a New York jeweler, to comply with nonimportation. In Boston the "Signs, Doors and Windows" of nonsubscribers "were daub'd over in the Night time with every kind of Filth, and one of them particularly had his person treated in the same manner." In October of 1769, Nathaniel Rogers finally agreed to comply "from principles of self-preservation" after his house had twice been "besmeared" with dung.[78] Nonimportation, originally touted as a nonviolent alternative to rioting, had come full circle to embrace mob actions.

The revolutionary implications of this sort of behavior were profound. Nonimportation committees commandeered police and judicial functions when they marched into merchants' quarters, inspected invoices, judged the offenders, and administered punishments.[79] The usurpation of such powers was validated by maintaining a broad political base: all actions became legitimate if they were performed in the name of "the whole body of the people." When the old laws weren't working, Sam Adams declared, the "will and pleasure of society" had to be imposed directly.[80] But who could speak for the will and pleasure of society? The people who came together to sign the agreements. The nonimportation associations—"binding on each and all" of the signers, in the words of the Virginia Association of 1770—functioned as legal compacts.[81] If governments were indeed social contracts as John Locke maintained, the associations could lay a stronger claim to legitimacy than the British Crown.

Nonimportation succeeded again, just as it had during the Stamp Act crisis: the Townshend duties, with the exception of a token tax on tea, were repealed in April of 1770. Having achieved its major goal, the nonimportation movement temporarily subsided. Early in 1774, however, when Parliament responded to the Boston Tea Party by passing the "Coercive Acts"—closing the Boston Harbor, making all Massachusetts officials responsible only to the Crown, and giving added powers to the occupying army—colonial resistance galvanized as never before. The Virginia assembly set aside June 1, the date of the Boston port closure, as a day of fasting and prayer. When the governor answered by dissolving the assembly, members moved to the Raleigh Tavern and continued their meeting. If Parliament could isolate Massachusetts and bring it to its knees, the assembly reasoned, they could subdue Virginia as well. It was time for the American colonists to stand together.

Patriots in other colonies agreed, and on September 5, 1774, the First Continental Congress convened in Philadelphia. Most history texts note the forceful manner in which the delegates petitioned the British government; of more significance than their rhetoric, however, was their decision to form a single "Continental Association" to implement—and enforce—a sweeping nonimportation, nonexportation, and nonconsumption agreement for all the colonies. Crossing regional boundaries and class distinctions, the association, as it came to be called, became the voice, and force, of revolutionary America.

The key to the association lay in its implementation, outlined in section eleven:

> That a committee be chosen in every county, city, and town, by those who are qualified to vote for representatives in the legislature, whose business it shall be attentively to observe the conduct of all persons touching this association; and when it shall be made to appear, to the satisfaction of a majority of any such committee, that any person . . . has violated this association, that such majority do forthwith cause the truth of the case to be published in the gazzette; to the end, that all such foes to the rights of British-America may be publicly known, and universally contemned as the enemies of American liberty; and thenceforth we respectively will break off all dealings with him or her.[82]

The association took effect immediately as "every county, city, and town" formed their committees. These committees commanded far greater power than the "Committees of Correspondence" which had been spreading patriot propaganda and organizing protests. Selected by "the body of the people," they claimed a quasi-legitimate authority over all matters pertaining to political conduct. And in 1774 nearly everything *did* pertain to politics—not only what people said, but what they bought or sold, produced or consumed. In each local community the "committee" enforced the standards of proper revolutionary behavior. No village, family, or individual would remain unaffected by the political, social, and economic convulsions sweeping the colonies.

Despite the wishful thinking of moderate Whigs, violence, both implied and real, lay behind the enforcement of the association by the committees—and the violence was intrinsic to its structure, even if not explicitly advocated. What was likely to happen to people who had been advertised in the newspapers as "enemies of American liberty"? The committee in Skenesborough, New York, published the name of an opponent of the association, announcing that "[we] hereby give notice to the public that he may be treated with all that neglect and contempt which is so justly his due."[83]

"Neglect" meant ostracism, but what might "contempt" entail? The "popular Punishment for modern delinquents" during the revolutionary era was tarring and feathering:[84]

> The following is the Recipe for an effectual Operation. "First, strip a Person naked, then heat the Tar untill it is thin, & pour it upon the naked Flesh, or rub it over with a Tar Brush. . . . After which, sprinkle decently upon the Tar, whilst it is yet warm, as many Feathers as will stick to it. Then hold a lighted Candle to the Feathers, & try to set it all on Fire; if it will burn so much the better. But as the Experiment is often made in cold Weather; it will not then succeed—take also an Halter & put it round the Person's Neck, & then cart him the Rounds." [85]

When the victim tried to remove the tar, he ripped off some skin as well, exposing himself to widespread infection. After John Malcolm was tarred and feathered because of his argument with George Hewes, Malcolm's doctors reported that "his flesh comes off his back in Stakes."[86]

Long after the crowd had dispersed and the wounds had healed, the social stigma lingered on. In an era when "shaming" was taken seriously, tarring and feathering served as the perfect instrument for humiliation. What could be more ridiculous than a human prancing about with feathers, like a silly goose? One Connecticut Tory was forced to walk twenty miles from New Milford to Litchfield, carrying his own live bird. He was then coated with tar and covered with the feathers he had plucked from his goose. After kneeling and thanking the crowd for its leniency, he was marched out of town to the beating of drums. Abner Beebe was coated with hog dung rather than feathers, an ingenious variation invented by the farmers of East Haddam. The feathers came from geese, the dung from pigs—these animals, low status even by barnyard standards, were chosen carefully in order to maximize the embarrassment.[87]

The mere threat of a tarring and feathering generally sufficed to procure a repentance. In Norfolk, Virginia, those accused of opposing the association were made to stand next to a pole, with a

bag of feathers attached to the top and a barrel of hot tar under-
neath.[88] In Bucks County, Pennsylvania, "a disciple of that species
of creatures called *Tories*" was "formally introduced to a tar-barrel,
of which he was repeatedly pressed to smell."[89] The confessions
offered under this sort of pressure were always made in public,
reaffirming the dominance of community values over private interests.[90] Often, the forced nature of the recantations sounded as unreal
as those procured years later under twentieth-century dictators. Six
men from Marblehead, Massachusetts, stated that they considered
the hostility of their community to have been a "cleansing force"
which, they hoped, would make them fit once again to participate
in public affairs.[91]

Despite the objections to the "mob" so often voiced by respectable
citizens, tarring and feathering gained a quasi-official acceptance as a
legitimate mode of punishment. A letter from a New Yorker, after describing the tarring and feathering of Thomas Randolph in Quibble
Town, New Jersey, boasted that "the whole was conducted with that
regularity and decorum, that ought to be preserved in all public punishments."[92] Members of the association's committees, duly elected by
the local populace, often administered the tarring and feathering
themselves; they nearly always gave their approval. Sometimes a few
gentlemen might try to intervene, but as the rebellion progressed, the
distinction between "committee" and "mob" became blurred. The patriotic press reported incidents with a patronizing and humorous tone,
identifying with the crowd rather than the victim. Participants were
complimented rather than condemned for behavior which normally
would be considered rowdy at best, criminal at worst—and they seem
to have enjoyed themselves in the festival-like atmosphere which accompanied the inflicting of bodily harm upon a common enemy.
They too evidenced a condescending and sardonic attitude when they
reported their activities: "[W]e apprehended a violent tory, whom we
tarred and feathered . . . and then left him to ruminate on the quality
of our manners."[93]

Tarring and feathering, however crude and sadistic, fostered a
sense of political involvement for the common people of the times,
allowing them to participate—and prevail—in public affairs. The
pot of tar at the bottom of a liberty pole: two potent symbols that

went hand in hand. Buttressed by a sense of righteousness and feeling secure in their numbers, plain farmers, laborers, seamen, artisans, apprentices, teenagers, and servants helped to determine the course of events. Many could not vote, but they could all engage in "out-of-doors" politics, a term denoting any form of civic activity that was not officially sanctioned by law: caucuses, conventions, committees, or street mobs.[94] The vigor with which the association was enforced, and the vitality of the military mobilization that followed, were due in part to the obvious pleasure which ordinary people took in exercising their new-found powers.

Richard Maxwell Brown notes that crowd activities, even when violent, assumed a sort of moral authority because they allegedly expressed the will of the majority:

> It was the Revolutionary generation that developed, intellectually, the majoritarian concept of popular sovereignty, and it was the Revolutionary generation that perfected techniques of violence to enforce popular sovereignty. . . . The idea of "the sovereignty of the people" gave an ideological and philosophical justification and an awesome dignity to the brutal physical abuse or killing of men that tarring and feathering, vigilantism, and lynching came to embody.[95]

Truly, this was power to the people—at least the majority of the people, or those who could convince themselves and others through forceful means that they acted in the name of the majority. One patriot from Virginia observed that immense powers were "lodged with Men whom I should think must themselves be surprised at the great authority they have stepd. into."[96]

Of particular surprise, no doubt, was the sanctioning of revolutionary activities by both church and tavern, the most important venues in the social lives of the colonists. In normal times, ordinary men walked a tight line between opposing demands: their preachers told them to behave themselves, while their friends in the "ordinaries" encouraged them to drink, swear, and fight. Now, quite fortuitously, men could prove themselves good by being bad. Particularly in Congregational New England, the "Black Regiment" preached patriotism on the Sabbath; at other times, in the taverns which served as meeting places for the local committees, men conducted their righteous business while drinking toast upon toast to manifest their virtue.[97] They freely engaged in the patriotic theater of the moment, however rowdy that might be, secure in the support of both their ministers and their drinking buddies. Exciting times, indeed.

By the close of 1774 the committees enforcing the association had assumed most of the functions of regular governments. They established standards for patriotic behavior, they determined who was not in compliance, and they meted out the appropriate punishments. Over the next two years they came to perform more routine services as well: the committees for Albany and Schenectady, for instance, provided water, fought fires, inspected chimneys, repaired bridges and pumps, ran ferries, maintained roads, licensed taverns, administered goals, forbade smallpox inoculations, mediated custody disputes, set the town clocks, and so on.[98]

At least 7,000 men were elected to the various local committees established to enforce the association, and these men came increasingly from the middle and lower economic ranks.[99] A letter from "A Poor Man" noted that the old governmental forms had proved inadequate and that New Yorkers had been "obliged to suspend the use of them, and have recourse to other forms"—meaning, of course, the committees. "In our new method," he boasted, "the people have all the weight and influence they ought to have, and are effectually represented."[100] In Albany, the move toward popular democracy extended so far that the committee made attendance at a public meeting compulsory for all men "whatsoever able to attend."[101]

But what about the "legitimate" governments of the British Crown? Increasingly, the old colonial regimes exercised no more than a paper power in areas which were not under direct military control. In December of 1774 Lord Dunmore reported regretfully: "There is not a justice of the Peace in *Virginia* that acts, except as a Committee-man."[102] Governor Josiah Martin of North Carolina admitted that his government was "absolutely prostrate, impotent, and that nothing but the shadow of it is left."[103] Throughout Massachusetts, aggrieved loyalists protested that they could not find a judge willing to hear their tales of distress. Even in Boston itself, with British troops patrolling the streets, Anne Hulton complained: "There's no Majistrate that dare or will act to suppress the outrages."[104] Dual authorities existed in all jurisdictions. Each passed laws, but which would be able to enforce them? That's what the Revolutionary War had to determine.

Yankees with Staves and Musick

The American Revolution did not start when the British marched toward Concord on April 19, 1775; it started the previous summer when farmers throughout Massachusetts flocked to their county seats to prevent the Crown-appointed judges from holding court. By showing up armed and in great numbers, these Yankees from the countryside effectively terminated British civil authority in their communities. When a group of influential planters, lawyers, and merchants met in Philadelphia almost two years later, they declared an independence that was already a fact of life for the common folk in the heartland of New England.

Worcester County was quintessential New England: wooded hills, stone walls, rocky soil, modest farms. According to social historian Jackson Turner Main, the overwhelming majority of inhabitants belonged to "a great middle class of small property owners."[105] Nearly all farmers possessed deeds to the land they worked. They tilled the soil with wooden plows and threshed grain on the barn floor with a flail. These were not fancy people; they worked hard on their lands, coming together mostly to pray or to drink.

Villages were scattered every six to eight miles, each consisting of a Congregational church, a tavern, a school, a small store, and perhaps a few artisans' shops. The town of Worcester was home to the county courthouse, where the Inferior Court of Common Pleas convened four times a year to hear countless suits, mostly for the nonpayment of debts.[106] When the court was in session, the town buzzed with gossip and neighborhood politics, not always friendly. Men gathered, men talked, men argued. Taverns flourished while the judges pondered—and then the farmers went home, for they could not afford to leave their fields untended.

To the people of Worcester, the Court of Common Pleas administered the greatest of all governmental powers: it could take or bestow private property. If you did not pay your debts, it forced you to give up a few acres or a cow; conversely, it helped you collect what was rightfully yours. The judges who served this court possessed an awesome power to change your life, for better or for worse; they seemed far more important than the members of Parliament 3,000 miles across the ocean. In 1773 and 1774 these judges heard 50 percent more cases than in preceding years; citizens of Worcester complained that the courts lent themselves to "the machinations of some designing persons in this Province, who are grasping at power, and the property of their neighbors."[107]

According to the 1691 charter for Massachusetts, the appointment of judges for the Court of Common Pleas required the approval of elected representatives; at least in theory, a judge who abused his power could be removed from office. Suddenly, that changed. In the spring of 1774 Parliament passed the Massachusetts Government Act, which tightened the reins of government to punish the patriots for the Boston Tea Party. As of August 1, 1774:

- All judges of the Court of Common Pleas and the Court of General Sessions, as well as local officials such as sheriffs, marshals, and justices of the peace, would be selected by the Crown-appointed governor and answerable only to him.

- The governor's counsellors, who served both as an upper house of the legislature and an executive check on the governor, would be appointed by the Crown rather than chosen by the elected assembly.

- Town meetings could not convene without the express consent of the governor, and once convened, they could discuss only agenda items approved by the governor.[108]

According to the new law, there was no way the people could remove dishonest officials. All pretense of accountability was replaced by patronage, with its great potential for abuse. Farmers feared their disenfranchisement would quickly result in economic ruin as harsh judges used small debts to justify foreclosures. Citizens of the town of Leicester, in Worcester County, warned that any "husbandman" could now be prohibited "from sowing grain, mowing grass, and feeding his pastures, so long as his majesty thinks proper."[109]

The first session of the newly constituted Court of Common Pleas for Worcester County was due to convene on September 6 and 7. If freeholders wanted to escape tenancy, if they had any hope of avoiding "a State of abject Slavery," they felt they had to prevent the new Massachusetts Government Act from taking effect.[110] Angry citizens from throughout the county gathered at the county seat, declared themselves a "Convention," and proclaimed "that the Courts should not sit on any terms." One week prior to the judges' appearance in Worcester, the convention recommended that "inhabitants of this County attend in Person," and in case any red-coated soldiers accompanied the judges, it suggested the people come "properly armed in order to repell any hostile force which may be imploied." The convention spelled out precisely what "properly armed" entailed: "that each member will purchase at least two pounds of powder in addition to any he may have on hand, and will use all his exertions to supply his neighbors fully."[111] General Thomas Gage, the new military governor, wrote nervously to the Earl of Dartmouth: "In Worcester they keep no terms; openly threaten resistance by arms; have been purchasing arms; preparing them; casting balls, and providing powder; and threaten to attack any troops who dare to oppose them."[112]

When the Crown-appointed judges showed up at the Worcester County courthouse to conduct routine business, they were greeted by an estimated 5,000 to 6,000 men from the surrounding country-side, including 1,000 armed militiamen organized neatly into rank-and-file on the town green. The crowd

> made a lane, & compelled ye. Judges, Sheriff, & Gentlemen of the Bar, to pass & repass them, Cap in Hand, in the most ignominious Manner; & read their Disavowall of holding Courts under the new Acts of Parliament, no less than Thirty Times in the Procession.[113]

With the dramatic closure of the Court of Common Pleas in September of 1774, the authority of the British government disappeared from Worcester County, never to return.

The Worcester County Convention quickly filled the power vacuum left by the termination of British rule. Assuming both legislative and executive authority, it ordered the sheriff to adjourn the Superior Court, freed all prisoners charged only with debt, and fired public officers who had refused to resign. It recommended that the towns keep the money they collected in taxes rather than turn it over to British-appointed authorities. Most significantly, the convention prepared to defend its actions by establishing seven militia regiments, to be led by newly elected officers pledged to the rebels' cause. It urged the towns to "provide themselves immediately with one or more field-pieces, mounted and fitted for use," and to form companies "ready to march at a *minute's* warning."[114] A few zealous activists from the American Political Society, seizing the initiative, went so far as to smuggle four cannons out of British-controlled Boston.[115]

Worcester was not alone. Great Barrington. Plymouth. Taunton. Concord. Springfield. Wherever a court was scheduled to meet, men assembled in great throngs to make sure that it did not. In town after town, judges with powdered wigs and long robes—important men, at least at one time—humbled themselves before farmers with mud on their boots.

In Great Barrington, 1,500 unarmed men "filled the Court-House and Avenues to the Seat of Justice, so full, that no Passage could be found for the justices to take their Places."[116]

In Concord, a "great Number of Freeholders and others" literally blocked the door to the courthouse. The officials retreated to Ephraim Jones's inn, then came up with a compromise proposal: if they were allowed to open the court, they promised to conduct no business. The judges waited all day for a response. At last, "after the Setting of the Sun," the "Body of the People" gave their reply: there could be no compromise. The court was to remain closed.[117]

In Springfield, "a great concourse of People, judg'd about 3000, assembled at the Court-House" and forced the judges and other appointed official to resign their posts.[118] Joseph Clarke of nearby

Northampton provided an eyewitness report which addressed not only the substance but the tone of the Springfield demonstration:

> Then the people paraded . . . to the meeting-house and demanded the appearance of the judges. The judges came according to their desire, and amidst the Crowd in a sandy, sultry place, exposed to the sun as far as they were able in such circumstances, gave a reasonable, &, to the major part, a satisfactory answer to such questions as were asked.
>
> It was also demanded of them that they should make a declaration in writing, signed by all the justices and lawyers in the County, renouncing in the most express terms any commission which should be given out to them or either of them under the new arrangement, which was immediately complied with and executed accordingly. . . .
>
> No man received the least injury, but the strictest order of justice were observed. The people to their honor behaved with the greatest order & regularity, a few individuals excepted, and avoided, as much as possible, confusion.
>
> The people of each town being drawn into separate companies marched with staves & musick. The trumpets sounding, drums beating, fifes playing and Colours flying, struck the passions of the soul into a proper tone, and inspired martial courage into each. [119]

From mid-August through mid-September of 1774, tens of thousands of plain folk from rural Massachusetts—mostly farmers, along with a few artisans from the villages—participated in a spontaneous uprising of unprecedented proportions. This was not a localized group of discontented tenants, nor a parochial crowd with particular interests. This was the "body of the people," if ever there was one. There were no special leaders. All decisions were made by the participants. Communications were conducted through ad hoc committees reporting directly back to the people.

The "body of the people" forced the resignations not only of judges but of Crown-appointed councillors. Timothy Paine of Worcester was visited at his home by some 2,000 or 3,000 people who demanded that he sign a resignation saying he was "very sorry" that he accepted the appointment "and thereby given any uneasiness to the People of this County, from whom I have received many favors." If Paine thought that signing a forced confession would be enough, he was mistaken: the people demanded that he make a personal appearance outdoors. A spokesman read Paine's resignation to the assembled throng, but even that was not enough:

> Numbers were dissatisfied, requiring that Mr. Paine should read it himself, and that with his hat off. . . . the people were drawed up in two bodies, making a lane between them, through which the committee and he passed and read divers times as they passed along, the said acknowledgment. [120]

John Murray was next. About 500 of the men who had visited Paine headed toward his home in Rutland, where they were joined by "about one thousand more from towns above." When told by his sons that Murray was away, the crowd "insisted upon searching the house, which was thoroughly done, as also the barns, out houses and stables." [121] How to proceed, with Murray nowhere to be found? The people decided to post a letter in the Boston newspapers. They proposed for Murray's "serious consideration"

> That you make an immediate Resignation of your Office, as a Counsellor. Your compliance as above, published in each of the Boston News Prints by the Tenth Day of September next, will save the People of this County the Trouble of waiting on you immediately afterwards. [122]

In some cases, the methods employed by the people were simple and nonviolent: when George Watson of Plymouth went to church, "a great number of the principal inhabitants of that town left the meeting house, where they used to worship, immediately upon his entering it." [123] But most of the time the crowds acted more forcibly:

- A crowd at Dartmouth ordered Timothy Ruggles "to depart forthwith, upon which the Colonel promised them he would go the next Morning by Sun an Hour high; but before that time the Brigadier's Horse had his Mane and Tail cut off, and his Body painted all over." [124]

- Joshua Loring complained to Governor Gage that he was visited twice in the night by a group of men, "their faces black'd and cutlasses in their hands," who warned him that if he did not resign "he must abide by the consequences, which would be very severe, that his house should be levelled to the ground."[125]

- Abijah Willard, while conducting routine business in Union, Connecticut, was captured by a crowd and returned to his home town of Brimfield, Massachusetts. There, the people

  called a Council of themselves, and Condemned Colonel Willard to Newgate Prison, in Symsbury; and a number set off and carried him six miles on the way thither. Colonel Willard then submitted to take the oath . . . , on which they dismissed him. One Captain Davis of Brimfield was present, who showing resentment, and treating the people with bad language, was stripped, and honored with the new fashion dress of tar and feathers; a proof this, *that the act for tarring and feathering is not repealed.* [126]

- Israel Williams, one of the powerful "River Gods" who had dominated politics in the Connecticut Valley, was placed in a closed room with the chimney stopped up. The patriots then started a fire and listened sadistically as their victim choked on smoke for hours on end.[127]

The most significant resignations occured in Cambridge. Before dawn on September 1 General Gage, hearing that the rebels were making away with powder from a provincial storehouse, sent out 200 men to retrieve what little remained and to seize a couple of cannons. The troops accomplished their missions and retreated quickly back to Boston. Soon, however, a crowd estimated at 4,000 gathered in Cambridge to prevent any further military activity by the British army. Since the redcoated soldiers had already withdrawn, the people expended their energy upon two local councillors, Samuel Danforth and Joseph Lee, who wisely agreed to resign their commissions. Later, the crowd visited the home of Thomas Oliver, the lieutenant-governor of Massachusetts and a member of the council. Although Oliver agreed to intercede on behalf of the people with General Gage, the assembled protestors demanded he resign from the council. Oliver refused at first, but he could not hold out forever:

> They began then to reason in their turn, urging the power of the people, and the danger of opposing them. All this occasioned a delay, which enraged part of the multitude, who, pressing into my back yard, denounced vengeance to the foes of their liberties. . . . They pressed up to my windows . . . swearing they would have my blood if I refused. . . . Part of the populace growing furious, and the distress of my family who heard the threats, and supposed them just about to be executed, called up feelings which I could not suppress. . . . I found myself giving way. . . . I cast my eyes over the paper . . . and wrote underneath the following words: "My house at Cambridge being surrounded by four thousand people, in compliance with their commands, I sign my name, THOMAS OLIVER." [128]

Ordinary men from Waltham, Watertown, Concord, Charlestown, Cambridge, and Framingham—not the famous Whigs from Boston—had forced the lieutenant-governor of Massachusetts, one of the most powerful men in the colony, to renounce an appointment to His Majesty's Council.[129]

Under intense pressure from "the body of the people," each of the thirty-six councillors either resigned or sought protection from the British army in Boston. No Crown-appointed officials would determine the fates of citizens to whom they could not be held accountable.

Great numbers of patriots, acting in concert, effectively dismantled the central provisions of the Massachusetts Government Act: they closed the courts and disempowered the council. They also made a mockery of the restrictions against town meetings. When General Gage tried to disband a meeting, the people would note wryly that each new meeting was only an extension of one that had started before the Massachusetts Government Act had gone into effect; in Marblehead, for instance, the same meeting was continued forty-six times in less than a year.[130]

In Danvers, according to merchant John Andrews, a meeting was held "directly under [the] nose" of General Gage. The people "continued it two or three howers longer than necessary, to see if he would interrpt 'em. He was made acquainted with it, but reply'd— 'Damn 'em! I won't do anything about it unless his Majesty sends me more troops.' " The spirit of open resistance was not to be contained. "The towns through the country are so far from being intimidated," Andrews wrote, "that a day in the week does not pass without one or more meetings, in direct contempt of the Act; which they regard as a blank piece of paper and not more."[131]

On August 24 a meeting was convened right in Salem, the seat of the British-controlled government. Gage ordered soldiers to march to the site; according to Andrews, "two companies from the 59th Regiment . . . proceeded within a few rods of the meeting." There, upon being confronted by numerous farmers who had gathered from the surrounding countryside, the British "halted, and marched back again immediately."[132] Later, Gage attempted to arrest members of the local committee of correspondence. Andrews reported:

> [T]here was upwards of three thousand men assembled there from the adjacent towns, with full determination to rescue the Committee if they should be sent to prison, Even if they were Oblig'd to repel force by force, being sufficiently provided for such a purpose; as indeed they are all through the country— every male above the age of 16 possessing a firelock with double the quantity of powder and ball enjoin'd by law. [133]

Gage dropped the case upon seeing, in his own words, "the people so determinate."[134]

Gage would have liked to dispatch troops into the countryside to repress the rebellion, but with the entire colony in a state of revolt, he was forced to admit "there was no knowing where to send them to be of Use."[135] Gage knew he had a revolution on his hands, not just a minor mob. He wrote to the earl of Dartmouth: "Tho' the People are not held in high Estimation by the Troops, yet they are numerous, worked up to a Fury, and not a Boston Rabble but the

Freeholders and Farmers of the Country."[136] And these "Farmers of the Country" were about to consolidate their local and spontaneous rebellions into a lasting and cohesive force.

Governor Gage tried to keep this from happening. Hoping to prevent a statewide meeting of representatives from the rebellious counties, he canceled the fall elections—but the people ignored the law once again and staged their elections. In October representatives from throughout Massachusetts met illegally and renamed themselves the Provincial Congress. Traveling from Salem to Concord to Cambridge as it conducted its business, the Provincial Congress commandeered public funds by declaring that all taxes must henceforth be paid to its own receiver general rather than to the old provincial treasurer. It assumed both the legislative and executive powers of government, and it recognized that those powers would have to be supported by armed force. It called for the acquisition of £20,000 worth of cannon and muskets, shot and powder—enough to equip an army of 5,000 soldiers. It formed a committee of safety with the authority to call up the militia, and it called upon all men of Massachusetts to drill and train for war.

Because the members of the Provincial Congress had been duly elected by the people, they felt justified in usurping the functions of government, both civil and military, from the officials appointed by the Crown. Operating outside and in contradiction to legally sanctioned institutions, the Provincial Congress gave a unified voice to the local resistance movements and thereby completed the Revolution of 1774: British authority in rural Massachusetts had been shattered at the local, county, and provincial levels, replaced by an assortment of crowds, committees, conventions, and congresses— all rooted firmly in the collective will of the majority of adult males. In the disapproving words of one loyalist, "Government has now devolved upon the people; and they seem to be for using it."[137]

According to the *Random House Dictionary of the English Language*, a revolution is "a forcible overthrow of an established government or political system by the people governed." In the late summer of 1774, the people of rural Massachusetts forcibly overthrew the established government. This was the first major shift of political authority from the British to the Americans. One government was overthrown, another quickly took its place. A new state was born, and eventually a new country.

Why is such a monumental event, this massive rising of the people, not included in the oft-told tale of our nation's beginnings? Such a serious lapse in reporting gives cause to wonder. Without bloodshed, without famous personalities, and without a singular event or unique location, the Massachusetts Revolution of 1774 has been neglected by history.

But let us not be misled: the crowd actions of 1774 constituted a very potent kind of revolution precisely because they *were* nameless and ubiquitous, aggressive yet bloodless.[138] The staggering power of "the body of the people" precluded serious resistance. Local Tories, overwhelmingly outnumbered, had no choice but to acquiesce.[139] Officers of the British army looked on helplessly, not knowing where, when, or how to deal with an uprising of such breadth and magnitude. All British troops withdrew to Boston, and General Gage reported back to London: "the Flames of Sedition" had "spread universally throughout the Country beyond Conception."[140]

These "flames of sedition" would soon spread to other colonies as well. The British government had tried to divide and conquer by focusing repression on Massachusetts; instead, its actions served to unite resistance as rebels from other colonies sent aid, engaged in protest, prepared for confrontation, and began to coordinate their activities and agendas. The massive revolt in Massachusetts served as a catalyst. Virginia, Pennsylvania, and the rest might have rebelled on their own without the lead of Yankee farmers, but the fact that one revolution was already in progress certainly hastened the day. When moderate delegates to the Continental Congress pushed for reconciliation in the fall of 1774, they were a bit too late: the American Revolution was already underway.

The people's revolution in Massachusetts set the standard for the "out-of-doors" political behavior so prevalent during the American Revolution. In the late summer of 1774 the common folk of Worcester and Springfield and the rest of rural Massachusetts perfected a form of political action that had been evolving for a decade. In 1765 rioters had hung effigies and conducted mock funerals; by 1774 ordinary farmers were forcing high-ranking government officials to resign.[141] By intimidating real people rather than toying with dummies, rank-and-file rebels effectively derailed all opposition. Without the loss of a single human life, the mightiest empire in the world was forced to withdraw from the Massachusetts countryside.

FIGHTING MEN AND BOYS

The Spirit of '75 . . . An American Crusade . . . Forging an Army . . . In the Face of the Enemy . . . Cannons Roaring, Muskets Cracking . . . Death or Victory . . . Beasts of Prey . . . Winter Soldiers . . . Summer Soldiers . . . Giting Thair Rights

The Spirit of '75

Predictably, marching with "staves and musick" soon gave way to the firing of guns and cannons. King George III declared Massachusetts to be in a state of rebellion, which it was, and he vowed to reassert his authority, as any deposed ruler would. "Blows must decide," he wrote to Lord North, whether the colonial governments "are to be subject to this country or independent."[1] The colonial rebels, understanding the king's intentions, stockpiled arms and ammunition and prepared for battle, while the Crown attempted to seize the rebel arsenals before they became too large. Step by step, the court closures of 1774 led to armed confrontation.

The Yankee farmers who started this revolution responded quickly to any reported initiatives by the British army. When red-coated soldiers threatened to shut down the town meeting at Salem, thousands of patriots faced them off. When the king's troops seized rebel magazines at Charlestown and Cambridge, great throngs of New Englanders (estimates range from 20,000 to 60,000), spurred by rumors that Boston had been bombarded, left their homes and headed towards the scene of the action.[2] According to one eyewitness, "For about fifty miles each way round there was an almost universal Ferment, Rising, seizing Arms & actual March into Cambridge . . . [T]hey scarcely left half a dozen Men in a Town, unless Old & decrepid."[3] The Reverend Stephen Williams recorded in his diary what happened when the news reached Longmeadow, where he was trying to conduct a service on the Sabbath:

[A]fter we had got to the meeting house in the afternoon—& just before the Exercise began Mr F- came in & informd that they had news from Boston—that the Ships in the Harbour of Boston, & the Army on the Land Side were allso fireing upon the Town so that it was like the Town was Demolishd. . . . people were put into a tumult & I closd the prayer—& Great numbers went out. . . . so many retird that it was difficult to cary on the Singing—I began my Srmon—but anon—a Signall was Given (or word Given) to the people at the windows—so that most of the males rushd out of the house—as if an Enemy was at the End of Parish—So that I Soon closd my Sermn, & administerd Baptism to a child—& dismissd the Assembly—thus we have had a disquietmt on the Sabboth day. . . .
      [A] number of men with arms—to be ready to move in an instant if needd—the blacksmith shop was opend—guns carrid to him to be mendd—horses to be Shod—& many Employd makeing Bullets—& a man Sent to Enfd to get powdr—in the Evening people met again, & repaird to the meeting house—& a number Gave in their names or listd & chose Some leader and were Getting ready to move—but while they were togather at the meeting house—Mr J. Sykes, came again to them & informd that the messenger was returnd & brot tideings—that all was well, and quiet at Boston—that there had been a tumult, or Squabble at Boston—& one man Killd—but now quiet & Still—oh how have we Sind away, & misimprovd Sabboths.[4]

The "Powder Alarm," as it came to be called, was over—a false alarm, to be sure, but a measure of things to come. According to one young farmer, "the People seemed rather disappointed, when the News was contradicted."[5]

The patriots, like the British, went after the magazines of their likely foes. In December of 1774 several hundred armed Yankees from New Hampshire took control of Fort William and Mary, commandeering cannons and powder. Four months before the British marched to Concord, American patriots, operating without orders from any higher authority, had taken the initiative and seized a British fort.

The following February 240 British troops embarked from Boston to seize more stored weapons, this time at Salem.[6] The marching soldiers halted at the edge of town, unable to continue because angry rebels refused to lower a drawbridge. Colonel Leslie, the officer in charge, engaged in an undignified shouting match with the assembled crowd and settled in the end for a face-saving compromise: the rebels would lower the bridge, but the troops would march no more than fifty rods on the other side. The mission came up empty, effectively thwarted by the citizens of Salem. But British officers would learn from their mistakes: when they went after the magazine in Concord two months later, they tripled the number of troops, they departed in the dead of night, and they chose a route that did not have a drawbridge.

Sometime, somewhere, one of these confrontations between men with muskets was likely to escalate beyond the puffing of chests. An hour before dawn on April 19, Sylvanus Wood of Woburn, Massachusetts, heard the bell ringing from the Lexington meeting house:

> [F]earing there was difficulty there, I immediately arose, took my gun and . . . went in haste to Lexington, which was about three miles distant. When I arrived there, I inquired of Captain Parker, the commander of the Lexington company, what was the news. . . . [W]hile we were talking, a messenger came up and told the captain that the British troops were within half a mile. Parker immediately turned to his drummer, William Diman, and ordered him to beat to arms, which was done. Captain Parker then asked me if I would parade with his company. I told him I would.
>
> By this time many of the company had gathered around the

captain at the hearing of the drum, where we stood, which was about half way between the meeting-house and Buckman's tavern. . . . Parker led those of us who were equipped to the north end of Lexington Common, near the Bedford road, and formed us in single file. I was stationed about in the centre of the company. While we were standing, I left my place and went from one end of the company to the other and counted every man who was paraded, and the whole number was thirty-eight, and no more.[7]

What did Sylvanus Wood and his sleepy-eyed compatriots expect might happen? Sylvanus had been asked to "parade," to display a military show of force; he had not been asked, and most likely did not expect, to engage in a pitched battle. Every time the Yankees had assembled to demonstrate their force, they had either prevailed against unarmed opponents or harangued British soldiers, shouting rather than shooting. But this time would be different:

The British troops approached us rapidly in platoons, with a general officer on horseback at their head. The officer came up to within about two rods of the centre of the company, where I stood, the first platoon being about three rods distant. They there halted. The officer then swung his sword, and said, "Lay down your arms, you damned rebels, or you are all dead men. Fire!" Some guns were fired by the British at us from the first platoon, but no person was killed or hurt, being probably charged only with powder.

Just at this time, Captain Parker ordered every man to take care of himself. The company immediately dispersed; and while the company was dispersing and leaping over the wall, the second platoon of the British fired and killed some of our men. There was not a gun fired by any of Captain Parker's company, within my knowledge. I was so situated that I must have known it, had anything of the kind taken place.[8]

British soldiers told a different story, claiming the rebels had pulled the trigger first. Although the truth will always remain hidden behind a veil of propaganda, we do know that "the shot heard 'round the world" had been fired, and many more would soon follow. British soldiers mowed down several of Wood's associates on the Lexington Green; later that day, upon their retreat from Concord, marching redcoats suffered heavy casualties as rebels took aim from the cover of trees and stone walls. The American Revolution had finally resulted in bloodshed.

As with the "Powder Alarm," response was immediate. By nightfall on April 19, militia units from Worcester, forty miles distant, arrived on the outskirts of Boston. Israel Putnam, it was said, heard the news while tending his fields in eastern Connecticut, jumped immediately on his horse, and headed toward Boston without returning to his house. Whether true or not, the Putnam tale expressed the spirit of the patriots. "The ardour of our people is such, that they can't be kept back," declared Connecticut's committee of correspondence.[9] Within a week, 3,716 men from Connecticut were marching to the aid of their neighboring colony, and by early summer an estimated 20,000 Americans surrounded Boston and trapped the British soldiers within the confines of the city.

What do these numbers mean? Who went, and who stayed home? How were people's lives affected by the onset of war?

Fourteen-year-old Joseph Plumb Martin, a Connecticut farmboy, recalled the day he heard the news:

> I was ploughing in the field about half a mile from home, about the twenty-first day of April, when all of a sudden the bells fell to ringing and three guns were repeatedly fired in succession down in the village. . . . I set off to see what the cause of the commotion was. I found most of the male kind of the people together; soldiers for Boston were in requisition. A dollar deposited upon the drumhead was taken up by someone as soon as placed there, and the holder's name taken, and he enrolled with orders to equip himself as quick as possible. . . . O, thought I, if I were but old enough to put myself forward, I would be the possessor of one dollar, the dangers of war to the contrary notwithstanding; but I durst not put myself up for a soldier for fear of being refused.[10]

During the following months soldiers from the surrounding area were billeted at Joseph's home, duly impressing the budding youth: "Their company and conversation began to warm my courage to such a degree that I resolved at all events to 'go a sogering.' " But his grandparents, with whom he lived, would not permit the lad to enlist. Joseph watched enviously as other hometown boys marched boastfully off to war:

> I accompanied them as far as the town line, and it was hard parting with them then. Many of my young associates were with them, my heart and soul went with them, but my mortal part must stay behind. By and by, they will come swaggering back, thought I, and tell me of their exploits, all their "hairbreadth 'scapes," and poor Huff will not have a single sentence to advance. O, that was too much to be borne with by me. [11]

Twelve-year-old Ebenezer Fox, sent by his poor family to work on a neighbor's farm, was also affected by the excitement of those days. Years later he recalled:

> Almost all the conversation that came to my ears related to the injustice of England and the tyranny of government. It is perfectly natural that the spirit of insubordination that prevailed should spread among the younger members of the community; that they, who were continually hearing complaints, should themselves become complainants. I, and other boys situated similarly to myself, thought we had wrongs to be redressed; rights to be maintained. . . . We made direct application of the doctrines we daily heard, in relation to the oppression of the mother country, to our own circumstances; and thought that we were more oppressed than our fathers were. I thought that I was doing myself great injustice by remaining in bondage, when I ought to go free; and that the time was come, when I should liberate myself from the thraldom of others, and set up a government of my own. [12]

With impeccable but accidental timing, Ebenezer Fox and a friend ran away on the very night of Paul Revere's ride to Lexington and

Concord. Hoping to ship out to sea, the boys journeyed secretly from Roxbury, Massachusetts, to Providence, Rhode Island—only to be hunted, in their eyes, by countless couriers and men-in-arms:

> Great anxiety was manifested in the country in the vicinity of Boston to know what was going on there. People were out in all directions to hear the "news from town." . . . Our fears induced us to think that the uncommon commotion that appeared to prevail must have some connexion with our escape, and that the moving multitudes we saw were in pursuit of us. [13]

But the grown men who were scurrying about let the boys be, unconcerned with two waifs on the run. As the fate of their country hung in the balance, Ebenezer and his pal arrived safely in Providence; the men, as it turned out, were all headed the other way to confront the redcoats near Boston.

Jeremiah Greenman, Jr., apparently the only son of a sailor from Newport, Rhode Island, turned seventeen on May 7, 1775—old enough to become a soldier without even lying about his age. Lacking, in his own words, any "mechanical art" or profession to pursue, he signed on with Rhode Island's "Army of Observation" on May 20: "I, Jeremiah Greenman, Jr., hereby solemnly engage and enlist myself as a soldier . . . for the preservation of the liberties of America." [14] Jeremiah Greenman, George Washington, and thousands of other boys and men would spend the summer of 1775 camped on the outskirts of Boston, where they demonstrated their determination to fight for their rights.

Thirty-one-year-old Joseph Hodgkins' seventh child, Joseph Jr., was born to his second wife, Sarah, only six weeks before the British marched on Concord. Joseph Sr., a cobbler from Ipswich, Massachusetts, had lost four previous children in their infancy, the last shortly before the death of his first wife, Joanna. This concerned father, however, would not remain at home to care for his wife and his infant son, for Joseph Hodgkins was a minuteman. On January 24, 1775, he had signed a covenant:

> We whose Names are hereunto subscribed, do voluntarily Inlist our selves, as Minute Men, to be ready for military operation,

upon the shortest notice. And we hereby Promise & engage, that we will immediately, each of us, provide for & equip himself, with an effective fire arm, Bayonet, Pouch, Knapsack, & Thirty rounds of Cartridges ready made. And that we may obtain the skill of compleat Soldiers, We promise to Convene for exercise in the Art Military, at least twice every week; and oftener if our officers shall think necessary. [15]

Late in the morning of April 19, Joseph Hodgkins was called upon to make good on his pledge; chosen to serve as the lieutenant for his unit, he really had no choice but to head toward Concord. Hodgkins and his fellow minutemen arrived too late to see action, but during their absence from home a rumor circulated throughout Ipswich that the British had landed nearby and were on the march. Panicking, and with few men left to protect them, the women and children of Ipswich fled their houses and headed north, Sarah and her brood presumably among them.

April 19 was only the beginning. Over the next several years these four Yankees—along with tens of thousands of other American males from throughout the colonies—were to assume long-term commitments as professional soldiers. Boys like Joseph Plumb Martin, Ebenezer Fox, and Jeremiah Greenman would come of age amid a military culture that defined—and threatened—their very existence, while men like Joseph Hodgkins would forsake their work and their family obligations to serve their country.

Joseph Martin and Ebenezer Fox wrote about their soldiering after the war had ended, as did James Collins, a teenager from the South who did not fight until later. Jeremiah Greenman kept a journal during the war, while Joseph Hodgkins wrote numerous letters home to his wife Sarah. These five men are special not because they performed heroic deeds or led the multitudes into battle; they are special because they recorded their experiences and their feelings. Traditionally, scholars have focused on the numerous accounts written by high-level leaders, both civil and military; this time, we will look at the Revolution through the eyes of privates and petty officers. The texture of war, as we shall see, changes dramatically when we look from the bottom up, not from the top down.

An American Crusade

Young Joseph Martin did not miss much in that summer of '75. The British remained within the confines of Boston, surrounded by a ragtag army of rebels who laid siege to the city but could not muster a direct assault. Neither army had sufficient strength to initiate an offensive. Only one battle was fought: on June 17 the British stormed and captured Breed's Hill at a cost of over 1,000 casualties; "a verry hot ingagement," Joseph Hodgkins called it.[16] Aside from this Battle of Bunker Hill, as it is mistakenly called, British and American soldiers simply loitered about, facing off intermittently in petty skirmishes and distant shellings which resulted in few injuries. Jeremiah Greenman, who would keep a journal for the remainder of the war, wrote nothing about his time around Boston—perhaps because there was little to say. It was a time of waiting.

With armed combat sparse, few soldiers had any "hair-breadth 'scapes" to report to their friends. Deaths were accidental, not heroic; the largest toll was exacted by "those putrid, malignant and infectious disorders"—typhoid fever and dysentery—caused by the unsanitary conditions in the crowded camps. Some of the stricken soldiers perished in hastily constructed military hospitals; more were transported back to their homes to die or recuperate—and to spread disease amongst their relatives and neighbors. These returning veterans of the siege of Boston, according to Benjamin Thompson, "have introduced such a general mortality throughout New England as was never known since its first planting."[17]

Joseph Hodgkins wrote frequently to Sarah from the encampments around Boston. On May 7 he wrote: "the Company is well I whant to know wether you have got a paster for the Cows for I cannot tell when I shall com home." On September 8 he wrote from Prospect Hill:

> I have know news to Rite to you only that the Enemy have not yet fired a gun nor sent a Bum at our People since I have Ben hear Except a few small armes at our People Who went Down on Chalstown Common after sum hoses.

And on October 6:

> I should Be glad if you could send me two striped shirts for
> the weather growes Cool we hear that Brothers child is very
> sick But I do not know as he can come home at Presant for
> our People are all most Bewitcht about getting home. [18]

By October the once-militant rebels, tired of hanging around for
half a year, were indeed "Bewitcht about getting home." Who
wouldn't be? With the approach of harvest, many simply packed
up and returned to their homes, where there was much work to be
done. Yankee farmers were willing to show up when needed for an
emergency, but most had no desire to turn professional. When eighteen men from New Hampshire headed for home, they announced
"that they didn't intend when they enlisted to join the Army"—
they had only wished to protect against a British invasion of the
New Hampshire coast.[19] With time, as the minutemen came to realize they would not really be *doing* anything around Boston, they
figured they had more important business to attend elsewhere.

Boredom, disease, economic necessity: little by little, the collective
spirit of the people, their furious patriotism, began to dissipate,
eclipsed by private lives and personal needs. At the end of July,
Benjamin Thompson reported, only 2,227 of the 4,207 men stationed
at the critical location on Prospect Hill "were returned fit for
duty."[20] On September 8 Washington complained that his men
wanted to go home; by September 21 he reported they were "not
far from mutiny."[21] On November 28 the commander-in-chief
wrote:

> [S]uch a dirty, mercenary spirit pervades the whole, that I
> should not be at all surprised at any disaster that may hap-
> pen. . . . Could I have forseen what I have, and am likely to
> experience, no consideration upon earth should have induced
> me to accept this command.[22]

In December, when their terms of enlistment expired, many of the
Connecticut troops, disregarding the pleas and threats of their of-

ficers, simply walked off the job, their arms in hand.²³ The glorious
"spirit of '76" was already on the decline during the second half of
'75. The rebels no longer behaved as a people possessed.

This waning of the spirit clearly bothered Joseph Hodgkins. On
November 28 he wrote to Sarah:

> Our men inlist very slow and our Enemy have got a Rein-
> forsment of five Regiments and if the New army is not Reased
> in season I hope I & all my townsmen shall have virtue anofe
> to stay all winter as Volentears Before we Will leave the line
> with out men for our all is at stake and if we Due not Exarte
> our selves in this gloris Cause our all is gon and we made
> slaves of for Ever But I pray god that it may never Be so.²⁴

Just a few days earlier Hodgkins had announced that he expected
to be back in Ipswich by the end of December, but now he was
not so sure. If everybody else went home, who would keep the
British at bay? Despite his obvious affection for his wife and children, Joseph decided to remain a soldier.

Jeremiah Greenman was not tempted to go home, but he did seek
a more active role. Early in September he volunteered, along with
eleven hundred other restless soldiers, to march through the Maine
wilderness, storm the city of Quebec, and take control of Canada.
This was to be the first major offensive of the Revolutionary War,
and the seventeen-year-old son of a sailor from Rhode Island was
just the sort of recruit that was needed for the job: young, unat-
tached, and hungry for adventure.

But why Canada, of all places? Hoping to revive the patriotic
fervor, American military leaders decided to grab the initiative by
striking where the British were weak. In retrospect, it is hard to see
how the invasion of a foreign colony related to the fight against
tyranny at home, but Yankees steeped in the Protestant faith had
little trouble drumming up the motivation to invade the stronghold
of Catholicism on their northern border. Britain had recently placed
all the lands west of the Appalachians under Canadian control, while
simultaneously granting official recognition to the Catholic Church
in Quebec. American Protestants of all denominations, from Yankee

Congregationalists to Southern Anglicans, noted the obvious parallels between the political tyranny of the British monarch and the religious tyranny of the Catholic pope: in each case, an authoritarian ruler was interfering with the freedom of individuals to live or worship as they pleased. The expedition into Canada, a continental cleansing in the name of political and religious liberty, promised to dethrone two tyrants at once. Here was the greatest Pope's Day riot of them all—and not only effigies would be burned this time. One army chaplain spoke for many when he wrote in his diary: "Had pleasing views of the glorious day of universal peace and spread of the gospel through this vast extended country, which has been for ages the dwelling of Satan, and reign of Antichrist."[25]

The Canadian expedition, under the command of Colonel Benedict Arnold, was scheduled to depart from Newburyport, Massachusetts, on September 18, 1775. The day before, on the Sabbath, Jeremiah Greenman and his fellow volunteers went to meeting under arms. Marching with flags flying into the First Presbyterian Church, they formed two lines and presented their guns. The preacher, after walking through the lines to the rolling of drums, told the soldiers what Moses said to the Lord, "If thy spirit go not with us, carry us not up hence." The men were moved. After the service, some of the officers convinced the sexton to open the tomb of George Whitefield, the famous revivalist of the Great Awakening, which lay within the church. Whitefield's body had decomposed in the five years since his death, but some of his clothes remained intact. The inspired zealots cut his collar and wristbands into small pieces which they used as relics to ensure success for their mission.[26]

Jeremiah Greenman, undoubtedly excited to be doing something at last, decided to chronicle the expedition. He started with the departure from Newburyport: "Early this morn. waid anchor with the wind at: SE a gale our Colours fliing Drums a beating fifes a plaing the hils and warfs a Cover biding thair friends fair well."[27] In the weeks that followed, Greenman mapped the progress of a daring journey through the great northern woods and described the difficulties the men encountered as they tried to navigate their flat-bottomed boats, called bateaux, up the Kennebec River to the Canadian border, then down the Chaudiere River to Quebec. The men rowed, dragged, and swam the boats, alternately buried in "mud and mire" or fighting against a current that was "very swift indeed." On several occasions they had to abandon the river altogether and portage over "carring places" which extended for miles. On October 7 Greenman reported: "this day left all Inhabitance & enter'd an uncultervated co and a barran wildernes." On October 8 "it began to wrain"; five days later "Sum small Spits of Snow" began to fall.

This was only the beginning. Five weeks into the journey Greenman wrote:

> T 24. our provision growing scant sum of our men being sick held a Counsel agreed to send the Sick and wekly men back & to send a Capt and 50 men forward to get in to the Inhabitance as soon as posabel that thay might send back provision . . . Colo Enoss with 3 Companys turn'd back took with them large Stores of provision and amunition wich made us shorter than we was before
>
> T 26. . . . the ground covered with Snow and very Cold . . . we expetckit to kill sum of our dogs to eat—
>
> F 27. . . . here it was agreed to leave our battoes and to fut it after being gratly fateg'd by carring over such hils mountain & Swamps such as men never pased before we carried two or thre battoes over this carring place to carry ye Sick down ye river Shedo . . .
>
> M 30. . . . got to Shedore river this river is very swift water rockey & shole overtook Liut Shaw that went forward with that batto was to carry Sick in but the river so raped and swift thay could no batto go down the river thare was one man lost by the battow a quanerty of amunition and guns with sum money
>
> T 31. Set out this morn very early left 5 sick men in the woods that was not abel to march left two well men with them but what litel provision thay had did not last them we gave out of our little every man gave sum but the men that was left was obliged to leave them to the mercy of wild beast . . . our provision being very Short hear we killed a dog I got a small peace of it and sum broth that it was boyled with a great de of trubel then, lay down took our blancots and slep very harty for the times

November 1775 by Shedore

W 1 . . . In a very misrabel Sittiuation nothing to eat but dogs hear we killed a nother and cooked I got Sum of that by good with the head of a Squirll with a parsol of Candill wicks boyled up to gether wich made very fine Supe without Salt hear on this we made a nobel feast without bread or Salt thinking it was the best that ever I eat & so went to Sleep contented . . .

T 2. this morn when we arose many of us so weak that we could hardly stand we stagerred about like drunken men how sumever we made shift to git our pack on them that did not thoro them away we marcht off hoping to see Sum Inhabitance by night I hap to git a pint of water that a partrig was boyled in about ten o Clock then I set out Strong hoping to find the Inhabitance by night but Sum of them so weak that a Small Stick as big as mans thumb would bring them to the ground . . . In the after noon we came in Sight of the Cattle wich the advanc party had sent out it was the Joifulest Sight that I ever saw & Sum could not refrain from crying from joy . . . hear we killed a creatur and Sum of ye men so hungrey before this Creater was dressed thay had the Skin and all entrels guts and every thing that could be eat on ye fires a boyling.

Of the 1,100 who departed from Newburyport, no more than 700 completed the journey to Quebec; the remainder either returned because of illness, returned because of choice, or succumbed in the wilderness. Those who went back home probably questioned the importance of the journey or the force of their convictions: was this march really necessary? Perhaps the men who devoured dogs also reevaluated their priorities: what really matters other than sheer survival? Those who were staggering about, and the few who were left on their own to die, might have pondered the meaning of life or simply focused on their immediate sorrows, but no doubt they were not contemplating the subtleties of political theory. Any problems they might have had with the king or the pope were no longer relevant.

Survivors like Jeremiah Greenman, on the other hand, had every reason to renew their devotion in order to give some purpose to the hardships they had just endured. They reached the banks of the St. Lawrence on November 9, and after a brief period of recovery they laid siege to Quebec. Since much of their arms and ammunition had been rendered useless during their journey through Maine, they did not storm the city until General Montgomery and 300 additional troops, traveling by an easier route, arrived with artillery, rifles, and powder. The delay proved costly: the British gained time to muster their forces, while many of the American soldiers came down with smallpox. Finally, on New Year's Eve, Benedict Arnold, General Montgomery, Jeremiah Greenman, and whoever else was healthy enough to wield a weapon mounted their attack: "at 2 oClock at night we turn'd out it snowing and blowing very hard got all in readyness with our laders Spears and So forth with hearts undanted to scale the wals." Arnold was wounded and Montgomery was killed on the first charge. Arnold's men penetrated into the lower town, but when Montgomery's forces failed to come to their aid, they were surrounded and captured.

Jeremiah Greenman was one of 426 Americans taken prisoner during the attack on Quebec. For half a year the prisoners were kept in a "dismal hole" where they ate "Stinking Salmond" and fought off the lice. Many succumbed to smallpox. In June the British General Carleton finally told the prisoners he would set them free if they signed a paper promising to "lay at home & not come thair to trubel him." Greenman and his comrades quickly assented: "we would sign'd any thing thay braught to us if that would carry us home." On August 11, after more than seven months, the prisoners set sail from Quebec. They arrived in Staten Island on September 12 and gained their freedom two weeks later at Elizabeth, New Jersey.

Despite the initial defeat at Quebec on New Year's Day, the Continental Congress, still hoping to conquer Canada, had sent several thousand reinforcements early in 1776. As soon as the new-comers arrived, however, they became weakened by the illnesses endemic to the Revolutionary War. The British, meanwhile, had sent fresh troops by sea, and by June the Americans withdrew from Canada via Lake Champlain. The retreat itself proved a disaster, described vividly by historian Charles Royster:

Along the line of retreat, at Isle-aux-Noix—a swampy, insect-infested island—and at Crown Point, the army paused while fifteen to thirty men died each day from smallpox, malaria, and dysentery. In foul sheds, lice fought maggots over the sick and the dead, while men yelled, sang, cursed, prayed, and died unheeded. [28]

It was an ignoble end to a once-grand design. When Captain Simeon Thayer returned to Elizabeth along with Jeremiah Greenman, he recorded poignantly in his diary that he was accompanied by only 10 of the original 87 members of his company. Three had deserted on September 25, early in the journey through Maine. Four went home sick the following day, and 17 more left with Colonel Enos late in October. Two were killed, 3 wounded, and 25 taken prisoner (including Thayer) during the attack on Quebec. Of the prisoners, 7 enlisted with the British to get out of jail, while 7 more succumbed to disease. Thayer, once in prison, lost contact with many of the rest. In his last entry, he noted only that his fellow patriots had "perish'd by different casualties, as dying by different diseases, such as in prison, some thro' hunger & fatigue, others running away, others listing with the British, others dying with the small pox, &c."[29]

This is not what the American patriots had bargained for. When thousands of Yankee farmers closed the Massachusetts courts in 1774, when tens of thousands from throughout the colonies swarmed Boston in 1775, the scenarios they envisioned for the future did not include eating dogs in the Maine woods or rotten fish in a distant prison, nor succumbing to smallpox in a foreign land. Was this what war was all about? And if so, who wanted it? Who would be willing to endure it?

Forging an Army

Some had expressed concern from the start. On May 31, 1774, Philip Vickers Fithian from the Northern Neck of Virginia recorded in his journal: "The lower Class of People here are in a tumult on the account of Reports from Boston, many of them expect to be press'd

& compell'd to go and fight the Britains!"[30] Not that these common folk were unpatriotic: when the alarm sounded a year later, they joined companies of volunteers in great numbers. But they didn't want to be *forced* into service. They didn't want to leave their homes for extended periods of time, nor to take orders from men who claimed to be their superiors.

In the spring and summer of 1775, during the height of the military fever, plain farmers from Virginia seized control of the volunteer companies which had originally been formed by slave-owning gentry. They rejected the blue uniforms "turn'd up with Buff; with . . . Buff Waist Coat & Breeches, & white Stockings" in favor of simple shirts and "a belt around them with a Tommyhawk or Scalping knife." These "shirtmen," as they came to be called, insisted on voting for their own officers. As volunteers, they also insisted on the right to come or leave as they pleased.[31]

The gentry did not approve. In August the Virginia Convention, acting as a legislative body, transformed the volunteer companies into units of minutemen organized on more traditional lines. No longer would privates elect their own officers. Recruits would be expected to march and drill. And most significantly, they would have to leave their homes and farms for eighty days the first year and sixty days in subsequent years, whether or not there was a war going on. The first twenty days of training would commence that fall—right in the middle of harvest season.

But the common folk refused to buy in. Plain farmers did not wish to subordinate themselves to officers who came from a different social class, nor did they see the point of training in "military anticks and ceremonies." One group protested that patriots should just "go and Fight the Battle at once, and not be Shilly Shally, in this way, until all the Poor people are ruined." Maybe the gentry could afford to leave their homes to play soldier, protested farmers from Chesterfield County, but not "the poorer sort who have not a slave to labour for them." When slave owners claimed they could not join the minutemen because they had to stay home to prevent insurrections, small farmers objected that service in the military was "calculated to exempt the gentlemen and throw the whole burthern on the poor" and that "the Rich wanted the Poor to fight for them, to defend there property, whilst they refused to fight for themselves."[32]

Enthusiasm for the war understandably dampened as common people evaluated the real consequences of military obligation. Lund Washington, who looked over his cousin George's estate at Mt. Vernon, reported that "our minute Scheme does not Equal the Conventions Expectation. the people do not come readily." By the fall of 1775 George Gilmer, Thomas Jefferson's physician and friend, complained in frustration: "I know not from what cause, but every denomination of the people seem backward. . . . We were once all fire, now most of us are become inanimate and indifferent."[33]

The shirtmen from Virginia were not alone: throughout the colonies most freeholding farmers and productive artisans—sensible people—chose not to pursue a military life beyond the first, quick response to Lexington and Concord. In the spring of 1775 thousands of eager volunteers had to be turned away for lack of supplies; by the end of that year, the Continental Congress was unable to raise half the number of troops it wanted and expected. But this could not continue. If patriots hoped to win their freedom, they would need to create some semblance of a professional army. With most plain farmers—the bulwark of the colonial population—unwilling to forget their plantings, forget their harvests, and become real soldiers, rebel governments had no choice but to hire the job out to lads like Jeremiah Greenman and to men so poor they had no other options—"those Lazy fellows who lurk about and are pests to Society," in the words of one gentleman from Virginia.[34]

In March of 1776 the British pulled out of Boston and headed toward New York. Who would oppose them there? Teenage boys like Joseph Plumb Martin, fearless in their innocence, incognizant of danger and pain:

> I was told that the British army at that place was reinforced by fifteen thousand men, it made no alteration in my mind; I did not care if there had been fifteen times fifteen thousand, I should have gone just as soon as if there had been fifteen hundred. I never spent a thought about numbers; the Americans were invincible in my opinion.[35]

By the time the second round of recruiters came through Milford, Connecticut, Joseph had turned fifteen—a year older and that much more determined to have his way. By threatening to run off and board a privateer, he managed to convince his grandparents to allow him to join the army. "I used frequently to go to the rendezvous, where I saw many of my young associates enlist," Joseph would write years later. After hearing "repeated banterings to engage with them," one evening he "went off with a full determination to enlist at all hazards." After some wavering, he set his name to paper. "I was now what I long wished to be, a soldier. I had obtained my heart's desire; it was now my business to prove myself equal to my profession."[36]

Why had this youth of fifteen decided to become a professional soldier? First and foremost, Joseph Plumb Martin became a soldier because he was a young male in Revolutionary America, and that was the thing to do. It was peer pressure pure and simple: "The old bantering began—come, if you will enlist I will, says one; you have long been talking about it, says another—come, now is the time."[37] Joseph Plumb Martin agreed to place his life in danger because he was scared *not* to.

Throughout the war, recruiters would target impressionable youths like Joseph, for they were the easiest to catch. Ebenezer Fox reported how the state of Massachusetts found sailors for its twenty-gun ship, the *Protector:*

A recruiting officer, bearing a flag and attended by a band of martial music, paraded the streets, to excite a thirst for glory and a spirit of military ambition. The recruiting officer possessed the qualifications requisite to make the service appear alluring, especially to the young. He was a jovial, good-natured fellow, of ready wit and much broad humor. Crowds followed in his wake when he marched the streets; and he occasionally stopped at the corners to harangue the multitude in order to excite their patriotism and zeal for the cause of liberty. When he espied any large boys among the idle crowd around him, he would attract their attention by singing in a comical manner the following doggerel:

> All you that have bad masters,
> And cannot get your due;
> Come, come, my brave boys,
> And join with our ship's crew.

A shout and a huzza would follow, and some would join in the ranks. [38]

Military recruiters took who they could get. In those days, with roughly 50 percent of the population under sixteen and most of the men over twenty already supporting families, teenagers constituted a disproportionate share of the available males. [39] Technically, boys under sixteen were to be excluded from the military; in reality, the army sought them out, for they were the easiest to train. As one recruiter observed, boys with little property, no marital ties, and romantic visions of glory were "very proper for service." [40] Very proper indeed, for the fighting force of the rebels would have been rather small without them: only about one-fifth of the professional soldiers who served in the Continental Army were married men. [41] Eager to accept any stout lad who was willing to bend the truth, recruiters rarely asked for proof of age. At age fifteen, Joseph Plumb Martin was nowhere near the youngest male to fight for his country. David Hamilton Morris of Pennsylvania's Third Regiment enlisted at the age of eleven. By the time Jeremiah Levering turned fifteen, he had already put in three years with the artillery. [42] In Eastern Virginia, naval recruiters were ordered to impress one-half of all male orphans. [43]

This was not ideal. Virtuous patriots did not really want to hire a standing army of any sort, let alone of boys. Ideally, the British would be repulsed by citizens-turned-soldiers, men who volunteered to take up arms when the need arose and then returned to their private lives. But when the volunteers and militiamen packed up to go home in the fall of 1775, somebody had to take their place, and the Americans were forced to pay for a job that should have been done for free. "The few who act upon Principles of disinterestedness," wrote George Washington, "are, comparatively speaking, no more than a drop in the Ocean." [44]

Washington himself preferred professional soldiers of any age to militiamen who would come and go as they pleased. He urged the government to offer a bounty to entice recruits to enlist, but the Continental Congress maintained that bounties were antithetical to republican principles. When the British made their move toward New York and not enough volunteers stepped forward, however, Congress changed its mind: on June 26, 1776 it voted to grant $10 to anyone who would enlist for three years. Still, not enough soldiers signed on, and on September 6 Congress upped the ante: $20, a new suit of clothes, and 100 acres of land to those who enlisted for the duration of the war. This proved sufficient to lure Jeremiah Greenman into the army once again, his previous experiences notwithstanding, and despite his promise, made under duress, never again to take up arms against the British.

But even this higher price could not entice most American farmers to sacrifice their lives to a military regime; perhaps they believed too sincerely in the cause of freedom, since they refused to give up their own. Ironically, the perennial shortage of soldiers forced all levels of government to intrude ever more deeply into the private lives of individuals—all in the name of liberty. Starting in 1777 Congress fixed the number of companies that each state had to recruit for the Continental Army; the states, in turn, assigned quotas to the various towns. Most state and local governments, unable to entice enough volunteers even by adding to the bounties, resorted in the end to the draft—just as the farmers from Virginia had feared. Free American citizens, because they would not fight willingly, were told by their government that they *had* to place a body on the line, either their own or somebody else's. Just as in modern times, a man's future could be determined by a brief notice in the mail:

To Dea. John Sail, SIR:

This is to inform you are this evening drafted as one of the Continental men to go to General Washington's headquarters, and you must go or find an able bodied man in your Room, or pay a fine of twenty pounds in law, money in twenty-four hours.

[Signed] Samuel Clark, Capt.[45]

Ebenezer Fox, having returned home from his short stint as a twelve-year-old sailor, was working in Boston as an apprentice barber when his master, John Bosson, was drafted. Years later, Ebenezer recalled Bosson's reactions:

> One day, while my fellow apprentice and myself were at work, Mr. Bosson entered the shop laboring under great agitation of mind. It was evident that something had happened to discompose his temper, which was naturally somewhat irritable. He walked rapidly about, occasionally stopping, and honing several razors that he had put in perfect order previous to his going out; and attempting to sharpen a pair of shears that at the time bore the keenest edge. . . .
>
> At length, from various ejaculations, and now and then a half-smothered curse upon his ill luck, we gathered the fact, that he was enrolled among the soldiers who were soon to take up the line of march for New-York. This was an unfortunate business for him; a reality he had not anticipated. The idea of shouldering a musket, buckling on a knapsack, leaving his quiet family, and marching several hundred miles for the good of his country, never took a place in his mind. Although a firm friend to his country, and willing to do all he could to help along her cause, as far as expressing favorable opinions and good wishes, yet there was an essential difference in his mind between the theory and the art of war. . . .
>
> But what was to be done? A substitute could not be obtained for the glory that might be acquired in the service; and as for money, no hopes could be entertained of raising sufficient for the purpose.
>
> Mr. Bosson continued to fidget about, uttering such expressions as his excited feelings prompted, allowing us to catch a disconnected sentence, such as: "Hard times—don't need two apprentices anymore than a toad needs a tail";—"If either of you had the spunk of a louse, you would offer to go for me." With this remark he quitted the shop apparently in high dudgeon.[46]

And so it was that Ebenezer Fox, with the spunk of a louse, became a teenage soldier.

Joseph Plumb Martin, in his second tour of duty, also served as a substitute:

> The inhabitants of the town were about this time put into what were called squads. . . . Each of these squads were to furnish a man for the army, either by hiring or by sending one of their own number. . . . One of the above-mentioned squads, wanting to procure a man, . . . attacked me, front, rear and flank. I thought, as I must go, I might as well endeavor to get as much for my skin as I could. Accordingly, I told them that I would go for them and fixed upon a day when I would meet them and clinch the bargain.
>
> The day, which was a muster day of the militia of the town, arrived. I went to the parade, where all was liveliness, as it generally is upon such occasions, but poor *I* felt miserably; my execution day was come. I kept wandering about till the afternoon, among the crowd, when I saw the lieutenant, who went with me into a house where the men of the squad were, and there I put my name to enlisting indentures. . . . The men gave me what they agreed to, I forget the sum, perhaps enough to keep the blood circulating during the short space of time which I tarried at home after I enlisted. They were now freed from any further trouble, at least for the present, and I had become the scapegoat for them.[47]

Military manpower was placed on the open market, and Joseph Plumb Martin was in high demand. As towns struggled to fulfill their quotas, as privateers cast about for sailors to hoist their sails, and as draftees of any substance searched for substitutes to fill their slots, boys and men of little property who were willing to sell their time and bodies found no shortage of takers. Some enlisted again and again, taking one bounty after another but not reporting for service. Recruiting officers, meanwhile, signed imaginary names and pocketed the bounties while claiming that the illusive recruits had deserted. Entrepreneurs purchased the services of boys and poor men, then hawked their human merchandise for a higher price to any individual, squad, or town that needed to produce a soldier. Local constables arrested poor men for vagrancy, then sold off their prisoners as substitutes—sometimes to more than one buyer.[48] Once money had become a factor, corruption followed in suit.

The net result of bounties and drafts was to ensure that the fighting men of the Continental Army came from an unrepresentative sample of the male population. With the exception of officers, most of the long-term soldiers were boys and men of little wealth. Most could not even vote, whether because of their age or their lack of property.[49] In the words of John Shy, "[T]he men who shouldered the heaviest military burden were something *less* than average colonial Americans. As a group, they were poorer, more marginal, less well anchored in society."[50]

Poor soldiers carried the burden not because they were more patriotic than the rest but because they were more available. Ironically, those whose property had been threatened by British policy were unable to fight precisely because that property—whether a farm, a blacksmith's shop, or a lawyer's office—needed constant attention. Most men of means, whether their holdings were modest or substantial, felt they could not afford the time, nor did they wish to give up the assistance of their own sons or apprentices. In June of 1777 a writer for the *Connecticut Courant* reported: "the inhabitants were busily employed in recruiting the children and servants of their neighbors, and forbidding their own to engage."[51] In May of 1776 John Adams had declared that "we must all be soldiers," but when his own law clerk wanted to enlist, he told him point blank: "We cannot all be soldiers."[52]

A revealing incident: when news of the Declaration of Independence reached Worcester, site of one of the original court closings in 1774, Isaiah Thomas, the patriotic printer of the *Massachusetts Spy,* presided over a celebratory reading of the document. After the official ceremony was over, the *Spy* reported with obvious approval, "a select company of the sons of freedom, repaired to the tavern, lately known by the sign of the King's Arms, which odious signature of despotism was taken down by order of the people." The zealous patriots raised twenty-four toasts, including "Perpetual itching without benefit of scratching, to the enemies of America" and "May the freedom and independency of America endure, till the sun grows dim with age, and this earth returns to chaos."[53]

Some of the more youthful participants in the events of the day and the drinking that evening became so animated that they decided to enlist in the Continental Army. As it so happens, one of the eager soldiers-to-be was Ben Russell, Isaiah Thomas's apprentice. Thomas didn't like that. Russell's father, a Boston stonemason, had sent the lad to apprentice at the *Spy* specifically to keep him from enlisting, and besides, Ben's services were sorely needed at the press. The patriotic Thomas had hoped the celebration of the Declaration of Independence would inspire new recruits—but not his own apprentice. Thomas took the case to court, where he managed to annul the enlistment because Russell was under sixteen.[54] (Later in the war, when Thomas himself was drafted, he sent Russell as his substitute.) Here in the hothouse of patriotism, Yankees looked to the other side of the stone wall for somebody else to do the fighting.

And that is exactly what made the men and boys who *did* do the fighting so important. Even if they were not the republican citizen-soldiers we would like them to have been, the rank-and-file of the Continental Army kept the British from reclaiming control of its colonies. But at what cost to themselves? Once boys and poor men had been transformed into troops on the march, how did they weather the storms of battle? What did they fear and feel?

In the Face of the Enemy

Throughout the summer of 1776 each side mustered its forces and prepared for a showdown in New York. By August over 30,000 British and Hessian troops, the largest single military force ever assembled in the eighteenth century, prepared to invade Long Island and Manhattan, defended by fewer than 20,000 Americans. "[I]t seams the Day is Come that in all Probility on which Depends the Salvation of this Countery," wrote Joseph Hodgkins. "But what will Be the Essue god only knows."[55]

As rebel soldiers arrived in Manhattan and British soldiers set up camp on Staten Island, many citizens departed from the city to avoid the imminent conflagration. "Everything wears the face of a Garrison Town," a Connecticut officer wrote to his wife.[56] With tens of thousands of men needing to be fed, housed, clothed, and supplied with rum, prices skyrocketed. "[I]t is Verry Expensive Living hear," Hodgkins complained from New York, much as visitors from the country have complained ever since.[57] Joseph Plumb Martin, unable to afford any rum, participated in the plunder of a wine cellar near his barracks. When Martin and his cohorts were apprehended, General Putnam himself threatened "to hang every mother's son of them." Young Joseph, not yet wise to the ways of the world, bore his admonishment heavily: "I took every word he said for gospel and expected nothing else but to be hanged before the morrow night."[58] This was the common stuff of life in an army town: privates drinking, officers growling. "But I hope god will Direct our ways and Presarve us from Every Evil Especialy from sin while we are absint from each other," Joseph Hodgkins wrote to Sarah when he first arrived in New York.[59]

As in Boston, it was a waiting game—but there was more uncertainty this time, for the enemy called the shots. When and where would they attack? On June 20, more than two months before the actual battle, Hodgkins boasted a nervous confidence: "I think they will meat with a Wharm reception for our men are in good Spirits and seem to be impatient & sick of waiting for them," he wrote. "I hope with the Blesing of god we shall Be able to keep our ground and let them know that yankeys can fite."[60] Good spirits, perhaps, but who could help but be afraid? Late in August, the British having landed on Long Island, Joseph Martin's regiment was called into action. Martin candidly recalled the emotions of an untested soldier:

Although this was not unexpected to me, yet it gave me a rather disagreeable feeling, as I was pretty well assured I should have to snuff a little gunpowder. However I kept my cogitations to myself, went to my quarters, packed my clothes, and got myself in readiness for the expedition as soon as possible. I then went to the top of the house where I had a full view of that part of the Island; I distinctly saw the smoke of the field-artillery. . . . The horrors of battle there presented themselves to my mind in all their hideousness. I must come to it now, thought I. Well, I will endeavor to do my duty as well as I am able and leave the event with Providence.[61]

This was the young lad's moment of truth: would he stand and fight, or would he cut and run? Not all of Martin's comrades-in-arms maintained their composure. One complained compulsively of thirst, causing his officer to point to Private Martin: " 'Look at that man,' said he, pointing to me; 'he is not thirsty, I will warrant it.' I felt a little elevated to be stiled a *man*." Another, in the prelude to a subsequent battle, announced repeatedly to all who could hear, "Now I am going out to the field to be killed"—which he was. A third reluctant warrior made a lasting impression on Joseph, demonstrating how *not* to behave:

> He ran round among the men of his company, snivelling and blubbering, praying each one if he had aught against him, or if *he* had injured any one, that they would forgive him, declaring at the same time that he, from his heart, forgave them if they had offended him. . . . Had he been at the gallows with a halter around his neck, he could not have shown more fear or penitence. A fine soldier you are, I thought, a fine officer, an exemplary man for young soldiers! I would have then suffered anything short of death rather than have made such an exhibition of myself. [62]

In his desire to be thought of as a man, there was no way young Joseph would become the laughing stock of his peers. Although he admitted that his first sight of wounded men—"some with broken arms, some with broken legs, some with broken heads"—left him "a little daunted," he really had no choice: he would have to prove himself a soldier by placing his life in danger. [63]

And danger he soon found. When the British landed in full force on Long Island, the Americans quickly retreated. As Martin and his company advanced to the front, they encountered some troops from Maryland who were caught in a millpond, trying to swim to the other side as the enemy poured grapeshot upon them "like a shower of hail."

> When they came out of the water and mud to us, looking like water rats, it was a truly pitiful sight. Many of them were killed in the pond, and more were drowned. Some of us went into

the water after the fall of the tide, and took out a number of corpses and a great many arms that were sunk in the pond and creek. [64]

The Americans, pushed to the westernmost edge of Long Island, managed to retreat to Manhattan where the British high command neglected to station any ships on the East River. (Had they done so, Washington might well have been forced to surrender.) On September 15, the British staged an amphibious attack at Kip's Bay, on Manhattan's East Side. Again the Americans retreated: "[T]he demons of fear and disorder seemed to take full possession of all and everything on that day," Martin reported. "Every man that I saw was endeavoring by all sober means to escape from death or captivity, which at that period of the war was almost certain death." Martin himself, separated from his company, hid in the bushes while enemy soldiers "came so near to me that I could see the buttons on their clothes." When he and a sick companion tried to catch up with their regiment, an American officer, trying to put brakes on the helter-skelter flight of the troops, commanded the men to stop. Martin argued that his companion needed shelter and medical attention, but the officer responded callously, "Well, if he dies the country will be rid of one who can do it no good."[65]

Men fleeing from battle, bent only on their own self-preservation—this was not how true patriots were supposed to behave. One army chaplain, while delivering a funeral address, strayed from praising the deceased in order to exhort his audience: "If you cannot maintain your ground, why fly in disorder? 'Tis unworthy of a soldier and a christian. Fear is a very thin shield, and betrays more than it defends."[66] Robert Cooper, delivering a sermon entitled "Courage in a Good Cause," went so far as to threaten those who succumbed to fear with the wrath of God:

> To draw back, if you were even before the cannon's mouth, would fix both awful guilt and indelible disgrace upon you. . . . If then you would escape deep guilt before God, and lasting contempt among men, forward you must go, wheresoever the

drum shall beat, and the trumpet sound for battle. You have, in a word, no alternative, but either to venture your lives bravely, or attempt to save them ignominiously; to run the hazard of dying like heroes, or be certain of living like cowards. [67]

Words similar to these were leveled repeatedly at Joseph Martin, Jeremiah Greenman, and all the other lads of the Continental Army—tender youths still formative and pliable. How, then, did they feel about themselves when they had no real choice but to run?

Not many of Cooper's "cowards" freely expressed their feelings. In an unusual disclosure, however, Garret Watts of North Carolina tried to make sense of his own flight during a different battle:

Amongst other things, I confess I was amongst the first that fled. The cause of that I cannot tell, except that everyone I saw was about to do the same. It was instantaneous. There was no effort to rally, no encouragement to fight. Officers and men joined in the flight. I threw away my gun, and, reflecting I might be punished for being found without arms, I picked up a drum, which gave forth such sound when touched by twigs I cast it away. [68]

Colonel Otho Williams, also present during a rout, noted the contagious nature of panic:

He who has never seen the effect of a panic upon a multitude can have but an imperfect idea of such a thing. The best disciplined troops have been enervated and made cowards by it. Armies have been routed by it, even where no enemy appeared to furnish an excuse. Like electricity, it operates instantaneously—like sympathy, it is irresistible where it touches. [69]

Such was the nature of war, regardless of what any preacher had to say.

Joseph Hodgkins, forced to flee during the battle for Long Island, "whas not without some happrehentions" when his company was almost surrounded: "we found the Enemy whar Endevering to Cut of our Retreet and in a grate measure Did for we whar obliged to go through fire & wharter But through the goodness of god we got cheafly in."[70] Hodgkins did not wish to dwell on his emotions: "I cant tel you how I felt," he wrote flatly to Sarah. He did, however, take care to explain the reasons for the retreat, prefacing his remarks with a defensive "I Dont know what most People think of it."[71] Joseph Martin likewise wrote defensively about his retreat from Kip's Bay, remarking that it "has been criticized so much" and "has since caused much 'inkshed.' "[72] The reputations of the participants were clearly at stake.

Although Hodgkins had his "sleave Buttin shot out and his skin a little grased," both he and Martin survived their first real fighting. But what of those who perished? The documentary record of history is skewed in favor of the survivors, those who lived to tell the tale. Soldiers who died, unlike Joseph Plumb Martin, could not relate their stories of escape. Howard Peckham, the military historian who has compiled a body count for every battle in the Revolution, estimates that around 400 Americans lost their lives in and around New York in the late summer and fall of 1776.[73] What did these men feel as they died? The British observer Nicholas Cresswell, in describing a later battle for New York, noted that not all of the men who had been shot behaved the same:

I never before saw such a shocking scene: some dead, others dying, death in different shapes; some of the wounded making the most pitiful lamentations, others that were of different parties cursing each other as the author of their misfortunes. One old veteran I observed (that was shot through both legs and not able to walk) very cooly and deliberately loading his piece and cleaning it from blood. I was surprised at the sight and asked him his reasons for it. He, with a look of contempt, said, "To be ready in case any of the Yankees come that way again."[74]

Of all wartime experiences, death is certainly the hardest to comprehend. Without first-hand documentation, and with no comparable experiences of our own, how can we possibly understand? If put in the place of the victims, whom would we curse, the enemy or the recruiting officer? Would we take solace in the fact that we had contributed to our cause, or curse our cause for contributing to our sorrow? Where would God be at that moment? Captain Joseph Jewett took thirty-six hours to perish of bayonet wounds suffered during the Battle of Long Island; on his last morning, he "was sensible of being near his End, often Repeating that it was hard work to die."[75]

More than 25,000 soldiers are said to have died on the American side during the Revolution: about 7,000 perished in battle, 10,000 died from disease, and another 8,500 in prison.[76] This total is not particularly large by modern standards, no more than the population of a small town in Ohio or Nebraska. But consider this: the per capita loss of lives, if applied to the present population of the United States, would come to a staggering two million. One out of every eight soldiers who served in the armed forces on behalf of the Revolution died; the percentage is far greater if we consider only the Continental army.[77] We know little about how these men experienced their last moments on earth.

Cannons Roaring, Muskets Cracking

Retreating from New York, the American army was tattered but not broken. Cold and hungry, Joseph Martin and his fellow soldiers were ordered to face off against the British once again at White Plains on October 28. The Americans made trenches which soon filled with chilly water, and many soldiers fell ill. Joseph Martin, separated from his belongings during the retreat on Manhattan, complained:

> To have to lie as I did almost every night (for our duty required it) on the cold and often wet ground without a blanket and with nothing but thin summer clothing was tedious. I have often while upon guard lain upon one side until the upper side smarted with cold, then turned that side down to the place warmed by my body and let the other take its turn at

smarting. . . . In the morning, the ground as white as snow with hoar frost. Or perhaps it would rain all night like a flood. All that could be done in that case was to lie down (if one could lie down), take our musket in our arms and place the lock between our thighs and "weather it out."

Martin became ill, and he was left on his own to get better:

I had the canopy of heaven for my hospital and the ground for my hammock. I found a spot where the dry leaves had collected between the knolls. I made up a bed of these and nestled in it, having no other friend present but the sun to smile upon me. I had nothing to eat or drink, not even water, and was unable to go after any myself, for I was sick indeed.

When his tour of duty ended in December of 1776 Joseph headed back to Connecticut, eager to enjoy the basic comforts of food, shelter, and dry clothing. His army days, he figured, were over: "I learned something of a soldier's life, enough, I thought, to keep me at home in the future."[78]

Joseph Hodgkins, meanwhile, was ordered to move southward through New Jersey, a few miles in advance of the pursuing British soldiers. "I Cannot Express the hardships & fetague we have under gone on our March from Place to Place," he wrote to Sarah. "But I desire to Be thankful that I am alive & well & in good spirits at Presant I hope god will still Presarve us & Carry us through all Defcltyes & Dangers we have to meet with in the way of our Duty."[79] Tom Paine, marching in the same army as Joseph Hodgkins, expressed similar sentiments in more dramatic terms:

These are the times that try men's souls: The summer soldier and the sunshine patriot will, in this crisis, shrink from the service of his country; but he that stands it *now*, deserves the thanks of man and woman. Tyranny, like hell, is not easily conquered; yet we have this consolation with us, that the harder the conflict, the more glorious the triumph.[80]

On Christmas night of 1776, even as Joseph Martin and 2,000 other "sunshine patriots" headed home, George Washington, Joseph

Hodgkins, and the rest of the Continental soldiers remaining on duty tried to cross the freezing Delaware River at three different locations in order to surprise the Hessians who had been celebrating the birth of Christ with hard drinking. Joseph described the maneuver briefly to Sarah:

> [O]n Chrismas night we marched with about 2000 Men to a ferry about 7 miles from Camp in order to Pass over to the Jersey side of the River to atack a Party of the Enemy that Lay at a Place Called Mount Holly But the Ise Prevented our Crossing that night But the Troops that Lay up about 20 miles up the River against Trintown got across the River & marched Round & Came in upon the Bak of Trentown about Dawning & Began a heavy fire with there field Peases which seprised the Enemy so they sirrendred the hole that whas took 925 Take about 20 kill & wounded Six Brass field Peases a grate quantity of small arms & Blankets this gave the Enemy a grate shock.[81]

Warmed by the Hessians' blankets and inspired by their success at Trenton, the Continental soldiers attacked once again at Princeton a week later, capturing 300 British troops. Joseph Hodgkins had intended to leave the army when his term expired at the end of 1776, but suddenly he changed his mind and signed up for three more years. Perhaps he was heartened by these first American victories, or, more likely, he was enticed by a very sweet offer: he was promoted to captain, and his first assignment was to go home and recruit more soldiers. That much he was certainly willing to do.

In the spring of 1777 Joseph Plumb Martin, a seasoned veteran at the age of sixteen, decided to enlist once again, as did Jeremiah Greenman. Initially, both Greenman and Martin were stationed on the Hudson River above New York City, but when the British made their move on Philadelphia, the seat of the Continental Congress, they marched south to reinforce the main body of the American army. As the British advanced, rebel soldiers tried to hold them off at Brandywine Creek. Private Elisha Stevens described the fighting there:

> Cannons Roaring muskets Cracking Drums Beating Bumbs Flying all Round. Men a dying wounded Horred Grones

which would Greave the Heardist of Hearts to See Such a Dollful Sight as this to See our Fellow Creators Slain in Such a manner.[82]

The Americans were overpowered, with over 1,000 soldiers either killed, wounded, or captured. Neither Martin nor Greenman had reached the main army in time to fight at Brandywine.

Two weeks later the British marched unopposed into Philadelphia. The Americans did not attack them there, but on October 4 they did challenge a large body of soldiers camped in nearby Germantown. General Washington ordered a complicated four-pronged attack, but two of the American divisions, lost in the fog and smoke, opened fire on each other. Joseph Martin, having arrived just in time for the battle, escaped injury, but 150 of his comrades were killed and 500 wounded—many by their own countrymen.

Just outside of Philadelphia two American forts, Mifflin and Mercer, flanked the Delaware River, effectively cutting off all supplies to the occupying army. The British, recognizing the strategic importance of these forts, brought out their heavy guns to dislodge the American troops. Jeremiah Greenman, now stationed at Fort Mifflin, catalogued the weaponry for each side according to the weight of its balls:

[T]he Enemys Batterys had got ready to play very smartly on the Fort, two bomb Battrys three 3 Gun Batteries, one of Six Guns 24 pounder, . . . the other at the Hospital Warf of 5–24 pounders . . . we all this time ware not inactive for we raised two 18 pounder batterys againts the Enemys Main Battery a nother of two 9 pounders to annoy the Batterys on the warf[83]

And Joseph Martin, also charged with the defense of Fort Mifflin, described the true-life nightmare which these batteries created for the soldiers:

During the whole night, at intervals of a quarter or half an hour, the enemy would let off all their pieces, and although we had sentinels to watch them and at every flash of their guns to cry, "a shot," upon hearing which everyone endeavored to take care of himself, yet they would ever and anon, in spite of all our precautions, cut up some of us. . . . I was in this place a fortnight and can say in sincerity that I never lay down to sleep a minute in all that time.

The British knew the situation of the place as well as we did. And as their point-blank shot would not reach us behind the wall, they would throw elevated grapeshot from their mortar, and when the sentries had cried, "a shot," and the soldiers, seeing no shot arrive, had become careless, the grapeshot would come down like a shower of hail about our ears. . . .

We had a thirty-two pound cannon in the fort, but had not a single shot for it. The British also had one in their battery upon the Hospital Point, which raked the fort. . . . The artillery officers offered a gill of rum for each shot fired from that piece, which the soldiers would procure. I have seen from twenty to fifty men . . . waiting with impatience the coming of the shot, which would often be seized before its motion had fully ceased and conveyed off to our gun to be sent back again to its former owners. When the lucky fellow who had caught it had swallowed his rum, he would return to wait for another, exulting that he had been more lucky or more dexterous than his fellows. [84]

At one point the British tried a direct charge, but according to Greenman they were repulsed in a "Great Slawter . . . leaving thear Dead wounded & a few prisoners . . . in all amounting to about three hundred in our hands."[85] Having failed to capture the fort by manpower, they mustered firepower instead: British artillery unleashed a continuous barrage of projectiles from the best warships in the world upon a sixteen-year-old lad from Connecticut and a nineteen-year-old from Rhode Island. Martin continued his account:

The enemy soon began their firing upon us and there was music indeed. . . . The cannonade was severe, as well it might be, six sixty-four-gun ships, a thirty-six-gun frigate, a twenty-four-gun ship, a galley and a sloop of six guns, together with six batteries of six guns each and a bomb battery of three mortars, all playing at once upon our poor little fort, if fort it might be called.

Some of our officers endeavored to ascertain how many guns were fired in a minute by the enemy, but it was impossible, the fire was incessant. In the height of the cannonade it was desirable to hoist a signal flag for some of our galleys that were lying above us to come down to our assistance. The officers inquired who would undertake it. As none appeared willing for some time, I was about to offer my services. . . . While I was still hesitating, a sergeant of the artillery offered himself. He accordingly ascended to the round top [and] pulled down the flag to affix the signal flag to the halyard. . . . The sergeant then came down and had not gone half a rod from the foot of the staff when he was cut in two by a cannon shot. This caused me some serious reflections at the time. He was killed! Had I been at the same business I might have been killed, but it might have been otherwise ordered by Divine Providence, we might have both lived. I am not predestinarian enough to determine it. The enemy's shot cut us up. I saw five artillerists belonging to one gun cut down by a single shot, and I saw men who were stooping to be protected by the works, but not stooping low enough, split like fish to be broiled. . . .

When the firing had in some measure subsided and I could look about me, I found the fort exhibited a picture of desolation. The whole area of the fort was as completely ploughed as a field. The buildings of every kind hanging in broken fragments, and the guns all dismounted, and how many of the garrison sent to the world of spirits, I knew not. If ever destruction was complete, it was here.[86]

Is this really the Revolutionary War? Where is Yankee Doodle, a feather in his hat? In the popular mind, the image of the American Revolution has been unduly shaped by its first two battles: at Concord untrained Yankee farmers hid behind trees and stone walls as they shot at redcoated soldiers foolish enough to march in the center of the road, while at Bunker Hill, where the rebels were told not to fire until seeing the whites of the eyes of the enemy, the battle was fought with sabers, bayonets, and the butts of the rifles, along with muskets fired at short range. The Revolution, we assume, was a close and personal affair—but it wasn't always that way. As in the larger conflicts of the nineteenth and twentieth centuries, many soldiers who died never saw their executioners, while those who fired long-range rifles or artillery did not always know whether or not they had terminated a human life. Cannons, mortars, howitzers, rocket launchers—these were all in common use, driving heavy iron balls toward enemy fortifications or filling the air with lead and scraps of metal intended to maim or kill.

As British and American armies fought for control of the capital at Philadelphia, other soldiers faced off well to the north. In the summer of 1777, 5,000 British troops, 3,000 Hessians, and over 1,000 women marched from Canada toward New York City in order to separate New England from the rest of the states. Spurred by rumors that the British were inciting the Indians to kill and scalp the Americans, thousands of patriots from New England and New York, primarily militiamen, gathered north of Albany to resist the invasion. The Americans chopped down trees and turned the roadways into swamps in order to slow the progress of the British; they also destroyed corn and drove off cattle to deny food to the enemy troops. Many of the invading troops, their provisions diminishing, deserted; these poor men from England, Scotland, and Germany decided to brave the American frontier or fight in the Yankee army rather than perish in battle or die of starvation. By mid-September the royal force had been reduced to 6,000. The British General, John Burgoyne, had expected support from the main army in New York, but support never came. Without enough provisions to stage a retreat, Burgoyne ordered his men to fight.

There were two major battles, both in the region between Bemis's tavern and Freeman's farm. Joseph Hodgkins's unit, including thirty-six men he had recruited from Massachusetts, fought in the first battle on September 19; one, Amos Spring, was killed.[87] According to military terminology, casualties were "heavy"—meaning that many men and boys suffered great pain and agony, and some lost their lives. In the aftermath of the fighting Thomas Anburey, a British lieutenant, reported "seeing fifteen, sixteen, and twenty buried in a whole"—and in some cases the gravediggers "left heads, legs and arms above the ground." In one grave the oldest of three officers was "not exceeding seventeen." Even so, Anburey was more upset by the plight of those who had not yet died:

> This friendly office to the dead, though it greatly affects the feeling, was nothing to the scenes in bringing in the wounded; the one were past all pain, the other in the most excruciating torments, sending forth dreadful groans. They had remained out all night, and from the loss of blood and want of nourishment, were upon the point of expiring. Some of them begged they might lay and die, others again were insensible, some upon the least movement were put in the most horrid tortures, and all had near a mile to be conveyed to the hospitals. [88]

After losing more men during the second battle on October 7, Burgoyne ordered a retreat; with no apparent alternative, he left 500 of the sick and wounded behind to fend for themselves. At Saratoga, surrounded by an estimated 13,000 to 17,000 Americans, Burgoyne finally surrendered.

The impact of the British defeat at Saratoga was profound. French leaders, assured that the Americans were strong enough to wage a real war, joined in the fight against Great Britain, their traditional enemy; for the remainder of the Revolution the patriots would depend heavily on France for money and supplies, arms and ammunition, soldiers and sailors. These strategic and diplomatic implications of Saratoga are often noted, but the more personal consequences are not often mentioned. About 150 Americans died in the fighting, while close to 1,000 of the foreign troops perished from battle wounds or illness. The families of the Americans heard about the loss of loved ones within weeks; the families of the Europeans not for months or even years. Indeed, since identification of the dead bodies was haphazard at best, how could anybody know for sure whether a missing soldier had deserted or died?

The Americans had won a major victory at Saratoga, but the war was far from over. Shortly after the British surrender Joseph Hodgkins wrote to Sarah:

> I am Prity Well now I have had somthing of the Camp Disorder & Lost most all my flesh But I hope soon to Pick up

my Crumes again we have had a Very fartagueing Campain
But as we have Don the Bisnes we Came hear for I hope None
of us will Complain of a little hardship I wish I Could inform
you that I thought our fartague was over for this year But to
the Contray I Expect we shall march to Morrow Morning
Down the River to wards the Pakskills & I Expect we shall
Be ordered towards Philledalpha to Take another winters
Camppain in the Jerseys Soldiers must not Complain.[89]

During the winter of 1777–1778 Joseph Martin, Joseph Hodgkins,
Jeremiah Greenman and the rest of the soldiers in the Continental
army set up camp at Valley Forge, in striking distance of the British army in Philadelphia. With neither force strong enough to dislodge the other, the British high command decided to abandon
Philadelphia in the late spring of 1778. As thousands of redcoated
soldiers marched towards New York, the American generals, despite an oppressive heat wave, ordered the troops under their command to attack at the courthouse in Monmouth, New Jersey.
Jeremiah Greenman reported that "a Number of our men died with
heat," while Joseph Martin, comparing the temperature to "the
mouth of a heated oven," noted that if "fighting is hot work in
cool weather, how much more so in such weather as it was on the
twenty-eighth of June, 1778. . . . [N]one can realize it that did not
feel it."[90] Over one hundred American soldiers perished that day,
thirty-seven of heatstroke.[91] At the end of the battle, despite severe
losses on both sides, the British simply continued on their way.

Between the fall of 1776 and the fall of 1778 many soldiers died
on both sides and many more suffered, yet the positions of the two
armies remained unchanged. The American Revolution, which both
sides had expected to win in a moment, had turned into a war of
attrition. This was a conflict that would be lost, not won.

Death or Victory

Having failed to advance into the interior of the northern or middle
states, the British commanders turned their attention to the South,
where they expected to receive support from local loyalists—

reportedly more numerous than in New England—and perhaps even from slaves, who had every reason to fight against their Whig masters. In 1776 the British had tried to take Charleston, but they had been repelled by patriots who built a fort with palmetto logs capable of absorbing the force of heavy artillery. This time the British determined to launch a much heavier assault, more like their move against New York. At the end of 1778 they took Savannah, the southernmost rebel port. During the following year they advanced into the interior of Georgia and South Carolina, and by the spring of 1780 a force of 10,000 men, ninety transport ships, and fourteen war ships combined to force the capitulation of Charleston, the only major city in the South. Over 5,000 Americans laid down their arms, the third largest surrender in United States history— only Bataan in World War II and Harpers Ferry during the Civil War yielded more prisoners.

After seizing Savannah, Charleston, and other southern ports, the British marched inland. At Camden they routed 3,000 patriots, killing or wounding about 1,000 and capturing another thousand. At Waxhaws redcoated cavalrymen commanded by Banastre Tarleton, not wishing to bother with prisoners, refused to "grant quarter" and hacked away with their sabres at the men in Abraham Buford's regiment who were flying a white flag. (In future battles victorious patriots would cry "Tarleton's quarter" or "Remember Buford" whenever they slaughtered men who had just surrendered.) As they advanced, British leaders insisted that local citizens pledge their allegiance to the king. Many did, for there were numerous loyalists in Georgia and the Carolinas, but others refused—including Daniel Collins and his sixteen-year-old son James.

In his autobiography James Collins revealed how the war in the South appeared from the inside. When fighting broke out in 1775 eleven-year-old James took no notice, but five years later, as the British marched toward his home on the border of North and South Carolina, he reported that "times began to be troublesome, and people began to divide into parties. Those that had been good friends in times past, became enemies; they began to watch each other with jealous eyes, and were designated by the names of, Whig, and Tory."[92]

One day, he recalled, his father came home in a rage, having just witnessed the destruction of a nearby ironworks which led to the deaths of several men. Daniel Collins announced to his family:

> I have come home determined to take my gun and when I lay it down, I lay down my life with it. My son you may prepare for the worst; the thing is fairly at issue. We must submit and become slaves, or fight.[93]

James, following in the same spirit, wanted to enlist in the army like his older brother, but his father, although certainly patriotic, advised him simply to volunteer so he could return home whenever he liked. (For the most part, this is how it was done in the South: men and boys, whether Whig or Tory, mustered for specific campaigns, then disbanded once their missions were completed.) James, a good horseman, started out "merely as a collector of news," an informal spy who rode through the countryside asking the people he knew about the whereabouts of opposition bands. Acting on information James provided, his company of patriots surprised a band of loyalists, killing eight and wounding sixteen; James fired his blue barrel shot gun twice, "but I suspect without effect." The young scout and his fellow patriots celebrated their victory by drinking peach brandy from the house they had raided.[94]

The next battle James witnessed came to the opposite conclusion: the slaughter of several patriots who could not retreat fast enough from the enemy. Collins himself did not fight in the main action, but he reported the results:

> The dead and wounded lay scattered in every direction over the field; numbers lay stretched cold and lifeless; some were yet struggling in the agonies of death, while here and there lay others, faint with the loss of blood, almost famished for water, and begging for assistance. The scene before me, I could not reconcile to my feelings. . . . Well, thought I, if this be the fate of war, I would willingly be excused. I devised several plans to get out of the scrape, but . . . the thing had gone too far, and there was no safety in retreating.

James did receive some consolation from the event: he acquired from one of the dead men "a good looking rifle, with a shot-bag and all the apparatus belonging."[95]

The big test for James Collins, and the first opportunity to use his new rifle, came at King's Mountain on October 7, 1780, where 1,000 back-country patriots faced off against an equal number of American loyalists commanded by a British major:

> The sky was overcast with clouds, and at times a light mist of rain falling; our provisions were scanty, and hungry men are apt to be fractious; each one felt his situation; the last stake was up and the severity of the game must be played; everything was at stake—life, liberty, property, and even the fate of wife, children and friends, seemed to depend on the issue; death or victory was the only way to escape suffering. Near two o'clock in the afternoon we came in sight of the enemy, who seemed to be fully prepared to give battle at all risks. When we came up, we halted, and formed in order of battle. . . .
>
> Each leader made a short speech in his own way to his men, desiring every coward to be off immediately; here I confess I would willingly have been excused, for my feelings were not the most pleasant—this may be attributed to my youth, not being quite seventeen years of age—but I could not well swallow the appellation of coward. I looked around; every man's countenance seemed to change; well, thought I, fate is fate; every man's fate is before him and he has to run it out. . . .
>
> We were soon in motion, every man throwing four or five balls in his mouth to prevent thirst, also to be in readiness to reload quick. The shot of the enemy soon began to pass over us like hail; the first shock was quickly over, and for my own part, I was soon in profuse sweat. My lot happened to be in the center, where the severest part of the battle was fought. We soon attempted to climb the hill, but were fiercely charged upon and were forced to fall back to our first position. We tried a second time, but met the same fate; the fight then seemed to become more furious. . . . We took to the hill a third time; the enemy gave way; when we had gotten near the top, some of our leaders roared out, "Hurrah, my brave fellows! Advance! They are crying for quarter."

By this time, the right and left had gained the top of the cliff; the enemy was completely hemmed in on all sides, and no chance of escaping—besides, their leader had fallen. They soon threw down their arms and surrendered. After the fight was over, the situation of the poor Tories appeared to be really pitiable; the dead lay in heaps on all sides, while the groans of the wounded were heard in every direction. I could not help turning away from the scene before me, with horror, and though exulting in victory, could not refrain from shedding tears.—"Great God!" said I, "Is this the fate of mortals, or was it for this cause that man was brought into the world?" . . .

Next morning, which was Sunday, the scene became really distressing; the wives and children of the poor Tories came in, in great numbers. Their husbands, fathers, and brothers, lay dead in heaps, while others lay wounded or dying; a melancholy sight indeed! while numbers of the survivors were doomed to abide the sentence of a court martial, and several were actually hanged. As regards the numbers that fell, authors have disagreed; yet none have overrated the number. I know our estimate at the time was something over three hundred.

We proceeded to bury the dead, but it was badly done; they were thrown into convenient piles and covered with old logs, the bark of old trees, and rocks; yet not so as to secure them from becoming a prey to the beasts of the forest, or the vultures of the air; and the wolves became so plenty that it was dangerous for anyone to be out at night, for several miles around; also, the hogs in the neighborhood gathered into the place to devour the flesh of men. . . . I saw, myself, in passing the place a few weeks after, all parts of the human frame lying scattered in every direction . . .

In the evening, there was a distribution made of the plunder, and we were dismissed. My father and myself drew two fine horses, two guns, and some articles of clothing, with a share of powder and lead; every man repaired to his tent, or home. It seemed like a calm, after a heavy storm had passed over, and for a short time, every man could visit his home, or his neighbor, without being afraid.[96]

James Collins did not stay home for long. Since "the British and Tories were still in strength," he wrote, "it became necessary for us to be again in motion; the Tories were mustering up in small parties, to seek revenge, and we again set out to chastise them."[97] On January 17, 1781, James Collins and the South Carolina militia joined with troops from the Continental Army to fight against British and loyalist soldiers commanded by Banastre Tarleton at a place called the Cowpens. The American commander, Daniel Morgan, placed Collins and the militiamen on the front line to absorb the charge of the British cavalry. When the militiamen retreated, as Morgan had expected, they drew the British horsemen straight into the firing line of the Continental regulars. The American strategy worked well—only Tarleton and a handful of his men managed to escape—but young James Collins had been sent as a sacrificial lamb, which caused him quite a scare. "Now my hide is in the loft," he thought to himself as he ran from the furious charge of British soldiers mounted on horses, lunging their bayonets at the frightened men and boys.

After the battle at Cowpens, Collins continued with his scouting missions, but he decided not to accompany the Continental Army as it moved northward, the British in hot pursuit. During the spring and summer of 1781 the British claimed victory in a string of battles, but at a severe cost: in the fighting at Guilford Court House and Eutaw Springs almost a thousand soldiers were killed or wounded, and several hundred more deserted. "Another such victory would ruin the British army," remarked a member of Parliament back in London.

Lord Cornwallis, the British Commander in the South, decided to focus his energy on Virginia, the richest and most populous of the former colonies. He marched his army to the Yorktown peninsula, where he hoped to establish control of the vast inland waterways of the Chesapeake Bay. Unaware that a French fleet from the Caribbean had just been dispatched to challenge the British command of the Chesapeake, Cornwallis mistakenly assumed that his men could be supplied at will by ships sent from New York. Sensing an opportunity to ensnare Cornwallis's army, George Washington ordered the northern force of the Continentals, along with several thousand French troops, to march quickly from New Jersey to Virginia. By the fall of 1781 7,000 British soldiers found themselves trapped inside of

Yorktown by almost 17,000 French and Americans, including Joseph Plumb Martin. (Jeremiah Greenman was just being released from a short stint as a prisoner, while Joseph Hodgkins, as we shall see, had left the army.) Deprived of food, shelled by heavy artillery, and weakened by an outbreak of smallpox within their ranks, the British could be saved only by relief from the sea, but twenty-four French battleships under the command of the Comte de Grasse delivered the coup de grace by turning away the British navy. On October 17 Lord Cornwallis ordered a white flag to be raised, and the following day the defeated soldiers lay down their arms. Although the British maintained control of New York, Charleston, and a handful of other seaports, the ruling politicians back in London, threatened at home by France and Spain, soon abandoned their efforts to reestablish control over the American colonies.

Beasts of Prey

The fighting in the South during the waning years of the American Revolution brought the logic of war to its natural conclusion. If the object was to eliminate opposing soldiers, why submit to artificial conventions? Unrestrained, the armies on both sides did what armies do best: maximize the killing of other human beings. Major William Pierce wrote:

> Such scenes of desolation, bloodshed and deliberate murder I never was a witness to before! Wherever you turn the weeping widow and fatherless child pour out their melancholy tales to wound the feeling of humanity. The two opposite principles of whiggism and toryism have set the people of this country to cutting each other's throats, and scarce a day passes but some poor deluded tory is put to death at his door. For the want of civil government the bands of society are totally disunited, and the people, by copying the manners of the British, have become perfectly savage.[98]

According to Pierce's commander, General Nathanael Greene, "The whole Country is in Danger of being laid waste by the Whigs and

Tories who pursue each other with as much relentless Fury as Beasts of Prey."[99]

Yet these "Beasts of Prey" were also human beings, men of common circumstances who found themselves caught in a conflict which had enveloped their personal worlds. Initially, few were any more bestial than Joseph Hodgkins, Joseph Plumb Martin, or any other soldier. But the peculiar character of a civil war, with its feedback cycle of escalating violence, inspired a passion for revenge, each atrocity justifying a more brutal response. After the Tories had beaten his mother, William Gipson of South Carolina admitted that he took "no little satisfaction" in torturing a prisoner who was placed in his charge: "He was placed with one foot upon a sharp pin drove in a block, and was turned round . . . until the pin run through his foot."[100] Years after the war had ended Moses Hall of North Carolina, in a statement of rare honesty, reported how he came to set aside his more humane sensibilities:

> The evening after our battle with the Tories, we having a considerable number of prisoners, I recollect a scene which made a lasting impression upon my mind. I was invited by some of my comrades to go and see some of the prisoners. We went to where six were standing together. Some discussion taking place, I heard some of our men cry out, "Remember Buford," and the prisoners were immediately hewed to pieces with broadswords. At first I bore the scene without any emotion, but upon a moment's reflection, I felt such horror as I never did before nor have since, and, returning to my quarters and throwing myself upon my blanket, I contemplated the cruelties of war until overcome and unmanned by a distressing gloom from which I was not relieved until commencing our march next morning before day by moonlight. . . .
>
> Being on the left of the road as we marched along, I discovered lying upon the ground something with appearance of a man. Upon approaching him, he proved to be a youth about sixteen who, having come out to view the British through curiousity, for fear he might give information to our troops, they had run him through with a bayonet and left him for dead. Though able to speak, he was mortally wounded. The sight

of this unoffending boy, butchered . . . relieved me of my distressful feeling for the slaughter of the Tories, and I desired nothing so much as the opportunity of participating in their destruction. [101]

Moses Hall and William Gipson, by reflecting upon the evolution of their own barbarous acts, revealed that their civilized sensitivities had merely been repressed, not lost forever; they had been monsters only for the moment. Soldiers, in order to perform their duty, must learn to ignore the prohibition against killing other human beings—but upon their return to civil society, they must place their violent deeds in some perspective. Joseph Plumb Martin, not a born killer, accepted his predatory role while serving in the war, only to question it later:

We overtook the enemy just as they were entering upon the meadow. . . . I could distinguish everything about them. They were retreating in line, though in some disorder. I singled out a man and took my aim directly between his shoulders. . . . He was a good mark, being a broad-shouldered fellow. What became of him I know not; the fire and smoke hid him from my sight. One thing I know, that is, I took as deliberate aim at him as ever I did at any game in my life. But after all, I hope I did not kill him, although I intended to at the time.[102]

James Collins, with hindsight, could recall the precise number of shots he had fired after each battle, but he always added a qualifying phrase: "whether with any effect or not, I do not know."[103] Collins, like Martin, did not wish to see himself as a murderer. Once, he reported in his autobiography, he "was put to a trial that I have not forgotten, nor will ever forget":

We had caught the old father of the clan that we were in search of; he was a very old, grayheaded man, and was brought before the colonel and threatened with instant death unless he would tell us where his sons were. The old man declared he did not know, but being still threatened, he fell on his knees, laid off his hat and began to beg for his life. . . . While he was in this situation a man in the company took me aside, and holding a long spear in his hand, with a handle perhaps six or eight feet long, said, "I want you to take this spear and run it through that d——d old Tory; he ought to die." "No," said I, "he is too old; besides the colonel would never forgive me; he is a prisoner and he don't intend to kill him." "Oh," said he, "I can easily plead you off with the colonel;" then putting his hand in his pocket he drew out a purse of money, saying, "Here is twenty dollars—(showing the silver)—I will give you this to kill him." I felt insulted. I thought he underrated my real character, and thought that through my youth and inexperience, he would bribe me to do a deed that he himself would be ashamed of. I turned away, saying, "It will take but one to do it, and you can do it as easily as I can." I thank God, I escaped the temptation, for I verily believe had I committed the deed, the ghost of that old man would have haunted me to this day; but I thank God, I never had a desire to take away the life of any man, even my worst enemy. A man in battle, or in the heat of passion, might deem it necessary, but after much reflection, I am inclined to think that no man, possessed of the spirit of patriotism, would seek revenge by taking away his enemy's life.[104]

James Collins, "after much reflection," recoiled at the thought of killing—but how did he really behave at the age of sixteen? Did he too, like so many others "in the heat of passion," take "no little satisfaction" in hurting the enemy? At the close of the war, Collins participated eagerly in the local sport of "ferreting out the Tories":

We would meet at a time and place appointed, probably at a church, schoolhouse, or some vacant building, generally in the afternoon, lay off our circuit and divide into two or more companies, and set off after dark. Wherever we found any Tories, we would surround the house, one party would force the doors and enter sword in hand, extinguish all the lights, if there were any, and suffer no light to be made, when we would commence hacking the man or men that were found in the house, threatening them with instant death, and occasionally making a furious stroke as if to dispatch them at once, but taking care to strike the wall or some object that was in the way, they generally being found crouched up in some corner, or about the beds. Another party would mount the roof of the house and commence pulling it down; thus, the dwelling house, smoke house, and kitchen, if any, were dismantled and torn down, at least to the joists. The poor fellows, perhaps expecting instant death, would beg hard for life, and make any promise on condition of being spared, while their wives or friends would join in their entreaties.

James seems to have felt no remorse for beating up on the Tories—since they "had been very troublesome," they now "had to pay the piper." But he was able to clear his conscience only by convincing himself that no lasting harm had been done: "There were none of the poor fellows much hurt, only they were hacked about their heads and arms enough to bleed freely."[105]

Few Revolutionary soldiers turned into pacifists, but many became aware that something was amiss: this was not life as it should be. Why, then, did they purposely train their rifles at men so much like themselves? Initially, they may have wished to defend liberty, or prove themselves worthy, or avenge the death of a friend—but quickly and inevitably, personal motivations were subsumed by a more pressing reality shared by all soldiers on both sides: "I fired without thinking," said Garret Watts, "except that I might prevent the man opposite from killing me."[106]

"Death was so frequent that it ceased to terrify," wrote James Morris while confined in a prison rife with disease. "It ceased to warn; it ceased to alarm Survivors."[107] Dr. Lewis Beebe, on the Canadian expedition, complained that death was "as little regarded as the singing of birds" and that soldiers were "cursing and swearing in the same tent with the corpse."[108] But cursing and swearing served a purpose: to help struggling soldiers face a reality which was far too grim. Revolutionary soldiers coined an expression for the swaggering jive, constant banter, and crude posturing which enabled them to move on: "camp feelings." Of necessity, they developed a hard outer crust.

The survivors, after all, needed to muster their own strength and carry on. A group of soldiers from New Jersey once dug two graves, then left momentarily to retrieve the bodies. Upon their return they discovered that some men from Pennsylvania had just deposited different corpses into the empty holes. The New Jersey men managed to win the ensuing argument and proceeded to remove the bodies buried by the Pennsylvanians, which they deposited under a shallow heap of brush and stones. Such were the last rites of four fallen patriots, for the gravediggers had to get on with the business of fighting a war.[109]

Winter Soldiers

Battles, although dangerous and memorable, were not routine affairs. The everyday lives of Revolutionary soldiers were marked more by marching, drilling, and sitting in camp cooking up "firecakes"—flour and water, fried on an open fire. They liked to gamble but had little money; they liked to drink but seldom had rum. According to Private William Burnett, a fifteen-year-old runaway servant from Virginia who discovered with some disappointment that life in the army was "not going to be a frolic," Revolutionary soldiers "took but little notice of anything else but the time, as it seemed slowly to pass."[110]

The fighting men of the Continental Army concerned themselves first and foremost with their daily necessities. Joseph Martin wrote obsessively about food, or the lack thereof. "We kept a continual Lent as faithfully as ever any of the most rigorous of the Roman Catholics," he joked. "But there was this exception, we had no fish or eggs or any other substitute for our commons. Ours was a real fast and, depend upon it, we were sufficiently mortified." Upon observing a starving squirrel he felt little remorse, noting that the squirrel "did not live to starve piecemeal six or seven years."[111] On another occasion he wrote:

Being pinched with hunger, I one day strolled to a place, where sometime before some cattle had been slaughtered. Here I had the good luck (or rather bad luck, as it turned out in the end) to find an ox's milt, which had escaped the hogs and dogs. With this prize I steered off to my tent, threw it upon the fire and broiled it, and then sat down to eat it, without either bread or salt. I had not had it long in my stomach before it began to make strong remonstrances and to manifest a great inclination to be set at liberty again. I was willing to listen to its requests, and with eyes overflowing with tears at parting with what I had thought to be a friend, I gave it a discharge.[112]

Toward the end of 1777, Martin recalled with considerable derision, Congress ordered a special Thanksgiving feast: "it gave each and every man *half* a *gill* of rice and a *tablespoon* of vinegar!"[113] That winter, with the main body of the Continental Army hunkered down at Valley Forge, the young private from Connecticut drew a most fortunate assignment: "to go into the country on a foraging expedition, which was nothing more nor less than to procure provisions from the inhabitants for the men in the army . . . at the point of the bayonet."[114] But two years later at Morristown, with soldiers prevented by the deep snow from raiding local farmers, there was simply no food to be had:

> We were absolutely, literally starved. I do solemnly declare that I did not put a single morsel of victuals into my mouth for four days and as many nights, except a little black birch bark which I gnawed off a stick of wood, if that can be called victuals. I saw several of the men roast their old shoes and eat them, and I was afterwards informed by one of the officers' waiters, that some of the officers killed and ate a favorite little dog.[115]

The eating of dog meat, once again, became the measure of hard times.

Raids on farmers in search of produce and livestock were far more frequent than attacks on enemy forces, for the soldiers, before they could fight, had to be fed. Typically, soldiers reported their little plundering expeditions with joking use of military terms. John Smith, on his retreat from New York, wrote in his diary on September 29, 1776, "This Evening our Visiting Rounds went out on a Patrole again & took up a sheep & two Large fat turkeys not Being able to give the Countersign & Brought to our Castel where they was tryd By fire & Executed By the whole Division."[116] Ebenezer Fox, the barber's apprentice, experienced no active combat during his first tour of duty in the militia, but he did participate in military maneuvers of some consequence:

> One afternoon some geese were discovered enjoying them-selves in a pond near the road; and one of the soldiers, thinking that a little poultry would not be an unacceptable addition to our bill of fare, threw a stone among them and killed one of the largest of the flock.
>
> The prize was secured and concealed by taking off the head of a drum and putting the goose into it, and then re-storing the instrument to its former appearance. The owner of the poultry followed and complained to the commanding officer of this depredation on his property. We halted long enough to have the wagons searched, but the goose was not found; and we were allowed to march on. When the camp fires were kindled at night, the goose was roasted, and our captain did not hesitate to eat a leg, wing, and a piece of the breast without troubling us with any questions respecting our right of possession.
>
> A few days subsequent to this event, we halted one evening, after a tiresome day's march, at a well-provided farming estab-lishment belonging to an old Quaker. . . . Late at night a party was sent out to search the premises and to seize whatever could be found capable of being converted to our benefit, or of con-tributing to our physical wants. In an orchard belonging to the Quaker a large number of fowls were found quietly roosting upon the trees, little dreaming of the murderous attack about to be made upon them. Between thirty and forty were captured, to whom no quarters were given, and brought into camp. The feathers were quickly plucked, and the bodies were scalded in the kettle. Afterwards they were stowed away in our knapsacks, and a party sufficient to carry the plunder were sent on in advance. [117]

Joseph Martin said it most succinctly: " 'Rub and go' was always the Revolutionary soldier's motto."[118]

Clothing was also in short supply. Recruits generally procured their own "uniforms," such as they were:

[T]hey wore small-clothes, coming down and fastening just below the knee, and long stockings with cowhide shoes ornamented by large buckles, while not a pair of boots graced the company. The coats and waist-coats were loose and of huge dimensions, with colors as various as the barks of oak, sumack and other trees of our hills and swamps could make them, and their shirts were all made of flax and, like every other part of the dress, were homespun.[119]

The informal attire of Revolutionary soldiers contrasted dramatically with the bright red uniforms of the British—and the rebel troops liked it that way. Americans, after all, did not like standing armies, and by limiting their identifying features to hunting shirts or sprigs of greenery in their hats, they appeared to play the part of citizen-soldiers. In the South, however, when small bands of patriots fought against similar groups of local loyalists who also wore no uniforms, the men on both sides found it difficult to distinguish friend from foe. James Collins, while on a scouting mission, once had to flee from his own company, who assumed he must be the enemy.[120] According to Moses Hall, a company of Tories marched right between two lines of Whigs at a place called the Race Paths, unaware of the true identity of their alleged allies until it was too late. On another occasion Hall donned the hat of a fallen foe, only to be told that a small red strap on the crown would target him as an enemy.[121]

In 1777 Congress offered a suit of clothes to new recruits, but how long would one set of clothing last? And what about the continuing soldiers whose shirts and britches had already turned to rags, and whose shoes had disintegrated from wear? Jeremiah Greenman's commanding officer, Colonel Israel Angell, complained of the condition of his men in August of 1777:

Not one half of them can not be termed fit for any duty in any immergency; of those, who of them went with me on a late expedition near to Kings bridge many were bare foot, in consequence of which its probable they won't be fit for duty again for many week . . . . [T]he Regiment is scandallous in its appearance in the view of every one—and has because of this incurred from . . . the inhabitants of Towns thro which they have lately passed, the disagreeable & provoking Epithets of the Ragged Lousey Naked Regiment. Such treatment, gentlemen, is discouraging dispiriting in its tendency: it does effectually unman the Man and render them almost useless in the Army.[122]

"Lousey" did not mean "terrible" but covered with lice. With only one set of clothing apiece the soldiers rarely did any laundry, and even when they did wash their clothes, the water they used was not hot enough to kill any bugs. Itching became a way of life, caused not only by lice but by scabies, fleas, or chiggers. "The Itch," as it was called, undoubtedly provided the most frequent occasion for the use of foul language in the Continental Army.

The low point, of course, was Valley Forge during the winter of 1777–1778. Joseph Plumb Martin remembered it well:

> The army was now not only starved but naked. The greatest part were not only shirtless and barefoot, but destitute of all other clothing, especially blankets. I procured a small piece of raw cowhide and made myself a pair of moccasins, which kept my feet (while they lasted) from the frozen ground, although, as I well remember, the hard edges so galled my ankles, while on a march, that it was with much difficulty and pain that I could wear them afterwards. The only alternative I had was to endure this inconvenience or to go barefoot, as hundreds of my companions had to, till they might be tracked by their blood upon the rough frozen ground.[123]

The soldiers' shelter, for the most part, was as ragtag as their attire. Privates slept in fields or barns when on the march, while officers secured whatever room and board they could find in local homes. Anytime the troops expected to remain in a camp for more than a few weeks, they erected cabins, huts, or tents to shed the elements, but their housing, like their clothing, revealed the absence of a military mold. The outskirts of Boston in July, 1775:

> They are as different in their form as the owners are in their
> dress; and every tent is a portraiture of the temper and taste
> of the persons what incamp within it. Some are made of boards,
> some of sailcloth, and some partly of one and partly of the
> other. Others are made of stone and turf, and others again of
> birch and other brush. Some are thrown up in a hurry and
> look as if they could not help it—mere necessity—others are
> curiously wrought with doors and windows done with wreaths
> and withes in the manner of a basket. [124]

Sails, sod, or brush might suffice for the summer months, but winter
demanded something more serious. Every December, as the temporary help went home, Continental soldiers busied themselves with
the building of log huts which sometimes, but not always, were
completed in time to afford some protection from the snow. In the
winter of 1779–1780, reported to be the coldest of the century,
Joseph Martin and Jeremiah Greenman and the rest of the hardcore regulars constructed an extensive garrison at Morristown, their
log cabins carefully notched at the corners and roofed with real
shingles.

The military encampment at Morristown, with barracks laid out
neatly in rows, was the culminating architectural achievement of the
Continental Army. In order to construct several hundred dwellings
in less than a month, however, the troops availed themselves of
"crosscut saws, handsaws, frows, augers, &c." belonging to local
farmers and craftsmen. "It is no concern of the reader's," Joseph
Martin wrote in jest, "by what means they procured their tools."[125]
Civilians did not relinquish their valuable belongings willingly, yet
how could the freezing soldiers, who might die without shelter, *not*
take what they needed? Herein lay the troubled relationship between
those who fought and those who stayed home: the men and boys
who put their lives on the line expected support, and when support
was not offered freely, they felt perfectly within their rights to seize
tools, blankets, firewood, food, or drink by threat or force; civilians,
meanwhile, resented the abuses they suffered at the crude hands of
haggard soldiers. "How disgraceful to the army is it," George
Washington once wrote, "that the peaceable inhabitants, our coun-

trymen and fellow citizens, dread our halting among them, even for a night and are happy when they get rid of us?"[126]

Conflict between citizens and soldiers grew increasingly acrid during the later years of the war. Citizens who never approved of a standing army were asked not only to tolerate an army but to support one, while soldiers who were asked to fight for the salvation of their country suspected, with good reason, that their fellow countrymen did not fully appreciate their efforts. Mutual suspicion evolved into outright enmity as soldiers who received few provisions resorted to plunder as a way of life, further alienating civilians who became even less likely to volunteer any assistance. The patriotic ideal—Americans coming together in defense of liberty and property—eroded rather swiftly in the face of these diverging interests.

The supreme insult, according to the beleaguered troops, was the infrequency of their pay. Sometimes they received their due, more often they did not. Rarely were they paid on time, and when money came late it lost much of its value. In January of 1778 $325 in Continental bills were required to redeem $100 in coin. A year later it was $742, and by January of 1780 it took $2,934 in Continentals to equal $100 in specie.[127] Inflation of this magnitude had many causes—scarcity of supplies, increased demand, lack of trust in the new currency, and British counterfeiting of Continental bills—but the end result was to render the soldiers' original contracts virtually meaningless. Congress could make adjustments for inflation if they wished, but they were not required to do so. Soldiers thus became dependent upon the whims of civilian politicians, who in turn were limited by the lack of public funds. If citizens paid their taxes in Continental currency, the bills would lose much of their value by the time they wound up in the hands of the troops, yet when states tried to collect hard dollars, many taxpayers could not, or at least did not, come forth. Towards the end of the war, with the public treasury empty, the fighting men of the Continental Army received nothing for months and even years on end. The economy was in a state of collapse, and soldiers—with no hard goods to peddle or barter—were the first to suffer.

While Jeremiah Greenman, Joseph Plumb Martin, Ebenezer Fox,

James Collins, and Joseph Hodgkins huddled around campfires or marched according to orders, many of their fellow Americans busied themselves with personal survival on a different level. In March of 1780 Dr. Robert Honyman described the mood in Virginia:

> The attention of the people of this state is very little taken up with the war at this time, or indeed for a year or two past. . . . The greatest part of the people are entirely taken up in schemes of interest of several kinds. Immense fortunes have been made by trade, or speculation . . . & almost all ranks are engaged in some sort of traffic or another. [128]

Farmers sold their grains and produce, milk and cheese, poultry and stock to the highest bidders—often the British army—while merchants hawked their wares for whatever price they could fetch. There is always money to be made by war, and the American Revolution, the longest declared war in our nation's history, saw no shortage of profiteers. Earlier, profiteers had been tarred and feathered, but by the end of the war they were too numerous to punish. Most civilians had learned to place their own personal interests ahead of the interests of their country—this, at least, was the perspective of those who continued to serve in the military. In July of 1780 Lieutenant Colonel Ebenezer Huntington expressed the views of many a soldier:

> The Rascally Stupidity which now prevails in the Country at large is beyond all description. . . . I despise my Countrymen, I wish I could say I was not born in America. I once gloried in it but am now ashamed of it. . . . I am in Rags, have lain in the Rain on the Ground for 48 hours past, and only a Junk of fresh Beef and that without Salt to dine on this day, recd no pay since last December, Constitution complaining, and all this for my Cowardly Countrymen who flinch at the very time when their Exertions are wanted, and hold their Purse Strings as tho' they would Damn the World, rather than part with a Dollar to their Army. [129]

What galled soldiers the most was the apparent well-being of those who chose not to fight. Although many civilians, like their counterparts in the army, suffered from shortages and high prices, the men who endured hunger, cold, and enemy fire on behalf of their country could not abide by those farmers and merchants who appeared to prosper—"Ye who Eat Pumpkin Pie and Roast Turkies," in the words of one disgruntled soldier. "As affairs are now going," wrote another, "the common soldiers have nothing to expect, but that if America maintain her independency, they must become slaves to the rich."[130]

Summer Soldiers

This was not the way it was supposed to be. According to Republican theory, "citizens" and "soldiers" should have been one and the same, militiamen who bore arms long enough to protect liberty and property but who never turned professional. The minutemen who responded to Lexington and Concord fit this description, as did the Virginia Volunteers and the farmers who closed the courts throughout Massachusetts. But in the fall of 1775 most of the militiamen went home to tend to their crops. Every spring the militias regrouped, but they would never again be trusted to defend the country by themselves. "Summer soldiers," Tom Paine called them, with obvious derision.[131]

The Continental regulars, a class apart, generally looked down on militiamen who could not, or at least would not, suffer the hardships which they themselves endured. Joseph Martin succinctly explained the difference between amateurs and professionals:

> That the militia did good and great service . . . on particular occasions, I well know, for I have fought by their side, but still I insist that they would not have answered the end so well as regular troops. . . . They would not have endured the sufferings the army did; they would have considered themselves (as in reality they were and are) free citizens, not bound by any cords that were not of their own manufacturing, and when the hardships of fatigue, starvation, cold and nakedness, which I have just mentioned, begun to seize upon them in such awful array as they did on us, they would have instantly quitted the

service in disgust, and who could blame them? I am sure I could hardly find it in my heart to do it. [132]

Officers of the American high command were not as understanding. General Nathanael Greene called his militia units "the worst in the world" and "of no more use than if they were in the moon." According to Greene, there were two basic problems with militiamen. First, they had no respect for the military hierarchy: "With the militia everybody is a general, and the powers of government are so feeble, that it is with the utmost difficulty you can restrain them from plundering one another."[133] Second, since they were not properly trained, they could not deal with the grim realities of a military campaign. "[P]eople coming from home with all the tender feelings of domestic life," Greene observed, were "not sufficiently fortified with natural courage to stand the shocking scenes of war. To march over dead men, to hear without concern the groans of the wounded, I say few men can stand such scenes unless steeled by habit or fortified by military pride."[134]

It takes a certain sort of training to turn peaceful, God-fearing civilians into warriors hardened to the horrors of death and destruction, and the militiamen never stayed around long enough to receive that instruction. They "come in you cannot tell how," Washington complained, "go, you cannot tell when; and act, you cannot tell where; consume your Provisions, exhaust your Stores, and leave you at last in a critical moment."[135] And they undermined military morale, exerting a bad influence on the regular soldiers. In the wake of the battle for New York, Washington wrote to John Hancock and the Continental Congress.

To place any dependence upon Militia, is, assuredly, resting upon a broken staff. Men just dragged from the tender Scenes of domestick life, unaccustomed to the din of Arms; totally unacquainted with every kind of Military skill, which being followed by a want of confidence in themselves, when opposed to Troops regularly trained, disciplined, and appointed, superior in knowledge, and superior in Arms, makes them timid, and ready to fly from their own shadows. Besides, the sudden change in their manner of living, (particularly in their lodging) brings on sickness in many; impatience in all, and such an unconquerable desire of returning to their respective homes that it not only produces shameful, and scandalous Desertions among themselves, but infuses the like spirit in others. Again, Men accustomed to unbounded freedom, and no control, cannot brook the Restraint which is indispensably necessary to the good order and Government of an Army; without which, licentiousness, and every kind of disorder triumphantly reign. To bring Men to a proper degree of Subordination, is not the work of a day, a Month or even a year; and unhappily for us, and the cause we are Engaged in, the little discipline I have been labouring to establish in the Army under my immediate Command, is in a manner done away by having such a mixture of Troops. . . . [I]f I was called upon to declare upon Oath, whether the Militia have been most serviceable or hurtful upon the whole; I should subscribe to the latter.[136]

The concerns expressed by Generals Washington and Greene were well founded. During the course of the war, an estimated one-half of all the men who served in the militias deserted at least once.[137] Maryland's General William Smallwood complained in October of 1777 that three-quarters of his regiment from Anne Arundel County had simply disappeared.[138] Most "deserters" did not sneak away stealthily in the dead of night; they packed up and went home by broad daylight, in stark defiance of orders from their superiors. And why shouldn't they go home? Instinctually inclined toward self-preservation, the deserters perceived that there was nothing to be gained by getting in the way of an army far superior to their own. Like most practical people, they chose to head home when the crops were ready to harvest; they preferred to spend the dead of winter indoors by hearth and family rather than huddled around campfires with other cold and hungry men, doing nothing.

And yes, as Washington suggested, many citizens were too "accustomed to unbounded freedom" to accept the "proper degree of Subordination" required of real soldiers. Americans liked to think and act for themselves—and generals didn't like this. General Schuyler, amazed that his troops did not "chose to move" when ordered to do so, complained bitterly: "Do not chose to move! Strange language for an army. But the irresistable force of necessity forces me to put up with it."[139] General Montgomery noted that the soldiers in his charge "carry the spirit of freedom into the field, and think for themselves," and that they even "felt it necessary to call a sort of town meeting" to plan any maneuvers. They demonstrated such a "leveling spirit, such an equality among them, that the officers have no authority," Montgomery reported. "The privates are all generals."[140] Baron von Steuben, while attempting to instill some sense of discipline in the Continental Army, observed that while in Europe an officer had only to say, " 'Do this,' and he doeth it," in America the officers had to say, " 'This is the reason why you ought to do that.' "[141] For some rugged Americans, even reason would not suffice to justify subordination. One potential recruit from South Carolina refused to serve under any man he could lick; another individualist from North Carolina promised "he would Shoot the first officer that would offer to Command him."[142]

Regulars and militiamen alike battled their superiors continuously over hats and hair, which they wished to wear as they pleased. Continental officers might try to resist these attempts at individual expression, but the hands of militia leaders were tied: if they failed to cede to the wishes of their men, they could be turned out of office. Since militia units in most cases elected their noncommissioned officers, the men who served in these positions could not be too harsh or arbitrary. Democracy in the army? A new and strange concept, indeed. But did the militias really constitute an "army"?

Although militiamen were not soldiers in the traditional sense—willing to abandon their homes and their private lives, suspend their civilized sensibilities, and follow their leaders without question—they still contributed significantly to the Revolution. American generals, even as they whined about the lack of military valor, did not hesitate to use militiamen for a first line of defense against the advancing enemy. If the militiamen stood their ground, they saved the regulars from facing danger, but even if they fled, rebel officers could use their flight to direct the overconfident pursuers into strategic traps, as they did at Cowpens, Guilford Court House, and Eutaw Springs. Regardless of their actual performance, militiamen also gave that extra boost that comes from large numbers. Their quick mobilization, even if for only short periods of time, swelled the ranks of the American forces at critical junctures—most notably at Saratoga, where British and Hessian troops found themselves overwelmed by patriot militiamen.

The militias did not have to take to the battlefield to prevent the occupation of the American interior by British troops. Because militiamen were so numerous, the British, with a finite pool of manpower, had to pick and choose a handful of locations where they could enforce their will. And what good did that do? Once the occupying troops departed, American militias would be back in control. John Shy explains: "A reservoir, sand in the gears, the militia also looked like a great spongy mass that could be pushed aside or maimed temporarily but that had no vital center and could not be destroyed."[143]

At home, the militias helped enforce revolutionary values and standards. Although militiamen hardly struck fear in the hearts of redcoated soldiers, their impact upon local Tories was far more profound: they wielded tar and feathers, an awesome power indeed. They forced reluctant citizens to declare allegiance to the cause, either by signing oaths or through military service. They intimidated merchants who appeared to be profiting from the war. They functioned, in essence, like a paramilitary government.

Increasingly, as the rich bought their way out of service, commoners who could not afford substitutes for the draft came to resent those who could. In some places, radical militiamen gave the revolution a sharper edge, infusing a certain class consciousness into the fight for independence. In Anson County, North Carolina, members of the militia were told by their state assembly to select five men to serve in the Continental Army. When nobody stepped forward voluntarily, the militiamen held an election—and rather than choose from among the ranks of ordinary farmers, they "elected" a lieutenant colonel from the militia, a judge, a justice of the peace, a deputy sheriff, and a planter. These five men, of course, had no intentions of serving in the Continental Army, and the superior officers quickly invalidated the results of the elections.

In Philadelphia militiamen pushed for a democratic reform of the military. The privates wanted to have a say in everything from the choice of uniforms to the selection of officers. They wanted privates, not officers, to decide on regulations and try offenses. They wanted better pay, and they opposed military exemptions for the rich. When one group is bound to service while another is not, the privates claimed, "the party bound is always considered as slaves to the party which is free." The militias, they believed, "can and ought to be conducted on the principles of Freedom." When Richard Peters, a company captain, was asked how many men he commanded, he responded wryly: "Not one, but I am commanded by ninety."[144]

In the spring of 1776 radical elements within the Philadelphia militia helped spark a provincial conference which unseated Pennsylvania's existing representatives, expanded the suffrage from 50 percent to 90 percent of the free adult males, and called for a convention to write a new state constitution. Militiamen, organized into a Committee of Privates, circulated a letter advising who should, and who should not, be selected as delegates: "great and over-grown rich Men will be improper to be trusted," it stated, while "Gentlemen of the learned Professions" were also to be shunned since they "are generally filled with the Quirks and Quibbles of the Schools."[145]

When the convention met in June, the first draft of the constitution included an intriguing clause:

> That an enormous Proportion of Property vested in a few individuals is dangerous to the Rights, and destructive to the Common Happiness, of Mankind; and therefore every free State hath a right by its Laws to discourage the Possession of such Property.[146]

Although this section was omitted from the final draft, the Pennsylvania constitution of 1776, following the push toward democracy by privates within the militia, placed more power in the hands of common people than any constitution for any state at any time in the history of this country. All governmental power was vested in a unicameral legislative body directly responsible to the electorate. Assemblymen, elected every year, could serve only four years in any seven-year period; members of the executive council who served three consecutive years would have to sit out the next four; congressional delegates could not serve more than two terms in a row. County positions which used to be appointed became elected, while all resident adult males who paid any taxes at all became eligible to hold office. In order to make representatives even more answerable to the people, the state was required to print weekly reports on roll-call votes, while the chambers were to "remain open for the admission of all persons who behave decently." Most significantly, "all bills of public nature" had to be "printed for the consideration of the people" before coming to a vote, and no bill could be passed until the meeting after it was introduced. This unique document, a blueprint for direct and democratic government, gave structure and form to the egalitarian sentiments of the militiamen who served as its primary advocates.[147]

Although militiamen from Philadelphia saw some active service (they crossed the Delaware with Washington in 1776 and they helped defend their city in 1777), they saved their most serious fighting for the home front—they even threatened they might use "Military power" and "take the direction into their hands in order to Save this Country from absolute Ruin."[148] This "ruin" was caused by runaway inflation: while militiamen were off fighting the British, they claimed, rich men who had shirked their duty were capitalizing on wartime shortages and jacking up prices. On May 23, 1779, the night before an exercise day, a broadside appeared throughout the city:

For our Country's Good!

The depreciation of our money and the high prices which every thing is got to, is one and the same thing. . . . In the midst of money we are in poverty, and exposed to want in a land of plenty. You that have money, . . . down with your prices, or down with yourselves. For by the living and eternal God, we will bring every article down to what it was last Christmas, or we will down with those who opposed.

We have turned out against the enemy and we will not be eaten up by monopolizers and forestallers.

[Signed]Come on Cooly[149]

That week militiamen seized over twenty wealthy men whom they accused of profiteering and threw them in jail. At the town meeting on May 25 they organized a price-fixing committee to seize over-priced items and sell them for a reasonable sum. Merchants and other opponents of price controls tried to oppose the committee at a town meeting two months later, but they were shouted down and driven out by "Two or Three Hundred Men of the lower Orders of the People armed with large Staves or Bludgeons."[150]

Prices continued to rise nonetheless, and on October 4 the militiamen decided to take more forceful action: they seized four more rich Philadelphians, whom they marched "about ye streets with the Drum after them, beating ye Rogue's March."[151] How this display of anger would stem inflation remained unclear, but it did lead to an armed confrontation as they paraded by the home of James Wilson, a conservative who had gathered together some friends for protection in case the mob came after him. As the militiamen marched by Wilson's house some men from within jeered at them, and shouting soon led to shooting. Joseph Reed, president of Pennsylvania, soon dispersed the crowd with a company of horsemen, and by the end of the day at least five militiamen had been killed and fourteen wounded in what came to be known as the "Battle of Fort Wilson."

Here was a revolution within the Revolution. The war had taken on a life of its own, wreaking havoc on the economy and causing the "lower sort" of Philadelphian "to rouse up as a Lyen out of his den" against "any person whatever" who was "puffed like a Toad, with a sense of his own consequence."[152] The "toads" were not British troops but "great and over-grown" American citizens. Philadelphia's part-time soldiers, when they returned home from their short tours of duty, carried their fight for justice with them. They might have lost at Fort Wilson, but they did manage to turn the sentiments of the lower classes into a genuine social movement. They undoubtedly believed, like Joseph Plumb Martin, that "every private soldier in an army thinks his particular services as essential to carry on the war . . . as the services of the most influential general."[153] Egalitarian in their beliefs, they expressed great anger that the burden of the war was shouldered so unevenly. After the fighting was over, when poor soldiers in the Continental Army mutinied because they had not been paid, Philadelphia militiamen had little difficulty in determining whose side they were on. As one mutineer reported, "The city militia with several troops of light horse were called out to disband us by force; but they would not obey their commanders,—and the general voice was 'Stand for your rights!' "[154]

Giting Thair Rights

In January of 1779, the same year as the showdown at Fort Wilson, Jeremiah Greenman wrote in his journal: "part of ye Regt this Evening peraded under arms under pertence of giting thair rights."[155] In April he noted again:

> F 23 . . . this Evening about ten oClock the biger part of the Regt. turn'd out in Muterny under arms paraded & took Comm'd of the artillery ware they stayed about two Hours gitting No Answer from the Colo. to satisfy them thay push'd off for providance marcht within two milds of the ferry ware thay halted & sent to Genl. Gates. Genl. Glover came to them Sum Incurrigement being given then thay return'd back to warren in the morning at Nine oClock and disband'd thay informed us that had sent a Commity to Providance to make a proper Complaint.
>
> S 24. thay return'd this after Noon inform the men thay was to be paid off by the 1st May the Regt. when paraded at Roll Call this evening behaved as well as hear to fore two of the Mutiners deserted.[156]

Starting in 1779 and continuing through 1783, two years after the surrender at Yorktown, dozens of minor mutinies such as this plagued the Continental Army. Most followed a similar pattern: hungry and frustrated men who had received no pay made a show of force, gained the attention of officers or politicians who offered them promises, and then backed off. On July 29, 1779, when "the biger part of the Regement had turn'd out in Muterny" and "marcht off for Greenwich," Jeremiah Greenman, by now a sergeant, went off with his men in hot pursuit; two days later the mutineers "all return'd to camp all pardined."[157]

Whereas Sergeant Greenman remained faithful to the established military order, Joseph Plumb Martin, still a private, defiantly joined with the protesters. In January of 1779, growing weary of "our old Continental line of starving and freezing," Martin and his colleagues "concluded that we *could* not or *would* not bear it any longer." They decided to parade in front of their huts with no officers, a clear violation of military rule. The officers "endeavored to soothe the Yankee temper . . . with an abundance of fair promises," but "hunger was not to be so easily pacified." Although the protesters disbanded, they harassed the officers through the night by the firing of arms, "making void the law." Rations improved slightly over the next few days, "but it soon became an old story and the old system commenced again as regular as fair weather to foul." The men paraded once more on their own, this time with arms, threatening to march to the state capital at Hartford and then to "disperse to our homes" if still unsatisfied. But they never made good on their threats: "[T]he old mode of flattery and promising was resorted to and produced the usual effect. We all once more returned to our huts and fires, and there spent the remainder of the night, muttering over our forlorn condition."[158]

On May 25, 1780, Martin's regiment took their protest one step further: they held bayonets to the breasts of their officers as they broke into open rebellion, "growling like soreheaded dogs" and "venting our spleen at our country and government."[159] These soldiers were not unpatriotic, nor were they making a concerted attempt to seize power or alter the existing order. They mutinied only because they had become tired, hungry, and desperate:

The men were now exasperated beyond endurance; they could not stand it any longer. They saw no alternative but to starve to death, or break up the army, give all up and go home. This was a hard matter for the soldiers to think upon. They were truly patriotic, they loved their country, and they had already suffered everything short of death in its cause; and now, after such extreme hardships to give up all was too much, but to starve to death was too much also. What was to be done? Here was the army starved and naked, and there their country sitting still and expecting the army to do notable things while fainting from sheer starvation.[160]

Finally, the protesters achieved some results: "Our stir did us some good in the end, for we had provisions directly after, so we had no great cause for complaint for some time."[161]

The Connecticut and Rhode Island mutinies were echoed by other regiments. On New Year's Day, 1781, over 1,000 Pennsylvania soldiers, emboldened by an extra issue of rum, seized artillery and marched towards Philadelphia, upset that they were expected to serve without pay beyond the terms of their enlistment. By the time they reached Princeton their numbers had swelled to about 1,700. Several hundred other soldiers simply packed up and went home, leaving scarcely 100 on active duty in the Pennsylvania line. If the generals and politicians wanted an army, they had no choice but to address the demands of the mutineers. But what had become of military order? Where would this wave of protest stop?

On January 20, 200 soldiers from New Jersey tried to follow suit: "Let us go to Congress who have money and rum enough but won't give it to us!"[162] Although the protesters soon agreed to return to camp, Washington did not let the matter stand. "Unless this dangerous spirit can be suppressed by force," he wrote to Congress, "there is an end to all subordination in the Army, and indeed to the Army itself."[163] Three days after a settlement had been reached, two leaders of the protest were seized and executed before a firing squad composed of their peers. And when Pennsylvania troops complained that promises from their own settlement had not been kept, twelve leaders were fired upon by troops loyal to General Anthony Wayne. Six of the men were killed instantly; observing that a seventh was maimed, Wayne ordered a soldier to finish him off with a bayonet. The soldier refused, pleading that the mutineer was his friend. Wayne held a pistol to the executioner's head, forcing him to complete the task. Wayne then ordered that the remaining five be hanged.

Even after the British had surrendered, Revolutionary veterans continued to express their discontent. In June of 1783 privates from the Pennsylvania line marched on Congress and demanded to be paid; the elected leaders of the young United States, fearful of a military takeover, sneaked out the back door. But the tired soldiers sought only money, not power. Throughout the war they had been told to wait until the end; now the end had arrived, but where was their recompense? What thanks had they received from their countrymen for the many sacrifices they had made?

Pay for past services came primarily in the form of depreciated currency and titles to land on the frontier. But since the worthless currency was not easily exchanged for food, drink, or shoes, veterans were forced to sell their land deeds at a pittance in order to purchase the hard stuff of daily living—or just to bankroll the trip back home. Although a handful of soldiers eventually found their way to new land and a new life, most of the ten million acres given to veterans wound up in the hands of speculators. The Revolutionary War had provided temporary employment for young males of the "lesser sort," but when the war was over, these boys-turned-men were left with little in the way of resources to establish themselves in a peacetime economy. "I may now go where I please," wrote a veteran from Virginia, "but where to go or what to do I am at a loss."[164] In April of 1783, after Elijah Fisher was released from the "old Jarsey preasen ship" in New York, he had to beg his way back to Boston. Once there, he found "there was so meny that Come from the army and from see that had no homes that would work for little or nothing but there vitels that I Could not find any Employment." On April 16 he wrote:

> I Com Down by the markett and sits Down all alone, allmost Descureged, and begun to think over how that I had ben in the army, what ill success I had met with there and all so how I was ronged by them I worked for at home, and lost all last winter, and now that I could not into any besness and no home, which you may well think how I felt; but then Come into my mind that there ware thousands in wors sircumstances then I was . . . and I . . . leave the avent to Provedance, and after that I felt as contented as need to be. [165]

The Revolutionary War had taken its toll, not only in lives but in dreams. Even Joseph Hodgkins, the once-ardent patriot who left his wife and children to help save his country, became disillusioned. Early in the war he had written to Sarah:

> I am willing to sarve my Contery in the Best way & mannar that I am Capeble of and as our Enemy are gone from us I Expect we must follow them. . . . I would not Be understood that I should Chuse to March But as I am ingaged in this glories Cause I am will to go whare I am Called.[166]

But as his fellow minutemen from Ipswich returned to their homes, and as he continued to expose himself to the rigors and dangers of military life without receiving what he felt to be a just recompense, Joseph lost his initial fervor. After writing repeatedly that "Soldiers must not Complain," he himself complained to Sarah: while troops suffered at Valley Forge, civilians back home had "Lost all Bowls of Compassion if they Ever had any." He hoped his neighbors might "maintain . . . there soldiers" more willingly, but he feared they "have Lost all there Publick Spirit I would Beg of them to Rouse from there studedity and Put on som humanity and stir themselves Before it is too Late."[167] On April 17, 1778, he wrote:

> when I think how I have spent three years in the war have Ben Exposed to Every hardship Venterd my Life & Limbs Broke my Constitution wore out all my Clothes & has got knothing for it & now not to be thanked for it seams two much for any man to Bare.[168]

That fall he declared that "the Continent in general . . . will Ever Be guilty of Ruening thousands unless they Due something more for them then what they Ever have Done yet," and the following spring Joseph Hodgkins, who spoke no more of "this glories Cause," resigned his commission.[169] Had he remained in the service only seven more months he would have been eligible for a life-long pension; perhaps he had lost all faith that it would ever be granted.

Joseph Plumb Martin, by nature so good humored, concluded the narrative of his war-time experiences on a caustic note:

> When those who engaged to serve during the war enlisted, they were promised a hundred acres of land, each, which was to be in their own or the adjoining states. When the country had drained the last drop of service it could screw out of the poor soldiers, they were turned adrift like old worn-out horses, and nothing said about land to pasture them upon. Congress did, indeed, appropriate lands under the denomination of "Soldier's lands," in Ohio state, or some state, or a future state, but no care was taken that the soldiers should get them. No agents were appointed to see that the poor fellows ever got possession of their lands; no one ever took the least care about it, except a pack of speculators, who were driving about the country like so many evil spirits, endeavoring to pluck the last feather from the soldiers. The soldiers were ignorant of the ways and means to obtain their bounty lands, and there was no one appointed to inform them. The truth was, none cared for them; the country was served, and faithfully served, and that was all that was deemed necessary. It was, soldiers, look to yourselves; we want no more of you. . . .
>
> We were, also, promised six dollars and two thirds a month, to be paid us monthly, and how did we fare in this particular? . . . I received the six dollars and two thirds, till (if I remember rightly) the month of August, 1777, when paying ceased. And what was six dollars and sixty-seven cents of this "Continental currency," as it was called, worth? It was scarcely enough to procure a man a dinner. . . . I received one month's pay in specie while on the march to Virginia, in the year 1781, and except that, I never received any pay worth the name while I belonged to the army. . . . The country was rigorous in exacting my compliance to *my* engagements to a punctilio, but equally careless in performing her contracts with me, and why so? One reason was because she had all the power in her own hands and I had none. Such things ought not to be. [170]

The fighting men and boys of the Revolution had become a class apart, and an underclass at that, powerless despite their arms.

Jeremiah Greenman did not express the disillusionment of Martin and Hodgkins. Promoted first to sergeant and eventually to the rank of first lieutenant and adjutant to the Rhode Island regiment, Greenman achieved a position of prominence which would have been hard to equal in civilian life. As an officer he served on court-martials of privates accused of "being Intoxicated with Liquor when a Sentinel," "stealing wood from the Publick," or "Damning Congress."[171] When soldiers deserted or mutinied, Greenman was dispatched to fetch them back. In May of 1781 he was taken prisoner for the second time, but as an officer he was not confined within prison walls as he had been in Quebec; no longer a private, he was treated as a gentleman and placed on parole for five months until an exchange could be arranged. Thanks to his career in the military, he appeared to be rising above his modest beginnings.

In March of 1783 Greenman reported in his journal that "the Gloreous Peaces is taken place." How would this seasoned veteran with no special trade make his living in peacetime? In the fall of 1785 Jeremiah Greenman, son of a sailor, signed on board a merchant ship headed for the West Indies; during his absence his wife Mary gave birth to his first child. For the next twenty years Jeremiah supported his family by shipping out to sea, first as a mate and later as a captain. During the 1790s he tried repeatedly to secure a commission in the United States Army, but the supply of experienced Revolutionary officers far exceeded the demand and he never received an appointment. In 1806 he emigrated with his wife and three of his four children to Ohio, where he procured 100 unimproved acres of rocky soil. He was landed at last, but he never became prosperous. In 1818, when Congress finally authorized monthly pensions to veterans in need, he applied for his share. He received a pension for two years, but in 1820 the government reviewed his case and concluded that his modest farm was sufficient to provide a living. Greenman protested, noting that by spending his youthful and productive years in the army he had been "deprived of the opportunity of acquiring any mechanical art" or "perfecting my self in any profession." He wrote directly to John C. Calhoun, secretary of war, calling attention to his "Eight years & siven months service together with three wounds received whilst in that service, & one of them rendering me incapable of *hard* labour." His first appeal denied, he tried again:

> My hopes & prospects to a future residence on this Terestiacal Globe, it seams are to be filled up with mortification of spirit & attended with hard labour what few remaining yeas I am permitted to tarry on it, being proscibed by the Laws of that Country I had faithfully served 8 years. [172]

This time the pension was granted, but Jeremiah Greenman, as faithful a soldier as one could imagine, had been reduced to groveling to receive his due.

James Collins left the war poor and propertyless, just as he was at the beginning. His father Daniel owned land, but Daniel had fathered twenty children and there was not enough to spread around. Having volunteered without formally enlisting, James was not authorized to receive the hundred acres promised to professional soldiers. Still only seventeen, he hired out as a laborer in order to earn the money to settle on the Georgia frontier. There, he joined the militia once again—to fight against the Creeks and Cherokees this time.

Our last young soldier, Ebenezer Fox, did not see active service until late in the war. While serving a brief term in the militia in 1779, he had learned enough about short rations and bare, cold feet to divest himself of any romantic notions about the life of a soldier. The sea, however, was another matter; pillaging valuable cargo from British ships offered greater potential than plundering geese from American farmers. By promising his master one-half of his wages and prize money, the seventeen-year-old apprentice secured permission to enlist on board the *Protector*, the pride of the Massachusetts state navy. Along with 330 men who "were carried, dragged, and driven on board, of all kinds, ages, and descriptions, in all the various stages of intoxication; from that of 'sober tipsiness' to beastly drunkenness," Ebenezer Fox shipped out in the spring of 1780. [173] On June 9 the *Protector* engaged in a heated battle with the

Admiral Duff; the *Duff* eventually surrendered, but Ebenezer was deafened for a week by the sound of his own cannon, and he never fully regained his hearing.

Later that summer, while the *Protector* was docked in Boston for repairs, Ebenezer's father died, leaving his mother with the care of eight children. Hoping to "contribute something to the maintenance of the family, who were left very destitute," the dutiful son enlisted for another cruise.[174] Over the next few months the *Protector* plundered one British ship after the next, but its very success proved its undoing, for it was soon overtaken by two enemy warships bent of exacting revenge and retrieving the lost goods.

Following the surrender of the *Protector,* the captured American sailors were sent to the infamous prison ship *Jersey,* a "floating Pandemonium" permanently docked on the Long Island shore. Fox recalled his first impressions upon being lowered into the hatch which housed the inmates:

> Here was a motley crew, covered with rags and filth; visages pallid with disease, emaciated with hunger and anxiety, and retaining hardly a trace of their original appearance. Here were men, who had once enjoyed life while riding over the mountain wave or roaming through pleasant fields, full of health and vigor, now shriveled by a scanty and unwholesome diet, ghastly with inhaling an impure atmosphere, exposed to contagion and disease, and surrounded with the horrors of sickness and death. [175]

The diet on board the *Jersey,* according to Fox, consisted of moldy bread filled with worms and meat that had been cooked in salt water fouled by human excrement. Prisoners passed the time by picking at their lice; once, for amusement, they collected the vermin in a snuff box which they emptied on one of their guards. Estimates of fatalities on board the *Jersey* during the course of the war range in the thousands, but since records were poorly kept, nobody can ever know how many young men "died in agony in the midst of their fellow sufferers, who were obliged to witness their tortures, without the power of relieving their dying countrymen, even by cooling their parched lips with a drop of cold water, or a breath of fresh air."[176]

After enduring several months in the hatch of the *Jersey*, Ebenezer Fox was offered a choice: he could remain where he was, or he could serve on a British ship. Ebenezer had tried to escape but failed, and he correctly assumed, since he was not an officer, that there was little hope for a prisoner exchange. Reasoning that the opportunities for escape would be far greater as a British sailor than an inmate, he agreed to help man a vessel sailing for Jamaica.[177] Once his ship had arrived at its destination, he plotted again to seek his freedom. He and four of his comrades trampled through the woods to the north side of the island, where they killed three local villagers who tried to capture the runaways for the reward. After five days of hiding in the bushes with little to eat or drink, the fugitives captured a small sailboat and made their way toward Spanish-controlled Cuba, pursued in the dead of night by a Jamaican schooner. From Cuba they went to St. Domingo, where Ebenezer signed on board the *Flora*, an American privateering vessel bound for France. Prior to his departure he and some new friends, who were observing the Sabbath by drinking at a public house on shore, were impressed onto a French ship. Before that ship could leave port, however, Fox jumped into the shark-infested harbor and swam back to the *Flora*, which then sailed across the Atlantic to France. Ebenezer was still in France when peace was announced.

Ebenezer Fox returned to Boston in May of 1783, only twenty years old but a seasoned adventurer. During his time at sea he had survived several battles, endured the hatch of the *Jersey*, and escaped from both the British and the French. His life had been endangered on numerous occasions, he had been wounded in the encounter on Jamaica, and he had lost part of his hearing. At the end of it all he received $80, his share of the *Flora*'s plunder. By prior agreement his master was to receive half of this, but upon Ebenezer's return Mr. Bosson demanded it all. Legally, that was his right. Despite more than three years of harrowing escapades and service to his country, young Ebenezer Fox was still apprenticed until his twenty-first birthday to a Boston barber who never went to war.

WOMEN

Expectations . . . A Duty We Owe . . . Women and the Army . . . Shaming . . . Where God Can We Fly from Danger? . . . What Was Done, Was Done by Myself

Expectations

There were few ladies of leisure in late colonial America. Most women worked, and worked hard. They grew vegetables, raised and butchered fowl, preserved food, cooked meals, tended the fire night and day, combed flax, carded wool, spun thread, wove and dyed cloth, sewed shirts and skirts, knitted socks and caps, washed and mended clothes, hauled water, made soap and candles, doctored the sick, gave birth to babies, tended toddlers, and instructed children in practical duties and moral obligations. As homemakers in the fullest sense, they endeavored to keep life moving along on an even keel, coordinating the varied activities which each household required to sustain itself.

In the prelude to the Revolutionary War, male patriots asked women to work even harder. American colonists had been taxed by Parliament without their consent, and they responded by boycotting British goods. But without British imports, where would the colonists acquire the manufactured products available only from Europe? Forbidden to trade directly with other countries, they developed two complementary strategies: make some of the goods themselves, and learn to do without. Both paths required the active participation of women. Women would have to weave by hand the cloth that had been woven by machine in England; they would also have to forsake the few imported luxuries which gave their modest homes the faintest hint of European culture.

But how could women, who had been systematically excluded from all aspects of the political arena, suddenly be persuaded to join in a political crusade? The task was not easy. If women were to add extra hours to their workdays, hours which did not really exist, they must become inspired; they too must become patriots.

During the peak of resistance to the hated Townshend duties of 1767, some visionary patriots seized upon an idea: why not commandeer the traditional New England "spinning bee" for political use? Customarily, a number of female churchgoers would gather from time to time at the house of their minister to spin for his personal wardrobe; after they finished the work of the day, they would listen to a sermon. These special events helped alleviate isolation and monotony as participating women conveniently combined work, socializing, and religion. Starting in 1768 and peaking in 1769, patriotic newspapers invested these spinning bees with new meaning (or, in our own parlance, a new spin): they became "ideological showcases" of the nonimportation movement as the women spun not only for their preachers but for the good of their country. Spinning bees, according to their new promoters, served both to advertise the making of cloth and to demonstrate that women could become patriots without departing from traditional concepts of femininity.[1]

Male editors, excited by the spinning bees, gave prominent billing to any and all evidence of "female industry" in the name of patriotism.[2] One advertisement in a Philadelphia paper noted the special excellence of homespun: "In this time of public distress, you have now, each of you, an opportunity not only to help to sustain your families, but likewise to cast your mite into the treasury of the public good."[3] The *Boston Evening Post* commented: "[T]he industry and frugality of American ladies must exalt their character in the Eyes of the World and serve to show how greatly they are contributing to bring about the political salvation of a whole Continent."[4] Ministers, likewise, heralded the virtues of homemade cloth. Peter Oliver, an embittered loyalist who opposed the "black regiment" of preachers-turned-patriots, described their efforts with obvious derision:

> Mr. Otis's black Regiment, the dissenting Clergy were also set to Work to preach up Manufactures instead of Gospel. They preached about it & about it, untill the Women and Children, both within Doors & without, set their Spinning Wheels a whirling in Defiance of Great Britain. The female spinners kept on spinning for 6 Days of the Week; & on the seventh, the Parsons took their Turns, & spun out their Prayers & Sermons to a long Thread of Politicks; & to much better Profit than the other Spinners; for they generally cloathed the Parson and his Family with the Produce of their Labor: This was a new Species of Enthusiasm, & might be justly termed, the Enthusiasm of the Spinning Wheel.[5]

Rebel leaders urged women to exhibit patriotism not only with their production but with their purchasing choices. If the boycott was to succeed, women as well as men would have to refrain from purchasing British imports. Christopher Gadsden of South Carolina, in an open letter addressed to "Planters, Mechanics, and Freeholders," explained in forthright terms why men should allow women to exert political leverage through the management of their household economies:

> I come now to the last, and what many say and think is the *greatest difficulty* of all we have to encounter, that is, to persuade our wives to give us their assistance, without which 'tis impossible to succeed. I allow of the impossibility of succeeding without their concurrence. But, for my part, so far from doubting that we shall have it, I could wish, as our political salvation, at this crisis, depends altogether upon the strictest oeconomy, that the women could, with propriety, have the principal management thereof; for 'tis well known, that none in the world are better œconomists, make better wives or more tender mothers, than ours. Only let their husbands point out the necessity of such a conduct, convince them, that it is the only thing that

can save them and their children, from distresses, slavery, and disgrace; their affections will soon be awakened, and co-operate with their reason. When that is done, all that is necessary will be done; for I am persuaded, that they will be then as anxious and persevering in this matter, as any the most zealous of us can possibly wish.[6]

To the extent that women became as "anxious" and "zealous" as male patriots, men like Gadsden could expect the female-run households to come to the aid of the nonimportation movement. Although he felt women's participation to be vital, the position he suggested they play was well within their sphere; it could be performed easily "with propriety." As much as men wanted women to become patriots, they did not expect any transgressions of traditional boundaries or demands for additional rights.

When imported tea became the major issue in 1773, William Tennent III told women that if they refrained from drinking tea, they could convince the British "that American patriotism extends even to the Fair Sex, and discourage any future Attempts to enslave us." Writing in the *South Carolina Gazette*, he exhorted: "Yes Ladies, You have it in your power more than all your committees and Congresses, to strike the Stroke, and make the Hills and Plains of America clap their hands."[7] Reporting on a gathering of New Hampshire women who "made their Breakfast upon Rye Coffee" instead of tea, the editors of the *New York Gazette and Weekly Mercury* cheerfully hoped that this example would inspire other women to follow in kind.[8]

When the fighting started in 1775, the drive to inspire female patriotism became still more compelling. As in all wars, men needed and expected women to continue with production on the home front, performing the tasks which they themselves could no longer accomplish. In World War II, the United States government invented Rosie the Riveter, that heroine of the factory who toiled happily in support of her loved ones overseas. In the American Revolution Rosie was only a farmer, but she still had to produce the goods—not only her usual output, but enough to compensate for a depletion of the male labor force and the continued absence of British imports. Ordinary farm wives, while continuing to fulfill their traditional obligations, would have to plant and harvest the fields, cut wood, fix fences, secure houses against rain and snow, forge and sharpen tools.

Women were also expected to feed and house the traveling armies. In later wars fought on foreign soil, these tasks were performed by military professionals, but during the Revolutionary War patriot soldiers depended on the support of the civilian population. When the Continental Army marched into town, soldiers slaughtered animals and commandeered corn, grain, and the produce from kitchen gardens. Although privates could sleep in the fields, warmed by blankets they "borrowed" from local residents, officers expected to be entertained in the homes of well-to-do patriots, where they assumed the right to be served by friendly mistresses. As necessity demanded, soldiers expropriated the labor of civilian women for military use without a second thought.

When men fell wounded or ill, they expected women to nurse them back to health. Whenever possible, they sought the aid of civilians with comfortable quarters; more often, they had to settle for less personal care within the barns and abandoned buildings that masqueraded as military hospitals. Typically, each hospital was staffed by one or two surgeons, a handful of "mates," and several nurses under the supervision of a "matron." Washington expressed clearly why nurses had to be female: if women could not be found to do the job, he would be "under the necessity of substituting in their place a number of men from the respective Regiments" who would therefore be "entirely lost in the proper line of their duty."[9] Washington himself delineated the tasks of these nurses, who functioned more like the nurses' aides and custodians of today:

> The NURSES, in the absence of the Mates, administer the medicine and diet prescribed for the sick according to order; they obey all orders they receive from the Matron; not only to be attentive to the cleanliness of the wards and patients, but to keep themselves clean they are never to be disguised with liquor; they are to see that the close-stools or pots are to be emptied as soon as possible after they are used; . . . they are to

see that every patient, upon his admission into the Hospital is immediately washed with warm water, and that his face and hands are washed and head combed every morning. . . . that their wards are swept over every morning or oftener if necessary and sprinkled with vinegar three or four times a day; nor are they ever to be absent without leave from the Physicians, Surgeons, or Matron.[10]

For their services, nurses received only a small fraction of the pay given to surgeons and mates: initially about 10 percent to 20 percent, and only 1 percent by the end of the war.[11]

The expectations placed upon women went beyond the conscious manipulations of politically motivated men. The Revolutionary War, of necessity, created new roles for women: they would have to work harder, they would have to provide food and shelter, they would have to care for the sick and wounded—and they would have to allow the men and boys to fight. But did women perform these tasks begrudgingly, or did they become active players in the revolutionary cause? How far did "American patriotism" extend "even to the Fair Sex"?

A Duty We Owe

Male patriots believed, and we would like to believe too, that women answered the patriotic call. There is much evidence suggesting that they did.

Women wrote poems:

Let the Daughters of Liberty, nobly arise,
And tho' we've no Voice, but a negative here,
The use of the Taxables, let us forebear. . . .
Stand firmly resolved and bid Grenville to see
That rather than Freedom, we'll part with our Tea.[12]

They signed petitions which competed favorably with the most flamboyant of male polemics: in 1770, more than 300 "mistresses of Families" from Boston promised to abstain from tea in order to "save this abused Country from Ruin and Slavery."[13] When fifty-one women of Edenton, North Carolina signed a nonimportation agreement in 1774, they noted that "it is a duty which we owe, not only to our near and dear relations and connections, but to ourselves."[14] Apparently, these women had embraced the cause as their own. Women had been invited to join the political arena, albeit in a limited fashion, and many accepted the invitation. "We possess a Spirit that will not be conquered," Abigail Adams wrote to her husband in September of 1776, when the Continental Army was floundering on the battlefield. "If our Men are all drawn off and we should be attacked, you would find a Race of Amazons in America."[15]

Some women could elucidate the rebels' rationale with absolute clarity. Not to be outdone by Sam Adams or Tom Paine, a "lady from Philadelphia" wrote to a British officer in Boston:

It is not a quibble in politics, a science which few understand, which we are contending for; it is this plain truth, which the most ignorant peasant knows, and is clear to the weakest capacity, that no man has a right to take their money without their consent. The supposition is ridiculous and absurd, as none but highwaymen and robbers attempt it. Can you, my friend, reconcile it with your own good sense, that a body of men in Great Britain, who have little intercourse with America, and of course know nothing of us, nor are supposed to see or feel the misery they would inflict upon us, shall invest themselves with a power to command our lives and properties, at all times and in all cases whatsoever? You say you are no politician. Oh, sir, it requires no Machivelian head to develop this, and to discover this tyranny and oppression. It is written with a sun beam.[16]

Patriotic women were willing to act in support of their beliefs. In 1774 the Boston Committee of Correspondence distributed a "Solemn League and Covenant" throughout the countryside, asking that it be "subscribed by all adult persons of both sexes."[17] The covenant was well received. According to a Boston merchant, it "went through whole towns with great avidity, every adult of both sexes putting their name to it, saving a few." The documents which have survived reveal that women signed sometimes next to their male kin and sometimes on their own.

Girls and single women, joining in the patriotic fervor, imbued their own drudgery with a romantic twist. Betsy Foote, a Connecticut farm girl, recorded in her diary for October 23, 1775, that after mending, spinning, milking, studying, and performing various other chores, she carded two pounds of wool and "felt Nationly."[18] Eleven-year-old Anna Winslow of Boston termed herself a "daughter of liberty" because she had learned to spin: "I chuse to wear as much of our own manufactory as pocible," she proudly proclaimed. Charity Clarke, a New York teenager, wrote to an English cousin that although "Heroines may not distinguish themselves at the head of an Army," the women of America constituted "a fighting army of amazones . . . armed with spinning wheels." Patriotism suited her well: "Though this body is not clad with silken garments," she declared, "these limbs are armed with strength, the Soul is fortified by Virtue, and the Love of Liberty is cherished within this bosom."[19]

Men and women alike—and boys and girls too—"felt Nationly," but they expressed their feelings differently: the men drank and caroused, while the women worked. Newport's Daughters of Liberty were willing to sacrifice for "the preservation and prosperity of their country"—but only if the men in their lives gave up "their dear and more beloved punch, renounce going so often to tavern, and be more kind and loving sweethearts and husbands."[20] Historian Laurel Thatcher Ulrich contrasts typical meetings of the Sons of Liberty and the Daughters of Liberty. On August 14, 1769, men from Boston gathered to celebrate the anniversary of the first Stamp Act demonstrations:

> Fourteen Toasts were drunk; After which they proceeded in Carriages to Mr. Robinson's at the Sign of Liberty-Tree in Dorchester; where three large Piggs barbicued and a Variety of other Provision were prepared for dinner. . . . After dinner 45 patriotic Toasts were drank, and the Company spent the afternoon in social Mirth.

In the same month in Brookfield, a group of ladies assembled for a spinning bee at the house of their minister, most of them working from five in the morning until seven in the evening. According to the host,

> Among the matrons there was one, who did the morning work of a large family, made her cheese, etc. and then rode more than two miles, and carried her own wheel, and sat down to spin at nine in the morning, and by seven in the evening spun 53 knots, and went home to milking. [21]

After the fighting commenced, women worked harder still. Elizabeth Adkins of Culpepper County, Virginia, recalled that when her husband went off to war in the summer of 1775, she "had to plough and hoe his corn and raise bread for his children."[22] Temperance Smith, a parson's wife from Sharon, Connecticut, described life back on the farm when her husband left to serve the troops at Fort Ticonderoga:

> [W]hen the exactions of the Mother Country had rendered it impossible for any but the wealthiest to import anything to eat or wear, and all had to be raised and manufactured at home, from bread stuffs, sugar and rum to the linen and woollen for our clothes and bedding, you may well imagine that my duties were not light, though I can say for myself that I never complained, even in my inmost thoughts. . . .
>
> [T]o tell the truth, I had no leisure for murmuring. I rose with the sun and all through the long day I had no time for aught but my work. So much did it press upon me that I could scarcely divert my thoughts from its demands, even during the family prayers, which thing both amazed and displeased me, for during that hour, at least, I should have been sending all my thoughts to heaven for the safety of my beloved husband and the salvation of our hapless country. Instead of which I was often wondering whether Polly had remembered to set the sponge for the bread, or to put water on the leach tub, or to turn the cloth in the dying vat, or whether wool had been

carded for Betsey to start her spinning wheel in the morning, or Billy had chopped light wood enough for the kindling, or dry hard wood enough to heat the big oven, or whether some other thing had not been forgotten of the thousand that must be done without fail, or else there would be a disagreeable hitch in the housekeeping.[23]

The effect of women's participation was profound, not only on the course of the Revolution, but on the women themselves. Mary Beth Norton, in a pioneering book called *Liberty's Daughters*, consulted the letters and diaries in 450 collections of family papers and concluded that the Revolutionary War had a revolutionary impact on women's "personal aspirations" and "self-assessments."[24] Because women performed on the home front while men went off to fight, because men asked for and received women's support, women felt personally strengthened by the wartime experience. Norton relates a small but telling example: in 1776, Mary Bartlett wrote to her husband Josiah, a congressman from New Hampshire perennially absent from home, about the state of "your farming business"; after 1778, all her letters referred to "our farming business."[25]

The Revolution, according to Norton, transformed traditional role definitions:

> Prior to the Revolution, when the private realm of the household was seen as having little connection with the public world of politics and economics, woman's secular role was viewed solely in its domestic setting. . . . [N]o one, male or female, wrote or thought about the possibility that women might affect the wider secular society through their individual or collective behavior. In theory, their sexual identity was a barrier that separated them from the public world. . . . The war necessarily broke down the barrier which seemed to insulate women from the realm of politics, for they, no less than men, were caught up in the turmoil that enveloped the entire populace.[26]

Suddenly entering the political domain, women displayed the zeal and zest of the newly converted. Norton cites a letter from Eliza Wilkinson from the sea islands of South Carolina:

[N]ever were greater politicians than the several knots of ladies, who met together. All trifling discourse of fashions, and such low little chat was thrown by, and we commenced perfect statesmen. Indeed, I don't know but if we had taken a little pains, we should have been qualified for prime ministers, so well could we discuss several important matters in hand. . . .

I won't have it thought, that because we are the weaker sex as to *bodily* strength, my dear, we are capable of nothing more than minding the dairy, visiting the poultry-house, and all such domestic concerns; our thoughts can soar aloft, we can form conceptions of things of higher nature; we have as just a sense of honor, glory, and great actions, as these "Lords of the Creation."[27]

A few female patriots became so politically conscious that they applied the message of the Revolution to their own situation: why not extend the fashionable concepts of "equality" and "representation" to women? On March 31, 1776, Abigail Adams wrote to her husband John, currently serving as a delegate to the Continental Congress in Philadelphia:

I long to hear that you have declared an independancy—and by the way in the new Code of Laws which I suppose it will be necessary for you to make I desire you would Remember the Ladies, and be more generous and favourable to them than your ancestors. Do not put such unlimited power in the hands of the Husbands. Remember all Men would be tyrants if they could. If perticular care and attention is not paid to the Laidies we are determined to foment a Rebelion, and will not hold ourselves bound by any Laws in which we have no voice, or Representation.[28]

Once politically awakened, women acted on their own to support the Revolution. In 1770, men had urged women to become patriots; ten years later, women were organizing patriotic activities without any guidance from male leadership. In June of 1780, Esther DeBerdt Reed, the wife of the governor of Pennsylvania, published a broadside entitled *The Sentiments of an American Woman*, in which she encouraged ladies "to wear a cloathing more simple," to dress their hair "less elegant," to forsake "vain ornaments," and to donate the money saved "for the relief of the armies which defend our lives, our possessions, our liberty."[29] Reed did not merely proselytize, she mobilized; three days after publication of her *Sentiments*, thirty-six Philadelphia women divided the city into districts and, traveling in pairs, canvassed every house, requesting contributions. In less than a month they collected more than $300,000 in Continental dollars, which translated to $7,500 hard currency. Women in other states organized similar campaigns, collecting significant sums in New Jersey, Maryland, and Virginia. This "Offering of the Ladies," as it was called, is often regarded as the culminating event in the political history of Revolutionary women: a patriotic campaign conceived and executed exclusively by the women themselves.

In the end, however, Esther Reed and her female activists were asked to cede control of their "offering." When they suggested to George Washington that he turn "the whole of the Money into hard Dollars & giving each Soldier 2 at his own disposal," Washington quickly vetoed their proposal; he assumed from past experience that the soldiers would trade in their hard cash for liquor, thereby leading to "irregularities and disorders." He preferred to use the money in a more practical manner: the purchase of shirts, to be made by the ladies themselves in order to save money. Washington got what he wanted. In December 1780, the ladies presented him with 2,000 shirts, the name of the individual maker inscribed on each. They told the general, "We wish them to be worn with as much pleasure as they were made." Two months later, Washington expressed his gratitude. The ladies deserved

> an equal place with any who have preceded them in the walk of female patriotism. It embellishes the American character with a new trait; by proving that the love of country is blended with those softer domestic virtues, which have always been allowed to be more particularly your own.[30]

Modern historians have been quick to observe how Washington managed to transform a public display of civic virtue into a reaffirmation of traditional female roles; the "offering" became, in effect, "General Washington's Sewing Circle."[31] Less often noted, however, is the distinctly upper-class orientation of the ladies' endeavors. Not many farm women or mechanics' wives could renounce fancy hairdos and "vain ornaments," since few had any to renounce—nor did they have much extra cash lying about the house to give to the cause. The "offering," touted both then and now as an example of the interest displayed by patriotic women in public affairs, was not very representative. For every woman who voluntarily contributed money, dozens more contributed only their labor to the Revolutionary cause—often involuntarily, or for a minimal price. In April of 1778 an army memorandum noted: "The wimen grumble at the price of shirts—make the best bargain you can with them."[32]

Although historically significant, the political awakening of women which culminated in the "Offering of the Ladies" needs to be placed in context. Many women of the times, unlike Esther Reed, Abigail Adams, and Eliza Wilkinson, were too occupied with their labors to meet together in parlors, trading in their "trifling discourse of fashions" for the "several important matters in hand." Eliza Wilkinson's slaves and the destitute Phoebe Ward (see Introduction) were in no position to have their "personal aspirations" and "self-assessments" heightened by patriotic words or deeds. Mary Beth Norton, although admitting that her research was "not based upon a representative cross section of the American female populace," still claimed that because of the "common experiences of femininity . . . it seems possible to allow the literate portion of the female population to speak for their illiterate counterparts."[33] Hardly. Eliza Wilkinson could not speak for those she held in bondage, nor Esther Reed, a governor's wife, for homeless refugees. We cannot rely upon femininity alone as the defining factor in a woman's life; we must also look at other contextual variables such as age, class, location, ethnicity, and race.[34]

The study of women in the American Revolution, based on the extant writings of contemporaries, is beset with dangers. First, because only a fraction of women in those times were literate, we are working with a biased sample. Less than half of the women who left wills could sign their names, and those who left wills came from the more prosperous and presumably more educated portion of the female population.[35] The percentage of women who could write diaries and letters was much smaller, while the women whose families were able to preserve these diaries and letters through the generations come from an extremely select group, heavily weighted on the upper end of society. Tenant farm wives in New York, Scotch-Irish from the hinterlands of the South, poor widows from the Northeastern seaports, frontier women, slaves—we learn little about these and other illiterate women, who constituted the majority, by reading the diaries and letters of those who lived in more comfortable circumstances.

A closer look at the evidence reveals *which* groups of women engaged in boycotting, petitioning, and other patriotic acts. According to the November 5, 1767, issue of the *Boston News-Letter*, a "large circle of very agreeable ladies," in support of the boycott of British goods, promised not to use "ribbons &c &c." When 300 "mistresses of Families" pledged to forego the use of imported tea three years later, the *Boston Evening Post* noted that the group was composed of "Ladies of the highest rank and influence."[36] These upper-class women sacrificed by giving up luxuries which others never had.

Also in 1770, in the artisan section of Boston, more than 100 "young ladies" signed another agreement to refrain from imported tea, describing themselves as "the daughters of those patriots who have and do now appear for the public interest."[37] Anna Winslow, Betsy Foote, Charity Clarke—the "army of Amazons" who "felt Nationly" while they spun was indeed a youthful brigade, female counterparts of the teenage boys who would follow fife and drum into battle. Many genteel ladies and teenage girls from patriotic families did indeed become politicized by the events culminating in the American Revolution, but these two groups do not adequately represent the wide range of American women living at that time.

We must also be wary of accepting the writings of patriotic men at face value. Since patriot leaders wanted women to fulfill certain roles, their pronouncements are often colored by political agendas. Witness, for example, the much-publicized spinning bees. Historian Laurel Thatcher Ulrich, in an exhaustive study, was able to document forty-six spinning bees throughout New England from 1768 through 1770; in only six of these was there any mention of "Daughters of Liberty." The participants were generally called "young women"; other designations included "Daughters of Industry," "the fair sex," and "noble hearted Nymphs." Of the 1,644 women attending the documented spinning bees, 1,539 (94 percent) met at the house of a minister. These women spun for the benefit of their particular preachers, not just to make political statements. In several cases, the motive seems to have been far more mundane than revolutionary: the recipients of the cloth were recently widowed and needed the help of women. In at least one instance, the spinning bee was defined as distinctly apolitical, even antipolitical: "The Ladies are impressed with such a nice Sense of their Liberties derived from their Maker, as not to be very fond of the tyrannic Restraints or the scheming Partisans of any Party." Politicians, the participants concluded, should behave more like women: "That People can never be ruined who thrive by their Losses, and conquer by being conquered." These particular women were not following the script as it was written by male patriots. Although patriotic men tried to commandeer spinning bees for their own purposes, Ulrich concludes that most of these events were more "an early form of women's religious or charitable activity" than conscious and concerted political statements by the participants.[38]

Women did work harder because of the Revolution, but they did not work only to display patriotic virtue—they worked because they *had* to, because there was more work to be done. The most frequent sacrifices came not from a rarified strata of polite society, but from housewives and farmwives who were burdened with extra chores without willing it that way. Sometimes, the extra work was even mandated by law. In order to clothe the soldiers, states set production quotas for each town. In 1776, for instance, the women of Hartford were told to come up with 1,000 coats and vests and 1,600 shirts.[39]

Women from the lower end of society participated in political activities that were at least as revolutionary as giving up tea and fancy ornaments: they rioted. In May of 1777, twenty-two women broke into a store in Poughkeepsie, New York, taking some tea which they claimed the owner was hoarding in order to drive up the price. Shortly thereafter, they entered the owner's home, accompanied by some men who broke into his casks of liquor.[40] In July of 1778, Abigail Adams reported a similar incident involving coffee instead of tea:

> An eminent, wealthy, stingy merchant (also a bachelor) had a hogshead of coffee in his store, which he refused to sell to the committee under six shillings per pound. A number of Females, some say a hundred, some say more, assembled with a cart and trunks, marched down to the Whare House and demanded the keys, which he refused to deliver. Upon which one of them seizd him by his Neck and tossed him into the cart. Upon his finding no quarter, he delivered the keys when they tipped up the cart and discharged him; then opened the Warehouse, hoisted out the Coffee themselves, put it into the trunks and drove off. . . . A large concourse of men stood amazed silent Spectators.[41]

Before the war, patriotic men had wanted women to contribute to "the political salvation of a whole Continent" by engaging in "virtuous" activities.[42] These instances of mob action, quite unladylike, could hardly be considered virtuous in the traditional sense, but ardent patriots did not seem to care as long as the results furthered their cause. Women acted outside the law, just as men did, but there was a difference: women focused most of their wrath on greedy shopkeepers, not British officials; their immediate intent was to change prices, not laws. In most cases, they actually paid the merchants for the items they confiscated—but they determined the prices themselves.

In fact, these rioters were operating within a well-established tradition: women in England had a long history of looting for food during hard times. Eighteenth-century female rioters, according to historian John Bohstedt, participated as "proto-citizens" in one form of "the common people's politics."[43] Barbara Clark Smith applied a similar concept to her study of food rioters and the American Revolution:

Excluded from the vote, unqualified to serve as jurors at courts of law, free women—together with servants, slaves, children, and propertyless men—were politically disabled by their dependent status. Yet women conducted nearly one-third of the riots. Here, then, were possibilities for political action that resistance and revolution opened for women, not as republican wives or mothers, but as social and economic actors within household, neighborhood, and marketplace. [44]

By rioting, ordinary women exercised power in a setting outside the narrow confines of their separate and individual households; they explored an intriguing interface between private and public realms. Even if they were not "perfect statesmen," these common folk engaged in collective action that made a difference.

Women and the Army

While upper-class women learned to make do with fewer luxuries, and while farm and working-class women stayed home and tended to business, those with no business to tend—thousands of poor wives or widows or runaway servants who had nowhere else to go—submitted to the harsh, migratory lifestyle of the professional army. "Camp followers," they were called. [45] They served the army as cooks, washerwomen, and nurses; during battles they carried messages and supplies and assisted with the artillery. These poor women cast their lots with the army because they had few other options. Since the vast majority were illiterate, and none left any diaries, we can only conjecture whether they felt liberated or exploited by the work they were required to perform.

Officers of the Continental Army were never quite sure how to deal with the women who followed the troops. On some level they sensed that women, particularly those who accompanied their husbands, were necessary to keep up the morale of the men; without women, Washington wrote, the army would "lose by Desertion, perhaps to the Enemy, some of the oldest and best Soldiers in the Service." [46] But should the army actually *support* these women? If it gave them no rations, the women would starve—yet rations were always scarce, even for the men. For most of the war, decisions concerning allocations to women were left to the discretion of local commanders; sometimes women received full rations, sometimes half, occasionally none at all. In 1780 officers at West Point were ordered to issue provisions to women only if they washed clothes at "a Reasonable Rate."[47] In 1783, as the war was winding down, the American high command was still debating the ticklish issue of rations for camp followers.[48]

In return for minimal support, the women performed the tasks of everyday living which fell within the domain of traditional female roles. Sarah Osborn, who cooked for Washington's army, explained the importance of her job succinctly when she applied for an army pension after the war: "It would not do for men to fight and starve too." In Osborn's deposition for a pension, the only extant testimony of a camp follower, she offers a revealing version of the victory at Yorktown:

> The drums continued beating, and all at once the officers hurrahed and swung their hats, and deponent asked them, "What is the matter now?"
> One of them replied, "Are not you soldier enough to know what it means?"
> Deponent replied, "No."
> They then replied, "The British have surrendered."
> Deponent, having provisions ready, carried the same down to the entrenchments that morning, and four of the soldiers whom she was in the habit of cooking for ate their breakfasts.[49]

As the men hooted and hollered, the women, as always, served them food.

Camp followers made invaluable contributions to the military effort, even if they were not always recognized or appreciated by the officers. John Shy has suggested that the Americans operated at a disadvantage since they maintained a smaller proportion of female support personnel than did the British.[50] They suffered from a shortage of nurses, and even the paucity of washerwomen took its toll.

The devastating effects of diseases and parasites relating to sanitation—dysentery, typhoid fever, typhus, lice, scabies—might have been reduced had the Continental Army paid more attention to the traditionally female job of maintaining adequate hygiene. Since men died of disease as often as they died in battle, the failure to take preventative measures must be counted as a military liability. On July 6, 1775, the Massachusetts legislature warned Washington that the soldiers it sent him were "youth" who had not yet learned "the absolute necessity of cleanliness in their dress, and lodging, continual exercise, and strict temperance, to preserve them from diseases."[51] According to an observer in the fall of 1775, only a few months after full mobilization:

> Many of the Americans have sickened and died of the dysentery, brought upon them in a great measure through an inattention to cleanliness. When at home, their female relations put them upon washing their hands and faces, and keeping themselves neat and clean; but, being absent from such monitors, through an indolent, heedless turn of mind, they have neglected the means of health, have grown filthy, and poisoned their constitution by nastiness.[52]

General Washington, however, believed there were too many women in his army, not too few. Women, in his mind, slowed the army down, inhibiting its ability to move. On August 4, 1777, he wrote:

> In the present marching state of the army, every incumbrance proves greatly prejudicial to the service; the multitude of women in particular, especially those who are pregnant, or have children, are a clog upon every movement. The Commander in Chief therefore earnestly recommends it to the officers commanding brigades and corps, to use every reasonable method in their power to get rid of all such as are not absolutely necessary.[53]

Washington seemed concerned, even obsessed, that taking care of the women would put an extra burden on the troops. On July 4, 1777, the first anniversary of the nation's independence, the commanding general of the Continental Army issued a proclamation of supreme military importance:

> That no women shall be permitted to ride in any waggon, without leave in writing from the Brigadier to whose brigade she belongs: And the Brigadiers are requested to be cautious in giving leave to those who are able to walk—Any woman found in a waggon contrary to this regulation is to be immediately turned out.[54]

A week later, Washington ordered again: "Women are to march with the baggage." Apparently these orders were ignored, for he had to issue them over and over:

> August 27—[W]omen are expressly forbid any longer, under any licence at all, to ride in the waggons.
> September 13—No Woman under any pretence whatever to go with the army, but to follow the baggage.[55]

Washington's frustration mounted; at first women could march *with* the baggage, while later they had to *follow* the baggage.

Despite all his decrees, soldiers continued to allow women in the wagons. The camp followers were often kin to some of the troops; in any case, the men paid them a modicum of respect in appreciation for the services they provided. Almost a year after the initial proclamation, Washington prefaced yet another edict with an admission that little had changed: "The indulgence of suffering Women to ride in Waggons having degenerated into a great abuse. . . ." Again, a year after that, he wrote: "[T]he pernicious practice of suffering the women to encumber the Waggons still continues notwithstanding every former prohibition."[56] All he could do, however, was issue another order which was not obeyed. At the close of the war, Sarah Osborn made part of the long journey to Yorktown in a wagon.[57]

Washington was concerned with style as well as function. Clearly, he viewed women who dressed in rags and tended their snot-nosed children as an embarrassment to the army. When the commander in chief led his men through Philadelphia on August 23, 1777, he ordered specifically that "Not a woman belonging to the army is to be seen with the troops on their march thro' the City." But the women did not obey his orders; after the soldiers had passed, they sprang loose from the alleys to which they had been confined and paraded defiantly through the main streets, demanding, by their very presence, their fair share of respect.[58]

Washington seemed concerned that the presence of certain women would corrupt his men. After his march through the city, he set up a guard "to prevent an inundation of bad women from Philadelphia" from reaching his troops.[59] In 1775 Artemas Ward, Washington's predecessor as commander in chief, had ordered "that all possible care be taken that no lewd women come into camp."[60] In 1780 officers at West Point were ordered to "without Delay make the Strictest inspection into the Carractor of the women who Draw [rations] in their Corps and Report on their honour."[61]

Whereas the British command not only allowed but facilitated prostitution, the American command, operating on the belief that citizen-soldiers ought to remain chaste, would not permit it. Prostitutes were certainly less visible among the Americans, and probably less common—not only because their trade ran counter to policy, but because common soldiers did not have any money to pay for their services. But officers did have money. In April and May of 1778 Lieutenant Benjamin Gilbert of Massachusetts reported that a woman named Marcy made repeated visits into the officers' tent, where she "lay all Nigt" with different men. On May 30, however, "Bragg and Marcy and Pol Robinson got under Guard and weir Tryed by a coart Martiall," and on June 5 "Polly Robinson Nel Tidrey was Drumed out of the Regt."[62] While prostitutes who worked within the camps were hired and then put to shame, those who managed to establish themselves off-base found greater security. During a six-month period in 1783 Gilbert recorded fifteen visits to a brothel he called "Wyoma," where he "drank Tea with the Girls, & staid all night."[63] Gilbert made no mention of "the Girls" of Wyoma running into any difficulties with army regulations.

Women camp followers during the American Revolution lived on the edge, lower in status than the teenage boys and poor men who themselves hovered on the brink of starvation. They performed whatever services were in demand and took whatever they could get in payment. They fended for themselves as best they could. Apparently, camp followers plundered the surrounding countryside, since official orders had to be issued forbidding them to do so.[64] Following the battle of Bemis Heights, just before the British surrender at Saratoga, American women were seen taking clothing from the dead and dying; it probably happened at other times as well.[65] Surely, these women would have preferred other methods of survival.

Camp followers shared many of the hardships, and some of the dangers, with the fighting soldiers. As she hustled about during battles carrying things this way and that, a camp follower was as likely as a regular gunner to be hit by artillery. Smallpox and dysentery knew no bounds of gender. When epidemic diseases swept through the camps, when food was scarce or shelter unavailable, women who accompanied the army suffered or died along with the men. These reluctant heroines forfeited much more than fancy ribbons, and they toiled longer hours, under far more trying circumstances, than the women and girls who might have "felt Nationly" while spinning for liberty.

Some American women became camp followers for the British. Unable to rely on support from nearby communities, the British army maintained a higher ratio of women in its ranks to provide for domestic needs. In 1777 the British army included 1 woman for every 8 soldiers; by 1781 there was 1 woman for every 4.5 soldiers.[66] These new recruits were primarily locals, not immigrants from abroad. Like the patriot camp followers, American women who cast their lot with the British army were primarily refugees with no other means of support. As armed men swept through and devastated the countryside, women who were widowed or made homeless joined the nearest army, offering their services more to avoid starvation than to further their political beliefs.

Despite their contributions, camp followers ranked on the very bottom of the social scale. Although the soldiers for whom they toiled may have appreciated their services, they received nothing but scorn from the upper classes. One officer, clearly not accustomed

to associating with the "lesser sort," described them in most un-
flattering terms. They were

> the ugliest in the world to be collected . . . their Visage dress
> etc every way concordant to each other—some with two others
> with three & four children & few with none . . . the furies who
> inhabit the infernal Regions can never be painted half so hid-
> eous as these women. [67]

Hannah Winthrop, in a letter to Mercy Warren, described British
camp followers who had been taken prisoner at Saratoga:

> I never had the least Idea that the Creation produced such a
> sordid set of creatures in human Figure—poor, dirty, emaci-
> ated men, great numbers of women, who seemed to be the
> beasts of burthen, having a bushel basket on their back, by
> which they were bent double, the contents seemed to be Pots
> and Kettles, various sorts of Furniture, children peeping thro'
> gridirons and other utensils, some very young infants who were
> born on the road, the women bare feet, cloathed in dirty rags,
> such effluvia filld the air while they were passing, had they not
> been smoking at the time, I should have been apprehensive
> of being contaminated by them. [68]

Camp followers were not the only women making military contributions. Female civilians gave aide in many ways. They hid men
and weapons. They moved provisions through hostile territory.
They spied, spreading valuable information which they overheard
from the officers who had taken over their homes. They carried
messages, moving about freely through a countryside sometimes
dominated by the enemy. Twenty-two-year-old Deborah Champion
rode for two days to deliver intelligence dispatches to George
Washington at Cambridge, Massachusetts. Sixteen-year-old Sybil
Ludington rode through the night for forty miles, banging on the
doors of militiamen to tell them that the British were on the march
toward Danbury, Connecticut. Jane Thomas galloped sixty miles to
warn a group of patriots, including her son, that some loyalists were
coming after them. [69]

Sometimes, when left at home alone, women guarded themselves, their children, and their belongings by force and cunning. For the women of the times, the most inspirational heroine was probably Nancy Morgan Hart of Georgia. Detained in her home by a half dozen loyalists who were looking for patriot fugitives, Hart told her daughter to fetch some water while she offered food and drink to the intruders. Once they were properly mellowed by her homemade whiskey, she grabbed their weapons, killed one of the men, and held the rest at gunpoint until her daughter returned with help.

A few women even fought on the battlefields. The most famous was Deborah Sampson, alias Robert Shurtless, who enlisted in the army disguised as a male. Sampson served for at least seventeen months before her identity was discovered. Margaret Corbin fought alongside her husband at Fort Washington on November 15, 1776; when he fell, she is said to have continued to fire his two-gun battery. Because she was wounded in the same battle, Corbin received the first U.S. Army pension awarded to a woman for a disability. A woman who was later called "Molly Pitcher" fought in the battle of Monmouth on June 28, 1778, carrying water for the thirsty men and overheated cannons.

These women make likely heroines, but their deeds, mythologized after the war, need to be placed in context. Much has been said but little is known about Deborah Sampson. In the 1790s she lectured to a curious public for a fee. A promoter named Herman Mann prepared a biography of sorts, written in a grandiose style which eclipsed its subject. These publicity stunts confused rather than clarified Sampson's story. One account states she was present at the siege of Yorktown, but this seems unlikely. According to military records she enlisted in April of 1781; a different set of records shows her enlisting in 1782. Yet another version has her signing up at a much earlier date under the name of Timothy Thayer. After receiving her bounty, she supposedly went on a drinking spree which led to her discovery. With so little known, it is easy to fantasize about this woman who performed as a soldier.[70]

According to military records, "Samuel Gay" of Massachusetts was "Discharged, being a woman, dressed in mens cloths. Augt. 1777."[71] There were probably a few more. Sally St. Clair, who supposedly kept her gender a secret until the end, was killed in the Battle of Savannah.[72] We have no way of knowing how many others might have served without being discovered. Once the truth came out, however, women disguised as men were hardly treated as heroines. One girl from New Jersey tried to enlist as a man when her father would not consent to her marriage; after she was exposed during a physical examination, an officer "orderd the Drums to beat her Threw the Town with the whores march."[73]

The name "Molly Pitcher" might or might not refer to a real person. In 1911 John Landis asserted that the legendary "Molly Pitcher" was Mary Ludwig Hays of Carlisle, Pennsylvania, but in 1976 Linda Grant De Pauw and Conover Hunt contended that although Hays was definitely present at Monmouth, "there is no reason to identify her with either of the two women who were seen handling weapons on that occasion."[74] According to De Pauw, "there was no 'real' Molly Pitcher, for like G. I. Joe, the name describes a group, not an individual."[75] What we do know is that some women like Mary Hays and Margaret Corbin participated in battles by performing whatever chores had to be done, including the carrying of water and ammunition.[76] Joseph Plumb Martin, the young private from Connecticut (see chapter 2), recalled a scene he witnessed personally during the fighting at Monmouth:

> A woman whose husband belonged to the artillery and who was then attached to a piece in the engagement, attended with her husband at the piece the whole time. While in the act of reaching a cartridge and having one of her feet as far before the other as she could step, a cannon shot from the enemy passed directly between her legs without doing any other damage than carrying away all the lower part of her petticoat. Looking at it with apparent unconcern, she observed that it was lucky it did not pass a little higher, for in that case it might have carried away something else, and continued her occupation.[77]

We do know that Mary Hays and Margaret Corbin were poor women who accompanied the army. As camp followers, they enjoyed little respect at the time, but in the mid-nineteenth century, long after the daily dirt of the war had been forgotten, they were turned into fighting heroines. Today, as we cast about for women to accompany men into our history texts, we once again exalt their deeds.

This is a disservice to the women of Revolutionary times, an implicit affirmation of a male-oriented writing of history which insists that in order to have a place, in order to count, women need to have participated as men did. For the most part, women did not participate in the same ways as men—indeed, they were not allowed to. When we focus on those few women who fought in the war, and when we further mythologize their deeds, we inadvertently downgrade the real lives of the mass of women who did not raise arms but who still played active and important roles in the Revolutionary War.

Shaming

"Sending sons and husbands to battle," according to Linda Kerber, was one of the ways (along with boycotting and rioting) "in which women obviously entered the new political community created by the Revolution." Kerber elaborates:

> Women who thrust their men into battle were displaying a distinctive form of patriotism. They had been mobilized by the state to mobilize their men; they were part of the moral resources of the total society. Sending men to war was in part their expression of surrogate enlistment in a society in which women did not fight. This was their way of shaping the construction of the military community. They were *shaming* their men into serving the interests of the state. . . . The pattern is far older than the American Revolution, but it was strengthened during that war.[78]

Alfred Young agrees: "If, in 1765, men had mobilized women, by 1775, women were mobilizing men." Women, he claims, "egged their menfolk into action."[79]

Several anecdotal tales lend support to this view. "Remember to do your duty!" a lady from New Jersey supposedly told her husband. "I would rather hear that you were left a corpse on the field than that you had played the part of a coward." A woman from Massachusetts "with her own hands bound knapsack and blanket on the shoulders of her only son, a stripling of sixteen, bidding him depart and do his duty." An "elderly grandmother" from Elizabethtown, New Jersey, reportedly told her children:

> My children, I have a few words to say to you, you are going out in a just cause, to fight for the rights and liberties of your country; you have my blessings . . . Let me beg you . . . that if you fall, it may be like men; and that your wounds may not be in your back parts. [80]

These accounts, however, come from sources with vested interests: the patriot press, which consciously encouraged women to sacrifice for the cause, and Elizabeth Ellet, the nineteenth-century author who wanted to establish respect for women by proving they were patriotic. Undoubtedly, many women wished their men well as they went off to war, but these embellished tales cannot be taken at face value.[81]

In fact, women of the Revolution had good cause *not* to dispatch their husbands, sons, and brothers to the battlefields. If the men left, more work—hard, physical work—would fall on their shoulders. If a husband was lost, the wife would be widowed, the children left fatherless—and in those days, finding a new husband and stepfather was not easy. If a son was lost, a mother could no longer count on his support in her old age. Any son who had made it to adolescence, furthermore, was a survivor; having escaped infant and childhood diseases, was he now to succumb to an unnatural death? Even if sons and husbands survived the war, women who sent them into the army would be abandoning their loved ones to an all-male community notorious for drinking and swearing; few women of the times relished that thought. For all these reasons, not to mention emotional attachments, Revolutionary women must have thought twice before "shaming men into service."

If we look at what women themselves had to say, we see that

many were not overly enthusiastic about their men leaving home. In depositions for pensions after the war had ended, several widows volunteered to discuss how they responded when their husbands joined the army. Unlike male patriots or Elizabeth Ellet, these women were not coloring their accounts to suit their best interests; in fact, if they wanted to receive their pensions, they might have done better to appear more supportive of their husbands' military careers.

- Hannah Dickinson testified that when her husband Samuel tried to leave home in June of 1781 to sail on a privateer, she "ingaged him in conversation and went a short Distance with him" so he might miss his ship. He did. Angry with Hannah "for Detaining him," Samuel enlisted on another ship.[82]

- On another occasion, Hannah Dickinson sent a neighbor with a message to Samuel, who was at that point in the service: "if he wished to see his wife alive he must go home immediately." The commanding officer gave Samuel a discharge, even though the message was no more than a ruse.[83]

- Hannah Robertson was hardly thrilled with her husband's going off to war:

    Indeed my said husband was gone in the United States service through a great part of the revolutionary war. I was troubled to think that he should love to be going so much in the war and leave me with helpless children in very poor circumstances.[84]

- Betsey Cross had the misfortune to be married to a recruiting officer. She recalled "that women were frequently complaining of him for drafting their husbands and friends."[85]

Other anecdotal evidence supports this more realistic picture:

- A drunken carpenter from Maryland enlisted on a privateer, but when the marines came to take him away his wife called the recruiting officer "every vile name she could think of." The carpenter's wife caused such a fuss that her husband was allowed to stay at home.[86]

- Sarah Hodgkins, as we shall see in more detail, wrote repeatedly to her husband Joseph, urging him to come home. "I think the time you ingaged for is now half out," she told him, "& if you Should live to See that out I hope you will Let Some body else take your Place."[87]

- William Moultrie of South Carolina recalled hearing a patriotic sermon in February of 1775

  which very much animated the men; whilst the female part of the congregation were affected quite in a different manner; floods of tears rolled down their cheeks, from the sad reflection of their nearest and dearest friends and relations entering into a dreadful civil war; the worst of wars! and, what was most to be lamented, it could not be avoided.[88]

- In September of 1776, "one very sick youth from Massachusetts" asked the Reverend Ammi R. Robbins: "Will you not send for my mother? If she were here to nurse me I could get well. O my mother, how I wish I could see her; she was opposed to my enlisting: I am now very sorry. Do let her know I am sorry!"[89]

- At Kingston in 1776 male patriots had seized a batch of tea, which some women demanded they release; if their demands were not met, the women pledged that "their husbands and sons shall fight no more."[90]

- On February 4, 1778, General Washington complained that women had been visiting Valley Forge "with an intent to entice the soldiers to desert." Washington's complaint spoke to a very real problem, for official records reveal that an average of eight to ten soldiers deserted each day—and the actual desertion rate was probably even higher.[91] We have no way of determining how many of these desertions can be attributed to fear, to the rigors of military life, to personal discomfort, or to the pleading of women, but we can safely say that letters from home presented serious impediments to the military force of the Continental Army as women wrote to their menfolk of the hardships they endured on their own: "I am without bread, & cannot get any, the Committee will not supply me, my Children will Starve . . . *Please Come Home.*"[92]

The notion that women were "displaying a distinctive form of patriotism" by "shaming" their men into battle oversimplifies the female experience of the Revolutionary War. Women did become more political, by necessity if not by choice—but this does not mean that the political goals of the state superceded personal commitments to family and natural instincts for survival. Particularly as the war dragged on, most farm and working-class women—the wives and mothers whose husbands and sons went to war—probably pulled rather than pushed when men and boys left home.

A Hessian prisoner from the battle of Trenton reported on the reception he and others received as they were paraded through Philadelphia: "The old women howled dreadfully, and wanted to throttle us all, because we had come to America to rob them of their freedom."[93] Although these women and many others of all classes lent their support to the Revolutionary cause, they did so in ways other than "mobilizing" their men and "thrusting" them onto the battlefield. This should come as no surprise: after the first rush in 1775, few of the men themselves wanted to sign up. To suggest that women proved their patriotism by willingly and enthusiastically placing their loved ones in harm's way is to force upon them an unnatural and unconvincing role. Like focusing too much attention on a handful of female soldiers or on privileged ladies who gave up "vain ornaments" which others never had, it steals the spotlight from the significant but less dramatic contributions made by ordinary women during a long and grueling war.

Where God Can We Fly from Danger?

The search for female participation in Revolutionary activities can mask the fear and the agony inflicted on women by men with guns. Many women suffered during the American Revolution, and some of their suffering was unique to their gender. History texts say much about spinning bees and boycotts—but why so little about women being looted, raped, widowed, and left homeless?[94]

The actual fighting during the American Revolution affected women in varying degrees. A few, like the women of Wyoming Valley on the Susquehanna River in July of 1778, watched helplessly as their male kin were slaughtered before their eyes.[95] Many, finding themselves within proximity of advancing and retreating armies, were forced to choose between two paths, each fraught with its own dangers: they might stay in their homes, protecting family and property as best they could, or they might flee from immediate danger to a fate unknown. The choice was not easy, for each alternative was frightful indeed.

Elizabeth Farmar chose to stay, even though her house lay between the lines of the British and Americans. She and her family endured frequent gunfire, food shortages, and "manny cold days" because soldiers confiscated their firewood. After the war, she proclaimed that she had made the right choice: "Most of the houses near us have been either burnt or pulled down as would have been the case with us if we had not stayd in it even at the hasard of our lives." In 1777 a woman from Pennsylvania told John Adams that "if the two opposite Armys were to come here alternately ten times, she would stand by her Property untill she should be kill'd. If she must be a Beggar, it should be where she is known."[96]

But the cost of standing firm could be high: homes were occupied by soldiers and property was looted. Even if the occupying army intended no harm to the female inhabitants, a military presence created many hardships. The officers, whether friend or foe, demanded to be quartered. Elizabeth Drinker, a Quaker from Philadelphia, was left alone when her husband was exiled for refusing to support the war effort. When the British captured the city in the fall of 1777, Mrs. Drinker found herself easy prey. On November 5 a soldier came to her door demanding blankets: "Notwithstanding my refusal, he went upstairs and took one." On November 25, she was intimidated by "an enraged, drunken Man . . . with a sword in his hand, swearing about the House." A Major Cramond then approached her asking for lodging, claiming "that it was a necessary protection at these times" to have an officer in the house. The major, who came across as a "thoughtful sober young man," promised "early hours and little Company." Despite her concerns, he moved himself in:

Cramond has 3 Horses 2 Cows 2 Sheep and 2 Turkeys with several Fowls in our Stable. He has 3 Servants 2 white Men and one

Negro Boy call'd Damon. . . . He has 3 Hessians who take their turns to wate on him as messengers or order men.

He soon took over most of the house, entertaining freely. Cramond and his entourage were not particularly abusive, but Mrs. Drinker felt her home was no longer her own: "they behave well and appear pleas'd—but I don't feel so."[97]

Some women quartered men willingly in times of distress. But if women helped men who were on the "wrong" side, they faced serious consequences. In Albany, Rachel Ferguson was sent to jail and held at £800 bail "for harbouring and entertaining a number of Tories," while Lidia Currey was jailed for "assisting in concealing and harbouring Persons from the Enemy."[98] Ironically, women were sometimes required to offer quarters while at other times they were prohibited from doing so; the legitimacy of a basic humanitarian act was entirely dependent on politics and power.

Women who stayed in their homes as an army approached were subject to abuses as well as intrusions. Rachel Wells of Borden Town, New Jersey, was robbed by troops on both sides.[99] Eliza Wilkinson, described in vivid detail the treatment she received from British soldiers:

> I heard the horses of the inhuman Britons coming in such a furious manner, that they seemed to tear up the earth, and the riders at the same time bellowing out the most horrid curses imaginable; oaths and imprecations, which chilled my whole frame. Surely, thought I, such horrid language denotes nothing less than death; but I'd no time for thought—they were up to the house—entered with drawn swords and pistols in their hands; indeed, they rushed in, in the most furious manner, crying out, "Where're these women rebels?" . . . making as if they'd hew us to pieces with their swords. . . . [T]hey then began to plunder the house of every thing they thought valuable or worth taking; our trunks were split to pieces, and each mean, pitiful wretch crammed his bosom with the contents, which were our apparel, &c. &c. &c.
>
> I ventured to speak to the inhuman monster who had my clothes. I represented to him the times were such we could not

replace what they'd taken from us, and begged him to spare me only a suit or two; but I got nothing but a hearty curse for my pains; nay, so far was his callous heart from relenting, that, casting his eyes towards my shoes, "I want them buckles," said he, and immediately knelt at my feet to take them out, which, while he was busy about, a brother villain, whose enormous mouth extended from ear to ear, bawled out, "Shares there, I say; shares!" So they divided my buckles between them.

The other wretches were employed in the same manner; they took my sister's ear-rings from her ears; hers, and Miss Samuells's buckles; they demanded her ring from her finger; she pleaded for it, told them it was her wedding ring, and begged they'd let her keep it; but they still demanded it, and, presenting a pistol at her, swore if she did not deliver it immediately, they'd fire. She gave it to them, and after bundling up all their booty, they mounted their horses. But such despicable figures! Each wretch's bosom stuffed so full they appeared to be all afflicted with some dropsical disorder. [100]

An incident such as this, not easily forgotten, might become the defining event in the victim's life for years afterwards. Wilkinson recalled the emotional aftermath of being looted:

The whole world appeared to me as a theater, where nothing was acted but cruelty, bloodshed, and oppression; where neither age nor sex escaped the horrors of injustice and violence; where the lives and property of the innocent and inoffensive were in continual danger, and the lawless power ranged at large. . . .

We could neither eat, drink, nor sleep in peace; for as we lay in our clothes every night, we could not enjoy the little sleep we got. The least noise alarmed us; up we would jump, expecting every moment to hear them demand admittance. In short, our nights were wearisome and painful; our days spent in anxiety and melancholy. [101]

Had Eliza Wilkinson been of a lower class, she might well have been raped. (The rape of "ladies" was strictly taboo, but this protection did not apply to women and girls without social standing.)

The fear of rape, as well as the actual experience, gave a unique twist to women's experience of the Revolutionary War. When armies came nearby, women and girls must have felt frightened and vulnerable.

Documentation of rape is difficult; frightened victims often failed to report it, while partisan men seized upon any indication of enemy depravity and recounted it widely, sometimes with considerable embellishment. Loyalists told how Flora MacDonald's daughters were taken prisoner in 1777 by rebels who put "their swords into their bosoms, split down their silk dresses and, taking them out into the yard, stripped them of all their clothing."[102] The patriotic *Pennsylvania Evening Post*, on the other hand, reported the sexual abuse by Cornwallis's troops in New Jersey:

> Besides the sixteen women who had fled to the woods to avoid their brutality and were there seized and carried off, one man had the cruel mortification to have his wife and only daughter (a child of ten years of age) ravished . . . [A]nother girl of thirteen years of age was taken from her father's house, carried to a barn about a mile, there ravished, and afterwards made use of by five more of these brutes.[103]

We do have some direct testimony which indicates not only that rape occurred, but that it was a common practice. After the British came through Hunterdon County, New Jersey, several women and girls gave official depositions to the Continental Congress. According to thirteen-year-old Abigail Palmer, possibly one of the subjects of the article in the *Evening Post:*

> A great many soldiers Belonging to the British Army came there [her home], when one of them said to the Deponent, I want to speak with you in the next Room & she told him she would not go with him when he seizd hold of her & dragd her into a back Room and she screamd & begd of him to let her alone, but some of Said Soldiers said they wou'd knock her Eyes out if she did not hold her tongue. . . . [H]er Grandfather also & Aunt Intreated . . . telling them how Cruel & what a shame it was to Use

a Girl of that Age after that manner, but . . . finally three of Said
Soldiers Ravished her. . . . [F]or three Days successively, Divers
Soldiers wou'd come to the House and Treat her in the Same
manner.

On the second day, the soldiers also raped her aunt, along with
Abigail's friend who had come to comfort her. On the third evening,
the soldiers found Abigail with another friend, who reported that
"the said Soldiers Ravished them both and then took them away to
their Camp, where they was both Treated by some others of the
soldiers in the same cruel Manner."[104]

All the women and girls from Hunderton County who reported
being raped signed their depositions with marks, suggesting they
were not literate. Officially, the British army did not permit rape;
in practice, officers tolerated the abuse of women if the victims were
not of their own class. Since upper-class women were employed in
the quartering of officers, they enjoyed a minimal level of respect;
lower-class females, on the other hand, received virtually no respect
from the occupying army. British soldiers saw them as fair game,
and their commanding officers did not dispute this.

In August of 1776 Lord Rawdon, a British officer, wrote proudly
to his uncle that 10,000 troops had landed on Staten Island, "as
healthy and spirited a body of men as ever took the field." The
soldiers, he reported, were happy to be on dry land, eating real
food, and pursuing sexual conquests:

The fair nymphs of this isle are in wonderful tribulation, as
the fresh meat our men have got here has made them as riotous as satyrs. A girl cannot step into the bushes to pluck a
rose without running the most imminent risk of being ravished, and they are so little accustomed to these vigorous
methods that they don't bear them with the proper resignation, and of consequence we have most entertaining courts-
martial every day.[105]

We can only guess how the victims must have felt when they reported their grievances to British officials such as Rawdon, who

regarded their tragedies as "entertaining" and who expected them to accept their unhappy fates "with the proper resignation." Rawdon continued his condescending remarks by noting with approval that a woman "to the southward . . . had behaved much better" after she had been raped by seven men, not complaining "of their usage" but demanding only that they return her old prayer book.

Victims of rape often suffered physically, either from the immediate trauma, from venereal disease, or from pregnancy. They invariably suffered psychologically. If their misfortune became public knowledge, they were stigmatized as well. As one man from Princeton reluctantly confessed, "[A]gainst both Justice and Reason We Despise these poor Innocent Sufferers." It was little wonder, he concluded, that "many honest virtuous women have suffered in this Manner and kept it Secret for fear of making their lives misserable."[106]

Many women, rather than face the prospects of plunder or rape, chose to flee as armies approached their homes. On April 20, 1775, the day after the first battle of the Revolution, a woman from Cambridge, herself seeking refuge, observed "the road filld with frighted women and children, some in carts with their tattered furniture, others on foot fleeing into the woods."[107] During the subsequent siege of Boston, about three-fourths of the civilians abandoned the city.[108] When the Americans tried to retake Newport in 1778, Mary Gould Almy reported that

> at 8 o'clock, in came some of my distressed relations into town, to get assistance to move their furniture inside the lines, as the order is given to burn all the houses, and every building within three miles of the town, the moment they see any force landing, to prevent their making barracks of them. Unhappy victims! they know not what to do; to come into town, they are undone; to go back, they are entirely ruined if they stay. Heavens! what a scene of wretchedness before this once happy and flourishing island! Cursed ought, and will be, the man who brought all this woe and desolation on a good people.[109]

Where would all these people go? When Helena Kortwright Brasher was forced to flee a British attack on Esopus, New York, she exclaimed: "Where God can we fly from danger? All places appear equally precarious."[110]

The poorest of the poor sometimes attached themselves to an army, for lack of any alternatives. The well-to-do often had friends or relatives in other locations with space to share; some even had country houses of their own to which they might escape. Those who were not rich also imposed on friends and relatives, even though there was neither room enough to house them nor extra food to offer them. Middle- and upper-class women who were forced to house refugees complained that "it is most too hard for me to have the Care of so Large a family at present" or that they had "not anything to eat but salt meat and hoe cake and no conveniences to dress them."[111] Imagine, then, how both hosts and guests of lesser circumstances must have fared. But these people left no records; we have no way of knowing how many barns were turned into sleeping quarters or how many appetites remained unsatisfied. Nor can we ascertain how many of the refugees literally had no place to turn.

Some refugees had been forcefully evicted by the men in power. Filer Dibblee, a loyalist lawyer from Stamford, Connecticut, fled with his family to Long Island in 1776, but the patriots there soon plundered the Dibblees' new home, imprisoned Filer, and turned Molly and her five children "naked into the streets."[112] Women frequently faced eviction because of the political beliefs of their husbands. Phebe Ward was left homeless because her husband had "firfeted his estate by Joining the British Enemy with a free and vollentary will."[113] During the British occupation of Charleston, Ann Hart confessed to her patriot husband that although she did not "condemn" him for his activities, she feared she was "liable to Banishment . . . for Actions not her own."[114]

Many women had to leave their homes; many more remained, sometimes without their male kin. Sally Logan Fisher, almost eight months pregnant, became stranded when her husband, a Philadelphia Quaker, was exiled: "I feel forlorn & desolate, & the World appears like a dreary Desart, almost without any visible protecting Hand to guard us from the ravenous Wolves & Lions that prowl about for prey."[115] Mary Donnelly was left alone to care for her children when her husband signed aboard a privateer. After his vessel was lost at sea, she received no income, "frequently being affraid to open my Eyes on the Daylight least I should hear my infant cry for Bread and not have it in my power to relieve him. The first meal I had eat for three days at one time was a morsel of dry bread and a lump of ice."[116]

Sometimes, husbands would never return. Women who were widowed by the war—often lower-class women, since most of the soldiers were poor—lost their minimal means of support. The Continental Congress, which could barely muster enough funds to keep its fighting men in the field, did not give high priority to the wives of dead privates. Even following the war, the national government refused to assume responsibility for widows unless their husbands had been officers. The wives of enlisted men had to wait until 1832, fifty years after the fighting had stopped, before receiving federal pensions; by then, of course, few were still alive.

State and local governments sometimes provided assistance, but not enthusiastically. A woman who qualified to obtain benefits was forced to make her way through a maze of official channels before receiving her due. Historians James Martin and Mark Lender describe the ordeal of Electra Campfield as she applied for relief:

> She first wrote to the county court, stating that her husband's death had left her "with one Child and without any kind of support," and that she had suffered "innumerable difficulties during the whole of the war." To receive benefits, she next had to find and then obtain depositions from her husband's former officers, establishing his service record in his New Jersey regiment. The minister of her local congregation also had to supply a deposition testifying to the legality of her marriage, and the local Overseer of the Poor then swore to her legal residency. All this information then went to the court, which approved her application and sent it to the state legislature. Widow Campfield then waited seven months for the assembly to approve her request and to authorize payment from the state treasury.[117]

What would Electra have done had she been unable to locate her husband's former officers? Undoubtedly, many qualified widows and orphans who could not master the complexities of the system slipped quietly through the cracks of a very weak safety net.

With official support spotty at best, widows sometimes petitioned individually for relief. It was a common practice in those days for destitute women to approach upper-class men with tales of distress, hoping to appeal to their sense of kindness. During and after the Revolution, women in need presented petitions to Congress, to state legislatures, or to important and influential men whom they hoped might become their patrons. Elenanor Healy, a former camp follower, complained to Congress that she "underwent the Severity of Cold and heat in the Service of her Country—besides A Greater, which was the loss of her Husband, who was killed. . . . [Y]our Petit[ioner] has lost the use of her Arm in the service and has two Orphans, the support of which puts [her]. . . . very much in dispair and Confusion." Healy received a response from George Washington, who suggested that she contact General Henry Knox. But Knox was "steping into his Carriage" when she called, leaving her with his clerk, who could do nothing for her.[118] Like other widows and camp followers, she was not legally entitled to any sort of recompense; when her appeal to charity faltered, she was left with nothing.

More often than not, widows and the mothers of deceased soldiers had to mourn without the presence of a body. Almost one-third of the men who died perished while in enemy hands; even those who succumbed to disease or could be retrieved from the battlefield were rarely returned to their distant families. Grieving was strangely abstract: no body, no grave, no physical manifestation of the loss— only the word of some messenger who could not always be trusted. A few women learned that their loved ones had perished, only to find out later that there had been some mistake. Many other women, after hearing of the death of a husband, sweetheart, son, or brother, must have waited in disbelief—for weeks, months, perhaps even years—for someone to tell them it wasn't so.[119]

The vast majority of women, even if they were not looted, raped, widowed, or left homeless, still experienced troubling times. Few locations remained untouched. The five largest cities—Boston, New York, Philadelphia, Charleston, and Newport—saw changes in occupying forces, and with each transition, countless families fled their homes to avoid persecution. Out in the countryside, as armies marched up and down the major valleys and deep into the hinterlands, women and children either scurried or remained, their lives deeply affected by a military culture in their midst.

What Was Done, Was Done by Myself

In 1980 Linda Kerber and Mary Beth Norton broke new ground with their extensive studies of women during the Revolutionary era. Kerber showed that we cannot overlook the women who served outside of any "institutional context" as "cooks, washerwomen, laundresses, private nurses, and renters of houses."[120] Norton demonstrated that by taking on work previously reserved for men, women began to break out of traditional gender roles:

> The war . . . dissolved some of the distinctions between masculine and feminine traits. . . . The link between male and female behavior, once apparently impenetrable, became less well defined. It by no means disappeared, but requisite adjustments to wartime conditions brought a new recognition of the fact that traditional sex roles did not provide adequate guidelines for conduct under all circumstances. When Betsy Ambler Brent looked back on her youth from the perspective of 1810, she observed, "[N]ecessity taught us to use exertions which our girls of the present day know nothing of." [121]

These were important insights; today, they must be extended to those portions of the female population who left few traces. Betsy Ambler Brent elaborated on what she meant by "necessity": "We Were forced to industry to appear genteely, to study Manners to supply the place of Education, and to endeavor by amiable and agreeable conduct to make amends for the loss of fortune." Other women had a very different concept of "necessity" as they struggled with the tasks of making a living during times of scarcity, often without the assistance of male labor. While upper-class women might have felt exhilerated by the partial breakdown of gender roles, lower-class women probably felt more oppressed: to take on the burdens of a man as well as a woman was no joy.

In the end, the most significant contribution of farm and lower-class women during the American Revolution can be stated quite simply: they toiled. "What was done, was done by myself," stated Azubah Norton of Connecticut, whose husband Benjamin was frequently absent from their farm.[122] Throughout the course of a war that lasted eight years, women did whatever they could to keep their households intact. Through their efforts, a society bordering on chaos did not fall apart. Even before the first battles, women produced at record speeds to compensate for the nonimportation of European goods. In the early stages of war, with goods scarce and an army of men to support, they stepped up an already feverish pace. Toward the end of the war, with the economy in collapse, women somehow managed to keep their households afloat.

During the early stages of the Revolution, when patriot leaders encouraged them to step up their efforts, women were much praised; by the end, the extra labors of women received little acclaim. Many hard-working women probably agreed with Rachel Wells of New Jersey, who complained after the war to the Continental Congress: "I have Don as much to Carrey on the warr as meney that Sett Now at ye healm of government & No Notice taken of me. . . . Now gentlemen is this Liberty?"[123]

Women who worked the hardest were mostly the illiterate, but one wife of a farmer and shoemaker left a moving account of how she felt about raising a family alone. Joseph and Sarah Hodgkins (the minuteman and his wife featured in chapter 2) corresponded frequently, and some of their letters have been preserved. Sarah Hodgkins neither signed petitions nor shamed men into battle; instead, she served her country, as most women did, within the context of her ceaseless labors and familial obligations.[124]

When Joseph left twenty-four-year-old Sarah and three children, including a six-week-old infant, to answer the call to duty in April of 1775, Sarah immediately assumed the responsiblities of head-of-household. She produced or purchased food for the table and kept the family, including her husband, in clothes. Since the army provided no uniforms, Joseph requested that Sarah supply him with shirts, britches, and stockings. He also sent Sarah his mending, along with requisitions for items which were cheaper in Ipswich than in military camps—coffee, sugar, cider, rum. He apologized repeatedly for burdening her with so many requests—"I fear I shall weary you in sending to have so much Done for me But I must tel you we live whare we have no woman do Due anything for us"—but he continued to ask for her help throughout his term in the army.

Sarah tried her best to fulfill his various orders. She also helped supply Aaron Perkins, her brother, and Thomas Hodgkins, Joseph's sixteen-year-old nephew, who served as cook in his uncle's company. As the men served their country, Sarah served the men: husband, brother, nephew, and even Joseph's eighty-three-year-old father, who lived nearby.

Whenever he could, Joseph sent home one-third of his salary, to be shared by Sarah and his father. (As an officer, Joseph had to pay for his own food and lodging while on duty.) But his pay was irregular, and Joseph apologized profusely when he had nothing to send. Sarah never complained, at least during her husband's first tour of duty. Instead, she offered him not only physical but emotional support:

> I rejoice to hear you are So well as I hear you are from time to time I feel quite concerned about you all these cool nights on account of your haveing no Better habetations to live in but I hope the Same that has preserved hitherto will stil be with you and preserve you from Cole and Storms & all the evels & Dangers to which you may exposed & in his own time return you home in Safty for which time I desire to waite patiantly.

After more than half a year in service, when Joseph went home on furlough during the second week in November, he and Sarah discussed his future plans: would he reenlist when his term expired on December 31? He said he would not, but in a letter dated November 28 he told Sarah that "if we Due not Exarte our selves in this gloris Cause our all is gon and we made slaves of for Ever." Fearing he might be wavering, Sarah braced herself for the possibility that he might change his mind: "I want to have you come home & See us I look for you almost every day but I dont alow myself to depend on any thing for I find there is nothing to be depended upon but troble & disapointments." Complaining no more, she told him she was sending along a shirt, a pair of britches, stockings, and some homespun shoe thread he had requested so he could make shoes for the officers.

By the end of December Joseph had decided to reenlist for another year. During this second term of service, the relationship between Joseph and Sarah began to change. Throughout 1775, Joseph had written home with instructions as to how to proceed with family business: get a pasture for the cow, dig the potatoes, buy some wood. Starting in 1776, his letters contained no more advice. Sarah, by now the household manager, must have figured it out on her own.

Perhaps because it might have been otherwise, Sarah began to feel Joseph's absence more keenly. Although he had written at least twice within the past week and six times within a month, Sarah wrote on February 1: "your Letters are Something of a rearity I wish you would write oftener if you can." She added in a postscript: "give regards to Capt Wade and tell I have wanted his bed fellow pretty much these cold nights that we have had."

On February 20, 1776, Sarah wrote:

> I want to See you very much I think you told me that you intended to See me once a mounth & it is now amonth & I think a very long one Since you left home & I dont hear as you talk of comeing but I must confess I dont think it is for want of a good will that you dont come home it is generaly thoght that there will be Something done amongst you very Soon but what will be the event of it God only knows o that we may be prepared for all events I am destressed about you my Dear but I desire to commit you to God who alone is able to preserve us through all the deficulty we have to pass through may he Strenghten your hands & incorage your heart to carry you through all you may be called in the way of your duty & that you may be enabled to put your trust in him at all times.

Revolutionary-era women coped with their many troubles by renewing their faith in God, and Sarah Hodgkins was no exception.

Women felt little control over their own destinies; always vulnerable, they placed themselves in the hands of a higher power. Rarely did a wife or mother write to a soldier without invoking the power of the Lord or making some reference to providence.

By trusting in God, Sarah was temporarily able to release her husband to his duty, while she fulfilled her own duties by continuing her daily labors:

> I have been very busy all day to day a making you a Shirte you Sent to me to Send you a couple & I had but one ready for the Cloth that I intended to make you Some Bodys of I have not got it Quite done So I was abliged to take one off of the Cloth I had in the house & I have got it done & washed and Sister Perkins is now a ironing of it. . . . I want to See you very much Sometimes I am almost impatient but considering it is Providence that has parted us I desire to Submite & be as contented as I can & be Thankfull that we can hear from one another So often.

With the passage of time, however, Sarah found it increasingly difficult to maintain her faith. With each new letter, she lobbied her husband more aggressively:

> I think I due really want to See you very much but dont understand as I am like to at present So I must be contented to Live a widow for the present but I hope I Shant always live So . . . I think the time you ingaged for is now half out & if you Should live to See that out I hope you will Let Some body else take your Place.

In the summer of 1776 their sixteen-month-old son, who had been an infant when his father left home, fell ill and died. Sarah's letter announcing the death has been lost, but her response to the tragedy was probably similar to her husband's: "it is heavy news to me But it is god that has Dun it therefore what can I say I hope it will Pleas god to santifie all these outward aflictions to us for our Best good."

On October 19, looking forward to the end of Joseph's second tour of duty, Sarah seemed apprehensive: would he enlist yet again?

> I want very much to See you I hope if we Live to See this Campaign out we shall have the happiness of liveing together again I dont know what you think about Staying again but I think it cant be inconsistant with your duty to come home to your family it will troble me very much if you Should ingage again I dont know but you may think I am too free in expressing my mind & that it would have been time enough when I was asked but I was afraid I Should not have that oppertunity So I hope will excuse my freedom.

Joseph did come home that winter—but not to stay. Despite Sarah's numerous entreaties, he enlisted for a third term of service, this time for three years instead of one. During Joseph's brief visit home they had conceived another child. But the father was soon gone, and Sarah gave birth in his absence. In 1775 Joseph had left a six-week-old son; in 1776 he was off in New York when their little boy died; in 1777 he was gone once again when the next son was born. As patient as she tried to be, Sarah began to hold Joseph accountable for his absence. Before, he had served in the army because external circumstances appeared to leave no choice; now, the choice had clearly been his own. None of Sarah's letters from 1777 survive, but a year later the wounds had clearly not healed. In February of 1778, when Joseph sent his regards without a written message, Sarah expressed her dissatisfaction:

> my Dear I must tell you a verbal Letter is hardly what I Should have expected from So near a freind at So greate a distance it seems you are tired of writing I am sorry you count it troble to write to me Since that is all the way we can have of conversing together I hope you will not be tired of receiveing letters it is true you wrote a few days before but when you was nearer you wrote every day Sometimes I was never tired of reading your Letters I Long to See you am looking for you every day if you Should fail of comeing my troble will be grate surely it will be atroble indeed.

And in April she wrote as a woman obsessed:

> I have Looked for you till I know not how to Look any longer
> but I dont know how to give over your not writing to me
> gives me Some uneasyness for I am sure it is not for want of
> oppertunities to Send for I have heard of a number of oficers
> coming home latly I wrote to you by a post about two months
> ago & have had no returns Sence I should be glad to know
> the reason of your not writing to me the first oppertunity you
> have if it is not too much troble for you
>
> Monday afternoon I am very Low in Spirits allmost despare
> of your coming home when I began I thoght I would write
> but a few lines & begun upon a Small piece of papeer but it
> is my old friend & I dont know how to leave off & Some is
> wrong end upwards & Some wright if it was not that I have
> Some hope of your coming home yet I believe I Should write
> a vollum I cant express what I feal but I forbear disappoint-
> ments are alotted for me . . . Sarah Hodgkins
>
> PS Brother Perkins & sister Sends their love to you Sister
> Chapman is got to bed with a fine Son I have got a Sweet
> Babe almost Six months old but have got no father for it.

Joseph finally left the army the following year. Perhaps unwisely, he quit with only a few months left in his three-year term, thereby nullifying the possibility of a pension. We do not know the extent to which his decision was based on Sarah's wishes.

We do know that in 1775 Sarah Hodgkins had supported her husband in every conceivable way as he went off to fight for the Revolution. In 1776 she had struggled, but she continued as best she could. In the final years she tried to get Joseph home—but until the end, she continued to send him clothing and manage the household in his absence. A heroine? Not in the traditional sense, but women like Sarah Hodgkins gave as much aid to the fledgling country as did the "several knots of ladies" who debated the politics of the day in genteel parlors.

Spurred by necessity, women of the Revolution helped keep a torn society from falling apart. A single entry from the diary of Temperance Smith, the parson's wife from Connecticut, reveals how religion, politics, work, and family, thoroughly interwoven, enabled women to carry on:

> On the third Sabbath in September Dr. Bellamy gave us a sound and clear sermon in which God's watchful providence over his people was most beautifully depicted and drew tears from the eyes of those who were unused to weeping. . . . On that night I went to bed in a calmer and more contented frame of mind than usual. I had, to be sure, been much displeased to find that our supply of bread (through some wasteful management of Polly's) had grown so small that the baking would have to be done on Monday morning, which is not good house-keeping; for the washing should always be done on Monday and the bakings on Tuesday, Thursday, and Saturday. But I had caused Polly to set a large sponge and made Billy provide plenty of firing, so that by getting up betimes in the morning, we could have the brick oven heated and the baking out of the way by the time Billy and Jack should have gotten the clothes pounded out ready for boiling, so that the two things should not interfere with each other. The last thought on my mind after committing my dear husband and country into our maker's care for the night, was to charge my mind to rise even before daylight that I might be able to execute my plans. [125]

LOYALISTS AND PACIFISTS

*Choosing Sides . . . The Dogs of Civil War . . . Tests of Faith . . . A
Rock and a Hard Place . . . A Lost Cause*

Choosing Sides

Nobody knows how many Americans remained loyal to the British during the American Revolution. John Adams once said
that a "full one third were averse to the Revolution. . . . An opposite
third conceived a hatred of the English. . . . The middle third . . .
were rather lukewarm"—a handy breakdown, often mentioned in
history texts, except for the fact that he was referring to American
attitudes towards the French Revolution many years later.[1] We tend
to grasp at numbers, even when none are available. How could we
possibly calculate the size of the loyalist and patriot factions when
many Americans at the time didn't even know how to classify themselves? We can try looking at those who signed oaths of allegiance
to each side, but we must keep in mind that oaths were often signed
under duress; we can look at those who volunteered to fight for the
British or the Americans, but even the willingness to serve in the
military, as we have seen, was affected by factors having little to
do with politics. Paul Smith, by a complex and intriguing process,
has estimated that about 20 percent of white Americans could be
classified as loyalists.[2] If we need a number, this is as good as any—
but the number itself, both tenuous and abstract, tells us little. It
only suggests what we already know: loyalists were plentiful enough

to turn the Revolution into a civil war, but not so numerous as to emerge the victors.

The literal definition of a loyalist—"a person who professed a continuing allegiance to the King of Great Britain"—is simultaneously too broad and too narrow. It includes people who passively accepted the legitimate authority of the British government, even though they might not have been willing to act in its defense, while it excludes a good number who contributed to the loyalist cause for self-serving reasons without cherishing any special feelings for monarchy in general or for George III in particular. Contemporary patriots seldom used the term "loyalist," with its positive connotations; they preferred to call their adversaries "Tories"—a word with a very British ring—often preceded by the adjective "damned." (Friends of the king, in a similar manner, liked to use the term "rebel," commonly preceded by the same adjective.) In the patriot vernacular, Tories were said to be "disaffected" to the American cause. Not signing the Association, toasting the king, quartering a British soldier—these were all marks of disaffection. The disaffected included anybody who failed to support the Revolution, even those who tried to stay neutral.

Several of the most vocal of the disaffected fit the classic image of the Tory: wealthy conservatives who were obligated to the British government and who felt threatened by republican theory and the rise of the common man.[3] In rural Massachusetts, where the Revolution began, loyalists came primarily from the ranks of the local elites, people like the Chandlers and Paines of Worcester County and the Williamses and Worthingtons of Hampshire County who had held power under the old order. In port towns like Boston, Newport, New York, Charleston, and Savannah, people who prospered by trading with the British had good reason to support the established government, even if they did not hold any political office.

But loyalists came in all shapes and forms, and they were not all rich. Edward Countryman writes:

New York's Tories numbered in the many thousands, and most of them were ordinary people rather than grandees. Among

twenty men taken up by the revolutionary authorities in New
York City in June 1776 were two tanners, five tavernkeepers,
four who called themselves laborers or apprentices, two leath-
erworkers, two smiths, a teacher, a pensioner, and a constable.
In the same year the committee of a Westchester County village, Salem, made inventories of the estates of men who had
fled to the British. It found that most of them were middling
farmers, like Ephraim Sanford. Sanford had a horse worth fifteen pounds, six cattle worth twenty-one pounds, five hogs and
fifteen bushels of corn valued at seventeen pounds, twelve loads
of hay worth eighteen pounds, and a forty-eight-acre farm valued at three hundred pounds. Sanford was thus in fair circumstances, but among the men who fled Salem there were also
some like Ezra Morehouse, a young man who owned only an
old mare, and Jacob Wallace, who possessed nothing at all.[4]

Antipatriot sentiments were shared by a wide variety of people
across a broad social spectrum. In New York, ironically, some of
those who opposed the Revolution were poor tenant farmers from
the 160,000-acre Livingston Manor in the Hudson Valley. Robert
Livingston, Jr., lord of the manor, was a Whig Revolutionary—
not because of deep philosophical convictions, but because his opponents in New York politics were all Tories. Livingston's tenants,
according to historian Staughton Lynd, saw in the Revolution a
chance to oppose their Lord and possibly take possession of the land
they worked. In May of 1777 the patriotic Committee for Detecting
and Defeating Conspiracies reported:

> Almost every body in the upper manor, particularly the eastern
> part of it, appears to have engaged with the enemy, first by
> taking an oath of secrecy, and then an oath of allegiance to the
> King of Great Britain; it appears to have been their design to
> have waited till the enemy came up, when they were to rise
> and take the whigs prisoners.[5]

Believing that they would be rewarded by the British with "Pay
from the Time of the Junction & each 200 Acres of Land," several
tenants signed a "Kings Book," promising to fight on behalf of the

Crown.[6] But the conspiracy was discovered and easily suppressed by militia units from neighboring areas. Precise records of the uprising were not kept, but from eyewitnesses and scattered official documents it appears that three to six tenants were killed and 100 to 300 taken prisoner during a week of armed skirmishes.

The tenants on Livingston Manor had a long history of expressing their discontent. In the early 1750s tenants who had refused to pay their rents took up arms to resist their eviction; in 1766 they again rose against their landlord, as discussed in chapter 1.[7] In the 1770s, instead of rallying to the side supported by the Livingstons, tenants tried to manipulate the Anglo-American conflict to their best advantage. In July of 1775 Robert R. Livingston wrote to John Jay: "many of the Tenants here refused to sign the association, & resolved to stand by the King as they called it, in hopes that if he succeeded they should have their Lands." Henry Livingston, meanwhile, wrote to Robert from the upper part of the Manor: "The Tenants here are Great Villains. Some of them are resolved to take advantage of the times & make their Landlords give them Leases forever." Were these really "loyalists"? If they sided with the king, they did so from defiant self-interest, not humble submission. Perhaps Jury Wheeler expressed the mood best when he pronounced that if he were forced to carry arms in the rebel army, his first target would be his captain.[8] In the Hudson Valley those most in need of a revolution failed to sign up for this one, while their landlords—members of the ruling elite—were classified as rebels.

This was not a unique situation. In New Castle County, Delaware, a mob of Tory refugees dragged a Whig constable from his home and forced him to be whipped by an African American—a potent symbolic act for those times.[9] Loyalist mobs in Delaware were branded by William Richardson, an officer in the Continental Army, as "poor ignorant illiterate people." In 1780 several hundred men from Sussex County, meeting at Black Swamp, banded together in an "Association" of their own to "fight against the Whigs because taxes was two high, and no man could live by such laws." These so-called Tories complained of the inequities of the draft: the rich could buy their way out, the poor could not. Historian Harold Hancock, by researching tax and probate records, discovered that many of the "Black Camp" loyalists were "men of small or no property," none had ever held any position of prominence, and almost half signed their names with Xs.[10]

In Baltimore County, Maryland, where patriots were the dominant creditors, "an ordinary farmer" named Alexander Magee claimed that "the American opposition to Great Britain is not calculated or designed for the defence of American liberty or property, but for the purpose of enslaving the poor people thereof."[11] Henry Guyton, also of Baltimore County, translated these thoughts into action: when a Whig official threatened to take him to court, Guyton told him "he would wipe his ass with his law," then "turned up his ass and said a fart for them." Vincent Trapnell, in a similar vein, told a member of the committee who had come to collect a fine to "kiss his arse and be damned, pulling his coat apart behind." Joseph Dashiell, a wealthy Whig from Worcester County, described local Tories as having

> a poor wretched hut crowded with children, naked, hungry and miserable without bread or a penny of money to buy any; in short they appear as objects almost too contemptible to excite the public resentment: yet these are the wretches, who set up to be the arbiters of government; to knock down independence and restore the authority of the British King.[12]

In Maryland as in Delaware and New York, common people who were disaffected turned the Revolution inside out. According to historian Ronald Hoffman,

> People in the lower orders, possibly the majority in some Eastern Shore communities, having lived with the economic and psychological disadvantages of being a subordinate class, now lashed out in anger at those figures dominating their immediate lives. The actions expressing this hatred varied. Some actively aided the British by taking up arms. Others pillaged locally with no particular direction. The majority openly, indeed defiantly, refused to be disciplined and showed contempt when their betters demanded respect and deference. Because of such a diverse pattern the resistance movement had the appearance

of an undirected social eruption so intensely passionate and yet so chaotic that it was not susceptible to any one form or explanation or to any clear political channeling.[13]

Hoffman studied the tax records for 100 people from Maryland who were tried during the Revolution for treason, insurrection, or riotous behavior. More than one in three had no land at all, while only one in seven possessed more than 300 acres. Only 3 percent of these vocal members of the disaffected possessed more than £750 in total taxable worth, while 37 percent had less than £100 and 82 percent less than £300. By and large, these were not wealthy people. Whig leaders, on the other hand, came primarily from the upper crust of local society.[14]

To the west of Livingston Manor in New York's Mohawk Valley, the tenant farmers on the Johnson estate also opposed the American Revolution, but for reasons that differed markedly from those of the Livingston tenants or the poor folk in Maryland and Delaware. In 1773 Sir William Johnson had imported 400 Catholic Scottish Highlanders to work his land, reasoning that people whose ethnic background, culture, and religion differed from that of their neighbors would look to him for protection and therefore be more obedient. His reasoning proved correct. Johnson's tenants did indeed seek refuge from Protestant Americans, not known for their tolerance. Although William died in 1774, the tenants remained loyal to his son, Sir John Johnson, who himself remained loyal to the Crown.

The Scottish immigrants must have hated the English, who had persecuted them in their homeland. But they feared their new neighbors, the American rebels, even more. With the onset of fighting in Massachusetts, Sir John Johnson and his tenants prepared for war. In May of 1775 the Revolutionary Committee from Tryon County reported that Johnson Hall was being fortified with "swivil-guns" and that "about one hundred and fifty Highlanders, (Roman Catholics) in and about Johnstown, are armed and ready to march."[15] In July 400 to 500 men from each side faced off at Johnson Hall, but negotiations prevented a major battle.[16] Early in 1776, with the rebels boasting greater numerical strength in the surrounding

region, "Six hundred men . . . the majority highlanders" were dis-
armed at Johnson Hall, with six of Johnson's men taken hostage.[17]
When the rebels came again in May to escort more prisoners to
Albany, Johnson and 130 Scotsmen fled to Canada. Those that remained, mostly women and children, continued to offer support to
the loyalists, relaying intelligence reports and harboring refugees
headed north. In 1777 the rebels tried to round up the rest of Johnson's former tenants, but they too escaped to Canada. For the remainder of the Revolution Sir John Johnson and his Scotsmen,
together with their Iroquois allies, engaged in protracted and violent
warfare with the American rebels along the northern frontier.[18]

Several other groups of recent immigrants remained loyal to the
Crown. Although many Dutch and Germans supported the Revolution, those who maintained their own language and culture did
not. Similarly, the Huguenots who settled in New Rochelle, the
only French immigrants who continued to speak their native tongue,
supported the British. William Nelson explains why:

> Taking all the groups and factions, sects, classes, and inhabi-
> tants of regions that seem to have been Tory, they have but
> one thing in common: they represented conscious minorities,
> people who felt weak and threatened. . . . Almost all the Loy-
> alists were, in one way or another, more afraid of America
> than they were of Britain. Almost all of them had interests that
> they felt needed protection from an American majority. Being
> fairly certain that they would be in a permanent minority (as
> Quakers or oligarchs or frontiersmen or Dutchmen) they could
> not find much comfort in a theory of government . . . based on
> the "common good" if the common good was to be defined
> by a numerical majority.[19]

Whether tenant farmers seeking their own land or cultural minorities fearful of persecution, many groups of Americans, upon sur-
veying the political landscape of the Revolution, sided with the
British for reasons that had little or nothing to do with political
philosophy. Articulate and vociferous Tories might preach on the
moral virtues of loyalty and the corresponding evils of revolution,

but many rank-and-file loyalists operated from concrete principles of survival and self-interest. Fur trappers wanted to keep the American farmers at bay; speculators feared that court closures would be bad for business; maritime workers opposed any disruption in trade; recent settlers worried that new revolutionary governments might not recognize their titles. For one reason or another, the patriotic cry of "liberty and property" did not always ring true.

Americans in the 1770s were sharply divided according to religion, national origin, location, and even language. Scots Irish Presbyterians in North Carolina, English American Anglicans in Virginia, Dutch and German Mennonites in Pennsylvania, Scottish Highlander Catholics in New York, native-born Congregationalists in Massachusetts—each group had its own culture, its own beliefs, its own set of interests. As political conflict regressed into outright warfare, each had to ask some fundamental questions: Who had granted their land? Who would protect it? What other groups coveted it? How might their own group acquire more? Each community approached the war influenced by a complex web of prior allegiances and antagonisms: were their friends Whigs or Tories? And even more critical, what about their enemies? As one group declared itself patriot, its opponents turned loyalist, and vice versa. The conflict between rebel colonists and Great Britain exaggerated preexisting differences, dividing Americans according to an intricate map of alliances which is difficult to decipher today.

Even within the same group, individuals differed in their perceptions of how best to play the Revolution. Most of the Green Mountain Boys, including Ethan Allen, cast their lot with the American rebels; they reasoned that only the British presented a strong enough force to challenge their own secession from New York. Justus Sherwood, a Green Mountain Boy who had intimidated his share of Yorkers, reasoned differently: since New York, their enemy, had joined the Revolution, the Green Mountain Boys must naturally favor the Crown. Sherwood, by default, became a loyalist; he fled to Canada, joined the British intelligence, and ran secret missions back to the Green Mountains, still trying to convince his neighbors to change sides. Toward the end of the war Ethan Allen himself toyed with the notion of siding with the British, just as Sherwood had done. Allen was not really a traitor, he was just playing at realpolitik, pitting one side against the other to further his immediate goal, independence for Vermont.

Within each regional, religious, or ethnic group differences of age, status, and class further complicated the choosing of sides. William Pencak, in his study of politics in provincial Massachusetts, found that loyalist leaders, on average, were fourteen years older than their rebel counterparts. Pencak explains:

> During the colonial period, younger inhabitants respected the elderly. . . . In part, the scarcity of old people accounted for their "veneration." However, as the number of elderly increased, they blocked young men's desires for land, families, and careers. Reverence for the elderly consequently declined. This process took an extraordinarily acute form in revolutionary Boston. . . . The loyalists, as revolutionary ideology revealed, appeared as greedy, power-hungry father figures who conspired to suppress the younger generation. The political crisis of Massachusetts in the mid-eighteenth century reflected the personal crises of many young men. A government monopolized by elderly men insisted on deference but proved unwilling to fulfill its obligations to a worthy, long-suffering populace. [20]

Pencak's thesis seems plausible, although it would be hard to prove for the overall population. Did common people as well as leaders display such an age discrepancy? Was a similar process at work in Rhode Island, Pennsylvania, or South Carolina? Did age figure as a factor in the choosing of sides along the northern frontier or in the southern backcountry? We have much yet to learn.

We do know that families were occasionally divided by differing allegiances. The Hessian Colonel Dincklage wrote that "Neighbors are on opposite sides, children are against their fathers."[21] Some partisans claimed that duty to one's country exceeded all familial obligations. John Adams maintained after the war, "I would have hanged my own brother had he taken part with our enemy in the contest."[22] Benjamin Franklin repudiated his son William for being a loyalist. When William was detained seventy feet underground in the infamous Simsbury dungeon, the most influential of patriots pulled no strings to mitigate the punishment.[23]

Mary Gould Almy, on the other hand, suffered great anguish as she watched her family fall apart. Mary was a Quaker with loyalist leanings; her husband Benjamin became a patriot soldier. In the summer of 1778, as Benjamin and the American forces prepared for an attack on his own family in British-controlled Newport, Mary kept a diary in the form of a letter addressed to her husband. One evening she ventured to a lookout where she could view the approaching army:

> And really, Mr. Almy, my curiousity was so great, as to wish to behold the entrenchment that I supposed you were behind. . . . Believe me, my dear friend, never was a poor soul more to be pitied, such different agitations as by turns took hold upon me. Wishing most ardently to call home my wanderer, at the same time filled with resentment for those he calls his friends, so that I returned home more distressed, my spirits more sunk than when I went out. Great enquiry was made at my return, to know the reason of my distressed countenance; but others who knew I had my share of sensibility, let me enjoy my sorrow that had no remedy.

And what about their children?

> Neither sleep to my eyes, nor slumber to my eyelids, this night; but judge you, what preparations could I make, had I been endowed with as much presence of mind as ever woman was; six children hanging around me, the little girls crying out, 'Mamma, will they kill us!' The boys endeavor to put on an air of manliness, and strive to assist, but step up to the girls, in a whisper, "Who do you think will hurt you! Arn't your pappa coming with them?' Indeed this cut me to the soul. After three years a lost wanderer, and could not meet a welcome.[24]

The Dogs of Civil War

Two months after fighting commenced in Massachusetts, the South Carolina provincial congress urged all citizens to sign a new association as proof of their allegiance to the Revolution. In July of 1775 the council of safety ordered Colonel Thomas Fletchall of the Ninety-Six district to muster his militia units so the men could inscribe their names. David Fanning, a young sergeant at the time, reported the results from his company:

> Col'n Thomas Fleachall of Fairforest ordered the Different Captains to call musters and present two papers for the Inhabitants to sign one was to see who was friends to the King and Government, and the other was to see who would Join the Rebellion. . . . There was 118 men signed in favor of the King, who Declard To Defend the same at the Risk of Lives and Property.[25]

Fletchall himself told the council of safety that the reading of the association was not a big hit: "I don't remember that one man offered to sign it." Instead, "it was agreed amongst the people in general to sign a paper of their own resolutions."[26]

The council of safety, disturbed by this incipient rebellion within the rebellion, dispatched William Henry Drayton, a leading figure in the provincial congress, and William Tennent, an influential minister, to convince these backcountry dissidents to change their minds. Drayton and Tennent found sympathetic ears in some areas, but in others they met with obstinate resistance. When they talked with German settlers congregated at the store of Evan McLaurin, they "did not procure one subscriber."[27] Upon meeting "the great and mighty nabob Fletchall," Tennent reported, they found "that reasoning was vain with those who were fixed by Royal emoluments."[28] According to Drayton, Fletchall stated "he would never take up arms against the King, or his countrymen; and that the proceedings of the Congress at Philadelphia were impolitic, disrepectful and irritating to the King." Fletchall's friends, Drayton reported, were even less agreeable. Joseph Robinson spoke with "impudence"; Robert Cunningham displayed "much venom"; Thomas Brown, evincing "bitterness and violence," insulted Drayton and almost provoked a duel.[29]

What made these men so obstinate? Why did they refuse to support the cause espoused by the majority of their compatriots?

The causes for disaffection in the South are difficult to ascertain. The backcountry farmers who opposed the Revolution did not justify their actions with well-reasoned arguments supporting Parliament or denouncing republican theory; in fact, most of them espoused the same republican values held by the Revolutionaries.[30] This was a conflict of interests and personalities, not ideologies. Yet southern loyalties cannot easily be explained by religion, nationality, or class. Anglican and Presbyterian, English and German, rich and poor appeared proportionately on both sides of the conflict. Some loyalists owned slaves while others did not, and the same held true for patriots. Robert Lambert, in his analysis of loyalists in South Carolina, found only one characteristic in common: they were all recent arrivals, making them "less likely to look favorably on a movement that was defying the authority from which they had obtained their lands."[31] Still, since other newcomers sided with the Revolution, additional factors must have come into play. Lambert suggests that prior friendships and animosities figured significantly, with frontier disputes over land and livestock escalating into feuds which were then superimposed upon revolutionary allegiances. Rachel Klein, noting the frequent contemporary use of the term "man of influence," argues that pockets of disaffection can be attributed to the loyalties of a few individuals who played key roles in their communities: Thomas Fletchall, a gristmill operator and militia colonel; Evan McLaurin, a prosperous store owner; Robert Cunningham, a ferryboat operator. Men occupying these key positions could not easily be opposed by backcountry farmers who wished to grind their wheat, purchase salt and sugar, or cross a river.[32]

But why did these "men of influence" themselves become loyalists?[33] Local revolutionaries, attempting to discredit their adversaries by ascribing dubious motives, offered their own explanations for the pockets of loyalism in the backcountry: key men, they claimed, harbored petty resentments for which they sought revenge, and these charismatic leaders convinced others to follow them. Robert Cunningham and Moses Kirkland, the first officers to lead armed loyalists into battle, had been passed over for promotions in the provincial militia. Robert Cunningham's cousin William turned against the Whigs after a superior officer who had promised him a promotion brought him to trial for insubordination. Daniel McGirt, the leader of a band of loyalist raiders, changed sides after a Whig officer falsely accused him of a crime in hopes of acquiring McGirt's prize mare. (The patriotic Drayton, on the other hand, had himself changed sides only a few years earlier when the Crown refused to appoint him to the position of chief justice; even Ben Franklin, some historians believe, became a revolutionary only after he had failed to secure a post within the British imperial system.[34])

Some of the resentments harbored by loyalist leaders were not so petty. David Fanning, according to popular tradition, "swore vengence on all whigs" after his pack train of trading goods had been pillaged by a militia band. William Cunningham did not go on the rampage which earned him the name of "Bloody Bill" until Whigs had killed his brother, a lame epileptic, and abused his father. Thomas Brown, for the crime of leading dinner toasts supporting the king, had been partially scalped, tarred and feathered, and branded on the bottom of his feet by a Revolutionary committee. These men had real cause for anger.[35]

For whatever reasons, the first year of the American Revolution in South Carolina was marked by civil war. Drayton and Tennent, in their attempt to convert the men who refused to sign the association, managed only to increase opposition. Early in September Robert Cunningham raised a force of 1,200 men to oppose the new Revolutionary government of South Carolina. On September 16 Drayton negotiated a treaty with Fletchall which granted the loyalists amnesty if they refused to aid the British and ceased criticizing the revolutionaries, but Cunningham, Brown, and others refused to abide by the treaty. Brown claimed that Fletchall's negotiations had been hampered by his "frequent recourse to the bottle," while Cunningham wrote to Drayton:

[T]hat peace is false and disgraceful from beginning to ending. It appears to me, sir, you had all the bargan making to yourself, and if that was the case, I expected you would have acted with more honor than taken the advantage of men (as I believe) half scared out of their senses at the sight of liberty caps and sound of cannon.[36]

Using this letter as evidence, Drayton was able to have Robert Cunningham arrested. Robert's brother Patrick tried and failed to spring him from jail, but Patrick and his friends did manage to seize a shipment of gunpowder which the council of safety was sending to the Cherokee Indians. The council claimed the gift of powder was simply for good will, but backcountry loyalists thought otherwise: the Revolutionary government, they were convinced, was arming the Indians to fight against them. In the wake of the powder incident, 2,000 loyalists from Ninety-Six rose up against the rebels. From November 19 through November 21 these men from the backcountry fought off the Revolutionary militias sent to subdue them. On November 22 the patriots agreed to withdraw, but within the next few weeks their numbers swelled to over 4,000 while many of the loyalists went back to their farms. On December 22 at a place called the Great Cane Brake the American Revolution squashed the local revolution of Ninety-Six. Most of the loyalists simply dispersed, but 135 were captured.

For the next four years loyalist resistance in the Deep South was scattered, but it never ceased. In 1778 Robert Cunningham, having been released from jail, won a seat in the state senate without even running. Although he never served his term since he would not take the loyalty oath, his election demonstrated the continuing opposition to the new state government. Thomas Brown and others who had fled to East Florida received plenty of local support when they ventured across the border to raid prominent Whigs in Georgia and South Carolina. David Fanning, along with many other backcountry loyalists, continued to strike back at the ruling party by teaming up with the Cherokee Indians. Operating with no central command and little aid from the British, these Americans refused to accept the domination of lowlanders who, in the name of liberty, insisted that all Americans submit to their new government.

David Fanning's narrative of his wartime experiences provides a vivid picture of loyalist activities in the southern backcountry. Fanning, orphaned at the age of nine, suffered during his childhood from a scalp disease which left him bald and caused him to don his most identifying accessory, a silk skull cap. He ran away from his court-appointed guardian, and at the age of eighteen he moved from

North Carolina to Raeburn's Creek in South Carolina, where he farmed and traded with the Indians. In 1775, at the age of twenty, he joined in the activities of loyalist dissidents. At Fletchall's he "signed in favor of the King," he helped seize the gunpowder, he fought in the battle at Ninety-Six, and he fled to the "Cherichee Indians" after being defeated at "the big Cane Brake." In January of 1776 he was finally captured. "I was made prisoner by a party of Rebels," he wrote, "who after Detaining me four days and Repeatedly urging me to take the Oath of Allegiance to the United States Stript me of Every thing and made me give Security for my future good Behaviour by which I got clear on the 10 of May 1776."[37]

Fanning's freedom did not last long. He was confined again for gathering "a Company of men Ready in order for to Join the Indians."[38] After he escaped, he did in fact organize twenty-five men to fight with the Cherokees against the patriots. He was taken prisoner once more, and then he escaped, and so on: fourteen times David Fanning was captured during a three-year period, and fourteen times he found some way to break loose.

In March of 1778 Fanning was elected to serve as the commander of a loyalist militia which raided Whigs in South Carolina and Georgia. Upon returning home, the rebels

> Raised a body of men for to take us and for the space of three months Kept so Constant a Look out that we were oblidged for to stay in the woods. Six weeks of which time I never saw a man except Samuel Brown who was afterwards Killed at Tigo-River, that shared my Sufferings and lived entirely without Either Bread or Salt upon what we Killed in the wilderness.[39]

Such was life for David Fanning throughout much of the Revolutionary War. A hunted man, he "Received two bullets in my Back one of which is not extracted." A reward of "Seventy Silver Dollars and 300 paper ones" was offered for his capture.[40] Somehow, David Fanning survived.

In the spring of 1780, with the British capture of Charleston, loyalists who had been dormant suddenly awoke and David Fanning no longer had to hide in the woods. When Fanning and William Cunningham set out to form a new company, they had no shortage of recruits. "We now found ourselves growing Strong," Fanning recorded, "Numbers flocking Daily to us."[41] For the next two years militia bands from both sides stalked the countryside of North and South Carolina, pillaging at will and trying to catch their opponents off guard. Inevitably some men were killed—and each death, of course, had to be avenged. Fanning's narrative continues:

[A]fter a little while nine of us had assembled at a friends house when we where surrounded by a party of 11 Rebels under the Command of Capt John Hinds we perceived their approach and prepared for to Receive them. when they had got quite near us we run out of the doors of the house, fired upon them and Killed one of them, on which we took three of their horses and some firelocks. We then took to the woods and unfortunately had two of our little Company taken, one of which the Rebels shot in cold Blood, and the other they hanged on the spot where we had Killed the man a few Days before.

We where exasperated at this that we determined for to have satisfaction and in a few Days I collected 17 men well armed and formed an ambuscade on deep River at Coxes Mill and sent out spies. in the Course of 2 hours one of my spies gave me information of a party of Rebels plundering his house which was about three miles off. I instantly marched to the place and Discovered them in a field near the house. I attacked them Immediately and Kept up a smart fire for half an hour, during which time we Killed their Capt and one private on the spot, wounded three of them and took two prisoners besides 8 of their horses well appointed and several swords. . . . the same day we pursued another party of Rebels and came up with them. the morning following we attacked them smartly and Killed 4 of them on the spot, wounded 3 dangerously and took one prisoner with all their horses and appointments. in about an hour after that we took two men of the same party and Killed one more of them—the same Evening we had Intelligence of another party of Rebels which where assembling about 30 miles off in order to attack us. as I thought it best to surprise them where they where collecting I marched all night and about 10 o'Clock next morning we came up with them. we commenced a fire upon each other which continued for about 10 minutes when they Retreated. We Killed two of them and wounded 7 and took 18 horses well appointed.[42]

Fanning and his comrades did indeed "have satisfaction" for their two buddies who were shot and hanged: in the course of three days they fought four skirmishes which yielded nine dead, thirteen wounded, and five taken prisoner—not to mention all the horses that were seized. But the dead and wounded rebels, of course, would someday be avenged in turn. "When Once the Dogs of Civil War are let loose," said Pierce Butler years later, "it is no easy matter to Call them back."[43]

John Ramsey, a local Whig leader, wrote to the Governor Thomas Burke: "from the daring Spirit of the Tories, almost all the whigs was gone to oppose Fanning. . . . what few there is of us, is Oblidge to be out Constantly or Lay in the woods."[44] By 1781 "laying out," as it was called, had become the way of life in the southern backcountry. James Collins reported:

There was much excitement through the whole country— scarce a man staid at home. Those that were not collected in parties, lay out in the woods; every article of furniture, clothing, or provisions—that was worth anything, was hid out; some in hallow trees, and often, hardware, that would stand it, was buried in the ground. A horse, that was worth any thing, was not to be seen, unless tied in some thicket . . . —and if a woman had but one quart of salt, to salt mush for her children, or a spoon to sup it with, she must keep it hid; or if she had any decent apparel, she would scarce dare wear it.[45]

David Fanning, once hunted by the rebels, was now the hunter. With an elite band of fifty-three hand-picked men Fanning continued to terrorize his opponents until "the worst of Rebels came to me beging protection for themselves and Property."[46] In September of 1781, even as Cornwallis was besieged at Yorktown, Fanning led a force of 950 against the North Carolina capital at Hillsborough, capturing the governor, his council, and several officers from the Continental Army. As the loyalists marched their prisoners toward Wilmington, which was still under British control, they were attacked at Lindley's Mill. Although dozens of men were killed and Fanning himself was wounded, they still managed to deliver Governor Burke and his council to the British authorities.

But when the British abandoned Wilmington on November 18, 1781, North Carolina loyalists were left with no outside support. Even so, disaffected backcountry farmers did not call off their war. In January of 1782 Fanning offered to lay down his arms, but only if "every friend of Government" were allowed to return to their homes "unmolested," exempt from any requirement to support the rebels or pay taxes.[47] These terms, of course, were rejected, and the endless cycle of revenge continued, as Fanning describes:

> In the course of this correspondence endeavoring to make peace I had reason to believe they did not Intend to be as good as their words, as three of their people followed Captain Linley of mine who had moved to Wottoguar and cut him to pieces with their Swords. I was immediately informed of it and Kept a look out for them. . . . after their Return I took two of them and hung them . . . by way of Retaliation, both on one limb of a tree.[48]

In March Fanning made another peace overture, but the response he received from Andrew Balfour, a rebel colonel, was direct: there would be "no resting place for a Toryes foot Upon the Earth." Fanning's response to Balfour was even more direct: he killed him. On March 11 Fanning's party embarked on what he called a "small scorge" of Randolph County. After firing two shots through Balfour—"which put an end to his commiting any more ill Deeds"— Fanning's band proceeded toward the home of Colonel Collier, "and on our way we burnt several Rebel houses, and catched several prisoners." Although Collier escaped, Fanning "took care to Distroy the whole of his plantation." Rebel Captain John Bryan, after seeing his house set on fire, "called Out to me and desired me to spare his house for his wife and Childrens sake." Fanning agreed, but only if Bryan would come out of his house and give up his arms. "[W]hen he came out," according to Fanning, "he Said here Damn you, here I am, with that he Received two Balls, the one through his head and the other through his Body—he came out with his Gun *cocked*." The scourge continued:

> from thence I pursued on to one Major Dugins House or Plantation and Distroyed all his property, and all the Rebel Officers property in the settlement for the distance of 40 miles, on our way I Ketched a Commisary from Salisbury who had some of my men prisoners and almost perished them and wanted to hang Some of them, which I carried him Immediately to a certain tree where they had hung one of my men by the name of Jackson, and I delivered him up to some of my men who had been treated ill when prisoners and they Immediately hung him. After hanging 15 minute cut him down. [49]

David Fanning's final terrorist act pales by comparison with the scourge of Randolph County, but it reveals his character in stark silhouette. In April of 1782 he and five friends "Set out for Chatham to where I heard of a weding that was to be that day." He crashed the festivities and lined up the males "to see if I Knew any of them that was bad men." None were, but he did find one of the guests hiding upstairs, a man named William Doudy. Fanning's men shot Doudy in the back of the shoulder as he tried to flee, and Fanning finished him off: "I then having pistols in my hand I Discharged them both at his Breast, with which he fell and that night Expired. I then paroled the rest."[50]

With the rebel government back in power and his band of followers reduced to a handful, Fanning could see that the end was in sight: "I concluded within myself that it was Better for me to try and settle myself being weary of the disagreeable mode of Living I had Bourne with for some Considerable time."[51] His search for a better "mode of Living" led David Fanning—after seven long years of running, hiding, and shooting—into the arms of sixteen-year-old Sarah Carr. They decided on a quick marriage, and to heighten the festivities Fanning convinced two of his friends, William Hooker and Sarah's brother William, to get married on the same day. This time, however, the rebels took their turn at bashing weddings, and Hooker's "horse was tied so fast he could not get him loose untill they catched him and murdered him on the spot." Fanning and Carr, however, were not to be deterred: "myself and Cap't Carr was married and Kept two Days meriment. the Rebels thought they was shure of me then, however I took my wife and concealed her in the woods."[52]

David and Sarah Fanning eventually made their way to Charleston, where the British army was still stationed, and from there they emigrated to Nova Scotia. In 1783 North Carolina's Act of Pardon stated specifically that "nothing herein contained shall extend to pardon Peter Mallet, David Fanning and Samuel Andrews, or any person or persons guilty of deliberate and wilful murder, robbery, rape or housebreaking." Although Fanning denied any rape, he could hardly argue with the rest. Even so, he maintained quite correctly that this sort of pardon made little sense, for "their Never was a man thats Been In Arms on Either Side But what Is gilty of Some of the Above Mentioned Crimes."[53]

What drove David Fanning to terminate the lives of so many human beings? Perhaps it was the pillaging of his pack train before the war, or his many stints in prison, or all that time "lying out" in the woods, or the cruel destruction of men who fought by his side. Or perhaps he was simply a "bad man," as he described others—a short-fused frontiersmen too prone to fury. In any case, it is unlikely that Fanning was driven to such extremes by a profound fondness for "his Majestys good Government," as he called it; his violent acts were much more personal.

If Fanning's destructive campaigns seem excessive to us today, they were only business-as-usual in the southern backcountry during the waning years of the Revolutionary War. William "Bloody Bill" Cunningham, after killing the man who murdered his brother, was said by his adversaries to have set houses on fire and then cut men "into pieces with his own sword" as they fled the flames.[54] Daniel McGirt wreaked havoc among southern patriots with his "corps of Indians, with negro and white savages disguised like them, and about 1,500 of the most savage disaffected poor people, seduced from the back settlements."[55] Thomas Brown also fought with Native Americans by his side, and the Indians, like the rebels who had tortured Brown, knew how to scalp.[56] By the 1780s loyalism in the southern interior had evolved into populist terrorism as Fanning, Brown, Cunningham, McGirt, and many more loyalists-turned-bandits killed and looted in the name of King and Country.

The torch of the British Empire in America was carried in the end by backcountry outlaws, strange friends indeed for Peter Oliver, Anne Hulton, and other well-heeled Tories who decried the breakdown of law and order. Tory prophecies of anarchy had been fulfilled, but at least some of the agents of anarchy fought on behalf of the Crown. "A mere rabble of undisciplined freebooters"—these particular words, written by a British officer, referred not to the revolutionaries in Boston but to Thomas Brown's Rangers, multicultural loyalists from East Florida.[57] Somehow, the Revolution had created its own mirror image, rebels against the Rebels, a mob within the Mob.

Tests of Faith

While backcountry planters in the South answered Revolutionary violence with violent acts of their own, several religious communities challenged the dominion of American rebels from the opposite direction: they refused to take up the sword. Quakers, Shakers, Moravians, Mennonites, Amish, Dunkers, Schwenkfelders—these radical spiritualists took the Reformation to heart by giving precedence to the life of the soul over the affairs of the state. Around 80,000 people, or one in every thirty free Americans, claimed membership in one of these communities at the eve of the Revolution.[58] Quakers, the original proprietors of Pennsylvania, were the largest group and also the most powerful; the others were composed primarily of industrious farmers who lived in small, cooperative communities. Many were German-speaking immigrants who had come to America from central and northern Europe in search of religious freedom and in some cases to escape military conscription. Rather than confront the secular authorities who persecuted them, these devout Christians had become proficient in the subtle art of avoiding all involvement in war and politics. In Revolutionary America, however, this would prove difficult to do.

In 1776 a group of Mennonites declared they were "a defenseless people and could neither institute nor destroy any government."[59] Since they did not deem it proper to oppose any civil authority, they could not possibly participate in an act of rebellion. They would pay their taxes, they would sell food to the army, they would even furnish wagons and teams free of charge—but that was as far as they could go in good conscience. When the rebels tried to get them to join the army, or pay extra taxes for the war, or at the very least sign a loyalty oath, the Mennonites just said no. But a movement dependent on popular support cannot accept no for an answer, and the American patriots, experienced in matters of coercion, brought the full force of the Revolution to bear on the Mennonites and other sects who would not join in their cause. As one contemporary commented, "The mad rabble said: 'If we must march to the field of battle, he who will not take up arms must first be treated as an enemy.' "[60]

Although pacifists were exempted from military service in some states, they were still required to hire substitutes. Those who refused were fined, and if they refused to pay the fine, they could be jailed. Religious dissidents, like everyone else, were also expected to sign oaths of allegiance to the Revolutionary government—and when they failed to do so, they were subjected to both formal and informal harassment:

- In the summer of 1777 George Kriebel's son, a Schwenkfelder, was fined for his failure to serve in the militia. When George appeared in court with proof that his boy was underage, his testimony was not accepted since he had not yet taken the oath—and he himself was then prosecuted.[61]

- In June of 1778 eleven farmers, nine of whom were Mennonites, were jailed for refusing to take the oath. They petitioned for relief, claiming that

    all their said personal estate, even their beds, bedding, linen, Bibles and books, were taken from them and sold by the Sheriff to the amount of about forty thousand pounds. That from some of them all their provisions were taken and even not a morsel of bread left them for their children. That as all their iron stoves were taken from them, ... they are deprived of every means of keeping their children warm in the approaching winter, especially at nights, being obliged to lie on the floor without any beds; that some of the men's wives were pregnant and near the time of deliverance, which makes their case the more distressing.[62]

- In August of 1777 General John Sullivan sent to Congress an important document he claimed to have captured from the enemy: the minutes of the Quaker Yearly Meeting at Spanktown, New Jersey, which depicted the position and movements of the Continental Army. Alarmed at this evidence that Quakers were acting as spies, Congress ordered the Supreme Executive Council of Pennsylvania to arrest eleven leading Friends, along with any other citizens suspected of being sympathetic to the British. In early September agents for the council detained thirty men in the Free Masons' lodge of Philadelphia. The prisoners, it was claimed, had demonstrated by their "conduct & conversation" that they were "highly inimical to the cause of America," but they were charged with no particular crime—they certainly had no connection with the Spanktown meeting, since there never *was* any Quaker meeting at Spanktown. Their writs of habeas corpus were suspended by an ex post facto act of the Pennsylvania assembly, and their requests for a hearing were flatly denied. With no opportunity to present a defense, seventeen Quakers and three Anglicans who refused to promise their allegiance to the Revolutionary government were exiled to Winchester, Virginia, where they had to be protected from outraged residents who resented the presence of known traitors in their community. Seven months later, after numerous petitions from around the country, Congress finally freed eighteen prisoners; the other two had died while in detention.[63]

- In April of 1778 Stephen Howell was fined fifty-two pounds and ten shillings for failing to serve in the militia or hire a substitute; upon refusing to pay the fine he was sent to jail. The minutes of the New Garden Monthly Meeting of Friends:

And being conducted there when he entered the prison
he felt such sweetness of mind as encouraged him to
persevere on in suffering for the testimony of a good
conscience. He was kept close prisoner upwards of three
months and favoured to bear his confinement with a
good degree of patience and resignation.[64]

The local officials, impressed with Howell's demeanor, eventually released him "without any demand for fees or otherwise."

- In July of 1780 the New York state "Commissioners for detecting and defeating Conspiracies" detained three Shaker
farmers who were driving sheep from their farms in New
Lebanon to the Shaker community in Niskeyuna, north of
Albany. The sheep, they feared, might be intended for the
enemy. When the Shakers proclaimed a "determined Resolution never to take up arms and to dissuade others from doing
the same," they were imprisoned, accused of being "highly
pernicious and of destructive tendency to the Freedom and
Independence of the United States of America." Later that
month six more Shakers were seized, including Mother Ann,
their spiritual leader. Charged with trying "to influence other
persons against taking up arms," the Shakers had to plead
guilty, since that was precisely what they were trying to do.
The authorities then sent Mother Ann to New York City
"for the purpose of being removed within the Enemy's
Lines." The British General Howe, of course, had no interest
in receiving this strange woman who would try to convince
his own soldiers not to fight, and Mother Ann wound up in
the Poughkeepsie jail, where she languished for several
months. Finally, in December, she was set free after posting
a bond of £200 and being told not to preach "any Matter or
Things inconsistent with the Peace and Safety of this the
United States."[65]

- On September 7, 1777, the war board moved over 200 prisoners into the Moravians' Family House at Bethlehem, Pennsylvania, and less than two weeks later the director general of
military hospitals commandeered the house of the Single
Brethren. Since the Moravians had "such fine large buildings," and since they appeared to live together "like one big
family," Revolutionary leaders reasoned that the displaced
people could squeeze in with neighboring communities. The

Moravians, of course, never gave their assent, but neither could they offer any resistance, for they were truly "a defenseless people." For nine months their once-sacred community became "a sewer of impurities," not just spiritually but physically: many of the Moravians died of the "camp fever" which spread from the hospital and prison.[66]

• In May of 1778 Andrew Giering, a Moravian shoemaker and farmer, was imprisoned because he had failed to take the oath. Although none of the other brethren from Emmaus had taken it either, Giering was singled out because of a private quarrel with John Wetzel, a former church member who had become a county official. Giering appealed his case, but his appeal was denied "unless he would take the test." Finally, in August, Giering wrote to the court:

> Sir,
>   I had great Scruples to take the prescribed Test & was resolved rather to suffer any Thing than to act against my Conscience and have been now 11 Weeks a Prisoner on that Account; I have made an Application to the Chief Judge, but I find I cannot be set free without taking the Test and as my poor Family is in great Distress by the Harvest Time & Fright of the Country on Account of the Indians; I am resolved rather to take the Test than to be longer separated from them. God knows my Heart & Circumstances & will in Mercy pardon me, if I do wrong & give Offence to any tender Conscience.

Each individual who was intimidated by the Revolutionary authorities had a choice to make—to acquiesce or resist, to obey a government which waged war or stay true to personal beliefs—and the choice was rarely easy. Stephen Howell, without a family to support, bore his confinement in jail with a "sweetness of mind," but Andrew Giering, with a wife and children, struggled. Did he act correctly in succumbing to the authorities? John Ettwein, a Moravian leader, had hoped that he would not cave in. He wrote to Giering during his imprisonment:

> I have been told that a certain man has said, if he could only persuade you to do it, the others would soon be attended to. For this

reason I sincerely trust you will not take the lead in this and thus
burden others with something, even though your own heart
might permit you to give way.

Yet how could Giering feel at peace with himself if he left his family
in distress? It was a difficult decision indeed, very similar to that
faced by thousands of other good men who wished only to do right
by their families, their neighbors, their churches, their country, and,
most of all, their Lord. Brother Ettwein, despite his own wishes,
knew that Giering had to decide for himself: "I leave it to your
heart to decide and trust the dear Saviour will make quite plain to
you the course which He would have you take."[67]

    When to comply and when to resist—this fundamental question
had to be faced not only by individuals but by communities. Most
of the pacifistic sects experienced internal dissension over where to
draw the line. In 1780 the Dunker annual meeting of Conestoga
forbade payment of "the substitute money," which contributed directly to war. Several members, under the threat of imprisonment,
chose not to follow this directive, and in 1781 the annual meeting
adjusted its policy accordingly: "in case a brother or his son should
be drafted . . . and he could buy himself or his son from it, such
would not be deemed so sinful, yet it should not be given voluntarily, without compulsion."[68] While some congregations wavered,
others held firm, refusing to adjust their expectations that their members not bear false witness or give aid to the war. In 1777, when
Congress levied a special tax of three pounds and ten shillings in
Continental currency, Christian Funk, a Mennonite bishop, argued
vehemently but unsuccessfully that the tax should be paid:

    [M]y fellow ministers were unanimously of the opinion, that
    we should not pay this tax to the government, considering it
    rebellious and hostile to the king; but I gave it as my opinion
    that we ought to pay it, because we had taken the money issued
    under the authority of congress, and paid our debts with it. . . .
    Were Christ here, he would say, Give unto *congress* that which
    belongs to congress, and to God what is God's.[69]

Another minister, Andrew Zigler, offered a terse response: "I would as soon go into war as pay the £3 10s." Funk, after losing the debate, was removed from the fellowship and forbidden to preach; even so, he continued to minister to a small group of followers, the Funkites.

The Quakers, despite their emphasis on the "inner truth" of each individual, insisted that members hold true to the pacifistic beliefs of the community as a whole—and those who did not were told they were no longer Friends. In 1776 the Philadelphia yearly meeting pronounced:

> It is our judgment that such who make religious profession with us, and do either openly or by connivance, pay any fine, penalty, or tax, in lieu of their personal services for carrying on war . . . do thereby violate our Christian testimony, and by doing so manifest that they are not in religious fellowship with us.[70]

By combing the minutes of Quaker meetings throughout the colonies from 1774 through 1783, Arthur Mekeel discovered that 2,347 members were disciplined for such causes as serving in the army, assisting the war effort, paying fines or taxes, taking an oath in support of the Revolution, or even just watching military exercises or celebrating Independence Day.[71] Nathaniel Scarlet of London Grove, described as an "ancient Quaker," apologized for having "through weakness . . . paid a tax tending to the encouragement of war and commotion," so he was allowed to remain with his meeting. Jeremiah Brown of Calvert confessed that he had received payment from the army when it commandeered his wagon and team, but he declared that his "compliance has not been easy to my mind," and he promised "for the future to give closer attention to the inward principles."[72] But the majority of the accused did not repent, and 1,720 of the errant Friends were actually disowned.[73] Most Quakers stayed true, many deviated, and all felt pressure from opposing directions: the Revolution demanded they join, their Meetings insisted they not. Cold and hungry rebels offered to pay for blankets and food, but the Friends dictated that they accept no money in the service of war. How, in all this, were they to respect their own "inner lights"?

The Moravians were more lenient. Although one of their principles was "not to fight with carnal weapons but with prayer," they still allowed that "a soldier could become and remain a member." Brethren were urged "not to mix in any party quarrels nor act in any way against their conscience," yet "whoever has done so despite this, him we refer to our d. Lord; we do not wish to pass judgment in matters of conscience." Perhaps because the Moravians were less restrictive than the Quakers, they could openly discuss the merits and dangers of all courses they might take. John Ettwein of Bethlehem, Pennsylvania, in his remarkable chronicle of "the Brethren's Conduct and Suffering" during the war, discussed the debates within his community concerning the proper response to the demands of the Revolution. According to Ettwein, when the local authorities started to collect fines from those who refused military service, some members argued that the young men be permitted to drill with the militia. Most, however, maintained that the Brethren should not be "induced by force or trickery or persecution to surrender their honorable freedom in the matter of bearing arms." But refusal to serve resulted in heavy fines, and this triggered another debate: some argued that all fines be paid by community funds, while others maintained that fines should be paid individually. In the end they agreed to raise a voluntary subscription for those who could not afford to pay.

In June of 1777 the Pennsylvania Assembly required that all male, white inhabitants above the age of eighteen, including the Moravians, take an oath:

> I _____ do Swear (or affirm) that I renounce & refuse all Allegiance to George the Third King of Great Britain his Heirs & Successors; and that I will be faithful & bear true Allegiance to the Common Wealth of Pennsylvania as a free & independent State.

The Moravians were being asked, point blank, to "mix in party quarrels" and rebel against the established government under which

they had lived and prospered. The vast majority chose not to submit. "The Test Act," claimed one of the brethren, "is a restraint
upon conscience; were I to abjure the King through fear, contrary
to the promptings of my heart, I should suffer from a bad conscience
[and] bear false witness against myself." When the Moravians and
many others failed to step forward to declare their allegiance, the
assembly clamped down. Any white male aged sixteen or over who
appeared "hostile to the freedom and independence of the country"
could be summoned to appear before a Justice to take the oath and,
should he refuse, he was to be imprisoned. Most of the brethren
held firm even in the face of this increased intimidation, yet they
disagreed sharply on whether they "should make some representation to the Assembly" or simply "do nothing in the matter." Rather
than take a vote they trusted God to make their decision for them,
and by a casting of lots they determined that "inaction leads to the
least harmful consequences in such gloomy times and circumstances." Brother Ettwein approved: "It is my duty," he wrote, "to
remain quiet and to evade the issue as long as I may."

In April of 1778 the assembly got tougher yet: failure to take the
oath could result not only in imprisonment but in the loss of citizenship, banishment, and the confiscation of property. On the day
the new law went into effect, nineteen Moravians were arrested and
"led through Bethlehem like sheep by a pack of wolves." Such stern
measures prompted a new debate within the community. Some said
they would submit if compelled to do so rather than "risk their all
and cause their dependents want and danger." Others responded,
"Even should all of you yield, we will not yield though we should
rot in jail." All agreed, however, that it was time to reconsider their
previous policy of inaction—encouraged, no doubt, by the biblical
watchword of the day: "I will also speak of Thy testimony before
kings, and shall not be put to shame." They decided to present their
grievances to the United States Congress. Their petition stated that
"we are by our Principles every where the most obedient Subjects
to all Laws, that do not run against our Conscience." And yet, they
asserted, "We have an awful Impression of all Oaths or Affirmations
and cannot say Yes! & think No! or No! & think Yes!"

Congress referred the brethren back to the Pennsylvania assembly, but the assembly refused to grant them an exemption from the Test Act. The oath of allegiance, it claimed, was "highly necessary to make a plain distinction by means of which to discern our friends from our foes," and one group could not be excluded without "arousing just suspicion and dissatisfaction" from other groups. Yet one year later, with most Moravians and all Quakers and many other useful and productive inhabitants of Pennsylvania still refusing to give ground, the assembly finally rescinded most of the penalties for noncompliance. As of April 1, 1779, those who refused to take the oath were barred from holding public office or serving on juries—and that was all. There would be no more imprisonment or threat of confiscation for the crime of not signing an oath. As much as the government wanted loyalty, it could not afford to lose tens of thousands of hard-working citizens for the lack of their names on a piece of paper. In their own modest way, the Moravians, who had tried to "evade the issue," helped to engineer a very peaceable revolution of their own.[74]

In 1774 the colonial rebels, in defense of liberty and property, had refused to submit to the arbitrary authority of the British Parliament. Only three years later the new state governments harassed, intimidated, and imprisoned people who were highly unlikely to stage the kind of revolt which they themselves had undertaken. It did not take long for the oppressed to become the oppressors. The intrusions upon the civil liberties of religious pacifists in the American Revolution revealed an ironic twist: the rebels who professed to carry the torch of freedom did their best to extinguish it, while those they accused of demonstrating a "destructive tendency" to subvert "freedom and independence" were the ones who kept that torch ablaze.

A Rock and a Hard Place

The American Revolution did not look kindly on those who hesitated. In 1777 seventeen men from Farmington, Connecticut, were jailed for failing to answer a militia call during a raid on nearby Danbury. Unlike the Quakers and other religious pacifists, these men seemed to have acted more from convenience than conscience;

they had probably hoped the war would simply go away. But it did not go away, and in order to procure their freedom they announced that "tho they have not altogether concured in Sentiment heretofore with every Step taken for the preservation of the Liberties of their Country," they were "ready to take up Arms & Step forth for its Relief, being now Convinced of the Justice of the American Cause." The state legislature freed the prisoners, who had learned to accept "that there was no such thing as remaining neuters."[75] Before their imprisonment the reluctant patriots from Farmington, by their inaction, had expressed the sentiments of countless Americans who wanted nothing more than to be left alone. Claiming they "never have in any respect interfered" with the Revolution, they appeared to have been motivated as much by inertia as by politics or philosophy. As James Allen reported from Philadelphia, "Many people who disapprove Independence have no other wish than to remain at peace, & secure in their persons without influencing the minds of others."[76]

But this was not one of the available options. The choice, really, was to join the Revolution or suffer the consequences. In Farmington, as in most communities, the alternative to the Revolution was jail or banishment, but in Morristown, New Jersey, it was the gallows. There, the local court sentenced 105 suspected loyalists to hang, but it reprieved all those who enlisted for the duration of the war. Four prisoners who refused to bend were in fact hanged, while the others chose the army over death. "The love of life prevailed," explained James Moody, a loyalist whose friends had been arrested.[77]

Punishment was not always this harsh, but those who did not willingly embrace American patriotism invariably faced a most unpleasant decision:

> To sign, or not to sign!—That is the question:
> Whether 'twere better for an honest man
> To sign—and so be safe; or to resolve,
> Betide what will, against "associations,"
> And, by retreating, shun them. To fly—I reck
> Not where—and, by that flight, t'escape
> Feathers and tar, and thousand other ills

That Loyalty is heir to: 'tis a consummation
Devoutly to be wished. To fly—to want—
To want?—perchance to starve! Ay, there's the rub!
For, in that chance of want, what ills may come
To patriot rage, when I have left my all,
Must give me pause! There's the respect
That makes us trim, and bow to men we hate.[78]

Most of the disaffected, with nowhere to fly, did in fact bow.

On November 15, 1775, George Washington wrote to Connecticut Governor Jonathan Trumbull:

Why should persons who are preying upon the vitals of their Country be suffered to stalk at large, while we know they will do us every mischief in their power? Would it not be prudence to seize of those Tories who have been, are, and that we know will be active against us?[79]

But how were these Tories to be identified, and under what legal pretext might they be seized? The identification, according to Thomas Paine, was easy: "He that is not a supporter of the Independent states of America . . . is, in the American sense of the word, A TORY."[80] The oaths of allegiance administered by each state turned this definition into law.

Most states, reflecting wartime fever, did not stop with oaths. In Virginia, wishing "health, prosperity, or success" to King George III constituted a crime; in Connecticut, declaring allegiance to the king could lead to a death sentence. In New York, "An Act More Effectually to Punish Adherents of the King" declared that "preaching, teaching, speaking, writing, [or] printing" opinions favorable to the Crown was a capital offense, commutable by a three-year tour on a ship of war. At the close of the war New York set the standard for discriminatory lawmaking: it declared that royalist creditors could not collect debts from Revolutionaries, and it excused any "Assault, Battery, or Trespass" which had been committed "with Intent to further the Common Cause of America."[81]

Even as state and local governments outdid themselves in their efforts to punish enemies of the Revolution, "out-of-doors" citizens continued to act on their own accord. The leading patriots of Bedford County, Virginia, with Colonel Charles Lynch presiding, conducted trials and meted out harsh sentences; typically, a prisoner received thirty-nine lashes, and those who refused to shout "Liberty Forever" were suspended by their thumbs until they did so. These were the first "lynchings," administered from a large walnut tree in Judge Lynch's own yard. As with many latter-day lynchings, government officials knew about the proceedings but did not care to stop them. After the war the Virginia legislature officially exonerated Colonel Lynch and his friends "from all pains, penalties, prosecutions, actions, suits, and damages" that might arise from their having inflicted harm on their "prisoners" without official sanction.[82]

Civil liberties, in the context of the Revolution, were perceived as unnecessary encumbrances to the administration of true justice. Samuel Seabury, a loyalist Anglican cleric from Westchester, New York, described the "trials" conducted by the early revolutionary committees:

> Here, gentlemen, is a court established upon the same principles with the *popish inquisition*. No proofs, no evidence are called for. The committee may judge from *appearances* if they please—for when it shall be made appear to a majority of any committee that the Association is violated, they may proceed to punishment, and *appearances*, you know, are easily *made;* nor is the offender's *presence* necessary. He may be condemned unseen, unheard—without even a possibility of making a defense. No jury is to be impannelled. No check is appointed upon this court;—no appeal from its determination.[83]

Later, after the war had magnified this "inquisition," an anonymous Tory wrote sarcastically:

> The Cry was for Liberty—Lord what a Fuss!
> But pray, how much liberty left they for us?[84]

And Mather Byles, one of the few Congregational ministers who remained loyal to the Crown, commented as he observed a large rebel gathering, "They call me a brainless Tory; but tell me, my young friend, which is better—to be ruled by one tyrant three thousand miles away, or by three thousand tyrants not a mile away?"[85]

Some patriots joined the loyalists in decrying the abuse of civil liberties. One Whig congressman, in arguing against censorship of a loyalist pamphlet, noted that it was "a strange freedom that was confined to one side of a question."[86] David Ramsey, the patriot who wrote a history of the Revolution, regretted that the war "could not be carried on without violating private rights." Although this was "unavoidable," he still felt it weakened the "moral character" of the new nation.[87]

Most patriots, however, were not too troubled by the persecution of their political opponents. Christopher Gadsden of South Carolina stated it succinctly: "The hardships of particulars are not to be considered, when the good of the whole is the object in view." According to George Mason of Virginia,

[E]very member of society is in duty bound to contribute to the safety and good of the whole, and when the subject is of such importance as the liberty and happiness of a country, every inferior consideration, as well as the inconvenience of a few individuals, must give place to it.[88]

Many patriots claimed that Tories were granted too many freedoms, not too few. On August 5, 1779 a writer for the *Pennsylvania Packet* held forth:

Among the many errors America has been guilty of during her contest with Great Britain, few have been greater . . . than her lenity to the Tories. . . . Rouse, America! your danger is great— great from a quarter where you least expect it. The Tories, the Tories will yet be the ruin of you! 'Tis high time they were separated from among you. They are now busy engaged in undermining your liberties. They have a thousand ways of doing it, and they make use of them all. Who were the occasion of this war? The Tories! Who persuaded the tyrant of Britain to prosecute it in a manner before unknown to civilized nations, and shocking even to barbarians? The Tories! Who prevailed on the savages of the wilderness to join the standard of the enemy? The Tories! Who have assisted the Indians in taking the scalp from the aged matron, the blooming fair one, the helpless infant, and the dying hero? The Tories! Who advised and who assisted in burning your towns, ravaging your country, and violating the chastity of your women? The Tories! . . .'Tis time to rid ourselves of these bosom vipers. An immediate separation is necessary. I dread to think of the evils every moment is big with, while a single Tory remains among us. [89]

This inflammatory rhetoric was not unusual. Those who sacrificed for the cause of freedom expressed more antagonism toward the Tories than toward the British. Joseph Hodgkins, the minuteman from Ipswich featured in chapter 2, could not abide the "Cursed Creaters Called Torys" who hindered the patriot soldiers in New York. On July 17, 1776, he wrote to his wife Sarah, "one of them was Tried on winsday Condemed on thusday and Exicuted on friday & I wish Twenty more whare sarved the same."[90] Hodgkins was a good man, a moral man, a religious man—but he did not wish to turn his other cheek, for the Tories were unworthy of Christian charity.

Hodgkins and other patriots felt hatred, and hatred could easily translate into cruelty. In Delaware in 1780 a jury of common citizens—good men, no doubt, like Joseph Hodgkins—concluded that Seagoe Potter, one of the Black Camp tax protestors, had been "seduced by the instigation of the Devil" into opposing the government. The jurors found Potter and seven others guilty of treason and told him,

[I]t is considered by the Court that you, Seagoe Potter, return to the prison from whence you came, from thence you must be drawn to the place of execution. When you come there you must be hanged by the neck but not till you be dead, for you must be cut down alive, then your bowels must be taken out, and burnt before your face, then your head must be severed from your body, and your body divided into four quarters, and these must be at the disposal of the Supreme Authority of the State.[91]

The jury which informed Potter he would be drawn and quartered was not an undisciplined mob but an official body representing the interests of the Revolutionary government. Humiliation with barnyard symbolism—goose feathers or hog's dung—had regressed to archaic forms of torture.

Loyalists behind British lines, strangely enough, often fared no better than those harassed by patriots. Witness, for instance, the fate of Queens County on the western tip of New York's Long Island. The people there had never been too sympathetic to the Revolution: prior to the British occupation, only 12 percent had publicly allied themselves with the rebel cause, while 27 percent had announced their support of the Crown—the remainder had not declared one way or the other in their public actions. In 1774 a countywide meeting repudiated a committee formed by a handful of radicals to enforce the association; the following year the county voted by a four-to-one margin to abstain from the Revolutionary provincial congress. When the British defeated the American army in August of 1776 and took control of Queens County, 1,300 citizens signed a letter of congratulations to the victorious officers while 800 volunteered to serve in a royalist militia.[92]

But the honeymoon between the British army and their American supporters in Queens County did not last long. Lord Rawdon, the officer who gave his tacit approval while his men raped the "fair nymphs" of Staten Island,[93] wrote sardonically, "we should (whenever we get further into the country) give free liberty to the soldiers to ravage it at will, that these infatuated wretches may feel what a calamity war is." Rawdon soon had his way as thousands of British and Hessian troops demanded food, firewood, and horses from the native inhabitants. Having no way of distinguishing between patriots and loyalists, most soldiers blithely assumed that all residents were to be treated as enemies. Although the withdrawal of the most ardent patriots had left the local population even more royalist than ever, that seemed to make little difference to British officers who regarded all Americans as "a Levelling, underbred . . . race of people." William Bamford maintained blindly that "the old Hatred for Kings and the seeds of sedition are so thickly sown against them, that it must be thrash'd out of them." Other officers, more objective and possibly less callous, reported the effects of this attitude: "those poor unhappy wretches who had remained in their habitation through necessity or loyalty were immediately judged . . . to be Rebels," wrote Charles Stuart, "neither their cloathing or property spared, but in the most inhuman and barbarous manner torn from them." And James Robertson later observed: "When I first landed I found in all the farms poultry and cows, and the farms stocked; when I passed sometime afterwards I found nothing alive."[94]

The presence of the British army altered the texture of daily living for the residents of Queens. Whether Whig, Tory, or neutral, the people suffered abuse in a thousand brief encounters—and they were called "damned rebels" if they dared complain. When passing the home of a commanding officer, they were told to dismount their horses and remove their hats. They cut their hay and threshed their grain according to command. They sold whatever livestock, produce, clothing, tools, or horses the British demanded, and they accepted whatever price the British offered. They watched helplessly as soldiers tore down their fences for firewood, setting animals free to trample and graze their crops. This is not what the people had expected. In 1776 loyalists had celebrated the arrival of the British army, assuming the tyranny of the Revolution had come to an end in Queens County, but by 1779 a loyalist officer reported "that the People in general are become indifferent, if not averse, to a Government which in place of the Liberty Prosperity safety and Plenty . . . has established a thorough Despotism." By treating all residents as American rebels, the occupying army made a false assumption come true. "Instead of destroying the Revolution," states historian Joseph Tiedemann, "the British army became one of its agents."[95]

The British army caused enormous disruptions wherever it went. People fled as it approached, fearful of armed confrontation or military rule. The population of New York City dropped from 21,000 to 5,000 when the British took over; Boston went from over 15,000 to 3,500.[96] Thousands of refugees had to find other places to live and some means of employment, while those who remained, like most of the residents of Queens, had to adjust to military occupation. The British, like the Americans, demanded oaths of allegiance, reasoning that anybody who signed would have a vested stake in British victory.

But when the Americans returned, what happened to those who had pledged loyalty to the Crown? After the British departed from Charleston in December of 1782, the state government of South Carolina confiscated the property of inhabitants accused of cooperating with the enemy during the occupation. In 1783, 250 people petitioned the house of representatives to have their property returned. Elizabeth Mitchell, a widow, pleaded that "for many years preceeding his death" her husband had been "a man of very distracted Mind and if he as been Guilty of any Acts to Occasion the displeasure of the Legislature, Such misconduct must have been the result of insanity only." Eleanor Cooper argued that her husband had complied only because "his simplicity and timidity made him a miserable Dupe to the Suggestions & persuasions of more artfull designing and malignant Men." David Bruce, a printer, maintained that his publication of Tom Paine's *Common Sense* had rendered him suspect to the British, and "hoping to avoid persecution" he was "prevailed upon by his fears & the insinuations of Artful Persons" to sign their loyalty oath.[97] Whoever appeared to have sided with the British needed to come up with some semblance of an excuse—and hope the new government would buy it.

Tens of thousands of Americans like David Bruce were willing to bend with the wind. William Greene of South Carolina, a captain in the patriot militia, switched sides when the British took Charleston; he served as a loyalist at King's Mountain, then moved to North Carolina to join with the patriots once again.[98] In New Jersey, as the rebel army retreated in the fall of 1776, the British guaranteed a pardon for all who pledged their allegiance to the king; 3,000 people, including one signer of the Declaration of Independence, took the oath, but after the American victories at Trenton and Princeton, some of these recent converts signed once again with the rebels. Others believed that a pledge made before God should not be broken; rather than perjure themselves before their Lord, they felt forced to honor whichever oath they had signed initially.

The American Revolution had a way of reaching out and grabbing the people who lived through it. With the political climate so highly charged, common folk uncommitted to either side would sometimes get ensnared. In the spring of 1777 Samuel Townsend, confined in the Kingston jail, petitioned for release:

> That ye petitioner some few days ago went from home upon some business and happened to get a little intoxicated in liquor, and upon his return home inadvertantly fell in company upon the road with a person unknown to yr petitioner and discoursing and joking about the Tories passing through there and escaping, this person says to yr petitioner that if he had been with the Wigs, [they] should not have escaped so. . . . To which your petitioner, being merry in liquor, wantonly and in a bantering manner told him that . . . five and twenty Whigs would not beat five and twenty Tories and, joking together, they parted, and yr petitioner thought no more of it. Since, he has been taken up and confined and he supposes on the above joke.
>
> Being conscious to himself of his not committing any crime or of being unfriendly to the American cause worthy of punishment . . . yr petitioner is extremely sorry for what he may have said and hopes his intoxication and looseness of tongue will be forgiven by this honorable convention as it would not have been expressed by him in his sober hours.[99]

A Lost Cause

At the close of the war defeated loyalists faced an uncertain future. Would they suffer any further persecution on account of their beliefs or prior actions? Would they be able to recover lost property? Could they find a place for themselves in the new order, or would they be forced to seek new homes?

Both British and American signatories to the Treaty of Paris, recognizing that the treatment of loyalists was a key issue, encouraged everybody to adopt a "spirit of reconciliation which, on the return of the blessings of peace, should universally prevail." In Article V the treaty stated that all persons "shall have free liberty to go to any part or parts of any of the thirteen United States, and therein to remain twelve months, unmolested in their endeavors to obtain the restitution of such of their estates, rights and properties as may have been confiscated." Article VI also provided:

> That there shall be no future confiscations made, nor any prosecutions commenc'd against any person or persons for, or by reason of the part which he or they may have taken in the present war; and that no person shall, on that account, suffer any future loss or damage, either in his person, liberty or property.[100]

It sounded good, but there was one major hitch: the United States Congress, which signed the treaty, had absolutely no powers of enforcement. All it could do was "earnestly recommend to the several states" that their citizens be granted these rights, and everybody knew that the states had no intention of returning lost property or insuring that people regarded as enemies remain "unmolested."

The Treaty of Paris, as expected, went unheeded. In many communities throughout the country the victorious patriots—some still angry, some coveting land, some just exercising the power now at their command—made it clear that loyalists would find no peace among them. In Danbury, Connecticut, a town meeting concluded that people who had supported the British should stay away "ever hereafter," for they would never be treated "as wholesome Inhabitants of this Town."[101] Stephen Jarvis, a Danbury native, undoubtedly knew he would not be welcomed back home after serving as an officer with the British, but he could not stay away from his fiancée, Amelia Glover:

> In April, 1783, peace was proclaimed. . . . On the 21st May, 1783, I reached my father's house, to the great joy of my aged parents and the rest of my family. . . . I had been absent for seven years without having the least communication with my home. And here I met the Young Lady to whom I was engaged. . . .
> There was then in Danbury a regiment of Dragoons belong-

ing to the American Army and commanded by a Colonel Jeamison. One of his Dragoons requested to speak with the British officer. I went down to the kitchen where he was and he apologised for the liberty he had taken: "For although you see me in this uniform I have a brother in the British Army and for his sake, sir, have come to warn you of the danger to which you are exposed." This gave me no small uneasiness and I began to consider how I should best defend myself. My father in the meantime walked out and went to where the Militia were embodied and in a few moments returned much agitated and said: "For God's sake, son, what will you do? They are certainly coming. What will be the consequence, God only knows."

My intended was also in the house as the mob arrived. I embraced her and desired her with the family to leave the room. . . . [I]n a few moments the house was filled, and for a short time great confusion. . . . I saw many whom I knew, went up to them and offered them my hand. Some shook hands with me. Others again damned me for a damned Tory. Others charged me with cutting out prisoners' tongues. This scene lasted for some time. At last one of them who seemed to be their leader addressed me in these words: "Jarvis, you must leave this town immediately. We won't hurt you now, but if you are seen within thirty miles of this by sundown you must abide the consequences."

I replied that it was impossible. From Danbury I would not go until my marriage with the lady in the next room. . . . "If I cannot remain in peace, give me a suitable time to make that lady my lawful wife and then I will leave you." . . .

[I]t was by some of our friends proposed to my father that the best mode to be adopted to tranquillise the mob was that I should be that evening married. . . . [A] parson was sent for, we retired to a room, and were that evening married. . . .

At daylight . . . my father knocked at my door and told me that Hunt had obtained a warrant for me and that the sheriff was coming to arrest me and to be on guard. As my door was fastened I felt secure, but I was mistaken, the door soon opened and the sheriff entered. My pistols were in my mother's room and I was unarmed. I however sprang from my bed and ordered him to retire or I would blow out his brains. He was so alarmed that in quitting the room he fell from the top to the bottom of the staircase. I then fastened the door more securely and returned to my bed.

In the meantime the sheriff raised a posse and surrounded the house. . . . I rose, dressed myself, raised one of the windows, and bade the posse "good morning." They looked sulky and made me no answer. I threw them a dollar and desired they would spend it drinking the bride's health. Their countenances now began to brighten and when they sent for a bottle of bitters they said I must drink their health first. But how to get the bottle up to me was a question. However, by tying together pocket handkerchiefs, that difficulty was got over and I received the bottle with a glass in a bucket. Nothing would do but the bride must make her appearance at the window also, which she at last did and touched her lips to the glass as we drank their health and then conveyed the bottle in the same way to them; and before they had emptied the bottle they swore I was a damned honest fellow, I had married the finest woman in the country, that my conduct had deserved her, and that they would protect me with their lives. [102]

Warmed by liquor and moved by romance, the crowd had softened, but Stephen Jarvis did not care to be around when the liquor wore off and the romance grew thin. After breakfast he escaped through the back door, with Amelia Glover Jarvis following the next day. The newlyweds would have to find somewhere else to settle and raise a family.

Jarvis's account is special for its fanciful touch, but countless loyalists who desired to see their families met with open hostility. In New York's Dutchess County John Cook returned from the war to his wife and eleven children, only to be greeted by the local committeemen:

You are hereby notified to Depart this County by the first day of September, as you are considered an Enemy to your Country—therefore take your all, and your Family, and follow your Friends to that Country that the King, your Master, has provided for those of your Character; or Else you may expect the Blood of your injured Country will fall on your head. [103]

Most people who were faced with this sort of ultimatum did not wait around to see if the threats were for real. Hastily gathering whatever belongings they could fit in a cart, they scurried to New York, Charleston, or Savannah, bidding farewell to friends, neighbors, and relatives whom they never expected to see again. If they were lucky, they found willing buyers for their land and the property they left behind; if not, or if they had been banished by law, their property was seized, without regard to the Treaty of Paris.

In the ports behind British lines, near chaos prevailed. Thousands of homeless refugees vied with each other for limited shelter, many having to settle for tents or other makeshift accommodations. Those without money or connections had nothing to do but wait as the Board of Associated Loyalists made arrangements for them to be carried away on British ships. Evacuation proceeded quickly and on a massive scale, with over 9,000 leaving Charleston at the end of 1782 and some 29,000 embarking from New York in 1783. Between 1775 and 1785 approximately 80,000–100,000 Americans left the country for political reasons; as a percentage of the overall population, this was five to six times the displacement created by the French Revolution.[104]

Where would they all go? Natives of the British Isles and rich, well-connected Americans chose to relocate in England. Although the new state governments confiscated their estates, the British government reimbursed those who could show proof of what they had lost. American émigrés in England expressed loneliness, and they rarely exercised the power or enjoyed the prestige of former times, but neither did they starve. Having declared their allegiance to the British Crown, they now lived under its protection, often supported by government pensions.

Most émigrés, lacking the resources to establish themselves in England, traveled to other British outposts in North America known only by maps and rumors. The most popular destination for loyalists in the deep South was East Florida, which grew from a population of 4,000 to 17,000 in a single year.[105] Within a few months of their arrival, however, the émigrés learned that Great Britain had ceded East Florida to Spain in the peace settlement. Not wishing to become Spanish subjects, the vast majority decided to move on. About one-third returned to the United States, some creeping back to their former homes, most settling on the frontier or some other location where their prior loyalties would not be known. Many others, including Thomas Brown and Robert Cunningham, sailed for the Bahamas, with a plantation economy based upon slavery. Those who carried their slaves to Jamaica, ironically, wound up protesting the trade policies of the British Parliament, just as their rebel opponents had done. Southern loyalists without slaves and nowhere better to go headed north to Canada, but many did not take well to the cold, and they too petitioned the British government, claiming it was "altogether impossible . . . to clear the ground, and raise the necessaries of life, in a Climate to southern Constitutions inhospitable and Severe."[106] They would prefer, they said, to trade in their homesteads in Canada for a small piece of the Bahamas.

The majority of loyalist émigrés from the North went to Canada. Three-quarters of these arrived in Nova Scotia, which at that time included all the maritime provinces. A few were real pioneers, hard workers in the prime of life, but their numbers also included small children, the elderly, city dwellers, and wealthy gentlemen like Joshua Chandler of Connecticut, who complained that "not one of the Famaly are used to Labour."[107]

In the spring of 1783, as the British evacuated their last stronghold in New York, thousands upon thousands of men, women, and children sailed into Port Roseway, Halifax, and St. John, having been assured by the loyalist press that the soil was good, the fish abundant, and "that Fevers and Agues are unknown."[108] Upon their arrival they discovered that the land had not even been surveyed, much less cleared, causing them to wait idly before receiving their lots. The poor were granted food, clothing, and a spade and an ax for each family, but during the first winter thousands of people who had not yet built their homes crowded together on ships in the harbor, the only available shelter. The soil proved thin, harbors froze in the winter, and Nova Scotia soon became known as "Nova Scarcity." In May of 1784 a British official complained from Halifax that he was hounded by "37,000 people crying for provisions."[109] In 1785, two years after settlement, two-thirds of the Canadian émigrés were still receiving rations from the government.[110] A disgruntled refugee reported back to the States:

> All our golden promises are vanished in smoke. We were taught to believe this place was not barren and foggy as had been represented, but we find it ten times worse. We have nothing but his Majesty's rotten pork and unbaked flour to subsist on. . . . It is the most inhospitable clime that ever mortal set foot on. The winter is of insupportable length and coldness, only a few spots fit to cultivate, and the land is covered with a cold, spongy moss, instead of grass, and the entire country is wrapt in the gloom of perpetual fog.[111]

Some émigrés, like William and Elizabeth Schurman, proved equal to the challenge of settling in this "inhospitable clime"; others, like Filer and Polly Dibblee, did not. William Schurman, a farmer and merchant from New Rochelle, New York, had tried to stay neutral at the outset of the war. His brother Jacob was a loyalist who had signed a protest against the Continental Congress; his wife's relatives were all patriots. When Jacob was harassed and eventually imprisoned, William declared in favor of the loyalists. During the war his first wife Jane died in childbirth, leaving William with three sons and a daughter; by the end of the war his second wife Elizabeth had given birth to two more boys. After the British defeat, William and Elizabeth decided to emigrate to Nova Scotia with their five sons, leaving their only daughter Mary with her mother's relatives.

Elizabeth had hoped to settle in the new town of Shelburne, but William saw greater opportunities on sparsely settled Prince Edward Island. While the Schurmans developed their homestead, William worked out as a logger, cooper, blacksmith, and bridge builder. They suffered adversity, but they quickly bounced back: when their house burned down, they put up a new one; when they lost one of their sons and a small trading boat in a storm, they started building ships of their own. Over the years they raised ten children and accumulated over 7,000 acres of land, two sawmills, one gristmill, a store, and a shipping business. They never returned to New Rochelle, but several of their descendants wound up in the United States, including a great-grandson, Jacob Gould Schurman, who served as the president of Cornell University for twenty-eight years. Expatriation, for the Schurmans, was certainly traumatic, but it was not a dead end.[112]

Filer and Polly Dibblee had lived in Stamford, Connecticut, where Filer, a lawyer and former member of the general assembly, was well known for his Tory leanings. In August of 1776 they fled to Long Island, seeking the protection of the British troops which had just landed. The protection was not good enough, however, for their house was soon plundered by rebels, with Polly and their five children turned "naked into the Streets." They moved to Oyster Bay on the Long Island Sound, but in 1778 rebels crossed the water, plundered the family again, and carried Filer back to Connecticut, where he was imprisoned for six months until exchanged. After two more plunderings the Dibblees were ready to leave the country, departing from New York in 1783. They survived the first winter in a log cabin, but they also went deeply in debt, and Filer, fearing imprisonment, "grew Melancholy, which soon deprived him of his Reason, and for months could not be left by himself." In March of 1784,

> whilst the Family were at Tea, Mr Dibblee walked back and forth in the Room, seemingly much composed: but unobserved he took a Razor from the Closet, threw himself on the bed, drew the Curtains, and cut his own throat.[113]

Three years later Polly Dibblee wrote to her brother from Kingston, New Brunswick:

> Since I wrote you, I have been . . . left destitute of Food and Raiment; and in this dreary Country I know not where to find Relief—for Poverty has expelled Friendship and Charity from the human Heart, and planted in its stead the Law of self-preservation—which scarcely can preserve alive the rustic Hero in this frozen Climate and barren Wilderness—
> You say "that you have received accounts of the great sufferings of the Loyalists for want of Provisions, and I hope that you and your Children have not had the fate to live on Po-

tatoes alone—" I assure you, my dear Billy, that many have been the Days since my arrival in this inhospitable Country, that I should have thought myself and Family truly happy could we have "had Potatoes alone—" but this mighty Boon was denied us—! I could have borne these Burdens of Loyalty with Fortitude had not my poor Children in doleful accents cried, Mama, why don't you help me and give me Bread? [114]

If relocating in the northern wilds was not appealing, neither was the alternative. Loyalists who wished to stay at home, along with those who tried to return, had no choice but to place themselves at the mercy of the patriot majority—"the body of the people"—and nobody knew what kind of retribution the neighbors might extract. Many soon discovered that mob actions did not end with the close of the war:

- One young New Yorker, while trying to return to the home of his parents, found that the patriots had not tired of barnyard amusements: "[H]is head and eyebrows were shaved, tarred and feathered, a hog yoke put on his neck, and a cow bell thereon; upon his head a very high cap of feathers was set, well plum'd with soft tar."[115]

- John Segee, the one-armed son of a loyalist soldier from Long Island, reported in a deposition to the British authorities in New York that he was assaulted by four men who

    flogged him the whole way from North Castle to the White Plains. . . . [T]hey cut his hair . . . gave him between twenty and thirty strokes with his cane and told him to go about his Business and let his Friends on Long Island know that every Rascal of them that attempted to come among them would meet with the same treatment.[116]

- Prosper Brown, upon returning home to New London, Connecticut, complained to officials that he was

    hung up by the neck with his hands tied . . . after which he was taken down, stript, and whipt with a Cat and nine tails in a most inhuman manner and then tarred and feathered and again hung up . . . as a public spec-

tacle where he continued naked about a quarter of an
hour exposed to the shame and huzzas of the most di-
abolic crew that ever existed on earth.[117]

- George Beckwith, who held a civil post with the British, testified from Simsbury, Connecticut:

  [T]the People rose in a mob and beat him cruelly, put
  him in a coal Basket, placed the Basket in a wheelbar-
  row, and wheeled him round the Town. . . . His Father,
  hearing how roughly the Son had been treated, rode
  to Town the succeeding day to reprimand the People;
  they put him in the same Basket, turned his wig round,
  and . . . wheeled him round the Town till they forced
  him to promise never to come there on such a business
  again.[118]

- The *Boston Gazette* reported approvingly what happened to a
loyalist soldier named Triest when he returned to his family:

  [H]aving forfeited the protection of the citizens of
  America, [he] was taken with a hard-spike under his
  crotch, and a halter round his neck, as the *only reward*
  of merit suitable for such traitors, he was hung at the
  mast head of a sloop from eight o'clock in the evening
  until twelve next day; he was then taken down, put in
  irons, and sent in a boat with his family to Badwaduce,
  having first signed a paper not to return on pain of
  death.

  N.B. Ropemakers are desired to reserve some hempen
  cravats, as they will soon be in fashion.[119]

Although many patriots displayed vindictive behavior, communities
which depended upon loyalists to fill an important economic role
tended to show more mercy. In 1774 a New Haven town meeting
invited loyalists who were "of fair character, and will be good and
useful members of society" to come back home. New Haven civic
leaders solicited wealthy Tory merchants from New York who
might want to relocate their businesses.[120] Animosities ran high in
New Haven, which had been troubled during the war by its proximity to the British forces on Long Island, and rancor did not dis-

appear at the end, but any desire for vengeance was subordinated to the interests of economic development.

In South Carolina, which was ravaged by civil war, patriots were sharply divided in their attitudes toward the defeated loyalists: most could not abide the enemy in their midst, but a few favored a policy of reconciliation. Judge Aedanus Burke, himself an ardent patriot, argued that "the experience of all countries has shewn, that where a community splits into a faction, and has recourse to arms, and one finally gets the better; a law to bury in *oblivion* past transactions is absolutely necessary to restore tranquility." Such ideas were not well received by those with personal accounts to settle. Burke wrote that he was warned before holding court "agt. admitting Lawyers to plead for the Tories, and as to myself, that I should be cautious how I adjudged any point in their favor." At some personal risk, Burke disregarded these warnings and endeavored to conduct proper trials. At Ninety-Six, a focal point of the civil war, Aedanus Burke presided over the trial of Matthew Love, accused of participating in "Bloody Bill" Cunningham's massacres. Burke refused to find Love guilty, reasoning that killing during time of war could not be tried as murder. Indeed, Burke was "shocked at the very idea of trying & condemning to death after so singular, so complicated & so suspicious a Revolution."[121]

The spectators at Love's trial, including friends and relatives of the victims, did not take such an enlightened view. Once Burke had left the room, they seized Matthew Love, who was no longer guarded by the court, and hanged him. People whose lives had been torn apart by the fighting could not, or at least would not, lay their bitter feelings to rest so easily. Francis Kinloch, a reasonably objective observer disgusted with both politics and war, complained of "the violent spirit of injustice" which prevailed at the end in South Carolina—"the same cruel joy," he said, that "animates a child to torment some helpless insect."[122]

Patriots who had lost their loved ones in the war found it difficult to forget. One woman from Georgia is said to have shadowed Thomas Brown after he had been taken prisoner, armed with a knife and looking for a chance to get even. Foiled in her attempt at assassination, she had to settle for a verbal assault:

> In the late day of your prosperity, I visited your camp, and on
> my knees supplicated for the life of my son, but you were deaf
> to my entreaties. You hanged him, though a beardless youth,
> before my face. These eyes saw him scalped by the savages
> under your immediate command. . . . When you resume the
> sword, I will go five hundred miles to demand satisfaction at
> the point of it. [123]

Patriots were sometimes willing to forgive—but only up to a point.
Most states enacted laws purporting to pardon past offenses by the
loyalists. The North Carolina general assembly, for instance, passed
"An Act of Pardon and Oblivion" which stated dramatically that
"all manner of treasons, . . . committed or done since the 4th day of
July, 1776, by any persons whatsoever, be pardoned, released and
put in total oblivion."[124] Loyalist officers or people who had left the
state, however, were not to be included in "any persons whatsoever," nor were those whose property had been confiscated, for the
patriots had no desire to return land they had already taken. Also
excluded were "persons guilty of deliberate and wilful murder, robbery, rape or housebreaking"—and that, as David Fanning observed, included nearly everybody who fought on either side.[125]
Vacuous pronouncements of good will meant little while "the violent spirit" ruled people's hearts. Time, and time alone, would heal
the many wounds of the Revolution.

But time did pass. Many of the refugees in Canada, unable or
unwilling to make a go of it there, drifted quietly homeward, one
family at a time, trying not to raise much of a stir. The boom town
of Shelburne, which had boasted a population of 10,000 in 1784,
dwindled to a ghost town of only a few hundred by the early 1800s.
Some emigrants, like William and Elizabeth Schurman, settled elsewhere in Canada, but a significant number—nobody knows how
many—eventually returned to the United States.[126]

When was it safe to come back? That varied from place to place
and from person to person. Martin Gay, a merchant and coppersmith
from Boston, was assured that it was safe to reunite with his family
in 1784, but when he did come home he found "there was so many
informations against me for the wicked speaches I had made" that

he could not "Expose myself at present in the publick Streets."[127]
He stayed a little more than a year as he tried to collect past debts,
but he soon retreated back to Canada; in 1792 he returned to Boston
once again, and this time he was left alone.

Immediately after the war Patrick Cunningham, who had played
a major role in South Carolina's disturbances of 1775, petitioned to
come home, but his request was denied; in 1785, upon petitioning
again, he was permitted to return after paying a fine amounting to
12 percent of his estate. Despite being legally disenfranchised, he
was soon elected to the legislature.

Also in 1785 Philip Barton Key, a loyalist officer from Maryland,
came home to resume his law practice. He was elected to the general
assembly in 1794—while still receiving his British pension. Twelve
years later, having finally renounced the pension, he was elected to
serve in the United States Congress. "Like the prodigal son to his
father," Key said, "I had returned to my country." He had been
"received, forgivin" by people who "knew me from my infancy."
Later, during the War of 1812, Philip's nephew Francis Scott Key
would write "The Star-Spangled Banner." [128]

The harsh treatment of loyalists during the Revolutionary period
was never formally repudiated, but at least some Americans tried
to prevent it from happening again. Freedom of speech, trial by
jury, the right of cross-examination, prohibition against bills of at-
tainder—these and other civil liberties, once denied to people called
Tories, were guaranteed to everyone under the new federal government. American schoolchildren have always been taught that the
Bill of Rights was meant to insure against the tyrannical abuses of
Old World governments, but the new American states had also been
abusive to basic civil liberties. Many of the Revolutionaries, once
the war had ended, recoiled at the consequences of popular fury,
the "tyranny of the majority" they had witnessed firsthand. The
War for Independence had proven that Americans needed protection—not just from kings, but from themselves.

NATIVE AMERICANS

Western Abenakis . . . Iroquois . . . Delaware and Shawnee . . . Cherokees . . . Catawbas . . . Chickasaws, Choctaws, Creeks, and Seminoles

Western Abenakis

In the fall of 1775, as American patriots prepared for their invasion of Quebec, Ethan Allen of the Green Mountain Boys sent a message to Native Americans who lived near the Canadian border:

> I always love Indians and have hunted a great deal with them I know how to shute and ambush just like Indian and want your Warriors to come and see me and help me fight Regulars—You know they stand all along close together Rank and file and my men fight so as Indians do and I want your Warriors to join with me and my Warriors like brothers and ambush the Regulars, if you will I will give you money, blankits Tomehawks Knives and Paint and the like as much as you say. . . . we are obliged to fight but if you our Brother Indians do not fight on either side still we will be Friends and Brothers and you may come and hunt in our woods and pass through our country in the Lake and come to our post and have Rum and be good friends.[1]

Colonel Christopher Greene, traveling through the northern wilderness with Benedict Arnold, Jeremiah Greenman, and other dedicated patriots on their way to Quebec (see chapter 2), also tried to enlist the support of the Indians he met on the way:

I feel myself very happy in meeting with so many of my brethren from the different quarters of the great country, and more
so as I find we meet as friends, and that we are equally concerned in this expedition. . . . We hear the French and Indians
in Canada have sent to us, that the king's troops oppress them
and make them pay a great price for their rum, &c. . . . By the
desire of the French and Indians, our brothers, we have come
to their assistance, with an intent to drive out the king's soldiers; when drove off we will return to our own country, and
leave this to the peaceable enjoyment of its proper inhabitants.[2]

This was a lie. Native Americans and French Catholics were hardly
"brothers" to the Yankees, whom they had been fighting for the
better part of a century. The New Englanders did not brave the
Maine wilderness in order to lower the price of rum in Canada, nor
did they intend to leave the land they hoped to conquer "to the
peaceable enjoyment of its proper inhabitants." The "Bostonians,"
as the local Indians called them, had come for their own reasons:
they wanted to strike a blow at the British, to eliminate enemy
access to the interior of the continent, to gain control of vast
stretches of land. To accomplish this task the American patriots
needed borderland inhabitants to supply them with food and with
fighting men as well. Just in case words were not enough to win
local support, Colonel Greene offered money: a two-dollar bounty
for signing up, and one "Portugese" gold piece for every month
served.

The British also tried to get Native Americans to fight on their
side. At the old mission of St. Francis, the principal town for the
Western Abenakis in southern Canada, residents complained that
redcoated soldiers were "very severe upon them to take up arms,"
refusing to sell them blankets or gunpowder unless they signed on.
An Abenaki chief from the Chaudiere River reported that the British
governor threatened to burn the village of Sartigan if the inhabitants
continued to communicate with rebel scouts.[3]

Historically, the Western Abenakis opposed all English-speaking
Europeans. Their homeland—present-day Vermont, New Hamp-

shire, and southern Quebec—lay between areas of English and French control. Situated on the eastern edge of Lake Champlain's "war road" connecting the Hudson and St. Lawrence rivers, they had become players in a global struggle for power between European rivals. In King William's War (1688–1697), Queen Anne's War (1702–1713), King George's War (1744–1748), and the French and Indian War (1754–1763), the native inhabitants had sided with the French, their trading partners who supplied them with guns, knives, blankets, and rum in exchange for furs. But now, with the French no longer in power, they had to choose between two groups of Englishmen: the regular soldiers who occupied Canada, and their American "children" from New England and New York. In May of 1775, shortly after the outbreak of war, one white settler reported the apparent confusion of the Abenakis:

> There are five or six families of *Indians* hunting at *Androscoggin*, about twenty-five miles north of my house. Several of the women and youngsters were at my house last week; one of them expressed much concern about the times; said their men could not hunt, eat, nor sleep; keep calling together every night; courting, courting, every night, all night. O, strange *Englishmen* kill one another. I think the world is coming to an end.[4]

Some of the Abenakis wound up fighting with the British when the Americans attacked Quebec.[5] Others, siding with the rebels, laid siege to Boston in 1775 and served in a special company of "Indian Rangers" from 1778 to 1781. What could these Native Americans possibly gain by placing their lives in jeopardy on behalf of men who meant them no good?

First and foremost, they gained jobs. The American Revolution, like most wars, was fought primarily by men and boys in need of the minimal recompense offered to soldiers. In 1775, a century and a half after their aboriginal ways had been altered by guns, liquor, and Europeans, the Abenaki Indians were struggling to survive. Before contact with the French and English, they had hunted deer and moose, fished, gathered wild foods from the forest, and culti-

vated corn, beans, and squash; after contact, they became increasingly dependent upon a market economy to obtain knives, guns,
blankets, and rum. They trapped for furs, drifting in and out of
trading posts and missions to peddle their wares. Although they
continued to hunt and fish, they had to compete with white settlers
for access to the forests; although they still planted corn, in times
of war they could not always wait around for the harvest. Under
the circumstances, many Abenaki males of fighting age deemed it
foolish to turn down the offers of money and goods proffered by
British or American recruiting officers.[6]

These Abenaki recruits did not go out of their way to sacrifice
their lives for either Congress or the king. The Western Abenakis
did not have a strong warrior tradition; young males preferred survival to honor at any price. But they played the war for what it
was worth. In 1777 several families left the British post at St. Francis
for the upper Connecticut River, then under American control. General Phillip Schuyler sent $800 to Colonel Timothy Bidel, the local
agent, to "supply them with every necessary they shod. want"—
adding, of course, that "we Expect that they hold themselves in
readiness to give us their aid should it be wanted." The following
year Bidel reported that twenty warriors were in his service, along
with several of their wives and fourteen children. These men saw
no active fighting during this time, but they still expected material
support for themselves and their families. That winter Bidel wrote,
"We have upwards of 30 Families of Indians here, almost naked,
am obliged to furnish them with Provisions, they are ready for any
service when called upon cod they be furnished with Blankets &c."
When government aid finally ran out, the Indians left to go hunting;
they also sent word to their relatives in St. Francis that they would
consider returning to the British if they could be assured of some
support. Unlike the soldiers at Valley Forge, these cold and hungry
people chose not to suffer undue hardship for a cause which was
not their own. The patriots, of course, expressed disappointment at
the "fickle disposition" of their allies.[7]

British General Guy Carleton, in a similar vein, observed that
the Abenakis always preferred the strongest side—defined in economic as well as military terms. Late in 1778 Governor Frederick

Haldimand complained that the Abenakis at St. Francis "are lately become very ungovernable," while the local commander, Lieutenant Wills Croft, wrote that whenever he tried to keep the Indians from going hunting, they "will not pay any attention to it." The problem, Croft explained, was "that when Indians go out hunting there is no preventing their going where they please."[8] Haldimand and Croft were worried that once the Abenakis came in contact with Americans from northern New England, they might be enticed to switch allegiances. Their concern was well founded, for the Abenakis did indeed make themselves available to the highest bidder.

In the eyes of British agents, the native people of northern New England and southern Quebec were notorious "wanderers."[9] Sir William Johnson once urged the Abenakis "to collect your people together on one Village, apply yourselves to your hunting, planting and Trade, and leave off Rambling about through the Country."[10] But this advice went unheeded, for the Abenakis refused to remain under the watchful eyes of Europeans. According to Colonel John Allan, an American agent,

> The very easy conveyance by the Lakes, rivers and Streams so Interspersed in this Country, they can easy take their women children & baggage, where ever their Interest, Curiosity, or caprice may lead them, & their natural propensity for roving is such that you will see families in the course of a year go thro' the greatest part of this extent.[11]

The Abenakis were not totally nomadic, but family bands, the basic units of their social structure, could move about with relative ease, whether to follow game or escape from danger. When invading armies entered their territory, Abenakis would take to the woods and become invisible.[12] With no large towns (other than the mission at St. Francis) which could be plundered or destroyed, these people could weather a war better than most.

Despite their service to both the British and the Americans, few Abenakis lost their lives while fighting in the Revolution. General Jacob Bayley reported to Washington in 1781 that seventeen men were still in his service, but "a much larger number has been here at times but are not steady." The Abenakis, he said, had for the most part been "rambling in the woods." A few had been "servicable as scouts," but that was the extent of their contribution. Bayley summed up the modest contribution of the Western Abenakis: "I do not think they have ever done us any damages."[13]

To navigate through the troubled waters of the Revolution, and to emerge with minimal casualties, was no easy feat. Joseph Louis Gill, an Abenaki chief, gave a masterful performance in the art of wartime survival. The son of two white captives, Gill was born into the Abenakis and rose to a position of prominence by marrying the daughter of a chief. Claiming to resent the heavy-handed pressure of the British at St. Francis, Gill originally sided with the Americans. Perhaps Gill also sought revenge for the deaths of his first wife and at least one child in a raid during the French and Indian War—but the raiders had come from New England, so his animosity could just as easily have been directed towards the Yankees. Possibly, his allegiance was affected by a desire to see his sons educated at Dartmouth College, although one son, Anthony, was sent home in 1777 because "he dont love his books, but loves play and idleness much better."[14] In any case, Joseph Louis Gill spent the first few years of the war drifting back and forth between the upper Connecticut River, under American control, and the village of St. Francis, still held by the British, gathering intelligence for the rebel army. In April of 1779 Congress rewarded Gill with a promotion:

> That a Commission of Major to be dated the 1st May 1779 be granted to Joseph Louis Gill an Indian Chief of the St. Francois Tribe & that all Indians of that Tribe who are willing to enter into the Service of the United States be collected & formed into a Company or Companies under the Command of the said Joseph Louis Gill & receive while in Service the like pay Subsistence & Rations with the officers and Soldiers of the Continental Army.[15]

"Like pay" with the Continental soldiers must have sounded good at the time, but in fact even the whites in 1779 were receiving little or no money for their service. The following year, when the financial support promised by the Americans failed to materialize, Gill moved back to St. Francis and took an oath of allegiance to the Crown, admitting that he "had been a very bad Subject."[16] Captain Alexander Fraser of the British Indian Department promised he would make Gill's son Anthony, whom the Americans had kicked out of college, the grand chief of St. Francis, provided that Gill would use his influence "to unite the Village and conduct them in a loyal and useful manner."[17] To prove his loyalty, however, Joseph would first have to conduct a successful raid against the Americans.

And so it was that Joseph Louis Gill, formerly a major in the Continental Army, led ten warriors into rebel country on the upper Connecticut, where they proceeded to take two prisoners. As the party returned toward St. Francis, however, the man they had gone after, an American officer named Benjamin Whitcomb, somehow managed to escape. The "escape," as it turned out, had been permitted by Gill in return for a promise: if the Americans ever invaded the Indian village at St. Francis, they would not burn it down. The British suspected that Gill might not have acted in good faith, but since he had brought in another prisoner, they were forced to admit that he had conducted a successful raid. The Abenakis who lived in British-held St. Francis were granted government support, while an American officer had promised protection in the event of a future invasion. Joseph Louis Gill, on behalf of his fellow Abenakis, had played both sides against the middle.[18]

But the Western Abenakis did not get off scot-free. At the close of the war Great Britain and the United States drew a boundary line at the forty-fifth parallel—right through the heart of their homeland. Abenaki society, traditionally dependent on travel and communications between the various bands and across the woods and rivers, was now split in two. The Abenakis of the Missisquoi region, whose community straddled the forty-fifth parallel, were particularly affected. Loyalist exiles settled just to the north of the line, while immediately south of the border, Ira and Ethan Allen, who had once invited the Indians to "have Rum and be goods friends," now claimed large tracts of Abenaki land which they hoped to sell for a profit.

The indigenous people, however, had no intention of relinquishing their homeland. In 1784 angry Abenakis ordered the settlers of the town of Swanton to depart, threatening to burn their houses and kill their cattle. One man simply loaded his canoe with corn from a settler's field, claiming it as "rent." The settlers didn't leave, but neither did the Indians; by 1786 they were living side-by-side in a state of tense coexistence. "If any one took possession of their lands," the Indians still huffed, "they would burn and destroy all Misiscouy." As late as 1793 a Yankee settler reported that the Abenakis "were a source of disquietude to the inhabitants, as they uniformly claimed the land as theirs, and often threatened the new comers, especially when they had been taking strong drink."[19]

But the number of settlers multiplied: during the 1790s the white population around Missisquoi increased from 74 to 858.[20] Most of the local Abenakis finally emigrated to the region near St. Francis, where the British government granted them 8,000 acres of land.[21] A few stayed where they were, continuing to live in their small family bands on the edges of white society. But they caused no more trouble as they eked out an existence on the borderlands of the old ways and the new. They hired out as laborers, sold baskets and trinkets, trapped for furs, and tracked the few remaining moose through the woods. This would be the pattern for most Native Americans in the wake of the Revolution: in order to survive, they had either to move away or become invisible. The Western Abenakis, already versed in moving about and keeping a low profile, actually fared better than most.

Iroquois

Traditional Iroquois society, unlike that of the Western Abenakis, was based on war. At the beginning of the sixteenth century, just prior to contact with Europeans, the people of the five Iroquois nations of New York—the Senecas, Cayugas, Onondagas, Oneidas, and Mohawks—lived in large settlements built in defensible positions and fortified with elaborate earthworks and palisades. According to the archaeological evidence from the town of Garoga, over 800 people crowded together for protection in nine longhouses within a fortress which was the size of only two football fields. While women raised corn, beans, and squash in nearby gardens, men journeyed far and wide to hunt and raid. Warriors returned not only with booty but with heads and scalps which they proudly displayed on poles, and with prisoners who were made to endure extreme forms of torture leading in the end to ritualistic cannibalization. Since any warriors who died in these raids had to be avenged, the Iroquois found themselves locked into a cycle of fighting and feuding.

Sometime in the late fifteenth or early sixteenth century, according to Iroquois oral tradition, the Peacemaker Deganawida, along with his disciple Hiawatha, convinced the Iroquois people to cease fighting each other and form the famous League of Five Nations. (In the early eighteenth century the league expanded to include the Tuscaroras, refugees from North Carolina who spoke an Iroquoian language.) Although fighting among the Iroquois ceased, warriors continued their raids on outsiders. With the arrival of the Europeans and the drastic decline in population due to introduced diseases, these raids took on a new significance: the Iroquois adopted prisoners into their society to take the place of lost relatives.

During the seventeenth and eighteenth centuries competition for the fur trade and alliances with warring European nations insured the continuation of warfare as a way of life. The sachems, or civil chiefs, assumed less and less authority, while the warriors assumed more. In 1762 a Seneca war chief pronounced at a conference with Sir William Johnson, the British Superintendent of Indian Affairs:

> The Reason that you do not see many of our Sachems at present here is that the Weather & Roads having been very bad, they were less able than we to travel, & therefore, we the Warriors, were made Choice of to Attend you & transact business; and I beg you will Consider that we are in fact the People of Consequence for Managing Affairs, Our Sachems being generally a parcell of Old People who say Much, but who Mean or Act very little, So that we have both the power & Ability to Settle Matters, & are now determin'd to Answer you honestly, & from our hearts to Declare all Matters fully to you.[22]

On the eve of the Revolutionary War, the Iroquois still had a reputation as a fearsome people. In 1773 Boston radicals pretended to be Mohawk warriors as they dumped tea into the bay. They freely expropriated the *image* of ferocious Indians for their own purposes.[23] Four years later the *reality* of Iroquois warfare would come back to haunt the patriots, who complained bitterly when actual Mohawks, having sided with the British, scalped white Americans.

European powers, pursuing their own interests, had always tried to channel the power of the Iroquois Confederacy, which they believed ruled a vast Indian empire extending well beyond their homeland in New York. In 1677 the English managed to form an alliance with the league, the historic "Covenant Chain." As with all Iroquoian treaties, wampum belts were exchanged to record the agreement so that future generations could be reminded of the bond that had been formed. A century later, two groups of Englishmen would claim to hold the other end of the original Covenant Chain.

In 1768 Sir William Johnson renewed the alliance with the Iroquois as he signed the Treaty of Fort Stanwix, which protected Indian lands by establishing a western boundary to white settlement:

> I do therefore by this Belt in the name of your Father the great King of England . . . renew and confirm the Covenant Chain subsisting between us, strengthening it, and rubbing off any rust which it may have contracted that it may appear bright to all Nations as a proof of our love and Friendship . . . so long as Grass shall grow or waters run.

Again in 1774, speakers for the League of Six Nations assured Johnson of the survival of the Covenant Chain, "which we have kept clean from rust, and held fast in our hands. This makes us remember the words that were told us when it was given, and which we always look upon, if any one offers to disturb that peace, and harmony subsisting between us."[24]

The colonial rebels, as they prepared for battle with Britain, naturally tried to interfere with that "harmony." White Americans, having repeatedly violated the line established by the Treaty of Fort Stanwix, were not popular with frontier Indians, but the rebels still hoped to keep the fierce Iroquois warriors from siding with the British. Although the Revolutionaries, as we have seen, did not usually advocate neutrality, sometimes that was the only realistic goal. "This is a family quarrel between us and Old England," they told the Iroquois in a meeting at Albany during the summer of 1775. "You Indians are not concerned in it. We don't wish you to take up the hatchet against the King's troops. We desire you to remain at home, and not join on either side."[25]

At least for a while, the patriots had their way. A Mohawk chief, Little Abraham, concluded the Albany council by declaring that "the determination of the Six Nations not to take any part; but as it is a family affair, to sit still and see you fight it out."[26] The following summer patriots feted a large contingent of Iroquois at German Flats in the Mohawk Valley in order to prove their good will. "The Consumption of provision and Rum is incredible," complained Philip Schuyler, the American general. "It equals that of an army of three thousand Men; altho' the Indians here are not above twelve hundred, including Men, Women and Children."[27] The Indians ate and drank, then repeated once again that it was in their best interests not to get involved.

John Butler, an agent for the British, tried to counter the American plea for neutrality:

> Your Father the Great King has taken pity on you and is determined not to let the Americans deceive you any longer . . . [T]hey mean to cheat you and should you be so silly as to take their advice and they should conquer the King's Army, their intention is to take all your Lands from you and destroy your people, for they are all mad, foolish, crazy and full of deceit—They told you . . . that they took the Tom Hawk out of your Hands and buried it deep and transplanted the Tree of Peace over it. I therefore now pluck up that Tree, dig up the Tom Hawk, and replace it in your hands with the Edge toward them that you may treat them as Enemies.

But Kayashuta, a Seneca chief, offered a pithy response:

> I now tell you that you are the mad, foolish, crazy and deceitful person—for you think we are fools and advise us to do what is not in our interest. . . . [Y]ou want us to assist you which we cannot do—for suppose the Americans conquer you what would they then say to us. I tell you Brother you are foolish and we will not allow you to pluck up the Tree of Peace nor raise the Hatchet. We are strong and able to do it ourselves when we are hurt. [28]

Most of the Iroquois, however warlike, suspected it was in their own best interests to sit this one out. But that was not easily done, for the pressures to become involved only intensified. At Albany and German Flats the Iroquois tried to get the Americans to recognize Mohawk land claims, but to no avail. Instead, local patriots from the Albany area started harassing the Mohawks who lived nearby; for their own safety, many of the native inhabitants packed up and moved to Canada, where they had no choice but to side with the Crown.

The anti-Indian rhetoric of the Americans, meanwhile, proved unbearable. In 1776 the wording in the Declaration of Independence—"the merciless Indian Savages, whose known rule of warfare, is an undistinguished destruction of all ages, sexes and conditions"—played well to a white audience, but it did not win any friends among Native Americans. Even as the patriots tried to convince the Iroquois to remain neutral, they pushed many into the enemy camp through hostile actions and attitudes. By the spring of 1777 a significant number of Mohawks, Onondagas, Cayugas, and Senecas appeared ready to join with the British.

The patriots did have some friends among the Iroquois. A Yankee missionary named Samuel Kirkland had worked hard to convince his congregation of Oneidas and Tuscaroras to side with the rebels. Having provided not only spiritual but material support for the Indians at his mission for many years, the popular purveyor of Christianity was able to extend his influence to political affairs. A few dissident Oneidas and Tuscaroras opposed Kirkland for refusing to baptize children unless their parents had already been saved, but for the most part these two nations yielded to the influence of their minister. As Seneca and Mohawk warriors contemplated fighting on one side, their counterparts at Kirkland's mission faced the prospect of confronting them in battle.

Pulled simultaneously in opposite directions, the ancient league no longer functioned harmoniously. In January of 1777, just when they needed it the most, the Iroquois extinguished their council fire at Onondaga, the site of the grand council of the Six Nations. Important decisions concerning war and peace would henceforth be made by the separate nations, villages, or individuals.

In 1777 the British finally managed to gain the assistance of a large number of Iroquois warriors. The persuasive arguments and activities of British agents were recorded in two separate accounts coming from Native American perspectives. Mary Jemison, a captive who married a Seneca warrior and lived as an Indian for more than seventy years, told in her autobiography how British speakers boasted

> that the King was rich and powerful, both in money and subjects; that his rum was as plenty as the water in lake Ontario; that his men were as numerous as the sands upon the lake shore; and that the Indians, if they would assist in the war, and persevere in their friendship to the king till it was closed, should never want for money or goods.[29]

British agents also "made a present to each Indian of a suit of clothes, a brass kettle, a gun, and tomahawk, a scalping-knife, a quantity of powder and lead, a piece of gold, and promised a bounty on every scalp that should be brought in." After treatment such as this, the Indians "returned home . . . full of the fire of war, and anxious to encounter their enemies."[30]

A more detailed account of the council with the British was reported by one of the participants, a Seneca warrior. Late in his life Blacksnake, as he came to be called, dictated a vivid narrative of his experiences in the Revolutionary War to another Seneca, Benjamin Williams, who had learned to write some English.[31] According to Blacksnake, when the British sent word that they wished to hold

a convention, "all the chiefs" agreed to attend, as did many others—
"the decision that whosoever wishes to go long they may go young
men and young females may also go if they wishes." The presence
of women at the Iroquois councils was standard procedure, common
to most of the matrilineal societies of the eastern woodlands. Although women rarely spoke in public councils, at least they attended; although they themselves did not hold positions of power,
they helped appoint those who did. Some women, like Molly Brant,
wielded considerable influence in the political sphere.

The large attendance at this council served two functions: it insured that decisions would be made with the full support of the
people, and it provided the opportunity for yet another party at the
expense of white hosts. The Indians would not be disappointed in
their expectations, for the British presented a truly lavish spread:

> [I]mmediately after arrival the officers came to see us to See
> what wanted for to Support the Indians with Provisions and
> with the flood of Rum. they are Some of the . . . warriors made
> use of this indoxicating Drinks, there was several Barrel De-
> livered to us for us to Drinked for the white man told us to
> Drinked as much we want of it all free gratus, and the goods
> if any of us wishes to get for our own use, go and get them,
> for and from our father gaven to you, and for the same the
> above gift, our chiefs began to think that the great Britain
> government is very Rich and Powerfull to his Dominion to
> force things and kind to his Nation, all things a boundantly
> provided for his people and for us too and Seval head of Cattle
> been killed for us to Eat and flour the our female Sect was
> very well please for the Kindness we Receive from our white
> Brithren.

Such generosity, of course, came with strings attached. Blacksnake
recalled a speech made by one of the commissioners:

> I was Send by father of old England to proceed the object
> the greatest important to be communicated with the Red Breth-
> ern. . . . he want you all the Six Nations and others Indians

Nations to turned out and joined with him and gave the American a Dressing and punishment for his Disobedience. . . . our
father will Support you all the Necessarys Such war utensils
gun and powder and leade and Tomahawk and Sharpe Edges
and provisions . . . will be well Supply in all times. . . . Now
here is your father offered you to take his axe and Tomehawk
to hold against American and here is the Bucherknife and Bow-
ieknife that you will also take for to take the American luck
and sculps and our father will pay So much Each one Sculp in
money &c. [32]

Blacksnake, at the time, did not think the people of the Six Nations
would agree to fight for the British, for he remembered "the Promiss
once made with american" to remain neutral. But his was only one
voice among many. Joseph Brant, the influential Mohawk who had
been educated in white schools and who had just returned from
London, spoke of the futility of trying to remain neutral:

Mr. J Brant came forward and Says that the offered is Reason
for all things that the King of great Britain is the father only
If we should Rebel and do nothing for him and Neither for
america do nothing for them, we appeared like a sleeping. . . .
there will be no peace for us any how to Either party if Should
be Down and Sleep we shoul be liable to cut our throat by the
Red coat man or By america. . . . I therefore Say and will Say
take up the offered By the Red coat man. [33]

To this the Seneca warrior Cornplanter, Blacksnake's uncle, replied,

warriour you must all marked and listen what we have to Say
war is war Death is the Death a fight is hard Business. . . . we
are a liable to make mistake moved I therefore full Desirious
to wait a little while for to heard more the consultation between
the two party.

But Joseph Brant, like all who favor war, offered a rebuttal which
was difficult to counter:

Brant than Said to cornplanter you are a very coward man it is not hardly worth while to take Notice what you have said to our people you have showed you cowardness &c. . . . the warriors had great Dail of controversy created amongst themselve Some for Brant and Some for Cornplanter appeared to creat it in two party . . . and at this time our Braved warriors they appeared to be had not like to be called Coward men they began to say we must fight for Some Body that they cannot Beared to be called coward.

Right at this point, the British played their final cards:

the Red coat officers found that Indian warriors are Split and also the female Sect likewise the began to use their influence over the warriors. . . . the Ship was landed at the mouth of Niargary fall or at fort george Brouthe in many Small articles for Suppose for the Indians to Bribe with, and to upset the Indians minde, Delivered them a Small Ginlings Bells and it was curiousity to our femals Eye and the Nois, and orstrich feathers, and the warriors also Never Did see such things. . . . and the British also Brought over what the called . . . ancient Belt of wampum, one of twenty Rows was called the old covenant between the Indians Nations and the whites wither is so or not I cannot tell nothings about it, But it Did appeared to me, By the whole multitude of Indians Believe what he Did said to us, in general Thing. [34]

The rum, the jingling bells, the ostrich feathers, the covenant belt— they all produced the desired effect. And with the advocates of moderation unable to counter the appellation of "coward," the war hawks eventually prevailed: those of the Six Nations who were present at the council agreed at last to side with their hosts.

As the British enlisted the support of the majority of Iroquois, military leaders from the United States abandoned their attempts to encourage neutrality. Instead, they asked for active military assistance from the minority faction, which included many Oneidas and Tuscaroras, as well as a few Onondagas. They tried to wine and dine the Native Americans in grand style, although they could not match the vast array of gifts offered by the British. [35]

Once they had declared their allegiances, Iroquois warriors on both sides were ordered into action. Oneida and Tuscarora men served as scouts in the American defense against Burgoyne's invasion from Canada. Senecas, Cayugas, and Mohawks, meanwhile, were placed in service during the siege of Fort Stanwix, which had fallen into rebel hands. The combined British, Hessian, Canadian, and loyalist forces besieging the fort came to about 650; the Indians matched that number, effectively doubling the strength of the king's army. When the rebels sent reinforcements, John Butler and Sir John Johnson led 70 white men and 400 Iroquois out to ambush them. At first many of the Iroquois held back. They suggested that the leaders of the warring parties hold a council to try to avert bloodshed, but Joseph Brant, knowledgeable in the ways of the whites, told them that was not the way things were done in European-style warfare; once men were in arms, they were bound to fight. Brant went forth with the white rangers, thereby shaming the rest of the Indians into following.

According to Mary Jemison, it was not supposed to happen this way:

> Previous to the battle at Fort Stanwix, the British sent for the Indians to see them come and whip the rebels; and, at the same time stated that they did not wish to have them fight, but wanted to have them just sit down, smoke their pipes, and look on. Our Indians went, to a man; but contrary to their expectation, instead of smoking and looking on, they were obliged to fight for their lives. [36]

And fight they did. On August 6, 1777, Indians led a furious charge on the unsuspecting rebels at a place called Oriskan, where they killed, wounded, or captured the majority of patriot soldiers. Blacksnake described the battle from the standpoint of the victors:

> as we approach to a firghting we had preparate to make one fire and Run amongst them we So, while we Doing it, feels no more to Kill the Beast, and killed most all, the americans army, only a few white man Escape from us . . . there I have Seen the most Dead Bodies all it over that I never Did see,

and never will again I thought at that time the Blood Shed a Stream Running Down on the Decending ground During the afternoon, and yet some living crying for help, But have no mercy on to be spared for them[37]

Although the British claimed to have won the battle at Oriskany, the Indians paid a heavy price. While Butler's rangers and Johnson's loyalists lost only six or seven men, over thirty Seneca warriors perished in one of the bloodiest battles of the American Revolution. Mary Jemison recalled the impact upon the Seneca community:

> Our Indians alone had thirty-six killed, and a great number wounded. Our towns exhibited a scene of real sorrow and distress, when our warriors returned and recounted their misfortunes, and stated the real loss they had sustained in the engagement. The mourning was excessive, and was expressed by the most doleful yells, shrieks, and howlings, and by inimitable gesticulations.[38]

To make matters worse, the opposing force of American rebels that caused such sorrow included about eighty Indians, mostly Oneidas. Iroquois had shed the blood of their brothers; the League of the Six Nations had been torn apart by the white man's war.

Iroquois warriors were no longer observers to the contest, nor incidental participants. Senecas and Oneidas alike suddenly embraced the war as their own and sought revenge for their losses. Rather than adopt any of the prisoners taken at Oriskany into their tribe, the Senecas chose to club them all to death as they ran the gauntlet. A band of warriors raided the Oneida settlement at Oriska, where they burned houses, destroyed crops, and drove away cattle. The Oriska residents countered by plundering the homes of Mohawks who lived within rebel-controlled territory, working side by side with the Tryon County committee of safety. The Mohawks, who had formerly prospered, were reduced to poverty and forced to seek assistance from the British.

In 1778 Seneca, Cayuga, Onondaga, and Mohawk warriors conducted numerous raids on white settlements in the Mohawk and upper Susquehanna valleys. At Wyoming 464 Iroquois Indians, along with a small force of Butler's rangers, routed the patriot militia and killed over 200 men. Rumors of the "massacre" circulated wildly among the Americans: innocent civilians, it was said, had been scalped and mutilated. This was untrue, but the much-maligned Indians, declaring "they would no more be falsely accused," did kill women and children later that year at Cherry Valley. Iroquois warriors complained that prisoners whom they had taken at Wyoming had violated their promise to refrain from further fighting, while four of the Mohawk war chiefs claimed that the patriot "Rables" had raided their own community "when we Indians were gone from our place, and you Burned our Houses, which makes us and our Brothers, the Seneca Indians angrey, so that we destroyed men, women, and Children at Chervalle."[39]

Blacksnake recalled his participation in one of the many raids during 1778, most likely either Wyoming or Cherry Valley:

> I just than took my tomehawk and Strok one and to another and so on Dont minde anything about criing woman and children and men some just Diing some fighting and all Shap there was not many gun fired that fight, and Did not last great while another I Did not know how many I kill, only I kill some many and I have gon By very norrow places to be Kill mysilfe.[40]

Recalling his actions years later, Blacksnake included some expression of humane feelings. He refused to participate in the plunder, he claimed, "because I think bad a Enouth to kill men and Distroyed their villege." He also voiced concern for the children who were left "un take care off." In his narrative, Blacksnake also seemed to struggle with the moral consequences of his behavior at Oriskany:

> I have Killed how many I could not telled for I pay no attention or to Kept it, account of it, its was great many for I never have it at all my Battles to think about Kepting account what ID Killed at one time
> But I have thought of its many that it was great sinfull by the sight of God. Oh I Do think so, it is Bad Enought to Spill

the human Blood But again might Doing in honour for protected our own country and So &c[41]

Were these the musings of a traditional Iroquois warrior? Formerly,
warfare had been much more personal, and all warriors certainly
would have known how many lives they had taken. Even the torture
and cannibalism had more of a human dimension: the prisoners were
expected to uphold their honor by enduring the pain, while those
who ingested parts of their bodies hoped to acquire the strength of
the victims. Now, with killing practiced on a much wider scale,
Blacksnake seemed confused about his role. Yes, he had to admit,
he had terminated the lives of many people, feeling "no more [than]
to Kill the Beast." That might be perceived as wrong—unless, perhaps, it was done to protect his people. In his later life, as he looked
back and pondered his actions, this Seneca warrior was not unlike
Joseph Plumb Martin and James Collins and other white Americans
who could never finally resolve whether killing was right or wrong.

The raids at Wyoming, Cherry Valley, and elsewhere forced
American settlers either to flee their homes or to endanger their
lives by staying. The board of war of the Continental Congress
correctly determined that it was impossible to fight a defensive war
on the frontier, where there would always be "an inadequate Security against the inroads of the Indians."[42] In 1778 they started
planning a major offensive against the Iroquois, and by the following summer over 4,500 soldiers commanded by General John Sullivan prepared to march toward native villages in the heartland of
New York state. At a Fourth of July banquet the officers offered a
special toast: "Civilization or death to all American Savages."[43] With
the Americans directing their offensive exclusively at the Indians,
the British provided little assistance; the outnumbered Iroquois were
left on their own to defend their homes. On the August 29 600
Iroquois warriors tried to stop the invasion at Newtown, but they
were unprepared to face a modern, heavily equipped army. When
cannons launched "bursting balls" in all directions, the Indians,
thinking they had been surrounded, abandoned the battlefield in
haste.[44] For the remainder of the "Sullivan expedition," as it was

called, the Iroquois harassed the invaders with sniper fire but offered no organized resistance.

The business of the American invasion was to destroy not only the homes of the Iroquois but their food stocks as well. Ordered by their officers to leave nothing edible, the troops slashed furiously with swords and sabers at crops ripe for the harvest. In the words of historian Barbara Graymont, this was "a warfare against vegetables."[45] Sergeant Moses Fellows recorded some of the "battles" of the Sullivan expedition:

> Sepr 9th . . . what Corn, Beans, peas, Squashes Potatoes, Inions, turnips, Cabage, Cowcumbers, watermilions, Carrots, parsnips &c. our men and horses Cattle &c could not Eat was Distroyed this Morning Before we march. . . . We totally Distroyed the town and orchard. . . .
>
> 15th at 6 o'clock the whole Army was turned out to destroy the Corn one Regt. from Each Brigade With the rifle men and artilery to guard the army while the Corn was Destroyed. We were from 6 to 2 o'clock Very Bussy until we completed our Work; it is thought we have Destroyed 15,000 Bushels of Corn, Besides Beans, Squashes, Potatoes in abundance. . . . the method we took to Gather it into the Houses Puting wood and Bark with it then set fire to the Houses; thus it was effectually Destroyed. Some we hove into the River.[46]

Another officer, George Grant, noted that the work on September 15 was accomplished "with the greatest cheerfulness," while on September 24 the troops chopped down "1500 Peach Trees, besides Apple Trees and other Fruit Trees."[47] At the conclusion of the expedition, General Sullivan boasted to Congress that

> The number of towns destroyed by this army amounted to 40 besides scattering houses. The quantity of corn destroyed, at a moderate computation, must have amounted to 160,000 bushels, with a vast quantity of vegetables of every kind. Every creek and river has been traced, and the whole country explored in search of Indian settlements, and I am well persuaded that,

except one town situated near the Allegana, about 50 miles from Chinesee there is not a single town left in the country of the Five nations.[48]

The timing of the Sullivan expedition, from the standpoint of the patriots, was perfect. In late August and early September the crops were just ripening, and it was much too late in the season to replant. The following winter turned out to be one of the coldest in history. While Continental soldiers were trapped by the snow and reduced to eating their dogs at Morristown (see chapter 2), the Iroquois Indians had to face the extremes of nature without any food stores from the previous summer. Mary Jemison recalled the impact of the Sullivan expedition on her people:

> Sullivan and his army arrived at Genesee river, where they destroyed every article of the food kind that they could lay their hands on. A part of our corn they burnt, and threw the remainder into the river. They burnt our houses, killed what few cattle and horses they could find, destroyed our fruit trees, and left nothing but the bare soil and timber. . . .
>
> [T]he succeeding winter . . . was the most severe that I have witnessed since my remembrance. The snow fell about five feet deep, and remained so for a long time; and the weather was extremely cold, so much so, indeed, that almost all the game upon which the Indians depended for subsistence perished, and reduced them almost to a state of starvation through that and three or four succeeding years. When the snow melted in the spring, deer were found dead upon the ground in vast numbers; and other animals, of every description, perished from the cold also, and were found dead in multitudes. Many of our people barely escaped with their lives, and some actually died of hunger and freezing.[49]

If the object of the Sullivan expedition was to make the Indians suffer, it was an unqualified success, but if the object was to subdue the warring Iroquois and secure the frontier, it was an unmitigated failure. As one American officer observed, "The nests are destroyed, but the birds are still on the wing."[50] The destruction of their homes and fields made the Senecas, Cayugas, Onondagas, and Mohawks even more dependent on the British, and during the winter of 1779–1780 several thousand Indians hovered around Fort Niagara hoping for some assistance.[51] The Onondagas, keepers of the wampum belts which served as records of past councils and treaties, delivered to the British seven belts they had received from the Americans, one of which they had cut to pieces in anger after their village had been destroyed by the Sullivan expedition. Once they had survived the winter and returned to the warpath, these Indians would not simply be fighting for the Crown—now, they had good reasons of their own to seek revenge against the American patriots.

By July of 1780, 830 Iroquois warriors were once again terrorizing white settlements in the Mohawk Valley. During the summer and fall they managed to kill or capture 330 white Americans, seize and destroy six forts, numerous mills, and over 700 houses and barns, and eradicate great quantities of food, just as their enemies had done the preceding year.[52] They also forced the Oneidas and Tuscaroras who had sided with the Americans either to seek protection at Fort Stanwix or to change sides and move to Niagara. Senecas, who were still angry at Oneidas for fighting against them at Oriskany, and Mohawks, who sought to avenge the plunder of their own villages by fellow Iroquois, set Oneida and Tuscarora settlements on fire. That winter hundreds of homeless refugees erected a make-shift village on the outskirts of Schenectady, where they had to beg first the Congress and then the state of New York for assistance. They also had to endure incessant harassment from American soldiers who, blinded by racism, seemed unable to distinguish between friend and foe. These refugees, in the end, were the only friends the Americans had among the former League of Six Nations; all the rest wound up firmly in the camp of the British.

By 1781, the year Cornwallis surrendered at Yorktown, the Iroquois were still not giving up. At least sixty-four separate parties—small bands of warriors who traveled light but inflicted great carnage—continued to work the frontiers of New York, Pennsylvania, and Ohio. These Indians were angry, and so were their white enemies. As with the civil war in the South at the close of the Revolution, barbarous acts perpetrated by each side inspired a passion for revenge, thereby escalating the conflict. Both Indians and whites scalped their dead opponents, and some of the live ones as well. According to Iroquois beliefs, a scalp served to replace a dead relative, "that he may be once more amongst you."[53] Scalping, for the warriors of European descent, was not supported by any particular tradition or set of beliefs, but it did provide a material expression for vengeance. For whites and Indians alike, scalping and other forms of mutilation reaffirmed the callous spirit necessary to military success. One American officer, Lieutenant William Barton, reported that he and Major Piatt, after killing some Indians, "skinned two of them from their hips down for boot legs."[54] The Indians, meanwhile, resorted to ancient methods of torture—this time, perhaps, for sadistic satisfaction as well as ritualistic purification. Some American soldiers, upon finding the bodies of a scouting party that had been ambushed, reported that they had been "mangled in a most inhuman and barbarous manner having plucked their nails out by the roots, tied them to trees and whipped them with Prickly Ash, whilst the rest threw darts at them, stabbed them with spears, cut out their tongues, and likewise cut off their heads."[55] Although this alleged sequence of events was not observed firsthand, the physical evidence of mutilated bodies certainly gave credence to the notion that this war had turned ugly indeed.

Only because their allies caved in did the Iroquois give up the fight. In July of 1782, 460 warriors embarked for yet another round of raids on the frontier, but they were recalled by Frederick Haldimand, the commanding general for Canada, pending the peace negotiations in Paris. Without British support in the form of arms, ammunition, and provisions, the Indians from New York, however fierce or dedicated, could not hope to hold their own against two and one-half million white Americans.

The Iroquois did not understand how their former allies, on whose behalf they had entered the war, could abandon and betray them at the end. According to the Treaty of Paris, Great Britain relinquished "all claims" and "territorial rights" south of the Great Lakes and east of the Mississippi to the United States. Although the treaty protected, at least nominally, the rights of white loyalists, it made no mention of Native Americans who lived within the territory which was being transferred from one white government to another. When Joseph Brant heard the news, according to Blacksnake, he "begun to sweare and stamp Down and . . . says we are Decieve by the King of the great Britain we are therefore will not stay here another manuit we will go back and we will not give up our lands as British did."[56] The Mohawk chief Kanonraron explained to the commander at Niagara that the people of the Six Nations were the "allies of the King of England, but not his subjects"— indeed, they were "a free People subject to no Power upon Earth." If "it was really true that the English had basely betrayed them by pretending to give up their Country to the Americans Without their Consent," he stated, "it was an act of Cruelty and injustice that Christians *only* were capable of doing."[57]

Kanonraron spoke just as defiantly to the Americans, who now claimed a right to the land the British had abandoned: "We are free, and independent, and at present under no influence. We have hitherto been bound by the Great King but he having broke the chain, and left us to ourselves, we are again free and independent."[58] To which the Americans offered a blunt response: "It is not so. You are a subdued people; you have been overcome in a war."[59] The Americans were correct: the nations which had been defeated were in no position to claim independence or dictate terms. At the Treaty of Fort Stanwix of 1784, Iroquois leaders had no choice but to agree to the provisions suggested by the victors. Representatives from the United States did not take all the Iroquois territory, but they did seize a part of it, and they issued no guarantee that they would not seize more. When the Iroquois delegates who had affixed their names to the treaty returned from Fort Stanwix, they were reprimanded by their people, who refused in council to ratify the agreement. But what did that matter? Leaders from the United States already had a paper in hand.

Many of the Iroquois, suspecting that any hold upon their former territory would be tenuous as best, decided to cast their lot with the British government across the Canadian border. Joseph Brant, cashing in on his many years of service to the Crown, negotiated for a large tract of land just north of Lake Erie on the Grand River; by 1785, 1,843 Native Americans, mostly Iroquois, had settled there.

Since these émigrés included members of each of the Six Nations, they resurrected the league council fire at Grand River. Although they no longer claimed ancestral ties to the land they inhabited, the Canadian Iroquois would not be subjected to the same degree of harassment they had experienced south of the border.

Other Iroquois refused to leave their homeland. According to Blacksnake, "they are not willing to give up their Rights of the Soil while they considerate actualy all belong to them."[60] Although the land of the Mohawks, the easternmost nation, had already been settled by the whites, the rest of Iroquois territory still lay on the frontier. Villages tried to rebuild after the war, but the people would never again become prosperous, let alone powerful. With white settlers pushing west over the following decades, the land base of the Iroquois eroded steadily as one tract after another passed from native hands. And Iroquois culture changed as well. The men, no longer able to make a living by hunting and raiding, had little choice but to farm, and that was women's work: only "squaws and hedghogs are made to scratch the ground," complained an Oneida man.[61] Both men and women lost status and self-esteem as they altered their traditional roles: the warriors were not to be feared, while the "mistresses of the soil" ceased to command the respect they had once held by virtue of providing most of the food for their people. Matrilineal descent, the cornerstone of Iroquois society, was not recognized in the world of the whites. Once heard and respected by the men whom they placed in power, Iroquois women no longer wielded political influence in a society dominated by Euro-American males.

At first glance it would seem that the Iroquois, with a culture based on warfare, might have adapted successfully to the war among the whites—but it didn't work out that way. The League of the Six Nations was torn apart by the American Revolution. During the war, when the nations developed opposing allegiances, the council fire had been extinguished. After the war, when the wounds might have healed, separate fires burned on either side of the Canadian border.

The split among the people was experienced on a local as well as a national level, with individual villages reduced to ashes by civil strife. Prior to the Revolution, the community at Oquaga on the upper Susquehanna had been a "cosmopolitan Indian town," in the words of Sir William Johnson, where Oneidas, Tuscaroras, Cayugas, Mohawks, and even Mahicans and Shawnees managed to live together in peace. The inhabitants, not in the least parochial, had offered refuge to outsiders who were experiencing trouble in other regions. But in the 1770s, as arguments became heated between white patriots and loyalists, Congregational and Anglican missionaries competed for influence and control at Oquaga. Political conflict was played out in religious terms as two groups of whites tugged at the souls of the Indians. Residents split into separate camps, and soon the village was caught in the paths of opposing armies. In 1778 a war party led by Joseph Brant appeared to take control of the area, causing the Americans to burn down Oquaga in order to deprive Brant's party of a base. The Sullivan expedition revisited the village the following year, while in 1780 and 1781 Iroquois warriors, together with Butler's rangers, marched through Oquaga. Situated in the middle of the war zone, Oquaga had ceased to be a haven for the dispossessed. Refugees flocked to Niagara or Schenectady, depending on their allegiances. In 1785 Oquaga, no longer a thriving community, was ceded to New York state.[62]

The American Revolution divided not only nations and communities, but families. Mary Jemison recalled two revealing incidents. Cornplanter, on a raiding campaign in 1780, took a prisoner known variously as John O'Bail or John Abeel. O'Bail, as Jemison called him, was a trader who had once fathered a child with an Indian squaw—and that child was Cornplanter. How would this fierce Seneca warrior treat his absentee father, who had neither nurtured nor supported him, who lived among the enemy, and who was now his captive? Jemison reported Cornplanter's response, as it was relayed directly to her:

"I am your son! you are my father! You are now my prisoner, and subject to the customs of Indian warfare. But you shall not be harmed—you need not fear, I am a warrior. Many are the scalps which I have taken. Many prisoners have I tortured to death. I am your son! I am a warrior. I was anxious to see you, and to greet you in friendship. I went to your cabin, and took you by force. But your life shall be spared. Indians love their friends and their kindred, and treat them with kindness. If now you choose to follow the fortune of your yellow son, and live with our people, I will cherish your old age with plenty of venison, and you shall live easy; but if it is your choice to return to your fields, and live with your white children, I will send a party of my trusty young men to conduct you back to safety. I respect you, my father; you have been friendly to Indians, and they are your friends." Old John chose to return. Cornplanter, as good as his word, ordered an escort to attend him home, which was done with the greatest of care. [63]

Jemison also told the story of two Oneida brothers who met under similar circumstances. One, the conqueror, fought for the British, while the other, the captive, had served as a guide for Sullivan's invading army.

"Brother, you have merited death! The hatchet or the war-club shall finish your career! When I begged of you to follow me in the fortunes of war, you was deaf to my cries—you spurned my entreaties!

"Brother! you have merited death; and shall have your desserts! When the rebels raised their hatchets to fight their good master, you sharpened your knife, you brightened your rifle, and led on our foes to the fields of our fathers! You have merited death, and shall die by our hands! When those rebels had driven us from the fields of our fathers to seek out new homes, it was you who could dare to step forth as their pilot, and conduct them even to the doors of our wigwams, to butcher our children, and to put us to death! No crime can be greater! But, though you have merited death and shall die on this spot, my hands shall not be stained in the blood of a brother. *Who will strike?*"

Little Beard, who was standing by, as soon as the speech was ended, struck the prisoner on the head with his tomahawk, and dispatched him at once. [64]

A father was saved, a brother was not—but why were these people placed in such awkward circumstances? None of this had anything to do with "taxation without representation" or trunks of tea in the Boston Harbor. Patriots disguised as Indians on a cold winter night in 1773 had not entertained the slightest notion that their actions might lead to such torment among the Iroquois people.

Delaware and Shawnee

Between 1742 and 1868 the Lenni Lenape people from New Jersey and Delaware moved first to the Susquehanna Valley in eastern Pennsylvania, then across the Allegheny Mountains to the upper Ohio Valley, then to Indiana, then to Missouri, then to Kansas, and finally to Oklahoma. During the American Revolution the Lenni Lenape were still near the beginning of their westward migration, inhabiting the upper Ohio along with several other Native American nations. The whites called these people and the region they inhabited "Delaware," after the third Lord de la Warr, governor of Jamestown in 1610.

The Shawnee, who neighbored the Delaware at the time, had also moved about. Their prewar history is more difficult to track, but at one point or another they had left some traces in the current states of Florida, Alabama, Georgia, South Carolina, North Carolina, Tennessee, Kentucky, Virginia, West Virginia, Pennsylvania, Ohio, Indiana, and Illinois. They appear to have lived on the upper Ohio, moved away in retreat from the aggressive Iroquois, and then returned.

During much of the seventeenth and eighteenth centuries the Iroquois exerted a powerful influence over the Delaware, the Shawnee, and many of the other Native Americans of the eastern woodlands by repeatedly raiding their settlements. The British, noting the military domination of the Iroquois, assumed that the "empire" of the Six Nations controlled and owned the land, not only in New York but in Pennsylvania, Ohio, western Virginia, and even Kentucky. And since they owned it, they had the power to give it away. In 1768, at Fort Stanwix in New York's Mohawk Valley, British Americans negotiated a treaty with the Six Nations which placed most of the Iroquois land off-limits to white settlement. In return, the Iroquois ceded all rights to the land south and east of the Ohio River—land which was inhabited by other groups of Native Americans, not themselves. Both parties to the treaty were pleased at the outcome: the Iroquois had preserved their own homes, while the whites now had a piece of paper purporting to give them some sort of legal title to land they coveted.

The Delaware, who were forced to move from the ceded Susquehanna, and the Shawnee, who relied on the hunting grounds to the south of the Ohio, were not so pleased. How was it that others could sell the land they used without their consultation? Indeed, how could *anybody* buy or sell the land? Like many Native Americans, they did not share the Europeans' concept of ownership. The missionary John Heckewelder, after scolding an Indian from the Ohio country for grazing horses in his meadow, reported the response he received:

> My friend, it seems you lay claim to the grass my horses have eaten because you had enclosed it with a fence: now tell me, who caused the grass to grow? Can you make the grass grow? . . . [T]he grass which grows out of the earth is common to all.[65]

Differing concepts of ownership, differing patterns of land use, differing cultures—these all would come to a head in the Ohio Valley during the Revolutionary War. As white settlers pushed west across the mountains, the Delaware, Shawnee, and other Native Americans who inhabited the region had to figure out how best to respond. Should they fight the whites or try to get along? Should they maintain their traditional culture or adapt to the ways of the newcomers? Each community debated these issues, and the people were not all of one mind. Nativists versus accommodationists, warriors versus civil chiefs, young people versus old—internal divisions threatened to tear the people apart as Native Americans had to decide which side, if any, they should support in the fight between the king and his rebellious subjects.

The British and the colonial rebels vied for the allegiance of the

Ohio Valley Indians, much as they did with the Iroquois and the
Western Abenakis. In the summer of 1775, after the outbreak of
fighting in Massachusetts, the British official Lord Dunmore tried
to turn White Eyes, a chief of the Delaware, against the rebels:

> you may rest satisfied that our foolish young Men shall never
> be permited to have your Lands but on the Contrary the Great
> King will Protect you and Preserve you in the Possession of
> them Our Young People in this country have been very foolish
> and done many Imprudent things for which they must soon be
> sorry and of which I make no doubt they have Acquanited you
> but I must desire you not to Listen to them as they wou'd be
> willing that you shou'd Act Equally foolish with themselves
> but rather Let what you hear pass in at one Ear and out of the
> other so that it may make no Impression on your Heart.[66]

The rebels, of course, told a different story. Later that fall representatives from the Delaware, Shawnee, and other western nations
met at Fort Pitt with a group of "Big Knives" (as they called the
colonists) who claimed to carry a message from "our great United
Council of Wise men now Assembled at Philadelphia." The Big
Knives made many speeches intended to persuade or intimidate the
Indians:

> *Brothers* you have no doubt heard of the dispute between us and
> some of our Fathers evil Counsellors beyond the Great Water, in
> this dispute your Interest is Involved with ours . . . the thirteen
> great Colonies of this Extensive Continent, Comprehending in
> the whole, at least One Million of Fighting Men, are now so
> firmly United and Inseparably bound together by one lasting
> Chain of Freindship, that we are no more to be Considered as
> Distinct Nations, but as one great and Strong Man, who if Mo-
> lested in any one of his Members, will not fail to Exert the Com-
> bined force of his whole Body to Punish the Offender. . . . If any
> other Nation or Nations shou'd take up the Tomhawk and En-
> deavour to Strike us it wou'd be Kind in you to give us Notice
> and Use your best Endeavours to Prevent the Stroke, for it must
> be your Interest to live in Peace and Amity with such near and

Powerfull Neighbours and this is all we Ask *A String to Each Nation.*[67]

This message seems to have been well received by several of the Indian delegates. Cornstalk, a Shawnee chief, promised to "live in peace," while White Eyes, a Delaware chief, stated:

> I am much rejoiced at what I have heard from our brother the bigknive. . . . I now for my part promise that if any of my foolish Young Men shou'd do any harm to your People that we will punish them as they deserve without delay as I wou'd wish to Comply with the dictates of the Christian Relegion and Commands of our Saviour whose hands were Nailed to the Cross and sides Peirced for our Sins as far as I am Capable in my Present Dark State A Belt.[68]

White Eyes, apparently converted, told the white Americans what they wanted to hear: he would pay homage to Christ and exert his influence to bring an end to frontier raids. Certainly, the Indians present at Fort Pitt in the fall of 1775 showed no signs of aiding the British.

Cornstalk and White Eyes, however, did not speak for all their people. Many Shawnee and Delaware warriors—"bad people" and "foolish young men," according to the chiefs—were not so keen on burying the hatchet with the white intruders. Nor were Native Americans to the west, who traded with the British at Detroit. The Miami, Wyandot, Chippewa, Ottawa, and Kickapoo all tried to convince the Shawnee and Delaware to join the fight against the Americans. So too did their immediate neighbors the Mingo, who still smarted over the cold-blooded murder of several of their people by Virginians in 1774.[69] Captain William Russell, an American, stated that

> The Corn Stalk . . . assured me, that the Mingoes behave in a very unbecoming manner Frequently upbraiding the Shawnees, in cowardly making the Peace; & call them big knife People; that the Corn Stalk can't well account for their Intentions. if this be true, and a rupture between England and America has

really commenced, we shall certainly Receive Trouble at the hands of those People in a short Time.[70]

And trouble there was. By October of 1776 raiding Mingo warriors had caused the whites in Kentucky to abandon all but three of their settlements. In February of 1777 the Mingos were joined by several Shawnee and Delaware, and together these Indians besieged the major towns of Wheeling and Boonesborough, running off horses and burning supplies. In March the executive council of Virginia resolved to raise a force of 300 men "to punish the Indians" by destroying a major Mingo town in central Ohio.

Just when armed confrontation seemed imminent, Colonel George Morgan, a United States Indian Agent, spoke out forcefully in opposition to the expedition:

> We could very easily chastise these People, was it not for . . . our desire to avoid offending other Nations; for to distinguish between a Party of one & the other in case of meeting in the Woods would be impossible in many cases; and a single mistake might be fatal. . . . I believe it is more necessary to restrain our own people & promote good order among them than to think of awing the different Nations by expeditions.[71]

Morgan, known by the Indians as Taimenend, the affable one, was a rare breed on the frontier: a white man who stood up for Native American interests. He insisted that the Indians be treated "in all respects with Justice, Humanity & Hospitality," while he worried that the settlers were likely "to massacre our known friends at their hunting camps as well as Messengers on Business to me." The real threat to peace on the frontier, Morgan maintained, came not from the native inhabitants but from white men who were driven by an "ardent desire for an Indian War, on account of the fine Lands those poor people possess."[72]

At least for the moment, George Morgan's arguments prevailed. Virginia Governor Patrick Henry, fearful of alienating the Shawnee and Delaware who had been friendly to the Americans, issued instructions to "support protect defend & cherish them in every Respect to the utmost. . . . Any Injury done them, is done to us while they are faithfull." The Continental Congress, concurring with Morgan and Henry, requested that Virginia abandon the march against the Mingo. On April 12 Governor Henry wrote a simple and direct letter to the commander: "SIR—The Expedition against Pluggys Town is to be laid aside by a Resolution of Congress."[73]

But frontier settlers, like the young Indian warriors, did not always abide by the policies of their "chiefs." Without government sanction, they commenced a series of raids against the Indians of the upper Ohio, and they even fired on Native Americans attending a treaty at Fort Pitt. As hostilities escalated, Brigadier General Edward Hand, recently appointed to take command in the region, proposed to lead an expedition of 2,000 men against the Mingos. Rumors circulated among the Indians "that an American general had arrived in Pittsburg, who denied quarter to any Indian, whether friend or foe, being resolved to kill them all."[74] George Morgan's pacifistic policies no longer prevailed; indeed, his continued advocacy of the Indians' interests were regarded with some suspicion. Late in 1777 Morgan was accused of being a Tory and placed under arrest.[75]

In the fall of 1777, upon hearing of Hand's new plan for an assault on the Indians of the upper Ohio, two Shawnee—Redhawk and Petella—paid a visit to Captain Matthew Arbuckle at Fort Randolph "with strong protestations of friendship . . . to know the reason of it."[76] Arbuckle, sensing that the Shawnee were becoming alienated from the Americans, decided to hold the men as hostages to insure the good behavior of their people. When Cornstalk, the moderate Shawnee chief, came to inquire why the two men were detained, he too was seized—and when Cornstalk's son, Elinipsico, arrived "to see his father and to know if he was alive," he was captured as well. While the four Shawnee were held in captivity, a white hunting party on the other side of the river was ambushed by Indians, and one man was killed. Although the Indians in question turned out to be Mingos, the enraged friends of the victim vented their anger on the most accessible targets: the four Shawnee prisoners. Captain John Stuart, stationed at Fort Randolph, described what happened:

the canoe was scarsely landed in the creek when the cry was raised let us kill the Indians in the fort and every man with his gun in his hand came up the bank pale as death with rage. . . . [Elinipsico] trembled exceedingly; his father incouraged him told him not to be afraid, for the great Spirit above had sent him there to be killed. the men advanced to the door, the Corn Stalk arose and met them, seven or eight bullets were fired into him, and his son was shot dead as he sat upon a stool. Redhawk made an attempt to go up the chimney but was shot down, the other Indian was shamefully mangled. I grieved to see him so long a dying. Thus died the great Cornstalk warrior who from personal appearance and many brave acts was undoubtedly a Hero. I have no doubt if he had been spared but he would have been friendly to the Americans.[77]

Governor Patrick Henry insisted on bringing the alleged murderers to trial, but in the court of Rockbridge County no witnesses were willing to testify and the suspects were acquitted.

With the murder of Cornstalk, who had tried so hard to avoid war, most of the Shawnee joined the British and the western tribes to fight against white Americans. In March of 1778 a number of Shawnee warriors accepted the war belt from Governor Hamilton, and the following month they brought in several prisoners to Detroit, including Daniel Boone. Over the next several years they proudly displayed the scalps they had taken to British officers who, like the Americans, paid bounties for these remnants of fallen enemies. By the end of the war the American General Daniel Brodhead called the Shawnee "the most hostile of any Savage Tribe."[78]

White Americans took to the warpath as well. In February of 1778 Patrick Henry agreed to increase the military support for frontier settlements, and in June, when a group of "young men" proposed "a scheme . . . of embodying themselves into a Company or two and marching at their own Expence into the Indian Country & there annoy the Enemy," Henry responded: "I greatly approve the Spirit of the young men who are to go to the Enemys Country. . . . It is bold of the men & commendable."[79]

The voices of moderation on both sides had been silenced. With no more opposition from within, American war hawks were free to do as they pleased. As the Virginia militia mobilized to raid the Ohio valley, Edward Hand finally got to lead his expedition from Fort Pitt. Having learned of a British cache of military stores on the Cuyahoga River, Hand set out with 500 militiamen to seize them. The spring thaw prevented Hand's troops from reaching their target, but as they returned they did run into one Delaware man and several women and children. After killing the man and one of the women, they learned of another party nearby. Hand reported dryly: "I detachd a party to Secure them, they turn'd out to be 4 Women & a Boy, of these one Woman only was Saved."[80]

Despite the murder of Cornstalk and the Shawnee hostages, and notwithstanding the barbarity of Hand's "squaw campaign" (as it came to be called) against the Delaware, Chief White Eyes remained loyal to the Americans. After Cornstalk's murder, he invited any of the Shawnee who sought refuge from the fighting to live at the Delaware town of Coshocton, where they might become "the same people" as their hosts. Even as most of the Shawnee migrated westward to join the British and their allies, seventeen families accepted the offer and moved to Coshocton, hoping to avoid the ravages of war.

But the people of Coshocton felt increasingly threatened by the pro-British Indians, who at this point were far more numerous than those who desired peace. White Eyes wrote almost pathetically to Morgan: "I spoke once more to the Wiondots but am sorry that I must inform you that they will not listen to me any more which they now have told me very plain." The "Tomhawk," he said, was being handed to all the Indians, and "whosoever would not take the Tomhawk he should be whipped." White Eyes then pleaded for help:

I am weak and am in need of your assistance. If you do not assist me now as soon as possible then I shall be ruined and destroyed. . . . I am blamed by the Nations that I betray them, therefore keep all what I tell you secret. . . . You can easily see that I am frightened and with my people in great danger, therefore consider and remember me for I rely now entirely on your help and assistance.[81]

Hoping that the Americans might provide them with some measure of security, three Delaware chiefs—White Eyes from the Turtle division, Hopocan (or "tobacco pipe") of the Wolf division, and Gelelemend (commonly known as Killbuck) of the Turkey division—ventured to Fort Pitt in 1778 for yet another council. The subsequent treaty spoke to the needs of both the Delaware and the patriots. The Delaware agreed to let an American army march through their country to fight the hostile tribes to the west, and they further agreed to feed the soldiers and supply them with guides. In return, the Americans agreed to build a fort to protect Coshocton and "to guarantee to the aforesaid nation of Delawares, and their heirs, all their territorial rights in the fullest and most ample manner." At the insistence of White Eyes, the final treaty also contained a most remarkable clause:

> And it is further agreed on between the contracting parties should it for the future be found conducive for the mutual interest of both parties to invite any other tribes who have been friends to the interest of the United States, to join the present confederation, and to form a state whereof the Delaware nation shall be the head, and have a representation in Congress: Provided nothing contained in this article to be considered as conclusive until it meets with the approbation of Congress. [82]

American Indians, led by the Delaware, forming a fourteenth state? The idea certainly appealed to White Eyes. Frequently subdued by Iroquois warriors, the Delaware were referred to as "women" by their neighbors from New York. Now, with new and powerful allies, the Delaware might be in a position to reverse that relationship. When a delegation from the Senecas tried to convince the Delaware to join the British, White Eyes told them he would stand by the Americans. With dramatic flare, he declared independence from Iroquois domination:

> You say you had conquered me that you had cut off my legs—had put a petticoat on me, giving me a hoe and cornpounder

in my hands, saying, "now woman! your business henceforward shall be, to plant and hoe corn, and pound the same for bread, for us men and warriors!" Look at my legs! if, as you say, you had cut them off, they have grown again to their proper size!— the petticoat I have thrown away, and have put on my proper dress!—the corn hoe and pounder I have exchanged for these fire arms, and I declare that I am a man. [83]

White Eyes' loyalty to white Americans, which appeared at times to border on the obsequious, can best be understood in a broader context: by siding with the "Big Knives," whom he perceived as mightier and more numerous than both the Iroquois and the British, the Delaware would never again be called women.

But the Fort Pitt treaty did not work out as the Delaware had expected, for Congress never seriously considered the notion of setting up a separate Indian state. This is not surprising to us, but it might have been to the Delaware; it is certainly possible that the translators neglected to include all the qualifying phrases. There was also a misunderstanding on the issue of building a fort. On paper the treaty promised to provide "for the better security of the old men, women, and children . . . whilst their warriors are engaged against the common enemy," but the Indians present, who had no recall of these last nine words, were truly amazed when the whites informed them that Delaware warriors were now obligated to join the army. Perhaps this was the fault of the translators, or perhaps, as George Morgan suggested, the whites had distributed so much liquor that the Indian delegates were not in their full senses during the proceedings: "There never was a Conference with the Indians so improperly or villainously conducted," Morgan wrote. Killbuck, the Turkey chief, later commented, "I have now looked over the Articles of the Treaty again & find they are wrote down false, & as I did not understand the Interpreter what he spoke I could not contradict his Interpretation." [84]

On November 10, 1778, less than two months after the signing of the treaty at Fort Pitt, the residents at Coshocton received some bad news: White Eyes, their chief, had just died of smallpox. According to George Morgan, who had been acquitted of being a Tory and was back on the job, this was a lie. Six years later he wrote a confidential letter to Congress:

> [White Eyes] was treacherously put to death, at the moment of his greatest Exertions to serve the United States in whose Service he held the Commission of a Colonel. I have carefully concealed and shall continue to conceal from young White Eyes the manner of his Father's death, which I have never mentioned to any one but Mr. Thomson, the Secretary, and 2 or 3 members of Congress. [85]

Today, that is all we know about the affair. Most likely White Eyes, like Cornstalk, had been murdered by Indian-hating whites who failed to distinguish friend from foe, although perhaps he was killed after calling the Americans to task for deceiving him. In any case, United States officials really had no choice but to cover up the murder. Had the Delaware learned the truth, many would undoubtedly have bolted to the other side.

Killbuck and many others bought the lie. Although they mourned the loss of White Eyes and expressed discontent with the manner and terms of the previous treaty, they continued to place their hopes in the Americans. In 1779 Killbuck led a delegation of fourteen Delaware to Philadelphia, where they were entertained at the home of George Morgan. They paid a visit to George Washington, who promised them nothing in particular—but having been betrayed by the translators at Fort Pitt the year before, the Indians requested a written transcript this time. Then they approached Congress with demands for the clothing and trade goods which had been promised them in each of the preceding four years. But Congress, unable at the time to clothe its own army, could spare nothing for the Delaware. Besides, the congressmen argued, how could whites be assured of the friendship of these Indians when many of their people had joined the other side? To this, a Delaware spokesman replied,

> We are told that there are in several of your states People you call Tories—but as that does not make those particular States your Enemies, so we hope you will make a proper Distinction

between our Nation and Individuals—who, on Account of
their Conduct have become Outcasts from it and whom we
will never receive again as Friends until you agree to receive
them as your Friends or you obtain full satisfaction for the
Injuries they have done you.[86]

To prove their trust and friendship, the Delaware left three of their
youths behind to be educated at Princeton in the ways of the whites:
White Eyes' son George, Killbuck's son John, and Killbuck's half-
brother Thomas.[87]

When the delegation came home empty from Philadelphia, Killbuck began to lose his influence. Other Indians, he complained,
"mock, and make all the Game of me they Can."[88] When the Americans, suffering from a lack of supplies, abandoned the fort that was
supposed to protect the friendly Delaware, Captain Pipe (Hopocan)
of the Wolf division convinced a majority of the council at Coshocton to join with the British, who seemed to offer greater opportunities for trade and prosperity. White Eyes and Killbuck had
looked to the Americans to provide the Delaware with wealth,
power, and prestige; now that the Big Knives could not even come
through with a few blankets, Pipe could argue convincingly that
they were no longer of any use. The logic was so clear that even
Daniel Brodhead, the American general, had to agree: "I conceive
they will be compelled to make terms with the British *or perish*,"
he wrote to Washington.[89]

The Coshocton council, having turned militantly anti-American,
did what it could "to blacken the Character of Killbuck" because
he had become "a Friend to the States."[90] Rejected by the majority
of their people, Killbuck and a few others who had become identified with the Big Knives had no choice but to seek refuge at Fort
Pitt. But western Pennsylvania was no haven for Indian refugees,
and the friendly Delaware were continually harassed by local whites
who assumed that all Indians were to be treated as enemies. While
Congress was wasting its time by "bestowing commissions on savages," one prominent settler complained, "the state of Pennsylvania
judged right by offering a bounty for their scalps."[91]

Now that the once-friendly town of Coshocton had changed allegiances, the Americans decided to destroy it. In the spring of 1781 Brodhead and 300 soldiers—guided by Killbuck and his fellow refugees—marched into the heart of Delaware territory. They found Coshocton defended by only fifteen warriors, whom they proceeded to kill and scalp. An American soldier, Martin Wetzel, murdered an Indian envoy who had been promised safe conduct to discuss terms of peace.[92] Militiamen fired on neutral Christians from a nearby Moravian mission who were trying to run away; one militia unit prepared to march on the mission itself, but Brodhead intervened. Killbuck and his friends witnessed all this; indeed, they were a part of it. They helped to shed their own people's blood. The scalps taken at Coshocton—anonymous "redskins" to the white soldiers— must have been recognized by the Delaware guides as neighbors, cousins, and former friends.

Indians from the various tribes in the Ohio Valley, the vast majority now united in opposition to the Americans, responded to the attack on Coshocton by stepping up their raids on frontier settlements. In September of 1781 Captain Pipe and a mixed party of 300 warriors from the Delaware, Shawnee, and several of the western tribes also paid a visit to the Moravian missions at Gnadenhutten, Schoenbrunn, and Salem. Suspecting that the missionaries had been sending intelligence reports to the Americans, the British and their Indian allies decided to cut off communications between the brethren and Fort Pitt by moving the mission farther west, beyond the reach of American influence. Pomoacan, a Wyandot, explained to the Christian Indians why it was in their own best interests to relocate:

My cousins, ye believing Indians, . . . I am no little troubled about you, for I see you live in a dangerous place. Two powerful and mighty spirits or gods are standing and opening wide their jaws toward each other to swallow, and between the two angry spirits, who thus open their jaws, are you placed; you are in danger, from one or from the other, or even from both, of being bruised and mangled by their teeth; therefore it is not advisable for you to remain here longer, but bethink ye to keep alive your wives, and children and young people, for here must you all die. Therefore I take you by the hand, raise you up and settle you there where I dwell, or at least near by me, where you will be safe and will live in quiet. . . . Ye will at once find food there, and will suffer no want.[93]

"For here must you all die"—a frightening prophesy, and not far off the mark. Although the missionaries resisted, Pomoacan and Captain Pipe and the rest of the warriors forced the residents of all three missions—almost 400 people—to travel westward for twenty days to the Sandusky River in Northwest Ohio.[94] But Pomoacan could not hold true to his promise of food, and the converted Indians did "suffer want." Toward the end of winter, on the verge of starvation, many dispersed into the woods to try to find some form of nourishment. Over 100 drifted back to their former villages at Gnadenhutten, Schoenbrunn, and Salem.

Meanwhile, Lieutenant Colonel David Williamson and 160 volunteers from the Pennsylvania militia, smarting over the latest wave of raids by hostile Indians who had murdered, scalped, or captured several frontier families, embarked on yet another punitive expedition into eastern Ohio. Failing to find any warriors, the militiamen vented their anger on the Christians who had just returned to their old settlements in search of food. Although the mission Indians were admittedly peaceful, the soldiers claimed they had harbored enemy warriors and therefore deserved to be punished.[95] David Zeisberger, one of the missionaries, reported the events as they were relayed to him by the two survivors:

> Our Indians were mostly on the plantations and saw the militia come, but no one thought of fleeing, for they suspected no ill. The militia came to them and bade them come into the town, telling them no harm should befall them. They trusted and went, but were all bound, the men being put into one house, the women into another. . . . Then they began to sing hymns and spoke words of encouragement and consolation one to another until they were all slain. . . .
>
> Two well-grown boys, who saw the whole thing and escaped, gave this information. One of these lay under the heaps of slain and was scalped, but finally came to himself and found

opportunity to escape. The same did Jacob, Rachel's son, who was wonderfully rescued. For they came close upon him suddenly outside the town, so that he thought they must have seen him, but he crept into a thicket and escaped their hands. . . . He went a long way about, and observed what went on. . . .

They made our Indians bring all their hidden goods out of the bush, and then they took them away; they had to tell them where in the bush the bees were, help get the honey out; other things also they had to do for them before they were killed. . . . They prayed and sang until the tomahawks struck into their heads. The boy who was scalped and got away, said the blood flowed in streams in the house. They burned the dead bodies, together with the houses, which they set on fire. [96]

Ninety-six men, women, and children—none of whom were warriors—perished at Gnadenhutten on March 8, 1782. [97]

Earlier in the war David Zeisberger, feeling vulnerable to the hostile Indians of the west, had contemplated moving the mission closer to Fort Pitt. The massacre at Gnadenhutten changed his mind:

But now we plainly see that if we had gone there with our Indians, we should, unwittingly, have gone into the greatest danger. Nowhere is a place to be found to which we can retire with our Indians and be secure. The world is already too narrow. [98]

Too narrow indeed—not only for David Zeisberger and the rest of the Moravian missionaries, but for many other groups, whites and Indians alike, who tried to navigate the troubled waters of the Revolutionary War. [99]

Cherokees

Early in 1776 Henry Stuart, a British Indian agent, ventured toward the heart of Cherokee country in the southern interior bearing "a full supply of ammunition and some presents to keep the Indians in good temper and to dispose them to pay attention to what we

might find necessary to recommend to them."[100] What would the
Cherokees do with the ammunition they received? Would they use
it on animals or people? And if people, which ones?

On August 25 Henry Stuart reported to his brother John, Superintendent for the Southern District, at great length on the progress
of his mission. The Cherokees, he said, were not of one mind. Upon
landing at Mobile, Stuart had been greeted by a young warrior
called Chiucanacina, or Dragging Canoe, who inquired about

> the cause of the present quarrel and disorders in the colonies
> and the reason why their supplies of ammunition and goods
> (which were formerly brought from Georgia and Carolina)
> were stopped. He told me that their nation was under very
> great apprehensions and uneasiness, and complained much of
> the encroachments of the Virginians and inhabitants of North
> Carolina. He said that they were almost surrounded by the
> white people, that they had but a small spot of ground left for
> them to stand upon, and that it seemed to be the intention of
> the white people to destroy them from being a people.

It was the Virginians, Stuart told Dragging Canoe, who were en-
croaching on Cherokee lands contrary to the king's orders. Stuart
also remined him that the preceding year at Sycamore Shoals the
Cherokee chiefs Attakullakulla (Dragging Canoe's father), Oconostota, and The Raven had signed away the rights to 27,000 square
miles—the heart of Kentucky and some of Tennessee—to a group
of land speculators who called themselves the Transylvania Company.

Dragging Canoe, who had walked out of those negotiations, insisted that he would not be bound by the terms of Sycamore Shoals:

> He made answer that he had no hand in making these bargains
> but blamed some of their old men who he said were too old
> to hunt and who by their poverty had been induced to sell
> their land, but that for his part he had a great many young
> fellows that would support him and that they were determined
> to have their land. [101]

While Dragging Canoe was belittling his elders, Stuart reported that the "principal Indians did not at all approve of the behaviour of the young fellows" who went out on raids, and that they "hoped we would not pay any regard to what any of their idle young fellows said." "Old men" versus "young fellows"—it seemed a major rift was in the making among the Cherokee.[102]

Shortly after his arrival at Chote in the heart of Cherokee country, Stuart witnessed firsthand the tensions between young and old. A delegation of fourteen black-painted warriors from the Iroquois, Shawnee, and other northern tribes tried to convince the Cherokee to join in a united attack against the American settlers. Stuart and Alexander Cameron, believing that an attack against the Americans was premature and doomed to failure, tried "to dissuade them from their intentions of attacking the settlements by representing to them the dangerous consequences that were likely to follow to their nation." Would the Indians heed the agents' warning? "All the principal chiefs assented very readily to everything, but the young warriors became impatient."[103]

The youthful, zealous militants were not to be deterred by words of caution. At a council of all the people from the surrounding villages, one of the visiting Mohawks "produced a belt of white and purple whampum"—a war belt, which he gave to Dragging Canoe. Other tribes gave other belts as they urged the Indians "to drop all their former quarrels and to join in one common cause." A Shawnee warrior, producing "a war belt about 9 feet long and six inces wide, of purple whampum, strewed with vermilion," argued persuasively

> that the red people who were once masters of the whole country hardly possessed ground enough to stand on; that the lands where but lately they hunted close to their nations were thickly inhabited and covered with forts and armed men; that wherever a fort appeared in their neighborhood they might depend there would soon be towns and settlements; that it was plain there was an intention to expirpate them, and that he thought it better to die like men than to dwindle away by inches.

How could any self-respecting youth resist talk like this? Few did. "Almost all the young warriors from the different parts on the nation" joined in singing a war song, "though many of them expressed their uneasiness at being concerned in a war against the white people." Uneasiness notwithstanding, they had their pride, their honor, and a very just cause. "After this day," Stuart observed, "every young fellow's face in the Overhill Towns appeared blacked and nothing was now talked of but war."

Much as patriotic white youths drilled with the militias during the spring and summer of 1775, these young Indians sang war songs and prepared their "spears, clubs and scalping knives." The elders—perhaps wiser, and certainly more cautious—had lost control: "The principal chiefs who were averse to the measure and remembered the calamities brought on their nation by the last war, instead of opposing the rashness of the young people with spirit, sat down dejected and silent."[104]

As old men and young drew farther apart, Cherokee women must have wondered and worried about the fate of their people. Although Henry Stuart, like most white males of the times, paid little attention to the words or deeds of women, we do know from a few scattered sources that Cherokee women, like Iroquois women, often accompanied men to large councils. According to Charles Robertson, a participant at Sycamore Shoals in 1775, "there was about one thousand in all counting big and little; and about one-half of them were men." Women and children presumably accounted for the rest, and at one point the women had to hide the guns of a handful of drunken warriors.[105] In a peace council with the Iroquois in 1768, Oconostota had offered

> a Belt from our Women to yours, and we know that they will hear us—for it is they who undergo the pains of childbirth and produce men, surely therefore, they must feel mother's pains for those killed in war, and be desirous to prevent it.[106]

Nancy Ward, the Cherokee ghigau, or "beloved woman," who helped prepare warriors for battle, is said to have pleaded for peace at this and other councils, although the documentation is sparse.[107] Later, in 1781, Ward would address commissioners from the United States:

You know that women are always looked upon as nothing; but we are your mothers; you are our sons. Our cry is all for peace; let it continue. This peace must last forever. Let your women's sons be ours; our sons be yours. Let your women hear our words. [108]

The circumstances were different at Chote in 1776, yet Nancy Ward and other Cherokee women must have known they would feel the effects of any war which the men decided to wage. They were undoubtedly concerned, and they probably expressed this concern. If so, their concerns went unheeded. The young warriors—their sons—would have their way.

During the late spring and summer of 1776 Cherokee warriors staged numerous raids on American settlers with the twenty-one horseloads of powder and lead Henry Stuart had given them. Although they managed to spread terror along the frontier, their timing could not have been worse. The patriots had just repelled a British attack on Charleston; facing no other threat in the region, rebels from the four southernmost states were free to vent their rage on Indians instead of redcoated soldiers. Griffith Rutherford, commander of the North Carolina council of safety, suggested that if "the Frunters, of Each of them Provances" worked together, they could bring about the "Finel Destruction of the Cherroce Nation." North Carolina's delegates to the Continental Congress announced that if their "duties as Christians" did not stand in the way, they ought "to extinguish the very race of them and scarce to leave enough of their existence to be a vestige in proof that a Cherokee nation once was." Thomas Jefferson, in a somewhat more subdued tone, hoped that "the Cherokees will now be driven beyond the Mississippi and that this in the future will be declared to the Indians as the invariable consequences of their beginning a war." And General Charles Lee, commander of the Continental Army in the South, stated it rather bluntly: "as these Cherokees are not esteem'd the most formidable Warriors, we can probably do it without much risk or loss." [109]

And so it was that 6,000 armed men from Virginia, North Carolina, South Carolina, and Georgia—having trained and mobilized for war, and with no other enemy to fight—marched against the Cherokee Indians during the late summer and early fall of 1776. William H. Drayton, a leading patriot in the South Carolina assembly, instructed members of the expedition.

> *And now a word to the wise.* It is expected you make smooth work as you go—that is, you cut up every Indian corn-field, and burn every Indian town—and that every Indian taken shall be the slave and property of the taker; that the nation be extirpated, and the lands become the property of the public.[110]

These directions were dutifully executed. In less than a month Colonel Andrew Williamson, commander of the South Carolina forces, reported to Drayton: "I have now burnt down every town, and destroyed all the corn, from the Cherokee line to the middle settlements."[111] The contingents from North Carolina and Virginia likewise torched villages and confiscated crops. Historian Tom Hatley notes that 3,000 head of cattle which accompanied the soldiers, together with all the horses and mules, added "a variation on scorched earth" as they devoured the forage. "Where we encamped," one of the soldiers recalled after the war, in "one night the beeves destroyed the whole of it even to the stumps, and destroyed the grass to the bare ground."[112]

Cherokee warriors, vastly outnumbered, could offer only sporadic resistance. At first they suffered severe losses in a handful of direct confrontations; later, according to British agent Alexander Cameron, "they fled with their wives and children to the woods" as the enemy approached each town.[113] This caused some frustration for the American troops: according to one soldier from South Carolina, "it grieves us that we should not have an engagement to get satisfaction of them Heathens, for the great Slavery and hardships they put us to."[114] When they failed to come upon warriors, the conquering soldiers had to make do with whomever they could find. William Lenoir of North Carolina recorded in his journal that on September 12 a party of patriots "killed & sculpt 1 Indian Squaw."[115] In a similar vein, some South Carolina troops "espied an Indian squaw; at her they fired two guns." The shots wounded her in the shoulder and leg. In an act they considered to be merciful, "some of our men favored her so far that they killed her there, to put her out of pain." Shortly thereafter, the men took another woman, "an easy prey because she was lame."[116]

American soldiers did not capture many of the "enemy" during the Cherokee campaign of 1776, but those they did take were not received as prisoners of war. William Lenoir reported that John Roberson, to avenge a death suffered during a frontier raid on his household, murdered "an old Indian prisoner, as he marched along under guard." When Roberson was imprisoned for this deed, "the troops were so incensed against the Indians that the thought of seeing Roberson punished seemed rather disgusting . . . and Roberson was released."[117]

Andrew Williamson, the South Carolina commander, requested of the legislature that "such of those Indians as should be taken Prisoners would become slaves and the Property of the Captors," just as William Drayton had suggested. His request was eventually denied for fear that whites who fell into Indian hands might suffer a similar fate, but in the meantime some of the soldiers sold their prisoners and pocketed the profits. One officer recalled how the capture of "two squaws and a lad" almost led to a mutiny:

> there arose a dispute Between me & the whole Body, Officers & all, Concerning Selling off the Prisoners for Slaves. I allowed it was our Duty to Guard Them to prison, or some place of safe Custody till we got the approbation of the Congress Whether they should be sold Slaves or not, and the Greater part swore Bloodily that if they were not sold for Slaves upon the spot they would Kill and Scalp them Immediately. Upon which I was obliged to give way. Then the 3 prisoners was sold for £242. The Whole plunder we got including the Prisoners Amounted Above £1,100.[118]

The war against the Cherokee was a short and lopsided affair. For the Americans, the campaign had served as good practice, a warmup for the fight against Britain; in the words of David Ramsay, a contemporary historian from South Carolina:

> The expedition into the Cherokee settlements diffused military ideas, and a spirit of enterprize among the inhabitants. It taught them the necessary arts of providing for an army, and gave them experience in the business of war. . . . [T]he peacable inhabitants of a whole state transformed from planters, merchants, and mechanics, into an active, disciplined military body.[119]

For the Cherokees, on the other hand, the 1776 raids by Dragging Canoe and other militants ended in disaster. The Cherokee people—old men, women, and children included—paid a heavy price because their young warriors were the first Native Americans to wage war against the fledgling United States. Within three months the vast majority of villages had been destroyed, and the people had been deprived of their autumn harvest. According to one of the American soldiers, the Cherokee "were reduced to a state of the most deplorable and wretched, being obliged to subsist on insects and reptiles of every kind."[120]

The Cherokees officially surrendered by signing two treaties—with South Carolina and Georgia at DeWitt's Corner on May 20, 1777, and with North Carolina and Virginia at Long Island of the Holston River exactly two months later. The treaty at DeWitt's Corner stated point blank that the South Carolina troops "did effect and maintain the conquest of all the Cherokee lands" and thereby acquired "all and singular the rights incidental to conquest."[121] At Long Island the Cherokee chiefs bemoaned the unfair arrangements made at DeWitt's Corner and tried to do better. When white delegates presented a proposal for a boundary, The Raven stated the line "binds verry close upon me," while Corn Tassel pleaded passionately:

> My elder Brothers have imposed much on me in the land way. if this and another house was packed full of goods they would not make satisfaction. . . . It seems misterious to me why you should ask so much land so near to me. I am sensible that if we give up these lands they will bring you more a great deal than hundreds of pounds. It spoils our hunting ground; but always

remains good to you to raise families and stocks on, when the goods we receive of you are rotten and gone to nothing. . . . you require a thing I cannot do, for which reason I return you the string of Beads to consider upon again.

The delegates from North Carolina responded bluntly:

We think the proposals made yesterday respecting the boundary line between our state and the Indians, ought not to be altered. We think it would be verry unjust to give up to the Indians any part of the settlements, that our state took under protection during the War . . . We have no intention to purchase any lands from the Indians; neither can we imagine that the General Assembly of our State will think it just to pay large sums of money for lands and settlements, which they have at a great expence, protected during the War.[122]

And so it would be. In the treaties negotiated at DeWitt's Corner and Long Island, the Cherokees signed away their rights to over five million acres, an area the size of the state of New Jersey. But what more could the old chiefs say or do to prevent it? Although forced to accept the line as it was first proposed, they did not really approve. The Raven told delegates from Virginia: "I depend on you to let the Governor of Virginia know that I had fixed a boundary, but that at your request I suffered it to go to the place you propose on my land." In name at least, The Raven continued to think of "my land." Corn Tassel conceded defeat with one last plea for recompense:

The land I give up, will ever hold good; it will ever be as good as it is now; and when we are all dead and gone it will continue to produce. Therefore I expect when you come to run the line, that you will bring some acknowledgement. You have come empty handed, with nothing to make us an acknowledgement for the land. . . .

Now I am done; I give up the land you asked; I shall say no more. If you ask for more, I will not give it. In confirmation I give you a string.[123]

The Raven and Corn Tassel, representing a conquered people, had no choice but to acquiesce—but how would they be received back home when they returned with nothing once again? "Some of my people that are ungovernable," Corn Tassel feared, "may say something when I go home."[124]

They certainly did: Dragging Canoe, for one, insisted that since he had not signed the treaty, he had not ceded any land. Dragging Canoe and Young Tassel and the other militants—the ones who had actually waged the war—refused to accept defeat. Calling themselves *Ani-Yunwiya*—"the real people"—they withdrew from the rest of the Cherokees, whom they contemptuously referred to as "Virginians." Led by young warriors rather than old chiefs, the inhabitants of four large towns which had been destroyed by the war decided to rebuild their settlements near Chickamauga Creek, to the south and west of their old homes, and start life anew. For the next seventeen years these Chickamaugas, as they came to be called, would continue to resist the westward thrust of white settlers, while the remaining Cherokees struggled to find some place in the vanishing middle ground between the Americans to the east and their militant relatives to the west—a space, once again, which was "already too narrow." The Cherokee Indians had split in two.[125]

With the Chickamauga refusing to surrender, American patriots executed a relentless series of search-and-destroy missions. A typical set of orders authorized the troops to burn the towns, "all the males therein to be killed, and the females captured for exchange; supplies captured to be divided among the soldiers participating."[126] Since frontier volunteers were not trained to make fine distinctions between the Chickamaugas and old-guard Cherokees, many people who had tried to stay out of trouble inevitably suffered from the consequences of the war waged by radical secessionists.[127] After each new wave of destruction, more and more of the people who were left homeless and destitute joined with the Chickamaugas for lack of other alternatives. One astute patriot wrote to Thomas Jefferson: "the burning of their huts, and destruction of their corn, will I fear make the whole Nation Our irreconciliable Enemies, and force them for Sustenances to live altogether by depredation on our frontiers, or make an open Junction with our foes."[128] By 1780 Joseph Martin, the Virginia agent who lived with the Cherokees, reported to Governor Jefferson that "most of their Chiefs and Warrioers of the old Towns" seemed ready to fight against the patriots.[129]

But just as the Cherokees seemed on the verge of reuniting in their opposition to white encroachment, the United States seized the upper hand in the war against Britain. With no hope of outside support, moderate leaders gave up the fight; they admitted to the Americans that they had acted like "Rougues," and they promised to behave in the future.[130] The Chickamauga militants, on the other hand, continued to resist. After their villages had been destroyed yet again, Dragging Canoe told a group of visiting Shawnee about their war with the "Virginians":

> They were numerous, and their hatchets were sharp. After we had lost some of our best warriors, we were forced to leave our towns and corn to be burned by them, and now we live in the grass as you see us. But we are not conquered.[131]

Dragging Canoe and the older chiefs—his father Attakullakulla, Oconostota, The Raven, Corn Tassel—personified the two basic alternatives open to a people who are being conquered by superior force: to fight to the bitter end, or to capitulate and then try to forge some sort of workable accommodation. The special circumstances presented by the American Revolution sharpened and exaggerated each response. The militants, armed and encouraged by the British, were able to maintain a viable military presence even though they were greatly outnumbered. The moderates, meanwhile, played to both sides of warring white men, much in the manner of Cornstalk (the Shawnee) or Joseph Louis Gill (the Abenaki). When the British captured Savannah and prepared to make their move into the southern interior, The Raven traveled to Georgia in order to tell Thomas Brown, the loyalist who had become an Indian agent, that "he was done with the Big Knife."[132] But when the Americans once again seized the initiative in 1781, three of the old chiefs journeyed to Williamsburg to cement their friendship with the patriots. Just to be safe, however, The Raven returned to Savannah at the same time to assure Brown:

Oconostata went to Virginia to make the Rebels believe the Nation meant Peace, but it was only to save the Corn upon the Ground & prevent our Towns being burnt when our Corn is made we will attack them with as much spirit as ever.[133]

The moderates tried to cover all bases; in fact, they covered none.

Both militants and moderates were doomed to fail. The Chickamaugas, too few in number to fight alone, were left stranded by the retreat of the British. For a period they gained support from the Spanish, who were struggling to maintain some presence along the Mississippi, and they also joined with the Indian Confederacy which followed the Revolution (see below). In 1794, however, they were finally subdued by military force. The moderates, meanwhile, watched in vain as the boundaries they established in each successive treaty were violated by westward-moving settlers. In 1787, ten years after the Treaty of Long Island had established a line "FOREVER AND EVER," Corn Tassel had to admit that all his negotiating, talking, and pleading had come to nothing: "It is well known that you have Taken almost all our Country from us without our consent," he complained to the governor of Virginia. "That Don't seem to satisfy my Elder Brother, but he still Talks of fire and sword. . . . For my part I love peace."[134] Although for years he had tried to "stand up like a wall" between warring parties, in 1788 Corn Tassel—while under a flag of truce—was killed by angry frontiersmen bent on avenging the death of relatives who had been squatting on Cherokee land.

The American Revolution, at the time, was described metaphorically as a fight between the British "Father" and his rebellious American "children." For the Cherokees, the rift between fathers and sons was no mere metaphor. Older men watched, hurt, as their boys, now grown, rejected their families and moved away to wage a war which the fathers deemed fruitless. Younger men, meanwhile, were forced to make a difficult choice between their duties to the elders and their own personal beliefs—and much like the rebellious colonists, they chose to fight for their freedom.[135] Once again, the conflict between warring nations of white men magnified the tensions within Native American communities. The bitter quarrel within the Euro-American "family" produced contorted reflections in other families as well.

Catawbas

By the time of the American Revolution, the Catawba Indians of the southern piedmont were already surrounded by white settlers. Their numbers severely diminished by disease, about 500 Catawbas lived on a reservation of 225 square miles along the border of North and South Carolina. With the frontier far to the west, they could no longer survive by hunting, trapping, and raiding; somehow, the Catawbas had to adapt to the realities of a more sedentary existence. They farmed, they rented out some of their land to white planters, and they produced a variety of handmade goods for the market. In the words of historian James Merrell,

> The old means of acquiring goods—presents, deerskins, perhaps plunder—were dead or dying, and pots, baskets, or land were the only substitutes that were at once available to the Nation and acceptable to its neighbors. A planter who chased Indian hunters out of his fields was unlikely to make a fuss when another party dug a little clay or cut a few canes. Even more important, marketing these commodities brought Catawba and settler together in a new, less confrontational arena. Through countless repetitions of the same simple exchange, a different form of intercourse emerged, a form based, not on suspicion and the expectation of conflict, but on consensus and a modicum of trust. When a farmer looked out his window and saw Catawbas approaching, he was now more likely to grab a few coins or a jug of whiskey than a musket or an axe. Indians now came, the planter knew, not to plunder or terrorize, but to collect rents or peddle pots.[136]

In former times, the Catawbas had been fierce warriors, viable opponents of the mighty Iroquois; according to one Iroquois man, the Catawbas had boasted "that they were men and double men for they had two P_____s."[137] But now, these once-virile warriors no longer presented a serious threat to the Iroquois, the Euro-American settlers, or anybody else. John Smyth, an Englishman who visited the Catawbas on the eve of the Revolution, described them as "a poor, inoffensive, insignificant people" who were "simple, submissive, and obliging."[138]

When fighting commenced between Britain and the colonies in 1775, the Catawbas were in no position to play off one side against the other: they were few in number, their region was dominated by patriots, and the British were nowhere in sight.[139] Their choice was not *who* to support—it had to be the rebels—but whether to give that support vigorously or begrudgingly. They opted for the first alternative. Unlike the Western Abenakis and others who sought to minimize their participation, the Catawbas joined the Revolution with spirit and determination. Old warriors who had not fought since their youths would get another chance, while the young, like the young of many cultures, saw only the romantic side of war. When their patriotic neighbors came to the reservation to sign them up for the army, proud Catawbas seized on the opportunity to shine once again.

In July of 1775 Joseph Kershaw, a storekeeper-turned-colonel, announced that the Catawbas were "hearty in our interest."[140] Later that year they formed into a company under the command of a white captain, Samuel Boykin, and in February of 1776 thirty-four Catawbas saw their first action: hunting down runaway slaves. On June 28 Boykin's company helped in the successful defense of Charleston, then in July and August they served as scouts in the war against the Cherokees. They saw no action in 1777 or 1778, quiet years in the South, but in 1779 the Catawbas ventured into Georgia to help fight against the British, who had just taken Savannah.

In 1780 the Catawba reservation became a focal point of rebel resistance, with General Thomas Sumter commanding 500 troops—mostly white, some Native American. Catawba men fought side-by-side with other patriots at Rocky Mount, Hanging Rock, and Fishing Creek, but they had to retreat after the British victory at nearby Camden. Men, women, and children abandoned the reservation and fled north to Virginia. Upon their return several months later, they found their towns had been destroyed and "all was gone; cattle, hogs, fowls, &c., all gone."[141]

Catawbas continued to serve until the end: they fought in the battles at Guilford Courthouse, Haw River, and Eutaw Springs. At the close of the war Catawbas helped raid maroon communities of runaway slaves.[142] A payroll dated June 21, 1783, lists forty-one Catawba Indians who received between £5 and £49 apiece, depending on their length of service; other men not mentioned were known to have fought at other times. In proportion to the size of their community, the Catawbas' contribution to the patriots' cause was outstanding. And in the spirit of the times, they changed the title of their leader from "king" to "general."[143]

Understandably, the Catawbas tried to cash in on their patriotism after the war was over. Hoping that their contributions would be noticed and appreciated, veterans donned old uniforms at the slightest pretext. Former soldiers visited Thomas Sumter frequently; one dropped by the home of Roger Craighead once a year to make sure that the captain would not forget who had saved his life at the Battle of Hanging Rock. What did these visiting Indians want? Whatever they could get—perhaps some rum, food, or clothes, and always a few diplomatic words. When Catawba soldiers returned home from the fighting, Joseph Kershaw greeted them warmly: "I . . . am happy to have it in my power to welcome you in peace to your native Land . . . after this Long and Bloody war in which you have taken so noble a part and have fought and Bled with your white Brothers of America."[144]

From the few scattered accounts which survive, it appears that the appreciation of the Catawbas' service was genuine. Native Americans who had fought at Rocky Mount and Fishing Creek were not referred to as "warriors," but as "Revolutionary soldiers." At the turn of the century whites still praised the Catawbas for being "the best friends and allies South Carolina ever had." Even after the Civil War, their reputation endured: one elderly man recalled his father telling him that the Catawbas "served the entire war under Sumter and fought most heroically."[145]

On one level, the Catawbas' participation in the Revolutionary War worked to their advantage. While most Native American nations had to face retribution for choosing the wrong side, the Catawbas fared somewhat better. In 1786 they complained to the legislature of

South Carolina that "some of our Men have been very Much beaten and abused for hunting on White peoples Land." In other circumstances, such a complaint would have fallen on deaf ears, but the Catawbas recalled that "during the late War we have Exerted our selves as good soldiers in behalf of this State," and the government wound up declaring that "the Catawba Indians have a right by Treaty to hunt in any part thereof without Molestation."[146] James Merrell concludes that the Revolution gave the Catawbas

> a permanent (if small) place in the pantheon of heroes honoring the nation's birth. If South Carolina often neglected Catawbas after the Revolution, at least it was usually a benign neglect, a far cry from the policies of other states toward their original inhabitants. At the same time patriotism became one more tool—along with pottery, land leases, and a less threatening countenance—Indians could use to carve a niche for themselves in the social landscape of the Carolina piedmont. . . . Had Catawbas chosen another path, had they opted for something other than a life as potters and patriots, they would not have survived the century.[147]

And yet their privileged position in the war—fighting for the winners, not the losers—did not guarantee an equal share of the spoils. In the wake of the Revolution many victorious Americans found land easier to acquire, but the land base of the Catawbas continued to diminish. White Carolinians might have been generous with their praise, but many still coveted the Catawba reservation. One by one settlers moved in; they promised to pay rent but did not always come through with the money. One arranged to lease fishing rights on a trial basis; the "trial," according to the written contract which illiterate Catawbas couldn't read, was for ninety-nine years. In 1791 a contingent of Catawbas paid a visit to President Washington, who was touring the countryside. They "seemed to be under some apprehension," Washington observed, "that some attempts were making or would be made to deprive them of part of the 40,000 Acres wch was secured to them by Treaty."[148]

The invention of the cotton gin in 1793 rendered land on the piedmont more valuable yet, and whites who hoped to establish plantations outdid themselves in scheming for a share of the diminishing reservation. In 1805 Catawbas complained to President Jefferson that "Sharp witted and designing Christians . . . Raise Quarrells with our people and commits little Slye crimes." The Indians, of course, had no recourse in the courts, where they were forbidden to testify; "[we are] not heard when we speak the truth," they protested.[149] By 1826 scarcely 100 Catawbas remained in two small villages, and in 1840 the remaining Catawbas signed away what little was left of their land in return for a tract in North Carolina which they never received. A decade later, after an abortive attempt to move in with the Cherokees, they drifted back home and crowded onto 630 acres—less than one square mile of the original 225-square-mile reservation.[150] Although the American Revolution did not lead directly to the decline of the Catawbas, it did establish the domination of the United States from the Atlantic to the Mississippi, thereby creating the conditions under which all Native Americans—even those deemed "friendly"—would be overwhelmed in the end.

One Catawba Indian, Peter Harris, left enough traces for historians to sketch a brief biography. Orphaned at the age of three when a smallpox epidemic claimed the lives of his parents, he was taken in by a nearby white family. Upon coming of age, however, he returned to the Catawbas, married, and had one son. In 1779, when twenty-three years old, Harris enlisted in the Third South Carolina Regiment, and on June 20 he was wounded at Stono Ferry. He fought under Sumter in 1780 and was one of the forty-one Catawbas listed in the 1783 payroll. Shortly before his death, he expressed some regret over his activities in the army. Once, he recalled, he had come across a British soldier who was drinking from a spring, defenseless. Harris shot the man. In retrospect, this seemed to him like an act of "a coward, rather than of a brave man."[151]

Immediately after the war a promoter named Adam Caruth persuaded Peter Harris and three other Catawba warriors to journey to England, where they performed traditional dances wearing breech clouts, war paint, and feather headdresses. The dancers were promised a share of the proceeds, but Caruth absconded with all the money. Wealthy patrons procured tickets for the four men to return home, but during the journey the other three reportedly became seasick and threw themselves overboard. Back home, Harris applied for and received 200 acres of land near Fishing Creek, payment for his services with the Third Regiment. (Catawbas who fought only in their own company received no such rewards.) Apparently, he did not thrive. In 1822, one year before he died, the sixty-six-year-old Harris asked for help from the state of South Carolina:

> I'm one of the lingering embers of an almost extinguished race, Our graves will soon be our only habitations, I am one of the few stalks, that still remain in the field, where the tempest of the revolution passed, I fought against the British for your sake, The British have Disappeared, and you are free, Yet from me the British took nothing, nor have I gained anything by their defeat. I pursued the deer for my subsistence, the deer are disappearing, & I must starve God ordained me for the forest, and my ambition is the shade, but the strength of my arm decays, and my feet fall in the chase, the hand which fought for your liberties is now open for your relief. In my Youth I bled in battle, that you might be independant, let not my heart in my old age, bleed, for the want of your Commiseration.[152]

The legislators, whether moved by pity or patriotism, granted Harris a pension of sixty dollars a year.

Chickasaws, Choctaws, Creeks, and Seminoles

The Chickasaws of northern Mississippi and western Tennessee, like the Catawbas of the Carolinas, were not plagued with indecision: they knew from the beginning which party to support. Historically, they had always favored the British against the French. British agents described the Chickasaws as "antient Friends" and "the Nation the most attached to the English of any in the Southern District."[153] In return for their allegiance, the Crown kept the Chickasaws well supplied with guns and ammunition, which they used to hunt game and ward off enemies. This alliance continued during the American Revolution; throughout the war, British agents boasted of the "friendly disposition" of their faithful allies, the Chickasaws.[154] Just as the Catawbas went along with those who held the power in their immediate vicinity, the Chickasaws took the easy path by siding with Great Britain, which controlled the Mississippi Valley north of Louisiana.

The Chickasaws, it appeared at the start, were likely to provide significant help for the British war effort. One Native American who had lived among several tribes proclaimed they were "real warriors, even braver than the Catawbas." A French governor once wrote, "These people breathe nothing but war." The Chickasaws themselves boasted that they had "only to beat drums in our cabins" to make the Choctaws, who were far more numerous, run away. Superintendent John Stuart was certainly pleased to have "the bravest Indians on the Continent" line up firmly in his corner. And these fine warriors wasted no kind words on the colonists. When Virginia sent a white belt of peace in May of 1779 asking for their allegiance, the Chickasaws sent a direct and undiplomatic response:

> We desire no other friendship of you but only desire you will inform us when you are Comeing and we will save you the trouble of Coming quite here for we will meet you half Way, for we have heard so much of it that it makes our heads Ach, Take care that we dont serve you as we have served the French before with all their Indians, send you back without your heads. We are a Nation that fears or Values no Nation as long as our Great Father King George stands by us for you may depend as long as life lasts with us we will hold him fast by the Hand.[155]

The Chickasaws talked tough, but did their warriors come to the aid of the British with energy, conviction, and enthusiasm, as the Catawbas did for the patriots? Late in 1776, when John Stuart asked their assistance in patrolling the Mississippi, the Chickasaws "refused to go out, assigning for reason that it would be prejudicial to their hunting at this season which is their chief support."[156] During the largest battle in the region, the defense of Pensacola early in 1781, 800 Indians rallied for the British—but the Chickasaws were represented by only six warriors.[157] Active support was so minimal that Peter Chester, the British governor of West Florida, pronounced: "I am firmly of the opinion that one British regiment, properly stationed upon the River Mississippi, would be of more real security to the colony in case of an attack from the rebels than the whole Chickisaw and Choctaw nations."[158] Charles Stuart, a deputy of the Indian department, complained that the Chickasaws were "a spoiled Nation, Proud and Insolent."[159]

Why didn't the Chickasaw warriors, so noted for their bravery, fight harder? Perhaps they were intimidated by the patriots, whose repression of the Cherokees early in the war dampened the willingness of neighboring Native Americans to seek a similar confrontation. As John Stuart explained in 1778, "the Rough Treatment which the Cherokees met with has had a bad effect upon the Southern nations," filling them with "dread of sharing the Same fate."[160] But Stuart himself thought there was more to it than fear:

> What I suppose to have been their real [reason] was the influence of the traders among them, who in every nation endeavour to prevent the Indians from going to war as it is diametrically opposite to their views of traffic by getting hides in barter for their goods.[161]

To hunt, trap, and trade—or to fight the king's war: these were the choices open to Chickasaw males during the Revolution. Whereas many Native Americans were tugged in opposite directions by emissaries of the British and the patriots, the Chickasaws were pulled on the one hand by official agents of the king who urged them to take up the hatchet, and on the other by traders who preferred they venture into the woods in search of furs and pelts.

A key weapon in this tug-of-war was liquor. West Indies rum flowed freely into Gulf Coast ports, offsetting the scarcity of European trade goods caused by wartime privateering on the Atlantic.

Traders therefore pushed rum instead of blankets and knives, and they found plenty of willing takers. Although the excessive consumption of liquor created problems in most Native American communities, abusive drinking—fueled by the marketplace—took a disproportionate toll in the southern interior and Gulf Coast region during the Revolutionary War. In 1776 John Stuart complained from Pensacola:

> The merchants concerned in the Indian trade find such an amazing profit in bartering rum for deerskins that they oppose every regulation by which this destructive commerce can be prevented: for one skin taken in exchange for British manufacture, there are five got in exchange for that liquor, the effect of which is that the Indians are poor, wretched, naked and discontented.[162]

A shipment of 30,000 gallons of rum, according to Stuart, had been distributed and consumed within three months. In 1777 Charles Stuart reported that in Choctaw and Chickasaw country he saw "nothing but Rum Drinking and Women crying over the Dead bodies of their relations who have died by Rum." One chief estimated that excessive drinking had taken over 1,000 lives within eighteen months—perhaps an exaggeration, but it doubtless felt that way. Stuart reasoned:

> Unless some Step is taken to put a Stop to this abuse we need not look for any assistance from this nation, for at the very time they may be wanted they may be all drunk and Rum flows into their land from all quarters and is in my Opinion the only source of all abuses and complaints.[163]

In 1778, at a council with the Chickasaws and Choctaws, Charles Stuart reported that one of the chiefs "spoke much against the carrying of rum into their land, said it was like a woman, when a man wanted her and saw her he must have her"; another chief, he said, "disapproves of so much rum coming from Mobile . . . and observed that if it was not stopped it would wash out beloved talks as rain would a man's track." To these complaints, Stuart added a few of his own:

[O]ne of the reasons why I could not get the Indians to fix a day for the talks was many of them being drunk. It was the cause assigned for the Chickesaws not going out with Colonel McGillivray; it is the cause of their killing each other daily; it is the cause of every disturbance in the nation; it is the cause of every depredation committed upon the settlements and of this town's being constantly in an uproar and the lives and properties of the inhabitants in perpetual danger.

Stuart once again argued that the British would never be able to "depend on Indians for any operation" until "the immoderate importation of rum into the Indian country" had ceased.[164] It did not. The drinking continued, Chickasaw warriors failed to rally to the king's cause, and men who might have been killed in battle died by the bottle instead.

On a different level, the failure of Chickasaws to come through for the British can be explained by simple geography: they were not in the direct line of fire. Through most of the war the Cherokees, Chickamaugas, Choctaws, and Creeks buffered the Chickasaws in the Mississippi Valley from the land-hungry rebels of the Atlantic colonies. When the patriots did venture to the northern edge of Chickasaw country in the spring of 1780, the "bravest Indians on the Continent" finally showed up to fight. Thomas Jefferson, then governor of Virginia, had ordered the building of a fort just below the confluence of the Ohio and Mississippi rivers. Shortly after the construction of Fort Jefferson, as it was called, Chickasaw warriors started harassing soldiers who ventured into the surrounding countryside. New settlers who counted on the fort for protection were forced to give up their plans. For almost a year an army of Chickasaws, with no help from British soldiers, laid siege to Fort Jefferson, cutting off supplies and trapping the soldiers inside. Rum did not seem to present much of a problem when it came to protecting their homeland. In June of 1781 the patriots abandoned the fort.

The Chickasaws emerged from the American Revolution with their land intact, but the outcome of the war did present serious problems. What would happen to the one southern tribe which had made no secret of its continuing allegiance to the Crown and unqualified animosity towards the patriots? With their patrons defeated, who would supply them with guns, knives, blankets, and rum? How would they be treated by white Americans whom they had insulted so brashly?

Some of the Chickasaws thought it best to make amends with the victors. In July of 1782 Piomingo, who had always supported the British, wrote to the Virginians on behalf of his people:

> Friends We Mean to Conclude A Peace With you. . . . Youl Observe at the Same time Our making A Peace with you doth Not Intitle Us to Fall out With Our Fathers the Inglish for we Love them as They were the First People that Ever Supported Us to Defend Our Selves Against Our former Enimys the French & Spaniards & All their Indians. And We are a People that Never Forgets Any Kindness done Us by Any Nation. . . .
>
> I this day Send you a Flagg for a Peace not To Renew Any more Battles As there never was much fight Between you & us, As to Our parts We Never Have done you much Harm. Its True Some Of Our young fellows has Stole Some of your Horses but Still they Never Went Of themselves their was Other Nations Creeks Cherokees Waupunockys &c Who Led Them Out And what damage Was done was by Reason you Settled A Fort in our Hunting ground without Our Leave And at that place you Suffered Most from Us. . . . Remmember That Our fore fathers On both Sides were allways friends, but as for Our parts we have had a Small difference but I dont know who was In the rong it is my desire that we Should Still be at Friendship With Each Other. [165]

Virginia, which at that point claimed land clear to the Mississippi, welcomed the idea of establishing some sort of peace with these potentially hostile people—but of course the Virginians also wanted some of their land. In the fall of 1783 a Virginia delegation ventured into Chickasaw country to negotiate for the territory in the vicinity of old Fort Jefferson. The Chickasaws would hear nothing of it. Rather than give up land, they kept the patriots at bay by offering a more complete repudiation of their prior actions and a full renunciation of their former friends, the British:

The English put the Bloody Tomahawk into our hands, telling us that we should have no Goods if we did not Exert ourselves to the greatest point of Resentment against you, but now we find our mistake and Distresses. The English have done their utmost and left us in our adversity. We find them full of Deceit and Dissimulation and our women & children are crying out for peace.[166]

At least for the moment, these words sufficed. The Virginia-Chickasaw Treaty of 1783 defined the eastern boundary of the Chickasaws, but this only reflected the existing settlement pattern. No new land changed hands.

While some leaders were negotiating with the Americans, others preferred to seek friendship with the Spanish. Following the demise of British influence in the west, Spain, hoping to gain control of the Mississippi Valley, offered to help the Chickasaws and other Native Americans resist the westward advance of settlers from the United States. In June of 1784 delegates from six Chickasaw villages granted a trade monopoly to Spain, which they assumed was in a better position to come through with guns, knives, and blankets than the war-impoverished United States. As one Spanish official boasted, "The Chickasaws are poor and there are no other white people except the Spaniards who can supply their necessities."[167]

But the United States would not remain poor forever, reasoned Piomingo and his faction. In 1786 these Chickasaw leaders granted a trade monopoly to the Americans at the Treaty of Hopewell. Both Spain and the United States could now claim an exclusive friendship with the Chickasaws—but they were not dealing with the same people. Two competing factions within a Native American nation, each looking for an alliance with a different set of Euro-Americans—the same type of internal dissension experienced by the Iroquois, Shawnee, Delaware, Cherokee, and other nations during the American Revolution was now experienced by the Chickasaws, who at one point had appeared united in their loyalty to Great Britain. Although it took the Chickasaws a little longer, they too succumbed to the divisiveness fostered by the peculiar logic of the Revolutionary War. The confusion among the Chickasaw was expressed most eloquently in a 1783 letter to Congress:

The Spaniards are sending talks amongst us, and inviting our young Men to trade with them. We also receive talks from Georgia to the same effect—We have had speeches from the Illinois inviting us to a Trade and Intercourse with them— Our Brothers, the Virginians Call upon us to a Treaty, and want part of our land, and we expect our Neighbors who live on Cumberland River, will in a Little time Demand, if not forcibly take part of it from us, also we are informed they have been marking Lines through our hunting grounds: we are daily receiving Talks from one Place or other, and from People we Know nothing about. We know not who to mind or who to neglect. [168]

In the mid-1780s the Chickasaws were also pressured to join the pan-Indian Confederacy organized by Alexander McGillivray of the Creeks. Just when the United States, with its large and land-hungry population, appeared to have the upper hand, Native Americans from other southern nations—Creeks, Choctaws, Cherokees, and the breakaway Chickamaugas—were joining together in resistance, supplied with Spanish arms. During the early stages of the Revolutionary War, the Creeks and Choctaws, like most Indian nations, had experienced serious divisions.[169] Historically, they were prejudiced against the colonists—the word for "Georgian" in one of the Creek languages was *Ecunnaunuxulgee,* or "people greedily grasping after the lands of red people."[170] Still, patriots like George Galphin wooed them, as he admitted, with "rum and good words."[171] (After the council at Augusta in May of 1776, Creeks from the single town of Coweta went home with ninety kegs of rum.)[172] Many Creeks and Choctaws, whether influenced by rum or fearful of suffering the fate of the Cherokees, agreed not to oppose the rebels; others provided support for the British in the fight against land-grabbing settlers. The anti-American factions prevailed when the British made their advances in the South in 1780. The British provided Creeks and Choctaws with an opportunity to strike out against the Georgians and Carolinians—but even after the British had been defeated, these Indians, now mobilized, vowed to keep up the good fight. Creeks and Choctaws, bitter enemies before the Revolution, were at last coming together to stave off the Ecunnaunuxulgee—and other Native Americans from across the south were joining in the crusade.

Would the Chickasaws become part of this movement? Piomingo and his friends thought not. In order to keep their land, the pro-American faction felt the Chickasaws had to treat the United States as an ally, not an enemy. This attitude enraged the militants of the new confederacy, who, according to McGillivray, "are all eager to chastize the Chickasaws for their defection from the general league."[173] In 1786 warriors from the confederacy started harassing the errant Chickasaws, and by the 1790s, isolated acts of violence escalated into full-scale hostilities. Once again, Native Americans wound up fighting each other because of their differences in strategies: whether to accommodate or resist the white Americans. Even as they strove to achieve unity, factions persisted. Piomingo and the pro-American Chickasaws never did sign up.[174]

The pan-Indian confederation in the South during the 1780s and 1790s was a direct consequence of the Revolutionary War. With Great Britain defeated, American settlers swarmed from Georgia, Virginia, and the Carolinas into the region between the southern Appalachias and the Mississippi. Alexander McGillivray, who was half Creek, worked tirelessly to coordinate the resistance to these white intruders. Somewhat sickly and not much of a warrior himself, McGillivray utilized his diplomatic, rhetorical, and organizational abilities to gain allegiance from the militant factions of all the southern tribes. He forged an alliance with Spain, which agreed to issue arms to any Indians carrying McGillivray's "slips of paper."[175] And he stood up to the Anglo-Americans, voicing the views of Native Americans without the use of an interpreter:

We Cheifs and Warriors of the Creek Chickesaw and Cherokee Nations, do hereby in the most solemn manner protest against any title claim or demand the American Congress may set up for or against our lands, Settlements, and hunting Grounds in Consequence of the Said treaty of peace between the King of Great Brittain and the states of America declaring that as we were not partys, so we are determined to pay no attention to the Manner in which the British Negotiators has drawn out the Lines of the Lands in question Ceded to the States of America—it being a Notorious fact known to the Americans, known to every person who is in any ways conversant in, or acquainted with American affairs, that his Brittannick Majesty was never possessed either by session purchase or by right of Conquest of our Territorys and which the Said treaty gives away. On the contrary it is well known that from the first Settlement of the English colonys of Carolina and Georgia up to the date of the Said treaty no tittle has ever been or pretended to be made by his Brittanic Majesty to our lands except what was obtained by free Gift or by purchase for good and valuable Considerations. . . .

The Americans altho' sensible of the Injustice done to us on this occasion in consequence of this pretended claim have divided our territorys into countys and Sate themselves down on our land, as if they were their own. . . . We have repeatedly warned the States of Carolina and Georgia to desist from these Encroachments. . . . To these remonstrances we have received friendly talks and replys it is true but while they are addressing us by the flattering appellations of Friends and Brothers they are Stripping us of our natural rights by depriving us of that inheritance which belonged to our ancestors and hath descended from them to us Since the beginning of time. [176]

Like the Mohawk Joseph Brant, who was organizing a similar resistance movement in the North, McGillivray could hold his own with the best of Euro-American lawyers and statesmen.

The confederations of both the South and the North managed to stave off defeat for more than a decade. The various postwar treaties ceding land to the United States were all rejected by these militant Native Americans who tried to put aside their tribal differences and traditional animosities. People like Dragging Canoe of the Chickamaugas, McGillivray of the Creeks, and Brant of the Iroquois sought out their counterparts among other groups. Acting together, they were sometimes able to repulse the waves of militiamen who ventured west to suppress them. In 1791, when the United States Army marched in full force into the Ohio country, warriors from across the North, and even some from the South, stood up to the intruders and killed 630 troops in a single battle.

The pan-Indian movement climaxed—and perished—in 1794 when 2,000 armed men from the various Indian nations, the largest and most diverse group of Native American warriors ever to assemble under arms at a single time and place, gathered at Fallen Timbers on the Miami River to confront a slightly larger army from the United States. The Indians, led to believe they would be supported by British soldiers from Canada, staged an abortive and inconclusive attack. When they learned the British would not in fact come to their aid, many went home. The Americans, after routing the warriors who had stayed, proceeded with their customary burning of cornfields throughout the surrounding countryside. The northern confederacy fell apart after the defeat at Fallen Timbers, and the southern branch began to wither away at approximately the same time. Perhaps if *all* the Indians had joined, perhaps if support from the British had materialized . . . but it didn't happen that way. As J. Leitch Wright has said of the southern movement, "the trend toward Creek centralization was just that: a trend, more of a hope than a reality."[177]

There was one group of Native Americans which not only survived but thrived in the aftermath of the American Revolution: the Seminoles from Florida. Several decades before the war, bands of Creeks from Georgia had migrated south and settled in lands which had been depopulated by introduced diseases. (Spaniards called these people *cimarron*—"wild and untamed." With no "r" sound in their native languages, the Creek émigrés came to speak of themselves as *Cimallon,* which evolved into *Simallone* and eventually *Seminole.*)[178] On the eve of the Revolution about 1,500 Seminoles, who were only beginning to see themselves as a separate people, inhabited the northern portions of East Florida. In 1774 William Bartram, a traveling naturalist from Philadelphia, noted that one of their settlements, Cuscowilla, consisted of sixty frame houses with productive gardens surrounded by a lush countryside inhabited by "innumerable droves of cattle," all sorts of wild game, and "squadrons of the beautiful, fleet Siminole horse."[179] Solid houses, rich farmland, healthy livestock, abundant wildlife—the community of Cuscowilla was not that different from many other Native American settlements on the eve of the Revolution. But Cuscowilla, unlike most Indian towns from Georgia to the Canadian border, still looked that way ten years later, twenty years later, thirty years later. Situated in a colony which passed from Spain to Great Britain and then back to Spain, the Seminoles were not pressured by white American settlers for several decades. Not until 1813 did the United States make its first concerted thrust into Florida. Many Seminoles at that point retreated to the South, where they continued to hold out against the intrusions of outsiders into the 1830s.

Not that the Seminoles didn't feel the presence of the Revolutionary War. They did. The British called on them for help, and the Native Americans from Florida responded. In 1777 John Stuart reported that "the Seminollies consist of 800 men bearing arms" who could be "depended upon in case of any sudden attack of East Florida."[180] Several of these "men bearing arms" worked with Thomas Brown's East Florida Rangers to stage attacks on rebel outposts in Georgia.[181] In 1778 Stuart again boasted "all the Seminollie Indians are firmly attached to His Majesty's interest: they consist of near one thousand gun-men."[182]

By fighting in the name of the Crown, the Seminoles pursued their own interests as well. Because British regulars, East Florida Rangers, and local Native Americans were able to keep the aggressive rebels from penetrating into Florida, the Seminoles remained secure in their own homes. With their settlements facing no immediate danger, warriors could seize the offensive by raiding plantations in Georgia—and they insisted on keeping the horses, cattle, and slaves they captured. Since the British had sent them on these missions, the warriors expected additional recompense. During the winter of 1778–89, those who had fought during the previous season traveled en masse to St. Augustine and demanded to be paid with goods and food. Yes, they would fight, but they would not fight for free. And they would fight in their own style. Despite complaints from their British allies, they continued to mutilate the bodies of fallen enemies.[183]

The Seminoles, like so many other Native Americans, became embroiled in a war that was not of their own making. A few warriors died, but there were no villages burned, crops destroyed, women and children left homeless. The war did cause disruptions in trade and the production of food; for a time, some people went hungry. But nobody seems to have starved, and the hard times ended rather swiftly. After the war was over, the people of Cuscowilla and other communities continued much as they had before. Indeed, Seminole villages expanded in the 1780s and 1790s. Many thousands of refugees flocked to Florida in 1782 and 1783—Euro-American loyalists, African American slaves, Native Americans whose homes had been seized or destroyed—and some of these joined Seminole communities or established their own maroons nearby. (The term maroon, like Seminole, derives from *cimarron*— "wild and untamed.")[184] While Native American populations in other areas east of the Mississippi plummetted, the number of Seminoles increased dramatically.

The Seminoles fared better than others because they lived in a colony which did not come under the jurisdiction of the land-hungry United States. This leaves us to wonder how other native peoples might have fared if the Revolutionary War had not been waged, or if the outcome had been different. If the new and expansionist United States had not prevailed, would Native Americans between the Appalachias and the Mississippi have been able to hold onto their lands? The Native Americans probably would not have kept their homes forever, but they might have held on longer than they did if not for the American Revolution. It took the English colonists a century and a half to dominate the countryside from the Atlantic to the Appalachias. In the wake of the Revolutionary War, it took white settlers scarcely a decade to conquer another equally large region.

The American Revolution, a fight for freedom from colonial rule, was also the most extensive and destructive "Indian war" in the nation's history. Whereas other wars affected individual nations, the Revolution affected *all* Native Americans east of the Mississippi. The effects were felt on many levels:

- It killed people—primarily warriors, but others as well. It burned their houses and destroyed their food, making them cold and hungry. It took away their land, hindering their ability to produce more food for the future. It—the war itself, whether its agents were white or Indian, Whig or Tory— made Native Americans suffer.

• It provoked serious dissension by exaggerating the differences between factions which normally occur within leadership groups, between generations, and among the various nations.

• It militarized Euro-Americans, the very people who would eventually dispossess the Native Americans from their homes. In the words of David Ramsay, it "diffused military ideas" among the rebellious colonists and "gave them experience in the business of war." Once the patriots had defeated the mightiest empire on earth, they assumed they could subdue a few scattered Indians.

• It changed the balance of power. Without the British, the French, and the colonists competing with each other, Native Americans could no longer play off one against the other. For a short period after the war Spanish agents from Florida and Louisiana, as well as British officials in Canada, helped check domination by the United States—but this didn't last. After the defeat at Fallen Timbers, Native Americans would no longer be courted by competing groups of whites who bid for their favors with presents or supplied them with the guns they needed to protect their lands.

With Native Americans weakened and divided by the war, and with militarized white Americans no longer hampered by competition from European powers, the victorious new nation faced west and started marching, relentlessly. Perhaps the settlers did not expect much opposition. If so, they were wrong—the pan-Indian movements in both the South and the North provided considerable resistance for more than a decade. But the odds were simply too great, the numbers heavily stacked against those who tried to fight back. For the patriots, the War of Independence signified a new beginning; for Native Americans, it only hastened the demise of their sovereign status.

6

AFRICAN AMERICANS

The Promise and the Panic of '75 . . . Liberty to Slaves . . . A Board Game . . . Two Émigrés . . . Patriots of Color . . . Toward Freedom?

The Promise and the Panic of '75

During the third week of April in 1775, just as throngs of Yankee farmers were facing off against redcoated soldiers at Lexington and Concord, a number of slaves in Virginia, on a smaller and more personal scale, faced off against their masters. On April 15, along the Appomattox River, a slave belonging to John Baulding was convicted of insurrection and conspiracy to commit murder. On April 21, according to the *Virginia Gazette,* two slaves were "tried at Norfolk, for being concerned in a conspiracy to raise an insurrection in that town"; the alleged insurgents, Emanuel (Matthew Phripp's slave) and Emanuel de Antonio (James Campbell's slave), were sentenced to hang.[1] On the same day, Edmund Pendleton alerted George Washington that the citizens of Williamsburg had just been aroused by "some disturbances in the City, by the *Slaves.*"[2] Frightened masters took guard. In Chesterfield County, a trader named Robert Donald reported that "we Patrol and go armed . . . alarm'd for an Insurrection of the Slaves."[3]

It was just at this moment—shortly before dawn on April 21—that Virginia's Governor John Murray, the Earl of Dunmore, dispatched his marines to seize the gunpowder stored in the magazine at Williamsburg and bring it to one of His Majesty's ships. On one

level the seizure of powder at Williamsburg paralleled the famous
raid on rebel stores at Concord two days earlier, but here in the
South the institution of slavery altered the context of all political
acts. When the citizens of Williamsburg discovered what had happened, they gathered in front of the governor's mansion to voice
their discontent. "By disarming the people," they complained, Dunmore had weakened "the means of opposing an insurrection of the
slaves . . . for the protection against whom in part the magazine was
first built."[4] Believing "that some wicked and designing persons
have instilled the most diabolical notions into the minds of our
slaves," they observed that now more than ever they had to pay
"the utmost attention" to their "internal security."[5] As one newspaper reported,

> The monstrous absurdity that the Governor can deprive the peo-
> ple of the necessary means of defense at a time when the colony
> is actually threatened with an insurrection of their slaves . . . has
> worked up the passions of the people . . . almost to a frenzy.[6]

That afternoon, when a committee presented the grievances of the
people to the governor, Dunmore defended his actions with a most
intriguing argument. Having heard of "an insurrection in a neighboring county," he told them, he had removed the powder "to a
place of security . . . lest the Negroes might have seized upon it."[7]
At least for the moment, Dunmore's preposterous defense seemed
to work, for the crowd withdrew. But when rumors circulated that
Dunmore was ready to make another move, the crowd reappeared
and threatened retribution unless the governor returned the powder.
Abruptly, Dunmore changed his stance: if any harm should come
to a British official, he pronounced, he would "declare Freedom to
the Slaves, and reduce the City of Williamsburg to Ashes."[8]

In this confrontation at Williamsburg we see the Revolutionary
politics of the South laid bare: both Whigs and Tories played the
"slave card" whenever and however they could. Dunmore alternately duped and intimidated patriot masters by referring to the
likelihood of slave insurrections, while the patriots used Dunmore's

seizure of the powder and his threat to free the slaves to foster a climate of alarm. The fear of slaves on the one hand, and the military potential of mobilizing slaves on the other, gave a peculiar twist to the logic of war in Virginia, North Carolina, South Carolina, Georgia, and Maryland.

For the slaves themselves—about 430,000 people in the southern colonies, and another 50,000 or so in the North—the coming of the Revolution brought new hopes and new dangers.[9] They could not have helped but notice the peculiar references to "freedom" and "slavery" voiced by their masters. The ironies were not lost on them, nor were the possibilities. With "freedom" in the air, they naturally sought ways of getting some of their own. Many appear to have been aware of the important decision in the Sommersett case back in Great Britain: in 1772 Lord Mansfield, Chief Justice of the King's Bench, determined that James Sommersett, who had been purchased in Virginia, taken to England, and then escaped, could not be forcibly returned to his master.[10] American slaves took this case to heart: if they could somehow reach the shores of England, they too would be set free. On September 30, 1773, a notice for a runaway couple posted in the *Virginia Gazette* stated that the fugitives might be on their way to Britain "where they imagine they will be free (a Notion now too prevalent among the Negroes, greatly to the Vexation and Prejudice of their Masters)." On June 30, 1774, another notice speculated that a runaway named Bacchus would probably try "to board a vessel for Great Britain . . . from the knowledge he has of the late Determination of Sommerset's Case."[11] Clearly, these people were paying attention to relevant events beyond the limits of their plantations.

No more than a handful of slaves actually found their way to freedom during the buildup to the Revolution, yet all slaves felt the weight of a new wave of repression. Scared that the British might instill insurrections, patriot masters—the so-called Revolutionaries— panicked. They feared slaves who "entertained ideas, that the present contest was for obliging us to give them their liberty."[12] They feared the British, who "have been tampering with our Negroes; and have held nightly meetings with them; and all for the glorious purpose of enticing them to cut their masters' throats while they are asleep."[13]

And with fear running rampant, so did rumors. On May 29 the *South Carolina Gazette* printed a report from London: "There is gone down to Sheerness, seventy-eight thousand guns and bayonets, to be sent to America, to put into the hands of N*****s, the Roman Catholics, the Indians and Canadiens."[14] John Stuart, the British Indian commissioner, reported that "Massacres and Instigated Insurrections, were Words in the mouth of every Child."[15] According to George Milligen, a prominent loyalist, "reports were daily circulated that the Negroes of this plantation had refused to work, that in another they had obtained arms and were gone into the woods, that others had actually murdered their masters and their families, etc."[16] Janet Schaw, a Scottish traveler, wrote from Wilmington that patriots believed the king was

> ordering the tories to murder the whigs, and promising every Negro that would murder his Master and family that he should have his Master's plantation. . . . Every man is in arms and the patroles going thro' all the town, and searching every Negro's house, to see they are all at home by nine at night.[17]

Although the rumors were certainly exaggerated, masters had real cause for concern. Why *wouldn't* the slaves rebel, if they were supplied by the British with arms? Worse yet, might they not be joined by hostile Indians? "Nothing can be more alarming to the Carolinians than the idea of an attack from Indians and Negroes," wrote John Stuart.[18]

And worst of all, what if lower-class whites rebelled with the rest? That would present the ultimate challenge to the authority of the slaveholders. At least in Maryland, where poor loyalists rose in opposition to the patriot elite, this seemed a real possibility. In May of 1775 James Mullineux told a grand jury of a conversation with John Simmons, a wheelwright from Dorcester County:

> [H]e understood that the gentlemen were intending to make us all fight for their land and negroes, and then said damn them

(meaning the gentlemen) if I had a few more white people to join me I could get all the negroes in the county to back us, and they would do more good in the night than the white people could do in the day. . . . [I]f the gentlemen were killed we should have the best of the land to tend and besides could get money enough while they were about it as they have all the money in their hands.

According to Mullineux, "Simmons appeared to be in earnest and desirous that the negroes should get the better of the white people."[19]

The dangers were real, and masters prepared for the worst. The general committee in South Carolina called out the militia. "[T]he threats of arbitrary impositions from abroad—& the dread of instigated Insurrections at home—are causes sufficient to drive an oppressed People to the use of Arms."[20] The committee called on Charleston inhabitants "to do Patrole Duty and to Mount Guard every night" in order to "guard against any hostile attempts that might be made by our domesticks," and it recommended that citizens bring arms and ammunition to church on Sundays.[21] In Williamsburg, patriot leaders doubled the slave patrol, and the patrollers reported nervously that "even the whispering of the wind was sufficient to rouse their fears."[22]

White apprehensions came to a head on July 8 in the Tar River region of North Carolina. Acting on a rumor "of an intended insurrection of the negroes against the whole people which was to be put into execution that night," the Pitt County safety committee took immediate action:

Resolved, that the Patrolers shoot one or any number of Negroes who are armed and doth not willingly surrender their arms, and that they have the Discretionary Power, to shoot any Number of Negroes above four, who are off their Masters Plantations, and will not submitt.[23]

After promising to reimburse the "owners of any Negro who shall be killed or Disabled in consequence of this Resolve," the committee dispatched over a hundred men to suppress the revolt. We have no firsthand accounts of the incident from slaves, but one week later John Simpson, chairman of the Pitt County safety committee, wrote a letter to Richard Cogdell, Chairman on the Craven County safety committee, in which he described the dangers, the fears, and the repression in some detail:

> We then separated to sound the alarm thro' this county and to apprehend the suspected heads. By night we had in custody and the gaol near forty under proper guard. Sunday the Committee sett and proceeded to examine into the affair and find it a deep laid Horrid Tragick Plan laid for destroying the inhabitants of this province without respect of persons, age or sex. By negro evidence it appears that Capt Johnson of White Haven . . . in consort with Merrick, a negro man slave . . . propagated the contagion. The contagion has spread beyond the waters. There are five negroes were whipt this day by order.
>
> Monday.—The Committee sat. Ordered several to be severely whipt and sentenced several to receive 80 lashes each to have both Ears crapd which was executed in presence of the Committee and a great number of spectators.
>
> In the afternoon we recd by express from Coll. Blount of negroes being in arms on the line of Craven and Pitt and prayed assistance of men and ammunition which we readily granted. We posted guards upon the roads for several miles that night. Just as I got home came one of Mr Nelson's sons from Pometo . . . and informed me of 250 negroes that had been pursued for several days but none taken nor seen tho' they were several times fired at . . . On Tuesday we sent off two companies of Light Horse . . . in order to find from whence the report arose and found the author to be a negro wench of William Taylor's on Clayroot, with design to kill her master and mistress and Lay it upon these negroes. She has received severe correction.
>
> Since that time we have remained as quiet as we could expect from the nature of things. We keep taking up, examining and scourging more or less every day; from whichever part of the County they come they all confess nearly the same thing, viz that they were one and all on the night of the 8th inst to fall on and destroy the family where they lived, then proceed from

House to House (Burning as they went) until they arrived in the Back Country where they were to be received with open arms by a number of Persons there appointed and armed by Government for their Protection, and as a further reward they were to be settled in a free government of their own. . . .

P. S. In disarming the negroes we found considerable ammunition.[24]

This vivid account raises many questions. By what standards of evidence did the safety committee conclude that Captain Johnson and Merrick were the instigators? Might the confessions of slaves have been influenced, directed, or even forced by the interrogators to confirm their worst fears? How did the white patrols shoot at 250 negroes who were the figment of the imagination of a "negro wench"? In sum, did the patriots of Pitt, Craven, and Beaufort Counties narrowly avert a slave insurrection of immense proportions, or had they engaged in a witch hunt? Quite possibly, real rumblings among the slaves were interpreted by fearful masters as "a deep laid Horrid Tragick Plan." Without intervention, that plan might or might not have materialized into a genuine insurrection on the night of July 8, 1775.

All slaves suffered under the climate of fear and repression which prevailed throughout the South at the outset of the war, and some, despite the dangers, sought to turn the Revolution to their own advantage. It was a pivotal time for those held in bondage. As white patriots and loyalists squabbled over the fate of the British Empire in North America, and as each side tried to capitalize on the specter of "domestick" insurrections, African Americans experienced the political conflict of 1775 directly and personally. From the scattered evidence left by white folks, some telling stories emerge:

- On July 20, 1775, Andrew Estave placed an advertisement in the *Virginia Gazette*. His message was unusual: he wished to justify the harsh punishment he had just administered to a fifteen-year-old girl, whose name he did not mention. He had purchased the girl on February 10, and within five months she had run away twelve times. On the first three occasions he administered forty lashes after she had been captured; later he did not bother, since it seemed to do no good. Then, he claimed, another slave discovered the girl "with her thumb thrust into the private parts" of his daughter. Before the enraged Estave could seize her, she ran off for the thirteenth time—this time to the governor's palace, where she sought asylum. But since Lord Dunmore himself had just retreated to his ships in the harbor, the slave patrol had no trouble seizing the girl. This time, Estave reported, "I gave her eighty lashes, well laid on, and afterwards applied to her back a handful of cold embers." All we know about this persistent runaway comes from this one public statement issued by her vengeful master, yet we can certainly imagine her horror and fright when she found nobody at home in the governor's residence. Her hopes for freedom, fostered in part by rumors that the British would free the slaves, were quickly shattered.[25]

• During the crackdown at Wilmington, according to Janet Schaw, a male slave belonging to Doctor Cobham was shot to death while sneaking around in the woods. Schaw reported the circumstances, as they were told to her by a local informant the following night:

> That poor Cobham had lost a valuable slave, and the poor fellow his life without the least reason, he was certain; for that it was a fact well known to almost every body that he met a Mistress every night in the opposite wood, and that the wench being kept by her Master, was forced to carry on the intrigue with her black lover with great secrecy, which was the reason the fellow was so anxious to conceal himself; that the very man who shot him knew this, and had watched him.[26]

We do not know the name of this lover who gave up his life in the early stages of the American Revolution.

• On July 5, 1775, Thomas Hutchinson reported from St. Bartholomew Parish to the South Carolina council of safety:

> In consequence of an Information made me that Several of the Slaves in the neighborhood, were exciting & endeavoring to bring abt a General Insurrection, I took the very earliest Opty to prevent the fatal consequences

thereof by Apprehending such as were said to be the Principal leaders of their Infernal designs, & immediately after convened a Court of Justices & Freeholders in order to proceed on their Examination & Tryal, & upon full proof of the Fact the Cort were under the disagreable necessity to Cause Exemplary punishmts.

Hutchinson included in his report a transcript of the trial.

Jemmy, a Slave belonging to John Wells, Saith, that the followg Slaves (to wit) George, Prince & Patience belonging to Francis Smith, Jack, Hector, & daphney, belonging to Wm. Smith, Shifnal, Quashey & Jupiter, belonging to his Master, Ben & Pearce, belonging to James Parson's Esqr. & Ben, belongg to Jno. E, Hutchinson, are Preachers, & have, (many of them) been preaching for two Years last past to Great crouds of Negroes in the Neighborhood of Chyhaw, very frequently, which he himself attended . . . that at these assemblies he had heard of an Insurrection intended & to take the Country by Killing the Whites . . . That he Jemmy, heard the Prisoner George Say that the old King had reced a Book from our Lord by which he was to Alter the World (meaning to set the Negroes free) but for his not doing so, was now gone to Hell, & in Punishmt—That the Young King, meaning our Present One, came up with the Book, & was about to alter the World, & set the Negroes free.[27]

For the alleged crime of preaching that the king intended to free the slaves, and on the testimony of a single man, "Prisoner George" was hanged. The others were "punish'd in a less degree."

• In December of 1775 a slave whose name was not recorded "was tried and found guilty of sheepstealing" by a patriot court in Lancaster County, Virginia. Although his crime was punishable by death, the prisoner was sentenced only "to be burnt in the hand." At the moment of his sentencing, instead of saying God save the King (as is usual upon such occasion) he roared out, with the greatest sincerity, "God d-n the K-g. and the Governor too." This man played to his audience; he had to in order to survive.[28]

- Joseph Harris, a "small mulatto man" belonging to Henry King of Hampton, Virginia, ran away in July of 1775 and managed to reach HMS *Fowey*, the ship which served as the temporary seat of the royal government of Virginia. An experienced pilot, Harris was immediately placed into service on a small vessel, the *Liberty*. When the *Liberty* ran aground during a hurricane on September 5, Harris and a British captain, Matthew Squire, escaped from the patriots in a canoe which Harris had obtained from a slave. Local patriots took all the valuable possessions from the beached *Liberty*, then set it on fire "in return for [Squire's] harbouring gentlemen's negroes, and suffering his sailors to steal poultry, hogs, &c."[29] When Squire demanded that the rebels return the pillaged goods, the Hampton committee responded that they would do so only after the British had returned Joseph Harris and all other blacks who had run away from their masters.

  On October 26 Squire forced the issue by leading an attack on Hampton with six small vessels, one no doubt piloted by Harris. It was the first full-scale battle of the Revolution in the South, and former slaves figured prominently in both the politics of the matter and the actual fighting. Several men lost their lives, black as well as white. The rebels, in repelling the attack, seized one of the boats with "3 wounded Men 6 sailors and 2 Negros."[30] The white prisoners were "treated with great humanity," while the black prisoners were "tried for their lives."[31] Joseph Harris seems to have survived the Battle of Hampton. After fleeing to the British he brushed twice with death, but at least he was no longer a slave.

- In mid-June of 1775 "Several Negroes" from Charleston were "Suspected & charged of plotting an Insurrection."[32] Some were given "slight corporal punishments," but a man named Jeremiah, a free black, was held prisoner for two more months pending further investigation.[33] Jeremiah was an important figure in the Charleston harbor—a fisherman, a firefighter, a boat pilot who had guided men-of-war in and out of their moorings. He was relatively wealthy, worth £1,000 sterling by one estimate, £700 by another.[34] He even owned some slaves. But the patriots of Charleston were concerned that since he had guided men-of-war in the past, he would prove useful to the British should they attempt to attack the city. They were also worried that Jeremiah might be the critical link between the British armed forces and the slaves of South Carolina.

Jeremiah was tried again on August 11. Based on the testimony of three slaves, he was charged with "sending firearms to Negroes in the country and advising them to go in to His Majesty's troops when any should arrive." There was no physical evidence, and one of the witnesses soon recanted his testimony. George Milligen, a loyalist, suspected that those who testified against him did so "only to save themselves from a whipping, the only punishment they were told would be inflicted on Jerry."[35] Despite his legal status as a freeman, Jeremiah was tried under the "Negro Act" which applied only to slaves. William Campbell, the royal governor, tried to intervene on Jeremiah's behalf, but this only served to inflame the patriots; "my attempting to interfere in the matter," Campbell reported, "raised such a clamour amongst the people as is incredible, and they openly and loudly declared if I granted the man a pardon they would hang him at my door."[36] Henry Laurens, one of the judges, admitted that "the Inhabitants are as suddenly blown up by apprehensions as Gun powder is by Fire." According to what he could gather from "the out of Door Secrets of the people," Laurens reported that "I had heard enough to fill me with horror from a prospect of what might be done by Men enraged . . . if a pardon had been issued."[37]

The two judges and five freeholders who served as a jury determined unanimously that Jeremiah "was guilty of a design & attempt to encourage our Negroes to Rebellion & joining the King's troops if any had been Sent here."[38] On August 18 Jeremiah was hanged and his body burned. He never admitted any guilt, even to a clergyman who hoped to extract a confession. As he was about to hang, according to Governor Campbell, he "told his implacable and ungrateful persecutors God's judgment would one day overtake them for shedding his innocent blood."[39]

Was Jeremiah the boatman guilty as charged? It seems highly unlikely that the British gave him arms to run to the slaves; at no other time during the course of the war did either the British or Americans give weapons to black men without putting white men in charge. Did he try to plot an insurrection? A prosperous man with connections in the white community, and a slave owner himself, Jeremiah did not fit the profile of a radical. His guilt, if we can call it that, was described succinctly by Campbell: "He had often piloted in men-of-war, and it was strongly suspected (which I believe was his only crime) that he would have had no objection to have been employed again in the same service."[40]

Many whites who were suspected of loyalties to the British were hounded, tarred and feathered, sent into exile—but they were not hanged on the mere suspicion of what they might do in the future. Something else was going on here, something with a distinctly racial twist. Jeremiah personified the worst fears of white patriots: what if black men, acting as their own agents, sided against them? Henry Laurens, while explaining his vote in favor of execution, offered a clue as to the true nature of Jeremiah's "crime": "Jerry was a forward fellow, puffed up by prosperity, ruined by Luxury & debauchery & grown to an amazing pitch of vanity & ambition & withal a very Silly Coxcomb."[41] Perhaps it was for this that Jeremiah died: there was no telling the dangers if blacks forgot their "place."

Jeremiah, Joseph Harris, the prisoner who damned the king, George the preacher, the unfortunate lover who was killed for sneaking toward his sweetheart, the fifteen-year-old-girl who ran in vain to Dunmore—these African Americans were more affected by events leading up to the Revolution than most so-called patriots. Death or freedom—these were the stakes. A far greater proportion of blacks would die in the Revolution than whites, while a few would manage to free themselves from masters much more oppressive than the British Parliament.

Liberty to Slaves

On November 14, 1775, Lord Dunmore, the royal governor of Virginia, made it official:

> And I do hereby further declare all indented Servants, Negroes, or others, (appertaining to Rebels,) free, that are able and willing to bear Arms, they joining HIS MAJESTY'S Troops as soon as may be, for the more speedily reducing this Colony to a proper Sense of their Duty, to HIS MAJESTY'S Crown and Dignity.[42]

The impact was profound on both masters and slaves. Although white patriots had sensed it was coming, they expressed shock and dismay nonetheless. In the words of David Ramsay, they were "struck with horror."[43] Instinctively, they translated their fear and trembling into anger. Patriots dubbed Dunmore "King of the Blacks," an insult which we can not even begin to fathom today. Congress accused him of "tearing up the foundations of civil authority and government."[44] In a letter to Richard Henry Lee, George Washington responded with venom to Dunmore's "diabolical Schemes":

> If my Dear Sir that Man is not crushed before Spring, he will become the most formidable Enemy America has—his strength will Increase as a Snow ball by Rolling; and faster, if some expedient cannot be hit upon to convince the Slaves and Servants of the Impotency of His designs. . . . I do not think that forcing his Lordship on Ship board is sufficient; nothing less than depriving him of life or liberty will secure peace to Virginia.[45]

From the tone of Washington's letter and from everything else that was written, said, or done by patriot masters, we can infer that Dunmore's proclamation hit a very sore nerve. Most slaves, they knew, would run to the British if given half a chance.[46] Lund Washington reported to George Washington from Mount Vernon that "there is not a man of them, but would leave us, if they believ'd they coud make there Escape."[47] Newspapers in several colonies reprinted a small but telling incident in Philadelphia. A "gentlewoman" was walking along a narrow sidewalk when she came upon a black man who refused to step into the muddy street to let her by. When she called him to task, the man replied: "Stay, you d_____d white bitch, till Lord Dunmore and his black regiment come, and then we will see who is to take the wall."[48] This one story confirmed the fears of many whites: Dunmore's proclamation had shaken the very roots of a society based on subordination.

To counter the thrust of Dunmore's proclamation, patriots developed a multipronged defense. First, they redoubled their efforts to insure that slaves would not escape. Masters kept slaves indoors at night, closely watched. They removed boats from the shores. In some cases, they relocated their slaves inland to lessen the likelihood of runaways reaching the British. The patriots of Maryland, ostrich-like, prohibited "all correspondence with Virginia by land or water" in hopes that news of Dunmore's proclamation could somehow be kept from the people they held in bondage.[49]

Patriots also publicized the proclamation in order to heighten anti-British sentiment. Patrick Henry, while recruiting for the militia, circulated a broadside with a copy of Dunmore's offer of freedom. Newspapers abounded with derogatory references to slaves who had fled to Dunmore—referring to them as "black bandetti" and the "Speckled regiment"—to arouse white citizens.[50] The strategy worked. Philip Fithian noted that in the Virginia backcountry the impact of the proclamation was "to quicken all in Revolution." Richard Henry Lee wrote that "Lord Dunmore's unparalleled conduct in Virginia has, a few Scotch excepted, united every Man in that large Colony." Edward Rutledge predicted from South Carolina that the proclamation would "more effectively . . . work an eternal separation between Great Britain and the Colonies,—than any other expedient, which could possibly be thought of."[51]

Finally, patriots tried to convince the slaves to remain with their masters. Within two weeks of the proclamation John Page, vice-president of the Virginia Committee of Safety, published an appeal to the slaves in several newspapers:

Long have the Americans, moved by compassion, and actuated by sound policy, endeavored to stop the progress of slavery. Our Assemblies have repeatedly passed acts laying heavy duties upon imported negroes, by which they meant altogether to prevent the horrid traffic; but their human intentions have been as often frustrated by the cruelty and covetiousness of a set of English merchants, who prevailed upon the king to repeal our kind and merciful acts, little indeed to the credit of his humanity. Can it then be supposed that the Negroes will be better used by the English, who have always encouraged and upheld this slavery, than by their present masters, who pity their condition? . . . No, the ends of Lord Dunmore and his party being answered, they will either give up the offending negroes to the *rigour* of the laws they have broken, or sell them in the West Indies, where every year they sell many thousands of their miserable brethren, to perish, either by the inclemency of the weather, or the cruelty of barbarous masters. Be not then, ye negroes tempted by this proclamation to ruin yourselves. I have given you a faithful view of what you are to expect and declare, before GOD, in doing it I have considered your welfare, as well as that of the country. Whether you will profit by my advice I cannot tell, but this I know, that whether we suffer or not, if you desert us, you most certainly will.[52]

Not many slaves were likely to read this verbose piece of propaganda nor be swayed by its twisted logic. Yet patriot masters apparently felt the need to fabricate such arguments, if only to relieve their own consciences. Understandably, they preferred to envision themselves as purveyors of freedom, the British as engineers of slavery. But it wasn't true, and the slaves undoubtedly knew this.

Taking a more personal approach, some masters talked directly to their slaves and tried to convince them not to flee. When his brother James was away, Henry Laurens gathered the people whom James claimed to own; he "admonished them to behave with great circumspection in this dangerous times" and "set before them the great risque of exposing themselves to the treachery of pretended freinds & false witnesses." According to Henry, the slaves responded according to script: "Poor Creatures, they were sensibly affected, & with many thanks promised to follow my advice & to accept the offer of my Protection."[53] Robert Carter reported receiving a similar reply after he had elicited the support of his slaves: "We all fully intend to serve you our master and we do now promise to use our whole might & force to execute your Commands."[54] But what else could they say to a man who might whip or sell them at will? On August 14, 1776, Henry Laurens boasted to his son John that his own slaves "all to a Man are strongly attached to me" and that "not one of them has attempted to desert"; on the same day, Lachlan McIntosh, Jr., reported to his father that one of his slaves had just escaped—along with five belonging to Henry Laurens.[55]

The slaves' actions spoke louder than words: Dunmore's proc-lamation triggered a mass escape. The Northampton committee of safety reported that about two hundred "immediately joined him," and on November 19, only five days after publication of the proc-lamation, Andrew Sprowel estimated that 300 had successfully made their way to Dunmore.[56] On November 24 John Page wrote to Thomas Jefferson, "Numbers of Negros and Cowardly Scoundrels flock to his Standard," and three days later Edmund Pendleton told Richard Henry Lee that "slaves flock to him in abundance."[57] By the end of November newspapers were announcing that "boatloads of slaves" had tried to reach the British ships.[58] By December 2 a dispatch from Williamsburg read:

> Since Lord Dunmore's proclamation made its appearance here, it is said he has recruited his army, in the counties of Princess Anne and Norfolk, to the amount of about 2000 men, including his black regiment, which is thought to be a considerable part, with this inscription on their breasts:—"Liberty to slaves."[59]

"Liberty to slaves"—it must have sounded so sweet. On planta-tions throughout the Chesapeake region African Americans held in bondage spread the news. ("The Negroes have a wonderfull Art of communicating Intelligence among themselves," two masters from Georgia told John Adams. "It will run severall hundreds of Miles in a Week or Fortnight.")[60] Undoubtedly, the possibility of fleeing to freedom was the talk of the fields and quarters. Those who had always wanted to escape—there were certainly many, far more than dared make the attempt—now had a better idea of where they might go.

On November 17 Robert Brent advertised for a runaway slave whose "elopement" stemmed from "a determined resolution to get liberty, as he conceived, by flying to lord Dunmore."[61] In the months following the proclamation, advertisements for runaways made numerous references to slaves who sought to join "the min-isterial army."[62] One master from Virginia, Landon Carter of Sabine Hall, recorded this in his diary:

> Last night after going to bed, Moses, my son's man, Joe, Billy, Postillion, John, Mullatto Peter, Tom, Panticove, Manuel & Lancaster Sam, ran away, to be sure, to Ld. Dunmore, for they got privately into Beale's room before dark & took out my son's gun & one I had there, took out of his drawer in my passage all his ammunition furniture, Landon's bag of bullets and all the Powder, and went off.... These accursed villains have stolen Landon's silver buckles, George's shirts, Tom Parker's new waistcoat & breeches. [63]

With arms and ammunition, clothes, and some valuables that might be traded for cash or favors, these ten men with dreams of freedom had issued a *de facto* declaration of independence. So did all 87 slaves belonging to John Willoughby, Jr.[64]

We do not know the full identities of the runaway slaves who managed to reach the British ships alive, although we do have some lists of first names: on board the HMS *Scorpion* on March 3, 1776, were three Thoms, three Dicks, two Johns, Abraham, Murphy, Abberdeen, Gilbert, Goosman, Bobb, Friday, Quash, Thena, Peggy, Jeffery, Morris, Ben, Betty, Rose, Claranda, Jacob, James, Arthur, Richard, Presence, Cato, Maryann, Peggy, Polly, Grace, Queen, and Patience.[65] We have no record of where these people came from, whether they had their husbands, wives, or children with them, or what became of them.

But we do know that Dunmore quickly made use of the "Stout Active Negro's" who offered their services.[66] On December 6 he wrote that he was arming refugee slaves "as fast as they came in."[67] He clad them in uniforms, dubbed them "Lord Dunmore's Ethiopian Regiment," and sent them to work pillaging patriot plantations along the shores of the Chesapeake to supply the British ships with food.[68] He also sent black recruits into battle: the "Ethiopian Regiment" participated in a prolonged confrontation at Great Bridge during early December. Two runaways who were captured by the patriots reported that three-quarters of the soldiers who manned the garrison were Negroes and that "all the blacks who are sent to the fort at the great Bridge, are supplied with muskets, Cartridges &c strictly ordered to use them defensively & offensively."[69] When the British were defeated on December 9, thirty-two African Americans were taken prisoner.

We also know that many who attempted to reach Dunmore never made it. Those who tried faced some very difficult tasks. First, they had to escape the ubiquitous patrols organized by nervous patriot masters; then they had to locate the British ships, maneuver secretly to an adjacent shore, and figure out some way of transporting themselves across the water. The water transport proved the toughest. One group was apprehended in a thirty-foot vessel navigating the James River; a party of thirteen, steering a schooner into the Chesapeake, was overtaken by a whale boat; seven men and two women were seized in an open boat on their way to Norfolk. Eleven runaways were placed in the "great gaol" of Williamsburg after being "discovered making off in boats, when our people attacked them, and wounded two, one it is thought mortally." Three men, upon boarding a vessel which they believed to belong to the British, "declared their resolution to spend the last drop of *their blood* in lord *Dunmore's* service"—and then discovered that the ship belonged to Virginia, not the British navy. Two of the men were sentenced to hang "as an example to others."[70]

Although a handful of the captured runaways were put to death, the state did not favor execution, which required compensation to the owners. Most captured runaways who were deemed too troublesome to return to their masters were either auctioned off in the West Indies or purchased from their owners at public expense and sent to work in the lead mines of western Virginia.[71] Either way, they were doomed to hard labor and harsh treatment for the rest of their lives. Some runaways, when captured, committed suicide rather than live with the consequences. Despite the financial loss to the state, a few were put to death with dramatic displays of vengeance and intimidation. In Maryland three slaves who had killed a white man while trying to reach Dunmore were sentenced by the Dorchester County Court:

> They were to be taken to the place of execution and there each
> of them to have their right hands cut off and to be hanged by

the neck until they were dead; their heads to be severed from
their bodies and their bodies to be divided each of them in
four quarters and their heads and quarters to be set up in the
most public places in the county.[72]

Other slaves, upon viewing the mutilated remains, would presumably be deterred from running away.

While slaves who failed in their escapes suffered terribly, those
who managed to reach Lord Dunmore experienced troubles of their
own. Crowded aboard ships, they were highly susceptible to the
usual array of serious diseases common among soldiers and sailors
of the eighteenth century: dysentery, typhus, typhoid fever, smallpox. In March of 1776 Dunmore reported that "a fever crept in
amongst them, which carried off a great many very fine fellows."[73]
After Dunmore had withdrawn his ships from the Elizabeth River,
Robert Honyman recorded in his diary that 150 dead blacks had
been left behind. By June many more had died, and patriot troops
along the shores reported sighting numerous bodies as they floated
in the water.[74]

Hoping to contain the epidemic, Dunmore established a "sick
house" on Gwynne's Island in the Chesapeake Bay. Recent recruits,
primarily black, were inoculated there against smallpox, yet many
still died. After the British had been driven from the island, American soldiers on the landing force described "the deplorable situation
of the miserable wretches left behind":

> Many poor Negroes were found on the island dying of the
> putrid fever; others dead in the open fields; a child was found
> sucking at the breast of its dead mother. In one place you might
> see a poor wretch half dead making signs of water, in another,
> others endeavoring to crawl away from the intolerable stench
> of dead bodies by their sides.[75]

Illness took a terrible toll. "Had it not been for this horrid disorder,"
Dunmore wrote on June 26, "I should have had two thousand
blacks; with whom I should have had no doubt of penetrating into
the heart of this Colony."[76]

As it was, only about 300 former slaves left with the British when they withdrew from the Chesapeake later that summer. A substantial majority of the "Ethiopian Regiment" had perished. Countless other slaves who had tried to gain their freedom by responding to Dunmore's proclamation had been captured. For most of those who seized the time to make their escape, the sweet dream of liberty turned into a nightmare.

Although Lord Dunmore, the governor of Virginia, was the only British official to promise emancipation, many slaves throughout the South assumed that if they offered their services to the British they would be set free. To some extent this was true. Governor Robert Eden of Maryland, upon his departure in the spring of 1776, granted asylum to slaves who managed to reach his ship. When a British fleet appeared off the mouth of North Carolina's Cape Fear River in March of 1776, former slaves from as far inland as 150 miles presented themselves for service. British Captain George Martin quickly organized these runaways into a company of "Black Pioneers" and put them to work as laborers, servants, and guides. In South Carolina a British captain anchored in the Charleston harbor admitted to angry patriots that he was harboring runaway slaves, and he boasted that he could have had 500 more had he accepted all who sought asylum.[77]

With limited space and supplies on their ships, British captains did not take on every man, woman, or child who came their way. But they did aid and encourage the runaways however they could. In the Charleston harbor about 500 former slaves sought refuge on Sullivan's Island, protected by British ships which were anchored nearby. Sullivan's Island, at that point in time, was not exactly prime real estate—it housed the "pest house" for imported slaves who had come down with communicable diseases. In December of 1775 it also housed an entire community of runaways who, by their very existence, appeared to threaten local patriots. Since any haven for slaves seeking their freedom would serve as a lure to those back on the plantations, the council of safety ordered William Moultrie to organize an attack. According to Charleston merchant Josiah Smith, Jr., Moultrie's force early in the Morning sett Fire to the Pest house, took some Negroes and Sailors Prisoners, killed 50 of the former that would not be taken, and unfortunately lost near 20 that were unseen by them till taken off the Beach by the Men Warrs Boats.

Henry Laurens boasted that the raid would "mortify" the British governor and "serve to humble our Negroes in general."[78]

Three months later, with 200 fugitives huddled on Tybee Island in the Savannah harbor, angry and fearful patriot slaveowners prepared to stage a similar attack. On March 14, 1776, Stephen Bull wrote to Henry Laurens:

It is far better for the public and the owners, if the deserted negroes . . . who are on Tybee Island, be shot, if they cannot be taken . . . for if they are carried away, and converted into money, which is the sinew of war, it will only enable an enemy to fight us with our own money or property. Therefore, all who cannot be taken, had better be shot by the Creek Indians, as it, perhaps, may deter other negroes from deserting, and will establish a hatred or aversion between the Indians and negroes.[79]

Laurens had some hesitations: "[I]t is an awful business," he wrote back, "notwithstanding it has the Sanction of Law to put even fugitive & Rebellious Slaves to death, the prospect is horrible." But practicality superseded morality, and on behalf of the South Carolina council of safety Laurens suggested that the patriots of Georgia proceed as Bull had suggested.

[W]e think the Council of Safety in Georgia ought to give that encouragement which is necessary to induce proper Persons to seize & if nothing else will do to destroy all those Rebellious Negroes upon Tybee Island or wherever they may be found, If Indians are best the most proper hands let them be employed on this service but we would advise that some discreet white Men were incorporated with or joined to lead them.[80]

On March 25 forty white patriots disguised as Indians, along with thirty Creeks, staged their raid on Tybee Island. We have no first-hand accounts of the attack, but the governor of Florida, Patrick Tonyn, complained that the raiding party showed "signs of the most savage barbarity"—including brutal beatings and scalpings—and that "the white people exceeded the ferocity of the Indians." [81]

Over the course of 1776 the royal governors in Georgia, South Carolina, North Carolina, Virginia, and Maryland abandoned their posts and all British ships withdrew to the North. Periodically over the next few years, British vessels would enter the Chesapeake Bay; whenever they did, runaway slaves would come "flocking down from the interior parts of the country." [82] But everywhere else in the South, slaves who still hoped to make their escape had no ready access to a liberating army. A few still fled, [83] and some daring individuals and groups entertained notions of armed insurrection [84]— but this had always been true, even before the special circumstances of the Revolutionary War. For the most part, with the British far away, slaves in the South reverted to traditional modes of coping. They engaged in work slowdowns, even as their masters urged them to pick up the pace of production to make up for wartime short-ages. [85] Many preached and practiced Judeo-Christian religions, with special emphasis on the Exodus theme. And no matter what they felt, they told their masters what the white folks wanted to hear. Until a better time should arrive, they did what they had to do to survive.

A Board Game

First to Georgia late in 1778, then to the Carolinas and Virginia in 1779 and 1780, the British returned. The royal army arrived in force this time, and slaves fled in far greater numbers than they had before. Henry Laurens estimated that 5,000 ran to the British during the first three months of the Georgia campaign—about one-third of the local black population. George Abbot Hall, a merchant and customs collector, figured that over 20,000 slaves fled in South Carolina; David Ramsay, the contemporary historian, placed the number at 25,000—at least one-quarter of the African Americans in that state. Josiah Smith, another merchant, reported that almost all the slaves within an eighty-mile radius of Charleston had deserted. Thomas Jefferson estimated that 30,000 ran away during 1781 in Virginia.[86] This was clearly an exodus of biblical proportions.

Some of those who ran came from the plantations of prominent patriot masters. When the British sailed up the Potomac in 1781, thirty slaves from Jefferson's Monticello estate seized the opportunity to escape from their master.[87] Seventeen fled from George Washington:

> Peter, an old man. Lewis, an old man. Frank, an old man. Frederick, a man about 45 years old; an overseer and valuable. Gunner, a man about 45 years old; valuable, a Brick maker. Harry, a man about 40 years old, valuable, a Horseler. Tom, a man about 20 years old, stout and Healthy. Sambo, a man about 20 years old, stout and Healthy. Thomas, a lad about 17 years old, House servant. Peter, a lad about 15 years old, very likely. Stephen, a man about 20 years old, a cooper by trade. James, a man about 25 years old, stout and Healthy. Watty, a man about 20 years old, by trade a weaver. Daniel, a man about 19 years old, very likely. Lucy, a woman about 20 years old. Esther, a woman about 18 years old. Deborah, a woman about 16 years old.[88]

The runaways, of course, expected to be liberated once they reached the British army. Like Lord Dunmore before him, General Henry Clinton issued a proclamation: "every NEGRO who shall desert the Rebel Standard" would enjoy the "full security to follow within these Lines, any Occupation which he shall think proper."[89] Unlike Dunmore, however, Clinton stopped short of proclaiming emancipation; he was trying to lure slaves without giving too much offense to white slaveowners. But neither masters nor slaves read the fine print. Whites took offense in any case, while slaves once again assumed that if they made it to the British they would be free.

This assumption was not entirely correct. British policy was cool and calculating, not humanitarian. In the words of historian Robert Olwell, "fugitive slaves were sheltered under the guise that they constituted contraband enemy property, rather than recognized as liberated persons."[90] Royal officers wanted slaves for the labor they might perform—and to deprive the rebels of that labor. The British put African Americans to work in a variety of capacities: sawyers and carpenters helped build ships, blacksmiths forged and mended tools, skilled and unskilled workers built and repaired roads. In South Carolina 5,000 slaves toiled on a hundred plantations seized from the rebels in order to supply the needs of the army.[91]

Officially, blacks who labored for the British received wages; in reality, they received little or nothing after deductions were made for their provisions. They were given inferior food; in times of scarcity, which of course were frequent, their rations were the first to be cut. They were housed in separate quarters. They were worked long and hard. Their former masters, not wishing to hurt or destroy their own property, had not worked the slaves beyond endurance; their new masters hardly seemed to care, for worn-out laborers could easily be replaced by new refugees at no extra expense. Indeed, the whole point of acquiring slaves was for blacks to perform labor that was too rough or hazardous or demeaning for whites to do themselves. People of African origins or descent, allegedly protected from the sun by their dark skins and accustomed to an equatorial environment, were ordered to cut trees and dig trenches during the "sickly season" when, in the words of General Cornwallis, "the heat is too great to admit of the soldiers doing it."[92] According to Lord Dunmore, supposedly the "Great Liberator," blacks constituted "the most efficatious, expeditious, cheapest, and certain means of reducing this Country to a proper sense of their Duty" because they were "fitter for service in this Warm Climate than White Men" and "may be got on much easier terms."[93]

British officers made no secret of commandeering runaways for their personal use. On June 21, 1781, the Hessian officer Johann Ewald wrote in his diary:

Since this army had been fighting continuously across the country for ten months, Lord Cornwallis had permitted each subaltern to keep two horses and one Negro, each captain, four horses and two Negroes, and so on, according to rank. But since this order was not strictly carried out, the greatest abuse arose from this arrangement. . . . Every officer had four to six horses and three or four Negroes, as well as one or two Negresses for cook and maid. Every soldier's woman was mounted and also had a Negro and Negress on horseback for her servants. Each squad had one or two horses and Negroes, and every non-commissioned officer had two horses and one Negro. Yes, indeed, I can testify that every soldier had his Negro, who carried his provisions and bundles.[94]

Politically, the British used runaways as hostages: if patriot masters would only agree to change sides, they could have their slaves back. When ninety slaves belonging to George Galphin escaped, British officers promised to return them if Galphin, an Indian commissioner for the rebels, agreed to provide crucial information; in the meantime, these slaves who had expected freedom were put to work on the plantation of the British general Augustine Prevost. After the British had captured Charleston in 1780, the board of police established a plan whereby any slaves belonging to masters who agreed to pledge their allegiance to the king would be returned. Using slaves as a lure, royal officials hoped to turn former patriots into loyalists. That the slaves had fled their patriot masters expecting to be freed was of no account.[95]

So many slaves fled to the British that they constituted something of a problem. Because of the "confusion" created by Negro desertions, in May of 1780 General Clinton actually requested Cornwallis to "make such Arrangements as will discourage their joining us."[96] The following month General James Patterson complained of the "very great Inconveniences . . . found from Negroes leaving the service of their masters and coming to the British Army."[97] Try as they might, the British could not find an immediate use for all the slaves—tens of thousands of them, women and children included—who requested protection and support.

What to do with the excess? At Camden General Cornwallis ordered that all blacks who were employed by the army be tagged, and he instructed the provost marshal to "take up, and flog out of the Encampment all those who are not Mark'd"—but he was forced to rescind his order under pressure from his officers, who wished to mine the available labor pool for personal servants. After gaining control of most of Georgia in 1778 and 1779, the royal government empowered the commissioner of claims to seize "all fugitive slaves found in the province" and to build "a strong and convenient house or prison" to hold those who were too "unruly" or tried to "abscond." In Charleston the board of police seized blacks who did not hold a pass from their master or a certificate of freedom and impressed them to labor for the government. Slaves who had escaped from loyalist masters were returned upon demand. Other refugees who were not deemed of use by the army were put to work on plantations owned by British officers or sold to the West Indies. If short of supplies, the British would sometimes trade back slaves for provisions. When the royal fleet retreated from Port Royal in 1780, Major General Alexander Leslie refused to take with him several hundred African Americans who had dared to escape and were requesting asylum.[98] According to David Ramsay, British ships cast off the runaway slaves like so much dead weight:

> [I]n order to get off with the retreating army, they would sometimes fasten themselves to the sides of the boats. To prevent this dangerous practice the fingers of some of them were chopped off, and soldiers were posted with cutlasses and bayonets to oblige them to keep their proper distances.[99]

Clearly, the British did not really care. The loyalist official John Cruden explained quite accurately that the thrust of British policy was not intended to undermine the slave system:

> 'Tis only changing one master for another; and let it be clearly understood that they are to serve the King for ever, and that those slaves who are not taken for his Majesty's service are to remain on the plantation, and perform, as usual, the labor of the field.

Cruden argued that by siphoning off "the most hardy, intrepid, and determined blacks," the British army was actually strengthening the institution of slavery. With the most troublesome slaves removed, masters would find it easier to "keep the rest in good order."[100]

Since numerous loyalists and British officials, including Lord Dunmore, were slaveowners themselves, they were understandably reluctant to place weapons in the hands of African Americans. William Bull opposed the arming of blacks because he believed "their savage nature" prompted them to commit "indiscriminate outrages," and also because of "the danger of the example to the rest of that class of people."[101] Yet however cautious and conservative, some officials could still perceive that arming slaves might prove useful in certain circumstances. If the goal was to intimidate white patriots, for instance, the performance of black men with bayonets could not be surpassed by the best of redcoated regulars. When Eliza Wilkinson's home was plundered by British troops, she reserved her strongest complaints for the "insolent" former slaves who accompanied the soldiers.[102]

When British officers placed rifles or muskets, bayonets or swords, in the hands of former slaves, they insisted on strict supervision. Blacks always served under white officers; usually they carried arms for specified tasks of limited duration, such as the defense of Savannah.[103] By and large, this strategy worked: armed African Americans served the purposes of the white officers who ordered them about, then gave up their arms in the end.[104]

But occasionally it backfired: when their missions were done, some former slaves refused to turn in the weapons they had been issued. Toward the end of the war bands of armed blacks who had escaped from Whig masters escaped once again—this time from Tory officers—into deep woods and dank swamps. Forming their own maroon communities, they survived by hunting and gathering, raiding plantations, and even farming. One group, calling themselves "the King of England's soldiers," lived until 1786 within a camp containing twenty-one houses and some cropland, all protected by a half-mile stretch of log and cane pilings in the Savannah River swamps. The commander of the militia unit which finally drove these people from their settlement reported that his men destroyed "about four acres of green rice" and "as much rough rice as would have made 25 barrels or more if beat out, and brought off about 60 bushels of corn."[105] Another group, referred to as "Negro Dragoons" or "Black Dragoons," pillaged in the war-torn region between the two armies in South Carolina. According to one report, written shortly before the British departed Charleston,

> the black dragoons . . . have been out four times within the last ten days plundering & robbing between the Quarter house and this place—last night they came as high as Mrs. Godins, where they continued from 11 o'clock till 4 this morning & carried off everything they could, except what was in the house which they did not enter—all her cattle, sheep, hogs, horses, & half the provisions she had was moved away. She thinks the number at least one hundred all Blacks.[106]

After the war, white loyalists joined with white patriots and Catawba Indians to destroy these and other black communities which had managed to take advantage of the turbulent times to fashion lives without masters, if only for a short period of time.[107]

In the closing years of the war tens of thousands of slaves participated in a revolution on their own behalf without running off to the British or to the swamps. Throughout the ravaged regions of the South, the collapse of normal channels of authority opened opportunities for defiance and self-assertion. In April of 1780 on the Silk Hope plantation in South Carolina, British soldiers "bound the overseer . . . & whipped him most unmercifully" in the presence of slaves. At the Pinckney plantation the previous year, "the overseer concealed himself in the swamp" while British troops "burnt the dwelling house & books destroyed all the furniture, china &ca." Upon his return from the swamp, the Pinckney overseer discovered that "the Negroes pay no attention to his orders." Why should they have? His authority had been based on crude power—a power he no longer possessed. According to Eliza Pinckney, the slaves who remained on her plantation considered themselves "perfectly free" and "quite their own masters." In 1780 Pinckney predicted her crop would be "very Small by the desertion of Negroes in planting and hoeing time." William Bull, a loyalist, wrote that slaves had become "ungovernable, absenting themselves often from the service of their

masters." The British Colonel Banistre Tarleton wrote that "upon
the approach of any detachment of the King's troops, all negroes,
men, women, and children . . . thought themselves absolved from all
respect to their American masters." Indeed they did—particularly
when the masters themselves fled from the British, leaving only the
slaves to tend to their plantations.[108]

How did slaves fare once left to their own devices on abandoned
plantations? We do not know. Almost all of our information concerning the actions of African American slaves during the Revolution must be inferred from the documents of white people: letters,
diaries, memoirs, reports, records, ledgers, newspaper accounts.
Comparable sources from the slaves themselves are scanty. "Given
the nature of slave societies," writes Robert Olwell, "the historical
record says least about the situations in which slaves were most
autonomous."[109] Even so, Olwell conjectures that the slaves on
abandoned plantations engaged in small, self-sufficient agriculture—
tending their gardens and poultry—just as they had done in their
limited free time when their masters had been present.[110] This seems
plausible, since they had to support themselves somehow. We do
know that they did not continue to bring in cash crops to benefit
their absent masters. They harvested what they could for themselves—"the best produce of the plantation," according to Thomas
Pinckney—while they allowed the rest to lie "rotting in the
fields."[111] For a week, a month, or perhaps even a year, they experienced a freedom of sorts. But it was not true emancipation.
Hungry and anxious, they might well have sensed it was too soon
to celebrate.

When the British invaded Georgia, the Carolinas, and Virginia,
enslaved African Americans had no way of knowing how things
would turn out. They were under the general impression that if
they could escape and offer their services to the invading redcoats,
they would be freed. But they had no assurances, nor was it certain
that the British would prevail. What if they ran away but were later
captured or defeated by their original owners, or what if the British
soldiers proved not to be an army of liberation after all, but just
one more set of white men ready to exploit black labor? Perhaps

the British would free some but not all of those who ran away. Perhaps families would be torn apart.

On the other hand, what would happen if slaves decided *not* to join the British? Patriot masters, fleeing the British army, might haul them away to places unknown, where they could be sold or hired out to strangers. If their masters ran and left them behind, they would have to survive on their own amidst economic chaos. And how would they be treated if they happened to be *captured* by the British, rather than joining them willingly? As prizes of war, they would belong to the conquerors. Very likely, they would be sold and sent to the West Indies.

Perhaps they should just run away without seeking support from either side. They could try to blend in with the small communities of free blacks in Savannah, Charleston, Wilmington, or Williamsburg. But in such numbers? How would they all make a living? Maybe they'd do better in the backwoods or the Dismal Swamp. Still, they would have to support themselves, and they'd run a great risk of being captured if they settled in one place and tried to produce some food.

Their fates were in the balance: they might wind up free or dead. In the fields and huddled in small groups at night, they pondered the alternatives. They had to project the consequences of their actions, to predict the most likely outcomes. They considered the various options. They evaluated possible strategies. They plotted and schemed. Imagine, just for a moment, that they had kept journals of their proceedings: we would read their speeches and arguments, we would learn about their caucuses, we would hear of their plans—three will go this way, four over there, the rest must wait to hear from those who lead the way. Imagine the talk within families: shall we take separate paths? And the tiny conspiracies, two or three cohorts acting with caution: we cannot tell a soul, for we might be betrayed.

Condemned to ignorance, we will never know what the slaves said to each other in those days of decision. But we can safely conclude that each and every man and woman—and the older children as well—processed the available information with interest, hope, and concern. Whatever paths they chose, we can be sure they took nothing for granted. Eliza Wilkinson boasted that the Revolution had turned her circle of lady friends into "politicians" and "perfect statesmen" as they discussed the pressing issues of the day in their parlors.[112] What then of these slaves, who not only talked but acted on questions of such monumental import to their lives? Were they not even greater politicians—and generals too?

White politicians and generals took no notice of these deliberations among African Americans, for they were hatching schemes of their own: how best to adapt the institution of slavery to the peculiar dynamics of the American Revolution. Both the British and American armies viewed slaves as mere pawns in the game of war. When British soldiers captured rebel plantations, they divided up the spoils—including the slaves. When patriot soldiers captured loyalist plantations, they too divvied up the take. As roving bands of partisans, both patriot and loyalist, plundered and pillaged throughout the countryside in the later years of the war, they commandeered all slaves they could find for their personal use or sale. Booty— including human beings—constituted an important component of a soldier's recompense. In 1781 the American General Thomas Sumter systematized the use of slaves as payment to the soldiers under his command: a lieutenant colonel who served ten months would receive three grown slaves and a child, a major would get three adults, a captain two adults, and so on according to rank; even the privates were given one slave each.[113] As governor of Virginia, Thomas Jefferson signed a bill granting every white male who enlisted for the duration of the war "300 acres of land plus a healthy sound Negro between 20 and 30 years of age or 60 pounds in gold or silver."[114] When patriot forces recaptured Georgia, slaves were given not only to soldiers but to public officials in lieu of salaries.[115] And loyalists answered in kind: "if the rebels will give one negro for one year's service," one suggested, "let us give two."[116]

The expendability of African Americans was nowhere more apparent than at Yorktown in 1781, where 4,000 to 5,000 slaves lent their support to Cornwallis in hopes of obtaining their freedom. Under siege, the British army suffered from severe shortages of food. Rather than share minimal provisions with everyone under their command, officers cut back on rations to blacks, who were forced to eat "putrid ships meat and wormy biscuits that have spoiled on the ships."[117] When even these ran out, starving and diseased African Americans were forced out from behind the barricades into a no-man's-land between the lines. What would become of these people, suddenly deprived of all support? If they somehow managed to survive, how would they be treated by their old patriot masters?

Most did not live long enough to face that event. Sarah Osborn, a camp follower for the Continental Army, recalled seeing "a number of dead Negroes lying round their encampment, whom . . . the British had driven out of the town and left to starve, or were first starved and then thrown out."[118] Joseph Plumb Martin also remembered the former slaves who had been cast out by the British:

> During the siege, we saw in the woods herds of Negroes which Lord Cornwallis (after he had inveigled them from their proprietors), in love and pity to them, had turned adrift, with no other recompense for their confidence in his humanity than the smallpox for their bounty and starvation and death for their wages. They might be seen scattered about in every direction, dead and dying, with pieces of ears of burnt Indian corn in the hands and mouths, even of those that were dead.[119]

From within British lines the Hessian Captain Johann Ewald wrote candidly:

> On the same day as the enemy assault, we drove back to the enemy all of our black friends, whom we had taken along to despoil the countryside. We had used them to good advantage and set them free, and now, with fear and trembling, they had to face the reward of their cruel masters. Last night I had to make a sneak patrol, during which I came across a great number of these unfortunates. In their hunger, these unhappy people would have soon devoured what I had; and since they lay between two fires, they had to be driven off by force.[120]

Literally and figuratively, this was the fate of many southern slaves in the Revolutionary War. They had scented freedom—some had even managed a taste—but here they were on a desolate plain, starving and diseased, cast out and abandoned between two sets of white men who had once used them to great advantage.

Two Émigrés

As the British withdrew first from Yorktown and Wilmington, then Savannah and Charleston, and finally New York and St. Augustine, they carried on their ships a great many African Americans. Estimates vary as to the numbers, but all contemporary observers and modern historians agree that it was in the tens of thousands.[121] At first glance, it might appear that such a mass exodus signaled freedom and new beginnings, but the vast majority—in the vicinity of 80 percent—were still slaves, the property of loyalist émigrés or British officials.[122] Some of these had always belonged to loyalist masters; others had escaped to the British to find freedom, only to be commandeered by army officers or given to loyalists as compensation for lost property. For the most part, the institution of slavery remained intact as ships departed to the Bahamas, Jamaica, or other islands in the West Indies. According to the British General Guy Carleton, ten families sailing from Savannah to Jamaica carried with them 1,568 slaves.[123] Thomas Brown, leader of a Tory band that terrorized patriots in the deep South, had come to Georgia in 1774 with 150 white indentured servants; at the close of hostilities, he wound up with 170 black slaves to work his new plantations on Caribbean islands.[124] In St. Augustine, as of July, 1783, merely eight of the 2,563 black refugees from South Carolina were free, and three of the 1,956 from Georgia.[125]

Only the hundreds who left for England and some (but scarcely all) of those headed for Canada did so as free men and women. Virtually all the emigrants to the British Isles wound up in London, where they lived in impoverished communities with few economic opportunities and no prospects for social advancement. Shortly after their arrival, many were persuaded or coerced into emigrating once again, to Sierra Leone this time. Unlike the later colonization from Nova Scotia, this early "Back to Africa" movement was promoted exclusively by whites who wanted to rid London of its people of color. For a host of reasons, the settlement failed. Former slaves from Virginia or South Carolina who had fled to the British army and finally arrived in a land of freedom wound up dying of tropical diseases or being sold back into slavery.[126]

According to official records, exactly 3,000 free African Americans departed from New York to Canada in 1783—1,336 men, 914 women, and 750 children.[127] Emigrants had to remain wary until the moment they sailed away. As they awaited their boats in New York, they hid from American slave catchers who threatened to take them back to their old masters. If caught by some white American—whether a former master or an impostor on the prowl—what could they say or do? On September 18, 1783, Judith Jackson petitioned General Carleton from New York:

> I came from Virginia with General Ashley When I came from there I was quite Naked. I was in Service a year and a half with Mr Savage the remaining Part I was with Lord Dunmore. Washing and ironing in his Service I came with him from Charlestown to New York and was in Service with him till he went away My Master came for me I told him I would not go with him One Mr. Yelback wanted to steal me back to Virginia and was not my Master he took all my Cloaths which his Majesty gave me, he said he would hang Major Williams for giving me a Pass he took my Money from me and stole my Child from me and Sent it to Virginia[128]

Unlike the tens of thousands of emigrants who were still enslaved and the hundreds of thousands of African Americans who remained in bondage in the new United States, a handful of free black émigrés left written accounts of their personal adventures. As usual, the evidence is skewed towards those who survived or prospered. Yet these tales, although not a balanced sample, give personality and texture to the African American experience of the Revolutionary War. Below is an excerpt from the two most extensive narratives written by contemporaries who had once been slaves in the South. Both pieces were prepared for and published in religious journals, and both the authors—Boston King and David George—were preachers.

Boston King was born around 1760 in the countryside outside Charleston. His father, born in Africa, was "beloved by his master" and became a "driver," or overseer, of other slaves; his mother was an herbalist. At the age of sixteen Boston King was sent out as a "bound apprentice" to a nearby carpenter. Despite his privileged status within the slave community back on the plantation, he received repeated beatings by his "master," the carpenter. Under normal circumstances Boston King would have no other option but to endure his beatings, but in 1780 the American Revolution—or more precisely, the presence of the British in Charleston—offered him a way out:

> My master being apprehensive that Charles-Town was in danger on account of the war, removed into the country, about 38 miles off. Here we built a large house for Mr. Waters, during which time the English took Charles-Town. Having obtained leave one day to see my parents, who lived about 12 miles off, and it being late before I could go, I was obliged to borrow one of Mr. Waters's horses; but a servant of my master's, took the horse from me to go a little journey, and stayed two or three days longer than he ought. This involved me in the greatest perplexity, and I expected the severest punishment, because the gentleman to whom the horse belonged was a very bad man, and knew not how to shew mercy.
>
> To escape his cruelty, I determined to go to Charles-Town, and throw myself into the hands of the English. They received me readily, and I began to feel the happiness of liberty, of which I knew nothing before, altho' I was much grieved at first, to be obliged to leave my friends, and reside among strangers. In this situation I was seized with the small-pox, and suffered great hardships; for all the Blacks affected with that disease, were ordered to be carried a mile from the camp, lest the soldiers should be infected, and disabled from marching. This was a grievous circumstance to me and many others. We lay sometimes a whole day without any thing to eat or drink; but Providence sent a man, who belonged to the York volunteers whom I was acquainted with, to my relief. He brought me such things as I stood in need of; and by the blessing of the Lord I began to recover.

By this time, the English left the place; but as I was unable to march with the army, I expected to be taken by the enemy. However when they came, and understood that we were ill of the small-pox, they precipitately left us for fear of the infection. Two days after, the waggons were sent to convey us to the English Army, and we were put into a little cottage, (being 25 in number) about a quarter mile from the Hospital.

Being recovered, I marched with the army to Chamblem.[129] When we came to the head-quarters, our regiment was 35 miles off. I stayed at the head-quarters three weeks, during which time our regiment had an engagement with the Americans, and the man who relieved me when I was ill of the small-pox, was wounded in the battle, and brought to the hospital. As soon as I heard of his misfortune, I went to see him, and tarried with him in the hospital six weeks, till he recovered; rejoicing that it was in my power to return him the kindness he had shewed me.

From thence I went to a place about 35 miles off, where we stayed two months: at the expiration of which, an express came to the Colonel to decamp in fifteen minutes. When these orders arrived I was at a distance from the camp, catching some fish for the captain that I waited upon; upon returning to the camp, to my great astonishment, I found all the English were gone, and had left only a few militia. I felt my mind greatly alarmed, but Captain Lewes, who commanded the militia, said, "You need not be uneasy, for you will see your regiment before 7 o'clock tonight." This satisfied me for the present, and in two hours we set off.

As we were on the march, the Captain asked, "How will you like me to be your master?"

I answered, that I was Captain Grey's servant.

"Yes," said he; "but I expect that they are all taken prisoners before now; and I have been long enough in the English service, and am determined to leave them." These words roused my indignation, and I spoke some sharp words to him. But he calmly replied, "If you do not behave well, I will put you in irons, and give you a dozen stripes every morning."

I now perceived that my case was desperate, and that I had nothing to trust to, but to wait the first opportunity for making my escape. The next morning, I was sent with a little boy over the river to an island to fetch the Captain some horses. When we came to the Island we found about fifty of the English horses, that Captain Lewes had stolen from them at different times while they were at Rockmount. Upon our return to the Captain with the horses we were sent for, he immediately set off by himself.

I stayed till about 10 o'clock, and then resolved to go to the English army. After travelling 24 miles, I came to a farmer's house, where I tarried all night, and was well used. Early in the morning I continued my journey until I came to the ferry, and found all the boats were on the other side of the river. After anxiously waiting some hours, Major Dial crossed the river, and asked me many questions concerning the regiment to which I belonged. I gave him satisfactory answers, and he ordered the boat to put me over. Being arrived at the headquarters, I informed my Captain that Mr. Lewes had deserted. I also told him of the horses which Lewes had conveyed to the Island. Three weeks after, our Lighthorse went to the Island and burnt his house; they likewise brought back forty of the horses, but he escaped.

I tarried with Captain Grey about a year, and then left him, and came to Nelson's-ferry. Here I entered into the service of the commanding officer of that place. But our situation was very precarious, and we expected to be made prisoners every day; for the Americans had 1600 men, not far off; whereas our whole number amounted only to 250: But there were 1200 English about 30 miles off; only we knew not how to inform them of our danger, as the Americans were in possession of the country.

Our commander at length determined to send me with a letter, promising me great rewards, if I was successful in the business. I refused going on horse-back, and set off on foot about 3 o'clock in the afternoon; I expected every moment to fall in with the enemy, whom I well knew would shew me no mercy. I went on without interruption, till I got within six miles of my journey's end, and then was alarmed with a great noise a little before me. But I stepped out of the road, and fell flat upon my face till they were gone by. I then arose, and praised the Name of the Lord for his great mercy, and again pursued my journey, till I came to Mums-corner tavern. I knocked at the door, but they blew out the candle. I knocked again, and intreated the master to open the door. At last he came with a frightful countenance, and said, "I thought it was the Americans; for there were here about an hour ago, and I thought they were returned again." I asked, How many were there? he answered, "about one hundred." I desired him to saddle his horse for me, which he did, and went with me himself. When we had gone about two miles, we were stopped by the picket-guard, till the Captain came out with 30 men: As soon as he knew that I had brought an express from Nelson's-ferry, he received me with great kindness, and expressed his approbation of my courage and conduct in this dangerous business. Next morning, Colonel Small gave me three shillings, and many fine promises, which were all that I ever received for this service from him. However he sent 600 men to relieve the troops at Nelson's-ferry.

Soon after I went to Charles-Town, and entered on board a man of war. As we were going to Chesepeak-bay, we were at the taking of a rich prize. We stayed in the bay two days, and then sailed for New-York, where I went on shore. Here I endeavored to follow my trade, but for want of tools was obliged to relinquish it, and enter into service. [130] But the wages were so low that I was not able to keep myself in clothes, so that I was under the necessity of leaving my master and going to another. I stayed with him four months, but he never paid me, and I was obliged to leave him also, and work about the town until I was married.

A year after I was taken very ill, but the Lord raised me up again in about five weeks. I then went out in a pilot-boat. We were at sea eight days, and had only provisions for five, so that we were in danger of starving. On the 9th day we were taken by an American whale-boat. I went on board them with a chearful countenance, and asked for bread and water, and made very free with them. They carried me to Brunswick [New Jersey], and used me well. Notwithstanding which, my mind was sorely distressed at the thought of being again reduced to slavery, and separated from my wife and family; and at the same time it was exceeding difficult to escape from my bondage, because the river at Amboy was above a mile over, and likewise another to cross at Staten-Island. I called to remembrance the many great deliverances the Lord had wrought for me, and besought him to save me this once, and I would serve him all the days of my life.

While my mind was thus exercised, I went into the jail to see a lad whom I was acquainted with at New-York. He had been taken prisoner, and attempted to make his escape, but was caught 12 miles off: They tied him to the tail of a horse, and in this manner brought him back to Brunswick. When I saw him, his feet were fastened in the stocks, and at night both his hands. This was a terrifying sight to me, as I expected to meet with the same kind of treatment, if taken in the act of attempting to regain my liberty. I was thankful that I was not confined in a jail, and my master used me as well as I could expect; and indeed the slaves about Baltimore, Philadelphia, and New-York, have as good victuals as many of the English; for they have meat once a day, and milk for breakfast and supper; and what is better than all, many of the masters send their slaves to school at night, that they may learn to read the Scriptures. This is a privilege indeed. But alas, all these enjoyments could not satisfy me without liberty! Sometimes I thought, if it was the will of GOD that I should be a slave, I was ready to resign myself to his will; but at other times I could not find the least desire to content myself in slavery.

Being permitted to walk about when my work was done, I used to go to the ferry, and observed, that when it was low water the people waded across the river; tho' at the same time I saw there were guards posted at the place to prevent the escape of prisoners and slaves. As I was at prayer one Sunday evening, I thought the Lord heard me, and would mercifully deliver me. Therefore putting my confidence in him, about one o'clock in the morning I went down to the river side, and found the guards were either asleep or in the tavern. I instantly entered into the river, but when I was a little distance from the opposite shore, I heard the sentinels disputing among themselves: One said, "I am sure I saw a man cross the river." Another replied, "There is no such thing." It seems they were afraid to fire at me, or make an alarm, lest they should be punished for their negligence. When I got a little distance from the shore, I fell down upon my knees, and thanked GOD for this deliverance.

I travelled till about five in the morning, and then concealed myself till seven o'clock at night, when I proceeded forward, thro' bushes and marshes, near the road, for fear of being discovered. When I came to the river, opposite Staten-Island, I found a boat; and altho' it was very near a whale-boat, yet I ventured into it, and cutting the rope, got safe over. The commanding officer, when informed of my case, gave me a passport, and I proceeded to New-York.

When I arrived at New-York, my friends rejoiced to see me once more restored to liberty, and joined me in praising the Lord for his mercy and goodness. But not withstanding this great deliverance, and the promises I had made to serve GOD, yet my good resolutions soon vanished away like the morning dew: The love of this world extinguished my good desires, and stole away my heart from GOD, so that I rested in a mere form of religion for near three years. [131]

About which time, (in 1783,) the horrors and devastation of war happily terminated, and peace was restored between America and Great Britain, which diffused universal joy among all parties, except us, who had escaped from slavery, and taken refuge in the English army; for a report prevailed at New-York, that all the slaves, in number 2000, were to be delivered up to their masters, altho' some of them had been three or four years among the English. This dreadful rumour filled us all with inexpressible anguish and terror, especially when we saw our old masters coming from Virginia, North-Carolina, and other parts, and seizing upon their slaves in the streets of New-York, or even dragging them out of their beds. Many of the slaves had very cruel masters, so that the thoughts of returning home with them embittered life to us. For some days we lost our appetite for food, and sleep departed from our eyes.

The English had compassion upon us in the day of distress, and issued out the Proclamation, importing, That all slaves should be free, who had taken refuge in the British lines, and claimed the sanction and privileges of the Proclamations respecting the security and protection of Negroes. In consequence of this, each of us received a certificate from the commanding officer at New-York, which dispelled all our fears, and filled us with joy and gratitude. Soon after, ships were fitted out, and furnished with every necessary for conveying us to Nova Scotia. [132]

The certificates which permitted the former slaves to embark on the ships were issued by Brigadier General Samuel Birch; the initials "G B C"—General Birch's Certificate—proved the ticket to freedom for Boston King and his fellow émigrés. In Nova Scotia, African Americans who did not feel welcome at Halifax, Shelburne, or Saint John congregated in a segregated settlement they called Birchtown. With 1,500 inhabitants, Birchtown became the largest separate community of free blacks in the Western Hemisphere.

David George, unlike Boston King, did not come from a family with favored status on the plantation:

> I was born [ca. 1743] in Essex county, Virginia, about 50 or 60 miles from Williamsburg, on Nottaway river, of parents who were brought from Africa, but who had not the fear of God before their eyes. The first work I did was fetching water, and carding of cotton; afterwards I was sent into the field to work about the Indian corn and tobacco, till I was about 19 years old. My father's name was John, and my mother's Judith. I had four brothers, and four sisters, who with myself, were all born in slavery: our master's name was Chapel—a very bad man to Negroes. My oldest sister was called Patty; I have seen her several times so whipped that her back has been all corruption, as though it would rot. My brother Dick ran away, but they caught him, and brought him home; and as they were going to tie him up, he broke away again, and they hunted him with horses and dogs, till they took him; then they hung him up to a cherry-tree in the yard, by his two hands, quite naked, except his breeches, with his feet about half a yard from the ground. They tied his legs close together, and put a pole between them, at one of which one of the owner's sons sat, to keep him down, and another son at the other. After he had received 500 lashes, or more, they washed his back with salt water, and whipped it in, as well as rubbed it in with a rag; and then directly sent him to work in pulling off the suckers of tobacco.

I also have been whipped many a time on my naked skin, and sometimes till the blood has run down over my waistband; but the greatest grief I then had was to see them whip my mother, and to hear her, on her knees, begging for mercy. She was master's cook, and if they only thought she might do any thing better than she did, instead of speaking to her as to a servant, they would strip her directly, and cut away. I believe she was on her death-bed when I got off, but I never heard since. Master's rough and cruel usage was the reason of my running-away. [133]

David George fled south to the Savannah River, where he found work with a man named John Green. But when his master from Virginia tracked him down, he fled again, this time deep into Indian country. He was captured by the Creeks and given to Blue Salt, a chief. "The people were kind to me," he recalled. But when his original master's son came to claim George as his property, Blue Salt agreed to trade his new "prize" for some "rum, linnen, and a gun."

Again George fled, again he was taken by Indians, and again he was pursued by his master's son. Finally George Galphin, the major white trader among the Creeks, purchased the fugitive by paying both his original master and his new Indian captors. David George worked for Galphin, whom he considered "kind," for several years. He married and converted to Christianity. A white itinerant preacher, Wait Palmer, encouraged George and seven other converts at the Silver Bluff trading post to organize an all-black Baptist Church, perhaps the first in history. [134] Despite his own misgivings, George was appointed an elder; by default, he would soon become the preacher.

I proceeded in this way till the American war was coming on, when the Ministers were not allowed to come amongst us lest they should furnish us with too much knowledge. The Black people all around attended with us, and as Brother Palmer must not come, I had the whole management, and used to preach among them myself. Then I got a spelling book and began to read. I used to go out to the little children to teach me a, b, c. They would give me a lesson, which I tried to learn, and then I would go to them again, and ask them if I was right? The reading so ran in my mind, that I think I learned in my sleep as really as when I was awake; and I can now read the Bible, so that what I have in my heart, I can see again in the Scriptures.

I continued preaching at Silver Bluff, till the church, constituted with eight, encreased to thirty or more, and till the British came to the city of Savannah and took it. My master was an Antiloyalist;[135] and being afraid, he now retired from home and left the Slaves behind. My wife and I, and the two children we then had, and fifty more of my Master's people, went to Ebenezer, about twenty miles from Savannah, where the King's forces were. The General sent us over the big Ogee-chee river to Savages' Plantation, where the White people, who were Loyalists, reported that I was planning to carry the Black people back again to their slavery; and I was thrown into prison, and laid there about a month, when Colonel Brown,[136] belonging to the British, took me out.

I stayed some time in Savannah, and at Yamacraw a little distance from it, preaching with brother George Liele.[137] He and I worked together also a month or two: he used to plow, and I to weed Indian-corn. I and my family went into Savannah, at the beginning ot the siege. A ball came through the roof of the stable, where we lived, and much shattered it, which made us remove to Yamacraw, where we sheltered ourselves under the floor of a house on the ground.

Not long after the siege was raised, I caught the small pox, in the fall of the year, and thought I should have died, nor could I do any more than just walk in the spring. My wife used to wash for General Clinton, and out of the little she got maintained us. I was then about a mile from Savannah, when the Americans were coming towards it a second time. I wished my wife to escape, and to take care of herself and of the children, and let me die there. She went: I had about two quarts of Indian corn, which I boiled; I ate a little, and a dog came in and devoured the rest; but it pleased God some people who came along the road gave me a little rice.

I grew better, and as the troops did not come so near us as

was expected, I went into Savannah, where I met my family, and tarried there about two years, in a hut belonging to Lawyer Gibbons, where I kept a butcher's stall. My wife had a brother, who was half an Indian by his mother's side, and half Negro. He sent us a steer, which I sold, and had now in all 13 dollars, and about three guineas besides, with which I designed to pay our passage, and set off for Charlestown; but the British light horse came in, and took it all away. However as it was a good time for the sale of meat, I borrowed money from some of the Black people to buy hogs, and soon re-paid them, and agreed for a passage to Charlestown, where Major P. the British commander, was very kind to me. When the English were going to evacuate Charlestown, they advised me to go to Halifax, in Nova Scotia, and gave the few Black people, and it may be as many as 500 White people, their passage for nothing.

We were 22 days on the passage, and used very ill on board. When we came off Halifax, I got leave to go ashore. On shewing my papers to General Patterson, he sent orders by a Serjeant, for my wife and children to follow me. This was before Christmas, and we staid there till June; but as no way was open for me to preach to my own color, I got leave to go to Shelburne (150 miles, or more, I suppose, by sea), in the suit of General Patterson, leaving my wife and children for a while behind. Numbers of my own color were here, but I found the White people were against me. I began to sing the first night, in the woods, at a camp, for there were no houses then built; they were just clearing and preparing to erect a town. The Black people came far and near, it was so new to them: I kept on so every night in the week, and appointed a meeting for the first Lord's-day, in a valley between two hills, close by the river; and a great number of White and Black people came, and I was so overjoyed with having an opportunity once more of preaching the word of God, that after I had given out the hymn, I could not speak for tears.

In the afternoon we met again, in the same place, and I had great liberty from the Lord. We had a meeting now every evening, and those poor creatures who had never heard the gospel before, listened to me very attentively: but the White people, the justices, and all, were in an uproar, and said that I might go out into the woods, for I should not stay there.

David George continued to preach, first to a congregation of six, then fifteen, and eventually fifty. But when George baptized a white couple, William and Deborah Holmes, he ran into trouble:

> Their relations who lived in town were very angry, raised a mob, and endeavored to hinder their being baptized. Mrs. Holmes's sister especially laid hold of her hair to keep her from going down into the water; but the justices commanded peace, and said that she should be baptized, as she herself desired it. Then they were all quiet.
>
> Soon after this the persecution increased, and became so great, that it did not seem possible to preach, and I thought I must leave Shelburn. Several of the Black people had houses on my lot; but forty or fifty disbanded soldiers were employed, who came with the tackle of ships, and turned my dwelling house, and every one of their houses, quite over; and the Meeting house they would have burned down, had not the ringleader of the mob himself prevented it. But I continued preaching in it till they came one night, and stood before the pulpit, and swore how they would treat me if I preached again. But I stayed and preached, and the next day they came and beat me with sticks, and drove me into the swamp. I returned in the evening, and took my wife and children over the river to Birch town, where some Black people were settled, and there seemed a greater prospect of doing good than at Shelburn. [George's narrative continues with further attempts to preach in a racially charged atmosphere, leading in the end to his emigration from Nova Scotia to Sierra Leone.]

For Boston King, David George, and thousands of other men, women, and children who had once been slaves, the American Revolution presented both danger and opportunity. Boston King escaped first from his master, then from the loyalist Captain Lewes, and once again from his American captors in New Jersey—people who claimed to be fighting for the cause of liberty. He dodged the Americans during his daring mission from Nelson's-ferry; later, he dodged the slave-catchers in New York City. David George escaped from his cruel master, then resumed life on the run each time his master's son tracked him down. He abandoned his new master, the patriot George Galphin, to place his life in the hands of the British; in consequence, he narrowly escaped harm during the siege of Charleston and was robbed of his passage money by British soldiers. Both men were compelled to put their lives in jeopardy on numerous occasions. Both men contracted smallpox but survived. Both men peddled their services to various white men along the tortuous road to freedom.

Boston King and David George were among the fortunate few (less than 1 percent of the slave population) who settled in Canada as free human beings. Yet Canada was no promised land. The climate was harsh, the land not bountiful. A few years after arrival, as support from the British government subsided, Boston King reported "a dreadful famine":

> Many of the poor people were compelled to sell their best gowns for five pounds of flour, in order to support life. When they had parted with all their clothes, even to their blankets, several of them fell down dead in the streets, thro' hunger. Some killed and eat their dogs and cats; and poverty and distress prevailed on every side.

Although life proved rough for whites as well as blacks, the pain was not distributed evenly. "Many of my black brethren at that time," wrote Boston King, "were obliged to sell themselves to the merchants, some for two or three years; and others for five or six years."

In the early 1790s, when African American émigrés were offered a chance to emigrate once again—to Sierra Leone this time, in Africa—many former slaves, including Boston King and David George, seized the opportunity. The Revolutionary War, through a most circuitous route, led almost 1,200 people who had been reared in bondage on American plantations not exactly back to their homelands (few, if any, had ancestors from Sierra Leone) but at least to a place where they would assume some command over their lives.[138]

Patriots of Color

The Revolutionary experiences of African Americans in the North were shaped by different circumstances. Although tens of thousands remained in bondage in the 1770s—some 6,000 in Pennsylvania, 9,000 in New Jersey, 20,000 in New York, and 13,500 in New England[139]—the institution of slavery did not buttress the entire socioeconomic system, as it did in the South. About 10 percent of African Americans in the North had already managed to become free (contrasted with less than 3 percent in the South),[140] while for those still enslaved, the Revolution opened legal as well as extralegal avenues towards liberation.

As in the South, some slaves with patriot masters considered running to the British. In June of 1774 Abigail Adams wrote to her husband: "There has been in town a conspiracy of the negroes . . . to draw up a petition to the Governor, telling them they would fight for him provided he would arm them, and engage to liberate them if he conquered."[141] A year later Thomas Gage, the royal governor of Massachusetts and commander of the British army, contemplated a course of action similar to that which Lord Dunmore would take in Virginia: "Things are now come to that Crisis, that we must avail ourselves of every resource, even to raise the Negroes, in our cause."[142] But Gage never did instigate a major recruiting drive aimed at blacks. Although some slaves escaped over the next few years to place themselves in the service of the British, African Americans from the North did not undertake the kind of mass exodus which characterized the war in the South.[143]

A far larger number, free as well as slave, tried to further their interests by siding with the patriots. The rebellious crowds on the streets of Boston and other port cities included many people of color—Negroes and mulattos, the so-called "rabble." Crispus Attucks, one of the victims of the Boston Massacre, seems to have been a former slave. Of Natick Indian and possibly African descent, Attucks was one of many seamen and laborers who had their own good reasons to oppose the redcoats.[144] According to John

Adams, who defended the British soldiers at their murder trial, "this Attucks . . . appears to have undertaken to be the hero of the night." The soldiers, Adams claimed, had good reason to fear this "stout Molatto fellow, whose very looks was enough to terrify any person." Although Adams was certainly attempting to prejudice the jury when he placed Attucks "at the head of such a rabble of Negroes, &c. as they can collect together," Crispus Attucks and others did actively participate in the Revolutionary events of the 1760s and 1770s.[145]

Several people of color fought as minutemen at Lexington and Concord: Peter Salem of Framingham, Pompy of Braintree, Prince of Brookline, Cato Stedman and Cato Bordman of Cambridge, Cato Wood and Cuff Whitemore of Arlington, Samuel Craft of Newton, Job Potama and Isaiah Bayoman of Stoneham, Pomp Blackman, and probably others. Some of these men were slaves, some free. The historical record gives neither an indication of their motivations nor a record of their performances, but we do know that at least one suffered injury: a broadside publicizing "The Bloody Butchery by the British Troops" listed "Prince Easterbrooks (a Negro Man)" as among the wounded.[146]

We also know that soldiers of color fought at the Battle of Bunker Hill. Shortly after the war Dr. Jeremy Belknap wrote in his diary that an eyewitness had told him that "A negro man belonging to Groton, took aim at Major Pitcairne, as he was rallying the dispersed British Troops, & shot him thro' the head." The first historian of the battle, Samuel Swett, wrote that "Salem, a black soldier, and a number of others," shot "the gallant Maj. Pitcairn." Swett also stated that Cuff Whitemore "fought bravely . . . to the last" and "had a ball through his hat." According to muster rolls, at least fourteen men listed as Negro or mulatto were present. John Trumbull, who viewed the battle from across the harbor, included two blacks in his famous painting, *The Battle of Bunker Hill*.[147] There is one direct and convincing account of an African American fighting with valor—a petition to the general court of Massachusetts signed by fourteen officers who were on the field:

The Subscribers begg leave to Report to your Honorable House, (which Wee do in justice to the Caracter of so Brave a Man) that under Our Own observation, We declare that A Negro Man Called Salem Poor of Col. Frye's Regiment—Capt. Ames. Company—in the late Battle at Charlestown, behaved like an Experienced officer, as Well as an Excellent Soldier, to Set forth Particulars of his Conduct Would be Tedious. Wee Would Only begg leave to Say in the Person of this said Negro Centers a Brave & galant Soldier. The Reward due to so great and Distinguished a Caracter, We Submit to the Congress.[148]

Field officers appreciated the military valour of soldiers like Salem Poor, but the American high command did not. Blacks, they feared, cast a bad light on what was supposed to be a republican army: it was in bad taste, they believed, for slaves (or people who looked like slaves) to be fighting for the "liberty" of whites. On July 10, 1775, less than one month after Salem Poor's heroics at Bunker Hill, Horatio Gates, the adjutant general for the rebel forces, instructed recruiting officers that they should not enlist "any stroller, negro, or vagabond."[149] On October 8 Washington convened a war council to determine "whether it will be adviseable to re-inlist any Negroes in the new Army—or whether there be a Distinction between such as are Slaves & those who are free?" The Council voted "unanimously to reject all Slaves, & by a great Majority to reject Negroes altogether."[150] Ten days later a congressional committee affirmed this decision, and on November 12 Washington proclaimed in his general orders that "Neither Negroes, Boys unable to bare Arms, nor old men unfit to endure the fatigues of the campaign, are to be inlisted."[151] Once the old enlistments had expired on December 31, all black soldiers were to be excluded from a whitewashed army.

By the end of the year, however, Washington suddenly reversed this decision. In his general orders of December 30 he announced this: "As the General is informed, that Numbers of Free Negroes are desirous of inlisting, he gives leave to the recruiting Officers, to entertain them, and promises to lay the matter before the Congress, who he doubts not will approve of it."[152] Why the sudden about-face? Why would the slave-owning commander-in-chief of the Continental Army cede to the wishes of African American soldiers who were "desirous of inlisting"? During the final two months of 1775, the dynamics of the war had changed significantly in two important respects: only half the expected number of American soldiers had volunteered to reenlist, and Lord Dunmore had issued his proclamation offering freedom to any slaves who joined the British service. Facing a shortage of manpower, and fearing that Dunmore's proclamation would influence slaves in the North as well as the South, Washington acted expediently to rescind his exclusion of African Americans. He explained to John Hancock, president of the Continental Congress, "as it is to be apprehended, that they may Seek employ in the ministrial Army—I have presumed to depart from the Resolution respecting them, & have given Licence for their being enlisted."[153] On January 16, 1776, Congress reluctantly resolved "that the free negroes who have served faithfully in the army at Cambridge, may be re-inlisted therein, but no others."[154]

During the course of 1776 all northern states issued some sort of restrictions on the recruitment of African American soldiers. New Hampshire exempted "lunatics, idiots, and Negroes" from signing a declaration to take up arms. One community in New Jersey ordered Negroes to turn in all weapons "until the present troubles are settled."[155] Even so, some African Americans continued in the army: veterans from 1775 reenlisted, while a few slaves accompanied their masters who had become officers. Prince Whipple, slave to a signer of the Declaration of Independence from New Hampshire, crossed the Delaware with Washington on December 25, 1776.[156]

Everything changed in 1777 when Washington convinced Congress to solicit long-term enlistments of at least three years. Since not many men of means proved willing to make that kind of commitment, men of no means wound up taking their place. Congress placed quotas upon the states, which in turn issued orders that each town come up with a certain number of recruits. In New Hampshire and Massachusetts, towns formed committees to find and hire people willing to serve at the least possible expense. Since free people of color, almost invariably poor, came cheaply, prior restrictions against their enlistment were either overturned or ignored. Despite national policy, even slaves were allowed to enlist; some towns paid bounties to masters who allowed their slaves to join the army. African Americans in the hinterlands of New England constituted a very small proportion of the population but a much larger proportion of the professional soldiers after January 1, 1777. In Concord, where slaves accounted for only 1 percent of the inhabitants and free blacks even less, African Americans filled 8 percent of the muster for the Continental Army.[157]

In Connecticut, the state with the largest slave population in New England, the legislature passed two important acts which paved the way for the recruitment of black soldiers: any two men who procured a substitute would be exempted from the draft, and former masters who freed their slaves to serve in the army would be relieved of any future obligation for support. Suddenly, men of color who had been seen as an embarrassment to the army became hot property. One slave who agreed to serve would suffice to exempt both a master and his son. Whites who were drafted but did not own slaves often cast about to buy one. A slave, on his part, had a strong incentive to serve: his freedom. This was not guaranteed by law, but it was a seller's market and many slaves were able to negotiate freedom as the price for their service. Some did not get this promise, however, while others failed to get it in writing. From military records and other scanty evidence, we learn the results of these business arrangements:

- After serving in both 1775 and 1776, Lebbeus Quy remained enslaved to Daniel Brewster of Norwich. But in 1777 his bargaining power increased, and on June 10 Brewster granted Quy his freedom "in consideration of his now Ingaging to serve in the Continental Service during the present Warr." Quy served "for the duration," as promised. He received his discharge in June of 1783 and lived as a free man for thirty-nine more years.[158]

- Aaron Carter was emancipated on May 28, 1777, by Christopher Comstock of Chatham. He enlisted the following day as a substitute for Salmon Root, also of Chatham. Carter paid Comstock £40 for his freedom—most likely the sum that Root paid Carter to take his place in the army. Carter received his discharge at the close of 1781. Aaron's brothers Jacob, Asher, Edward, and Esau also served in return for their freedom.[159]

- Jack Arabas of Stratford enlisted in 1777 at the instigation of his owner, Thomas Ivers, and served in the all-black second company, fourth regiment, of the Connecticut line of the Continental Army. Although Ivers had probably agreed to emancipation, Arabas had nothing on paper.

  When Arabas left the army in 1783, Ivers reclaimed his former property. Arabas fled. After he was captured, he took his case to court. The result: Arabas was set free because of his long-term of service in the Revolution.[160]

- Joseph Mun of Waterbury also sued for his freedom after the war. Mun claimed that his former master, William Nicholls, had agreed to free him in return for service. But Nicholls sold Mun while Mun was fighting in the war, and the new "owner" did not honor the alleged agreement for emancipation. This time the court decided to return Mun to slavery. Perhaps it was swayed by the fact that Mun had sustained a broken arm during the war; should he prove incapacitated as a freeman he would become a ward of the state, while if he were to remain a slave, his master would have to care for him.[161]

- Selah Hart of Farmington drove a hard bargain with his slave Pharoah: he would free Pharoah after the war, but only if Pharoah gave Hart a portion of the wages he received as a soldier. Pharoah fought at Germantown and Monmouth, then in the southern campaigns during the later years. At the close of the war Hart asked the state to send Pharoah's back wages directly to him, and the state agreed to do so.[162]

- Chatham Freeman of Wallingford received his freedom from his owner, Noah Yale, in return for taking the place of Noah's son in the draft. After the war Yale did not try to reclaim Freeman, but he did still own the veteran's sweetheart. For seven more years Chatham Freeman toiled for Noah Yale to earn the hand his fiancée.[163]

A disproportionate number of these African American soldiers served long tours of duty. Robert E. Greene, in his analysis of black pension claims compiled for the Daughters of the American Revolution, found that three-quarters remained on duty for three or more years.[164] Free blacks tended to enlist for "three years or the duration" while slaves promised to serve until the end as a condition of obtaining their freedom.

But not all made it to the end. The military record for Zachery Prince of Simsbury reads simply: "Rec'd his freedom . . . now Ded."[165] Thomas Sackett of Cornwall enlisted in March of 1778, became free in April, fell ill by September, and died in November; after the war an officer from his unit, falsely claiming Sackett had been his slave, petitioned the government for the back wages of the deceased veteran.[166] In 1781 two slaves—Lambert Latham and Jordan Freeman—died while joining the white patriots of Groton in defending Fort Griswold. Survivors of the battle stated that Freeman killed a British major and that Latham was slain with Colonel Ledyard while Ledyard was offering his sword in surrender. After the war the town erected a monument to the fallen martyrs of Fort Griswold; at the bottom of the list, separated from all the rest, were the names of "Lambo" Latham and Jordan Freeman.[167]

Lambert Latham, Jordan Freeman, Joseph Mun, Zachery Prince, Thomas Sackett—these African American patriots from Connecticut never enjoyed the fruits of freedom. Neither did Private Jehu Grant, at least during the war years. The slave of a Tory master from Rhode Island, Grant escaped and joined the rebel army in Danbury, Connecticut. For ten months he served as a teamster and a personal servant, typical roles for black soldiers. Then his master came to claim him. In 1832 Grant, eighty-years old and blind, petitioned for a routine pension, but his petition was denied: "services while a fugitive," the government claimed, were not covered by the Pension Act of 1832. Grant appealed the decision:

I was then grown to manhood, in the full vigor and strength of life, and heard much about the cruel and arbitrary things done by the British. Their ships lay within a few miles of my master's house, which stood near the shore, and I was confident that my master traded with them, and I suffered much from fear that I should be sent aboard a ship of war. This I disliked. But when I saw liberty poles and the people all engaged for the support of freedom, I could not but like and be pleased with such thing (God forgive me if I sinned in so feeling) . . . These considerations induced me to enlist into the American army, where I served faithful about ten months, when my master found and took me home. Had I been taught to read or understand the precepts of the Gospel, "Servants obey your masters," I might have done otherwise, notwithstanding the songs of liberty that saluted my ear, thrilled through my heart. [168]

Apparently this appeal, with its ironic self-effacement, was either ignored or denied, for there is no record of Grant receiving a pension.

In 1778 Rhode Island exceeded Connecticut in its zeal for recruiting slaves. With the Continental Army withering away at Valley Forge, Congress issued high quotas to the states: Rhode Island would have to raise enough men to fill two battalions. Since Newport, the hub of the state, was in British hands, the pool of eligible prospects had diminished, while the slave trade, the staple of the economy, had ground to a halt due to the British blockade, so the state had little money to offer for bounties. Desperate, political leaders suddenly wondered, why not turn slaves into soldiers? The proportion of slaves in Rhode Island was higher than anywhere else in New England; if black men would serve, the state could meet its quota.

Since it would be impossible to fill the two battalions "without arming the slaves," the legislature declared in February, "every able-bodied Negro, Mulatto or Indian Man slave, in this State may enlist." The slaves would receive their freedom and "all the Bounties, Wages, and Encouragements" given to any other soldier; the masters would be recompensed for the loss of their slaves by money coming from Congress. [169] Fearful of the implications and doubtful they would ever get paid, influential masters opposed the new law, and within four months they managed to get it repealed. But the precedent had been set: over the course of the war, approximately 225 to 250 African Americans enlisted in the all-black First Rhode Island Regiment of the Continental Army under the command of Colonel Christopher Greene. [170] Many of these joined after the act had been overturned; illegally or not, recruiters still took who they could get.

No sooner had the First Regiment congealed than it was called into action. In August of 1778 an American attack on Newport backfired when the French fleet, which was supposed to offer support, became crippled by a storm. The British-Hessian forces staged a counterattack as the Americans retreated, and they drove particularly hard at the regiment of new black recruits. But the First Regiment, showing no weakness, inflicted heavy casualties on the enemy.[171] Years later a white veteran of the Battle of Rhode Island described the First Regiment's heroics during the retreat:

> There was a *black* regiment in the same situation. Yes, a regiment of *negroes*, fighting for *our* liberty and independence,—not a white man among them but the officers,—stationed in the same dangerous and responsible position. Had they been unfaithful, or given way before the enemy, all would have been lost. *Three times in succession* were they attacked, with most desperate valor and fury, by well disciplined and veteran troops, and three times did they successfully repel the assault, and thus preserve our army from capture. They fought through the war. They were brave, hardy troops.[172]

The First Regiment saw action in several other battles: Red Point, Yorktown, Fort Oswego. Colonel Greene and several black soldiers were killed in a British surprise attack at Points Bridge, New York, on May 14, 1781. In July of 1781 a French officer reviewing the troops reported that "Three-quarters of the Rhode Island regiment consists of negroes, and that regiment is the most neatly dressed, the best under arms, and the most precise in its maneuvers."[173]

The First Regiment continued in service until June 13, 1783, when the troops were sent home without pay. In his farewell address the new commanding officer, Lieutenant Colonel Jeremiah Olney, praised his men for their "fortitude and patience" and for their "valour and good conduct displayed on every occasion when called to face the enemy in the field." He regretted they had not been paid but assured the troops that the government would come through shortly and that he himself would do whatever he could to help them "obtain their just dues from the public."[174] Yet when some black soldiers, who knew no other way of making a living, tried to reenlist, he told a different story:

It has been found, from long and fatal experience, that Indians, Negroes and Mulattoes, do not (and from a total Want of Perseverance, and Fortitude to bear the various Fatigues incident to an Army) cannot answer the public Service; they will not therefore on any Account be received. [175]

Many white veterans—young men like Jeremiah Greenman—also hoped to continue with military careers—and whites had first priority. Once jobs had become scarce and recruits plentiful, the army saw no further need for soldiers of color.

Outside of New England, other states tried to take advantage of black manpower. New York offered a bounty of 500 acres to "any person who shall deliver one or more of his or her able-bodied male slaves to any warrant officer" to "serve for the term of three years or until regularly discharged."[176] New Jersey offered a land bounty as well, with the precise amount to be determined in each case by two freeholders and a county judge.[177] In 1780 Maryland energetically sought the services of free blacks, who comprised a large percentage of those poor enough to consider joining the army. "Our recruiting business in this County goes on much worse than I expected," wrote Richard Barnes from St. Mary's. "The greatest part of those that have enlisted are free Negroes & Mulattoes." The following year Maryland started drafting all free men "although blacks and mulattoes," and the legislature contemplated forcing masters who owned six or more male slaves of military age to furnish one for the army; the measure failed because planters protested that the price they were to be paid "is not equal to the value of a healthy, strong, young negro man."[178]

White resistance to putting African Americans under arms was strongest in areas with the greatest concentrations of slaves. But even in Virginia, the heart of tobacco land, patriots could not ignore the possibilities for exploiting black manpower. More than half the free Negro males of military age in Virginia joined the army, probably for the same reason that freemen from the North enlisted: it was the best or only job available. But with fewer than 1,000 free blacks available for service in the entire state, patriots would not gain a significant military advantage unless they tapped into the pool of 50,000 male slaves of appropriate age.[179]

White leaders, however, did not want slaves in their army for two reasons: it appeared to contradict republican principles, and they feared slaves with weapons. In 1777 the general assembly required any "Negro or mulatto" who enlisted to "produce a certificate from a justice of the peace that he is a free man."[180] This law might have prevented runaways from joining the American army, but it did not stop white owners from making use of slaves to fulfill their military obligations. Masters who had been drafted still enlisted their bondsmen, claiming them to be free; recruiting officers, eager to swell their numbers, winked knowingly.

Virginia slaves fought at Brandywine, Germantown, Monmouth, Charleston, Savannah, Camden, Yorktown. James LaFayette and Saul Matthews served as spies. Caesar Tarrant piloted armed vessels, while Pluto served as a sailor. Richard Pointer warded off a company of Indians singlehandedly.[181]

These men, when they agreed to enlist, did not have the bargaining power of northern slaves. No law stated they were to receive their freedom at war's end; indeed, the law stated very clearly that they should not even be in the army. They procured no written contracts with their masters; if they arranged oral contracts, these were easily violated. After the war, most of these veteran patriots were slated to return to slavery—unless the state interfered. In 1783, flushed with victory and a sense of moral righteousness, the Virginia assembly declared that all slaves who had "faithfully served agreeable to the terms of their enlistment, and have thereby of course contributed towards the establishment of American liberty and independence, should enjoy the blessings of freedom as a reward for their toils and labors."[182] But how much good did it do? In the late 1780s and 1790s the assembly received numerous petitions from individual slaves requesting to be freed by separate resolutions: James LaFayette and Caesar Tarrant in 1786, Saul Matthews in 1792, Richard Pointer in 1795, Pluto in 1796, and many others.[183] Apparently, many black veterans had not received any direct benefit from the Emancipation Act of 1783.

North or South, slaves were never *guaranteed* freedom-for-service. Even where freedom was stipulated by law, former slaves would sometimes have to petition governmental authorities to escape the grasp of masters who tried to reclaim their property. Petitions to the government, the only extant testimonies from African Americans who fought with the rebels, bear witness to the precarious nature of the so-called freedom earned by patriots of color:

To the General Assembly of the State of North Carolina

The Petitioner of Ned Griffin a Man of mixed Blood Humbley Saieth that a Small space of Time before the Battle of Gilford a certain William Kitchen then in the Service of his Countrey as a Soldier Deserted from his line for which he was Turned in to the Continental Service to serve as the Law Directs—Your Petitioner was then a Servant to William Griffin and was purchased by the said Kitchen for the purpose of Serving in His place, with a Solom Assurance that if he your Petitioner would faithfully serve the Term of Time that the said Kitchen was Returned for he should be a free Man—Upon which said Promise and Assurance you Petitioner Consented to enter in to the Continental Service in said Kitchens Behalf and was Received by Colo: James Armstrong at Martinborough as a free Man Your Petitioner furter saieth that at that Time no Person could have been hired to have served in said Kitchens behalf for so small a sum as what I was purchased for and that at the Time that I was Received into Service by said Colo: Armstrong said Kitchen Openly Delcaired me to be free Man—

The Faithfull purformance of the above agreement will appear from my Discharge,—some Time after your Petitioners Return he was Seized upon by said Kitchen and Sold to a Certain Abner Roberson who now holds me as a Servant— Your Petitioner therefore thinks that by Contract and merit he is Intitled to his Freedom I therefore submit my case to your Honourable Body hoping that I shall have that Justice done me as you in your Wisdom shall think I am Intitled to and Desarving of & Your Petitioner as in duty bound Will Pray

N Carolina his	his
Edgecomb County	Ned X Griffin
April 4th 1784	mark[184]

The General Assembly responded to this petition the same day: "Ned Griffin, late the property of William Kitchen shall forever hereafter be in every respect declared to be a freeman, and he shall be, and he is hereby enfranchised and forever delivered and discharged from the yoke of slavery."[185]

Only in South Carolina and Georgia was the fear of armed black men so great as to inhibit all efforts to recruit African Americans for military service. Not that the idea wasn't considered: John Laurens argued that "Men who have the habit of Subordination almost indelibly impress'd on them, would have one very essential qualification of Soldiers."[186] On March 29, 1779, the national Congress actually resolved "That it be recommended to the States of South Carolina and Georgia, if they shall think the same expedient, to take measures immediately for raising three thousand able-bodied negroes."[187] Ironically, Congress argued that South Carolina must arm blacks because it was unable to meet its quotas "by reason of the great proportion of citizens necessary to remain at home to prevent insurrection among the negroes."[188]

But most white gentry took great offense. "We are much disgusted here at Congress recommending us to arm our Slaves," Christopher Gadsden wrote to Sam Adams, "it was received with great resentment, as a very dangerous and impolitic Step."[189] One opponent explained the response with candor: "A strong, deep-seated feeling, nurtured from earliest infancy, decides, with instinctive promptness, against a measure of so threatening an aspect."[190] The South Carolina general assembly overwhelmingly opposed Congress's recommendation; instead, it decided to alleviate the shortage of military manpower by offering slaves as bounties to white recruits.

On September 14, 1779, shortly after the South Carolina general assembly had rejected the idea of recruiting African Americans for the army, the South Carolina navy commissioners issued an order: "Endeavor by Every means in Your Power to Enlist Seamen and able bodied Negro Men to Serve on board the Rutledge Galley for Six Months."[191] Why recruit black sailors but not black soldiers? Soldiers carried their own arms; sailors did not. And sailors plied their trade on board ships, where they posed no immediate threat to white civilians. Black men who rowed oars and hoisted sails were no more likely to engage in insurrections than slaves who planted tobacco or cleaned stables. According to Virginia law, "not more than one-third of the persons employed in the navigation of any bay or river craft . . . shall consist of slaves."[192]

Many ship captains and navy recruiters preferred to hire blacks, who came cheaper: when issued rum, whites received a pint and blacks only a gill.[193] Blacks were easily cheated out of their prize money. Slaves or former slaves, with no means of redress, complained less than whites about injustice or abysmal living conditions. They could not resist when assigned undesirable tasks. They rarely deserted, fearful of being caught and returned to plantation slavery. If ever they appeared to get out of line, they were told they would fetch a good price in the West Indies. In short, any African American who signed onto a vessel could be subdued by his captain and intimidated by his mates. One white man from Virginia received threats that officers and sailors would "cut him and staple him and use him like a Negro, or rather, like a dog."[194]

Blacks put up with this sort of treatment only because the alternatives appeared even worse. The sea offered the most realistic means of escape from chattel slavery, even though, in the words of historian W. Jeffrey Bolster, runaways merely exchanged "the lifetime domination of one owner for the crap-shoot of a series of captains."[195] Newspaper advertisements, noting that refugees would "endeavor to get on board some vessel," warned captains not to enlist runaway slaves who tried to pass themselves off as free.[196] But the warnings often went unheeded; many captains, hard pressed for manpower, did not ask too many questions when a desperate prospect, willing to work for little recompense, stood before him.[197]

The seafaring life actually presented more opportunities for advancement than any other field open to slaves. Navigating the channels of the Carolina low country and the hundreds of rivers and inlets of the Chesapeake Bay, some slaves had already learned to master the water. These pilots, called "patroons," came in high demand during the Revolution. Some defected to the British, others served the patriots.[198] Government documents, although very incomplete, reveal that the Virginia state navy employed at least four slaves as pilots: "Captain" Starlins, Caesar Tarrant, Cuffee, and Minny. Starlins led the crew of the *Patriot* in an attack on a British sloop. Tarrant guided his vessel through several engagements; he remained a slave at war's end, but in 1786 he received his freedom and eventually he acquired some property. Cuffee and Minny died in action.[199] Minny's owner petitioned the state:

> A petition of Lucretia Pritchett . . . setting forth that in a late attack on a piratical tender in Rappahannock river, Minny, a negro man . . . voluntarily entered himself on board a vessel commanded by Mr. Hugh Walker, and being used to the water, and a good pilot, bravely and successfully exerted himself against the enemy, until he was unfortunately killed, whereby the estate of the said Joseph Pritchett was deprived of a valuable slave.[200]

Pritchett requested recompense for "the value thereof," and she was awarded $100.

Toward Freedom?

On May 25, 1774, several African Americans held in bondage appealed to the governor and council of Massachusetts:

> The Petition of a Grate Number of Blackes of this Province who by divine permission are held in a state of Slavery with the bowels of a free and christian Country
> Humbly Shewing
> That your Petitioners apprehend we have in common with all other men a naturel right to our freedoms without Being depriv'd of them by our fellow men as we are a freeborn Pepel and have never forfeited this Blessing by aney compact or agreement whatever. But we were unjustly dragged by the cruel hand of power from our dearest frinds and sum of us stolen from the bosoms of our tender Parents and from a Populous Pleasant and plentiful country and Brought hither to be made slaves for Life in a Christian land.
> Thus we are deprived of every thing that hath a tendency to make life even tolerable, the endearing ties of husband and wife we are strangers to for we are no longer man and wife than our masters or mistresses thinkes proper marred or on-

marred. Our children are also taken from us by force and sent
maney miles from us wear we seldom or ever see them again
there to be made slave of for Life which sumtimes is vere short
by Reson of Being dragged from their mothers Breest. Thus
our Lives are imbittered to us on these accounts. . . .

We therfor Bage your Excellency and Honours will give this
its deer weight and consideration and that you will accordingly
cause an act of the legislative to be passed that we may obtain our
Natural right our freedoms and our children be set at lebety at
the yeare of twenty one. . . . [201]

These slaves articulated and personalized John Locke's "social contract" theory of government, which would soon serve as the foundation for the Declaration of Independence. Six weeks later the same
petitioners added that they would like to receive "some part of the
unimproved land, belonging to the province, for a settlement, that
each of us may there sit down quietly under his own fig tree." The
legislature heard the petitions and voted to let "the matter now
subside."[202] Throughout the Revolutionary era African Americans
from New England petitioned their government with similar appeals, but they were all denied.

Echoing the petitions which patriots submitted to Parliament,
slaves and freemen deftly and ironically applied republican theory
to their own circumstances.[203] At first only a handful of Quakers
seemed to get the point, but as white patriots repeated the idiom of
their "enslavement" by the King and Parliament *ad infinitum*, they
found it increasingly difficult to escape the obvious implications of
their own rhetoric. In Worcester, where thousands of farmers had
gathered to depose Crown-appointed judges in 1774, a county convention in June of 1775 responded favorably to a petition it had
received from the "negroes of Bristol and Worcester":

That we abhor the enslaving of any of the human race, and
particularly of the negroes in this country, and that whenever
there shall be a door opened, or opportunity present for anything to be done towards the emancipation of the negroes, we
will use our influence and endeavor that such a thing may be
brought about.[204]

Two years later Worcester representatives, among others, pushed for an abolition bill in the state assembly, but the measure was tabled because of "an apprehension that our brethren in the Other Colonies" might object.[205]

The push for emancipation gained support wherever the local economy and social structure did not depend heavily on slavery. No doubt influenced by the ubiquitous cries for "liberty" which defined the era, northern states moved slowly toward abolition.

- In 1777 Vermont (which would not be admitted as a state until 1791) declared this in its constitution:

  > All men are born equally free and independent, and have certain natural, inherent, and inalienable rights; among which are the enjoying and defending life and liberty . . . *therefore* no male person, born in this country or brought from over sea, ought to be holden by law to serve any person as a servant, slave, or apprentice, after he arrives to the age of twenty-one years; nor female, in like manner, after she arrives to the age of eighteen years; unless they are bound by their own consent after they arrive to such age, or bound by the law for the payment of debts, damages, fines, costs, or the like.[206]

  Although it still allowed for bound apprenticeships, the new government created by the freedom-loving Green Mountain Boys dealt the first official blow to chattel slavery in North America.

- In Pennsylvania the assembly passed a bill for gradual abolition in 1780. In order to address the "sorrows of those who have lived in undeserved bondage," the bill freed all slaves born after 1780—but not until they had reached the age of twenty-eight. Clearly a compromise measure, the bill satisfied nobody. Slaveowners resisted its implementation and tried to get the law reversed, while abolitionists noted that since most people "used to hard labour without doors begin to fail soon after thirty," slaves who were freed at the age of twenty-eighty would have few years left to enjoy their freedom.[207]

- The Massachusetts legislature never did act on the issue of emancipation, but a series of court cases between 1781 and

1783 effectively abolished slavery throughout the state. Quok Walker from Worcester County and Elizabeth Freeman from Berkshire County, in separate cases, sought freedom from masters who beat them. Both were freed by the court, and in the Walker case Chief Justice John D. Cushing declared that the institution of slavery was "wholly incompatible and repugnant" to the Declaration of Rights contained in the 1780 state constitution.[208] Slavery in New Hampshire was terminated by a later series of court rulings.

- The legislatures of both Connecticut and Rhode Island enacted gradual emancipation measures in 1784. As in Pennsylvania, slaves were to be freed only after a certain age: twenty-five in Connecticut, twenty-one for males and eighteen for females in Rhode Island. (The following year, Rhode Island raised the age for females to twenty-one.) The impact of these gradual emancipation procedures was minimal: by the 1800s, when the first slaves would have been freed according to law, legal slavery had for the most part been replaced by other means of racial subjugation.[209]

- In New York and New Jersey, the states with the highest proportion of slaves outside the South, abolition proceeded more slowly yet. In 1785 both states considered proposals to terminate slavery: in New York a measure failed because the legislators could not agree whether free blacks should vote, while in New Jersey the opposition successfully derailed the abolitionist movement by associating it with the unpopular and unpatriotic Quakers. In 1799 New York finally provided for the emancipation of males at twenty-eight and females at twenty-five. In 1804 New Jersey declared it would free male slaves at twenty-five and females at twenty-one. Since the laws only applied to people not yet born, no slave would be freed under either act until half a century after the start of the Revolution. When the time for emancipation grew near, the number of slaves diminished rapidly in both states as masters sold off their human property or relocated southward.[210]

Despite the snail's pace of forced abolition, the institution of slavery in the northern states was considerably weakened after the Revolution. Changing economic factors, the humanitarian concerns of some masters, and the refusal of many slaves to accept their status led to an increase in the number of free blacks during the decades following the war. According to the 1790 census approximately 40 percent of African Americans in the northern states were free (listed as "all other free persons"), while by 1810 about 74 percent of African Americans in the North were free (listed as "all other free persons, except Indians not taxed"). Sometimes aided by white abolitionists and free blacks, those still held in bondage found more opportunities to flee their masters. According to one estimate, over half of the young male slaves in Philadelphia ran away during the 1780s.[211]

Several African Americans attained some degree of wealth or recognition in the wake of the Revolution. Paul Cuffe, who had signed a 1780 protest against taxation without representation, became a prominent sea captain, merchant, and advocate of black colonization in Africa.[212] James Forten, once a prisoner of war, accumulated a fortune of $100,000 from his sail-making business and became a significant voice in the push for abolition. Richard Allen and Absalom Jones helped form the Free African Society in Philadelphia and the African Methodist Episcopal Church, still a major feature in many African American communities today. In Boston, Prince Hall, who had signed several of the petitions for emancipation, established a black Freemasons' lodge; in Newport veterans from the First Regiment helped form the Free African Union Society, the first all-black benevolent association. The mathematician Benjamin Banneker put out an almanac, while the poet Phillis Wheatley impressed her white audience, including George Washington. Tom Peters, who like Boston King and David George had joined with the British, helped establish the Sierra Leone colony. Without the Revolutionary emphasis on "liberty," these people might not have achieved what they did.[213]

But the few who were able to excel cannot be considered representative of the great mass of African Americans during that time. While the war gave some impetus to emancipation in the North, it had the reverse effect in the South, where nine of every ten black people resided. Once peace had been restored, slaves who had dared to defy their masters during the Revolution could do so no longer. African Americans, like Native Americans, lost power when Euro-

Americans ceased to fight against each other. Notwithstanding the rhetorical cries of "liberty," the institution of slavery remained firmly entrenched. Despite the wartime exodus and epidemics, the number of slaves increased from less than 500,000 in 1770 to almost 700,000 in 1790.[214] From the onset of the Revolution to 1800, the slave population nearly doubled in the Chesapeake region.[215] Indeed, the sale of slaves to trans-Appalachian settlers became a major industry in Virginia.

Southern planters had waged war to preserve a basic Lockean principle: the protection of property as a prerequisite for liberty.[216] Since property, for them, meant slaves, the Revolution, far from terminating slavery, rigidified it. Historian John Shy explains:

> By 1783, Southern slave owners, previously content to run a system more flexible and less harsh in practice than it appeared in the statute books, realized as never before how fragile and vulnerable the system actually was, and how little they could depend on the cowardice, ignorance, and gratitude of their slaves. Troubled by the agitation, even within themselves, created against slavery by the rhetorical justification of the Revolution, slaveowners set about giving legal and institutional expression to a new level of anxiety about the system. New rules governing slavery and a new articulation of racist attitudes may have been one of the most important, enduring, and paradoxical legacies of the Revolutionary War.[217]

The prospects for freedom had triggered a backlash, and those who had not managed to escape would suffer all the more. Even many who did escape fared badly: Thomas Jefferson claimed that at least twenty-seven of the thirty slaves who had left him for the British died of "the small pox and putrid fever," and he estimated that "the state of Virginia lost under Ld. Cornwallis's hands that year [1781] about 30,000 slaves, and that of these about 27,000 died of the small pox and camp fever."[218] Although some southern slaves found their way to freedom, many more perished in the attempt.[219] Comprising only 15 percent of the population of the United States, African Americans who fled to the British suffered approximately as many fatalities (primarily from disease) as were incurred by all patriot soldiers throughout the war.[220] Death and continued slavery were the most frequent outcomes.

But we should take care not to generalize. Each experience was unique, with its own particular mix of promise and pain. Witness, for instance, what happened to the slaves belonging to William Hooper of Wilmington, North Carolina. Early in 1782, upon returning to his pillaged home, Hooper learned that "three fellows of mine had gone off with the British; one had been forced away by the militia, and I had lost five other negroes by the small-pox." Hooper quickly set about gathering "my few negroes that remained, and who were straggling in the town and its vicinity." His wife had also abandoned their home, and on her way back she reunited with their slave John, "a boy about my house, to whom I was partial." According to Hooper,

> everything was attempted to attach him to the service of the British. He was offered clothes, money, freedom—every thing that could captivate a youthful mind. He pretended to acquiesce, and affected a perfect satisfaction at this change of situation; but in the evening of the day after Mrs. Hooper left the town, he stole through the British sentries, and without a pass, accompanied by a wench of Mrs. Allen's, he followed Mrs. Hooper seventy miles on foot, and overtook her, to the great joy of himself and my family. His sister, Lavinia, . . . pursued a different conduct. She went on board the fleet after the evacuation of the town, and much against her will was forced ashore by some of my friends, and returned to me.[221]

So what was the final tally? John returned on his own accord; Lavinia would have preferred to stay away. Three departed with the British, one with the militia, five died of smallpox, and the "few" who did not make definitive attempts to leave found themselves back in slavery. Here in a microcosm we see how the Revolutionary War affected the slaves in the South.

William Hooper must have been upset to lose nine slaves, but he was undoubtedly pleased with the loyalty shown by John. And proud: John's flight home reflected well on Hooper's behavior as a master.[222] William Withers, on the other hand, spoke for countless disgruntled masters when he complained of "the treachery of the Negroes beyond expectation" when his slaves ran off to the British.[223] "Loyalty" versus "treachery"—these terms are mirror images of the same egocentric orientation; they reflect the feelings of the master, not the character of the slave. When a person held in captivity chose to stay or to run, he or she did so for motives much deeper than simply pleasing or punishing the master and mistress. John might or might not have loved Mr. and Mrs. Hooper; in either case, a life of some comfort within the plantation household held more appeal for this particular fellow than following the orders of strange white men whom he had no reason to trust, and perhaps dying in battle or succumbing to disease. John's sister Lavinia, meanwhile, must have had her own good reasons for not wanting to return. For the slaves themselves, the issues at stake were far more profound than white masters bothered to ponder.

This appears evident to us now, and the skewed vision of the masters somewhat reprehensible. But is not our modern vision skewed as well as we rewrite our texts to include the "contributions" which African Americans made to the Revolutionary cause? This too reveals an egocentric orientation. Black patriots were not fighting in support of national independence or opposition to Parliament, and black loyalists were not endangering their lives on behalf of the king. First and foremost, African Americans of the Revolutionary era "contributed" to their own quests for freedom. Everything else pales by comparison.

However distorted by the eyes of white masters, the courageous struggles for black freedom during the American Revolution are still evident in the historical sources. Behind every advertisement for a runaway slave lies a saga of heroic proportions:

• On November 7, 1775, Joshua Eden placed a notice in the *South-Carolina Gazette:*
   Absented himself from the Subscriber, the 4th of this Instant, a NEGRO Man, named LIMUS; he is of a yel-

low Complexion, and has the Ends of three of his Fingers cut off his left Hand; he is well known in Charles-Town from his saucy and impudent Tongue, of which I have had many complaints; therefore, I hereby give free liberty, and will be also much obliged to any Person to flog him (so as not take his Life) in such Manner as they shall think proper, whenever he is found out of my Habitation without a Ticket; for though he is my Property, he has the audacity to tell me, he will be free, that he will serve no Man, and that he will be conquered or governed by no Man.—I forwarn Masters of Vessels from carrying him off the Province, and all Persons from harbouring him in their Houses or Plantations.[224]

Limus, with his "saucy and impudent Tongue," said no more than white patriots were saying to the British: he refused to be governed by others. Under different circumstances, this attitude would have made him a hero instead of an outlaw.

• Ten years later Peregrine Thorn advertised in the *Maryland Gazette:*

TWENTY POUNDS REWARD
Charles County, near Newport, July 18, 1785.
RAN away from the subscriber, the 14th instant, a likely negro man named SAM, alias SAMUEL JOHNSON, and has frequently passed under the names of James Willis and Samuel Perkins, by the latter he had a pass by a person in Baltimore, under the appellation of a magistrate. Sam is about 23 years old, near 6 feet hight, of a yellowish complexion, has a down impudent look, is pitted with the small-pox, and has a remarkable cut with an ax on one of his legs, which may not yet be well; had on when he went off, an old pair of trousers, osnabrig shirt worn through at the elbows, an old short blue jacket without sleeves, and an old hat; he is an artful rogue, born on the eastern shore, and is well know there and in Baltimore, where he ran away from his master in time of the war, was taken up in Philadelphia, after making several voyages to the West-Indies, has been latterly sent to Baltimore for sale, he then made his escape for several days, but was luckily apprehended,

and is now, I understand, making for that place, and it is more than probable will pass by many other names, as he has informed several, since gone, that he is free, and others that he has a master in Baltimore, and is going home to inform him of his being wrecked down the bay, carrying him a parcel of goods. Whoever takes up the above negro, and brings him to me, shall receive the above reward.[225]

From this remarkable portrait, however biased, we learn much and wonder more: Where did he get that cut with an ax? How did this lad, a teenager during the war, manage to escape? How did he fare in the West Indies, where he could always be sold as a slave by his captain or his mates? Imagine the adventures he must have had, his "tales of hair-breadth 'scapes." But Sam, unlike Joseph Plumb Martin, Ebenezer Fox, and other white survivors, was in no position to write his memoirs after the war; he had more pressing business at hand. We do not know whether Samuel Johnson was captured or not, but at that point in time, with the British no longer a factor, his prospects were not bright.

- Also in 1785, ten years to the day after British soldiers marched on Lexington and Concord, Henry Laurens enlisted the support of Alexander Hamilton in the retrieval of a runaway slave named Frederic, who had just been captured. Frederic maintained that John Laurens, Henry's son, had set him free shortly before John was killed in 1782. Henry claimed that made no sense, since John "was too tenacious of propriety to have manumitted a Slave not his own." Calling Frederic's statements "a tissue of lies," Henry Laurens tried to set the record straight:

> During the Seige of Charleston, when he pretends he carried arms & to have acted in the Trenches, he was at my Mepkin Plantation, whence some time after the Town fell, he joined the temporary Conquerors; he also seduced his Wife, she thro' the persuasion of faithful Scaramouch returned, he was afterward captured by an American Cruizer, carried into George Town & claimed by one of my Attornies, he broke thro' & escaped and had not been heard of till now We learn he is in the Jail of New York. . . . [H]e was always a very good Lad

before the War, contaminated no doubt by bad Examples in that dreadful Scene.[226]

As Laurens tells it, the Revolutionary War had corrupted his once-docile slave. As Frederic would likely tell it, the Revolution had created the opportunity to pursue his dream of freedom. But now the war was over, and with it the openings it had presented. For a brief moment in the long epoch of North American slavery, a seam had torn loose in the cloak of oppression; by 1785 that seam was sewn shut, and Frederic had nowhere to go. The prisoner was sent from New York back to Charleston. Five months later Laurens grumbled: "There he goes carrying a little dirt out of the Garden, not earning his Victuals."[227] Frederic could no longer escape, but he was not about to submit.

Limus, Sam, Frederick, and many like them had struggled for the cause of liberty: their own. These fighters for freedom were heroes, every bit as much as Crispus Attucks at the Boston Massacre or Salem Poor at Bunker Hill. With their saucy tongues and impudent looks, they were viewed at the time as renegades—but were not George Washington and Sam Adams regarded that way by the British? Freedom was in the air, and blacks as well as whites sought their portion. "Give me liberty or give me death," said Patrick Henry, soon to be governor of Virginia. That's what Limus and Sam and Frederick thought as well, and they acted accordingly.

7

THE BODY OF THE PEOPLE

People's History and the American Revolution . . . Who's In and Who's Out . . . The Human Face of Freedom

People's History and the American Revolution

People make history, complex human beings from varying circumstances who pull together, drive apart, and interact in countless ways. Not just a few people, but all of them. Common people—men and women without the special privileges afforded by wealth, prestige, or political authority—participate in the historical process on several levels:

They do the work, carrying on the business of everyday life.

They bear the brunt when things go wrong.

They manipulate the system as best they can, trying to improve their lot within the parameters of the world as it is presented to them.

They fight the wars.

They grant or withhold support.

They test the limits of authority in everyday contexts.

Since they pose a never-ending threat to the elites who control the circumstances of their lives and profit at their expense, they force people in positions of power to engage in constant supervision and periodic repression.

Sometimes they strive to redefine existing hierarchies, working collectively to challenge those who would keep them down. Occasionally, they rise up and rebel.

Common people have always made history on the first seven levels. Even when they have not challenged and rebelled, they have helped determine the fabric and the future of their societies. But at certain times, they have gone beyond mere participation and consciously endeavored to reconstruct their societies according to their own designs. The American Revolution was one of those times.

Although the involvement of ordinary people in the actual rebellion was of great historical import, we should not allow high drama to eclipse the participation of common folk on all levels:

Work. The business of war required a hardworking people to work even harder. During the various waves of nonimportation, both women and men stepped up the pace of production to compensate for the absence of goods from abroad. With the advent of armed combat, they picked up the pace yet again. Artisans and laborers made tools and weapons. Women, freemen who stayed home, and slaves grew food and furnished necessities not only for themselves and their usual markets, but for tens of thousands of soldiers who had ceased to contribute productive labor.

Bearing the brunt. As hard as they worked, common folk had less to consume. Time and again, they made do without—at first voluntarily, later not. The temporary hardships of nonimportation were followed by severe wartime scarcities which spanned the better part of a decade. The colonies, with a limited manufacturing capacity, made ships, arms, and ammunition instead of useful tools and consumer goods. Salt, required to preserve food, was requisitioned by the American, British, German, and French armies; people rioted over what little was left for civilian use. Foodstuffs—meat, milk, grain, produce—were in high demand and short supply. The prices on salt, food, clothing, and everything else skyrocketed because of shortages and the inflated Continental currency. With the collapse of the domestic economy, the common people, as always, were the first to know it in their stomachs.

Common people endured the ravages of war. They were pillaged by the various armies in their midst. Women were raped. Homes were commandeered for the use of officers. Houses were burned, fences destroyed. Diseases ran rampant: more people died of illnesses spread by the war than did from enemy fire.

These great troubles, although affecting the rich along with the poor, did not affect rich and poor alike. The rich, when pillaged, had more to fall back on. "Ladies" were rarely raped. When loyalists were exiled at the end of the war, the well-to-do went to England or island plantations, the others to cold and often barren regions in Canada. Commissioned officers, when taken prisoner, were generally placed on parole and allowed to continue with everyday life, while privates languished in the hulls of prison ships. Few rich people and many poor people suffered from diseases related to the unsanitary conditions of camp or prison life. People of means generally chose to inoculate themselves against smallpox, much to the dismay of commoners who were thereby exposed to the disease but did not wish to engage in the practice themselves.

Many Native Americans lost their fields and crops, their homes and villages, and finally their land. White Americans waged war not simply against warriors but against populations. And it worked: Indian women, children, and old men starved to death and froze.

While a few African Americans gained their freedom, the vast majority did not. Nervous masters clamped down more tightly than ever on slaves who did not escape. A great number of those who did manage to get away perished to disease. As the British surrendered to the Americans at Yorktown, former slaves were cast out to die in the no-man's-land between the armies. This was the fate of many among the underclasses: to be caught within the gears of war, then abandoned in the end.

Manipulating the system. Native Americans and African Americans, although victimized, hardly remained passive. Using a variety of strategies, they tried to take advantage of the rift between colonists and the mother country: some sought employment with whichever army promised the most opportunity; most, perceiving a brighter future for themselves if the British prevailed, opposed the American rebels; a few, like the slaves from the North who seized on republican principles to demand their own freedom, called the shots the opposite way and sided with the patriots. Whichever path they chose, Native Americans and African Americans were motivated neither by monarchical beliefs nor republican principles, but by their own self-interest. They played the game for what it was worth to them.

Many whites did the same. As in most times, the drive for survival prevailed—perhaps not in the beginning, but definitely by the end. When patriots called for short-term boycotts of British goods prior to the outbreak of war, they received overwhelming support. When Revolutionary committees demanded that people sign the association, most went along with the crowd. But when the committees demanded that people continue their sacrifices year after year, many balked. Farmers as well as merchants charged whatever prices they could get. Facing disease, military conscription, runaway inflation, and a severe scarcity of food and goods, common people with common sense concluded that charity must start at home. The net effect of so many people looking out for themselves was economic collapse. Ordinary Americans, not just wealthy speculators, made this happen.

Fighting the wars. Common people, as usual, did most of the actual fighting. According to republican theory, all men would serve in militias to help protect their liberty and property—but it didn't work out that way. Men of means, when called, bought their way out; men without means could not. The poor served in place of the rich, just as they did in European armies. Officers gained the fame, but common folk pulled far more than their share in the struggle for military superiority. Independence was declared by wealthy merchants, planters, and lawyers; independence was won by poor men and boys while those who were better off gave but grudging assistance.

Granting or withholding support. During the French and Indian War, common people showed up for parades and drank toasts to the king. Even in the early 1770s, the king's birthday was celebrated with gusto throughout the colonies. Later, it was not. People always have the power to deny consent. At the very least they can drag their heels, even if they dare not defy. Between 1776 and 1779 slaves who had lost hope of fleeing to the British engaged in ad hoc slowdowns, despite their masters' attempts to speed them up. In their boycotts, common people as well as leaders withheld support from the royal government. Whether by acting or declining to act, men and women who were not rich made their presence felt.

Testing the limits of authority. On the eve of the Revolution many tenant farmers spoke ill of their landlords; urban crowds taunted British soldiers; slaves, according to folkloric evidence, played subtle tricks on their masters. Those on the bottom, as usual, found ways to heckle those on top. These minor acts of personal disobedience—a glance, a grunt, or some other sign of displeasure, barely detectable—congealed during the Revolutionary era into a genuine social movement, or series of movements, based on defiance.

Supervision and repression. And through their defiance, common people forced elites to clamp down. In the decade before the war, British authorities sent soldiers into the streets of Boston and New York to stifle protests by the "mob"—but this exacerbated rather than alleviated the hostilities. When the Massachusetts Government Act effectively disenfranchised the citizenry as punishment for the Boston Tea Party, ordinary farmers would not stand for it and they closed the courts. Common people, by expressing their discontent, had triggered acts of repression, but these in turn stimulated an outright rebellion. The attempts by those who held political power to restrain the common people backfired. The result was the American Revolution.

In the South repression played a special role. Why would a conservative planter who owned substantial real estate and 15 slaves, or maybe even 150, be driven to revolution? Because he feared that his slaves, lured by the British with promises of freedom, might revolt. To prevent slave insurrection and social upheaval, the southern elite mobilized against Lord Dunmore while tightening the reins on the people they held in bondage. Because of the presence of slavery, political disputes between ruling elites metamorphosed into revolution, with a peculiar southern twist: masters fashioned themselves as rebels. And once fighting had commenced, the need to keep armed guards at home depleted the manpower available to the army. Because they needed to be watched, slaves constituted an awesome political force despite the fact that they lacked arms, the vote, and the freedom to organize.

Rise up and rebel. Resistance spurred repression, which fueled yet more resistance. British authority tumbled, and with it all notions of aristocracy in the new United States. Common people rose up as never before, questioning the special privileges of their "betters." After a decade of political ferment and eight more years of war, free white Americans ceased to bow.

The "transforming hand of revolution," as J. Franklin Jameson once called it, profoundly affected the nature of the political conflict with Great Britain.[1] Common people functioned as key operatives at all stages: they started the war, they ran the committees, they fought the battles. Laborers and seamen dumped tea into the Boston harbor. Thousands of nameless farmers closed the courts in Massachusetts, terminating British rule. Crowds gathered anywhere and everywhere, armed with buckets of tar and baskets of feathers to enforce revolutionary standards. Even within the rigid structure of the military, common soldiers exercised more power than usual. They elected their own noncommissioned officers. Often, they refused to obey orders; occasionally, they mutinied. They deserted almost at will. More so than in most wars, they challenged or ignored traditional lines of command: try as he might, George Washington was never able to force his men to kick women camp followers out of the wagons.

The "transforming hand" was felt on the other side as well. In Maryland, Delaware, and New York's Hudson Valley, common people fancied themselves loyalists because the elites they opposed were patriots. In North and South Carolina, loyalist settlers from the backcountry contested the power of low-country patriots. These "friends of the king" were actually rebels, albeit in a convoluted manner. So were hundreds of thousands of slaves who rooted for or sided with the British, hoping to become free. Native Americans, meanwhile, fought their own wars of independence, mostly against the American patriots. The spirit of Revolution prevailed throughout, with common people on each side fighting a war in order to challenge what they perceived as the forces of oppression.

Why did this wave of rebellion sweep across the British colonies of North America between 1765 and 1783? Economic interests, political rivalries, demographic developments, and the evolution of republican ideology obviously played their parts. How these factors combined to initiate revolutionary fervor varied according to location, ethnicity, and a host of other variables.

A people's history, however, goes beyond this question of causality to focus on *how* this happened. When we investigate the ways in which people experience history, we must do as they did: deal with the situation as it was. Farmers in Massachusetts, artisans in Philadelphia, or slaves in South Carolina did not spend great amounts of time pondering the origins of their restive sentiments. They did not ask *why* they wanted liberty; they simply tried to achieve it.

By choosing to look at the actions of specific groups and individuals, a people's history helps us reevaluate our generalizations and fine-tune the telling of history; by pointing the camera in new directions, it reveals fresh images which must then be incorporated into the overall picture. The story of our nation's founding, told so often from the perspective of the "founding fathers," will never ring true unless it can take some account of the Massachusetts farmers who closed the courts, the poor men and boys who fought the battles, the women who followed the troops, the loyalists who viewed themselves as rebels, the pacifists who refused to sign oaths of allegiance, the Native Americans who struggled for their own independence, the southern slaves who fled to the British, the northern slaves who negotiated their freedom by joining the Continental Army.

Who's In and Who's Out

Although not all these groups were included in "the body of the people" as conceived by the patriots, the wheels set in motion by the Revolution were moving rapidly. According to historian Gordon Wood,

> The Revolution resembled the breaking of a dam, releasing thousands upon thousands of pent-up pressures. There had been seepage and flows before the Revolution, but suddenly it was as if the whole traditional structure, enfeebled and brittle to begin with, broke apart, and people and their energies were set loose in an unprecedented outburst. Nothing contributed more to this explosion of energy than did the idea of equality. Equality was in fact the most radical and most powerful ideological force let loose in the Revolution. Its appeal was far more potent than any of the revolutionaries realized. Once invoked, the idea of equality could not be stopped, and it tore through American society and culture with awesome power. . . . Within decades following the Declaration of Independence, the United States became the most egalitarian nation in the history of the world, and it remains so today, regardless of its great disparities of wealth.[2]

According to Wood's critics, however, this "idea of equality" left many in the lurch: women who could not vote, almost half a million slaves, somewhere between 110,000 and 150,000 Native Americans, about 80,000 to 100,000 loyalists who had to leave their homes (as well as hundreds of thousands of others who remained where they were but faced repercussions for their prior allegiances), and even many patriots who remained without property at war's end.[3] In 1780 white radicals in Virginia proposed a scheme to spread the wealth: take one out of every twenty slaves from the rich and give them to the poor whites who enlisted in the army.[4] Clearly, the concept of "equality" had a long way to go. "The Revolution flattered to deceive," writes Duncan MacLeod, "it promised more than it achieved."[5] In the words of Michael Meranze, "the accomplishments of the Revolution and of liberal society are inseparable from its repressions and exclusions."[6]

So was the cup of the Revolution half full or half empty? How can we assess its inclusions and omissions?

In rural Massachusetts, where British authority was first over-

thrown, ordinary farmers and artisans appeared to transform the
political landscape when they humiliated and forced out of office
local elites. As elites lost power, plain folk took their place. Jackson
Turner Main, in his comparison of the wealth of legislators before
and after the Revolution, found that in three northern states the
percentage of lawmakers worth over £5,000 declined from 36 percent to 12 percent, while those worth less than £2,000 increased
from 17 percent to 62 percent. Even in the South, where large
slaveholders still held power, legislators worth over £5,000 decreased from 52 percent to 28 pecent, while those worth under
£2,000 increased from 12 percent to 30 percent.[7]

This broadening of political representation was due in part to the
participation of common people in Revolutionary activities before
and during the war. After serving in militias or on local committees
which ferreted out loyalists, people who had once viewed the exercise of power as beyond their reach could no longer be awed or
intimidated into leaving the political process in the hands of the
elite. As John Shy observes, once common folk "had seen and even
taken part in hounding, humiliating, perhaps killing men known to
them as social superiors, they could not easily re-acquire the un-
thinking respect for wealth and status that underpinned the old order."[8] The American Revolution spelled an end to deference among
the free population. No longer would mud-caked farmers feel compelled to yield the way to dandy gentlemen. Hundreds of thousands
of Euro-American males could now enjoy the fruits of freedom,
much as they had anticipated: they could farm new land, drink hard
cider, and argue politics without being intimidated by redcoated
soldiers or a handful of men who wielded power with the blessing
of the Crown.

But we must take care not to exaggerate these democratic gains.
In the aftermath of the war, throughout the hinterlands of the young
nation, even free white males felt left out, betrayed by the unfulfilled
promises of the Revolution. In the late summer and fall of 1786
thousands of farmers from western Massachusetts gathered to close
the courts, just as they had done twelve years earlier. Once again,
these people felt threatened by judges who could seize their property
for debts or unpaid taxes—and once again, Revolutionary farmers

formed as "the body of the people," met in taverns, marched to fife and drum with sprigs in their hats, and promised "to turn out at a minute's warning" to fight for what they felt was rightfully theirs.[9] Appealing to the same logic of rebellion that had worked the first time, these farmers declared their readiness to fight the Revolution all over: "Whenever any encroachments are made either upon the liberties or property of the people, if redress cannot be had without, it is virtue in them to disturb the government."[10]

And Massachusetts farmers did "disturb the government" in 1786. They closed courts at Worcester, Springfield, Northampton, Great Barrington, Taunton, and Concord—the same places as in 1774. When local militias were called out to oppose the angry farmers, the militiamen refused to raise arms against their neighbors. But just as the rebels were about to seize a federal armory at Springfield, an army sponsored by rich men from Boston managed to push them back. The insurgents were pursued from town to town, and Shays' Rebellion, as it came to be called, was soon squashed.[11]

The popular discontent of the mid-1780s was not limited to western Massachusetts. Other New England farmers protested in Connecticut, New Hampshire, and Vermont. In Rhode Island the debtor movement actually gained control of the legislature and forced the state to issue paper money. Governmental leaders in New York, North Carolina, and Georgia debated whether to circulate paper money in their own states in order to escape the wrath of indebted farmers. In New Jersey debtors attacked the courts at several locations; near Morristown, the Reverend Joseph Lewis wrote that "a spirit of rebellion caught hold of the greatest part of the community." In York, Pennsylvania, 200 men armed with guns and clubs took back cattle that had been seized by the government in lieu of taxes. In Maryland "a tumultuous assemblage of the people" closed the Charles County court. Debtors stopped court proceedings in the Virginia counties of King William, Greenbrier, and Amelia; James Madison wrote that "prisons and courthouses and clerk's offices" throughout the state were "willfully burnt." After the court was closed in Camden, South Carolina, Judge Aedanus Burke believed that not even "5,000 troops, the best in America or Europe, could enforce obedience to the Common Pleas."[12]

The distress of the farmers, who still thought of themselves as "the body of the people," was real and widespread—and so was the distress of Native Americans devastated by war, as well as slaves held under tighter control. Euro-American women were not set back by the Revolution, but neither did they see a significant change in their political status.[13] In 1785 Hannah Griffitts wrote an intriguing poem in her diary:

> The glorious fourth—again appears
> A Day of Days—and year of years,
>   The sum of sad disasters,
> Where all the mighty gains we see
> With all their Boasted liberty,
>   Is only Change of Masters.[14]

Who were these new "Masters"? Men lording over women? Upper-class leaders continuing to rule the lower classes? Regardless of Griffitts's intent, the poem can be read either way. In the mid-1780s there were still many Americans, male and female, who felt bypassed by the "mighty gains" celebrated on the Fourth of July. Gordon Wood's "idea of equality" which had been "let loose in the Revolution" had not yet done them much good.

And yet, although many people were left out, we commit the fallacy of hindsight if we judge the achievements of the Revolutionary Era according to modern standards of justice. "All men are created equal," at the time, was certainly not intended to include women, slaves, or Indians. It was a radical concept for its day, regardless of its limited scope. Beyond that, as Wood and others have maintained, the concept of equality served as a blueprint for the future, pointing in a direction which would eventually extend across the lines of gender and to all racial, ethnic, religious, or political minorities.

But there is danger in these musings, even if true. What good was some "blueprint" to the people who were alive back then? We do not have to condemn the patriots for failing to transcend the prevailing ethic of their day, but we do have to acknowledge that only a minority of the people of that time—males of European descent—were in a position to benefit politically or socially from the American Revolution, and that even many of these did not feel that the Revolution had delivered the goods. In our eagerness to embrace the ideological significance of the Revolution, we should not forget to pay some attention to the numerous contemporaries who did not live to see a personal advantage accruing to the notions of "liberty" and "equality."

There is another danger in treating the idea of "equality" in modern terms. Today, "equality" is generally interpreted to include protection for the rights of minorities; during the Revolution, "the body of the people" referred exclusively to the majority. "The hardships of particulars are not to be considered," wrote Christopher Gadsden, "when the good of the whole is the object in view."[15] In each separate town, "the people"—that is, the patriots—enforced their own standards of behavior on everyone else. In 1776 patriots from Longmeadow, Massachusetts, raided the store of Samuel Colton to protest exorbitant prices. Toward the end of the war Colton, in a petition for restitution, claimed that "a Great Number of Persons Blackt and in Disguise" had "Carried away the whole of his Rum and Salt &c, Except a Trifle Left for private use, Ransacking and Searching his house from top to bottom Plundering and Carrying away what they Saw fit."[16] In response, 126 citizens (including 16 with the last name of Colton) signed a petition which justified the raid in the name of "the body of the people":

[A]t the Beginning of the present Contest between Great Britain and the American States there was a Considerable Time when the courts of Justice were shut up and the Operation of the Laws of the Land suspended and all Power having originated from the Body of the people reverted back to its source and Fountain and was in Fact exercised by them in some Instances and in others by committes appointed by the People for that Purpose: That it was found absolutely necessary at that Time to guard against Evils and Mischiefs which then threatened the Destruction of the whole Body, that for that Purpose it was found Necessary to hinder some Members of the Community from acting Contrary to the general Welfare Just as their Humor or Malice should Direct, as to imprison those that were hostile, to seize on Private property where necessary, and in some Instances to prevent People from using their Property in such a Manner as essentially to injure the whole. . . . [A]t those Times many Things were done by the Body of People and by their committes, which could not be justified at a Time when Justice was administered by the Law of the Land, tho at the Time of doing them they were not only Justifiable but necessary and commendable as being done for the General Good. [17]

The state Assembly decided to grant immunity to these raiders who had acted "for the General Good."

Ordinary people gained power through their Revolutionary activities, and they did not hesitate to use it. Patriots of Longmeadow seized goods which they thought were priced too high; Massachusetts farmers forced Crown-appointed officials to take off their hats and recite their resignations to the assembled throng; local crowds harassed Mother Ann, the Shaker, because of her pacifistic preachings; white settlers laid waste to Indian villages; mobs tarred and feathered or smeared dung over people they branded as Tories— these groups all operated in the name of a "General Good" which their adversaries appeared to threaten. Too much attention to the rights of their victims would be self-defeating. We ought not to forget that Judge Lynch himself was a patriot who administered his makeshift justice from a walnut tree in his own yard.[18]

It is one of the supreme ironies of the American Revolution that the assumption of authority by "the body of the people"—probably its most radical feature—served to oppress as well as to liberate. This was a real revolution: the people did seize power, but they exercised that power at the expense of others—loyalists, pacifists, merchants, Indians, slaves—who, although certainly people, were not perceived to be a part of the whole. This was, after all, a war. It would not be the last time Americans sacrificed notions of liberty and equality in the name of the general good. Frontier vigilantism, night-riding in the South, the internment of Americans of Japanese descent during World War II, red-baiting in the 1950s—these extreme manifestations of majoritarian rule did not violate our beginnings but reflected them. However crude, they echoed the tarring and feathering, the forced administration of loyalty oaths, and the general subjugation of unpopular minorities which characterized the American Revolution.

And yet the opposite is true as well. When women marched for the right to vote, when workers sat down in their factories for the right to form unions, when African Americans engaged in mass demonstrations to terminate Jim Crow in the South—these extensions of democracy also reflected our beginnings, mirroring the Yankees who paraded "with staves and musick" during the court closures of 1774. Our Revolutionary heritage works both ways. "The body of the people," the dominant force during the 1770s, has empowered and deprived.

The Human Face of Freedom

Revolutionary soldiers were freedom-loving sorts. They "carry the spirit of freedom into the field, and think for themselves," complained General Richard Montgomery, who could not understand why the troops called "a sort of town meeting" every time a maneuver was planned. "The privates are all generals," he reported bitterly.[19] This "spirit of freedom" did not mesh well with the dictates of war. "Men accustomed to unbounded freedom, and no control," George Washington observed, "cannot brook the Restraint which is indispensably necessary to the good order and Government of an Army; without which, licentiousness, and every kind of disorder triumphantly reign."[20]

If freedom was to be won in the end, the men who fought for their freedom had to be reined in. Upon assuming command during the siege of Boston, Washington attempted to bring the soldiers "to a proper degree of Subordination." The Reverend William Emerson described the impact of Washington's imposition of military discipline:

> There is a great overturning in camp as to order and regularity.
> New lords new laws. The Generals Washington and Lee are

upon the lines every day. New orders from his Excellency are read to the respective regiments every morning after prayers. The strictest government is taking place, and great distinction is made between officers and soldiers. Everyone is made to know his place and keep it.[21]

Throughout the remainder of the war, Washington did everything within his power to establish subordination within the ranks. Not hesitant to administer punishment, he asked Congress repeatedly for permission to increase the maximum number of lashes from 100 to 500. Although he commuted some death sentences, he allowed others to stand. How else could he proceed? Free-spirited patriots had to be transformed into soldiers who did as they were told.

Fighting men and boys were not the only ones who had to sacrifice freedom in order to attain it. The institution of war, like that of slavery, had a way of entrapping all of its participants, even at the highest levels. George Washington himself was not exempt. Because he had chosen a military role, he found himself forced to behave in ways which he himself came to regard as suspect. Witness:

At the close of the war, after the British had surrendered at Yorktown but before tempers had cooled, a group of New York patriots captured and killed a Tory named Philip White. Enraged loyalists quickly retaliated by hanging a patriot whom they held as prisoner, Joshua Huddy. "Up goes Huddy for Philip White," read a sign pinned to his chest. George Washington, outraged by the vengeful killing of a helpless prisoner, announced to British authorities "that unless the Perpetrators of that horrid deed were delivered up I should be under the disagreeable necessity of Retaliating, as the only means left to put a stop to such inhuman proceedings."[22] When his pleas for justice were ignored, Washington ordered that a prisoner be chosen at random, then executed. Only if Huddy's murderers were punished would the execution be waved.

The victim turned out to be Charles Asgill, a nineteen-year-old British captain who had surrendered at Yorktown. Did this young officer really deserve to die for a crime in which he had played no part? Perhaps not, but Washington had decided to use Asgill as a hostage, and he remained firm in his resolve. On June 4, 1782, he wrote to his brigadier general:

396   A PEOPLE'S HISTORY OF THE AMERICAN REVOLUTION

> I am deeply affected with the unhappy Fate to which Capt Asgill is subjected, yet . . . in the Stage to which the Matter has been suffered to run, all Argumentation on the Subject is entirely precluded on my part, that my Resolutions have been grounded on so mature Deliberation, that they must remain unalterably fixed.[23]

One week later Washington added, "The Enemy ought to have learnt before this, that my Resolutions are not to be trifled with."[24] The week after that, in response to a flood of entreaties begging for mercy, Washington admitted that he felt "exceedgly distressed on this Occassion," but he then explained that "Justice to the Army and the Public" and "my own Honor" required that his orders "be carried into full execution."[25]

During the course of the summer the Asgill affair mushroomed into an international cause célèbre. When the victim, a young man of Washington's own class, made a personal appeal, the general found it difficult to maintain his resolve. Asgill's letter and the entreaties of his family "work too powerfully upon my humanity," Washington finally conceded.[26] Originally, he had treated the matter as "purely of a Military nature and reducable to this single point," but now his feelings seemed to be getting in the way.[27] Since he could not alter his public position without appearing weak, he found himself trapped by the uncaring logic of military necessity. To escape, he abdicated responsibility and asked Congress to "chalk a line for me to walk by in this business."[28] Despite his prior resolve, he confessed privately that he hoped Congress would decide that Asgill be "released from his Duress and that he should be permitted to go to his Friends in Europe."[29] In the end, after the intervention of the French king and queen (Asgill's mother was French), Congress determined to set the prisoner free. Washington expressed relief. Congress and the French had bailed him out, liberating not only Asgill but Washington himself from the strange dictates of military reasoning.

In the Asgill affair George Washington, a man of sound moral character, had been compelled to act against his own better judgment. Just as the institution of slavery dehumanized masters as well as slaves,[30] so did the dictates of war lead men of high principles into embarrassing and uncomfortable positions. The "Father of our Country," unquestionably the most powerful man of his times, was held prisoner within the confines of his role as commander-in-chief.

If we focus on the *process* of the Revolutionary War rather than its *outcome*, we find that almost everybody had to give up, at least for a time, the very freedom they hoped to achieve. For most Americans, the experience of a war fought on home ground was not expansive but restrictive. Options were limited, and all possibilities seemed fraught with danger, discomfort, or dishonor. The peculiar logic of the American Revolution, with its heavy demands as well as its violence, had a way of boxing people into corners. In the words of missionary David Zeisberger, "Nowhere is a place to be found to which we can retire. . . . The world is already too narrow."[31]

The American Revolution forced all sorts of people to make hard choices between unsavory alternatives. Joseph Plumb Martin and Jeremiah Greenman had to decide whether to violate military discipline and demand their due, or to take up arms against their cold and hungry comrades who mutinied. Andrew Giering, the Moravian shoemaker, had to decide whether to remain in jail, allowing his family to go hungry, or to betray his religious beliefs by taking an oath. Boston King, David George, and Judith Jackson had to decide whether to abandon their homes and risk their lives by running to the British, or to submit to the increasingly harsh repressions of their masters.

For some, there was no freedom at all, no meaningful choices to be made. Many African Americans, under closer guard, were kept in slavery, no matter how much Lord Dunmore entreated them to run away. Mothers saw their sons go off to war, regardless of what they said or did. Native American villagers starved and froze through no fault of their own. What could Polly Dibblee and her five children do when they were thrown "naked into the Streets" on Long Island? Or when Polly's husband Filer left his family stranded in exile, having cut his own throat at the end of a harsh Canadian winter?

Over the course of the war, many people must have wondered: All this over a tax on tea? How did this happen? Nobody really knew. The American Revolution, like every war, took on a life of its own. At least for a time, it ensnared the very people who yearned for liberation. If freedom was the end, the war itself signaled a very tenuous beginning. Just as the "accomplishments of the Revolution and of liberal society are inseparable from its repressions and exclusions," so are the results of the Revolution inseparable from the actual experience of the war, with all its attendant sorrows. In a people's history based on real lives, this flesh and blood of the past cannot be ignored.

Yet many slaves, Indians, pacifists, women, and poor folk on both sides functioned as active agents, not just passive victims. In the American Revolution, the "total war" of its day, virtually everybody played a role. Although common people have always had a hand in history, there was something special going on during those times, a level of involvement that was simultaneously frightening and exciting. Everyday life—the very foundation of social existence—became politicized. Ordinary folks, not just leaders, engaged in a compelling drama which enveloped the entire populace.

The merging of public and private worlds was the most pervasive feature of the American Revolution. There is a telling tale from the revolution in Massachusetts during the summer of 1774:

Jesse Dunbar, of Halifax, in Plymouth County, bought some fat Cattle of Mr. Thomas, the Counsellor, and drove them to Plymouth for sale; one of the Oxen being skinned and hung up, the Committee came to him, and finding he bought it of Mr. Thomas, they put the ox into a cart, and fixed Dunbar in his belly, and carted him four miles, and then made him pay a dollar, after taking three more Cattle and a Horse from him; the Plymouth mob delivered him to the Kingston mob, which carted him four miles further, and forced from him another dollar, then delivered him to the Duxbury mob, who abused him by throwing the tripe in his face, and endeavoring to cover him with it, to the endangering his life, then threw dirt at him, and after other abuses, carried him to said Thomas's house, and made him pay another sum of money: and he not taking the beef, they flung it in the road and quitted him. [32]

This was the Revolution that the farmers made: Jesse Dunbar was carted about in an oxen's belly because he had chosen to do business with the wrong person. Everyday events like buying or selling an ox took on new meanings in those tumultuous times as each and every American redefined his or her place in the rapidly transforming social landscape and charted some course midst the evolving ideologies, political alignments, and economic realities of the Revolutionary era. In order to survive, everybody had to pay attention to public happenings, project how their own personal actions might be construed, and calculate how those actions might affect the course of events. Some Americans could vote, most could not—but they all took part in the political process, whether they wanted to or not. The people of the Revolution had become players.

NOTES

Introduction

1. Charles K. Bolton, *The Private Soldier Under Washington* (Williamstown, MA: Corner House, 1976), 179; Charles Royster, *A Revolutionary People at War: The Continental Army and American Character, 1775–1783* (Chapel Hill: University of North Carolina Press, 1979), 166.
2. Herbert Aptheker, ed., *A Documentary History of the Negro People in the United States* (New York: Citadel Press, 1969), 7.
3. Mary Beth Norton, *Liberty's Daughters: The Revolutionary Experience of American Women, 1750–1800* (Boston: Little, Brown & Co., 1980), 204–5.
4. Joseph Plumb Martin, *Private Yankee Doodle: Being a Narrative of Some of the Adventures, Dangers and Sufferings of a Revolutionary Soldier*, ed. George F. Scheer (Boston: Little, Brown & Co., 1962), 18–23. Originally published in 1830 in Hallowell, Maine, under the title *A Narrative of Some of the Adventures, Dangers and Sufferings of a Revolutionary Soldier, Interspersed with Anecdotes of Incidents That Occurred Within His Own Observation*.
5. Douglas Adair and John A. Schutz, eds., *Peter Oliver's Origins and Progress of the American Revolution: A Tory View* (Stanford, CA: Stanford University Press, 1967), 157.
6. Henry S. Commager and Richard B. Morris, *The Spirit of 'Seventy-Six: The Story of the American Revolution as Told by the Participants* (Indianapolis and New York: Bobbs-Merrill, 1958), 63–4.
7. Wallace Brown, *The Good Americans: The Loyalists in the American Revolution* (New York: William Morrow, 1969), 140.
8. William Moultrie, *Memoirs of the American Revolution* (New York: David Longworth, 1802), 355; Robert M. Weir, " 'The Violent Spirit,' The Reestablishment of Order, and the Continuity of Leadership in Post-Revolutionary South Carolina," in Ronald Hoffman, Thad W. Tate, and Peter J. Albert, eds., *An Uncivil War: The Southern Backcountry during the American Revolution* (Charlottesville: University Press of Virginia, 1985), 76.

9. John Shy, *A People Numerous and Armed: Reflections on the Military Struggle for American Independence* (Ann Arbor: University of Michigan Press, 1990), 26.

10. Royster, *Revolutionary People at War*, 365. Some historians claim that elite patriots had a particular interest in selective recall: they hoped to erase "the popular side of the Revolution" from the public memory. [Alfred F. Young, *The Shoemaker and the Tea Party: Memory and the American Revolution* (Boston: Beacon Press, 1999), 121.]

11. Philip S. Foner, *Labor and the American Revolution* (Westport, CT: Greenwood Press, 1976), 202.

12. Foner, *Labor and the American Revolution*, 203. For more invocations of the American Revolution, see Len Travers, *Celebrating the Fourth: Independence Day and the Rites of Nationalism in the Early Republic* (Amherst: University of Massachusetts Press, 1997).

13. Richard M. Brown, "Violence and the American Revolution," in Stephen G. Kurtz and James H. Hutson, eds., *Essays on the American Revolution* (Chapel Hill: University of North Carolina Press, 1973), 113.

14. Brown, "Violence and the American Revolution," 113.

15. Commager and Morris, *The Spirit of 'Seventy-Six*, 1295. Many recent historians, of course, have been more sensitive to the ways in which the war affected its people. Edward Countryman, for instance, expresses a more empathetic attitude when he declares: "The glory did not come free. It had a price, and Americans ought to be comfortable enough with ourselves to recognize that the price and the glory cannot be pried apart." ["Indians, the Colonial Order, and the Social Significance of the American Revolution," *William and Mary Quarterly*, 3rd series, 53 (1996): 362.] In a similar vein, Michael Meranze states that "the accomplishments of the Revolution and of liberal society are inseparable from its repressions and exclusions." ["Even the Dead Will Not Be Safe: An Ethics of Early American History," *William and Mary Quarterly*, 3rd series, 50 (1993): 378.]

16. Historians of the Revolution have always reflected the dominant views of their times. From 1776 to the early twentieth century, American historians saw the Revolution as a righteous war of independence. The Revolution, they said, was to be accepted as it was put forth by the Revolutionaries themselves: a struggle for American liberty against oppressive British rule. Although most school textbooks continued to be based on the patriotic perspective until very recently, serious scholars began questioning this simplistic stance almost a century ago. The Progressive school of historians, starting in the early 1900s and lasting through the Depression, viewed the war in economic as well as political terms. Influenced by the economic conflicts of their own world, the Progressives looked back to discover similar conflicts in the Revolutionary period. Carl L. Becker (*The Spirit of '76* and *The History of Political Parties in the Province of New York*) commented memorably that the "question of home rule" was accompanied by the "question of who should rule at home." Louis M. Hacker (*The Triumph of American Capitalism*) stated, "The struggle was not over high-sounding political and constitutional concepts; over the power of

taxation or even, in the final analysis, over natural rights. It was over colonial manufacturing, wild lands and furs, sugar, wine, tea, and currency."

After World War II, when economic and class warfare seemed in abeyance, consensus historians focused once again on the political motivations of the Revolutionaries. Robert E. Brown (*Middle-Class Democracy and the Revolution in Massachusetts, 1691–1780* and *Virginia, 1705–1786: Democracy or Aristocracy?*) argued that most colonists were middle-class, not rich or poor, and that they had enjoyed the privileges of democracy well before the Revolutionary era. The war, he claimed, was fought more to defend the democracy that already existed than to achieve some radical change. Clinton Rossiter (*Seedtime of the Republic*) and Edmund S. and Helen M. Morgan (*The Stamp Act Crisis* and *The Birth of the Republic*) held that the Americans were basically united in their opposition to colonial rule, that the rebels were consistent and justified in their resistance to "taxation without representation," and that economic motivations, although present, were not very significant.

The turbulent 1960s ushered in two new waves of historical research, each reflecting an aspect of the contemporary mood. Radical historians began to focus again on class conflict, paying specific attention this time to underclass Americans who traditionally had been left out of the Revolutionary story: African Americans, Native Americans, women, poor white men. Jesse Lemisch popularized the notion of "history from the bottom up" with his essay on seamen entitled "Jack Tar in the Streets." [*William and Mary Quarterly*, 3rd series, 25 (1968): 371–407.] Alfred F. Young's collection of essays, *The American Revolution: Explorations in the History of American Radicalism*, may have been the pivotal publication in this school of thought. Meanwhile, Bernard Bailyn (*The Ideological Origins of the American Revolution* and *Pamphlets of the American Revolution*) and Gordon Wood (*The Creation of the American Republic*) viewed the Revolution as the ideological transformation of an aroused populace. Claiming that the real conflict was about how people thought, Bailyn chose to focus his research on works of propaganda.

Recently, Gordon Wood (*The Radicalism of the American Revolution*) has attempted to synthesize the political and social perspectives while answering the radical critique that the Revolution did not go far enough in democratizing American society. One of Wood's reviewers, Edmund S. Morgan, wrote:

> The Revolution did revolutionize social relations. It did displace the deference, the patronage, and social divisions that had determined the way people viewed one another for centuries and still view one another in much of the world. It did give to ordinary people a pride and power, not to say an arrogance, that have continued to shock visitors from less favored lands. It may have left standing a host of inequalities that have troubled us ever since. But it generated the egalitarian view of society that makes them troubling and makes our world so different from the one in which the Revolutionists had grown up.

Not all historians have accepted Wood's synthesis. Michael Zuckerman, for one, feels that Wood "denies class at every turn," that he "disregards race, gender, and ethnicity almost completely," and that he "has shrunk America to a country without slaves, women, families, or the South." ["Rhetoric, Reality, and the Revolution: The Genteel Radicalism of Gordon Wood," *William and Mary Quarterly*, 3rd series, 51 (1994): 697–8.]

More recently still, perhaps reflecting the increased realism of the 1990s, Theodore Draper has written a book on the Revolutionary Era entitled simply *A Struggle for Power*. All the commotion over rights and liberties, according to Draper, masked a more fundamental antagonism: who would gain control over the North American continent? The question of "who was right," he claims, "cannot be answered without asking another question: Right for whom?"

An excellent treatment of the evolving treatments of the Revolution appears in Alfred F. Young, "American Historians Confront 'The Transforming Hand of Revolution,' " in Ronald Hoffman and Peter J. Albert, eds., *The Transforming Hand of Revolution: Reconsidering the American Revolution as a Social Movement* (Charlottesville: University Press of Virginia, 1995), 346–492.

17. Some of the people I will discuss in this book do not conform strictly to this literal defintion of "common people." A few of the women were wealthy, as were some loyalists and pacifists, while Native American leaders commanded political power. Even so, women possessed no political standing, loyalists and pacifists were politically persecuted, while all Native Americans were prevented from participating in any significant way within the new United States—and all these groups have been neglected in the traditional telling of the American Revolution. My use of the term "common people" should be interpreted in this historiographic context.

1 Rank-and-File Rebels

1. For the Knowles Riot and other crowd actions of seamen and port laborers see John Lax and William Pencak, "The Knowles Riot and the Crisis of the 1740s in Massachusetts," *Perspectives in American History* 19 (1976): 163–214; Jesse Lemisch, "Jack Tar in the Streets: Merchant Seamen in the Politics of Revolutionary America," *William and Mary Quarterly*, 3rd series, 25 (1968): 371–407; Marcus Rediker, "A Motley Crew of Rebels: Sailors, Slaves, and the Coming of the American Revolution," in Ronald Hoffman and Peter J. Albert, eds., *The Transforming Hand of Revolution: Reconsidering the American Revolution as a Social Movement* (Charlottesville: University Press of Virginia, 1996), 155–198; Gary B. Nash, *The Urban Crucible: Social Change, Political Consciousness, and the Origins of the American Revolution* (Cambridge: Harvard University Press, 1979), 221–2.

2. Historian Pauline Maier has observed:

> Eighteenth-century Americans accepted the existence of popular upris-ings with remarkable ease. Riots and tumults, it was said, happened "in all governments at all times." . . . Not that extra-legal uprisings were encouraged. They were not. But in certain circumstances, it was un-derstood, the people would rise up almost as a natural force, much as

night follows day, and this phenomenon often contributed to the public welfare. [Pauline Maier, *From Resistance to Revolution: Colonial Radicals and the Development of American Opposition to Britain*, 1765–1776 (New York: Alfred A. Knopf, 1972), 3.]

3. Richard Walsh, *Charleston's Sons of Liberty: A Study of the Artisans, 1763–1789* (Columbia: University of South Carolina Press, 1959), 37.

4. Rediker, "Motley Crew of Rebels," 155.

5. Nash, *Urban Crucible*, 301–2. In Wilmington, North Carolina, class antagonisms were displayed yet contained. A crowd of 500 burned an effigy of an "HONOURABLE GENTLEMAN," then visited the various gentlemen of the town, inviting them to the bonfire where demonstrators and the "better sort" joined in offering toasts to liberty, property, and an end to the stamp tax. "They continued together until 12 of the clock, and then dispersed, without doing any mischief." [Ann Withington, *Toward a More Perfect Union: Virtue and the Formation of American Republics* (New York: Oxford University Press, 1991), 55.]

6. Hutchinson also insulted the lower classes by blaming the Knowles impressment riot on "Foreign Seamen, Servants, Negroes, and Other Persons of Mean and Vile Condition" [Gordon Wood, *The Radicalism of the American Revolution* (New York: Vintage, 1991), 34; Gary B. Nash, "Social Change and the Growth of Prerevolutionary Urban Radicalism," in Alfred F. Young, ed., *The American Revolution: Explorations in the History of American Radicalism* (De Kalb, IL: Northern Illinois University Press, 1976), 20.] Marcus Rediker argues convincingly that Hutchinson was correct: seamen and African Americans did figure prominently in the Knowles Riot; indeed, they remained at the forefront of radical crowd actions throughout the Revolutionary era. (Rediker, "Motley Crew of Rebels," 155–98.)

7. Nash, *Urban Crucible*, 294–7. Pauline Maier notes that this second riot had little to do with the Stamp Act and was more likely "inspired by a group of merchants who feared they had been named in a set of recent depositions about smuggling" (Maier, *Resistance to Revolution*, 58). Even if the rioters had an interest in destroying some papers, however, the severity with which they destroyed everything else remains relevant to their feelings of underlying hostility.

8. Nash, *Urban Crucible*, 294.

9. Nash, "Social Change," 7. In Philadelphia, the changes were even more dramatic. The share of the richest 5 percent increased from 33 percent to 55 percent between 1693 and 1771, while the share of the poorest half declined from 10.1 percent to 3.3 percent.

10. Nash, *Urban Crucible*, 263.

11. William Pencak, *War, Politics, & Revolution in Provincial Massachusetts* (Boston: Northeastern University Press, 1981), 272–5; Maier, *Resistance to Revolution*, 83–7, 297–312.

12. Maier, *Resistance to Revolution*, 57, 59. Throughout the Revolutionary era, patriot leaders would continue their attempts to dampen popular actions, although with diminishing success. In 1768, when a Boston crowd protesting the seizure

of John Hancock's sloop *Liberty* threw stones at the comptroller's house, "some prudent gentlemen" persuaded them to stop; when a mob burned the pleasure boat belonging to a customs official, "some gentlemen who had influence" tried to intervene, but too late. [Maier, *Resistance to Revolution*, 124–5.] In Baltimore in 1776, an angry crowd led by David Poe, a recent immigrant from Ireland who "seemed at the head of the lower class," was quieted by James Nicholson, a merchant and ships captain who served as president of the Whig Club. [Charles G. Steffen, *The Mechanics of Baltimore: Workers and Politics in the Age of Revolution, 1763–1812* (Urbana and Chicago: University of Illinois Press, 1984), 68–9.]

13. According to Peter Oliver, brother of the deposed stamp collector, "If a Whisper was heard among his Followers, the holding up of his Finger hushed it in a Moment: & when he had fully displayed his Authority, he marched his Men to the first Rendevouz, & order'd them to retire peacably to their several Homes; & was punctually obeyed." [Douglas Adair and John Schutz, eds., *Peter Oliver's Origin & Progress of the American Rebellion* (Stanford: Stanford University Press, 1961), 54.] Oliver's coverage of MacIntosh's command of the crowd has to be read in light of his tendency to attribute all crowd actions to the manipulation of leaders. When I suggest below that MacIntosh and others had been "bought," I do not mean to imply that they had actually been "hired" to perform the "dirty Jobs" of more respectable Revolutionary leaders, as Oliver claimed. Aside from Oliver's blanket statement there is no evidence suggesting that MacIntosh was a mercenary, but there is ample evidence that would lead us to believe that MacIntosh and others were co-opted for this particular event.

14. Several historians have suggested that African Americans did indeed play a prominent role in crowd actions throughout the Revolutionary era, most likely participating in their fair share of destruction. This will be discussed in chapter 6. Certainly, they were prominent at the Boston Massacre, although Paul Revere pretended it wasn't so: his famous engraving of the event showed not a single black face, not even Crispus Attucks's. Although blacks could not be prevented from participating, some white leaders still considered their presence to be an embarrassment. (Rediker, "Motley Crew of Rebels," 193.)

15. Nash, *Urban Crucible*, 351; Edward Countryman, *The American Revolution* (New York: Hill & Wang, 1985), 103.

16. Dirk Hoerder, "Boston Leaders and Boston Crowds, 1765–1776," in Young, ed., *American Revolution*, 246.

17. Edward Countryman, *A People in Revolution: The American Revolution and Political Society in New York, 1760–1790* (Baltimore: John Hopkins University Press, 1981), 37.

18. Countryman, *People in Revolution*, 37, 40; Paul A. Gilje, *The Road to Mobocracy: Popular Disorder in New York City, 1763–1834* (Chapel Hill: University of North Carolina Press, 1987), 51. Gilje observes that

> This disturbance again revealed a combination of whig and plebian elements. The impact of whig rhetoric appeared in the shouts of "Liberty, Liberty." Of more significance, however, were the plebian ele-

ments ... [including] a distinct resentment of wealth. The items of clothing lost "thro' Mistake" were obvious symbols of ostentation, and Weyman's *Gazette* commented that the bonfire in the Common, a typical plebian action in the eigtheenth century, was "much to the Satisfaction of Many at this destressed Time." ... Those New Yorkers who stood in the dancing shadows of the raging bonfire that night were participating in a public theater far more meaningful than the stage show planned by New York's would-be entertainers.

19. Countryman, *People in Revolution*, 61.

20. Barbara Clark Smith, "Social Visions of the American Resistance Movement," in Hoffman and Albert, eds., *Transforming Hand of Revolution*, 36. Smith goes on to present an interesting contrast with rum drinking: "The site was often public: taverns, streets, or militia mustering fields. The occasion was generally hospitable to wide participation, although sometimes rum drinking enlivened all-male gatherings. Rum drinking required little or no material culture; it was possible and common merely to pass the bottle."

21. One yeoman from Virginia recalled his childhood: "We made no use of tea or coffee for breakfast, or at any other time; nor did I know a single family that made any use of them. ... I suppose the *richer sort* might make use of *those* and other luxuries, but to such people I had no access." [Rhys Isaac, *Transformation of Virginia, 1740–1790* (Chapel Hill: University of North Carolina Press, 1982), 46.]

22. Benjamin W. Labaree, *The Boston Tea Party* (New York: Oxford University Press, 1964), 8, 28, 164.

23. William Lincoln, *History of Worcester, Massachusetts, from its Earliest Settlement to September, 1836* (Worcester, MA: Charles Hersey, 1862), 70.

24. Labaree, *Boston Tea Party*, 266. During the siege of Yorktown, Sarah Osborn served the weary soldiers "beef, and bread, and coffee (in a gallon pot)." [John C. Dann, *The Revolution Remembered: Eyewitness Accounts of the War of Independence* (Chicago: University of Chicago Press, 1980), 244.]

25. Labaree, *Boston Tea Party*, 261. Jones maintained that he thought his tea had been smuggled and was therefore acceptable. The crowd remained unconvinced, forcing him to make public apologies and to admit that his tea was obtained from England, even though it probably was not. To distinguish between smuggled tea and tea that had been taxed proved impossible; all tea was suspect, and to be suspect was proof enough.

26. Alfred F. Young, "George Robert Twelves Hewes (1742–1840): A Boston Shoemaker and the Memory of the American Revolution," *William and Mary Quarterly*, 3rd series, 38 (1981): 590.

27. Labaree, *Boston Tea Party*, 141; L. F. S. Upton, ed., "Proceedings of Ye Body Respecting the Tea," *William and Mary Quarterly*, 3rd series, 22 (1965): 298.

28. Young, "George Hewes," 591.

29. Maier, *Resistance to Revolution*, 276.

30. The British Admiral watched from a house at the foot of the wharf, but he did not interfere. He wrote the next day: "I could easily have prevented the Execution of this Plan but must have endangered the Lives of many innocent

People by firing upon the Town" [Labaree, *Boston Tea Party*, 145]. The silent onlookers, in this context, insured the safety and success of those who cut open the crates of tea and dropped them into the shallow water.

31. Labaree, *Boston Tea Party*, 145. Adams also appeared to understand the seriousness of the Boston Tea Party. His diary continues: "This Destruction of the Tea is so bold, so daring, so firm, intrepid, & inflexible, and it must have so important Consequences and so lasting, that I cannot but consider it as an Epocha in History."

32. Oliver, *Origin and Progress of American Rebellion*, 65, 74–5.

33. Anne Hulton, *Letters of a Loyalist Lady* (Cambridge: Harvard University Press, 1927), 11.

34. In 1833 a writer named James Hawkes met the ninety-one-year-old Hewes, a participant in both the Boston Massacre and the Boston Tea Party, in upstate New York. After telling his life story to Hawkes, Hewes journeyed to Boston to reconnect with his patriotic past. There, having become something of a celebrity in his old age, he was interviewed again by Benjamin Bussey Thatcher, a gentleman reformer and abolitionist. Both Hawkes and Thatcher published Hewes's memoirs, well adorned with their own digressions. [James Hawkes, *A Retrospect of the Boston Tea Party, with a Memoir of George R. T. Hewes, a Survivor of the Little Band of Patriots Who Drowned the Tea in Boston Harbour in 1773* (New York: S. Bliss, Printer, 1834); Benjamin Bussey Thatcher, *Traits of the Tea Party; Being a Memoir of George R. T. Hewes, One of the Last of Its Survivors; With a History of That Transaction; Reminiscences of the Massacre, and the Siege, and Other Stories of Old Times* (New York: Harper & Brothers, 1835).] In 1981 Hewes was rediscovered by Alfred F. Young, a scholar who has labored for decades to bring ordinary people to the center stage of historical inquiry. (Alfred F. Young, "George Hewes," 561–623.) With the Hawkes and Thatcher books serving as his basic texts, Young encountered two major problems: "separating [Hewes] from his biographers and sifting the memories of a man in his nineties." Young noted that Hawkes "had a tendency to use Hewes as an exemplar of the virtues of Benjamin Franklin and selfless patriotism," while Thatcher imbued Hewes with a nineteenth century reformist's "compassion for the lowly." Hewes himself had a personal agenda in the 1830s, "both monetary and psychic," which may have influenced his selective memory: he had recently applied for a military pension, while he basked in the notoriety that accrued to his tales. Hewes' memory "also displayed common weaknesses. . . . He had trouble with sequences of events and with the time between events." Yet by consulting tax rolls, wills, church and court records, relief rolls, muster rolls, newspaper accounts, and other personal narratives, Young was able to cross-check much of the evidence and piece together an intriguing portrait of a commoner in the thick of the Revolutionary struggle. Recently, Young has incorporated his article into a book, *The Shoemaker and the Tea Party: Memory and the American Revolution* (Boston: Beacon Press, 1999). Below, all of Hewes's quotations come from Young's *William and Mary Quarterly* article.

35. Young, "George Hewes," 588–9.

36. Gary B. Nash, *The Urban Crucible*, 361.
37. Young, "George Hewes," 589–90.
38. Young, "George Hewes," 591–2.
39. *Massachusetts Gazette and Boston Weekly News-Letter*, January 27, 1774. Reprinted in Young, "George Hewes," 593–5. According to Thatcher, Hewes tried to defend Malcolm from these crowd actions. It seems unlikely, however, that Hewes was particularly nonviolent at this stage of his life. Young seems to embrace Thatcher's view that Hewes was too nice a fellow to want his enemies (Malcolm and the British soldiers) to get punished. He states, without qualification, "The man who could remember the whippings of his own boyhood did not want to be the source of pain to others" [596]. Young accepts Thatcher's reporting and interpretation at face value; he says "the story rings true," despite his own warnings against accepting too soft a view of the younger Hewes. Twice he tells us not to confuse the "Good Samaritan" in his nineties, by then a devout Methodist, with the streetwise revolutionary in his thirties [578, 596]. He also notes that Thatcher, who reports the various incidents of mercy, is too eager "to dissociate Hewes from the 'mob' " [567]. He even states succinctly, "One suspects he had been a much more angry and aggressive younger man than he or his biographers convey" [569]. Ironically, Young himself might be one of the genteel biographers he warns us against when he states, point-blank, that Hewes was "reluctant to inflict pain on others" [578] and that he reacted with "horror" to the sentencing of a soldier who had cheated him out of money [586].
40. Young concludes that Hewes "was moved to act by personal experiences that he shared with large numbers of other plebeian Bostonians" and that "he took action with others of his own rank and condition—the laboring classes who formed the bulk of the actors at the Massacre, the Tea Party, and the Malcolm affair." ["George Hewes," 597–98.] Young's conclusion seems valid, firmly rooted in the evidence he presents. Yet perhaps he stretches beyond his reach by framing the article between two events which he forces into too neat a pattern: in 1762 or 1763, before the Revolutionary furor, Hewes bowed in deference as he delivered a pair of shoes to John Hancock, but later, in 1778 or 1779, Hewes actually changed ships when his lieutenant "ordered him one day in the streets to take his hat off to him—which he refused to do for any man" [561–2]. Young then asks: "What had happened in the intervening years?" In response, Young offers a one-dimensional, causal explanation: Hewes had "cast off the constraints of deference." His experiences in the Revolution had "transformed him, giving him a sense of citizenship and personal worth." Young concludes: "These two incidents . . . measure the distance he had come: from the young man tongue-tied in the presence of John Hancock to the man who would not take his hat off to the officer of the ship named *Hancock*" [599].

These incidents, however, are too dissimilar to be measured against each other. In no way can a voluntary encounter in the parlor of a respected gentleman, a pillar of civil society, be compared to a butting of egos out on the streets between two waterfront toughs, an arrogant officer and a hardened sailor. We can easily imagine George Hewes, the wayward student and mischievous apprentice, reacting to an officer in 1763 in a defiant manner; the type of defiance might have differed because of his age, but there is no reason to believe he would have displayed the deference he gave to Hancock. Similarly, we can imagine that if Hewes were invited into the Hancock parlor in 1778, he might still have bowed, just as he did fifteen years earlier. The difference here lies more with the circumstances than with a transformation of Hewes's personality. And even if we assume that his personality had been transformed, how could we separate the impact of the Revolution from the normal changes in personality structure accruing to age? How can we compare a man at two different stages in his life, and then conclude that whatever changes we find are attributable to a single extrinsic factor?

In a similar vein, Young overstates his case when he reads Revolutionary import into Hewes' tendency in his memoirs "to place himself closer to some of the great men of the time than is susceptible to proof" [570]. Such a tendency is very common during the process of "life review," as Young calls it, whether or not one has experienced the leveling influence of revolution. As with Young's "framing," this does not invalidate his conclusions nor even weaken his argument, which is strong enough to stand without these artificial supports. The Revolution was indeed a pivotal period in Hewes's life, probably his defining moment. Without it, this man who could not even vote would scarcely have wielded much influence upon the course of events, and he certainly would not have enjoyed his late-life fame. George Robert Twelves Hewes was a revolutionary "everyman"—unique, to be sure, as are we all, but also a person who can speak for his times just as well as his more famous coevals. Alfred Young has done a dual service by bringing Hewes to the attention of modern students: he has enabled us to become acquainted with a twice-forgotten Revolutionary, and he has demonstrated how a common man's life story can be superbly reconstructed from biased and scattered sources.

41. Philip S. Foner, *Labor and the American Revolution* (Westport, CT: Greenwood Press, 1976), 130.

42. Foner, *Labor and the American Revolution*, 147.

43. Jack P. Greene, ed., *Colonies to Nation, 1763–1789: A Documentary History of the American Revolution* (New York: W. W. Norton, 1975), 96–7.

44. Greene, *Colonies to Nation*, 99–100.

45. Marvin L. M. Kay, "The North Carolina Regulation, 1766–1776: A Class Conflict," in Young, *American Revolution*, 86, 91.

46. Kay, "North Carolina Regulation," 103; A. Roger Ekirch, *"Poor Carolina": Politics and Society in Colonial North Carolina, 1729–1776* (Chapel Hill: University of North Carolina Press, 1981), 165.

47. Edward Countryman, " 'Out of the Bounds of the Law': Northern Land Rioters in the Eighteenth Century," in Young, *American Revolution*, 46.

48. Countryman, "Out of Bounds of the Law," 44–5.

49. Sung Bok Kim, *Landlord and Tenant in Colonial New York: Manorial Society, 1664–1775* (Chapel Hill: University of North Carolina Press, 1978), 387–8.

50. Countryman, *People in Revolution*, 40.

51. Kim, *Landlord and Tenant*, 398.
52. Countryman, *People in Revolution*, 40.
53. Countryman, "Out of Bounds of the Law," 45; Countryman, *People in Revolution*, 49.
54. Countryman, *People in Revolution*, 54.
55. Countryman, *American Revolution*, 80.
56. Paul A. Gilje, *Rioting in America* (Bloomington and Indianapolis: Indiana University Press, 1996), 44–5; Patrick Henderson, "Smallpox and Patriotism: The Norfolk Riots, 1768–1769," *Virginia Magazine of History and Biography*, 73 (1965): 413–24; Keith Mason, "A Loyalist's Journey: James Parker's Response to the Revolutionary Crisis," *Virginia Magazine of History and Biography*, 102 (1994): 150–2.
57. Gilje, *Rioting in America*, 4, 35.
58. Michael A. Bellesiles, *Revolutionary Outlaws: Ethan Allen and the Struggle for Independence on the Early American Frontier* (Charlottesville: University Press of Virginia, 1993), 22.
59. Charles A. Jellison, *Ethan Allen: Frontier Rebel* (Syracuse, NY: Syracuse University Press, 1983), 61.
60. Jellison, *Ethan Allen*, 59.
61. Jellison, *Ethan Allen*, 38; Bellesiles, *Revolutionary Outlaws*, 82.
62. Jellison, *Ethan Allen*, 52.
63. Bellesiles, *Revolutionary Outlaws*, 91; Jellison, *Ethan Allen*, 53–4.
64. Bellesiles, *Revolutionary Outlaws*, 78.
65. Bellesiles, *Revolutionary Outlaws*, 89.
66. Bellesiles, *Revolutionary Outlaws*, 97.
67. Jellison, *Ethan Allen*, 53.
68. Bellesiles, *Revolutionary Outlaws*, 212.
69. According to Bellesiles, the organization of the Green Mountain Boys was always open—"anyone could account himself a member by sticking a fir twig in his hat and opposing the authority of New York"—and once one had participated in what amounted to outlaw actions, there was no turning back. (*Revolutionary Outlaws*, 83.)
70. Maier, *Resistance to Revolution*, 75.
71. Greene, *Colonies to Nation*, 66–7.
72. Nash, *Urban Crucible*, 360.
73. Maier, *Resistance to Revolution*, 118.
74. Maier, *Resistance to Revolution*, 121.
75. Mary Beth Norton, David M. Katzman, Paul D. Escott, Howard P. Chudacoff, Thomas G. Peterson, and William M. Tuttle, Jr., *A People and a Nation: A History of the United States* (Boston: Houghton Mifflin, 1990), 134.
76. Maier, *Resistance to Revolution*, 121.
77. Maier, *Resistance to Revolution*, 126.
78. Maier, *Resistance to Revolution*, 126–7.
79. Maier, *Resistance to Revolution*, 135–6; Nash, *Urban Crucible*, 360.
80. Maier, *Resistance to Revolution*, 138.
81. Maier, *Resistance to Revolution*, 136.

82. Greene, *Colonies to Nation*, 249. Note the inclusion of "her" in the last sentence. The Continental Congress, in suggesting that women might be treated as enemies, seems to have acknowledged that women could be treated as political actors.

83. Wallace Brown, *The Good Americans: The Loyalists in the American Revolution* (New York: William Morrow, 1969), 131.

84. *Boston Evening-Post*, Nov. 6, 1769. Cited in Brown, "Violence and the American Revolution," 104.

85. Oliver, *Origin and Progress of American Rebellion*, 94.

86. Hulton, *Letters of a Loyalist Lady*, 71. Here is Hulton's complete version of the Malcolm incident:

> [H]e was stipt Stark naked, one of the severest cold nights this Winter, his body coverd all over with Tar, then with feathers, his arm dislocated in tearing off his cloaths, he was drag'd in a Cart with thousands attending, some beating him w'th clubs & Knocking him out of the Cart, then in again. They gave him several severe whipings, at different parts of the Town. This Spectacle of horror & sportive cruelty was exhibited for about five hours. . . . They bro't him to the Gallows & put a rope about his neck say'g they woud hang him he said he wishd they woud, but that they coud not for God was above the Devil. The Doctors say that it is imposible this poor creature can live They say his flesh comes off his back in Stakes.

87. For a discussion of the symbols of humiliation, see Ann Withington, *Toward a More Perfect Union: Virtue and the Formation of American Republics* (New York: Oxford University Press, 1991), 226. Barnyard symbolism was taken to the extreme by New York patriots who tarred and feathered both Edward Short and his horse. [Philip Ranlet, *The New York Loyalists* (Knoxville: University of Tennessee Press, 1986), 141.]

88. Smith, "Social Visions," 41.

89. Frank Moore, *The Diary of the American Revolution* (New York: Washington Square Press, 1967), 31.

90. A typical example: In January of 1775, the *Boston Gazette* reported from Portsmouth, New Hampshire: "About 60 pounds of TEA was publicly burnt on the Parade in the Town at 8 o'clock in the Evening, last Wednesday, belonging to a person who bro't it from Salem, who was so far convicted of his own Error in attempting the Sale of that condemn'd Commodity, that he put it in the Fire himself in presence of a large Number of Spectators." [Jan. 23, 1775; cited in Smith, "Social Visions," 46.]

91. Robert M. Calhoon, "The Reintegration of the Loyalists and the Disaffected," in Jack P. Greene, ed., *The American Revolution: Its Character and Limits* (New York: New York University Press, 1987), 52. The goal of the local committees was not so much to punish as to insure compliance. "The great end of discipline," said one committee, was "to take away the sin and save the sinner." [Smith, "Social Visions," 48.] Typically, someone who had violated the terms of the Association was ostracized, both socially and economically, "until he,

by his future behaviour, convinces his countrymen of his sincere repentance for his past folly." [Maier, *Resistance to Revolution*, 282.] The "apology" of Enoch Bartlett from Haverhill, Massachusetts, revealed very pragmatic reasons for his change in attitude: "As My comfort in life does so much depend on the regard and good will of those among whom I live, I hereby give it Under my Hand that I will not buy or Sell Tea or Act in Any public office Contrary to the Minds of the people in General . . . and will yet hope that all My errors in judgment or Conduct meet with their forgiveness and favour which I humbly ask." [Calhoon, "Reintegration of Loyalists," 52.]

92. Morton Borden and Penn Borden, *The American Tory* (Englewood Cliffs, NJ: Prentice-Hall, 1972), 72–3.

93. Kenneth Roberts, ed., *March to Quebec: Journals of the Members of Arnold's Expedition* (New York: Doubleday, Doran, & Co., 1938), 507. Some committees made token attempts to contain outright violence, but these were often more formal than real. A few tried self-consciously to dissociate themselves from extreme or disorderly behavior, seeking "the discouragement of all licentiousness, and suppression of all mobs and riots." A handful even tried to regulate the use of liquor and profane language while engaging in group activities. [Maier, *Resistance to Revolution*, 280.] One New York committee officially disapproved of all "unlawful assemblies . . . unless judged necessary by the major part of the Committee of the said Town or District." [Maier, *Resistance to Revolution*, 281.] Seldom, however, would the majority of a committee fail to give its approval for any actions intended to reprimand Tories.

94. See Gordon Wood, *Creation of the American Republic, 1776–1787* (Chapel Hill: University of North Carolina Press, 1969), 319–21; Brown, "Violence and the American Revolution," 108.

95. Richard Maxwell Brown, *Strains of Violence: Historical Studies of American Violence and Vigilantism* (New York: Oxford University Press, 1975), 56; Brown, "Violence and the American Revolution," 103.

96. Smith, "Social Visions," 47.

97. Drinking was such an accepted feature of political meetings that the patriotic American Political Socity of Worcester felt the need to regulate its extent: "That in all and every of our monthly meetings, our expenses for liquor, &c., shall not exceed six pence per man upon an average, and in our quarterly meetings, it shall not exceed two shillings per man." [Records of the American Political Society, manuscript at the American Antiquarian Society, Worcester, MA, reprinted in Albert A. Lovell, *Worcester in the War of the Revolution* (Worcester, MA: Tyler & Seagrave, 1876), 23.]

David W. Conroy, in his book *In Public Houses: Drink & the Revolution of Authority in Colonial Massachusetts* (Chapel Hill: University of North Carolina Press, 1995), discusses the relationship between taverns, with their "rituals of fellowship, and webs of connection," and a revolutionary frame of mind. Drinking in groups, he maintained, fostered a spirit of rebellion and loosened the grip of the old social order:

Slowly, unevenly, but relentlessly a new political culture had emerged in colonial Massachusetts. The concept and practice of hierarchy had been

strained, altered, and finally eroded by the restiveness, by the ready assertion of ordinary men shedding traditional constraints on their political
behavior. They were mostly ready to do so in companies at taverns. . . .
Informal meetings in public rooms had contributed to the expansion of
men's capacity to criticize, berate, and even move to foil those leaders to
whom deference in posture and speech was customarily due [263, 241].

98. Countryman, *People in Revolution*, 178.
99. David L. Ammerman, *In the Common Cause: American Response to the Coercive
    Acts of 1774* Charlottesville: University Press Virginia, 1874, 106–10; Smith,
    "Social Visions," 39; Countryman, *People in Revolution*, 126–7. Countrymen
    concludes, "In New York, as in the Philadelphia committees studied by Richard Ryerson, the make up after each new committee election moved downwards socially and to the left politically."
100. Countryman, *People in Revolution*, 145.
101. Countryman, *People in Revolution*, 145.
102. Maier, *Resistance to Revolution*, 279.
103. Norton et. al., *People and a Nation*, 135.
104. Hulton, *Letters of a Loyalist Lady*, 72.
105. Jackson Turner Main, *The Social Structure of Revolutionary America* (Princeton,
    NJ: Princeton University Press, 1965), 22.
106. "In the period 1761–1765 the annual number of suits in five rural counties
    equalled 22 percent of the adult male population, most of them for debt. . . .
    For some men 'all problems of government revolved about the necessity of
    saving the land from creditors.' Even though the actual number of foreclosures
    (a difficult figure to recover) may not have been high, debt hung over farmers
    like a dark cloud ready to envelope them in impoverishment and ruin." [Richard L. Bushman, "Massachusetts Farmers and the Revolution," in Richard M.
    Jellison, ed., *Society, Freedom, and Conscience: The American Revolution in
    Virginia, Massachusetts, and New York* (New York: W. W. Norton, 1976),
    119.]
107. American Political Society, "Rules and Regulations," January 3, 1774, manuscript, American Antiquarian Society, Worcester, MA; reprinted in Lovell,
    Worcester in the War of the Revolution, 22, and William Lincoln, *History of
    Worcester, Massachusetts, from its Earliest Settlement to September, 1836*
    (Worcester, MA: Charles Hersey, 1862), 72.
108. For the full act, see L. Kinvin Wroth, ed., *Province in Rebellion: A Documentary History of the Founding of the Commonwealth of Massachusetts, 1774–1775*
    (Cambridge: Harvard University Press, 1975), document 148, 507–19. An
    abridged version appears in Greene, *Colonies to Nation*, 204–7.
109. John L. Brooke, *The Heart of the Commonwealth: Society and Political Culture
    in Worcester County, Massachusetts, 1713–1861* (New York: Cambridge University Press, 1989), 140.
110. Bushman, "Massachusetts Farmers and the Revolution," 82.
111. Worcester County Convention, Resolves, August 30–1, 1774, and Worcester
    County Convention, Proceedings, September 6–7, 1774, Wroth, *Province in
    Rebellion*, documents 316 and 318, 895–6, 904. Nobody knew where this would

lead, but the people were certainly concerned. One patriot wrote to the *Massachusetts Spy:* "Blood will probably be spilt in this Contest. . . . [T]o suffer these novel courts to go on and establish themselves is treasonably to give up our constitution; to spill our dearest blood in its defence is . . . a duty for the neglect of which we demerit ETERNAL DAMNATION." [*Massachusetts Spy,* August 25, 1774.]

112. Governor Gage to the Earl of Dartmouth, August 27, 1774, M. St. Clair Clarke and Peter Force, *American Archives* (Washington, D.C., 1837), 4th series, 1:742. In the face of these preparations, Gage decided not to force a confrontation. Even if the soldiers succeeded in allowing the judges to convene the court, it was obvious that no jurors would consent to participate. [See Stephen E. Patterson, *Political Parties in Revolutionary Massachusetts* (Madison: University of Wisconsin Press, 1973), 100.]

113. Oliver, *Origin & Progress of the American Rebellion,* 153. Oliver's account, which I use here because of its tone, was taken almost verbatim from an anonymous letter addressed to the Provincial Congress of Massachusetts and published in various newspapers, including the Boston *Weekly News-Letter,* February 23, 1775, and New York's *Rivington's Gazette,* March 9, 1775. This account has been reprinted in Clarke and Force, *American Archives,* 4th series, 1:1261; Frank Moore, *The Diary of the American Revolution* (New York: Washington Square Press, 1967), 8. See also William E. Lincoln, ed., *The Journals of Each Provincial Congress of Massachusetts in 1774 and 1775, with an Appendix containing the Proceedings of the County Conventions* (Boston, 1838), 635–9; Lincoln, *History of Worcester,* 88; Lee N. Newcomer, *The Embattled Farmers: A Massachusetts Countryside in the American Revolution* (New York: Columbia University, 1953), 46. Although we have no definitive eyewitness account of the Worcester court closure, the report used here agrees in its essentials with related incidents which were better documented, notably the court closure at Springfield and the forced resignation of Counsellor Timothy Paine. The number of people is clearly an estimate. Oliver uses the 5,000 figure, while Lincoln, in both his texts, calls it 6,000, without citing any sources. In any case the number was massive, particularly considering the decentralized settlement pattern of rural Worcester County.

114. The various resolves of the Worcester County Convention are reprinted in the *Massachusetts Spy,* October 6, 1774; Lincoln, *History of Worcester,* 88–90; Wroth, *Province in Rebellion,* documents 316, 318, and 323.

115. Ellery B. Crane, *History of Worcester County, Massachusetts* (New York: Lewis Historical Publishing Co., 1924), 1:506.

116. *Boston Evening-Post,* August 29, 1774; *Massachusetts Spy,* August 25, 1774; *Providence Gazette,* August 27, 1774.

117. *Boston Gazette,* September 19, 1774; Robert A. Gross, *The Minutemen and Their World* (New York: Hill & Wang, 1976), 53–4.

118. *Boston Gazette,* September 12, 1774; Wroth, *Province in Rebellion,* document 314, 885–6; Clarke and Force, *American Archives,* 4th series, 1:747. The newspaper account of the Springfield court closure included the exact words of the resignations:

We, the Subscribers, do severally promise and solemnly engage to all People now assembled at 5p., in the County of Hampshire, on the 30th Day of August 1774, that we will never take, hold, execute, or exercise any Commission, Office, or Employment whatsoever, under, or in Virtue of or in any Manner derived from any Authority, pretended or attempted to be given by a late Act of Parliament, entitled, "An Act for better regulating the Government of the Province of Massachusetts-Bay, in New England.

119. James R. Trumbull, *History of Northampton, Massachusetts, from its Settlement in 1654* (Northampton: Press of Gazette Printing Co., 1902), 346–8. Since this is the most detailed eyewitness account of the court closures, and since it is not reproduced in a readily available source, here is the portion of Clarke's letter, dated August 30, which follows the first two paragraphs:

The People then reassembled before Mr. Parsons's house. Your uncle Catlin falling into a personal quarrel, at length gained the attention of the people. They considered him as an object worthy of their malice, as he was an officer of the court. He was treated with candor and too mildly to make any complaint. His boasted heroism failed him in the day of trial, and vanished like a puf of smoak. He and O. Warner, who came to his assistance in the quarrel, made such declarations as were requested of them, and then were dismissed, unhurt, and in peace. Your uncle may say what he pleases with regard to their abuse of him, but I was an eye witness to the whole, and you I believe will be satisfied that no abuse was intended when I tell you what easy terms they requested & were satisfied with, namely, only a declaration that he would not hold any office under the new act of parliament.

Col. Worthington was next brought upon the board. The sight of him flashed lightening from their eyes. Their spirits were already raised and the sight of this object gave them additional force. He had not refused his new office of counsellor. For that reason especially he was very obnoxious. But the people kept their tempers. He attempted to harangue them in mittigation of his conduct, but he was soon obliged to desist. The people were not to be dallied with. Nothing would satisfy them but a renunciation in writing of his office as Counsellor and a recantation of his address to Gov. Gage, which last was likewise signed by Jona. Bliss & Caleb Strong, Jun.

Jonathan Bliss next came upon the floor, he was very humble and the people were very credulous. He asked their pardon for all he had said or done which was contrary to their opinions; and as he depended for his support upon the people, he beged to stand well in their favor.

Mr. Moses Bliss was brought into the ring, but the accusation against him was not well supported, and he passed off in silence. The Sheriff was the next who was demanded; he accordingly appeared. He was charged with saying some imprudent things, but none of them were proved, & he departed.

Col. Williams took the next turn. He went round the ring and vindicated himself from some accusations thrown upon him and denied some things that were laid to his charge. He declared in my hearing that "altho he had heretofore differed from the people in opinion with regard to the mode of obtaining redress, he would, hereafter, heartily acquiesce in any measures, that they should take for that purpose, and join with them in the common cause. He considered his interest as embarked in the same bottom with theirs, and hoped to leave it in peace to his Children."

Capt. Merrick of Munson was next treated with for uttering imprudent expressions. I thought they would have tarred & feathered him, and I thought he almost deserved it. He was very stubborn, as long as he dare be, but at length he made some concessions. But not till after they had carted him.

After the last two paragraphs quoted in my text, Clarke concludes: "I kept all the time amongst the people, and observed their temper and dispositions. . . . The people will probably be condemned for preventing the sitting of the court but their conduct yet is comendable. I wait till morning, hope nothing will be transacted rashly tonight, for it is given out by the fearful that there is a number looking."

120. Correspondence Proceedings, Boston, August 29, 1774, Clarke and Force, *American Archives*, 4th series, 1:745. *Boston Evening-Post*, September 5, 1774. All accounts of the incident are in basic agreement as to the nature and tenor of the proceedings, but estimates of the crowd's size vary. The *Evening-Post* said 3,000. The account reprinted in *American Archives* states 1,500. That day, Paine himself said "more than fifteen hundred," while the following day he revised his estimate to "more than Two Thousand." That was a large enough crowd in any case, particularly from a rural area on one day's notice. The only other disagreement among the accounts is that Paine says the people at the common "were drawn up in the form of a hollow square" rather than in two lines. This difference is easy to understand: the ends of the lines might well have collapsed towards the middle as people strained for a view of the principal actor, causing Paine himself to perceive a closed figure.

121. *Boston Evening-Post*, September 5, 1774.

122. *Boston Evening-Post*, September 5, 1774; *Boston Gazette*, September 5, 1774.

123. *Massachusetts Spy*, August 25, 1774.

124. *Boston Evening-Post*, August 29, 1774; Clarke and Force, *American Archives*, 4th series, 1:732. According to a loyalist's letter to the Massachusetts provincial congress in February of 1775, "Afterwards he had his arms taken from his dwelling-house in Hardwick, all of which are not yet returned. He had at another time a very valuable English horse, which was kept as a stallion, poisoned, his family disturbed, and himself obliged to take refuge in Boston, after having been insulted in his own house, and twice on his way, by a mob." [Clarke and Force, *American Archives*, 4th series, 1260–1; Moore, *Diary of the American Revolution*, 7.]

125. Joshua Loring to Thomas Gage, August 31, 1774, Wroth, *Province in Rebellion,* document 160, 537–8.

126. Clarke and Force, *American Archives,* 4th series, 1:731–2.

127. Clarke and Force, *American Archives,* 4th series, 1:1263; Moore, *Diary of American Revolution,* 11; Gregory H. Nobles, *Divisions Throughout the Whole: Politics and Society in Hampshire County, Massachusetts, 1740–1775* (Cambridge: Cambridge University Press, 1983), 169. Nobody seems to have believed Williams when he told the crowd at Springfield that he would engage with them "in the common cause," for Williams was the object of other crowd actions as well. [Nobles, *Divisions Throughout the Whole,* 172.] Nobles suggests that Williams was punished not only for being a Tory but "for his pride and power of former years." [178] As farmers rebelled against the harsh and arbitrary decrees issued by a distant king and parliament, they vented their anger on members of their own communities who had enjoyed power, wealth, and prestige by virtue of British rule.

128. For Oliver's resignation and accompanying statement see *Boston Evening-Post,* September 5, 1774; *Boston Gazette,* September 5 and 12, 1774; *Massachusetts Spy,* September 8, 1774; Clarke and Force, *American Archives,* 4th series, 1: 764–6; Lorenzo Sabine, *Biographical Sketches of Loyalists of the American Revolution* (Port Washington, NY: Kennikat Press, 1966; originally published in 1864), 2:130–3. Additional sources for the Cambridge incident can be found in Clarke and Force, *American Archives,* 4th series, 1:761–70, and Letters of John Andrews, Esq., of Boston to William Barrell of Philadelphia, handwritten copy, Massachusetts Historical Society, 52–9.

129. It was fortunate that Oliver went along with the crowd, for an estimated 20,000 to 60,000 additional patriots from Massachusetts and other New England colonies, upon hearing rumors of a British offensive, were headed towards Cambridge and Boston in what would later be called the "Powder Alarm."

130. Dirk Hoerder, *Crowd Action in Revolutionary Massachusetts, 1765–1780* (New York: Academic Press, 1977), 285. This little ruse, in addition to demonstrating an in-your-face attitude toward British authority, reveals how frequently town meetings were held. With so much business to transact, once a week barely sufficed.

131. Andrews, Letters, August 26, 1774, 48. See also Hoerder, *Crowd Action,* 286.

132. Andrews, Letters, August 25, 1774, 46.

133. Andrews, Letters, August 26, 1774, 48.

134. Hoerder, *Crowd Action,* 285; Clarke and Force, *American Archives,* 4th series, 1:730. The officer who served notice on the Committee was soon forced to resign "all his posts of *honor* and *profit*" because nobody would sell him any food, which led his family to the edge of starvation.

135. Gage to Dartmouth, September 2, 1774, *The Correspondence of General Thomas Gage, 1763–1775,* Clarence E. Carter, ed. (New Haven: Yale University Press, 1931), 1:370.

136. Gage to Dartmouth September 2, 1774, Gage, *Correspondence,* 1:371.

137. Hoerder, *Crowd Action,* 293.

138. The demonstrators wished to be viewed not as drunken rabble but as up-
standing citizens acting for the good of their country. During the proceedings
of September 2 the participants asked Samuel Danforth and Joseph Lee, the
counsellors who had just resigned, whether they had been treated respectfully.
Lee gave the crowd the answer they wanted: they were "the most extraordinary People that he ever saw for Sobriety and Decency etc." [Hoerder,
Crowd Action, 289–90.] All the county conventions which met in the wake of
the court closures decried mob violence as a matter of public record. Yet for
all their disavowals of mobs and riots, the insurgents were still participating
in illegal activities, backed implicitly by force. The rebels of 1774 played on
the edge, and the obsessive concern they expressed for their image suggests
that they knew it. Throughout the turmoil in Massachusetts in the late summer
of 1774, a double standard prevailed: during town meetings or when deposing
judges, the rebels took special care to act according to "the strictest order of
justice"—but bands of night-riders, more radical or more rowdy, still felt free
to terrorize opponents after hours. A lawyer from Great Barrington, for
"threatening to execute the new Acts," was covered with grease ("for want
of tar") and feathers and "placed down an empty well." [Andrews, Letters,
August 23, 1774, 45.] Even so, when we consider that tens of thousands of
people were involved in public actions, that British authority was overthrown,
and that ruling elites were deposed from power, we can only marvel at so
small a casualty count. As John Andrews observed of the many thousands
who flocked toward Cambridge during the first few days of September, "It's
greatly to their credit that in all the different parties that were collected, and
in all their various movements, there was as much good order and decorum
observ'd, as when attending church on Sundays." [Andrews, Letters, September 6, 61.]

Occasionally, even the nighttime vigilantes exhibited concern over proper
behavior. A crowd from Braintree, after intimidating an unpopular sheriff,
voted on the issue of "whether they should huzza, . . . it being Sunday evening." These farmers, however fond of raising toasts, decided not to break
the Lord's peace. [Abigail Adams to John Adams, September 14, 1774, *Adams
Family Correspondence*, L. H. Butterfield, ed. (Cambridge, MA: Belknap Press,
1963), 1:153.]

139. Although a few notable Tories fled to Boston, most conservatives, rather than
abandon their stores or estates, huddled in their homes, muzzled and fearful.
Jonathan Judd, Jr., from Southampton, kept a diary through the turbulent
days of late August and early September, 1774:

> Fryday. 19. Barrington Court Stoped by a Mob. Confusion coming
> on. . . . Monday. 22. a Noise begins about Springfield Court. . . . Sun-
> day. 28. probably the Court will be stoped. great zeal to the west. . . .
> Tuesday. 30. . . . vast numbers gone from the West by Westfield for
> Springfield. Captn. Bancroft had a triming for his Language about
> them—Wednesday. 31. hear this Morning that 3, or 2,000 People were
> collected that they would not let the Court Sit. afterwards they trimed
> some of the Court. all opposition was in vain every Body submitted

to our Sovereign Lord the Mob—Now we are reduced to a State of Anarchy. have neither Law nor any other Rule except the Law of Nature which much vitiated and Darkened to go by . . . Saturday. 3. nothing new unless that the Mob Party are likes to be the Strongest what is like to be the event of these things none knows. the most miserable Situation is probable. people seem to be infatuated to our Destruction. [Jonathan Judd, Jr., Diary, volume 2 (1773–82), Forbes Library, Northampton, MA.]

140. Gage to Dartmouth, September 2, 1774, Gage *Correspondence*, 1:370.

141. See Withington, *Toward a More Perfect Union*, 225–8. This time comparison is not neat and tidy: in 1765 the crowds had forced the stamp collectors to resign, while the August 26 mob had also intimidated the powerful Thomas Hutchinson. But these actions did not materially affect the functioning of government, and there were no alternative institutions trying to usurp British authority. The intimidation of Hutchinson, unlike the actions of 1774, did not enjoy overwhelming support, and nobody even suggested that he must resign. The riots of 1765, involving only a small fraction of the population, challenged an isolated act of Parliament and specific individuals; the revolution of 1774, involving the vast majority of males in rural Massachusetts, used mass intimidation to overthrow a government.

To date, there has been no comprehensive narrative of the Massachusetts farmers' revolution of 1774. The best treatment, although brief, is in Richard D. Brown, *Revolutionary Politics in Massachusetts: The Boston Committee of Correspondence and the Towns, 1772–1774* (Cambridge: Harvard University Press, 1970), 210–36.

2 Fighting Men and Boys

1. Henry S. Commager and Richard B. Morris, *The Spirit of 'Seventy-Six: The Story of the American Revolution as Told by the Participants* (Indianapolis and New York: Bobbs-Merrill, 1958), 61. The king's declaration that Massachusetts was in a state of rebellion is generally seen as an indication of blind intransience to the appeals of the Continental Congress, but it can also be interpreted as a very realistic assessment of the true state of affairs.

2. Franklin B. Dexter, ed., *The Literary Diary of Ezra Stiles* (New York: Charles Scribner's Sons, 1901), 1: 484–5; Lyman H. Butterfield, ed., *Diary and Autobiography of John Adams* (Cambridge: Belknap Press, 1961), 2: 124, 160; Stephen E. Patterson, *Political Parties in Revolutionary Massachusetts* (Madison: University of Wisconsin Press, 1973), 103.

3. Stiles, *Diary*, 1: 480–2.

4. Diary of Reverend Stephen Williams (typescript copy), Richard Salter Storrs Library, Longmeadow, MA, Book 8, 311–3. Williams soon learned that "not one man . . . was killed."

5. John Adams, *Diary and Autobiography*, 2: 160. An account of what actually

happened in Cambridge to trigger the "Powder Alarm" is given in chapter 1 above.

6. See introduction above. Another dress rehearsal for military confrontation occurred at dawn on March 30, when

> the troops at Boston beat to arms, and five regiments marched out. . . . It was supposed they were going to Concord, where the Provincial Congress in now sitting. A quantity of provisions and warlike stores are lodged there. Several expresses were immediately sent away to give notice of their marching. Important consequences were apprehended; but, happily, they only went a few miles out, and then returned. . . . The troops went out of the common road, marched over the people's land, where their grain was sown, and through their gardens, broke down their fences, walls, &c., and did other injuries. ["Letter from Boston," April 1, in *Pennsylvania Journal*, April 12, 1775. Reprinted in Frank Moore, *The Diary of the American Revolution* (New York: Washington Square Press, 1967), 15–6.]

7. Commager and Morris, *The Spirit of 'Seventy-Six*, 82; Hugh F. Rankin, *The American Revolution* (New York: Putnam, 1964), 27. See also a similar account in John C. Dann, ed., *The Revolution Remembered: Eyewitness Accounts of the War of Independence* (Chicago: University of Chicago Press, 1980), 6–9. Most accounts say that more than thirty-eight rebels had assembled at Lexington; the British, not wishing to appear as the bullies, claimed that they faced as many as 200 or 300. Other rebel versions place the number at between fifty and seventy. This is probably the number that answered the call, but according to Wood, many were still in the process of arming themselves at the meeting house when the British arrived.

8. Commager and Morris, *The Spirit of 'Seventy-Six*, 82–3; Rankin, *The American Revolution*, 27.

9. Richard Buel, Jr., *Dear Liberty: Connecticut's Mobilization for the Revolutionary War* (Middletown, CT: Wesleyan University Press, 1980), 36.

10. Joseph Plumb Martin, *Private Yankee Doodle: Being a Narrative of Some of the Adventures, Dangers and Sufferings of a Revolutionary Soldier*, ed. George F. Scheer (Boston: Little, Brown & Co., 1962), 6–7. Originally published in 1830 at Hallowell, Maine, under the title *A Narrative of Some of the Adventures, Dangers and Sufferings of a Revolutionary Soldier, Interspersed with Anecdotes of Incidents That Occurred Within His Own Observation.*

11. Martin, *Private Yankee Doodle*, 8–9.

12. Ebenezer Fox, *The Revolutionary Adventures of Ebenezer Fox of Roxbury, Massachusetts*, reprinted in Hugh F. Rankin, ed., *Narratives of the American Revolution* (Chicago: R. R. Donnelley & Sons, 1976), 10–11. Originally published in 1838.

13. Fox, *Revolutionary Adventures*, 13–14.

14. Jeremiah Greenman, *Diary of a Common Soldier in the American Revolution, 1775–1783*, ed. Robert C. Bray and Paul E. Bushnell (De Kalb, IL: Northern Illinois University Press, 1978), xiv, 8.

15. Herbert T. Wade and Robert A. Lively, *This Glorious Cause: The Adventures of Two Company Officers in Washington's Army* (Princeton: Princeton University Press, 1958), 9. Minutemen were not new to the American Revolution. In 1645 thirty men from each militia unit were expected to be ready for duty "at halfe an howers warning." By 1756 some of the men in the French and Indian War described themselves as "minnit men," a term that would spread throughout New England as militiamen prepared to be called to action upon short notice. [*Glorious Cause*, 5–6.]

16. Joseph Hodgkins to Sarah Hodgkins, June 18, 1775 Wade and Lively, *Glorious Cause*, 168–9.

17. Commager and Morris, *The Spirit of 'Seventy-Six*, 154. The mass movement of men to and from the Boston area precipitated the spread of smallpox as well as diseases related to sanitation. During the winter of 1775–1776 smallpox epidemics broke out in many New England towns, causing high mortalities and great consternation. In Fitchburg, the epidemic was blamed on a Dr. McCarthy, the close friend of a prominent loyalist, who allegedly introduced the disease in order to drum up business. [Lee N. Newcomer, *The Embattled Farmers: A Massachusetts Countryside in the American Revolution* (New York: Columbia University, 1953), 69.]

18. Joseph Hodgkins to Sarah Hodgkins, May 7, September 8, and October 6, 1775, Wade and Lively, *Glorious Cause*. 167, 172, 178.

19. Charles Royster, *A Revolutionary People at War: The Continental Army and American Character, 1775–1783* (Chapel Hill: University of North Carolina Press, 1979), 60–1.

20. Commager and Morris, *The Spirit of 'Seventy-Six*, 154.

21. Allen Bowman, *The Morale of the American Revolutionary Army* (Port Washington, NY: Kennikat Press, 1943), 47.

22. Washington to Joseph Reed, November 28, 1775, John C. Fitzpatrick, ed., *The Writings of George Washington from the Original Manuscript Sources, 1745–1799* (Washington: United States Government Printing Office, 1931–44), 4:124–5; Commager and Morris, *The Spirit of 'Seventy-Six*, 162.

23. Buel, *Dear Liberty*, 55. Symeon Lyman described in vivid detail the intense pressure brought to bear by the officers:

> We was ordered to parade before the general's door, the whole regiment, and General Lee and General Solivan came out, and those that would not stay 4 days longer after their enlistments was out they was ordered to turn out, and there was about 3 quarters turned out, and we was ordered to form a hollow square, and General Lee came in and the first words was "Men, I do not know what to call you; are the worst of all creatures," and flung and curst and swore at us, and said if we would not stay he would order us to go on Bunker Hill and if we would not go he would order the riflemen to fire at us, and they talked they would take our guns and take our names down, and our lieutenants begged of us to stay and we went and joined the rest, and they got about 10 of their guns, and the men was marched off, and the general said that they should go to the work house and be confined,

and they agreed to stay the four days, and they gave them a dram, and the colonel told us that he would give us another the next morning, and we was dismissed. There was one that was a mind to have one of his mates turn out with him, and the general see him and he catched his gun out of his hands and struck him on the head and ordered him to be put under guard. [Commager and Morris, *The Spirit of 'Seventy-Six*, 158–9.]

24. Joseph Hodgkins to Sarah Hodgkins, November 25, 1775, in Wade and Lively, *Glorious Cause*, 185.
25. Royster, *Revolutionary People at War*, 99.
26. Royster, *Revolutionary People at War*, 23–4.
27. Greenman, *Diary of Common Soldier*, 13. These words and the many that followed, according to Jeremiah, "were penn'd intirely for my Own Amusement at the time of writing and as a Memorial of Facts which, I suppos'e might elt me Some Pleasure Recollection . . . I don't look upon them of Suffeceint Consqunce to merit the Public View." (Greenman, *Diary*, 12.) Although Greenman did not write with an eye to publication, I take issue with his assessment that his journal was of little consequence. Since so few words were "penn'd" by the common soldiers of the Revolution during the war itself, and since fewer still have been preserved, Greenman's journal, which he continued for the better part of a decade, stands as an important record of the "real-life" experiences of fighting men who should not be forgotten. All entries concerning the Quebec expedition are taken from pages 13–35. Several other firsthand accounts, all by officers, appear in Kenneth Roberts, ed., *March to Quebec: Journals of the Members of Arnold's Expedition* (New York: Doubleday, Doran & Co., 1938).
28. Royster, *Revolutionary People at War*, 100. John Trumbull gave an eyewitness report from Crown Point: "At that place I found not an army, but a mob, the shattered remains of twelve or fifteen very fine battalions, ruined by sickness, fatigue and desertions. . . . Among the few we have remaining, there is neither order, subordination, nor harmony, the officers, as well as the men, of one colony insulting and quarreling with those of another." [Commager and Morris, *The Spirit of 'Seventy-Six*, 221.]
29. Roberts, *March to Quebec*, 34, 293–4.
30. Michael A. McDonnell, "Popular Mobilization and Political Culture in Revolutionary Virginia: The Failure of the Minutemen and the Revolution from Below," *Journal of American History* 85 (1998): 952.
31. McDonnell, "Popular Mobilization in Virginia," 956. The social impact of this popular mobilization on Virginia society was profound. In the words of historian Rhys Isaac, "social distance was inevitably reduced, special advantages derived from cosmopolitan education were diminished, and distinctions of rank were rendered less sharp." [Rhys Isaac, "Dramatizing the Ideology of Revolution: Popular Mobilization in Virginia, 1774 to 1776," *William and Mary Quarterly*, 3rd series, 33 (1976): 383.]
32. McDonnell, "Popular Mobilization in Virginia," 965–8.
33. McDonnell, "Popular Mobilization in Virginia," 964.

34. McDonnell, "Popular Mobilization in Virginia," 975.
35. Martin, *Private Yankee Doodle*, 16.
36. Martin, *Private Yankee Doodle*, 16–17. Martin's full account is set forth in the introduction, above.
37. Martin, *Private Yankee Doodle*, 16.
38. Fox, *Revolutionary Adventures*, 39–40.
39. According to the 1790 census, 51 percent of the white population of the United States was 16 or older while 49 percent was 15 or younger. In 1774 over 57 percent of the total population of the thirteen colonies was 20 or younger. In Connecticut in 1774 less than 1 percent of the males between 10 and 20 were married while over 76 percent of the males between 20 and 70 were married. [Thomas L. Purvis, *Almanacs of American Life: Revolutionary America, 1763 to 1800* (New York: Facts On File, 1995), 123, 124, 126, 144.] In Boston in 1765 there were 4,109 boys under 16 compared with only 2,941 adult males. Although the adult male population had been affected by the preceding war, girls outnumbered women 4,010 to 3,612. Children were more numerous than adults regardless of wartime casualties. [Alfred F. Young, "The Women of Boston: 'Persons of Consequence' in the Making of the American Revolution, 1765–76," in Harriet B. Applewhite and Darline G. Levy, eds., *Women and Politics in the Age of the Democratic Revolution* (Ann Arbor: University of Michigan Press, 1990), 183.] In 1790 Dr. Benjamin Rush figured that for every 100 people born in Philadelphia only 46 lived to the age of 16, while only 16—roughly one in six—lived past the age of 36. [Linda Grant De Pauw and Conover Hunt, *Remember the Ladies: Women in American, 1750–1815* (New York: Viking, 1976), 35.]
40. James K. Martin and Mark E. Lender, *A Respectable Army: The Military Origins of the Republic, 1763–1789* (Arlington Heights, IL: Harlan Davidson, 1982), 90.
41. Royster, *Revolutionary People at War*, 296. Theodore J. Crackel has estimated that about 40 percent of men of "military age" served in the militias or Continental Army at some time during the war, but almost three-fourths of the males born in 1760—those who were fourteen or fifteen years old at the outset of the fighting—served in the military. ["Revolutionary War Pension Records and Patterns of American Mobility, 1780–1830," *Prologue: Journal of the National Archives* 16 (1984): 161.]
42. Don Higginbotham, *The War of American Independence: Military Attitudes, Policies, and Practice, 1763–1789* (Bloomington: Indiana University Press, 1971), 391. Higginbotham notes that of the 144 nonofficers on John Paul Jones's *Bon Homme Richard*, 41 were listed as "boys" [338]. Since anyone who shaved and whose voice had deepened was probably deemed a man rather than a boy, this crew must have been youthful indeed.
43. L. P. Jackson, "Virginia Negro Soldiers and Seamen in the American Revolution," *Journal of Negro History* 27 (1942): 256. How far down did they go? A historical marker near Golden Pond, KY, states that Nathan Futrell, at age seven, was "reputed to be the youngest drummer boy in War of the Revolution."
44. Washington to John Hancock, September 24, 1776, Fitzpatrick, *Writings of Washington*, 6: 107–8.

45. Higginbotham, *War of American Independence*, 393. Americans continued to use British pounds as well as the new United States dollars throughout much of the war.

46. Fox, *Revolutionary Adventures*, 31–2.

47. Martin, *Private Yankee Doodle*, 60–61.

48. Ronald Hoffman, *A Spirit of Dissension: Economics, Politics, and the Revolution in Maryland* (Baltimore: John Hopkins University Press, 1973), 232.

49. In August of 1776, soldiers of the celebrated "Flying Camp" complained "that they could not vote unless they were worth 40 sterling at least," whereas "the whole company was not worth 40 sterling." [Hoffman, *Spirit of Dissension*, 172.]

50. John Shy, *A People Numerous and Armed: Reflections on the Military Struggle for American Independence* (Ann Arbor: University of Michigan Press, 1990), 173. Based on his study of tax rolls in nine New Jersey towns after the war, Theodore Crackel concludes veterans were "quite representative of the whole adult male population" in terms of taxable wealth. ["War Pension Records and Mobility," 162.] But his results are misleading. Crackel's figures do not distinguish between the long-term professionals of the Continental Army and men who served single terms with militia units. Crackel himself observes that the "relative distribution of veterans when measured in terms of land holdings" broke down at the top: among the richest 3 or 4 percent, only 23 percent were veterans, as opposed to about 40 percent of all other categories. These figures should be interpreted with caution, since the sample was small and local. Other local studies suggest a clear lower-class orientation. In his look at Peterborough, New Hampshire, Shy found that although most adult males "at one time or another carried a gun in the war," the few who served long terms

> were an unusually poor, obscure group of men, even by the rustic standards of Peterborough. Many—like John Alexander, Robert Cunningham, William Ducannon, Joseph Henderson, Richard Richardson, John Wallace, and Thomas Williamson—were recruited from outside the town, from among men who never really lived in Peterborough. Whether they lived *anywhere*—in the strict legal sense—is a question. Two men—Zaccheus Brooks and John Miller—are simply noted as "transients." At least two—James Hackley and Randall McAllister—were deserters from the British army. At least two others—Samuel Weir and Titus Wilson—were black men, Wilson dying as a prisoner of war. A Few, like Michael Silk, simply appear, join the army, then vanish without a documentary trace. Many more reveal themselves as near the bottom of the socioeconomic ladder: Hackley, Benjamin Allds, Isaac Mitchell, Ebenezer Perkins, Amos Spofford, Jonathan Wheelock, and Charles White were legal paupers after the Revolution, Joseph Henderson was a landless day-laborer, Samuel Spear was jailed for debt, and John Miller was mentally deranged. [Shy, *People Numerous and Armed*, 172.]

See also John P. Resch, "The Continentals of Peterborough, New Hampshire: Pension Records as a Source for Local History," *Prologue: Journal of the National Archives*, 16 (1984), 169–83.

Studies from Maryland, Virginia, Massachusetts, and Pennsylvania reveal similar results. [Shy, *People Numerous and Armed*, 322–3, n 6.] In New Jersey Mark Lender found that "at least 90 percent of the Continentals with available socioeconomic data represented the poorest two-thirds in society," 46 percent held "no taxable property whatsoever," while 57 percent were landless—"not an attractive condition in that state's agricultural economy." [Martin and Lender, *Respectable Army*, 90–1.] William Pencak, in his study of Boston, found that 57 percent of the soldiers had real estate assessed at less than ten pounds per year of rental value, compared with only 12 percent of the Sons of Liberty, the vocal political leaders in support of the war. The poor were more likely to fight, while those who were not so poor did the talking. [William Pencak, *War, Politics, and Revolution in Provincial Massachusetts* (Boston: Northeastern University Press, 1981), 273.]

51. Royster, *Revolutionary People at War*, 135.
52. Royster, *Revolutionary People at War*, 39.
53. *Massachusetts Spy*, July 24, 1776. Reprinted in William Lincoln, *History of Worcester, Massachusetts, from its Earliest Settlement to September, 1836* (Worcester: Charles Hersey, 1862), 103.
54. W. J. Rorabaugh, " 'I Thought I Should Liberate Myself from the Thraldom of Others': Apprentices, Masters, and the Revolution," in Alfred F. Young, ed., *Beyond the American Revolution: Explorations in the History of American Radicalism* (De Kalb, IL: Northern Illinois University Press, 1993), 191, 211.
55. Joseph Hodgkins to Sarah Hodgkins, August 28, 1776, in Wade and Lively, *Glorious Cause*, 215.
56. Joy D. Buel and Richard Buel, Jr., *The Way of Duty: A Woman and Her Family in Revolutionary America* (New York: W. W. Norton, 1984), 113.
57. Joseph Hodgkins to Sarah Hodgkins, June 10, 1776, Wade and Lively, *Glorious Cause*, 205.
58. Martin, *Private Yankee Doodle*, 21; Commager and Morris, *The Spirit of 'Seventy-Six*, 425–6.
59. Joseph Hodgkins to Sarah Hodgkins, April 24, 1776, Wade and Lively, *Glorious Cause*, 199.
60. Joseph Hodgkins to Sarah Hodgkins, June 20 and July 17, 1776, Wade and Lively, *Glorious Cause*, 207, 209.
61. Martin, *Private Yankee Doodle*, 22–3; Commager and Morris, *The Spirit of 'Seventy-Six*, 441.
62. Martin, *Private Yankee Doodle*, 24, 54, 24–5; Commager and Morris, *The Spirit of 'Seventy-Six*, 442.
63. Martin, *Private Yankee Doodle*, 24.
64. Martin, *Private Yankee Doodle*, 26. Michael Graham, an eighteen-year-old private, recalled that rout in greater detail:

> It is impossible for me to describe the confusion and horror or the scene that ensued: the artillery flying with the chains over the horses'

backs, our men running in almost every direction, and run which way they would, they were almost sure to meet the British or Hessians. And the enemy huzzahing when they took prisoners made it truly a day of distress to the Americans. I escaped by getting behind the British that had been engaged with Lord Stirling and entered a swamp or marsh through which a great many of our men were retreating. Some of them were mired and crying to their fellows for God's sake to help them out; but every man was intent on his own safety and no assistance was rendered. At the side of the marsh there was a pond which I took to be a millpond. Numbers, as they came to this pond, jumped in, and some were drowned. . . . Out of the eight men that were taken from the company to which I belonged the day before the battle on guard, I only escaped. The others were either killed or taken prisoners. [Dann, *Revolution Remembered*, 50.]

65. Martin, *Private Yankee Doodle*, 36–41. Martin himself commented sarcastically: "Pretty fellow! thought I, a very compassionate gentleman! When a man has got his bane in his country's cause, let him die like an old horse or dog, because he can do no more!"

66. Royster, *Revolutionary People at War*, 226–7.

67. Royster, *Revolutionary People at War*, 225.

68. Dann, *Revolution Remembered*, 195.

69. Commager and Morris, *The Spirit of 'Seventy-Six*, 1131.

70. Joseph Hodgkins to Sarah Hodgkins, August 28, 1776, Wade and Lively, *Glorious Cause*, 215.

71. Joseph Hodgkins to Sarah Hodgkins, September 5, 1776, Wade and Lively, *Glorious Cause*, 218.

72. Martin, *Private Yankee Doodle*, 33, 40.

73. Howard H. Peckham, *Toll of Independence: Engagements & Battle Casualties of the American Revolution* (Chicago: University of Chicago Press, 1974), 22–26. According to Peckham, over 4,000 were taken prisoner during this time.

74. Richard Dorson, ed., *America Rebels: Narratives of the Patriots* (Westport, CT: Greenwood Press, 1953), 130.

75. Royster, *Revolutionary People at War*, 33.

76. Peckham, *Toll of Independence*, 130.

77. Derived from Shy, *People Numerous and Armed*, 248–9; Martin and Lender, *Respectable Army*, 198–9; Peckham, *Toll of Independence*, 130.

78. Martin, *Private Yankee Doodle*, 47, 55, 57.

79. Joseph Hodgkins to Sarah Hodgkins, December 31, 1776, Wade and Lively, *Glorious Cause*, 228–9.

80. Tom Paine, *The American Crisis*, reprinted in Jack P. Greene, ed., *Colonies to Nation, 1763–1789: A Documentary History of the American Revolution* (New York: W. W. Norton, 1975), 406.

81. Joseph Hodgkins to Sarah Hodgkins, Dec. 31, 1776, Wade and Lively, *Glorious Cause*, 229.

82. Royster, *Revolutionary People at War*, 225.

83. Greenman, *Diary*, 81.

84. Martin, *Private Yankee Doodle*, 88–90.

85. Greenman, *Diary*, 82.

86. Martin, *Private Yankee Doodle*, 90–2.

87. Wade and Lively, *Glorious Cause*, 114–15, 229–33. Hodgkins did not describe the fighting in his letters to Sarah, noting only that "I have nothing new to write as the Compleet Victory gained over our enemy in this Part of the world is By this time an old story it will Be Needles for me to say much about it Espechaly as you will have the Perticklers By them that whare hear on the spot But I think there is a Remarkable hand of Providence in it & we shall Due well to ackowledge it." Since Hodgkins reported being ill with "the Camp Disorder," it is possible he did not participate in the active combat.

88. Rankin, *American Revolution*, 141–2.

89. Joseph Hodgkins to Sarah Hodgkins, October 27, 1777, Wade and Lively, *Glorious Cause*, 232.

90. Greenman, *Diary*, 122; Martin, *Private Yankee Doodle*, 127, 131.

91. Peckham, *Toll of Independence*, 52.

92. James Collins, *Autobiography of a Revolutionary Soldier*, John M. Roberts, ed. (Clinton, LA: Feliciana Democrat, 1859; reprinted New York: Arno Press, 1979), 22.

93. Collins, *Autobiography*, 25.

94. Collins, *Autobiography*, 22, 28–38.

95. Collins, *Autobiography*, 43–4.

96. Collins, *Autobiography*, 51–4.

97. Collins, *Autobiography*, 55.

98. William Pierce to St. George Tucker, July 20, 1781, cited in Sylvia R. Frey, *Water from the Rock: Black Resistance in a Revolutionary Age* (Princeton, NJ: Princeton University Press, 1991), 133.

99. A. Roger Ekirch, "Whig Authority and Public Order in Backcountry North Carolina," in Ronald Hoffman, Thad W. Tate, and Peter J. Albert, *An Uncivil War: The Southern Backcountry During the American Revolution* (Charlottesville: University Press of Virginia, 1985), 107–8.

100. Dann, *Revolution Remembered*, 188–9. This punishment, called "spiceting," was a brutal variation of the common practice of picketing, in which the prisoner, like a horse, was merely tied to a stake in the ground.

101. Dann, *Revolution Remembered*, 202–3.

102. Martin, *Private Yankee Doodle*, 130.

103. Collins, *Autobiography*, 58.

104. Collins, *Autobiography*, 55–6.

105. Collins, *Autobiography*, 66–7.

106. Dann, *Revolution Remembered*, 195.

107. Dennis P. Ryan, ed., *A Salute to Courage: The American Revolution as Seen Through Wartime Writings of Officers of the Continental Army and Navy* (New York: Columbia University Press, 1979), 105.

108. Commager and Morris, *The Spirit of 'Seventy-Six*, 821–2.

109. Charles K. Bolton, *The Private Soldier Under Washington* (Williamstown, MA: Corner House, 1976), 178.

110. Dann, *Revolution Remembered*, 373.

111. Martin, *Private Yankee Doodle*, 98–9.

112. Martin, *Private Yankee Doodle*, 75.

113. Martin, *Private Yankee Doodle*, 100. Half a gill is equal to one-quarter of a cup.

114. Martin, *Private Yankee Doodle*, 104.

115. Martin, *Private Yankee Doodle*, 172.

116. John Smith, Diary, 1776–1778, volume 2, manuscript, American Antiquarian Society, Worcester, MA.

117. Fox, *Revolutionary Adventures*, 34–6.

118. Martin, *Private Yankee Doodle*, 285.

119. Commager and Morris, *The Spirit of 'Seventy-Six*, 568.

120. Collins, *Autobiography*, 59–64.

121. Dann, *Revolution Remembered*, 201–4.

122. Ryan, *Salute to Courage*, 90; Greenman, *Diary*, 63.

123. Martin, *Private Yankee Doodle*, 101. The most striking and emotive description of the suffering at Valley Forge appears in the December 14, 1777, entry of the diary of a surgeon, Albigence Waldo, reprinted in Ryan, *Salute to Courage*, 113–4, and Hugh F. Rankin, ed., *Narratives of the American Revolution* (Chicago: R. R. Donnelley & Sons, 1776), 181–3.

124. Commager and Morris, *The Spirit of 'Seventy-Six*, 153.

125. Martin, *Private Yankee Doodle*, 167.

126. Royster, *Revolutionary People at War*, 73.

127. Newcomer, *Embattled Farmers*, 210.

128. Rhys Isaac, *The Transformation of Virginia, 1740–1790* (New York: W. W. Norton, 1982), 276.

129. Royster, *Revolutionary People at War*, 314–5.

130. Royster, *Revolutionary People at War*, 191, 296.

131. See above, "Cannons Roaring Muskets Cracking."

132. Martin, *Private Yankee Doodle*, 290.

133. Bowman, *Morale of Revolutionary Army*, 14, 30.

134. Don Higginbotham, "The Strength and Weaknesses of the Militia," Richard D. Brown, ed., *Major Problems in the Era of the American Revolution, 1760–1791* (Lexington, MA: D. C. Heath, 1992), 239.

135. Bowman, *Morale of Revolutionary Army*, 70.

136. Washington to Hancock, September 24, 1776, Fitzpatrick, ed., *Writings of George Washington* 6: 106–15; Commager and Morris, *The Spirit of 'Seventy-Six*, 480–4. If Washington felt the militias were bad, the "volunteer" units were even worse: "Those who engage in Arms under that denomination . . . are uneasy, impatient of Command, ungovernable; and claiming to themselves a sort of superior merit, generally assume, not only the Priviledge of thinking, but to do as they please." [Washington to Patrick Henry, April 13, 1777, *Writings of Washington*, Fitzpatrick, ed. 7: 407–9, cited in McDonnell, "Popular Mobilization in Virginia," 974.]

137. Bowman, *Morale of Revolutionary Army*, 70.

138. Hoffman, *Spirit of Dissension*, 204.

139. Broadus Mitchell, *The Price of Independence: A Realistic View of the American Revolution* (New York: Oxford University Press, 1974), 117.

140. Bowman, *Morale of Revolutionary Army*, 30; Mitchell, *Price of Independence*, 117–8.

141. Bowman, *Morale of Revolutionary Army*, 30.

142. Royster, *Revolutionary People at War*, 84; Jeffrey J. Crow, "Liberty Men and Loyalists: Disorder and Disaffection in the North Carolina Backcountry," in Hoffman et al., *Uncivil War*, 149.

143. Shy, *People Numerous and Armed*, 238. For another positive view of the contributions by the militias, see Mark V. Kwasny, *Washington's Partisan War, 1775–1783* (Kent, OH: Kent State University Press, 1996).

144. Steven Rosswurm, *Arms, Country, and Class: The Philadelphia Militia and "Lower Sort" during the American Revolution, 1775–1783* (New Brunswick, NJ: Rutgers University Press, 1987), 57, 55, 73. In Philadelphia, as elsewhere, the rich found ways of avoiding military service. Rosswurm reports that the average taxable wealth of those who twice hired substitutes for the Philadelphia militia was nine times as much as those who served two tours of duty. [208.]

145. Rosswurm, *Arms, Country, and Class*, 101–2.

146. Rosswurm, *Arms, Country, and Class*, 104.

147. The Pennsylvania Constitution of 1776, passed on September 28, is reprinted in Greene, *Colonies to Nation*, 339–45.

148. Rosswurm, *Arms, Country, and Class*, 133.

149. Rosswurm, *Arms, Country, and Class*, 178.

150. Rosswurm, *Arms, Country, and Class*, 191.

151. Rosswurm, *Arms, Country, and Class*, 213.

152. Rosswurm, *Arms, Country, and Class*, 206.

153. Martin, *Private Yankee Doodle*, xxiv.

154. Rosswurm, *Arms, Country, and Class*, 247.

155. Greenman, *Diary*, 133.

156. Greenman, *Diary*, 135.

157. Greenman, *Diary*, 138.

158. Martin, *Private Yankee Doodle*, 150–3.

159. Martin, *Private Yankee Doodle*, 183, 186.

160. Martin, *Private Yankee Doodle*, 182.

161. Martin, *Private Yankee Doodle*, 187.

162. James K. Martin, "A 'Most Undisciplined, Profligate Crew': Protest and Defiance in the Continental Ranks, 1776–1783," in Ronald Hoffman and Peter J. Albert, eds., *Arms and Independence: The Military Character of the American Revolution* (Charlottesville: University Press of Virginia, 1984), 136.

163. Martin, "Most Undisciplined Crew," 136.

164. Royster, *Revolutionary People at War*, 344.

165. Bolton, *Private Soldier Under Washington*, 247–8.

166. Joseph Hodgkins to Sarah Hodgkins, March 20, 1776, Wade and Lively, *Glorious Cause*, 195.

167. Joseph Hodgkins to Sarah Hodgkins, February 22, 1778, Wade and Lively, *Glorious Cause*, 236.

168. Joseph Hodgkins to Sarah Hodgkins, April 17, 1778, Wade and Lively, *Glorious Cause*, 238.

169. Joseph Hodgkins to Sarah Hodgkins, October 13, 1778, Wade and Lively, *Glorious Cause*, 244.

170. Martin, *Private Yankee Doodle*, 283, 287–8.

171. Greenman, *Diary*, 242–3.

172. Greenman, *Diary*, xiv, xxxi, xxxii.

173. Fox, *Revolutionary Adventures*, 41.

174. Fox, *Revolutionary Adventures*, 56.

175. Fox, *Revolutionary Adventures*, 68, 72.

176. Fox, *Revolutionary Adventures*, 102.

177. Charles Royster, noting that "rather than serve the king, thousands of American soldiers and sailors chose almost certain death" as prisoners, argues that the reluctance of Americans in confinement to defect bears witness to their devotion to their cause. [Royster, *Revolutionary People at War*, 377–8.] Jesse Lemisch, referring to captured sailors, draws a similar conclusion: "To a striking extent prisoners remained patriots, and very self-consciously so. . . . Under these intolerable conditions, seamen from all over the colonies discovered that they shared a common conception of the cause for which they fought." ["Jack Tar in the Streets: Merchant Seamen in the Politics of Revolutionary America," *William and Mary Quarterly*, 3rd series, 25 (1968): 371–407.] These arguments are neither necessary nor convincing. Prisoners such as Ebenezer Fox could still be patriotic even as they agreed to serve on British ships, looking for their chance to escape so they might continue to serve their country. Jeremiah Greenman noted that many of those who defected in the Quebec prison ran away from the British shortly thereafter. The fact that most prisoners remained in prison, meanwhile, does not prove anything. The British did not extend their offer to every sick soldier or sailor who rotted away under their care, but only to a handful of healthy, stout men whom they thought might do them some good. And these men might have based their decisions on a host of variables that had little to do with love of country: the conditions they endured, their health at the time, the health of their fellow inmates, their prospects while serving on British ships, peer pressure, etc. To treat the actions of men in such desparate circumstances in an ideological context does not do justice to the prisoners themselves, who should neither be blamed nor praised for doing what came naturally: trying to survive, whatever that entailed. Often, they had no choices to consider, and even when they did, we ought to refrain, given our very limited information and distant perspective, from passing judgment or drawing hasty conclusions about their reasoning.

3 Women

1. Mary Beth Norton, *Liberty's Daughters: The Revolutionary Experience of American Women, 1750–1800* (Boston: Little, Brown, 1980), 163, 168. The expression "ideological showcases" is Norton's.

2. Norton reports: "The *Boston Evening Post*, which carried only one previous account of female domestic industry, printed twenty-eight articles on the subject between May and December 1769, and devoted most of its front page on May 29 to an enumeration of these examples of female patriotism." [Norton, *Liberty's Daughters*. 166.]

3. Linda K. Kerber, *Women of the Republic: Intellect and Ideology in Revolutionary America* (Chapel Hill: University of North Carolina Press, 1980), 42.

4. Norton, *Liberty's Daughters*, 166. Three weeks later, the *Post* expressed the hope that "the ladies, while they vie with each other in skill and industry in their profitable employment, may vie with the men in contributing to the preservation and prosperity of their country and equally share in the honor of it." [Norton, *Liberty's Daughters*. 167.]

5. Douglas Adair and John A. Schutz, eds., *Peter Oliver's Origins and Progress of the American Revolution: A Tory View* (Stanford, CA: Stanford University Press, 1967), 63–4.

6. Christopher Gadsden, "To the Planter, Mechanics, and Freeholders of the Province of South Carolina, No Ways Concerned in the Importation of British Manufactures," Richard Walsh, ed., *The Writings of Christopher Gadsden* (Columbia: University of South Carolina Press, 1966), 83.

7. Norton, *Liberty's Daughters*, 159.

8. Norton, *Liberty's Daughters*, 159.

9. Kerber, *Women of the Republic*, 58–9.

10. Kerber, *Women of the Republic*, 59.

11. Kerber, *Women of the Republic*, 60.

12. "Patriotic Poesy" [1768], *William and Mary Quarterly*, 3rd series, 34 (1977): 307–8. Reprinted in Kerber, *Women of the Republic*, 38, and Norton, *Liberty's Daughters*, 160.

13. Norton, *Liberty's Daughters*, 160–1; Alfred F. Young, "The Women of Boston: 'Persons of Consequence' in the Making of the American Revolution, 1765–76," in Harriet B. Applewhite and Darline G. Levy, eds., *Women and Politics in the Age of the Democratic Revolution* (Ann Arbor: University of Michigan Press, 1990), 196.

14. Kerber, *Women of the Republic*, 41; Linda Grant De Pauw, *Founding Mothers: Women in America in the Revolutionary Era* (Boston: Houghton Mifflin, 1975), 159.

15. Kerber, *Women of the Republic*, 67.

16. Henry S. Commager and Richard B. Morris, *The Spirit of 'Seventy-Six: The Story of the American Revolution as Told by the Participants* (Indianapolis and New York: Bobbs-Merrill, 1958), 95.

17. Young, "Women of Boston," 204.

18. Norton, *Liberty's Daughters*, 169; DePauw, *Founding Mothers*, 155.

19. Norton, *Liberty's Daughters*, 169.

20. Philip S. Foner, *Labor and the American Revolution* (Westport, CT: Greenwood Press, 1976), 78.

21. Laurel Thatcher Ulrich, " 'Daughters of Liberty': Religious Women in Revolutionary New England," in Ronald Hoffman and Peter J. Albert, eds.,

Women in the Age of the American Revolution (Charlottesville: University Press of Virginia, 1989), 226–7. Similar examples from New Hampshire and Connecticut are cited in Norton, *Liberty's Daughters*, 215.

22. Constance B. Schulz, "Daughters of Liberty: The History of Women in the Revolutionary War Pension Records," *Prologue: Journal of the National Archives*, 16 (1984): 146.

23. Helen Evertson Smith, *Colonial Days and Ways, As Gathered from Family Papers* (New York: Frederick Ungar, 1966; originally published in 1900), 226–7; this quotation is reprinted in Milton Meltzer, ed., *The American Revolutionaries: A History in Their Own Words* (New York: Thomas Y. Crowell, 1987), 70.

24. Norton, *Liberty's Daughters*, xv.

25. Norton, *Liberty's Daughters*, 219.

26. Norton, *Liberty's Daughters*, 297.

27. *Letters of Eliza Wilkinson During the Invasion and Possession of Charleston, S. C. by the British in the Revolutionary War*, Caroline Gilman, ed. (New York: Samuel Colman, 1839; reprint edition by Arno Press, 1969), 17, 61, 66. Selections cited in Norton, *Liberty's Daughters*, 188–9, and Kerber, *Women of the Republic*, 226.

28. For the complete exchange between John and Abigail Adams on this matter, see Richard D. Brown, ed., *Major Problems in the Era of the American Revolution* (Lexington and Toronto: D. C. Heath, 1992), 302–5.

29. Reprinted in Brown, *Major Problems*, 305–6.

30. Norton, *Liberty's Daughters*, 186–7.

31. Norton, *Liberty's Daughters*, 187.

32. Edward C. Papenfuse, *In Pursuit of Profit: The Annapolis Merchants in the Era of the American Revolution, 1763–1805* (Baltimore: John Hopkins University Press, 1975), 90.

33. Norton, *Liberty's Daughters*, xv, xvi. Sixteen years after the publication of *Liberty's Daughters*, in her preface to the 1996 edition, Norton explained why she had not said much about camp followers and other special groups: "Always I would try to focus on the experiences that characterized the lives of most women at that time" [xiii]. Again, she assumed that the experiences of "most" women could be deduced from the records of the those who could and did write.

34. The "common experiences of femininity" have not seemed to bind together women of the late twentieth century on the abortion issue; nor did the common experiences of masculinity—hunting, for instance—bind together men of varying backgrounds and political persuasions in the Revolutionary era. Too often, "women" are treated as a single, undifferentiated group. A recent American history text, appropriately inclusive of women and minorities, observes: "Women, who had previously regarded politics as outside their proper sphere, now took a part in resisting British policy." This text is only a survey, but still: what does the term "women" imply? Imagine: "Men now took a part in resisting British policy." Would the term "men" include loyalists as well as patriots? Slaves as well as masters? Clearly, we must be more specific than that. [Mary Beth Norton, David M. Katzman, Paul D. Escott, Howard P.

Chudacoff, Thomas G. Peterson, and William M. Tuttle, Jr., *A People and a Nation: A History of the United States* (Boston: Houghton Mifflin, 1990), 121.]

35. Joel Perlmann and Dennis Shirly, "When Did New England Women Acquire Literacy?" *William and Mary Quarterly*, 3rd series, 48 (1991): 51–2.

36. Feb. 12, 1770. Cited in Young, "Women of Boston," 196. During the crisis that culminated in the Boston Tea Party, a Newport paper reported: "We can assure the Publick, that a Lady in this Town, of affluent Circumstances, and equal to any One in it for good Sense, Politeness and Consequence, last Week came to the Resolution to have no India Tea drank in her Family until the Duty upon that Article is taken off." [De Pauw, *Founding Mothers*, 158.] The frequent use of the term "ladies" in the reporting of female participation in the boycotts is telling: not all women of the times merited this appellation; indeed, most did not.

37. *Boston Gazette*, Feb. 12, 1770. Cited in Young, "Women of Boston," 196.

38. Ulrich, "Religious Women in Revolutionary New England," 215–22. Despite Ulrich's research, most current texts which mention spinning bees ignore the church-based context which shaped the experience for the participants. The textbook cited above, for example, states: "In towns throughout America, young women calling themselves Daughters of Liberty met to spin in public in an effort to spur other women to make homespun and end the colonies' dependence on English cloth." [Norton et al., *A People and a Nation*, 121.]

39. Joan R. Gundersen, *To Be Useful to the World: Women in Revolutionary America, 1740–1790* (New York: Twayne, 1996), 67.

40. Kerber, *Women of the Republic*, 43–4.

41. Kerber, *Women of the Republic*, 44; Foner, *Labor and the American Revolution*, 188.

42. Norton, *Liberty's Daughters*, 166.

43. John Bohstedt, "The Myth of the Feminine Food Riot: Women as Proto-Citizens in English Community Politics, 1790–1810," in Harriet B. Applewhite and Darline G. Levy, eds., *Women and Politics in the Age of Democratic Revolution* (Ann Arbor: University of Michigan Press, 1990), 21–60.

44. Barbara Clark Smith, "Food Rioters and the American Revolution," *William and Mary Quarterly*, 3rd series, 51 (1994): 5. Smith, taking issue with Bohstedt, questions whether the rioting was really a precursor of "citizenship" as we understand it today, since the rioters were not trying to influence the affairs of state. Instead, they operated within a realm which was simultaneously public and private, based on a "multiplicity" of "horizontal linkages . . . created by kinship, fellowship, neighboring, and local exchange." [Smith, "Food Rioters," 30.]

45. Linda Grant De Pauw objects to applying the term "camp follower" to the women travelling with the army: "A camp follower is a civilian who follows an army usually to sell goods or services, including prostitution. The key word here is *civilian*. A camp follower is not subject to military discipline, is not listed on muster rolls, does not draw pay or rations, and has no assigned military functions. Indeed a camp follower is expected to disappear when bullets begin to fly." ["Women in Combat: The Revolutionary War Experience,"

Armed Forces and Society, 7 (1981): 210.] Instead, De Pauw prefers to call the women who accompanied the Continental forces "women of the army." This seems to go too far in the other direction. Although women were subject to military discipline and they did sometimes help on the battlefield, they were not recruited, many did not appear on the muster rolls, they were rarely paid, and the issue of whether they should receive full rations, as we shall see, was still being debated at the close of the war. They could hardly be considered a "women's branch of the Continental Army," as De Pauw contends. I will continue to use the accepted term "camp follower," noting that it does not necessarily connote prostitution, nor does it preclude, with respect to the Revolutionary War, some functions relating to battle: relaying messages, carrying food and water during the fighting, moving ammunition, or even loading artillery.

46. Washington to Robert Morris, January 29, 1783, John C. Fitzpatrick, ed., *The Writings of George Washington from the Original Manuscript Sources, 1745–1799* (Washington: United States Government Printing Office, 1931–44), 26: 78–80.

47. Kerber, *Women of the Republic*, 56.

48. Washington to Morris, January 29, 1783, Fitzpatrick, ed., *Writings of Washington*, 26: 78–80; Washington to Henry Know, March 8, 1783, Fitzpatrick, ed., *Writings of Washington*, 26: 199–200; Holly A. Mayer, *Belonging to the Army: Camp Followers and Community during the American Revolution* (Columbia: University of South Carolina Press, 1996), 129–34; Walter H. Blumenthal, *Women Camp Followers of the American Revolution* (New York: Arno Press, 1974), 78–82.

49. *The Revolution Remembered: Eyewitness Accounts of the War of Independence*, John C. Dann, ed. (Chicago: University of Chicago Press, 1980), 244–5.

50. John Shy, *A People Numerous and Armed: Reflections on the Military Struggle for American Independence* (Ann Arbor: University of Michigan Press, 1990), 32.

51. Charles Royster, *A Revolutionary People at War: The Continental Army and American Character, 1775–1783* (Chapel Hill: University of North Carolina Press, 1979), 59.

52. Blumenthal, *Camp Followers*, 83.

53. Blumenthal, *Camp Followers*, 64.

54. General Orders, July 4, 1777, Fitzpatrick, ed., *Writings of Washington*, 8: 347.

55. Blumenthal, *Camp Followers*, 73.

56. General Orders, May 31 and June 19, 1778, and June 7, 1779, Fitzpatrick, ed., *Writings of Washington*, 11: 498, 12: 94, 15: 240; Blumenthal, *Camp Followers*, 74.

57. Dann, *Revolution Remembered*, 243. In her deposition, the most complete testimony we have by a camp follower, Osborn stated very explicitly when she walked, when she rode a horse, and when she rode in a wagon. In light of the importance Osborn placed on her mode of transportation, Washington's fixation against women in wagons seems particularly significant.

58. Blumenthal, *Camp Followers*, 65–6; Kerber, *Women of the Republic*, 57.

59. Blumenthal, *Camp Followers*, 66. Washington's need to issue a guard suggests that some "bad women" were indeed infiltrating the ranks.

60. Blumenthal, *Camp Followers*, 59.

61. Kerber, *Women of the Republic*, 56.

62. Rebecca D. Symmes, ed., *A Citizen-Soldier in the American Revolution: The Diary of Benjamin Gilbert in Massachusetts and New York* (Cooperstown: New York State Historical Association, 1980), 30–2.

63. John Shy, ed., *Winding Down: The Revolutionary War Letters of Lieutenant Benjamin Gilbert of Massachusetts, 1780–1783* (Ann Arbor: University of Michigan Press, 1989), 67, 86–7, 98. On March 1 Gilbert wrote: "fine Kippen Issued immediately on application," using a slang term for prostitutes [87].

64. Mayer, *Belonging to the Army*, 135–6.

65. Blumenthal, *Camp Followers*, 84–5.

66. Blumenthal, *Camp Followers*, 19, 93.

67. Mayer, *Belonging to the Army*, 126. The identity of the author is unknown, although Mayer states he "may have been Elias Parker."

68. Blumenthal, *Camp Followers*, 27–8.

69. Paul Engle, *Women in the American Revolution* (Chicago: Follett, 1976), xvi; DePauw, *Founding Mothers*, 163–4.

70. A Citizen of Massachusetts, *The Female Review: or, Memoirs of an American Young Lady*, (Dedham, MA: Nathaniel and Benjamin Heaton, 1797) published again under the title *The Female Review: The Life of Deborah Sampson*, John Adams Vinton, ed. (Boston: Wiggin & Lunt, 1866). The 1866 edition, with Vinton's extensive introduction, was reprinted by Arno Press in 1972. See also Elizabeth Ellet, *The Women of the American Revolution* (New York: Haskell House, 1969; originally published in 1850), 2: 127; Elizabeth Evans, *Weathering the Storm: Women of the American Revolution* (New York: Scribners, 1975), 303–4; Julia Ward Stickley, "The Records of Deborah Sampson Gannett," *Prologue: Journal of the National Archives*, 4 (1972); 233–41. Most references to Sampson use her married name of later years, Gannett, since that is the name she used in her pension petitions; I deem it more appropriate to use her true name at the time of her service.

71. Linda Grant De Pauw, "Women in Combat: The Revolutionary War Experience," *Armed Forces and Society*, 7 (1981): 218; Janice E. McKenney, " 'Women in Combat': Comment," *Armed Forces and Society*, 8 (1982): 688.

72. De Pauw, "Women in Combat," 218.

73. Mayer, *Belonging to the Army*, 20.

74. John B. Landis, "Investigation into American Tradition of Woman Known as Molly Pitcher," *Journal of American History*, 5 (1911): 83–96; Linda Grant De Pauw and Conover Hunt, *Remember the Ladies: Women in America, 1750–1815* (New York: Viking, 1976), 90. Once again I have chosen to use the surname "Hays" rather than the surname of a later husband, "McCauly."

75. De Pauw, "Women in Combat," 215. See also John T. White, "The Truth About Molly Pitcher," in James K. Martin and Karen R. Stabaus, eds., *The American Revolution: Whose Revolution?* (Huntington, NY: Robert E. Krieger, 1981), 99–105. White, like DePauw and Hunt, questions the notion that "Molly Pitcher" was a single identifiable woman.

76. Historians De Pauw and McKenney disagree as to whether the water was to quench the thirst of the men or cool the artillery. [De Pauw, "Women in

Combat," 215; McKenney, "Comment," 689.] I suspect it was both, and for the present purposes the debate is irrelevant. In either case, women did perform support services during battle.

77. Joseph Plumb Martin, *Private Yankee Doodle: Being a Narrative of Some of the Adventures, Dangers and Sufferings of a Revolutionary Soldier*, ed. George F. Scheer (Boston: Little, Brown & Co. 1962), 132–3.

78. Linda Kerber, " 'History Can Do It No Justice': Women and the Reinterpretation of the American Revolution," in Hoffman and Albert, eds., *Women in the Age of the American Revolution*, 21, 22, 26. Italics in the original.

79. Young, "Women of Boston," 206; Alfred F. Young, *The Shoemaker and the Tea Party: Memory and the American Revolution* (Boston: Beacon Press, 1999), 105.

80. Kerber, "History Can Do It No Justice," 21–2.

81. Charles Royster offers other examples from the patriot press, including a poem: "Go act the hero, every danger face/Love hates a coward's impotent embrace." [*Revolutionary People at War*, 30–1.] Young cites two examples of women sending men into battle. The first comes from Ezra Stiles, a future president of Yale College, who reported that an eyewitness to the 1774 "powder alarm" told him:

> The Women kept on making Cartridges, & after equipping their Husbands, bro't them out to the Soldiers which in Crowds passed along & gave them out in handfuls to one and another as they were deficient, mixing Exhortation & Tears & Prayers & spiriting the Men in such an uneffeminate Manner as even would make Cowards fight. He tho't if anything the Women surpassed the Men for Eagerness & Spirit in the Defence of Liberty by Arms. . . . The Women . . . gave up their Husbands Sons &c to Battle & bid them fight courageously & manfully & behave themselves like Men & not like Cowards. [*The Literary Diary of Ezra Stiles*, Franklin B. Dexter, ed., (New York: Charles Scribner's Sons, 1901), 1: 480. I have included here a more complete quotation than did Young.]

Although this is the most convincing evidence we have for shaming, it still comes to us filtered twice through the eyes of male patriots. Significantly, this event occurred over seven months before fighting broke out, and we have no reason to suspect that these women thought they were sending off their men to become soldiers. The blind, euphoric charge during the buildup to war never tells the whole story.

Young's other example also comes from the early stages of the Revolution. In 1775 a loyalist reported from Massachusetts that "a certain epidemical phrenzy runs through our fair country women which outdoes all the pretended patriotic virtue of the more robustic males:—these little mischief making devils have entered into an almost unanimous association that any man who shall basely and cowardly give up the public cause of freedom, shall from that moment on be discarded [from] their assemblies, and no further contrition shall be able to atone for the crime." [Young, "Women of Boston," 206.] Here, the "fair country women" who banished men from their "assemblies" were not patriotic women expressing their serious commitment to the cause; they were "little mischief making devils" who exercised the power at their command, as do teenagers everywhere. Like their male counterparts, these girls were more susceptible than adults to the seductive appeal of wartime rhetoric. When the *rage militaire* swept through the colonies in 1775, boys who were sixteen, and younger still, rushed to be a part of the action—and girls did too. More like high school cheerleaders than the League of Women Voters, they banded together as they might at a carnival, aflame with excitement, understandably eager to be a part of it all.

Sarah Wister, a well-to-do teenager from Philadephia whose family retreated to a country home not far distant from Valley Forge, wrote a fascinating daily chronicle of her flirtations with officers. The war filled Sarah with dreams "of bayonets and swords, sashes, guns, and epaulets." Young Sarah, if anyone, was the type of girl to "shame" men into battle. Wister's journal was published serially in the *Pennsylvania Magazine of History and Biography*, IX (1885–6). In 1902 Albert Cook Myers published the manuscript as a book, *Sally Wister's Journal, a True Narrative* (Philadelphia: Ferris & Leach). Myers's version, altered to achieve correct grammar, spelling, and punctuation, has been reprinted in Evans, *Weathering the Storm*, 112–48, and Richard M. Dorson, ed., *America Rebels: Narratives of the Patriots* (New York: Pantheon, 1953), 219–36. A more accurate rendition of the original appears in Kathryn Zabelle Derounian, ed., *The Journal and Occasional Writings of Sarah Wister* (Rutherford, Madison, Teaneck, NJ: Fairleigh Dickinson University Press, 1987), 41–75.

82. John C. Dann, "The Revolution Remembered—By the Ladies," *American Magazine* 3 (1987–8): 71. As with his book, *The Revolution Remembered*, Dann presents verbatim accounts from pension requests.

83. Dann, "Revolution Remembered—By the Ladies," 71.

84. Dann, "Revolution Remembered—By the Ladies," 74.

85. Dann, "Revolution Remembered—By the Ladies," 73.

86. Mary Beth Norton, " 'What an Alarming Crisis Is This': Southern Women and the American Revolution," in Jeffrey J. Crow and Larry E. Tise, eds., *The Southern Experience in the American Revolution* (Chapel Hill: University of North Carolina Press, 1978), 217.

87. Herbert T. Wade and Robert A. Lively, *This Glorious Cause: The Adventures of Two Company Officers in Washington's Army*, (Princeton, NJ: Princeton University Press, 1958), 208.

88. William Moultrie, *Memoirs of the American Revolution* (New York: David Longworth, 1802; Arno Press reprint, 1968), 1: 57.

89. Charles K. Bolton, *The Private Soldier Under Washington* (Williamstown, MA: Corner House, 1976), 179; Royster, *Revolutionary People at War*, 166. See my introduction for the full quotation.

90. Smith, "Food Rioters," 18.

91. Royster, *Revolutionary People at War*, 196. According to Royster, the desertion rate throughout the course ofthe war ran about 20 percent to 25 percent [71]. For a more extended discussion of desertions, see chapter 2 above.

92. Joan Hoff Wilson, "The Illusion of Change: Women and the American Revolution," in Alfred F. Young, ed., *The American Revolution: Explorations in the History of American Radicalism* (De Kalb: Northern Illimois University Press, 1976), 424–5.

93. Royster, *Revolutionary People at War*, 31.

94. One could argue, of course, that there is nothing new or noteworthy about the suffering of women during wartime, so we need not dwell on the subject. The failure to discuss the impact of a war on its people, however, constitutes a falsification of history. Although political leaders treat individual lives as if they were expendable in order to wage their wars, historians ought not to follow suit.

95. The American farmer Hector Saint-John de Crevecoeur described the scene as it was told to him:

> Each wife, each father, each mother could easily distinguish each husband and son as they fell. But in so great, so universal a calamity, when each expected to meet the same fate, perhaps they did not feel so keenly for the deplorable end of their friends and relations. . . . What a spectacle this would have exhibited to the eyes of humanity: hundreds of women and children, now widows and orphans, in the most humble attitude, with pale, dejected countenances, sitting on the few bundles they had brought with them; keeping their little unconscious children as close to them as possible; hiding by a mechanical instinct the babies of their breasts; numbers of aged fathers oppressed with the unutterable sorrow; all pale, all trembling, and sinking under the deepest consternation, were looking towards the door—that door through which so many of their friends had just passed, alas! never to return. [Commager and Morris, *The Spirit of 'Seventy-Six*, 1009.]

Although Crevecoeur himself was not an eyewitness, the basic outline of his description is confirmed by the writings of British soldiers. (Commager and Morris, *Spirit of 'Seventy-Six*, 1006–7.) These precise descriptions and attributions of particular emotions were speculative—but they do seem plausible. Most people under similar circumstances would undoubtedly appear "all pale, all trembling, and sinking under the deepest consternation."

96. Norton, *Liberty's Daughters*, 199–200.

97. Norton, *Liberty's Daughters*, 63–4.

98. Kerber, *Women of the Republic*, 49.

99. Gundersen, *Useful to the World*, 154.

100. Wilkinson, *Letters*, 28–30. The looting occurred on both sides. In Connecticut, patriots hiding behind a stone wall shot a girl who was carrying clothes to her father; they stole her bundle and cut off her finger for a ring. [Evans, *Weathering the Storm*, 28.] Throughout the later years, when civil war raged rampantly throughout the South, Whigs and Tories alike plundered and looted at will, fueled by escalating animosities as each side sought to avenge the atrocities of the other. See chapter 2.

101. Wilkinson, *Letters*, 31, 46.

102. Kerber, *Women of the Republic*, 46.

103. De Pauw and Hunt, *Remember the Ladies*, 86. Other patriot accusations of the abuse of women by British soldiers can be found in Frank Moore, *The Diary of the American Revolution* (New York: Washington Square Press, 1967), 217, 378, 431–4.

104. Kerber, *Women of the Republic*, 46; Norton, *Liberty's Daughters*, 203.

105. Commager and Morris, *The Spirit of 'Seventy-Six*, 424.

106. Norton, *Liberty's Daughters*, 202–3.

107. Kerber, "History Can Do It No Justice," 6; Norton, *Liberty's Daughters*, 197.

108. Young, "Women of Boston," 206.

109. Evans, *Weathering the Storm*, 255.

110. Norton, *Liberty's Daughters*, 197–9; Gundersen, *Useful to the World*, 156. In his memoirs, William Moultrie recalled thousands of "poor women and children" in Georgia "travelling to they knew not where." [*Memoirs of the American Revolution* (New York: David Longworth, 1802), 2: 259.]

111. Norton, *Liberty's Daughters*, 200.

112. Wallace Brown, *The Good Americans: The Loyalists in the American Revolution* (New York: William Morrow, 1969), 140.

113. Brown, *Good Americans*, 140.

114. Norton, "Alarming Crisis," 220–1. Mary Morris, the wife of patriot financier Robert Morris, noted with consternation the eviction of women from Philadelphia whose husbands had already been exiled: "My feelings [are] . . . wounded for the sufferings of a Number of my Sex in this State, who are compelled to leave it, by that Cruell Edict of our Counsel: a resolve which Oblidges all the women whose Husbands are with the enemy, and Children whose parents are there, to repair to *them* Immediately; a determination like this which admits of no Exception, is unjust. . . . [T]here is many whose conduct has not Merited it, tho there is others that have, yet why not discriminate between the innocent and the guilty?" [Kerber, *Women of the Republic*, 53.]

115. Norton, *Liberty's Daughters*, 218.

116. Brown, *Good Americans*, 140.

117. James K. Martin and Mark E. Lender, *A Respectable Army: The Military Origins of the Republic, 1763–1789* (Arlington Heights, IL: Harlan Davidson, 1982), 198.

118. Kerber, *Women of the Republic*, 93.

119. When soldiers died in battle, other soldiers had to secure their own survival before hauling about dead bodies, or even trying to identify them. While wandering about the site of a battle in central New York six years after the fighting, Alexander Thompson came upon "a vast number of human skulls and bones scattered through the woods"—the bodies had been left to rot on the ground, or had perhaps been covered quickly with a thin layer of duff. [Dennis P. Ryan, ed., *A Salute to Courage: The American Revolution as Seen Through Wartime Writings of Officers of the Continental Army and Navy* (New York: Columbia University Press, 1979), 282. See also Blumenthal, *Camp Followers*, 85.] During the battle of Saratoga, American camp followers

stripped the dead of all belongings and clothing—a scavenger's bounty indeed—making identification difficult. [Blumenthal, *Camp Followers*, 84–5.] Sometimes the only "evidence" of a soldier's demise was his failure to report for duty. Under conditions such as these, some who were reported dead did in fact resurface later.

120. Kerber, *Women of the Republic*, 73.

121. Norton, *Liberty's Daughters*, 225.

122. Norton, *Liberty's Daughters*, 215.

123. Norton, *Liberty's Daughters*, 225–6; Kerber, *Women of the Republic*, 87–9. Kerber includes a reproduction of the original petition. Wells, once well off but no more so, was petitioning for the payment of interest on her loans, which had been invalidated because she was forced to flee from New Jersey during the war.

124. All the following selections come from the letters of Joseph and Sarah Hodgkins, reprinted in Herbert T. Wade and Robert A. Lively, *This Glorious Cause: The Adventures of Two Company Officers in Washington's Army* (Princeton, NJ: Princeton University Press, 1958), 167–245. These letters, faithfully transcribed, should be read by any serious student of the American Revolution. They paint a full, multidimensional portrait of the war's impact over an extended time.

125. Smith, *Colonial Days and Ways*, 228–9; Meltzer, *American Revolutionaries*, 71–2. Mrs. Smith, like many other women who wrote about their wartime experiences, had household slaves to assist her.

4 Loyalists and Pacifists

1. Charles F. Adams, ed., *The Works of John Adams* (Boston: Charles C. Little and James Brown, 1850), 10: 110. Adams was writing about the political sentiments of Americans towards the European conflict between England and France in 1797. The complete passage reads: "I should say that full one-third were averse to the revolution. These, retaining that overweening fondness, in which they had been educated, for the English, could not cordially like the French; indeed, they most heartily detested them. An opposite third conceived a hatred of the English, and gave themselves up to an enthusiastic gratitude to France. The middle third, composed principally of the yeomanry, the soundest part of the nation, and always averse to war, were rather lukewarm both to England and France." Adams did say, on another occasion, that although the colonies had been nearly "unanimous" in their "universal" opposition to the Stamp Act in 1765, by 1775 the British had "seduced and deluded nearly one third of the people of the colonies." [Adams, *Works*, 10; 192–3.] These two quotations from his writings in 1815 have somehow blended together in popular historiography to make Adams the definitive contemporary source on the strength of the loyalists.

2. Paul H. Smith, "The American Loyalists: Notes on their Organization and Numerical Strength," *William and Mary Quarterly*, 3rd series, 25 (1968): 269.

By consulting official records, Smith found that about 19,000 men from the thirteen colonies actually took up arms on the British side. He then examined Lorenzo Sabine's nineteenth-century compilation of loyalist biographies and found that 895 of the 6,025 men mentioned by Sabine took up arms, or roughly 15 percent. If Sabine's sample represented a true cross section of the loyalist population, then the 19,000 fighting men represented 15 percent of the adult male loyalists, which would be 128,000. Since there were about four people to a family, Smith concludes that around 500,000 families could be classed as loyalist. Comparing this with the total white population of the colonies, and adjusting for the factor of time (not all the loyalist soldiers served simultaneously), Smith concluded: "[M]y final estimate is that the loyalists comprised about 16 per cent . . . of the total population, or 19.8 per cent of the white Americans." The weakest link in this chain of reasoning is the assumption that Sabine's sampling of biographies "suffiently represent[s] a cross section of the loyalists." Smith believes it does, claiming that "the diversity of his sources and the size of his sample contribute to its remarkable accuracy." I believe it does not. Using Smith's own figures, the sample represents less than 5 percent of the total—and these people were selected specifically for their prominence; I do not see how the most famous 5 percent of any population can ever represent the whole. In this case, the prominent loyalists might have been more willing to join the king's forces, since they were the leaders and presumably more devoted to their cause, or less willing to take up arms, as we have seen with the patriots. Perhaps, with any luck, the eagerness of some leaders to take up arms offset the hesitancy of others, rendering the sample accurate after all. Only this we know: Smith's figures, the best we have, are still highly speculative.

3. For insights into the minds of these loyalists, and their resistance to the increasing democratization of their society, see Anne Hulton, *Letters of a Loyalist Lady* (Cambridge: Harvard University Press, 1927), and Douglass Adair and John A. Schutz, eds., *Peter Oliver's Origin & Progress of the American Rebellion* (Stanford, CA: Stanford University Press, 1961).

4. Edward Countryman, *A People in Revolution: The American Revolution and Political Society in New York, 1760–1790* (Baltimore: John Hopkins University Press, 1981), 116–7. The roundup of Tories in New York City also included the mayor and some gentlemen, as well as one man described simply as "a damned rascal." [William H. Nelson, *The American Tory* (Oxford: Clarendon Press, 1961), 86.] Countryman also reviewed the records of 350 people detained by the revolutionaries in Albany County between 1778 and 1781: "Two hundred fifty-two of these people were farmers, yeomen, and farm laborers, and among the rest were twelve innkeepers, thirty-one artisans and youths, nine professional men, and two merchants. Four were women, and the occupations of nineteen of the men were not given" [121]. Harold Hancock conducted a similar review of the backgrounds of forty-six people specifically excluded from "An Act of Free Pardon" passed by Delaware's rebel government in 1778: "Three persons had 'Esq.' attached to their names, and the list included two captains of militia and one militia man, a former sheriff, one lawyer, and three physicians, but a variety of occupations were represented: two laborers, one weaver, two

inkeepers, two coopers, one cordwainer, one coppersmith, one hatter, one saddler, one bricklayer, one tailor, five mariners or shallopmen, and three pilots. Nine husbandmen or yeomen were included." [*The Loyalists of Revolutionary Delaware* (Newark: University of Delaware Press, 1977), 84.] Note that these were the loyalist *leaders*, yet they did not constitute anything resembling a ruling elite.

5. Staughton Lynd, "The Tenant Rising at Livingston Manor, May 1777," in Lynd, *Class Conflict, Slavery, and the United States Constitution: Ten Essays* (Indianapolis and New York: Bobbs-Merrill, 1967), 72. Lynd's essay was originally published in *The New-York Historical Society Quarterly*, 48 (1964): 163–77.

6. Lynd, *Class Conflict*, 69, 73.

7. For the 1766 uprising, see chapter 1 above, "Country Rebellions." For uprisings of the 1750s, see Lynd, *Class Conflict*, 65.

8. Lynd, *Class Conflict*, 68, 69. Historians Philip Ranlet and Sung Bok Kim argue that the reluctance of Livingston's tenants to support the patriots stemmed not from class antagonisms but from fears that rival New Englanders, who were Whigs, coveted the land they worked. Ranlet and Kim also maintain that Staughton Lynd has exaggerated the extent of the tenants' "loyalism," accepting at face value the statements of paranoid Revolutionaries who saw "Tories behind every bush." [Philip Ranlet, *The New York Loyalists* (Knoxville: University of Tennessee Press, 1986), 120–136; Sung Bok Kim, "Impact of Class Relations and Warfare in the American Revolution: The New York Experience," *Journal of American History* 69 (1982): 326–46.] Historians can argue over the motives of the tenants precisely because these illiterate farmers left but scanty evidence of their true thoughts and feelings. Again, the stories of ordinary people are hard to retrieve, but this much is clear and undisputed: many poor people who worked the soil on the Livingston Manor, acting according to what they perceived as their own best interests, sided at least momentarily with the British.

9. Hancock, *Loyalists of Delaware*, 96; Robert M. Calhoon, "The Reintegration of the Loyalists and the Disaffected," in Jack P. Greene, ed., *The American Revolution: Its Character and Limits* (New York: New York University Press, 1987), 60.

10. Hancock, *Loyalists of Delaware*, 90–5.

11. Ronald Hoffman, *A Spirit of Dissension: Economics, Politics, and the Revolution in Maryland* (Baltimore: John Hopkins University, 1973), 157, 191; Ronald Hoffman, "The 'Disaffected' in the Revolutionary South," in Alfred F. Young, ed., *The American Revolution: Explorations in the History of American Radicalism* (De Kalb, IL: Northern Illinois University Press, 1976), 285.

12. Hoffman, *Spirit of Dissension*, 205, 192, 198; Hoffman, " 'Disaffected' in the Revolutionary South," 286, 288–9. According to George Dashiell, commander of the Somerset County militia, so many of the common people were disaffected that they outnumbered the patriots in the militia "more than three to one." Consequently, Dashiell refused to pass out arms to his own militiamen. [Hoffman, *Spirit of Dissension*, 233.]

13. Hoffman, *Spirit of Dissension*, 224.

14. Hoffman, *Spirit of Dissension*, 225. Hoffman qualifies his conclusion: "Too much importance should not be attached to these statistics. The economic profile of the men indicated differs little from that of the colony in general. Still the lot of most of them was not a pleasant one. Even the most cursory examination of their estates indicates that they possessed little, and because of this condition, their frustrations were sharp. Feelings of dissatisfaction inhere in any class of subordinate people, but except in times of marked social disorder, these attitudes rarely find overt expression. The Revolution created such an abnormal situation" [225–6]. Although the disaffected were of average means for the colony, that average was not itself very high. Most of the people tried for treason, insurrection, or riotous behavior possessed little indeed when compared with the men who tried to make them fight against the Crown.

15. J. P. MacLean, *An Historical Account of the Settlements of Scotch Highlanders in America Prior to the Peace of 1783* (Cleveland: Helman Taylor Company, 1900), 199.

16. Countryman, *People in Revolution*, 147.

17. MacLean, *Scotch Higlanders*, 205.

18. See chapter 5, "Iroquois."

19. Nelson, *American Tory*, 91.

20. William Pencak, *War, Politics, and Revolution in Provincial Massachusetts* (Boston: Northeastern University Press, 1981), 205–6, 214.

21. John Shy, *A People Numerous and Armed: Reflections on the Military Struggle for American Independence* (Ann Arbor: University of Michigan Press, 1990), 23. Gold Selleck Silliman, a Connecticut militia officer, reported that "A great Number of those who are at Bottom Friends to their Country among us, and who would take it excessively ill to be thought otherwise, have Brothers, Fathers, Sisters, Sons, & in short every kind of Relationship that you can mention among the Enemy." Although "the tender Sensations" of intimate relations were "inconsistent with the Character of the Patriot," Silliman was sympathetic when relatives of loyalists opposed "vigorous Measures . . . that perhaps may be the Means of taking or slaying a Father, a Son, &c." [Joy D. Buel and Richard Buel, Jr., *The Way of Duty: A Woman and her Family in Revolutionary America* (New York: W. W. Norton, 1984), 133–4.]

22. Wallace Brown, *The Good Americans: The Loyalists in the American Revolution* (New York: William Morrow, 1969), 144.

23. In his will, Benjamin Franklin explained why he bequeathed to his only son only a small part of his property: "The part he acted against me in the late war, which is of public noteriety, will account for my leaving him no more of an estate he endeavored to deprive me of." [Lorenzo Sabine, *Biographical Sketches of Loyalists of the American Revolution* (Port Washington, NY: Kennikat Press, 1966; originally published in 1864), 1: 444.] For in-depth treatments of the relationship between Ben and William Franklin, see Willard S. Randall, *A Little Revenge: Benjamin Franklin and his Son* (Boston: Little, Brown & Co., 1984), and Sheila L. Skemp, *Benjamin and William Franklin: Father and Son, Patriot and Loyalist* (Boston: Bedford Books of St. Martin's Press, 1994).

24. Elizabeth Evans, *Weathering the Storm: Women of the American Revolution* (New York: Scribners, 1975), 255, 261. Evans reprints the entire letter, a most revealing document.

25. Lindley S. Butler, ed., *The Narrative of Col. David Fanning* (Davidson, NC: Briarpatch Press, 1981), 19–20.

26. Tho. Flethcall to President of Council of Safety, July 4, 1775, in R. W. Gibbes, ed., *Documentary History of the American Revolution* (New York: D. Appleton & Co., 1855), 123.

27. Drayton to Council of Safety, August 16, 1775, Gibbes, *Documentary History*, 141.

28. Tennent to Henry Laurens, August 20, 1775, Gibbes, *Documentary History*, 145.

29. Drayton to Council of Safety, August 21, 1775, Gibbes, *Documentary History*, 150–151.

30. Rachel Klein writes that Charles Woodmason, an Anglican minister, "admonished lowcountry rebels who made 'such a noise about Liberty! Liberty! Freedom! Property! Rights! Privileges! and what not; And at the same time keep half their fellow subjects in a State of Slavery.' Woodmason was not referring to black slaves but to the thousands of white frontiersmen who remained all but unrepresented in the South Carolina assembly. Inland and coastal leaders spoke the same political language, but on the frontier republican rhetoric could accommodate the loyalist as well as the patriot position." [Rachel Klein, "Frontier Planters and the American Revolution: The South Carolina Backcountry, 1775–1782," in Ronald Hoffman, Thad W. Tate, and Peter J. Albert, eds., *An Uncivil War: The Southern Backcountry during the American Revolution* (Charlottesville: University Press of Virginia, 1985), 40–1.]

31. Robert S. Lambert, *South Carolina Loyalists in the American Revolution* (Columbia: University of South Carolina Press, 1987), 28.

32. Klein, "Frontier Planters," 45–6. For additional treatments of the localized causes of loyalism in the South, see Paul D. Escott and Jeffrey J. Crow, "The Social Order and Violent Disorder: An Analysis of North Carolina in the Revolution and the Civil War," *Journal of Southern History* 52 (1986): 373–402; Albert H. Tillson, Jr., "Localist Roots of Backcountry Loyalism: An Examination of Popular Political Culture in Virginia's New River Valley," *Journal of Southern History* 54 (1988): 387–404; Keith Mason, "Localism, Evangelicalism, and Loyalism: The Sources of Discontent in the Revolutionary Chesapeake," *Journal of Southern History* 56 (1990): 22–54. For a study of how all sorts of factors—"ethnic background, economic interest, family ties, social and geographic circumstances, personal psychology, and underlying beliefs and values"—affected one loyalist, see Keith Mason, "A Loyalist's Journey: James Parker's Response to the Revolutionary Crisis," *Virginia Magazine of History and Biography* 102 (1994): 139–166.

33. Klein suggests they may have been responding to the desires of their communities, which leads us back where we started.

34. See Gordon S. Wood, "Not So Poor Richard," *New York Review of Books*, June 6, 1996.

35. Klein, "Frontier Planters," 47, 58, 60; Butler, *Narrative of David Fanning*, 3, 24; Lambert, *South Carolina Loyalists*, 207; Sabine, *Biographical Sketches of Loyalists*, 1: 261; Edward J. Cashin, " 'But Brothers, It Is Our Land We Are Talking About': Winners and Losers in the Georgia Backcountry," in Hoffman et al., *Uncivil War*, 248.

36. Lambert, *South Carolina Loyalists*, 41–42; Robert Cunningham to Drayton, October 5, 1775, Gibbes, *Documentary History*, 200.

37. Butler, *Narrative of David Fanning*, 22.

38. Butler, *Narrative of David Fanning*, 23.

39. Butler, *Narrative of David Fanning*, 25–6.

40. Butler, *Narrative of David Fanning*, 29.

41. Butler, *Narrative of David Fanning*, 31.

42. Butler, *Narrative of David Fanning*, 35–6.

43. Robert M. Weir, " 'The Violent Spirit,' The Reestablishment of Order, and the Continuity of Leadership in Post-Revolutionary South Carolina," in Hoffman et al., *Uncivil War*, 76.

44. Butler, *Narrative of David Fanning*, 6.

45. Collins, *Autobiography*, 65.

46. Butler, *Narrative of David Fanning*, 43.

47. Butler, *Narrative of David Fanning*, 64.

48. Butler, *Narrative of David Fanning*, 68.

49. Butler, *Narrative of David Fanning*, 71–3.

50. Butler, *Narrative of David Fanning*, 76.

51. Butler, *Narrative of David Fanning*, 76.

52. Butler, *Narrative of David Fanning*, 76–7.

53. Butler, *Narrative of David Fanning*, 103, 106. Fanning was here referring to an earlier pardon, but the list of "Above Mentioned Crimes" is basically the same, and Whigs were certainly responsible for their fair share of the killing and plundering. The British Colonel Robert Gray described this stage of the war in clear and vivid terms: "[T]he tories in many places ... hid themselves in the swamps from whence they made frequent incursions upon their enemies. When opposed by a superior force they dispersed, when the storm blew over they embodied and recommenced their operation. ... [W]higs and tories, both parties equally afraid of the other, dared not sleep in their houses but concealed themselves in swamps. This is called lying out. Both parties were in this condition in general all over Ninety-Six District and every other part of the province wherever it was checquered by the intersection of whig and tory settlements." [Hoffman, " 'Disaffected' in the Revolutionary South," 295.]

54. Sabine, *Biographical Sketches of Loyalists*, 1: 349. See also John S. Pancake, *This Destructive War: The British Campaign in the Carolinas, 1780–1782* (University, AL: University of Alabama Press, 1985), 88.

55. Klein, "Frontier Planters," 60–61.

56. The rebels were so fearful of the Indians that they once surrendered a fort upon hearing "a few war whoops" from Brown's allies. [Cashin, " 'Brothers, It Is Our Land,' " 254.]

57. Cashin, " 'Brothers, It Is Our Land,' " 258.

58. Arthur Mekeel, who canvassed the minutes of all the Friends' meetings, estimates there were 61,000 Quakers. There were also around 10,000 Mennonites and Amish in Pennsylvania alone, with other communities of significant size in New York and Virginia. In 1774, there were 2,295 Moravians listed in Pennsylvania, representing about half the total number in America; other Moravians lived in North Carolina, New York, Rhode Island, and Maryland. The Dunkers numbered about 800, and the Schwenkfelders were probably in a similar range. The Shakers were just beginning to gain converts at the end of the Revolution. Other sects, like the Nicholites, Rogerenes, and Sandemanians, remained fairly small. [Peter Brock, *Pacifism in the United States, From the Colonial Era to the First World War* (Princeton, NJ: Princeton University Press, 1968), 21, 163, 170, 178, 278; Kenneth G. Hamilton, *John Ettwein and the Moravian Church during the Revolutionary Period* (Bethlehem, PA: Times Publishing Co., 1940), 6–7; Arthur J. Mekeel, *The Relation of the Quakers to the American Revolution* (Washington: University Press of America, 1979), 330.] I will not discuss religious minorities, such as the Jews, who did not collectively oppose the war.

59. Brock, *Pacifism in the United States*, 262.

60. Brock, *Pacifism in the United States*, 270.

61. Robert M. Calhoon, *The Loyalists in Revolutionary America, 1760–1781* (New York: Harcourt Brace Jovanovich, 1973), 387.

62. Brock, *Pacifism in the United States*, 263; John Ettwein, "A Short Account of the Disturbances in America and of the Brethren's Conduct and Suffering in This Connection," in Kenneth G. Hamilton, *John Ettwein and the Moravian Church during the Revolutionary Period* (Bethlehem, PA: Times Publishing Co., 1940), 213.

63. Brock, *Pacifism in the United States*, 252–3; Calhoon, *Loyalists in Revolutionary America*, 388–9; Mekeel, *Relation of the Quakers to the American Revolution*, 173–9; Anne M. Ousterhout, *A State Divided: Opposition in Pennsylvania to the American Revolution* (New York and Westport, CT: Greenwood Press, 1987), 165–8.

64. Brock, *Pacifism in the United States*, 239–40.

65. Brock, *Pacifism in the United States*, 274; Paul Engle, *Women in the American Revolution* (Chicago: Follett Publishing Company, 1976), 165–6, 177.

66. Hamilton, *John Ettwein*, 172–173, 180–1, 185.

67. Hamilton, *John Ettwein*, 212.

68. Brock, *Pacifism in the United States*, 268–9.

69. Brock, *Pacifism in the United States*, 264; Calhhon, *Loyalists in Revolutionary America*, 386.

70. Brock, *Pacifism in the United States*, 200.

71. Mekeel, *Relation of Quakers to American Revolution*, 334, 336.

72. Brock, *Pacifism in the United States*, 211, 223.

73. Mekeel, *Relation of Quakers to American Revolution*, 335.

74. Hamilton, *John Ettwein*, 132, 136, 163, 168, 169, 276, 177–8, 138, 193, 196–8, 210–1, 276. For a breakdown of the increasing stringency of Pennsylvania

oaths, see Claude Halstead Van Tyne, *The Loyalists in the American Revolution* (New York: Peter Smith, 1929), 321–2.

75. Catherine S. Crary, ed., *The Price of Loyalty: Tory Writings from the Revolutionary Era* (New York: McGraw-Hill, 1973), 188–9; Shy, *People Numerous and Armed*, 238. The legislature, in its need to attribute blame, concluded that the men had been misled by their minister, who was subsequently tried for treason.

76. Nelson, *American Tory*, 144–5.

77. Crary, *Price of Loyalty*, 225; James K. Martin and Mark E. Lender, *A Respectable Army: The Military Origins of the Republic*, 1763–1789 (Arlington Heights, IL: Harlan Davidson, 1982), 93.

78. Michael Kammen, "The American Revolution as a *Crise de Conscience:* The Case of New York," in Richard M. Jellison, ed., *Society, Freedom, and Conscience: The American Revolution in Virginia, Massachusetts, and New York* (New York: W. W. Norton, 1976), 143.

79. Pauline Maier, *From Resistance to Revolution* (New York: Alfred A. Knopf, 1972), 278.

80. Thomas Paine, *Crisis* papers, reprinted in Morton Borden and Penn Borden, *The American Tory* (Englewood Cliffs, NJ: Prentice-Hall, 1972), 65–7.

81. Emory G. Evans, "Trouble in the Backcountry: Disaffection in Southwest Virginia during the American Revolution," in Hoffman et. al., *Uncivil War*, 182; Richard Buel, Jr., *Dear Liberty* (Middletown, CT: Weslyan University Press, 1980), 265; Countryman, *People in Revolution*, 174.

82. James E. Cutler, *Lynch-Law: An Investigation into the History of Lynching in the United States* (New York: Longman, Green, & Co., 1905), 23–31; Richard Maxwell Brown, *Strain of Violence: Historical Studies of American Violence and Vigilantism* (New York: Oxford University Press, 1975), 59–60; Richard MaxwellBrown, "Violence and the American Revolution," in Stephen G. Kurtz and James H. Hutson, eds., *Essays on the American Revolution* (Chapel Hill: University of North Carolina Press, 1973), 107–8.

83. Kammen, "The American Revolution as a *Crise de Conscience*," 139.

84. Brown, *Good Americans*, 126.

85. Brown, *Good Americans*, 74.

86. Brown, *Good Americans*, 144.

87. David Ramsey, *History of the American Revolution* (Philadelphia, 1789), reprinted in *The American Revolution: Two Centuries of Interpretation*, ed. Edmund S. Morgan (Englewood Cliffs, NJ: Prentice-Hall, 1965), 18.

88. Maier, *Resistance to Revolution*, 137, 138.

89. Borden and Borden, *American Tory*, 75–6.

90. Herbert T. Wade and Robert A. Lively, *This Glorious Cause: The Adventures of Two Company Officers in Washington's Army* (Princeton, NJ: Princeton University Press, 1958), 210, 228.

91. Borden and Borden, *American Tory*, 89–90; Hancock, *Loyalists of Delaware*, 92. An account of a similar sentence in Maryland is given in North Callahan, *Royal Raiders: The Tories of the American Revolution* (Indianapolis and New York: Bobbs-Merrill, 1963), 239.

92. Countryman, *People in Revolution*, 148–49; Joseph S. Tiedemann, "Patriots by Default: Queens County, New York, and the British Army, 1776–1783," *William and Mary Quarterly*, 3rd series, 43 (1986): 36–7.

93. See chapter 3 above, "Where God Can We Fly from Danger?"

94. Tiedemann, "Patriots by Default," 38–9, 49.

95. Tiedemann, "Patriots by Default," 38–50.

96. Stanley K. Schultz, "The Growth of Urban America in War and Peace, 1740–1810," in William M. Fowler, Jr., and Wallace Coyle, eds., *The American Revolution: Changing Perspectives* (Boston: Northeastern University Press, 1979), 130.

97. Weir, "Violent Spirit," 92–4.

98. Pancake, *This Destructive War*, 82.

99. Crary, *Price of Loyalty*, 150–2; Kammen, "The American Revolution as a *Crise de Conscience*. 188. Townsend was soon freed by the council of safety. Perhaps they believed his excuse of intoxication, perhaps they sympathized with his statement that he was of "indigent circumstances" and had to support his wife, their two children, and his "helpless mother," or perhaps they felt he had already served his term by the time his petition was addressed.

100. The full treaty is reprinted in Jack Greene, ed., *Colonies to Nation, 1763–1789: A Documentary History of the American Revolution* (New York: W. W. Norton, 1975), 418–22.

101. Jean F. Hankins, "Connecticut's Sandemanians: Loyalism as a Religious Test," in Robert M. Calhoon, Timothy M. Barnes, and George A Rawlyk, eds., *Loyalists and Community in North America* (Westport, CT: Greenwood Press, 1994), 35.

102. Crary, *Price of Loyalty*, 376–9.

103. Crary, *Price of Loyalty*, 364.

104. Gordon S. Wood, *The Radicalism of the American Revolution* (New York: Vintage, 1993), 176; Brown, *Good Americans*, 192, 227.

105. Lambert, *South Carolina Loyalists*, 260. Many of the refugees in East Florida, according to Governor Tonyn, were poor farmers from the backcountry. [Kenneth Coleman, *The American Revolution in Georgia, 1763–1789* (Athens: University of Georgia Press, 1958), 145.]

106. Brown, *Good Americans*, 204.

107. Brown, *Good Americans*, 205.

108. Brown, *Good Americans*, 202; Van Tyne, *Loyalists*, 292–3.

109. Crary, *Price of Loyalty*, 404.

110. Van Tyne, *Loyalists*, 294, 300.

111. Van Tyne, *Loyalists*, 293–4; Neil MacKinnon, "The Nova Scotia Loyalists: A Traumatic Community," in Calhoon et al., *Loyalists and Community*, 221.

112. Donald Wetmore, "William Schurman of Bedeque, Prince Edward Island," in Phyllis R. Blakeley and John N. Grant, eds., *Eleven Exiles: Accounts of Loyalists of the American Revolution* (Toronto: Dundurn Press, 1982), 169–94.

113. Brown, *Good Americans*, 140–1.

114. Brown, *Good Americans*, 206–7.

115. Borden and Borden, *American Tory*, 92; Brown, *Good Americans*, 175–6.

116. Crary, *Price of Loyalty*, 369.
117. Crary, *Price of Loyalty*, 370.
118. Crary, *Price of Loyalty*, 370.
119. Brown, *Good Americans*, 176.
120. Hankins, "Connecticut's Sandemanians," 37; Brown, *Good Americans*, 177.
121. Robert M. Weir, " 'The Violent Spirit,' the Reestablishment of Order, and the Continuity of Leadership in Post-Revolutionary South Carolina," in Hoffman et al., *Uncivil War*, 87, 89–90, 98; Brown, *Strain of Violence*, 81.
122. Weir, "Violent Spirit," 80.
123. Sabine, *Biographical Sketches of Loyalists*, 1: 263.
124. Cited in Butler, *Narrative of David Fanning*, 103.
125. See above, "Dogs of Civil War."
126. Crary, *Price of Loyalty*, 419; Wallace, *Good Americans*, 203.
127. Crary, *Price of Loyalty*, 441–444.
128. Brown, *Good Americans*, 179; Sabine, *Biographical Sketches of Loyalists*, 601–602.

5 Native Americans

1. Charles A. Jellison, *Ethan Allen: Frontier Rebel* (Syracuse, NY: Syracuse University Press, 1983), 137.
2. "Journal of Dr. Isaac Senter," in Kenneth Roberts, ed., *March to Quebec: Journals of the Members of Arnold's Expedition* (Garden City, NY: Doubleday, 1947), 220–1.
3. Colin G. Calloway, *The Western Abenakis of Vermont, 1600–1800: War, Migration, and the Survival of an Indian People* (Norman: University of Oklahoma Press, 1990), 214–15.
4. Colin G. Calloway, ed., *Dawnland Encounters: Indians and Europeans in Northern New England* (Hanover, NH: University Press of New England, 1991), 172.
5. Some historians think that Abenakis also marched with Burgoyne in 1777 and raided the Champlain Valley and the town of Royalton in 1780 on behalf of the British, but others find no concrete evidence that Western Abenakis were among the Indians participating in these actions. See Gordon M. Day, *The Identity of the Saint Francis Indians* (Ottawa: National Museum of Man, 1981), 55.
6. The same held true for other Native Americans from New England, people who had long since been forced to abandon traditional ways of making a living. Virtually all the male Naticks of eastern Massachusetts, only a few miles from Boston, joined the army once the opportunity presented itself. In 1806 a handful of Natick survivors petitioned the general court of Massachusetts: "almost all that were able did go into the Service of the United States and either died in the service or soon after their return home. We your petitioners are their widows, there not being one male left now that was then of age to go to war." [Daniel R. Mandell, *Behind the Frontier: Indians in Eighteenth-Century Eastern Massachusetts* (Lincoln: University of Nebraska

Press, 1996), 167.] In 1776 Gideon Hawley, a missionary working among the Mashpee in southeastern Massachusetts, wrote: "what can they do but list with the army!" [Mandell, *Behind the Frontier*, 181.]

7. Calloway, *Dawnland Encounters*, 173; *Western Abenakis*, 214, 215, 208.

8. Calloway, *Western Abenakis*, 208, 217–18.

9. Calloway, *Western Abenakis*, 202.

10. Colin G. Calloway, *The American Revolution in Indian Country: Crisis and Diversity in Native American Communities* (Cambridge and New York: Cambridge University Press, 1995), 66.

11. Calloway, *American Revolution in Indian Country*, 83.

12. Day, *Identity of Saint Francis Indians*, 54.

13. Day, *Identity of Saint Francis Indians*, 54; Calloway, *American Revolution in Indian Country*, 79.

14. Calloway, *Dawnland Encounters*, 243.

15. Calloway, *Western Abenakis*, 213. One could easily argue that Indian chiefs like Gill do not conform to the definition of "common people" set forth in the introduction, since they exercised some form of power and enjoyed prestige among their people. Techinically this is true, yet in our study of the history of Native Americans we have no choice but to include the stories of chiefs and famous warriors. Theirs were the only words recorded; they are virtually the only personalities whose histories have been preserved. That is why I include their stories in this book, although I do not mean to imply that their experieces are representative of all Native Americans.

16. Calloway, *American Revolution in Indian Country*, 77.

17. Calloway, *Western Abenakis*, 219.

18. John C. Hudden, "The White Chief of the St. Francis Abnakis," *Vermont History*, 24 (1956): 343–5; Calloway, *American Revolution in Indian Country*, 76–8.

19. Calloway, *Western Abenakis*, 228, 230; Day, *Identity of Saint Francis Indians*, 56.

20. William A. Haviland and Marjory W. Power, *The Original Vermonters: Native Inhabitants, Past and Present* (Hanover, NH: University Press of New England, 1981), 246.

21. Calloway, *Western Abenakis*, 230, 233.

22. Barbara Graymont, *The Iroquois in the American Revolution* (Syracuse, NY: Syracuse University Press, 1972), 45.

23. Throughout the Revolutionary War, frontier rebels tried to tap into the ferocity, real or imagined, of the Indians. Daniel Brodhead had his men donned war paint, while George Rogers Clark encouraged the imitation of Indian war dances. Once, when trying to inspire his troops to cross a dangerous river, Clark reported he "suddenly took some water in my hand, poured powder over it, blacked my face, gave the war whoop, and marched into the water without saying a word. The party gasped and fell in one after another like a flock of sheep." [Richard M. Dorson, ed., *America Rebels: Narratives of the Patriots* (Westport, CT: Greenwood Press, 1953), 243, 247.]

24. Graymont, *Iroquois in the American Revolution*, 48, 50.

25. Graymont, *Iroquois in the American Revolution*, 72.

26. Anthony F. C. Wallace, *The Death and Rebirth of the Seneca* (New York: Alfred

A. Knopf, 1970), 127. Several Oneidas, meanwhile, were proclaiming their neutrality to Governor John Turnbull of Connecticut in similar terms: "We cannot intermeddle in this dispute between two brothers. The quarrel seems to be unnatural. You are *two brothers of one blood*. We are unwilling to join on either side in such a contest, for we bear an equal affection to both you Old and New England. Should the great king of England apply to us for aid, we shall deny him; if the Colonies apply, we shall refuse." [Colin G. Calloway, ed., *The World Turned Upside Down: Indian Voices from Early America* (Boston: St. Martin's Press, 1994), 149.]

27. Graymont, *Iroquois in the American Revolution*, 106. Joseph Bloomfield, a captain in the New Jersey line of the Continental Army, gave a detailed description of the Iroquois at the German Flats council. [Mark E. Lender and James K. Martin, eds., *Citizen Soldier: The Revolutionary War Journal of Joseph Bloomfield* (Newark: New Jersey Historical Society, 1982), 81–6.]

28. Graymont, *Iroquois in the American Revolution*, 97–8.

29. James E. Seaver, ed., *A Narrative of the Life of Mary Jemison* (Norman: University of Oklahoma Press, 1992), 98–9. The text, originally published in 1824 and reprinted numerous times, was transcribed from Jemison's oral telling of her life story when she was eighty years old. Although Jemison herself had adopted the customs and outlook of the Senecas, her story was not transcribed verbatim, as indicated by occasional lapses into the third person and a style more akin to the written than the spoken word. Even so, many of the events she describes can be verified by other sources, and some of the descriptions and insights reveal a decidedly Native American perspective. At first a captive, Jemison remained with the Iroquois by choice and referred to them often as "our people."

30. Seaver, *Mary Jemison*, 99.

31. Thomas S. Abler, ed., *Chainbreaker: The Revolutionary War Memoirs of Governor Blacksnake, as told to Benjamin Williams* (Lincoln: University of Nebraska Press, 1989). In 1777 Blacksnake was still known by his childhood name of Dahgayadoh, or "The Boys Betting." After he had established his reputation as a warrior, he was given a new name which translates into English as "Chainbreaker." In his later years he became known as Governor Blacksnake. Since the name Blacksnake was used both by Williams and the nineteenth-century historian Lyman Draper, who interviewed the venerable old man when he was well into his nineties, and since that is the name found in historical citations, I will follow tradition and use that name here.

32. Abler, *Chainbreaker*, 71, 72–3.

33. Abler, *Chainbreaker*, 74. Barbara Graymont is puzzled by this passage, since Brant was known to be elsewhere during the conference at Irondequoit, which she believes Blacksnake to be describing. [*Iroquois in the American Revolution*, 121–2, 126–7.] Thomas Abler counters by suggesting that Blacksnake is discussing a different conference at Oswego, at which Brant was present. [*Chainbreaker*, 65–9.]

34. Abler, *Chainbreaker*, 75–8.

35. For a vivid account of a 1777 council between United States Commissioners

and the friendly Iroquois, see James Thacher, *A Military Journal of the American Revolutionary War* (Boston, 1827), 114–15, reprinted in Colin G. Calloway, ed., *Revolution and Confederation* (Bethesda, MD: University Publications of American, 1994), 58–9.

36. Seaver, *Mary Jemison*, 100.

37. Abler, *Chainbreaker*, 128–30

38. Seaver, *Mary Jemison*, 100.

39. Graymont, *Iroquois in the American Revolution*, 190.

40. Abler, *Chainbreaker*, 136.

41. Abler, *Chainbreaker*, 131, 137. At one point, Blacksnake did profess to Draper that he had killed ten men in the Revolution, but since his narrative states dramatically at two different points that he could not remember how many he killed, it seems possible that Blacksnake was responding to the probing questions of Draper, filling in the gaps of his memory in order to provide the required answers. [Abler, *Chainbreaker*, 99.]

42. Graymont, *Iroquois in the American Revolution*, 167.

43. James H. Merrell, "Declarations of Independence: Indian-White Relations in the New Nation," in Jack P. Greene, ed., *The American Revolution: Its Character and Limits* (New York: New York University Press, 1987), 198.

44. Graymont, *Iroquois in the American Revolution*, 212.

45. Graymont, *Iroquois in the American Revolution*, 213.

46. Frederick Cook, ed., *Journals of the Military Expedition of Major General John Sullivan against the Six Nations of Indians in 1779* (Auburn, NY: Knapp, Peck, and Thomson, 1887), 90–1.

47. Cook, *Journals of Sullivan*, 112–13. Additional accounts of the destruction of food can be found on pages 70–7 (Henry Dearborn) and 172–5 (John Jenkins). For a recent analysis of the Sullivan campaign, see Joseph R. Fischer, *A Well-Executed Failure: The Sullivan Campaign against the Iroquois, July–September 1779* (Columbia: University of South Carolina Press, 1997).

48. Cook, *Journals of Sullivan*, 303. Some people of the times still refered to the Iroquois Confederacy as the Five Nations rather than the Six Nations, apparently ignoring the relatively recent addition of the Tuscaroras.

49. Seaver, *Mary Jemison*, 104–5.

50. Major Jeremiah Fogg, in Cook, *Journals of Sullivan*, 101.

51. Although British agents tried to minimize their costs at Niagara by providing only minimal rations, they did pander to the chiefs, whom they assumed would keep their people in line. Historian Colin Calloway notes that gifts to important figures included "real Gold and Silver Lace" to "the principal people of the Mohawks," "a fine blue Coat, trimmed with Gold-lace, and a gold-embroidered Waist Coat" for the Seneca chief Sayengeraghta, a scarlet coat with gold epaulets to his son, "a few Silver Works and Cloathing" to Cornplanter's daughter, "a Scarlet Coat & Waistcoat" to a Cahuga chief, "a Rich Brocade Waistcoat to Seyanderacta," and "a Ruffled Shirt & Feathers to Christian, an Oneida." [Calloway, *American Revolution in Indian Country*, 143–6.]

52. Graymont, *Iroquois in the American Revolution*, 240.

53. Graymont, *Iroquois in the American Revolution*, 232. This phrase comes from a

speech delivered by Kayashuta during a 1780 council at Niagara: "Brothers! This is the Flesh of a Virginian, taken by your Brothers the Shawnese and Delawares of Sciota, which they have sent to you to replace your Chief Sekanade, that he may be once more amongst you."

54. Cook, *Journals of Sullivan*, 8.

55. Cook, *Journals of Sullivan*, 112. General Sullivan offered a similar discription: "It appeared that they had whipped him in the most cruel manner, pulled out Mr. Boid's nails, cut off his nose, plucked out one of his eyes, cut out his tongue, stabbed him with spears in sundry places, and inflicted other tortures which decency will not permit me to mention; lastly, cut off his head, and left his body on the ground with that of his unfortunate companion, who appeared to have experienced nearly the same savage barbarity" [301].

56. Abler, *Chainbreaker*, 163–4.

57. Graymont, *Iroquois in the American Revolution*, 260.

58. Graymont, *Iroquois in the American Revolution*, 280.

59. Peter Marshall, "First Americans and Last Royalists: An Indian Dilemma in War and Peace," in Esmond Wright, ed., *Red, White and True Blue: the Loyalists in the Revolution* (New York: AMS Press, 1976), 49; Graymont, *Iroquois in the American Revolution*, 281–2.

60. Abler, *Chainbreaker*, 170.

61. Merrell, "Declarations of Independence," 210.

62. Calloway offers a full discussion of the civil war at Oquaga in *American Revolution in Indian Country*, 108–28.

63. Seaver, *Mary Jemison*, 107.

64. Seaver, *Mary Jemison*, 102–3.

65. C. A. Weslager, *The Delaware Indians: A History* (New Brunswick, NJ: Rutgers University Press, 1972), 37.

66. Reuben G. Thwaites and Louise P. Kellogg, eds., *The Revolution on the Upper Ohio, 1775–1777* (Madison: Wisconsin Historical Society, 1908), 73–4.

67. Thwaites and Kellogg, *Revolution on Upper Ohio*, 83, 94–7.

68. Thwaites and Kellogg, *Revolution on Upper Ohio*, 99–100, 103, 109–10. We have no way of knowing whether this reference to Jesus on the cross was made in sincerity or to please the whites—or perhaps it was an embellishment by the translator. In any case, its function was the same: to reinforce the promise of peace.

69. See Randolph C. Downes, *Council Fires on the Upper Ohio: A Narrative of Indian Affairs in the Upper Ohio Valley until 1795* (Pittsburgh: University of Pittsburgh Press, 1968), 162–4.

70. Thwaites and Kellogg, *Revolution on Upper Ohio*, 14–15.

71. Downes, *Council Fires*, 199–200.

72. Downes, *Council Fires*, 200; Gregory E. Dowd, *A Spirited Resistance: The North American Indian Struggle for Unity, 1745–1815* (Baltimore: John Hopkins University Press, 1992), 75. Morgan, who had traded with the Indians for years, was particularly close with the Delaware, helping White Eyes write some of his speeches. See Max Savelle, *George Morgan: Colony Builder* (New York: Columbia University Press, 1932), 135.

73. Thwaites and Kellogg, *Revolution on Upper Ohio*, 244, 247.

74. Downes, *Council Fires*, 205.

75. In March of 1778 Morgan was fully exonerated. He continued to serve as an Indian agent until 1779, when he resigned because of the aggressive policies pursued by the military command. For a summary of Morgan's arrest and subsequent acquittal, see Savelle, *George Morgan*, 148–51.

76. Reuben G. Thwaites and Louise P. Kellogg, eds., *Frontier Defense on the Upper Ohio, 1777–1778* (Madison: Wisconsin Historical Society, 1912), 126.

77. Thwaites and Kellogg, *Frontier Defense*, 159–60. Stuart reasoned that Cornstalk was friendly because "nothing would have induced him to make the visit to the garrison at that critical time, but to communicate the temper and disposition of the Indians, and their design of taking part with the British." Upon his arrival at the fort, Cornstalk had "made no secret of the disposition of the Indians declaring that he was opposed to joining the war on the side of the British, but that all the rest of the nation but himself and his wife were determined to engage in it; and of course he should have to run with the stream." [*Frontier Defense*, 157.] After the murder, General Hand admitted that "Cornstalk appeared to be the most active of his nation to promote the peace." [*Frontier Defense*, 176.]

78. Calloway, *American Revolution in Indian Country*, 172.

79. Downes, *Council Fires*, 209; Louise P. Kellogg, ed., *Frontier Advance on the Upper Ohio, 1778–1779* (Madison: State Historical Society of Wisconsin, 1916), 100.

80. Downes, *Council Fires*, 211.

81. Colin G. Calloway, ed., *Revolution and Confederation* (Bethesda, MD: University Publications of America, 1994), 155–6.

82. Weslager, *Delaware Indians*, 305. The full text of the treaty is reprinted in Calloway, *World Turned Upside Down*, 190–3.

83. Weslager, *Delaware Indians*, 301; Downes, *Council Fires*, 185. Some scholars have recently questioned the extent to which the Iroquois dominated the Delaware militarily. Although the Delaware were called women, Delaware tradition holds that the term was used to refer to peacemakers, not people who are weaker. According to Francis Jennings, "Now archaeologists find that tribes on the north and south of the Delawares lived in concentrated fortified villages, always prepared for war, but that the Delawares themselves lived dispersed, without fortifications. Obviously from such evidence, they were spared the fear of war, a finding that perfectly supports their own version of what 'women' status meant." [Robert S. Grumet, *Historic Contact: Indian People and Colonists in Today's Northeastern United States in the Sixteenth through Eighteenth Centuries* (Norman: Oklahoma University Press, 1995), xxii. See also pp. 232, 237.] Even if the Delaware had been peacemakers rather than a subdued people during earlier times, the fact that the Iroquois had successfully given away Delaware land in 1768 indicates that in the years preceding the Revolution, the Delaware had plenty of reasons to resent the treatment they received from their powerful neighbors. White Eyes certainly had good reason to feel he had

been emasculated, and an understandable desire to turn things around. Perhaps the Delaware were not subservient to the Iroqoius at the point of European contact, but the fact that Europeans recognized Iroquois dominance made it come true.

84. Kellogg, *Frontier Advance*, 203; Weslager, *Delaware Indians*, 304–5; Downes, *Council Fires*, 216–17. Killbuck elaborated: "The Tomhawk was handed to me at Fort Pitt but not in a Warlike manner, we all standing & at no Council Fire, neither did I understand the meaning of it. I neither desired any Implements of War, all what I agreed to was to pilot the Army 'till beyond our bounds, & my great Capt White Eyes with several others to go before the Army & convey them to the Enemy in order to be of use to both Parties, in case they should desire to speak or treat with one another." Eight months after the signing of the treaty, Killbuck and seven others issued an official complaint to Congress and General Washington: "That in the year 1778 Genaral McInosh and the Commissioners of Congress put a War Belt and Tomhawk into the Hands of the said Delaware Nation and induced some of their Chiefs to sign certain Writings, which to them were perfectly unintelligible and which they have since found were falsely interpreted to them and contained Declarations and Engagements they never intended to make or enter into. The said Delaware Nation have since returned the said Tomhawk and Belt into the Hands of the Agent for the United States and desired him to bury them as they have created great cunfusion among us." [Calloway, *Revolution and Confederation*, 177–8.]

85. Weslager, *Delaware Indians*, 306. Upon his death, White Eyes' belongings were listed as

1 Breech Clout fully trim'd
1 Bundle of blue and Red Ferreting.
1 Paint Bag with some paint in it
1 Silver Medal Effigee of Geo. the 3d of Great Britain
1 Large bet Wampum 11 Rows
1 Quill Back'd Comb 1 pr. Scissars 3 yards Gartering
1 Printed Linen Jacket, 1 Bundle Sundry Papers
1 Pr Saddle bags
1 Green Coat fac'd with Red with an Apatch
1 old Do Do Cotawy 1 Crib & Bridle ["Do" stands for "ditto"]
1 P Old Buch Skin Leggons. 1 plain Scarlet Jacket new
1 Do Old, 1 p Scarlet Breeches. 1 P of Buck Skin do
1 Scarlet Silk Jacket Trim'd with Gold Lace
1 small Red Pocket Book with some papers & needles
1 Fur Cap 1 pair plated Buckles 3 p Shoes viz 1 new & 2 Old
1 Old blue Breech Clout 1 P of white Legons bound
1 Knife Case, & belt 1 Match Coat
1 New Saddle & Saddle Cloth 1 Beaver Hat 1 Rifle, pouch, & Horn
1 Broach & Ear Ring 1 pipe Tomahawk 1 P Knee buckles
1 p Spectacles [Kellogg, *Frontier Advance*, 168.]

For a man of his time and place, whether white or Indian, he was quite well off. This was the kind of material prosperity, White Eyes must have conjectured, which the Americans could provide for his people.

86. Weslager, *Delaware Indians*, 310.

87. Weslager provides a followup to the education of these three young Delaware: "The two older lads were soon having trouble in the white man's world. Thomas Killbuck became addicted to 'Liquor & to Lying'; and, just as he was beginning to show an aptitude for geography, mathematics, and Latin, John Killbuck had an affair with one of Colonel Morgan's maids and became the father of her child. In 1785 Thomas and John returned to their people in Ohio, John bringing his wife and child with him. Meanwhile, George White Eyes progressed to Virgil and Greek and even won a prize at his grammar school commencement. But when he reached the college level he neglected his studies and sold his clothes, books, maps, and instruments to obtain money to return to Ohio." [*Delaware Indians*, 310–11.]

88. Kellogg, *Frontier Advance*, 254; Dowd, *Spirited Resistance*, 80.

89. Weslager, *Delaware Indians*, 313.

90. John Heckewelder to Daniel Brodhead, February 26, 1781, in Louise P. Kellogg, ed., *Frontier Retreat on the Upper Ohio, 1779–1781* (Madison: Wisconsin Historical Society, 1917), 338.

91. Kellogg, *Frontier Retreat*, 356–7.

92. Kellogg, *Frontier Retreat*, 376–80.

93. Eugene F. Bliss, trans. and ed., *Diary of David Zeisberger, a Moravian Missionary among the Indians of Ohio* (Cincinnati: Historical and Philosophical Society of Ohio, 1885), 1: 4.

94. From the Sandusky the missionaries were summoned to Detroit to face charges of treason. In fact, the missionaries had communicated frequently with Fort Pitt. Because of their connection to the central Moravian church in Bethlehem, Pennsylvania, they were forced to maintain relations with the American authorites. (See chapter 4, "Tests of Faith.") Nevertheless, the missionaries managed to convince British officials that their interests were spiritual rather than political, and the charges against them were dismissed.

95. The Christian Indians had in fact given food to the enemy—but they had also fed the Americans. While trying to remain neutral, these pacifists had little choice but to yield to any warring people who entered their settleements.

96. Zeisberger, *Diary*, 1: 79–81.

97. The soldiers had collected the people they found at Salem and moved them to Gnadenhutten. Those at Schoenbrunn fled toward Sandusky after being told that the others had been captured.

98. Zeisberger, *Diary*, 1: 86. For more on Zeisberger and the Moravian mission, see Earl P. Olmstead, *Blackcoats among the Delaware: David Zeisberger on the Ohio Frontier* (Kent, OH: Kent State University Press, 1991) and Earl P. Olmstead, *David Zeisberger: A Life among the Indians* (Kent, OH: Kent State University Press, 1997).

99. It was certainly too narrow for all the Moravians, as described in chapter 4, and especially narrow for Killbuck. In 1788 Killbuck arrived at Zeisberger's

new mission in Canada, "very meek and outwardly very poor," asking to be accepted into the church. Despite being commissioned as an officer (he was called Captain William Henry) things had never worked out for Killbuck in the white community of western Pennsylvania. According to Zeisberger, "in Pittsburg, where he retired during the war, he was often no day sure of his life, on account of the militia; when then he thought of going to us over the lake, he knew not how to come because of the Indians, who likewise wished his life." [*Diary*, 1: 420.] Years after the war had ended, this new convert could still find no peace—even in a Christian mission. Rejected first by his own people and then by the whites at Pittsburg, Killbuck now found himself living amongst the friends and relatives of victims who had succumbed to his former friends, the Big Knives. His new neighbors did not easily forgive Captain William Henry, who lived in fear of retaliation for the remainder of his days. Killbuck, White Eyes, Cornstalk—they all learned in the end that befriending the victors did not guarantee power, a share in the spoils, or even a taste of the elusive "liberty" which had inspired men to kill. The strange logic of the Revolutionary War was not that simple.

100. Henry Stuart to John Stuart, August 25, 1776, in K. G. Davies, ed., *Documents of the American Revolution 1770–1783* (Dublin: Irish University Press, 1976), 12: 197. With the usual land route cut off by patriots, Stuart had to sail around Florida and land at Mobile.

101. Davies, *Documents of the American Revolution*, 12: 192. The chiefs later claimed they had been tricked into signing the Sycamore Shoals Treaty without a clear understanding of its terms, and the American courts invalidated the agreement because it had been made by private parties, not the government. Most of the white settlers who had moved into the disputed area, however, simply remained where they were, even without valid claims.

102. Davies, *Documents of the American Revolution*, 12: 198, 200.

103. Davies, *Documents of the American Revolution*, 12: 199–200.

104. Davies, *Documents of the American Revolution*, 12: 199, 202–3.

105. Other contemporary observers of various Native American peoples commented on the hiding of weapons. See, for example, John F. D. Smyth, *A Tour in the United States of America* (New York: Arno Press, 1968; originally published in 1784), 188–9; "Tatham's Characters among the North American Indians," in Samuel C. Williams, *Tennessee during the Revolutionary War* (Knoxville: University of Tennessee Press, 1944), 269. Mary Jemison recalled that "knives, tomahawks, guns, and other instruments of war" were stashed away whenever Iroquois men drank liquor. [Seaver, *Mary Jemison*, 158–9.] Jemison noted further that before the Revolution "women never participated" in the drunken "frolics," but after the war "spirits became common in our tribe, and has been used indiscriminately by both sexes; though there are not so frequent instances of intoxication amongst the squaws as amongst the Indians." Jemison herself suffered personally from male drinking habits: her son John killed her son Thomas while intoxicated; later, John killed his other brother Jesse, also when drinking.

106. Tom Hatley, *The Dividing Paths: Cherokees and South Carolinians through the*

Era of Revolution (New York and Oxford: Oxford University Press, 1993), 220–1.

107. Norma Tucker, "Nancy Ward, Ghighau of the Cherokees," *Georgia Historical Quarterly*, 53 (1969); 193–4; John P. Brown, *Old Frontiers: The Story of the Cherokee Indians from Earliest Times to the Date of their Removal to the West, 1838* (Kingsport, TN: Southern Publishers, 1938), 195, 250; Grace S. Woodward, *The Cherokees* (Norman: University of Oklahoma Press, 1963), 91. One other speech from Nancy Ward survives, delivered at the Treaty of Hopewell in 1785. There, she told the Americans: "I am glad there is now peace. I take you by the hand in real friendship. I look upon you and the red people as my children. I have a pipe and a little tobacco to give to the commissioners to smoke in friendship. I have seen much trouble in the late war. I have borne and raised up warriors, I am now old, but hope yet to bear children who will grow up and people our Nation, as we are now under the protection of Congress and shall have no more disturbance." [Brown, *Old Frontiers*, 250.]

108. Williams, *Tennessee during the Revolutionary War*, 201.

109. Hatley, *Dividing Paths*, 193; Calloway, *American Revolution in Indian Country*, 197.

110. William Drayton to Francis Salvador, July 24, 1776, in R. W. Gibbes, ed., *Documentary History of the American Revolution* (New York: D. Appleton, 1857), 2: 29. Drayton continued: "For my part, I shall never give my voice for a peace with the Cherokee Nation upon any other terms than their removal beyond the mountains." This marked a dramatic turnaround in Drayton's relations with the Cherokee. The previous year, he had addressed the Cherokee chiefs: "Friends and Brother Warriors, I take you by the hand, in witness of the Peace and friend ship which has so long subsisted between your brothers the white people of this country and you and your People. . . . So shall we act to each other like Brothers—so shall we be able to support and assist each other against our common enemies." [Calloway, *Revolution and Confederation*, 206–7.] Hoping to cement their friendship, he had arranged to ship them some gunpowder. The powder, however, was seized by loyalists. Ironically, the loyalists gained many followers at that time by accusing the patriots of arming the Indians to raid frontier settlers. (See chapter 4, "Dogs of Civil War.")

111. Williamson to Drayton, August 22, 1776, in Gibbes, *Documentary History*, 2: 32.

112. Hatley, *Dividing Paths*, 219.

113. John Stuart to Lord George Germain, November 24, 1776, in Davies, *Documents of the American Revolution* 12: 253–4.

114. Hatley, *Dividing Paths*, 195.

115. J. G. de Roulhac Hamilton, ed., "Revolutionary Diary of William Lenoir," *Journal of Southern History*, 6 (1940): 255.

116. Hatley, *Dividing Paths*, 196.

117. Lenoir, "Diary," 256; Hatley, *Dividing Paths*, 201.

118. Rachel N. Klein, "Frontier Planters and the American Revolution: The South Carolina Backcountry, 1775–1782," in Ronald Hoffman, Thad W. Tate, and

Peter J. Albert, eds., *An Uncivil War: The Southern Backcountry during the American Revolution* (Charlottesvile: University Press of Virginia, 1985), 67; Hatley, *Dividing Paths*, 196.

119. Cited in Hatley, *Dividing Paths*, 199–200.

120. Hatley, *Dividing Paths*, 195.

121. Archibald Henderson, ed., "The Treaty of Long Island of Holston, July, 1777," *North Carolina Historical Review* 8 (1931): 76.

122. Henderson, "Treaty of Long Island," 87, 90–1, 94–5.

123. Henderson, "Treaty of Long Island," 98, 103, 102. When it came time to affix his mark to the Treaty of Long Island of Holston, Old Tassel balked, recalling his experience with the Transylvania Company at Sycamore Shoals. "Ever since I signed a paper for Col. Henderson I am afraid of signing papers," he stated. "He told me many lies and deceived us. He never showed me but one paper and I hear he has eight or nine" [110].

124. Henderson, "Treaty of Long Island," 111.

125. In the words of John Stuart, "The Cherokees are rather divided. A great number of them for the purpose of obtaining permission to return to their towns have patched up a peace with the rebels, while a far greater number of them have moved near one hundred miles lower down the river where they have built a large town and made considerable settlement, and although threatened by the rebels with destruction are not intimidated." [John Stuart to Lord George Germain, December 4, 1778, in Davies, *Documents of the American Revolution*, 15: 284–285.]

126. Brown, *Old Frontiers*, 199.

127. John Brown reports an incident which must have been paralled, with minor variations, many times: "Several frontiersmen tried their marksmanship on one who was endavoring to get away by lying low and propelling the canoe with one hand. It looked as though he would escape when Colonel Whitley said, 'Let me try.' At the discharge of his rifle, blood spurted from the arm of the warrior, but he continued to row. With tomahawk in his belt, Joseph Brown swam out to the canoe. The wounded Indian begged for his life, saying, 'I am a Cherokee,' meaning that he was not one of the hostile Chickamaugas. 'What are you doing at Nickajack?' asked Brown. 'To visit some friends,' he replied. Brown tomahawked him." [Brown, *Old Frontiers*, 426.]

128. James H. O'Donnell III, *Southern Indians in the American Revolution* (Knoxville: University of Tennessee Press, 1973), 109.

129. O'Donnell, *Southern Indians*, 106.

130. O'Donnell, *Southern Indians*, 117.

131. Brown, *Old Frontiers*, 176.

132. Calloway, *American Revolution in Indian Country*, 204.

133. O'Connell, *Southern Indians*, 119.

134. Calloway, *American Revolution in Indian Country*, 210.

135. In the words of anthropologist Fred Gearing, the schism between "amiable old men" and "violent young men" wreaked havoc on Cherokee culture: "The old men saw their priestly government crumble; the young men had

thrown the political structure away. Neither one found an adequate substitute." [Calloway, *American Revolution in Indian Country*, 201.]

136. James H. Merrell, *The Indians' New World: Catawbas and Their Neighbors from European Contact through the Era of Removal* (Chapel Hill: University of North Carolina Press, 1989), 211.

137. James H. Merrell, "Their Very Bones Shall Fight: The Catawba-Iroquois Wars," in Daniel K. Richter and James H. Merrell, eds., *Beyond the Covenant Chain: The Iroquois and Their Neighbors in Indian North America, 1600–1800* (Syracuse, NY: Syracuse University Press, 1987), 123.

138. John F. D. Smyth, *A Tour in the United States of America* (New York: Arno Press, 1968; originally published in 1784), 192, 194.

139. In September, the British Superintendent John Stuart admitted that he held no hope for convincing the Catawba to side with the Crown: since "they are domiciled and dispersed thro' the Settlements of north and South Carolina," he explained, "it is no wonder that they should be practised upon and seduced by the Inhabitants with whom they live." [Merrell, *Indians' New World*, 215.]

140. Douglas S. Brown, *The Catawba Indians: The People of the River* (Columbia: University of South Carolina Press, 1966), 261.

141. Brown, *Catawba Indians*, 271.

142. The Catawbas participated in the raids in anticipation of bounties. In 1787 South Carolina offered "a reward of Ten pounds sterling for each of said Negroes killed or taken," and early the following year state records show the payment of forty pounds to "Capt. Patton for scalps taken by Catawbas under his command." [Herbert Aptheker, *To Be Free: Studies in American Negro History* (New York: International Publishers, 1948), 13–14.]

143. Brown, *Catawba Indians*, 268–71, 276. One of the men on the paybill, Willis, was listed as "dec'd. Killed at Rocky Mount, (his wife and children alive)." Presumably, they were to receive his pay.

144. Merrell, *Indians' New World*, 218.

145. Merrell, *Indians' New World*, 218–20.

146. Brown, *Catawba Indians*, 279–80.

147. Merrell, *Indians' New World*, 222, 224. Chosing the winning side did not always have this benign effect. Although the Oneidas and Tuscaroras had sided with the patriots, their land was seized even faster than that of the other Iroquois nations in the aftermath of the war, while the "friendly" Stockbridge Indians, who had lost many men while fighting on behalf of the patriots, lost their land as well immediately following the Revolution. [See Calloway, *American Revolution in Indian Country*, 85–107.]

148. Merrell, *Indians' New World*, 229.

149. Merrell, *Indians' New World*, 224.

150. Charles M. Hudson, *The Catawba Nation* (Athens: University of Georgia Press, 1970), 63–6; Merrell, *Indians' New World*, 250–57.

151. Brown, *Catawba Indians*, 273–75.

152. Brown, *Catawba Indians*, 274–75. Merrell suggests that this petition was written with the help of Senator William Crafts. [*Indians' New World*, 218.]

Perhaps so, but the letter still demonstrates the power of referring to Revolutionary service.

153. Calloway, *American Revolution in Indian Country*, 219.

154. Davies, *Documents of the American Revolution*, 13: 169, 195; 15: 212.

155. Calloway, *American Revolution in Indian Country*, 216–7, 226.

156. Davies, *Documents of the American Revolution*, 12: 277.

157. Calloway, *American Revolution in Indian Country*, 228.

158. Davies, *Documents of the American Revolution*, 15: 188.

159. O'Donnell, *Southern Indians*, 63.

160. O'Donnell, *Southern Indians*, 70.

161. Davies, *Documents of the American Revolution*, 15: 183–4.

162. Davies, *Documents of the American Revolution*, 12: 241.

163. O'Donnell, *Southern Indians*, 63.

164. Davies, *Documents of the American Revolution*, 15: 155, 157–8.

165. The complete letter is reprinted in Calloway, *Revolution and Confederation*, 270–1. See also Arrell M. Gibson, *The Chickasaws* (Norman: University of Oklahoma Press, 1971), 75; Calloway, *American Revolution in Indian Country*, 231. The letter, drafted by an Englishmen named Simon Burney, was signed by Piomingo and three other Chickasaw leaders, but it was written in the singular: "this Comes from my Mouth Who is King of this Nation." The "King," presumably, was Piomingo.

166. Calloway, *Revolution and Confederation*, 276; Calloway, *American Revolution in Indian Country*, 232. See also Robert S. Cotterill, "The Virginia-Chickasaw Treaty of 1783," *Journal of Southern History* 8 (1942): 483–96.

167. Calloway, *American Revolution in Indian Country*, 230.

168. The full text is reprinted in Calloway, *World Turned Upside Down*, 164–6, and Calloway, *Revolution and Confederation*, 370–1. The letter continues, further expressing their confusion: "We are told that the Americans have 13 Councils Compos'd of Chiefs and Warriors. We Know not which of them we are to Listen to, or if we are to hear some, and Reject others, we are at a loss to Distinguish those we are to hear. We are told that you are the head Chief of the Grand Council, which is above these 13 Councils: if so why have we not had Talks from you,—We are head men and Chiefs and Warriors also: and have always been accustomed to speak with great Chiefs & warriors."

169. Divisions among the Creeks were accentuated by the fact that the so-called "Creeks" were not actually a nation, but simply a conglomeration of neighbors which included the Yamasee, Tuckabatchee, Hitchiti, Koasati, Alabama, Timucua, Natchez, Yuchi, some of the Shawnee, and many others. They did not speak the same language; they did not call themselves "the people." The term "Creek" was a catchall by Euro-Americans used to denote any southern Indians west of the Appalachias and east of the Mississippi who were neither Cherokee, Choctaw, nor Chickasaw. [J. Leitch Wright, Jr., *Creeks and Seminoles: The Destruction and Regeneration of the Muscogulge People* (Lincoln: University of Nebraska Press, 1986), 1–3.]

170. James H. Merril, "Delcarations of Independence," in Jack P. Greene, ed.,

The American Revolution: Its Character and Limits (New York: New York University Press, 1987), 200.

171. O'Donnell, *Southern Indians*, 15.

172. Martha C. Searcy, *The Georgia-Florida Contest in the American Revolution, 1776–1778* (University: University of Alabama, 1985), 29; David H. Corkran, *The Creek Frontier, 1540–1783* (Norman: University of Oklahoma Press, 1967), 297.

173. McGillivray to Miro, June 24, 1789, in John Walton Caughey, ed., *McGillivray of the Creeks* (Norman: University of Oklahoma Press, 1938), 240.

174. In 1791 Piomingo and fifty other Chickasaws actually fought for the United States army, which at the time was marching against the northern Indians. They were rewarded for their efforts with medals and "rich uniform clothes," while George Washington, by then president, proclaimed "how desirous he is of promoting the happiness of the Chickasaws." [Gibson, *Chickasaws*, 86.] Two years later, the pro-American Chickasaws tried to cash in on their support, requesting the aid of white settlers in their fight against the Creeks: "When you get this talk, speak strong to your young warriors, and let us join, to let the Creeks know *what war is.* You made whiskey; If war, it is good to take a little at war talks; please send me some." [Gibson, *Chickasaws*, 87]

175. Caughey, *McGillivray*, 30–1.

176. Caughey, *McGillivray*, 91–2.

177. Wright, *Creeks and Seminoles*, 117.

178. Wright, *Creeks and Seminoles*, 4.

179. Francis Harper, ed., *The Travels of William Bartram* (New Haven: Yale University Press, 1958), 119–23. (188–94 in the original 1791 edition, entitled *Travels through North & South Carolina, Georgia, East & West Florida.*)

180. Davies, *Documents of the American Revolution*, 14: 148.

181. Searcy, *Georgia-Florida Contest*, 29; Edward J. Cashin, *The King's Ranger: Thomas Brown and the American Revolution on the Southern Frontier* (Athens: University of Georgia Press, 1989), 61–2.

182. Davies, *Documents of the American Revolution*, 15: 34. When the Americans threatened a combined land and sea assault on Florida that summer, the British Governor Patrick Tonyn reported, "Soon after nigh five hundred Seminoly Indians advanced within a days march of the enemy. . . . Upon the first report of invasion the Seminoly Indians took into their charge the defence of St John's River from Black Creek upwards. These Indians, our neighbours, have upon this and every occasion shown their attachment to His Majesty and have given the fullest assurances that upon the slightest intimation they are ready to come to our assistance." [Davies, *Documents of the American Revolution*, 15: 168.]

183. Searcy, *Georgia-Florida Contest*, 113.

184. Wright, *Creeks and Seminoles*, 86.

6 African Americans

1. Woody Holton, " 'Rebel Against Rebel': Enslaved Virginians and the Coming of the American Revolution," *Virginia Magazine of History and Biography* 105 (1997): 168; Philip J. Schwarz, *Twice Condemned: Slaves and the Criminal Laws of Virginia, 1705–1865* (Baton Rouge: Louisiana State University Press, 1988), 184.

2. Edmund Pendleton to George Washington, April 21, 1775, in W. W. Abbot and Dorothy Twohig, eds., *Papers of George Washington* (Charlottesville: University Press of Virginia, 1983–), Colonial series, 10: 340.

3. Holton, "Rebel Against Rebel," 168.

4. Holton, "Rebel Against Rebel," 169.

5. Municipal Common Hall to Governor Dunmore, April 21, 1775, in William J. Van Schreeven, Robert L. Scribner, and Brent Tarter, eds., *Revolutionary Virginia: The Road to Independence, A Documentary Record* (Charlottesville: University Press of Virginia, 1973–83), 3: 55.

6. *South Carolina Gazette and Country Journal*, June 6, 1775, cited in Holton, "Rebel Against Rebel," 176; Peter H. Wood, " 'Taking Care of Business,' in Revolutionary South Carolina: Republicanism and the Slave Society," in Jeffrey J. Crow and Larry E. Tise, eds., *Southern Experience in the American Revolution* (Chapel Hill: University of North Carolina Press, 1978), 282.

7. Governor Dunmore to Municipal Common Hall: An Oral Reply, April 21, 1775, *Revolutionary Virginia*, Van Schreeven et al., eds., 3: 55; Governor Dunmore to Earl of Dartmouth, May 1, 1775, in K. G. Davies, ed., *Documents of the American Revolution* (Dublin: Irish University Press, 1975), 9: 108. For Dunmore's public defense of the powder seizure, see his "Proclamation" in *Virginia Gazette* (Pinkney), May 4, 1775: "I think proper to declare that the apprehensions which seemed to prevail throughout this whole country of an intended insurrection of the slaves, who had been seen in large numbers, in the night time, about the magazine, and my knowledge of its being a very insecure depository, were my inducements to that measure." Later, in a letter to the Earl of Dartmouth, he admitted he had removed the powder to prevent any attempt by the rebellious patriots to seize it themselves. [Davies, *Documents of the American Revolution*, 9: 108.]

8. *Revolutionary Virginia*, Van Schreeven et al., 3: 6.

9. For the number of slaves in 1774, see Thomas L. Purvis, *Almanacs of American Life: Revolutionary America, 1763 to 1800* (New York: Facts on File, 1995), 123, 126, 150, 161.

10. For a full discussion of *Sommersett v. Stuart*, see A. Leon Higginbotham, Jr., *In the Matter of Color: Race and the American Legal Process, the Colonial Period* (New York: Oxford University Press, 1978), 333–68. The *Sommersett* decision did not actually outlaw slavery in England; it held that slavery could not exist unless specifically prescribed by law. Since there were no laws in England itself (unlike the colonies) providing for the existence of slavery, the practical effect

was that as soon as a slave reached England, he or she was no longer obliged to remain in bondage. According to Mansfield; "So high an act of dominion [slavery] must be recognized by the law of the country where it is used. . . . The state of slavery is of such a nature, that it is incapable of being introduced on any reasons, moral or political, but only by positive law which preserves its force long after the reason, occasion, and time itself when it was created, is erased from memory. It is so odious that nothing can be suffered to support it, but positive law." [Higginbotham, *Matter of Color,* 354.]

11. Gerald W. Mullin, *Flight and Rebellion: Slave Resistance in Eighteenth-Century Virginia* (New York: Oxford University Press, 1972), 131. In November of 1774, according to James Madison, a gathering of slaves selected a leader "who was to conduct them when the English troops should arrive, which they foolishly thought would be very soon and that by revolting to them they should be rewarded with their freedom." [Sylvia R. Frey, *Water from the Rock: Black Resistance in a Revolutionary Age* (Princeton, NJ: Princeton University Press, 1991), 53.]

12. John Drayton, *Memoirs of the American Revolution* (Charleston, WV: A. F. Miller, 1821), 1: 231.

13. Ronald Hoffman, *A Spirit of Dissension: Economics, Politics, and the Revolution in Maryland* (Baltimore: John Hopkins University Press, 1973), 148.

14. *South Carolina Gazette,* May 29, 1775, cited in Robert Olwell, *Masters, Slaves, and Subjects: The Culture of Power in the South Carolina Low Country, 1740–1790* (Ithaca, NY: Cornell University Press, 1998, 229. Olwell suggests that the elliptical reference to "N*****s" instead of "Negroes" marked an attempt, however feeble, to keep this news from the slaves themselves. "Canadiens" refers to the French Acadians, over 1,000 in number, who were expelled from Nova Scotia and sent to South Carolina in 1756. At that time, as in 1775, whites worried that the Acadians might "join with the Negroes." [Robert A. Olwell, " 'Domestick Enemies': Slavery and Political Independence in South Carolina, May 1775–March 1776," *Journal of Southern History* 55 (1989): 26.]

15. John R. Alden, "John Stuart Accuses William Bell," *William and Mary Quarterly,* 3rd series, 2 (1945): 320.

16. Narrative of George Milligen, September 15, 1775, in Davies, *Documents of the American Revolution,* 11: 110.

17. Janet Schaw, *Journal of a Lady of Quality; Being the Narrative of a Journey from Scotland to the West Indies, North Carolina, and Portugal, in the years 1774 to 1776,* Evangeline Walker Andrews, ed. (New Haven: Yale University Press, 1922), 199–201.

18. John Stuart to Earl of Dartmouth, July 21, 1775, in Davies, *Documents of the American Revolution,* 11: 53.

19. Hoffman, *Spirit of Dissension,* 147.

20. Henry Laurens to John Laurens, May 15, 1775, *The Papers of Henry Laurens,* David R. Chestnutt and C. James Taylor, eds. (Columbia: University of South Carolina Press, 1968), 10: 118. The full text of this association is reprinted in Milligen's Narrative, Davies, *Documents of the American Revolution,* 11: 109–10.

21. Alden, "John Stuart Accuses William Bull," 318; Josiah Smith, quoted in Ol-
    well, *Masters, Slaves, and Subjects*, 238.
22. Holton, "Rebel Against Rebel," 173.
23. Proceedings of the Safety Committee in Pitt County, July 8, 1775, *The Colonial
    Records of North Carolina*, William L. Saunders, ed. (Raleigh, NC: Printer to
    the State, 1890; reprinted New York: AMS Press, 1968), 10: 87.
24. John Simpson to Richard Cogdell, July 15, 1775, *Colonial Records of North
    Carolina*, Saunders, ed., 10: 94–5. Paragraph separations added.
25. *Virginia Gazette* (Pinkney), July 20, 1775.
26. Schaw, *Journal of a Lady of Quality*, 199–201.
27. Thomas Hutchinson to Council of Safety, July 5, 1775, Chestnutt et al., *Papers
    of Henry Laurens*, 10: 205–7.
28. *Virginia Gazette* (Dixon and Hunter), January 6, 1776, cited in Rhys Isaac,
    "Dramatizing the Ideology of Revolution: Popular Mobilization in Virginia,
    1774 to 1776," *William and Mary Quarterly*, 3rd series, 33 (1976): 357. Isaac
    observes: "We do not know whether the cry was drawn forth primarily by
    relief at the mercy shown by the court, or pain at the impress of the hot iron,
    or whether a different exclamation on the part of the slave was distorted by
    nervous slaveowners into the form reported. . . . Masters were understandably
    anxious to believe that their slaves were faithful to them, sharing their hatred
    of the governor." True, we have no way of choosing between these varying
    explanations of the brief report in the *Virginia Gazette*, but in each of these
    scenarios, the slave conveyed the impression of favoring the patriots, which of
    course is what they wanted to hear.
29. Deposition of George Gray, September 4, 1775, Van Schreeven, *Revolutionary
    Virginia*, 4: 70; Holton, "Rebel Against Rebel," 158.
30. John Page to Thomas Jefferson, November 11, 1775, *The Papers of Thomas
    Jefferson*, Julian P. Boyd, Lyman H. Butterfield, and Mina R. Bryan, eds.
    (Princeton, NJ: Princeton University Press, 1950), 1: 257.
31. Holton, "Rebel Against Rebel," 158. One of the wounded was a painter be-
    longing to George Washington, either a slave or an indentured servant who
    had escaped to Dunmore the previous summer. Lund Washington, George
    Washington's manager at Mount Vernon, revealed the anger and frustration
    of white patriots when he wrote: "I suppose there is very little Chance of getg
    the painter from Lord Dunmore, if he comes up here and indeavors to Land
    at mt Vernon Raising the rest, I will shoot him, that will be some Satisfaction."
    [Lund Washington to George Washington, November 5, 1775, Abbot and
    Twohig, *Papers of George Washington*, Revolutionary War Series, 2: 306.]
32. Henry Laurens to John Laurens, June 18, 1775, Chestnutt et al., *Papers of
    Henry Laurens*, 10: 184.
33. William Campbell to Earl of Dartmouth, August 31, 1775, Davies, *Documents
    of the American Revolution*, XI: 95.
34. Campbell to Dartmouth, August 31, 1775, and Narrative of George Milligen,
    September 15, 1775, Davies, *Documents of the American Revolution*, 11: 95 and
    12: 111.
35. Milligen, "Narrative," 110, 111.

36. Campbell to Dartmouth, August 31, 1775, Davies, *Documents of the American Revolution*, 11: 96.

37. Henry Laurens to John Laurens, June 23 and August 20, 1775, Chestnutt et al., *Papers of Henry Laurens*, 10: 191 and 10: 321.

38. Henry Laurens to John Laurens, August, 20, 1775, Chestnutt et al., *Papers of Henry Laurens*, 10: 321.

39. Campbell to Dartmouth, Davies, *Documents of the American Revolution*, XI: 96–7.

40. Campbell to Dartmouth, Davies, *Documents of the American Revolution*, XI: 95.

41. Henry Laurens to John Laurens, August, 20, 1775, Chestnutt et al., *Papers of Henry Laurens*, 10: 321–2.

42. Facsimile of original broadside from Tracy W. McGregor Library, University of Virginia, in Holton, "Rebel Against Rebel," 183. Dunmore had actually drafted his proclamation one week earlier on November 7, but he waited until his forces prevailed in a skirmish at Kemp's Landing before publishing it. In that skirmish Joseph Hutchings, a commanding rebel officer, was captured by one of his former slaves who had escaped to Dunmore's service. [John E. Selby, *Revolution in Virginia, 1775–1783* (Williamsburg: Colonial Williamsburg Foundation, 1988), 64; Benjamin Quarles, "Lord Dunmore as Liberator," *William and Mary Quarterly*, 3rd series, 15 (1958): 502; Holton, "Rebel Against Rebel," 182.]

43. Quarles, "Dunmore as Liberator," 494.

44. Frey, *Water from the Rock*, 63.

45. Washington to Lee, December 26, 1775, Abbot and Twohig, *Writings of George Washington*, Revolutionary War series, 2: 611.

46. By examining lists of former slaves from Philadelphia who departed for Nova Scotia with the British in 1783, Gary Nash found that virtually all were in the prime of life and single, and two-thirds were male. Conversely, of those who remained behind in Philadelphia, only one-third were between the ages of seventeen and fourty-four, and Nash conjectures that many of these were probably married with children. The implications of these sets of numbers are significant: those who could leave did, while those too young, too old, or too encumbered stayed where they were. [Gary B. Nash, *Forging Freedom: The Formation of Philadelphia's Black Community, 1720–1840* (Cambridge: Harvard University Press, 1988), 57–8.]

47. Lund Washington to George Washington, Dec. 3, 1775, Abbot and Twohig, *Papers of George Washington*, Revolutionary War series, 2: 480. From the context of the letter, it seems that Lund was actually referring to "white Servts" in this passage, but if the servants escaped, he feared, the slaves might follow.

48. Originally published in the *Pennsylvania Evening Post*, December 14, 1775. Cited in Gary B. Nash and Jean R. Soderlund, *Freedom By Degrees: Emancipation in Pennsylvania and Its Aftermath* (New York: Oxford University Press, 1991), 77; Peter H. Wood, " 'The Dream Deferred': Black Struggles on the Eve of White Independence," in Gary Y. Okihiro, ed., *In Resistance: Studies in African, Caribbean, and Afro-American History* (Amherst: University of Massachusetts Press, 1986), 177–8. Although Benjamin Quarles wonders whether

this story is fact or fiction [*The Negro in the American Revolution* (Chapel Hill: University of North Carolina Press, 1961), 31], there is no doubt that many blacks responded differently to whites after the proclamation had raised their hopes, while whites felt threatened by tales such as these, whether real or fabricated.

49. Hoffman, *Spirit of Dissension*, 148.
50. Mullin, *Flight and Rebellion*, 134.
51. Holton, "Rebel Against Rebel," 185, 187.
52. *Virginia Gazette* (Pinkney), November 23, 1775; *Virginia Gazette* (Purdie), November 17, 1775; *Virginia Gazette* (Dixon and Hunter), November 25, 1775. Reprinted in Van Schreeven et al., *Revolutionary Virginia*, 4: 459–62. It is true that many Virginia politicians opposed the slave trade, but not for humanitarian reasons. Virginia itself already had as many slaves as it could use, and the presence of more both threatened social instabilility and lowered the price of slaves on the market. White Virginians, some of whom, like Thomas Jefferson, profited handsomely by breeding slaves for sale, tended to oppose the importation of slaves for the same reason domestic suppliers of any product or commodity oppose importation: to restrict competition from foreign sources.
53. Henry Laurens to James Laurens, June 7, 1775, Chestnutt et al., *Papers of Henry Laurens*, 10: 162–3.
54. Ellen Gibson Wilson, *The Loyal Blacks* (New York: G. P. Putnam's Sons, 1976), 26–7.
55. Henry Laurens to John Laurens, August 14, 1776, Chestnutt et al., *Papers of Henry Laurens*, 11: 223, footnote on 224.
56. Quarles, "Dunmore as Liberator," 501; Quarles, *Negro in the American Revolution*, 26. Although these numbers constitute but a small percentage of Virginia's slave population, they must be seen in the context of the extreme dangers and difficulties in making the escape, as discussed below.
57. John Page to Thomas Jefferson, November 24, 1775, Boyd et al., *Papers of Thomas Jefferson*, 1:265; Quarles, "Dunmore as Liberator," 498, 501.
58. *Virginia Gazette* (Pinkney), November 30, 1775, cited in Wood, "Dream Deferred," 178.
59. *Maryland Gazette*, December 14, 1775, cited in Wood, "Dream Deferred," 185.
60. L. H. Butterfield, ed., *Diary and Autobiography of John Adams* (Cambridge: Belknap Press, 1961), 2: 182–3.
61. *Virginia Gazette* (Purdie), November 17, 1775, cited in Mullin, *Flight and Rebellion*, 133.
62. Such ads appeared not only in Virginia and other southern states but in Pennsylvania as well. Mark Bird, for instance, advertised for a runaway named Cuff Dix: "He has often run away, changed his name, denied that the subscriber was his master, and been confined in several goals in this province. . . . As Negroes in general think that Lord Dunmore is contending for their liberty, it is not improbably that said Negroe is on his march to join his Lordship's own black regiment." [Billy G. Smith and Richard Wojtowicz, *Blacks Who Stole Themselves: Advertisements for Runaways in the Pennsylvania Gazette, 1728–1790* (Philadelphia: University of Pennsylvania Press, 1989), 129–30.]

63. "Diary of Landon Carter," *William and Mary Quarterly,* 1st series, 20 (1912): 178–9, cited in Quarles, "Dunmore as Liberator, 502, and Quarles, *Negro in the American Revolution,* 27.

64. Holton, "Rebel Against Rebel," 186; Sylvia R. Frey, "Between Slavery and Freedom: Virginia Blacks in the American Revolution," *Journal of Southern History* 49 (1983): 378.

65. Jeffrey J. Crow, *The Black Experience in Revolutionary North Carolina* (Raleigh, NC: Department of Cultural Resources, 1977), 71.

66. Lieutenant Colonel Archibald Campbell, cited in Frey, *Water from the Rock,* 69.

67. Quarles, "Dunmore as Liberator," 502; Quarles, *Negro in the American Revolution,* 27.

68. One party which was captured by the patriots consisted of "one white and sixteen blacks." [Quarles, "Dunmore as Liberator," 504; Quarles, *Negro in the American Revolution,* 29.]

69. Quarles, "Dunmore as Liberator," 502; Quarles, *Negro in the American Revolution,* 27–8.

70. *Virginia Gazette* (Pinkney), November 30, 1775; Frey, "Virginia Blacks in the Revolution," 384; Quarles, "Dunmore as Liberator," 501–2; Quarles, *Negro in the American Revolution,* 26–7; Mullin, *Flight and Rebellion,* 133; Patricia Bradley, *Slavery, Propaganda, and the American Revolution* (Jackson: University Press of Mississippi, 1998), 143.

71. Frey, "Virginia Blacks in the Revolution," 384–5.

72. Hoffman, *Spirit of Dissension,* 185.

73. Quarles, "Dunmore as Liberator," 504; Quarles, *Negro in the American Revolution,* 30.

74. Frey, "Virginia Blacks in the Revolution," 391; Wilson, *Loyal Blacks,* 27.

75. *Virginia Gazette* (Dixon and Hunter), July 20, 1776.

76. Mullin, *Flight and Rebellion,* 132.

77. William Moultrie, *Memoirs of the American Revolution* (New York: David Longworth, 1802), 1: 112; Hoffman, *Spirit of Dissension,* 152; Jeffrey J. Crow, "Slave Rebelliousness and Social Conflict in North Carolina, 1775–1802," *William and Mary Quarterly,* 3rd series, 37 (1980): 86; Olwell, "Domestick Enemies," 42; Wood, "Dream Deferred," 179.

78. Moultrie, *Memoirs of the American Revolution,* 1: 113–15; Henry Laurens to Richard Richardson, December 19, 1775, Chestnutt et al., *Papers of Henry Laurens,* 10: 576; David Ramsay, *History of the Revolution in South Carolina* (Trenton: Isaac Collins, 1785), 1: 50–1; Olwell, *Master, Slaves, and Subjects,* 239–41; Wood, "Dream Deferred," 178–9.

79. Stephen Bull to Henry Laurens, March 14, 1776, R. W. Gibbes, ed., *Documentary History of the American Revolution* (New York: D. Appleton, 1855), 1: 268. This letter also appears in Chestnutt et al., *Papers of Henry Laurens,* 11: 163.

80. Council of Safety to Stephen Bull, March 16, 1776, Chestnutt et al., *Papers of Henry Laurens,* 11: 172.

81. Patrick Tonyn to David Taitt, April 20, 1776, Davies, *Documents of the American Revolution*, 12: 108–9.

82. William Paca to Governor Johnson of Maryland, September 26, 1777, cited in Frey, *Water from the Rock*, 148.

83. Despite the disappearance of a British presence during the middle years of the Revolution, the war did give more of a direction to a small number of the slaves who fled. Gerald Mullin, in his research of advertisements for runaway slaves in Virginia, found that prior to 1775 only one in 316 mentioned that the fugitive might be headed northward. After 1775, 7 percent (19 of 283) stated that the refugees were probably headed north. [Mullin, *Flight and Rebellion*, 129.] The fugitive population doubled in Philadelphia and quadrupled in New York during the war. [Ira Berlin, *Many Thousands Gone: The First Two Centuries of Slavery in North America* (Cambridge: Harvard University Press, 1998), 231.]

84. In March of 1777 eleven slaves in Essex County, Virginia, were suspected of plotting an insurrection and placed on trial. One was hanged, several received lashes, and three had their ears nailed and cut off. [Schwarz, *Twice Condemned*, 184–7.]

85. During the war many plantations increased production of basic foodstuffs at the expense of cash crops like tobacco. They also increased the manufacture of cloth. These changes required additional work from the slaves, but slaves also learned new skills "such as weaving cloth, churning butter, molding candles, cobbling shoes, boiling salt, and carding wool. A visitor to Virginia noted that spinning was 'the chief employment of the female negores.'" [Berlin, *Many Thousands Gone*, 262.]

86. Frey, *Water from the Rock*, 86, 120; Abbott Hall, Custom House Report, December 31, 1784, Boyd et al., *Papers of Thomas Jefferson*, 8:199; Ramsay, *History of the Revolution in South Carolina*, 2: 382; Thomas Jefferson to William Gordon, July 16, 1788, Boyd et al., *Papers of Thomas Jefferson*, 13: 364. Although all figures are approximations, this was certainly the largest flight of slaves until the Civil War.

87. Thomas Jefferson to William Gordon, July 16, 1788, Boyd et al., *Papers of Thomas Jefferson*, 13: 363. Richard Henry Lee wrote: "Col. Taliaferro and Col. Travis lost every slave they had in the world, and Mr. Paradise has lost all but one. . . . This has been the general case of all those who are near the enemy. [Berlin, *Many Thousands Gone*, 260.]

88. John C. Fitzpatrick, ed., *The Writings of George Washington from the Original Manuscript Sources, 1745–1799*, (Washington, D.C.: United States Government Printing Office, 1931–44), 22: 14; Fritz Hirschfeld, *George Washington and Slavery: A Documentary Portrayal* (Columbia: University of Missouri Press, 1997), 23. Frederick, Frank, Gunner, Sambo, and Thomas were "recovered" in Philadelphia, while Lucy and Esther were "recovered" after the surrender at Yorktown. At least some of the others seemed to have sailed with the British from New York at the close of the war. On April 28, 1783, Washington wrote to Daniel Parker: "Some of my own slaves may probably be in N York but I am unable to give you their Descriptions; their Names being so easily changed,

will be fruitless to give you. If by Chance you should come at the knowledge of any of them, I will be much obliged by your securing them, so that I may obtain them again." [Fitspatrick, *Writings of Washington*, 26: 364–5; Hirschfeld, *George Washington and Slavery*, 26–7.]

89. Olwell, *Masters, Slaves, and Subjects*, 249.
90. Olwell, *Masters, Slaves, and Subjects*, 249.
91. Frey, *Water from the Rock*, 124–5.
92. Frey, "Virginia Blacks in the Revolution," 390.
93. Wilson, *Loyal Blacks*, 27. According to the Hessian officer Johann Ewald, "three hundred Negroes had to work head-over-heels at once" to build works for the defense of Savannah against a Franco-American assault in October of 1779. During the siege of Charleston the following year, Ewald reported that Negroes dragged things about "for lack of horses," while he himself supervised a crew of thirty who worked with axes and shovels. [Captain Johann Ewald, *Diary of the American War*, Joseph P. Tustin, trans. and ed. (New Haven: Yale University Press, 1979), 186, 221, 203.]
94. Ewald, *Diary*, 305. Some young women and girls became not ordinary servants but mistresses or prostitutes. A loyalist from Charleston wrote that "it was not uncommon for persons to let out the Negro girls to British Officers," while a patriot complained that he was unable to retrieve a slave named Esther from the British at Camden because "she was hid in an Officers room." [Olwell, *Masters, Slaves, and Subjects*, 255.]
95. Frey, *Water from the Rock*, 88, 121.
96. Clinton to Cornwallis, May 20, 1780, cited in Crow, *Black Experience in Revolutionary North Carolina*, 73.
97. Olwell, *Masters, Slaves, and Subjects*, 252.
98. Ramsay, *History of the Revolution in South Carolina*, 2: 384; Frey, "Virginia Blacks in the Revolution," 380, 394–7; Frey, *Water from the Rock*, 92, 95, 119–23, 131, 153, 163.
99. Ramsay, *History of the Revolution in South Carolina*, 2: 32–3.
100. Frey, *Water from the Rock*, 140. Cruden, a South Carolina merchant, served as Commissioner of Sequestered Estates starting in September of 1780. He was empowered to dispose of all "capital stock, consisting of land and Negroes," seized from the rebels. [125]
101. William Bull to George Germain, March 25, 1782, Davies, *Documents of the American Revolution*, 21: 50.
102. "But it's not in my power to describe the scene," Wilkinson wrote. "It was terrible to the last degree; and, what augmented it, they had several armed negroes with them, who threatened and abused us greatly." [Caroline Gilman, ed., *Letters of Eliza Wilkinson During the Invasion and Possession of Charleston, S. C. by the British in the Revolutionary War* (New York: Samuel Colman, 1839; reprint edition New York: Arno Press, 1969), 29, 42.]
103. In 1780, when the royal governor of Georgia asked the assembly "to arm and employ Negroes for our defense," the lawmakers agreed so long as the blacks remained armed only for the "time of Alarms actually fixed." [Frey, *Water from the Rock*, 100.]

104. From the flood of former slaves who came their way, British officers selected several hundred strong young men to become regular soldiers. Serving in units called the Black Pioneers, the Black Brigade, or the Black Carolina Corps, these recruits complied with military discipline and performed all the tasks normally expected of enlisted men, including armed combat. After the war these veterans, already trained and experienced, went on to serve first in the West Indies and later in the Napoleonic wars. Although they no longer toiled in the fields, they continued to obey the orders of their superiors and to perform difficult and/or dangerous tasks without significant reward or recompense. With no realistic possibilities to explore alternatives, they remained to all intents and purposes in a state of slavery. For the fate of African Americans who continued as British soldiers after the war, see Roger N. Buckley, *Slaves in Red Coats: The British West India Regiments, 1795–1815* (New Haven: Yale University Press, 1979).

105. Olwell, *Masters, Slaves, and Subjects*, 259; Michael Mullin, "British Caribbean and North American Slaves in an Era of War and Revolution, 1775–1807," in Jeffrey J. Crow and Larry E. Tise, eds., *The Southern Experience in the American Revolution* (Chapel Hill: University of North Carolina Press, 1978), 240–1.

106. Olwell, *Masters, Slaves, and Subjects*, 259.

107. For Catawba participation see chapter 5, "Catawbas," and Herbert Aptheker, *To Be Free: Studies in American Negro History* (New York: International Publishers, 1948), 13–4.] For the campaigns against various maroon communities, see also Jerome J. Nadelhaft, *The Disorders of War: The Revolution in South Carolina* (Orono, ME: University of Maine Press, 1981), 72, 132; Mullin, "British Caribbean and North American Slaves," 241; Olwell, *Masters, Slaves, and Subjects*, 277–9; Herbert Aptheker, *American Negro Slave Revolts* (New York: Columbia University Press, 1943; reprint New York: International Publishers, 1963), 207–8.

108. Olwell, *Masters, Slaves, and Subjects*, 248, 261–2, 265; Berlin, *Many Thousands Gone*, 301; William Bull to George Germain, March 22, 1781, Davies, *Documents of the American Revolution*, 20: 94–5.

109. Olwell, *Masters, Slaves, and Subjects*, 264.

110. The tending of gardens and poultry were particularly widespread in the lowcountry of South Carolina and Georgia, where the task system allowed slaves some time to labor on their own behalf. See Betty Wood's extensive treatment in *Women's Work, Men's Work: The Informal Slave Economics of Lowcountry Georgia* (Athens: University of Georgia Press, 1995), and Philip D. Morgan, *Slave Counterpoint: Black Culture in the Eighteenth-Century Chesapeake and Lowcountry* (Chapel Hill: University of North Carolina Press, 1998), 179–87.

111. Olwell, *Masters, Slaves, and Subjects*, 262, 265.

112. See chapter 3 above, "A Duty We Owe."

113. Richard Maxwell Brown, *Strains of Violence: Historical Studies of American Violence and Vigilantism* (New York: Oxford University Press, 1975), 77–8.

This handy formula, because it was stated so explicitly, became known as "Sumter's Law."

114. John C. Miller, *The Wolf by the Ears: Thomas Jefferson and Slavery* (New York: The Free Press, 1977), 24.

115. Quarles, *Negro in the American Revolution*, 110.

116. Frey, *Water from the Rock*, 136–7.

117. Frey, "Virginia Blacks in the Revolution," 394.

118. John C. Dann, ed., *The Revolution Remembered: Eyewitness Accounts of the War of Independence* (Chicago: University of Chicago Press, 1980), 244. For more on Sarah Osborn, see chapter 3 above, "Women and the Army."

119. Joseph Plumb Martin, *Private Yankee Doodle: Being a Narrative of Some of the Adventures, Dangers and Sufferings of a Revolutionary Soldier*, ed. George F. Scheer (Boston: Little, Brown & Co., 1962), 241. On October 4 James Thacher, a surgeon for the Continental Army, wrote in his journal: "The British have sent from Yorktown a large number of negroes sick with the small pox, probably for the purpose of communicating the infection to our army." [James Thacher, *A Military Journal during the American Revolutionary War, from 1775 to 1783* (Boston: Richardson and Lord, 1823), 337.] Three days later Robert Honyman recorded in his diary that the British "have turned several hundred Negroes out of the town in a most deplorable condition, perishing with famine and disease." [Frey, "Virginia Blacks in the Revolution," 394.]

120. Ewald, *Diary*, 335–6. Another German soldier, George Daniel Flohr, reported that blacks constituted "the majority" of the dead at Yorktown. [Robert A. Selig, "A German Soldier in America, 1780–1783: The Journal of Georg Daniel Flohr." *William and Mary Quarterly*, 3rd series, 50 (1993): 584.]

121. Frey, *Water from the Rock*, 169, 174–85, 193, 211; Wilson, *Loyal Blacks*, 21, 37; Quarles, *Negro in the American Revolution*, 163, 173; Robin W. Winks, *The Blacks in Canada: A History* (New Haven: Yale University Press, 1971), 32–3; Kenneth Coleman, *The American Revolution in Georgia, 1763–1789* (Athens: University of Georgia Press, 1958), 145–6; Nadelhaft, *Disorders of War*, 62; No figure even approaching exactitude can ever be derived, not only because of incomplete records, but because many evacuees departed from two or more ports in succession; thus, a mere total of the numbers from the various points of departure will not produce an accurate figure.

122. Frey, *Water from the Rock*, 172, 182.

123. Coleman, *American Revolution in Georgia*, 145.

124. Edward J. Cashin, *The King's Ranger: Thomas Brown and the American Revolution on the Southern Frontier* (Athens: University of Georgia Press, 1989), 174.

125. Quarles, *Negro in the American Revolution*, 173.

126. Mary Beth Norton, "The Fate of Some Black Loyalists of the American Revolution," *Journal of Negro History* 58 (1973): 402–26.

127. Winks, *Blacks of Canada*, 33. According to Article VII of the Treaty of Paris, the British were supposed to leave without "carrying away any negroes or other property of the American inhabitants." [Jack P. Greene, ed., *Colonies*

to Nation, 1763–1789: A Documentary History of the American Revolution (New York: W. W. Norton., 1975), 422.] General Carleton, claiming he was bound by prior commitments made to former slaves, maintained that he did not have to return the blacks under his command since they had come to the British as free people, not slaves. The Americans, arguing that slaves could not legally free themselves, pushed to enforce Article VII according to a more literal interpretation: the British should refrain from "carrying away any negroes" who had run from patriot masters. Washington leaned on Carleton to return what he regarded as stolen property, but Carleton held firm and thousands of liberated men, women, and children embarked to new lands and new lives.

128. *The Price of Loyalty: Tory Writings from the Revolutionary Era*, Catherine S. Crary, ed. (New York: McGraw-Hill, 1973), 374.

129. Probably Cambden, which at that point served as British headquarters.

130. He means here not military service but personal service: working for another man, as he had so often.

131. In order for the chronology of the narrative to make sense, this three-year fall from grace must have included his whole stay in New York, from when he arrived in 1780 until he left 1783.

132. Boston King's narrative was originally published under the title "Memoirs of the Life of BOSTON KING, a Black Preacher. Written by Himself, during his Residence at Kingswood-School," *The Methodist Magazine For March, 1798* [London, 1798]. It is reprinted in Vincent Carretta, ed., *Unchained Voices: An Anthology of Black Authors in the English-Speaking World of the Eighteenth Century* (Lexington: University of Kentucky Press, 1996), 351–66. The text here is based on the Carretta reprint.

133. David George's narrative, "An Account of the Life of Mr. David George, from Sierra Leone in Africa; given by himself in a Conversation with Brother Rippon of London, and Brother Pearce of Birmingham," appeared in John Rippon, ed., *Baptist Annual Register, 1790–1793* (London, 1793), 1: 473–84. It is reprinted in Carretta, *Unchained Voices*, 333–46, and Grant Gordon, *From Slavery to Freedom: The Life of David George, Pioneer Black Baptist Minister* (Huntsport, Nova Scotia: Lancelot Press, 1992), 168–83. The text here is based on the original source.

134. See Gordon, *From Freedom to Slavery*, 27–8.

135. George Galphin, a prominent patriot, would soon become the American Indian commissioner for the southern district. See chapter 5 "Chickasaws, Choctaws, Creeks, and Seminoles."

136. Probably Thomas Brown, leader of the multiracial "King's Rangers." See chapter 4, "Dogs of Civil War."

137. Liele had known George in Virginia, and while at Silver Bluff he had proved instrumental in George's conversion. His own narrative, "AN ACCOUNT of several Baptist Churches, consisting chiefly of NEGRO SLAVES: particularly of one at *Kingston*, in JAMAICA; and another at *Savannah* in Georgia," refers to the Revolution only briefly. [Carretta, *Unchained Voices*, 325–31.] The narrative of a fourth preacher, John Marrant, likewise deals minimally with the Revolution. ["A NARRATIVE OF THE LORD'S wonderful

DEALINGS WITH JOHN MARRANT, A BLACK, (Now going to Preach the GOSPEL in Nova-Scotia) Born in NEW YORK, in NORTH-AMERICA," Carretta, *Unchained Voices*, 110–27.]

138. The second settlement of Sierra Leone, unlike the first, survived—but that is another story. See Wilson, *Loyal Blacks*, 217–401; James W. St. G. Walker, *The Black Loyalists: The Search for a Promised Land in Nova Scotia and Sierra Leone, 1783–1870* (London: Longman and Dalhousie University Press, 1976), 145–397.

139. Gary B. Nash and Jean R. Soderlund, *Freedom by Degrees: Emancipation in Pennsylvania and Its Aftermath* (New York: Oxford University Press, 1991), 7; Purvis, *Revolutionary America*, 126; Arthur Zilversmit, *The First Emancipation: The Abolition of Slavery in the North* (Chicago: University of Chicago Press, 1967), 4.

140. Purvis, *Revolutionary America*, 126, 150, 161.

141. Sidney Kaplan and Emma Nogrady Kaplan, *The Black Presence in the Era of the American Revolution* (Amherst: University of Massachusetts Press, 1989), 15.

142. Kaplan and Kaplan, *Black Presence*, 17.

143. Graham R. Hodges and Alan E. Brown found 288 advertisements for runaways in New York and New Jersey newspapers from 1775 to 1783, compared with 387 over the preceding sixty years. [*"Pretends to Be Free": Runaway Slave Advertisements from Colonial and Revolutionary New York and New Jersey* (New York: Garland, 1994), xxxiii.] Although the rate had certainly increased, this was a small fraction of the 29,000 slaves from New York and New Jersey—even though these two states were in close proximity to the British army throughout the war.

144. See chapter 1, "A Shoemaker's Tale." We know that Attucks's mother was Natick; whether or not his father was African has not been ascertained. According to Thomas Doughton, the term "mulatto" in 1770 did not signify race but color; people used the term to refer to anyone who was not clearly identifiable as white or black. [Publication forthcoming.] According to Joanne Pope Melish, "slaves and their descendants throughout New England became quickly a people of mixed African, Native American and European descent—'of color' but not necessarily 'African' or 'black.' " [Joanne Pope Melish, *Disowning Slavery: Gradual Emancipation and "Race" in New England, 1780–1860* (Ithaca, NY: Cornell University Press, 1998), 10.] It does seem likely that Attucks was a former slave from Framingham, the "Crispas" who was sought as a runaway in an advertisement in 1750. [*Boston Gazette*, October 2, 1750, reproduced in Kaplan and Kaplan, *Black Presence*, 6.]

145. Quarles, *Negro in the American Revolution*, 6; Kaplan and Kaplan, *Black Presence*, 8.

146. Quarles, *Negro in the American Revolution*, 10; Kaplan and Kaplan, *Black Presence*, 17–20; Philip S. Foner, *Blacks in the American Revolution*, (Westport, CT: Greenwood Press, 1975), 42. The records of these men and others throughout the war are traced in *Massachusetts Soldiers and Sailors of the Revolutionary War*, 17 volumes (Boston: Wright & Potter, 1896–1908).

147. The "Salem" who was alleged to have shot Major Pitcairn was Peter Salem, not the Salem Poor mentioned below. Quarles, *Negro in the American Revolution*, 10–1; Kaplan and Kaplan, *Black Presence*, 20–3; Foner, *Blacks in American Revolution*, 42. Swett published his account in 1826, fifty-one years after Bunker Hill. Although time and tradition had undoubtedly altered the story, Swett did still have access to people who had participated in the battle themselves.

148. A photocopy is reproduced in Kaplan and Kaplan, *Black Presence*, 23.

149. Quarles, *Negro in the American Revolution*, 15.

150. Abbot and Twohig, *Papers of George Washington*, Revolutionary War series, 2: 125.

151. Abbot and Twohig, *Papers of George Washington*, Revolutionary War series, 2: 354.

152. Abbot and Twohig, *Papers of George Washington*, Revolutionary War series, 2: 620.

153. Abbot and Twohig, *Papers of George Washington*, Revolutionary War series, 2: 623.

154. Abbot and Twohig, *Papers of George Washington*, Revolutionary War series, 2: 625.

155. Quarles, *Negro in the American Revolution*, 17.

156. Bill Belton, "Prince Whipple, Soldier of the American Revolution," *Negro History Bulletin* 36 (1973): 126–7. Emanuel Leutze's painting, *Washington Crossing the Delaware*, depicts a black oarsman, but there is no reason to believe that Whipple himself was that person, nor that there was exactly one black oarsman. There could have been none—or perhaps they were all black.

157. Robert A. Gross, *The Minutemen and Their World* (New York: Hill and Wang, 1976), 3, 151, 185, 217.

158. Barbara W. Brown and James M. Rose, *Black Roots in Southeastern Connecticut, 1650–1900* (Detroit: Gale Research Co., 1980), 332; David O. White, *Connecticut's Black Soldiers, 1775–1783* (Chester, CT: Pequot Press, 1973), 19. For a compilation of all records of Connecticut soldiers, see Adjutants-General, *Record of Service of Connecticut Men during the War of Rebellion* (Hartford: Case, Lockwood and Brainard, 1889).

159. Brown and Rose, *Southeastern Connecticut*, xiv, xvii–xxi, 64–7. In a similar manner Beriah Hill of Norwich purchased Backus, a slave belonging to Ezekiel Fox. Hill freed Backus, who then immediately enlisted as "a free Negro, Private, Hired by 2 men." [Brown and Rose, *Southeastern Connecticut*, 129; White, *Connecticut's Black Soldiers*, 24–6.] The list goes on: "Samuel Deates Negro Bo't by two men for £70 and is to have his freedom at the end of the war" [White, *Connecticut's Black Soldiers*, 24]; Nehemiah Lyon of Woodstock purchased Cato from Ebenezer White, then freed him in return for military service. When Cato enlisted he gave his last name as Freeman. [Brown and Rose, *Southeastern Connecticut*, 136.]

160. White, *Connecticut's Black Soldiers*, 21. A payroll for the second company, captained by David Humphreys, lists fifty-six African American soldiers, including Arabus. [William C. Nell, *Colored Patriots of the American Revolution* (Boston: Robert F. Wallcut, 1855; reprint New York: Arno Press, 1968), 134.]

161. White, *Connecticut's Black Soldiers*, 22.

162. White, *Connecticut's Black Soldiers*, 22–3.

163. White, *Connecticut's Black Soldiers*, 24.

164. Robert E. Greene, *Black Courage, 1775–1783: Documentation of Black Participation in the American Revolution* (Washington: Daughters of the American Revolution, 1984), 337–8.

165. White, *Connecticut's Black Soldiers*, 21.

166. White, *Connecticut's Black Soldiers*, 24, 40. The officer, John Sedgwick, was successful in his claim although he could show no proof he had purchased Sackett from Joseph Wadsworth, Sackett's former owner who had freed him in return for service.

167. Nell, *Colored Patriots*, 136–9; Brown and Rose, *Southeastern Connecticut*, 144, 221–2; White, *Connecticut's Black Soldiers*, 29. For the story of Ledyard's surrender, see William Abbatt, ed., *Memoirs of Major-General William Heath* (New York: William Abbatt, 1901), 282–4, reprinted in Henry S. Commager and Richard B. Morris, eds., *The Spirit of 'Seventy-Six: The Story of the American Revolution as Told by the Participants* (Indianapolis and New York: Bobbs-Merrill, 1958), 730–1.

168. John C. Dann, ed., *The Revolution Remembered: Eyewitness Accounts of the War of Independence* (Chicago: University of Chicago Press, 1980), 27–8. Many slaves of Tories, like Grant, were returned to slavery once discovered or captured. If their owners did not or could not claim them (many had been sent into exile), they were put up for public auction. Julius Friedrich Wasmus, a German surgeon who had been taken prisoner by the patriots, wrote in 1781 from Massachusetts: "The good slaves, who as Royalists have sought protection with the English at the beginning of this war, have been confiscated by Congress and will now be on public sale for the one offering the most. This is very hard!" [*An Eyewitness Account of the American Revolution and New England Life: The Journal of J. F. Wasmus, German Company Surgeon, 1776–1783*, Helga Doblin, tr., Mary C. Lynn, ed. (New York: Greenwood Press, 1990), 236.] The sale of these slaves helped pay the costs of the Revolutionary War.

169. Lorenzo J. Greene, "Some Observations on the Black Regiment of Rhode Island in the American Revolution," *Journal of Negro History* 37 (1952): 142–3, 152. The complete text of the legislation is reprinted in Nell, *Colored Patriots*, 50–1.

170. Greene, "Black Regiment of Rhode Island," 165. Greene notes that prior estimates varied from 130 to 300, but Quarles argues that "Greene's estimate seems sound." [Quarles, *Negro in the American Revolution*, 73.]

171. Quarles, *Negro in the American Revolution*, 81.

172. Nell, *Colored Patriots*, 130. Nell identifies the speaker only as "Dr. Harris."

173. Evelyn M. Acomb, ed., *The Revolutionary Journal of Baron Ludwig Von Closen, 1780–1783* (Chapel Hill: University of North Carolina Press, 1958), 92. Kaplan and Kaplan [*Black Presence*, 65] report erroneously that Closen offered his observations "when the victorious American army passed in review at Yorktown"; in fact, he observed the regiment near White Plains on July 9, several months before the victory at Yorktown.

174. Greene, "Black Regiment of Rhode Island," 1781–2.
175. *Providence Gazette*, March 30, 1783. I thank Thomas Doughton for this reference.
176. George Livermore, "An Historical Research Respecting the Opinions of the Founders of the Republic on Negroes as Slaves, as Citizens, and as Soldiers," *Proceedings of the Massachusetts Historical Society* 6 (1862–3): 210–1.
177. Quarles, *Negro in the American Revolution*, 70.
178. Quarles, *Negro in the American Revolution*, 56–7.
179. L. P. Jackson, "Virginia Negro Soldiers and Seamen in the American Revolution," *Journal of Negro History* 27 (1942): 257.
180. Jackson, "Virginia Soldiers and Seamen," 251.
181. Jackson, "Virginia Soldiers and Seamen," 272–5. William Flora, a freeman, was the last man to retreat from the breastworks during the Battle of Great Bridge.
182. Livermore, "Historical Research," 235.
183. Jackson, "Virginia Soldiers and Seamen," 274–5, 283.
184. Herbert Aptheker, ed., *A Documentary History of the Negro People in the United States* (New York: Citadel Press, 1969), 13–4.
185. Foner, *Blacks in the American Revolution*, 72.
186. Gregory D. Massey, "The Limits of Antislavery Thought in the Revolutionary Lower South: John Laurens and Henry Laurens," *Journal of Southern History* 63 (1997): 510. See also Livermore, "Historical Research," 214–7.
187. Livermore, "Historical Research," 217; George H. Moore, *Historical Notes on the Employment of Negroes in the American Army of the Revolution* (New York: Charles T. Evans, 1862), 11–2, reprinted in Foner, *Blacks in the American Revolution*, 181–2.
188. Over the course of the war South Carolina was able to muster only 25 percent of the quotas issued by Congress; all other states except North Carolina met at least 50 percent of their quotas. [Calculated from yearly schedules of "Requisitions and Troops Provided for Continental Army, 1775–1783," Purvis, *Revolutionary America*, 234–40.]
189. Massey, "Limits of Antislavery Thought," 517.
190. Livermore, "Historical Research," 232.
191. Quarles, *Negro in the American Revolution*, 90–1.
192. Jackson, "Virginia Soldiers and Seamen," 262. That the legislature would see the need to pass this law suggests that a significant percentage of sailors were African Americans.
193. Quarles, *Negro in the American Revolution*, 91.
194. W. Jeffrey Bolster, *Black Jacks: African American Seamen in the Age of Sail* (Cambridge: Harvard University Press, 1997), 71; Jesse Lemisch, "Jack Tar in the Streets: Merchant Seamen in the Politics of Revolutionary America," *William and Mary Quarterly*, 3rd series, 25 (1968): 381–2.
195. Bolster, *Black Jacks*, 157.
196. The wording varied; this particular phrase appeared in ads in the *Maryland Gazette* for "two MULATTO LADS, the one named DICK, and the other Jack Smith" (August 18, 1780) and "a negro man named Caesar" (August

25, 1780), reprinted in Lathan A. Windley, ed., *Runaway Slave Advertisements: A Documentary History from the 1730s to 1790* (Westport, CT: Greenwood Press, 1983), 2: 126–7.

197. Throughout the eighteenth century blacks in search of an alternative to slavery had hired on as seamen. Whether runaways seeking distance from their owners or poor freemen in search of employment, they had embraced a life at sea, with all its dangers and discomforts, as the best available option. In the years leading up to the Revolutionary War seamen of color, like Crispus Attucks, had constituted a fair share of the urban crowds—the "Rabble of boys, sailors, and negroes"—who protested impressment, the Stamp Act, and the presence of British soldiers in Boston, Charleston, New York, Newport, and other port towns. For a discussion of blacks and seamen in pre-revolutionary crowds, see Marcus Rediker, "A Motley Crew of Rebels: Sailors, Slaves, and the Coming of the American Revolution," in Ronald Hoffman and Peter J. Albert, eds., *The Transforming Hand of Revolution: Reconsidering the American Revolution as a Social Movement* (Charlottesville: University Press of Virginia, 1995), 155–98.

198. Joseph Harris was one who fought for the British; see above, "The Promise and the Panic of '75."

199. Jackson, "Virginia Soldiers and Seamen," 264, 267–8; 274, 283–4.

200. Kaplan and Kaplan, *Black Presence*, 61.

201. Aptheker, *Documentary History of Negro People*, 8–9.

202. Quarles, *Negro in the American Revolution*, 39–40.

203. In 1777 a "Great Number of Blackes detained in a State of slavery" wrote: "[Following] the Lawdable Example of the Good People of these States your petitioners have Long and Patiently waited the Evnt of petition after petition By them presented to the Legislative Body of this state and cannot but with Grief Reflect that their Sucess hath ben but too similar they Cannot but express their Astonishment that It have Never Bin Consirdered that Every Principle from which Amarica has Acted in the Cours of their unhappy Dificultes with Great Briton Pleads Stronger than A thousand arguments in favours of your petioners." [Aptheker, *Documentary History of Negro People*, 10.] And in 1780 seven black residents of Dartmouth imbued the cry of "no taxation without representation" with new meaning: "[B]y Reason of Long Bondag and hard Slavery we have been deprived of Injoying the Profits of our Labouer or the advantage of Inheriting Estates from our Parents as our Neighbouers the white peopel do. . . . [W]e are not alowed in voating in the town meating in nur to chuse and oficer Neither their was not one ever heard in the active Court of the General Asembly the poor Dispised miserable Black people. . . . Contrary to the invariable Custom & Practice of the Country we have been & now are Taxed both in our Polls and that small Pittance of Estate which through much hard Labour & Industry we have got together to Sustain our selves & families." The petition therefore urged "That these the Most honouerable Court we Humbley Beseech they would to take this into Consideration and Let us aside from Paying tax or taxes." [Aptheker, *Documentary History of Negro People*, 15.] The argument was sound—these

people were clearly being taxed without political representation—yet revolutionary lawmakers took no action. Aptheker has reprinted additional petitions on pages 5–15; I cite one above in the Introduction. In 1776 Lemuel Haynes, son of a black father and white mother, wrote an extensive antislavery tract entitled, "Liberty Further Extended: Or Free thoughts on the illegality of Slave-keeping." Haynes, who would eventually become a prominent minister, used scripture in support of natural rights. The document, the longest antislavery argument extant from an African American author during the Revolution, is reprinted in Ruth Bogin, " 'Liberty Further Extended': A 1776 Antislavery Manuscript by Lemuel Haynes," *William and Mary Quarterly*, 3rd series, 40 (1993): 85–105.

204. William Lincoln, *History of Worcester, Massachusetts, from its Earliest Settlement to September, 1836* (Worcester, MA: Charles Hersey, 1862), 99.

205. Arthur Zilversmit, *The First Emancipation: The Abolition of Slavery in the North* (Chicago: University of Chicago Press, 1967), 111. The assembly actually sent the measure to Congress, wary that there might be "an impropriety in our determination on a question which may . . . be of extensive influence, without previously consulting your Honors." Congress made no reply and the bill was never revived.

206. Livermore, "Historical Research," 110.

207. Gary B. Nash and Jean R. Soderlund, *Freedom by Degrees: Emancipation in Pennsylvania and Its Aftermath* (New York: Oxford University Press, 1991), 103–4.

208. Zilversmit, *First Emancipation*, 113–5; Kaplan and Kaplan, *Black Presence*, 244–8.

209. The most comprehensive treatment of the demise of slavery and the reconstitution of racism in southern New England is Joanne Pope Melish, *Disowning Slavery: Gradual Emancipation and "Race" in New England, 1780–1860* (Ithaca, NY: Cornell University Press, 1998).

210. Edgar J. McManus, *A History of Negro Slavery in New York* (Syracuse, NY: Syracuse University Press, 1970), 161–79; Shane White, *Somewhat More Independent: The End of Slavery in New York City, 1770–1810* (Athens: University of Georgia Press, 1991); Graham R. Hodges, *Slavery and Freedom in the Rural North: African Americans in Monmouth County, New Jersey, 1665–1865* (Madison: Madison House, 1997); Zilversmit, *First Emancipation*, 139–52, 175–200, 208–22.

211. Ira Berlin, *Slaves Without Masters: The Free Negro in the Antebellum South* (New York: Pantheon, 1974), 46–7; Berlin, *Many Thousands Gone*, 233.

212. Cuffe had been one of the seven signers of the "taxation without representation" petition quoted in footnote 203, above.

213. Sidney and Emma Nogrady Kaplan offer a comprehensive treatment of the achievements of these and other African Americans in *Black Presence*, 85–236, with an extensive bibliography on pages 284–90. For Newport's Free African Union Society, see Ralph E. Luker, " 'Under Our Own Vine and Fig Tree': From African Unionism to Black Denominationalism in Newport, Rhode Island, 1760–1876," *Slavery and Abolition* 12 (1991): 23–48. For a more contex-

tualized treatment of James Forten's remarkable career, treated only briefly by Kaplan and Kaplan, see Gary B. Nash, *Forging Freedom: The Formation of Philadelphia's Black Community, 1720–1840* (Cambridge: Harvard University Press, 1988).

214. Kenneth M. Stampp, "Slavery—the Historian's Burden," in Harry P. Owens, ed., *Perspectives and Irony in American Slavery* (Jackson: University of Mississippi Press, 1976), 153–7; Robin Blackburn, *The Overthrow of Colonial Slavery, 1776–1848* (London: Verso, 1988), 128; Purvis, *Revolutionary America*, 123–4. The proportional increase of slaves was approximately the same as that of the overall population of the United States. [Purvis, *Revolutionary America*, 123.]

215. Berlin, *Many Thousands Gone*, 264.

216. See Winthrop D. Jordan, *White Over Black: American Attitudes Toward the Negro, 1550–1812* (Chapel Hill: University of North Carolina Press, 1968), 350–1.

217. John Shy, *A People Numerous and Armed: Reflections on the Military Struggle for American Independence* (Ann Arbor: University of Michigan Press, 1990), 257. Duncan MacLeod shows how "a consciously racist society" could emerge from the rhetoric of freedom:

> Until the middle of the eighteenth century the Negro's place in American society had been firmly institutionalized: he was a slave. The ideas central to the Revolution subjected that definition to severe strains. Coupled with broad humanitarian and religious impulses, they brought under fire the institution of slavery and promoted a destruction of the identity of slave and Negro. This demanded, especially of the South, a re-definition of society and of its values. . . . The Revolutionary debate promoted an articulation of ideas which had previously existed largely on the level of assumption. The process of articulation hardened and rationalized those assumptions and thereby made them more difficult to dislodge. . . . Articulation and definition gave them an authority and respectability which firmly established them as societal norms. [Duncan J. MacLeod, *Slavery, Race and the American Revolution* (London: Cambridge University Press, 1974), 8, 183.]

Although the entrenchment of slavery based on a more explicit racism was the dominent trend, a perceptible minority of masters in the upper South (but not the lower South) internalized revolutionary theory to the point of manumitting their slaves, most commonly in their wills but occasionally during their lifetimes. By 1790 the estimated number of free blacks in Virginia had increased to 12,766, or 4.2 percent of the total Negro population, up from only 1,800 in 1782. In the lower South (South Carolina and Georgia) free blacks still numbered only about 2,200, or 1.6 percent of the total Negro population, not a signficant change from the prewar years when free blacks such as the boat pilot Jeremiah congregated in Charleston. [Berlin, *Slaves Without Masters*, 46–9.]

218. Jefferson to William Gordon, July 16, 1788, Boyd, *Papers of Thomas Jefferson*, 13: 363–4. Since Jefferson had a vested interest in exaggerating the death toll,

and since he could not have relied on official records (there weren't any) and had no access to direct sources, we should not accept his estimate uncritically. But as shown below, there are other indications that approximately half the slaves who fled died from disease.

219. As shown above, 3,000 free blacks emigrated to Canada from New York, a few hundred left for the British Isles, an indeterminate number (more likely in the hundreds than the thousands) forged a temporary freedom in maroons, while some found refuge in the free black communities. ("There is reason to believe," white Virginians complained in 1781, "that a great number of slaves which were taken by the British Army are now passing in this Country as free men," yet at the close of the war there were only about 1,800 free blacks living in Virginia, not a significant change from before the war. [Berlin, *Slaves Without Masters*, 18, 46.]) Altogether, it is unlikely that more than 5,000 or 6,000 southern slaves acquired their freedom by flight during the Revolutionary War. Disease, as I show below, claimed the lives of several times that number. After the war the number of free blacks did rise dramatically in both the North and the upper South from a combination of humanitarian and economic causes. [Berlin, *Slaves Without Masters*, 46–7.]

220. With no appropriate records, we cannot say exactly how many blacks died in the war; we must be content with ballpark guesses. As we have seen, contemporary estimates of the number of slaves "lost" in Virginia, South Carolina, and Georgia (including the slaves of loyalists) added up to at least 60,000. This might appear a bit high (particularly Jefferson's figure), but it does not even include slaves from North Carolina, Maryland, and Delaware. Sylvia Frey thinks the figure is reasonably close to the truth. Frey also notes that far less than half that number departed with the British. [Frey, *Water from the Rock*, 174, 177, 179.] What happened to all the others? A Hessian officer, Carl Leopold Baurmeister, wrote during the evacuation from New York that half the slaves who responded to Clinton's proclamation "are no longer alive." [Frey, *Water from the Rock*, 192.] This estimate of one-half is certainly a very rough guess, but it would help explain how the 60,000 (or somewhat less) who were "lost" dwindled to the 15,000 or 20,000 who departed on ships. From the frequent accounts of epidemics, it does not seem unlikely that somewhere in the neighborhood of 25,000 African Americans perished. But 25,000 is the commonly accepted estimate for the total number of soldiers on the American side who were killed in battle, died from wounds, and succumbed to disease. (See chapter 2, "In the Face of the Enemy.") When we compare the two estimates, we see that approximately as many African Americans might have perished as whites who fought with the patriots.

221. William Hooper to James Iredell, February 17, 1782, Don Higginbotham, ed., *The Papers of James Iredell* (Raleigh, NC: Division of Archives and History, 1976), 2: 328–9.

222. In a similar vein, William Moultrie boasted of his slaves' reactions upon his return home:

> [T]here was immediately . . . an outcry throughout the plantation, that "Massa was come! Massa was come!" and they were running from

every part with great joy to see me. I stood in the piazza to receive them: they gazed at me with astonishment, and every one came and took me by the hand, saying, "God bless you, massa! we glad for see you, massa!" and every now and them some one or other would come out with a "ky!" And the old Africans joined in a war-song in their own language, of "welcome the war home." It was an affecting meeting between the slaves and the master: the tears stole from my eyes and run down my cheeks . . . I then possessed about two hundred slaves, and not one of them left me during the war, although they had had great offers. [Moultrie, *Memoirs of the American Revolution*, 2: 355–6.]

In fact, on March 14, 1781, Charleston's *Royal Gazette* listed the names of eight men and twelve women who had once belonged to Moultrie and had fled to the royal army. [Olwell, *Masters, Slaves, and Subjects*, 275.]

223. Frey, "Virginia Blacks in the Revolution," 382.
224. *South-Carolina Gazette*, November 7, 1775.
225. Windley, *Runaway Slave Advertisements*, 2: 154–5.
226. Henry Laurens to Alexander Hamilton, April 19, 1785, Harold C. Syrett, ed., *The Papers of Alexander Hamilton* (New York: Columbia University Press, 1962), 3: 606–7.
227. Massey, "Limits of Antislavery Thought," 529.

7 The Body of the People

1. J. Franklin Jameson, *The American Revolution Considered as a Social Movement* (Princeton, NJ: Princeton University Press, 1926). Jameson's phrase serves as the title of a recent volume of essays exploring the revolutionary implications of the war: *The Transforming Hand of Revolution: Reconsidering the American Revolution as a Social Movement*, Ronald Hoffman and Peter J. Albert, eds. (Charlottesville: University Press of Virginia, 1995).
2. Gordon S. Wood, *Radicalism of the American Revolution* (New York: Vintage, 1993), 232–3.
3. For estimates on the numbers of Native Americans at the time of the Revolution see Thomas L. Purvis, *Almanacs of American Life: Revolutionary America, 1763 to 1800* (New York: Facts on File, 1995), 24–5. According to Purvis, there were over 480,000 slaves in the thirteen colonies in 1774. [*Revolutionary America*, 123.] Wood himself uses the 80,000 figure for the number of loyalist exiles. [*Radicalism of the American Revolution*, 176.]
4. Michael A. McDonnell, "Popular Mobilization and Political Culture in Revolutionary Virginia: The Failure of the Minutemen and the Revolution from Below," *Journal of American History* 85 (1998): 978–9. One advocate of the proposal argued that "Negroes were a desireable Property, and it would be obliging to the Wealthy, who perform little personal duty, to contribute largely." The proposal was narrowly defeated due to stiff opposition by slave-

owners who argued that the proposal "bears hard upon those wealthy in Negroes."

5. Duncan J. MacLeod, *Slavery, Race and the American Revolution* (Cambridge: Cambridge University Press, 1974), 184. MacLeod refers here to the impact of the Revolution on slavery: "The historian is faced with the sad paradox that the first great onslaught on slavery in America was impelled by egalitarianism and by a belief in universal and natural rights: but it helped to produce a positive racism and an explicit denial of those rights." (See chapter 6.)

6. Michael Meranze, "Even the Dead Will Not Be Safe: An Ethics of Early American History," *William and Mary Quarterly*, 3rd series, 50 (1993): 378. Michael Zuckerman, another critic, holds that Wood's research was unduly influenced by "the rhetoric in the elite archives," leading him to focus too much attention on "affluent white northeastern males." ["Rhetoric, Reality, and the Revolution: The Genteel Radicalism of Gordon Wood," *William and Mary Quarterly*, 3rd series, 51 (1994): 697–8.]

7. Jackson Turner Main, "Government by the People: The American Revolution and the Democratization of the Legislatures," in Jack P. Greene, ed., *The Reinterpretation of the American Revolution, 1763–1789* (New York: Harper & Row, 1968), 336. [Originally published in *William and Mary Quarterly*, 3rd series, 23 (1966): 391–407.] In the northern three states, the proportion of farmers in legislative bodies increased from 23 percent to 55 percent, while merchants and lawyers decreased from 43 percent to 18 percent.

8. John Shy, *A People Numerous and Armed* (Ann Arbor: University of Michigan Press, 1990), 242–3. Shy adds another interesting explanation for the end of deference in the political process: "The military performance of the typical American officer in the Revolutionary War was not good; after all, very few had been schooled to lead men into eighteenth-century battle, or even to keep them clean, clothed, fed, sheltered, and sober under field conditions. Discipline was poor, and the junior officers were obviously to blame. So after eight years in which about 200,000 of the masses watched perhaps 20,000 of the so-called elite perform more or less incompetently, the postwar voter had lost much of his habitual deference to men allegedly 'better' than he was" [261].

9. David P. Szatmary, *Shays' Rebellion: The Making of an Agrarian Insurrection* (Amherst: University of Massachusetts Press, 1980), 77, 97; Robert A. Feer, *Shays's Rebellion* (New York: Garland, 1988; reprint of Ph.D. dissertation, Harvard University, 1958), 248.

10. Szatmary, *Shays' Rebellion*, 97.

11. The term "Shays' Rebellion" misleadingly suggests that Daniel Shays either initiated the insurrection or exerted some kind of controlling influence over it. Neither is the case. Shays was not even present at the first court closure, nor at some of the later ones. He seems to have risen to a leadership position because of his military experience: he had been a captain during the Revolution. The insurgents, recognizing they were in an armed confrontation, called upon him to make military decisions, not to represent them politically. He filled an important role, but we should be careful to note that he in no way owned the movement. Shays himself recognized this when he said to General Rufus Put-

nam, "I at their head! I am not. . . . I never had any appointment but that at
Springfield, nor did I ever take command of any men but those of the county
of Hampshire; no, General Putnam, you are deceived, I never had half so
much to do in the matter as you think." [Feer, *Shays's Rebellion,* 212.] The
term "Shays' Rebellion," I suspect, is commonly accepted for two reasons:
innocently, it is convenient, substituting the name of an individual for a complex social movement; not so innocently, it is intended to belittle the significance of the insurgents, and imply a mass of people unquestioningly following
their leader rather than acting for reasons of their own. Implicitly, it steers us
away from the real grievances of the insurgents. This problem is magnified
when the rebellious farmers are labeled "Shaysites," as if they were in some
type of cult. The failure to recognize the true importance of the farmers'
rebellion of the mid-1780s is due in part to the general acceptance of this
simplistic and misleading nomenclature. It has also been misunderstood because
its connection with the very successful rebellion waged twelve years earlier by
many of the very same people has consistently been overlooked.

12. Szatmary, *Shays' Rebellion,* 57–9, 123–6. Curiously, in 369 pages devoted to
the dramatic changes in the United States during the latter years of the eighteenth century, Gordon Wood makes not a single reference to the most significant social movement of the 1780s, the local rebellions of indebted farmers.

13. According to Mary Beth Norton,

> In the late 1780s and 1790s women whose appetite for public affairs
> had been whetted by the events of the Revolution kept themselves
> abreast of political happenings through newspapers, conversations, and
> correspondence. "I am turned a great politician," Margaret Manigault
> typically told her husband, Gabriel, in 1792; "I read the papers, & talk
> learnedly about them all." Similar statements may be found in the
> diaries or correspondence of nearly every white woman in late
> eighteenth-century America. . . . From the French traveler who in 1791
> encountered two young Virginia women eagerly taking part in political
> debates, to the New England girl who at a 1788 dance proudly pro-
> nounced herself a "politician" to a youth wishing to discuss the new
> Constitution, . . . the indications are unanimous: after the Revolution
> women no longer regarded politics as falling outside their sphere. As
> Abigail Adams put it in 1799, "If a woman does not hold the reigns of
> Government, I see no reason for her not judging how they are con-
> ducted." [Mary Beth Norton, *Liberty's Daughters: The Revolutionary Ex-
> perience of American Women, 1750–1800* (Boston: Little, Brown and Co.,
> 1980), 189.]

But even if we admit these changes in attitude among educated women who
kept diaries and wrote letters, we must note that there were no *structural*
changes in women's political roles attributable to the Revolution, nor is there
any indication that the change of consciousness noted by Norton extended
beyond elite circles.

14. Linda K. Kerber, *Women of the Republic: Intellect and Ideology in Revolutionary America* (Chapel Hill: University of North Carolina Press, 1980), 84.

15. Pauline Maier, *From Resistance to Revolution: Colonial Radicals and the Development of American Opposition to Britain, 1765–1776* (New York: Alfred A. Knopf, 1972), 137.

16. Appendix I, "Merchant Samuel Colton Documents," *Proceedings at the Centennial Celebration of the Incorporation of the Town of Longmeadow, October 17th, 1883, with numerous Historical Appendices and a Town Genealogy* (Longmeadow, MA: Centennial Committee, 1884), 217.

17. Petition of Nathaniel Ely, Festus Colton, and Azariah Woolworth, to the Senate and House of Representatives of the Commonwealth of Massachusetts, January 7, 1781, Massachusetts Archives, 231: 136; reprinted in *Centennial Celebration of Longmeadow*, 213.

18. See chapter 4 above, "A Rock and a Hard Place."

19. Allen Bowman, *The Morale of the American Revolutionary Army* (Port Washington, NY: Kennikat Press, 1943), 30; Broadus Mitchell, *The Price of Independence: A Realistic View of the American Revolution* (New York: Oxford University Press, 1974), 117–18.

20. Washington expressed his frustrations with the soldiers at great length in George Washington to John Hancock, September 24, 1776, *The Writings of George Washington from the Original Manuscript Sources, 1745–1799*, John C. Fitzpatrick, ed. (Washington, D.C.: United States Government Printing Office, 1931–44), 6: 106–15. Significant excerpts from this letter are reprinted in *The Spirit of 'Seventy-Six: The Story of the American Revolution as Told by the Participants*, Henry S. Commager and Richard B. Morris, eds. (Indianapolis and New York: Bobbs-Merrill, 1958), 480–4.

21. Commager and Morris, *The Spirit of 'Seventy-Six*, 153.

22. Washington to Moses Hazen, May 3, 1782, *Writings of Washington*, Fitzpatrick, ed., 24: 217.

23. Washington to Elias Drayton, June 4, 1782, *Writings of Washington*, Fitzpatrick, ed., 24: 307.

24. Washington to Elias Drayton, June 11, 1782, *Writings of Washington*, Fitzpatrick, ed., 24: 330.

25. Washington to John Dickinson, June 19, 1782, *Writings of Washington*, Fitzpatrick, ed., 24: 365.

26. Washington to James Duane, September 30, 1782, *Writings of Washington*, Fitzpatrick, ed., 25: 223.

27. Washington to William Heath, August 3, 1782, *Writings of Washington*, Fitzpatrick, ed., 24: 456.

28. Washington to James Duane, September 30, 1782, *Writings of Washington*, Fitzpatrick, ed., 25: 223.

29. Washington to the Secretary of War, October 7, 1782, *Writings of Washington*, Fitzpatrick, ed., 25: 241.

30. Thomas Jefferson issued the classic statement in this regard: "There must doubtless be an unhappy influence on the manners of our people produced by the existence of slavery among us. The whole commerce between master and

slave is a perpetual exercise of the most boisterous passions, the most unremitting despotism on the one part, and degrading submission on the other." [Thomas Jefferson, *Notes on the State of Virginia* (Chapel Hill: University of North Carolina Press, 1955; first published in 1785), 162–3.]

31. Eugene F. Bliss, trans. and ed., *Diary of David Zeisberger, a Moravian Missionary among the Indians of Ohio* (Cincinnati: Historical and Philosophical Society of Ohio, 1885), 1:86. See chapter 5 above, "Delaware and Shawnee."

32. M. St. Clair Clarke and Peter Force, *American Archives* (Washington, D.C., 1837), 4th series, 1: 1261; Frank Moore, *The Diary of the American Revolution* (New York: Washington Square Press, 1967), 9–10. See also Douglas Adair and John Schutz, eds., *Peter Oliver's Origin & Progress of the American Rebellion* (Stanford: Stanford University Press, 1961), 154–5. Oliver added, "And in the Month of February following, this same *Dunbar* was selling Provisions at *Plimouth,* when the Mob seized him, tied him to his Horse's Tail, & in that Manner drove him through Dirt & mire out of the Town, & he falling down, his Horse hurt him."

INDEX